P9-EDQ-988

THE JOURNAL OF
Richard Henry Dana, Jr.

THE JOURNAL OF
Richard Henry Dana, Jr.

VOLUME III

Edited by Robert F. Lucid

E
415.9
D15
A16
V.3

CAMBRIDGE, MASSACHUSETTS

The Belknap Press of Harvard University Press

1968

© Copyright 1968 by the Massachusetts Historical Society

© Copyright 1968 by the President and Fellows
of Harvard College

All rights reserved

Distributed in Great Britain by Oxford University Press, London

Library of Congress Catalog Card Number 68-14264

Printed in the United States of America

Contents

PART IV. A VOYAGE ROUND THE WORLD — 1859–1860

   1. Out to California   841

   2. At Sea and Hawaii   857

   3. California and to the Orient   895

   4. China   940

   5. Japan   1001

   6. China Again   1032

   7. The Voyage Back   1065

   Genealogies   1141

   Index   1155

Illustrations

(*Following Page 1022*)

The last page of the last volume of the *Journal* manuscript. *Courtesy of the Massachusetts Historical Society.*

Richard Henry Dana, Jr., in 1879. *Courtesy of the Massachusetts Historical Society.*

Sarah Watson Dana in 1876. *Courtesy of Longfellow House.*

The Yosemite Valley, and Steamer Day in San Francisco. *Courtesy of the Library of Congress.*

John C. Frémont. *Courtesy of the Library of Congress.* Bernice Pauahi Bishop, King Kamehameha IV, and Queen Emma, of Hawaii.

The three Richard Henry Danas. *Courtesy of Longfellow House.*

Hilo, Hawaii, and a view of Canton. *Courtesy of the Massachusetts Historical Society.*

Drawing of Josiah Tattnall in action, from *Harper's Illustrated Weekly.*

Two Oriental impressions of Westerners. *Courtesy of the Library of Congress.*

Sarah Watson Dana with Elizabeth Ellery Dana and Angela Henrietta Channing Dana. *Courtesy of Longfellow House.*

Two views of the *Journal's* author in later life. *Courtesy of Longfellow House.*

Title page of first edition of *Two Years Before the Mast. Courtesy of the Houghton Library, Harvard University.*

PART IV

A Voyage Round the World
July 1859 - September 1860

1. Out to California

MEM. OF JOURNAL OF MY VOYAGE FROM NEW YORK TO PACIFIC
OCEAN & C. R. H. D. JR.*

1859 JULY 20. WED. Sailed from N. York in the steam-ship Star of the
West, Gray, commander, for Aspinwall.[1] Between 4 & 500 passengers,
(1st. & 2d. Cabin & Steerage).

Mr. [George] Ripley, John Hodge & Capt. [James D.] Bulloch of the
Cahawba, down to take leave. Sailed at 1 P. M.

JULY 21. & 22D. Very heavy weather, & great discomfort of passengers from seasickness & want of room. Three in my small stateroom, with
three trunks, three valises, hat-box, guitar case, champagne basket &c.

Passengers — Capt. Poor U. S. N., going to take command of U. S.
Sloop-of-War St. Louis, at Aspinwall, Lt. Myers & wife & child, going to
Oregon, to join his Regt., 9th Infantry — Major Leonard & wife (a French
woman) Qu. Master U. S. Army, Locke & Pope, merchants of S[an]
Fr[ancisco], Miss Price of Cincinn., going to S. Fr. to marry a Mr.
Lawler, Miss Dexter, niece of Rich. Hildreth, a Miss Payne of Me., going
to marry in S. Fr., & a cousin of Capt. Poor, a Miss West, of Norfolk Va.
A Miss Dana of Oswego N. Y., niece of A. H. Dana, of N. Y., & a Mrs.
Gastner of S. Francisco.[2] These are all I knew. Several Jews, who clanned
together.

This ship was *filthy*. No care of water-rooms, poor ventilation, & no
discipline over servants. We, at Capt.'s table, good attention — rest, little
or none. Suffering of Steerage passengers, & 2d. Cabin passengers. In
1st cabin, no change of bed linen for whole passage — 11 days — no
cleaning out. Bad smell of dining-room, scarcely tolerable.

*The remainder of the *Journal* deals with the round-the-world trip. The text, up
to the entry for September 15, 1859, was rewritten by Dana from notes, letters,
and memories, due to the loss of the original in the sinking of the clipper ship *Mastiff*.

[1]Alfred G. Gray (1818–1876), veteran of the Navy in the Mexican War, was
probably commanding Dana's ship. Aspinwall was the eastern port of the Panama
trans-Isthmus railroad.

[2]Charles Henry Poor (1808–1882) commanded the *St. Louis*, 1860–1861, and other
Union Navy vessels during the Civil War. William Myers (1830–1887), West Point,
1852, had just left the U. S. Coastal Survey for frontier duty at Ft. Dallas, Oregon.
Hiram Leonard (d. 1883), whose name Dana spelled "Lennard," was paymaster, not
quartermaster. Miss Dexter's uncle was Richard Hildreth (1807–1865), writer on the
Orient, whose work is noted later. Alexander Hope Dana (1807–1887) can be found
in the Genealogy.

Hot weather begins, after passing Hatteras.

JULY 26.   At sundown make Morro Castle, & lie to all night.

[JULY] 27TH.   At sunrise, enter Havana Harbor. Familiar scene, Morro, Cabaña, Ceasar Blanca, houses, palm-trees, boats & boatmen.

Breakfast at Le Grand's. Cordially received by Le Grand. (Domingo & Antonio also).[3] Drive in volante. Guide of party. Cathedral, Mass, market, Dominica. On board at 10 o'ck, & sail out at noon.

Beautiful afternoon off coast of Cuba. Thunder storms over the island. Some yellow fever there, but not epidemic. One yellow fever man on board, — recovering.

Great heat from Havana to Aspinwall. No air, in state-rooms. Heat of mattresses. Up at day break ev. morning, & washed down by hose, refreshing bath, great use. Lie down on deck in shade.

Great deal of drinking, iced drinks, early & late. I drink nothing but tea & water, & am never thirsty.

Capt. Gray's chart-room, & our party gathering there, ev. evening. Negro steward singing —

> "It may be for years,
> And it may be forever".

Steerage passengers always singing Nellie Gray —

> "Sweet Nellie Gray,
> They're taking me away,
> And I'll never see my darling any more".

Excep. hot & disagr. work selecting luggage from lower cabin.

No relig. service on board. I read the morn. service, Sunday, to abt. dos. persons in Chart-Room, the milit. people & a few others.

AUG. 1. THURSD. Arrived at Aspinwall before day-break. Dismal place. Swamp, torrid marsh, hot, damp, a mist of vapors, like smoke, at sun-rise, all full of miasma. People on shore (whites) thin, shriveled, sallow, — effect of fever & ague. Negroes flourishing.

Find U. S. Frigate Roanoke, & Sloop St. Louis. Leave Capt. Poor there. (He feels dismal at the prospect of 2 or 3 years in this region.) Aspinwall not intended to be lived in by whites. Worst place I ever saw. Rich fruits, oranges, limes, bananas, pears, &c. &c.

Take cars at 9 A. M. & are discharged at Panama in 3 hours. On my birth-day cross a Continent. In morning, afloat on Atlantic, in evening, afloat in Pacific. Aspinwall & Panama are in *South* America.

[3]Le Grand was the proprietor of Le Grand Hotel in Havana, where Dana stayed during his earlier Cuban trip. Domingo and Antonio were servants at the hotel.

First half of passage across Isthmus is low swampy ground, decaying & growth of vegetation of richest character, going on at once. Very unhealthy. Population nearly all Negroes. Small Negro villages on the way. Negro women paddling in mud, with 4 flounces on white dresses, & barefooted! Latter half of passage across is hilly, mountainous, dry, picturesque. Grand view of Pacific Ocean. Picturesque character of Panama Bay — small mountainous islands, sprinkled over it. Ranges of mountains behind, connecting Andes & Cordilleras.

On board steam-ship Golden Gate, Whiting Master. Noble boat. Good regulations. Kept clean. Inspection of all parts daily.

Gossip & scandal in these boats. Passage long, & people not of highest style. Reputations often suffer, & sometimes justly, on these passages. So told by all, & believe it, from what I saw. Kept much by myself, & not intimate with any.

Picturesque character of all the Pacific Coast seen on this passage. Mountainous. Contrast with Atlantic, wh. is flat.

SUNDAY. AUG. 7. Acapulco, for coal. Best small harbor 1 ever saw — as good as possible. Breakfast ashore. Excellent Sp[anish] breakfast. Boat surrounded by boys swimming, naked in water, & diving for small coin. "Catch'ee one dime, Mistee". These boys dive & never failed to catch the coin thrown, & kept in water hours, without resting. Boats selling oranges, bananas &c.

SAT. EV. AUG. 13TH.   Make headlands off San Francisco. Enter "Golden Gate" by moonlight. Lighthouses, large shipping, great Clippers at anchor, large city of 80,000 people. Contrast with the S. Fr. of 1836, in the Alert — not one house — a solitude.[4]

Great crowd at landing. Little after midnight, reach Oriental Hotel.

SUNDAY. AUG. 14TH.   Walk in city. Church, morning service — large congregation. No afternoon service in any relig. soc. Most have service at 7½ P. M., — but custom is mostly to go to but one service.

[4]In *Two Years Before the Mast*, p. 281, Dana records his first sight of San Francisco, in December of 1835: "This large bay, which lies in latitude 37°58', was discovered by Sir Francis Drake, and by him represented to be (as indeed it is) a magnificent bay, containing several good harbors, great depth of water, and surrounded by a fertile and finely wooded country. About thirty miles from the mouth of the bay, and on the southeast side, is a high point, upon which the Presidio is built. Behind this point is the little harbor, or bight, called Yerba Buena, in which trading-vessels anchor, and near it, the Mission of Dolores. There was no other habitation on this side of the Bay, except a shanty of rough boards put up by a man named Richardson, who was doing a little trading between the vessels and the Indians."

Dana used the sections of the *Journal* dealing with California to compose an appendix to later editions of *Two Years* called "Twenty-Four Years After," which is included in the Houghton Mifflin edition of 1911.

Meet Felton — Fabens. Called on by S. Adams, brother of Rev. N. Adams, D. D.[5]

Dine with Felton, at Martin's. French Hs. Dinner as luxurious as in Paris. *Company* — Lt. Mowry, late of Army, now Del. elect fr. Arisona, Ex. Judge Parsons of a local court, Whitcomb, a lawyer, Judge Hagar.[6] All are Northern men, with Southern, pro-slavery, duelling principles. Anecdotes of S. Fr. in early times. Judge Parsons' adjourning his Court to go & see the Morissey prise fight, on pretense of death of Judge McKinley of U. S. Supr. C't.[7] Judges of Supreme C't. of Cal. attend opening of great gambling houses. Judiciary toasted, Ch. J. [S. C. Hastings] too drunk to reply, & Judge Wells gave "Success to Vice".[8]

Dr. Hastings, Dr. Holman, Pringle, Wm. Duer, Bishop Kip, Hall McAllister, Bayley Peyton, &c.[9]

[5]John Brooks Felton, brother of C. C. Felton, has been noted earlier. He moved to California in the middle of the decade and was a brilliantly successful lawyer, called "the Evarts of the Pacific slope." Active in Republican politics, once mayor of Oakland, he lost his fortune, and died in 1877. Francis Alfred Fabens, noted earlier as Dana's classmate at Harvard, moved to San Francisco in 1854, where he had a successful law practice. He died in 1872. Samuel Adams, a druggist, was the brother of Nehemiah Adams, noted earlier as pastor of the Union Congregational Church in Salem, Massachusetts.

[6]Sylvester Mowry (1830–1871), West Point, 1852, served on frontier duty in the Army and explored the territory from Utah to California, 1854–1855, served at Fort Yuma, and resigned in 1858. He was elected as a territorial delegate from Arizona, but the status of the territory was unclear and he was never seated. President Buchanan appointed him as California–Nevada boundary commissioner, but his Southern political sympathies caused his removal, his trial on disloyalty charges (acquitted), and his removal to England. Levi Parsons (1822–1877), a Little Falls, New York, lawyer, arrived in San Francisco in 1849 and was elected judge of the San Francisco District Court in 1850. He made a fortune building the Missouri, Kansas, and Texas Railroad, retired in 1866, and resided in New York City, where he was noted as a philanthropist. John S. Hagar was a judge of the 4th District Court of San Francisco in 1859. Mr. Whitcomb remains unidentified.

[7]At Mare Island on August 31, 1852, John Morrissey met George Thompson in a non-title prize fight which Thompson lost, on a foul, in the twelfth round. John McKinley (1780–1852) was an associate justice of the U. S. Supreme Court, 1837–1852.

[8]Alexander Wells (d. 1854) was a justice of the California Supreme Court, 1852–1854.

[9]Paragraphs like this one — catalogues or phrases without sentence syntax — are common in the early section of the round-the-world journal. They may be attributed to the fact that Dana was rewriting the earlier, lost journal, and seems at times to be jotting notes for purposes of later, fuller recollection. No doubt he originally intended to publish this section of the *Journal* as a sequel to *To Cuba and Back*. That he never did so is understandable, since he returned home to a United States which had as little time for reading travel narratives as he had for composing them. The names in this paragraph, in any case, must be a list of memorable people he met in the early, hurried days he spent in San Francisco. Serranus C. Hastings (1814–1893), originally from New York, came to California from Iowa in 1849. He was the

Invitation to lecture before Mercantile Library. Ditto, to deliver the anniversary oration of Pioneer Society to celebrate the setlt. of S. Francisco. Decline both.

Offer fr. a liquor house to supply my side-board with best wines &c. during my stay, *gratis*, — declined of course. Attentions — interest shown in my revisit to California, notices in the newspapers &c.

Dine with Bishop Kip — present, B. & lady, Wm. Duer, Col. Turner, & Mr. Blanding, a lawyer, ex. U. S. Att'y., & Capt. in Palmetto Regt. in Mex. War.

Dine with Felton again — present, Parsons, Pringle, & Edmund Randolph, of Va., a leading lawyer here.[10]

The Southern men, Blanding, Randolph, Pringle, &c. better than the N. men of S. principles I meet here.

Dine with Wm. Duer. Present, Mr. & Mrs. Duer, daughter & son, B'p. Kip & Baily Peyton. Anecdotes of early California life.

Visit U. S. Marine Hospital. Political jobbing, neglect of furniture for sick, failure of apparatus for heating &c., enormous money jobs, waste, & nothing done.

Visit City Hospital, not much better, but not so large expenses.

Deliver letter to Archb. Alemany.[11] Large R. C. Church of St. Mary. Working Cath. clergy & sisterhoods. Gen. respect & popularity of Bsh. Alemany. Visit School & Orphan Hs. of Sisters of Charity. School of Presentation Nuns, & Hospital of Sisters of Mercy. All creditable institutions.

Went to R.C. Ch. on Fest. of Assumption. Sermon sd. was not article

----

first chief justice of the California Supreme Court. Francis A. Holman was visiting physician to the City and County Hospital, San Francisco. Edward J. Pringle was a partner in a local legal firm. William Duer, of New York, was county clerk in San Francisco at the time. William I. Kip (1811–1893), Episcopal Bishop of the Diocese of California since 1857, came from New York to California as a missionary in 1853. Hall McAllister (1826–1888), son of Matthew D. and brother of Samuel W. McAllister, developed a great reputation as a lawyer. Bayley Peyton remains unidentified. Some of the biographical information in these and later notes dealing with Californians was drawn from John H. Kemble's edition of *Two Years* (Los Angeles: Ward Ritchie, 1964), 2 vols., which contains appendices dealing with Dana's California experiences and quotes portions of the *Journal*, as well as accompanying letters which Dana sent home at the time.

[10]Daniel Turner was chief engineer at Mare Island in 1859. His wife was a daughter of Francis Scott Key. Mr. Blanding, a member of the legal partnership of Lewis and William Blanding, was from South Carolina. Edmund Randolph (1819–1861), grandson of the statesman, settled in California in 1849 and gained fame as a lawyer and as a defender of the slave system.

[11]José Sadoc Alemany (1814–1888) came to America from Spain in 1841, as a Dominican missionary. He was consecrated Bishop of Monterey in 1850.

of Faith, but *gen. & pious* belief that the B. V. M. resumed her body, at death, & it was taken with her.

Windmills in gen. use here to raise water for irrigation & household purposes. More than 200 in the city.

Ch. R. Bond, assessor of taxes, attentive — takes me to ride. Go to the Mission.[12] This looks like 1836, & is the only thing that does.

Felton takes me to San Mateo. Visit the fort, at entrance of harbor. Great work — not completed.

Ditto, the fortifications on Alcatrass Island.

Part of S. F. is built over the water on piles, streets, shops & all, the sea flowing under them. Part is on made land. Rest is on sand hills. No grass, no trees. Some flower gardens, with artif. irrigation in summer. Dreary sandhills form the background. Bay is capacious & grand.

Strong wind fr. sea, ev. day at abt. 11 o'ck., & blows until night — very strong, — dust. Climate cold, all summer. People wear woolen clothes, & thick flannel underclothes. Overcoats worn a good deal in afternoon. Thin clothes — never. Very healthy except for consumptives or rheumatics. Children strong & healthful.

From the test[imon]y of the best citisens, I think the Vigilence Committee was a necessity. It certainly was effectual. As a gen. rule, ev. good cit. is in its favor, & ev. bad citisen against it.[13]

Jews & Chinese very numerous here. Jews, a business & political power. Chinese disfranchised, but very numerous — chiefly in the lighter labors & in trade. Signs in streets, of Chinese names. Generally, are under 5 year contracts with China companies & merchants, who pay them & employ & let them out. These contracts are legal & respected — I think.

Lawyers practice champerty & maintainance.[14] Not illegal. Injurious to the profession. Land-title lawyers been a curse to the city. Professional morals low — very low.

SAT. AUG. 20. Steamer Senator, for the leeward ports — to visit S. Diego, S. Barbara &c. Among passengers is Capt. John Wilson, who commanded

---

[12]Mr. Bond has not been identified, except for the fact that he was from New England. Dana refers to the Mission of Dolores.

[13]The first Committees of Vigilance were formed in San Francisco during June–September 1851, and were composed of eight hundred citizens, organized to combat widespread criminal disorder in the community. This group served as the nucleus of the great Committee, formed in August 1856 and composed of six to eight thousand citizens. The group summarily tried and punished criminals and deported or intimidated suspicious characters. The effort was relatively successful in bringing criminal activity within some acceptable limits, though the Committee was, in fact, itself operating outside the law.

[14]Champerty is the practice of bargaining to aid the defense or prosecution of a legal action for a share of the fee. Maintenance (note spelling) is an officious or unlawful intermeddling in a cause in law by assisting either party with money or other means to carry it on.

the brig Ayacucho in 1835-6 (Two Years before Mast) — long talks over old times.[15] He is now one of the richest & most respected rancheros in Cal. I was at his wedding, in S. Barbara — to Donña Ramona. He has large family — rancho in S. Luis Obispo.

Point Conception! What recollections associated with it! Now has lighthouse![16]

AUG. 21. Santa Barbara. The first place I saw in Cal. in 1835. Land in the surf, on the beach. Amphitheatre of mountains — Mission in the rear — islands on the sea side, & roaring surf! Call on Mr. Alfred Robinson. Lives at house of Noriego. Now (the children) called De la Guerra. Don Pablo de la Guerra, (Two Years &c.) receives me. Robinson's daughter, a belle.[17]

Call on Donña Angustias, (Two Years &c. danced at Robinson's wedding) still a fine looking woman. My book gives her great celebrity, on the coast.[18]

Judge Fernald, a young lawyer of S. Barbara, attentive.[19] Grapes, olives, wine making, & sheep raising.

AUG. 22. San Pedro. The point — the beach — the hill! This was our hated spot — place of toil & exposure. There, too, is the Dead Man's Island.

Good deal of trade here — now Steamer to carry freight to an upper landing at head of creek. Phineas Banning,[20] owner of the steamer & line of coaches to Los Angeles — very attentive to me. Coaches; six horses each, half wild, — run all the way. Level pampa for 30 miles to Los

---

[15]John Wilson (1795–1860) is mentioned frequently in *Two Years* as the expert captain of Dana's favorite brig, the *Ayacucho*. The 1911 edition of *Two Years* is indexed, and page citations here and in subsequent references to people, places, and events in that book, will be given only in special cases.

[16]Point Conception, about fifty miles north of Santa Barbara, was the first point of California land Dana's ship sighted in 1835. It is mentioned often in *Two Years*.

[17]Alfred Robinson (c. 1806–1895) was purchasing agent on board Dana's *Pilgrim*. In *Two Years* Dana suggested that Robinson's California wedding feast deprived the ship of stores. Robinson had good-humoredly answered the accusation in his own book, *Life in California* (1846), reprinted (Oakland, Calif., 1947), p. 83. Robinson married Donna Anita de la Guerra Noriego y Corillo, daughter of Don José de la Guerra. Her brother, Don Pablo (1819–1874), a noble of Spain by right of birth, was serving in the California legislature in 1860.

[18]Alfred Robinson's sister-in-law, Donna Angustias (1819–1874), was one of the great beauties of California. At this time she was married to Don Manuel Jimeno. Dana had praised her beauty in *Two Years*.

[19]Charles Fernald (b. 1830), a Maine man, was a county judge in 1859, having come to California in 1849.

[20]Phineas T. Banning, a resident of Los Angeles, laid out the town of Wilmington, California, in 1858. He came later to own large land interests, including Catalina Island.

Angeles. Few trees, no grass, alive with squirrels. (Told that snake, squirrel & bird occupy the same hole.)

Los Angeles, prosperous, growing. All engaged in grape growing. Vineyards everywhere. Hot, but dry, & not unpleasant. Meet here Henry Mellus,[21] my shipmate in Pilgrim, & his brother Frank, both settled here. Married sisters, Mex. women.

Dine with Mellus. Takes me to ride, to visit the vineyards. Grapes, olives, figs, peaches, pears & melons. Can raise fruits & flowers in ev. month in the year. Excellent climate for such, but too dry for wheat.

Of the people of Los Angeles of 1835-6, see John Temple, Stearns & Warner.[22] Two former become immensely rich. At Stearns', met Don Juan Bandini (Two Years &c.) & his wife, Donña Refugio, still beautiful, daughter of Don Santiago Argüello, (then, 1836, Commandante of S. Diego.)[23]

Meet here a brother of Geo. B. Emerson, who has been much abroad. Return in P. M., on a run of 30 miles, — tearing rate — to San Pedro.

TU. AUG. 23. San Diego. Familiar scenes. The great point (Loma), now Lighthouse on it, the little point, the beach, & the hills behind. All the hide houses gone! Also the Kanaka Oven. In their place, two or three shanties for use of people now there. In the stream, moored, a hulk, loaded with coal, to supply steamers in need — under charge of Capt.—— & his boy Tom. Steamer went up to a place called New S. Diego, at head of Bay. Got her to put me ashore on the Beach. Landed alone, & spent 2 or 3 hours wandering on beach & hills, in meditation. Causes eno' for reflection. 23 years ago, curing hides, cutting wood — 4 houses full of men — all gone — most dead. Found site of Kanaka oven, few bricks. Wandered over hills.

Walked up to the town, as so often before. "Black Ground". Village, familiar. Old adobe house of the Muchachos, large houses of Bandini & Estudillo & Arguello—Tomasa Pico still living. Estudillo dead. Bandini, I saw at Los Angeles.

Found here a shipmate of the Alert, Jack Stewart, now married &

[21]Mellus was Robinson's assistant on the *Pilgrim* and kept an annotated copy of *Two Years*, disagreeing with Dana's account in a great many particulars. James D. Hart has published an analysis of Mellus's commentary (of which Dana, it seems, was never aware), "An Eyewitness of Eight Months before the Mast," *New Colophon* 3: 128–131 (1950).

[22]John Temple (c. 1798–1866) had come to California in 1827. Dana met him there in 1836. Abel Stearns, noted much earlier in the *Journal,* was a California pioneer who made his fortune in livestock. Jonathan Trumbull Warner had come to Los Angeles as a trapper in 1834.

[23]Don Juan Bandini, mentioned in *Two Years* and noted earlier, died this same year. Don Santiago Argüello (1791–1862) and his daughter are not specifically mentioned in *Two Years.*

family — temperate & regular. Tom Wrightington, who kept the shop for Fitch, fell fr. his horse when drunk, & was found eaten by cayotes. Fitch dead. No one here but Stewart, that I remember.

Visit house of fellow passengers, in steamer, Doyle & wife.[24] He is agent for mail coach line — nice people.

Horse, & ride to Mission. All gone to decay. Large gardens, — now only cactuses & willows & few olive trees. Aqueduct in ruins. Buildings delapidated. Barracks for U. S. troops close by, abandoned & in ruins. Full run back to town, as Ben S[timson] & I did, in 1835.[25]

Took steamer in evening. Landed on Beach again & got shells, for memorials. One man fishing with Kanaka, on shores, who 5 years ago brot out large ship fr. Boston, — "Whisky did it.".

Steamed out of S. Diego — last look of Beach, hills, point &c.

WED. 24. AUG.   S. Pedro again. Master set me ashore at the old landing, I to walk to the new. Searched out the old spots. The landing & hill nearly gone, by land-slides. Old house still standing. Stood on old spot where spent so many dreary hours — imagined little Pilgrim at anchor in offing, & old work, & shipmates.

Up to Los Angeles again. Breakfast with [P. T.] Banning — *present*, 2 Melluses, Capt. Hancock (U. S. A.) & wife, Lt. Merchant (?) U. S. A. just retd. fr. an exped. to the desert. (News of Major Armistead battle just come in.)[26] Mr. Emerson, & others.

Lunch at Mellus'. Nearly same people — [John] Wilson also. Down to S. Pedro in 3 hours — full run all the way. Ran one mile without lynch-pin.

Last looks at S. Pedro, at sundown.

Stopped at S. Barbara, for an hour. Judge [Charles] Fernald sent me off box of S. B. wine.

Point Conception. Stopped at S. Luis Obispo & landed Wilson. Cordial invitation to visit him at his ranch — obliged to decline it. Passengers fr. S. Diego to S. Francisco, a Dr. Hoffman,[27] intelligent man, & a German

---

[24]Dana probably met Manville Doyle (1831–1916) and his wife. Doyle arrived in California from Illinois in 1850. He ran a livery business from 1855 to 1864 and later became a successful businessman and banker.

[25]In *Two Years,* pp. 142–147, Dana tells of visiting the Mission with his shipmate Ben Stimson (noted earlier), and of returning on their horses at a dead run.

[26]Winfield Scott Hancock (1824–1886), West Point, 1844, made a distinguished military record during the Civil War and in 1880 ran for president against Garfield. Charles Spencer Merchant (1795–1879), West Point, 1814, was a lieutenant colonel at this time. Major Lewis A. Armistead was stationed on the frontier and achieved note as an Indian fighter. Dana's news may have concerned an action against the tribes of the Southwest.

[27]David B. Hoffman (b. 1827), a physician from Bainbridge, New York, came to California in 1849. After 1853 he was coroner and postmaster of San Diego, served two terms in the state legislature, was a field surgeon during the Civil War, and later became president of a railroad.

gentleman by name of ——, a man of extr. acquirements & knowledge of Belles lettres & science, in all languages. His English is scientifically good. Valuable infn. fr. him as to history & condition of Calif.

FRID. EV. 26. AUG.   Enter Golden Gate again. Fort, Light hs., Alcatrass Island, Angel Island, Sausolito Bay, clipper ships at anchor, town, opp. coast of Contra Costa. Oriental Hotel again.

SAT. AUG. 27.   After full consultn., start for the mines & Big Trees & Yosemite Falls. Steamer to Stockton. Almost perpetual fogs & chilly winds in S. Fr. Bay. Over coat necessary. Stop at Benicia — small place — a failure — sustained only by U. S. Barracks & drydock for Pan. Co.'s boats. Up the S. Joaquin to Stockton. At Stockton take coach for Bear Valley & Mariposa. All day fr. Stockton to little Sp[anish] mining town of Hornitos. Excep. hot & dusty, all day. Sometimes not see the horses fr. driver's seat. Miserable looking country — parched up. Thousand sq. miles of dust, struggling herbage, no trees, no grass, no flowers, no birds, no water! Windmills everywhere, to raise water — only mode — whether for house use or for irrigation. Artif. irrig. fr. May to October.

High country very healthy — but low lands about the river beds — called "River Bottoms" subject to fever & ague, & a bilious fever known as Tulare fever, fr. Tulare Lake, or Tule fever, fr. the *Tule,* a kind of reed that covers the low river lands of S. Joaquin &c. Cross the Stanislaus, the Tuolumne, & the Merced. The Stanislaus by a bridge built of timber brot fr. Puget Sound to S. Fr. & thence here. Cheaper than to get fr. mountains of Calif. (comment on timber of Cal.) At the Tuolumne, a ferry, & at the Merced a tavern known as Snelling's (?), a place of very bad repute — frequented by fighters, & murders very common. I mean *free-fight* killings. Three men killed here in fight, short time since. Later, was a fandango, & 3 men wounded — few words & revolvers & knives. If killed, only say "ought to have been in better luck".

Usual Calif. rig, out of cities, is belt with a revolver in holster & a knife in sheath, both suspended fr. belt. Every rider & most coach travellers so prepared.

Now in region of gold digging — placer diggings. Country *rooted up,* as by beaver, on all sides. Here & there men digging, or washing out, with washbowls & rockers &c. Stage coach & 6 horses & 18 passengers turn out, on highway, for a man digging gold in a trench!

Night at Hornitos — very hot. Chiefly Mex. & Chinese here.

Chief topic in Mariposa Co. is "*The* Col.". The Col.'s mines, & the Col.'s mill, & the Col.'s struggles with the Merced Co. Half the personable men are colonels, but *"the Col."*, fr. Stockton to the Sierra Nevada, is Frémont.[28]

Breakfast at Bear Valley. Small & increasing village, created by Frémont's mining operations. F's house in the outskirts of the village. Here meet Col. —— a polit. & business friend of Frémont, & others. Take horse & ride to F.'s mines. Mountainous country, mountains nearly bare of grass & trees, except scrub oaks & small pines — a kind of chaporal. Dreary looking, but full of gold quartz, the famous Mariposa Grant, one of the 3 richest in the world. Meet Frémont on the mountain side, on a trail, just mounting his horse, wh. was tied to a bush. Introduced myself. Cordial welcome. Ride with him to his quartz mills, "Benton Mills".[29] Has dammed the Merced River, & has two mills & building a 3d, & one steam mill.

Returned to his house & lunch. Mrs. Frémont,[30] daughter, Miss Lilly, about 16, & sons, Charles, 8, Frank, 4, both bareheaded, sunburnt, hardy courageous boys — full of the speech & habits of the back woods. Frank rides mule to town. Before he cd. have a watermelon, was obliged to sing a song —

> "Oh don't you remember sweet Betsy fr. Pike.
> She came over the mountains with her brother Ike.
> She'd 2 shanghai roosters, & one spotted hog,
> A pair of brown heifers & one yellow dog.
> Tu ral lal &c. &c.

F.'s house beautifully situated, on slope, plenty water, well shaded with trees, only shaded house I've seen in Cal., — view of Sierra Nevada, in distance.

TU. 30TH. AUG. Started on horseback for the Sierra Nevada, with a guide — one Biddle Boggs, who knows the country — he also mounted, saddle bags, 2 blankets apiece. Very dusty & hot — downright beat of sun on head — dust in mouth & eyes & ears — cloud of dust after each horse. Dinner at Mariposa, Co. town, house of people named Hays (?) nice

---

[28]John Charles Frémont (1813–1890), whose name Dana spelled "Freemont," unsuccessful Republican candidate for president in 1856, had explored California in 1843 and held large grants, rich with gold, along the Merced River. He was to serve as a general officer during the Civil War, but without notable success. At this time he was unquestionably one of the most important men in the West.

[29]The mills were named after Frémont's father-in-law and longtime patron, Thomas Hart Benton (noted earlier).

[30]Mrs. Frémont, formerly Jessie Benton (1824–1902), married Frémont in 1841. She assisted him in writing the accounts of his explorations and in all the crises of his career. After 1871 she wrote regularly for popular periodicals.

Massach[usetts] people. Mariposa Gasette, Holmes editor, — 2500 subscribers. Abt. 2 P. M. horses again. Even the trail in pine forest so dusty that ride far behind my guide — not like to follow a rabbit on a trail, for the dust lies thick under leaves or stones. At length, coveted shade of Pine Forest, mountain sides & streams of running water. Water grateful to man & horse. I drink no spirit — only cold tea in flask, or brook water. Stop at a lonely house, where only a shockingly deformed, hunch back young woman, & get water melon — how refreshing! Graceful, unsurpassable manner in wh. she declines pay. Natural lady! American.

Grows dark, trail dim, no moon — lose trail, light match to find trail, obliged to stop — find nice running stream, the Can. . ., & little grass, & camp there. Tether the horses — build fire in stump of tree. Lie down, saddle bags for pillow, blankets, & look up into clear sky & stars. Delightful. No rain for 6 mos., earth dry, mountain air neither hot nor cold — & so very pure! Sleep sound.

Guide stupid, no prov. laid in, but bottle of quince preserves fr. Mrs. Frémont — eat that. Boggs' only topic is Col. Frémont, Mrs. Frémont, & the young ladies, & the trip they made to the Yosemite last May. Miss Nina & Miss Lilly &c.

Rose early, bath in the brook, horses, & on to Clark's. Clark an intellt. hunter & woodsman, who has camp here, near Big Trees, on South Fork of the Merced.

Breakfast with him. Indian Camp by his. Indians go off to get venison & trout for our dinner, & we go to the trees. Go on horseback, Clark our guide — abt. 5 miles off.

Measured one tree, bark gone — fr[om] fire, & it measured 97 feet circ. If allow for bark, wd. be 103 f. or 104. Measured about 1 f. above ground, & clear of roots. Its lowest branch is about 160 f. fr. ground, & about 3 or 4 f. in diameter. One tree, lying on ground, inside all rotted out, bark & shell remaining, rode through it, sitting upright in saddle, — about 40 f. of trunk remaining, in length. Another tree, standing, burnt into, rode into the cavity, turned horse round & rode out. Names put on some trees. Dr. Gwin named one for himself, wh. a zealous Republican tore off, & substituted name of Horace Greeley.[31] Agreed to name the 97 f. tree the "Giant Humboldt", & put up on it this card — "This tree is dedicated to the memory of Baron Humboldt, & is named the 'Giant Humboldt' — Aug. 31. 1859, Rich. H. Dana, Jr., Galen Clark, Biddle Boggs".[32] To save

[31]William McKendree Gwin (1805–1885), whose name Dana spelled "Gwyne," was Democratic senator from California, 1850–1861. Greeley's weekly editions of the *New York Tribune* had a wide circulation in the West and was, of course, Republican in politics.

[32]Friedrich H. A. Humboldt (1769–1859), famous naturalist and author of *Cosmos* (1845–1862), had just died, and Dana's dedication was meant to show a seriousness which would prevent people from defacing the tree with merely popular sentiments.

it from sport of wits & politicians. Another fallen tree, 167 f. long, abt. 33 f. diameter at base, & 4 f. diameter at end — broken off — like stranded ship — named by Mrs. Frémont — the Fallen Monarch.

Big trees are of a species of the redwood, a soft porous wood, & soft dry bark — leaves like our white cedar, — evergreen.

The pine trees have a bark of pale chocolate color.

Supper at Clark's Camp. Indians brot in deer & trout. Indians lasy, sleep in open air, with fire & plain cooking on coals, & gather acorns & sugar-pine cones &c. Chief do servile work for Clark, to get food. Sleep under boughs. Bath at night & morning in the Merced, rapids over stones.

Breakfast, start for Yosemite. At Mountain Meadow, a camp of 2 brothers named Woodfall (?), & a China woman to cook. Been a grissley bear here last night & killed 3 pigs. The men been out after her.

Just before sundown, reached the high rocks that overhang the Yosemite Valley — "Inspiration Rock" &c. View of Valley beneath & Bride Veil Falls. Rocks over 2000 f. of perpend. height — bold, clear of trees, rising right from Valley.

Ride down into the Valley, slowly, sun-down, twilight, moonlight. Glorious views. One mountain, a bold perpend. bluff, white stone, abt. 2500 f. high, called El Capitan, but by the Indians — Tu-toch-a-nu-lah. Arrive at the camp, at abt. 8 o'ck. Supper — bright moonlight, star-light, in midst of mountain precipices — romantic in extreme. The Sisters, "Udola, Tulula" — very high.

Party of young mechanics fr. Stockton, camped near us, each a horse & blankets, a pack mule with cooking app. & stores — 13 in all — sensible, well behaved men, making a sensible trip to see Falls, Big Trees &c.

SEP. 1. Excursion up the Valley. The Vernal Falls & Nevada Falls. These are the Merced. The falls on sides of Valley, are snow falls, & all dry in summer, except the "Bridal Veil", wh. is small. Yosemite is dry now. In spring & winter, all the valley full of sound of falling water. Also visited a lake of green water, fr. wh. high mountains ascend almost perpendicularly.

Indians been out & speared trout, sold to us. Beautiful evening. Camp fires of whites & Indians. Indians gathering berries & acorns. Make a flour of the acorns.

Yosemite Valley is a long narrow valley, 12 or 15 miles long, & from ½ to ¼ miles wide, very rich & green, with the Merced winding thro' it, a deep green gentle stream, trees growing from the open ground without undergrowth, like Eng. park scenery, with the contrast of steep, awful cliffs rising on all sides directly to the sky. The most perfect valley possible. Some of the perpend. heights exceed 3000 & sev[eral] exceed 2000 f. & the falls vary fr. 800 to 2500 f. plunge.

SEP. 3. Left the valley early, wound round & over the mountain, & along the ridge, where are fine views of Valley & the highest peaks of Sierra Nevada. Rattlesnake crossed my path, jumped off horse & killed him with stones & stick, & saved his rattles. Seven in number.

Long & rather tedious day's ride — of 45 miles. At Deer Flat, a camp of mule train going to Walker's River, mules tethered, packs off, fires lighted, & people at supper. Dark, & go on by moon-light. Each of these days see tracks of brown bears — none of grisly. Go on until near 9 o'ck., & then reach North Fork of Merced, at place of man named——. Here a collection of miners — one a Supervisor of the Co., all gambling & drinking. Drink, for everything. "Take a drink on it".

(Story of the member of Legisl. fr. the district, who carried round the head of Joaquin, the robber,[33] & exh[ibite]d for 2 bits apiece, & the head sold on exn. to pay his rent for rooms.)

(Frequent stories of fights, wh. are all with revolvers, among leading men, & the only qu[estion] seem to be wh. showed most pluck, & the qu. whether both are culpable is not raised.)

"Bit" is the univ. name for the 12½ or 10 cent piece.

SEP. 4. Bath in the N. Fork, & resume journey. Stop at a cave, a dome open at top, trees growing fr. the bottom, tops of branches just reaching the level of the ground. Leave the Coulterville trail on the right, and go over the ridge, the famous "Gantry's Gulch" on the left, & the ridges of Sierra Nevada beyond, — & before us — Mt. Bullion, & the hills of Frémont's Grant in Mariposa. (Gulch, is a narrow deep ravine.)

Reach Fremont's Mills at 3 P. M. — rest, & reach his house at a beautiful sunset. Delightfully refreshing warm bath & change of clothes — (my carpet bag brot up fr. Bear Valley Tavern). Supper & delightful ev.

(A woman here is cook who lived with me sev. months, named Mary *Collins* (?).[34]

SEP. 5. Spend the day with Fremont, visiting his mines & shafts. Specimens of quartz.

Frémont's energy & industry — his own chemist & engineer — his conflict with the Merced Co., drawn up in battle array, for three days, revolvers & knives, & one word wd. put all into a blase of firearms. His courage & dogged resolution prevail. His victory over all obstacles.[35] All the country accord to him these qualities in a remarkable degree.

[33]Joaquin Murietta, notorious highwayman, had been killed a few years earlier.

[34]It has been noted earlier that Dana lived with various native girls when he was on the coast in 1835–1836.

[35]After numerous challenges, Frémont's title to his rich Mariposa property (valued by some at the time as worth $10 million) was confirmed by the U. S. Supreme Court in 1855.

Courage & spirit of Mrs. Frémont – her influence over people, & power of creating enthousiasm in all work.

Take even. coach for Hornitos. Hot, but much less dusty, as wind ahead. Night at Hornitos.

SEP. 6. Coach at midnight for Stockton. Recross Merced, Tuolumne & Stanislaus & enter Stockton at 2 P. M.

All tell me that this dry, soil-less country, in the winter & spring is knee deep in grass & flowers – a garden. Miss Frémont gathered 21 diff. specimens of wild flowers in January.

Election in a few days. All the country placarded by advertisement bills of candidates – announcing themselves for diff. offices – posted on trees & houses, & along the trails.

Much of the placer mining done by Chinese. 2500 Chinese in Maraposa Co. alone.

Stockton, on a dead level, not on the S. Joaquin, but on a slue, or (set-up) fr[om] the S. Joaquin, the banks & marshes filled with rank growth of tule. River & slue wind 7 miles in 1½. Called "City of Windmills", (fr. gr. number of windmills for raising water).

Steamer [for] S. Fr[ancisco] at 4 P. M. & reach S. Fr. next day, Sep. 7, early. Great change fr. extr. heat of interior to cold of the Bay. Change all clothing – danger of rheum. & fever if not change clothing. Mt. Diabolo & the islands of the Bay. Coast Range.

Oriental Hotel again. Mrs. Frémont & children there. Also Bayard Taylor & wife – he on a lecture excursion.

Dine with [J. B.] Felton again. *Present,* Judge McAllester of U. S. C. C't., his son Hall McAllester, Judge Baldwin[36] of Supr., C't. of Cal., Mr. —— formerly M[ember of] C[ongress] fr. Ohio, [Levi] Parsons & Whitcomb (Judge M.'s story of Webster & the "demurrer" to a Bill for an acct., by an old man, ag[ainst] the B'k. of Geo.)[37]

S. Fr. a great fruit & flower market. Glutted with fruits – peaches, pears, melons & grapes – of the largest richest & sweetest kind. Hortic. show, & great stories of the rapid growth & productiveness of trees & shrubs & vines. Can raise fruits & flowers in open air in ev. m[onth] in the year. Great int. & pride in the cultivn. of fruits & flowers.

---

[36]Matthew Hall McAllister (1800–1865) was U. S. circuit judge in California, 1855–1862. His son is noted earlier. Joseph Glover Baldwin (1815–1864), frontier humorist and jurist, settled in California in 1854, served on the state Supreme Court, 1858–1862, and then retired to private practice. He published *The Flush Times of Alabama and Mississippi* in 1853.

[37]This parenthesis, like several which appear in the *Journal,* is a memorandum Dana has made to himself of a story he has heard.

Since Vig. Commee. & triumph of "People's Party", S. Fr. a quiet & well governed city — been out all hours, & fewer signs of crime & dissipation than New York.

Election to-day. Good order at polls. Only want is a Reg[istration] Law, & all wd. be easy & peaceable. All business suspended, & best people make point to go to polls & give their day to it. Bad people wd. make a holiday anyhow — & best people must agree for one. Still, great amt. of drinking near the polls, at exp. of candidates & pol. parties.

Desire to see two things wh. must leave unseen for want of time. The Almeden Quicksilver mines, & the hydraulic mining in the North, near Folsom & Nevada. Seen almost all else.

European hours in S. F. — dine late, lunch.

2. At Sea and Hawaii

SAT. SEP. 10. 10 A. M. set sail, in the noble clipper ship "Mastiff" for Sandwich Islands. This ship is bound to Hong Kong, stops at the Islands to land mail & few passengers, & has 175 Chinese steerage passengers on board. Wm. O. Johnson, master. His wife on board. Cabin passengers — Geo. Clifford of S. F., merchant — (br. of Gov. Clifford of Mass.), Chas C. Harris, Esq., of Honolulu, a lawyer, young Mr. Jas. H. C. Richmond of N. Bedford, going to Honolulu to enter into business, & a Jew (?) named Shanburn.[38] Ship of about 1200 tons, & said to be one of the best Am. ships afloat, & capt. a high reputation.

Beats out of harbor exceed. well. Quick in stays. Last view of S. Fr. hills, islands, forts, lighthouses, Golden Gate — & its fogs & strong N. E. winds.

First three days of passage; the coast fogs & cold hold on. Then clear, fair, Pacific Ocean weather, & light winds.

Enjoy highly life in a sailing vessel — so much better than a steamer. No noise, no smell of oil, no tremor, as still as country after city, & the int[erest] in the sails, winds, duties of seamen &c. Become intimate with Capt. Johnson. German by birth, well educated — a library on board wh. cost some 12 or $1500, & all other things to match — plate, cutlery, furniture, provisions &c. The ship his home & his idol & chief subject of conversation. He owns ¼ of her, & took her fr. the stocks, built in Donald McKay's best manner.[39]

Chief Mate is —— Bailey of N. Bedford, Second Mate Johnson of Salem, 3d Mate a Frenchman, & crew of abt. 20 men. All newest fashions of rigging.

Capt. J. & wife very fond of animals — has on board a large Engl. mastiff, of 125 lbs. weight, "Watch", two Engl. spaniels, two spaniel pups, a King Charles spaniel — two tame Kangaroos, two walloughbees (?)[40] a Java cat, pigeons, hens &c., a cow & calf, large number pigs &c. "Boy Tap" to take care of stock. "You Tap". "You Tap". "Kangaroos had no hay". "That dog no water". Constant attention to these animals. The mastiff follows Johnson everywhere, a perfect guard.

[38]John Henry Clifford, Governor of Massachusetts in 1853, has been noted earlier. None of the others mentioned have been identified.

[39]Donald McKay (1810–1880), Boston shipyard director, was a master builder of Clipper ships, which he first began producing in 1850.

[40]Dana's question mark is over the spelling of walaby, the Australian miniature kangaroo.

Interest myself & recall old times by watching working of ship, & work on rigging. Songs of sailors. Go below. Chinese burn lamps & smoke — Capt. J. forbids it.[41]

THURSDAY. SEP. 15. At abt. 5 P. M., quiet afternoon, good breese, all easy & happy, work going on. Capt. J. "Here, Mr. Bailey — fire in the ship!" Startled all. Smoke immediately pours up after ventilator & hatch. Call all hands aft. Rig hose to pump. Mates jump down the hatch aft, in the Lasarette (?)[42] & smoke pours up in volumes, stifling. Officers spring up & report that between-decks all on fire, & hay taken fire in lower hold. Capt. J. immed. gives up all hope of saving ship, & stops pump & all hands go to work in clearing boats for lowering. "Is there powder on board?" "Yes". Capt. J. has gone below to get it. Magasine brot up & thrown overboard, & Capt. J. armed with revolver. Chinese are alarmed & rush for the boats — beat them back by belaying pins & threats, & presenting pistol. Steward shows presence of mind & stands by Capt. Gig is lowered first. Mrs. Johnson comes up, prepared to go in boat.

A British ship has been in sight the last 2 days, sailing with us. She is sev. miles astern. Set our ensign Union down, & half mast & back after yards. Capt. J. asks me to see his wife safely in boat. She goes over side on rope. Ch[ief] M[ate] & I help her in. Chinese rush for the boat — beaten back — take in Chinese women, Cabin passengers, & few Chinamen, who rush in. Excellent boat. 2d Mate takes command, 4 oars — & I help at one. Pull over 2 miles & put all safely on board the Engl. ship. Ship Achilles, bound to Sydney. Calmness of Mrs. Johnson.

Soon, 2 more boats come fr. the Mastiff, each full of Chinamen, one in charge of 3d Mate — other has no officer, — so I volunteer & take charge of the boat, with a steering oar. Pull for the Mastiff. Smoke pouring out, but flames not burst out yet. Put her alongside, & take in Chinese, hanging fr. the rails & ropes & chains. Great noise & attempts to get in, but as they cannot swim are afraid to jump in. Keep boat well off — & get her full. Men lie in bottom, & crouch down. Order 'em aft. Gentle, & ready to obey. Put them all safely on board the Achilles. My boat leaks & keep one hand bailing. Put off again for the Mastiff.

Five boats now employed — 4 of Mastiff & one of the Achilles, under charge of her 2d mate. These boats all flying to & fro. Remarkable that with the alarm, & so many (175) ignorant, useless men, not knowing our language, unaccustomed to boats — struggling for life — we should have launched every boat safely, none swamped or stove, & loaded, transported & put on board all — everyone — without an accident.

[41]The last two sentences in this entry appear to have been added at a later time.
[42]The lazaret is the storage space between decks in some merchant ships.

When got alongside last time found all the Chinese had been taken off. Boats now take off baggage of passengers & crew. We had taken none before, for afraid to leave the deck & boats, lest Chinese take them.

Steward saves all my luggage with trifling exceptions,[43] as it was all in my room on deck & that was to windward. Nothing cd. be got from below or fr. lee side. Sailors house being on deck, save most of their clothes. Capt. J. saves the specie, $76,000, in gold, in boxes, & Ch[ief] M[ate] takes it to the Achilles, also 2 chronometers. The Capt. saves nothing of his own. Steward saves some trunks for him & for Mrs. Johnson. (Steward's name is Edw. Trofater.) Most of luggage in upper house is saved.

Now attempts to save the animals. The cat & one pup are smothered. Cow & one hog too large. The 2 wallabees are smothered. Save the two Kangaroos, all the large dogs, & number of poultry, pigs & pigeons. Capt. J. asks me to come on board & have a *calm conference* to see if anything more can be done. I do so. Very much fatigued by exertions in my boat, especially the steering oar, & head & lungs full of smoke. Capt. J. says all betw. decks a mass of fire, & will soon burst out thro' deck. Cannot get out longboat. Been trying it while we were in boats — too few men — & now of no use. All other boats out, & nothing more can be got fr. deck. Has been trying to get at the bread, but cannot cut thro' the deck. (Carpenter of no use — as seemed to lose his powers). Nor cd. it have been done — as too near fire. Nothing more can be done. My boat is full of luggage, & push off again — put all safely on board — 2 boats remain by side of the Mastiff — & Capt. J., the Chief Mate, Steward, are the last to leave her — Not until ordered — Capt. last to leave.

Flames burst out thro' deck, at main mast. Now, nearly dark, & flames glow over the Ocean. Mrs. J. anxious lest her husband stay too long. Two figures on the quarter deck. Now disappear & the last two boats come off. Capt. J. comes on board, & the poor, noble Mastiff is abandoned.

Flames mount the rigging, catch the sails, & all a mass of fire. Main & missen mast fall. Foremast stands long, then drops, & only a burning hull.

Capt. Hart of the Achilles, a generous, frank British sailor, takes Capt. J. by hand. Now the excitement over & his duty done — the magnitude of the loss comes over him, & he says over & over — "My ship Mastiff! My ship Mastiff! Is it possible she is gone!" Like the mourning of David over Absalom.

All agree in a sense of the wonderful nature of our relief. Just 6.45 P. M. when Johnson leaves his ship. Not over 2 hours fr. time alarm first given, until she is an uninhabitable mass of fire — yet all saved. If no

---

[43]One of the exceptions was the original draft of this portion of the *Journal*, which went down with the ship, requiring rewriting up to this point.

ship in sight, could not have been saved. Boats not hold half the people.[44]
(Was abt. 1000 lbs. bread & 6 bbls. water, on deck.) On delib. reflection
believe that very doubtful if could have saved one life. Chinese wd. have
been restrained with greater difficulty fr. the boats.[45]

Place of fire was Lat. 30.46 N. Long. 128.35 West. Achilles gets under
way again, & leaves the burning wreck of the poor Mastiff. For hours,
we see the bright light over the Ocean.

All feel the kind Providence of God that we are saved fr. fearful
suffering & death, & by common consent we have relig. service in the
Cabin. I read passages fr. Scripture & portions of the Service. Thanks-
givings & Prayers fr. the Service at sea. (Conv. with Capt. J. last night
on board the Mastiff.)

Ascertained that one Chinaman is lost. He went below to save his box
of money & was suffocated. All counted, & found only one missing.

Capt. Hart makes generous prov. for our comfort. He has his wife on
board, & 3 passengers. Newman & wife, & Ryan — all Irish. Hart & wife
are English.

Ch. Mate is Jarvis, Englishman from Essex, & 2d m. is Harley, Scotchman fr. Lanark. Capt. & both mates are good sailors, & solid, hardy men.
Achilles a ship of 500 tons, fully loaded with wheat, betw. decks full,
bound fr[om] S. Fr. to Sydney Austr. Our crew go forward, & no place
for the 174 Chinese but the open deck. Only 5 Chinese women, & they
huddle together under the steps aft. Rest get on spars, boats, gratings &c.,
& what with blankets saved, & old sails wh. Hart gives them, make
themselves as comf. as possible.

Very little rice on board, & give them boiled wheat, fr. the A.'s cargo,
& bread, & allowance of water.

Hart agrees to bear off for S[andwich] Islands.

SEPR. 18. Get the N. E. trades, & go on as fast as we can, lest get
short of water or bread. All sails set.

SEP. 22. THURSD. One week since the fire. Still it is the only subject
deep in our thoughts. Poor Johnson thinks & talks of scarcely anything
but his poor ship, & a kind Providence that gave us a ship in sight, — wh.
alone saved us. He fully feels that, & may also well pride himself on
having saved ev[ery] life, all the money, without an accident or mishap.[46]

[44]Dana excised the following lines: "& no water or bread would have been put in
the boats, for the fire took between decks, probably no efforts cd. have got out the
bread or water."

[45]Dana excised the following lines: "even if boats safely launched & filled, what
cd. we have done without bread & water, 500 miles fr. land?"

[46]Dana wrote up an account of the *Mastiff's* loss for the *Daily Alta California,*
where it was published on November 5, 1859. The piece was reprinted in the *Boston
Weekly Courier,* November 18, 1859.

We live very well on board the Achilles, the cooking good, provisions abundant, & the most cordial hospitality. All like Hart. In heavy seas & rain, Chinese get wet. Entertainment 3 times a day, to see water, bread & food served out to them. Queer [old] cove of a Chinaman, in Mr. Cifford's hat, whom we call "Clifford". The laughing girl & the small footed woman.

TUESD. SEP. 27. At daylight, see island of Molokai, on port hand, & soon Oahu is right ahead. Land high, & often rising to mountains. Pass down Channel between Molokai & Oahu. Diamond Head, a bold picturesque point, at S. E. end of Honolulu Roads. Pilot boats, rowed by bare headed Kanakas. Come to anchor in outer roads. Coral reefs, with bright surf breaking over them, between us & shore. Go ashore in Kanaka boat. Lateen sail.⁴⁷ Glorious surf each side of channel. Great many ships inside, chiefly whalers. Honolulu reminds me of S. Barbara, except the reefs, & the feature that the hills behind are rent by a deep valley, through wh. the trade winds blow. Town larger & more Am[erican] than I expected, abt. 14000 inhab. native & foreign. Lower part looks like any Am. seaport town.

Ex[aminatio]n of crew before Judge Platt, Am. Consul. No suff[icient] proof of stealing ag[ainst] any.⁴⁸ Excitement in the town on our news.

Judge [C. C.] Harris takes me, Capt. J. & wife, & all the dogs but the K[ing] Ch[arles] spaniel, wh. was lost or stolen after landing, to his house, up the valley — fine prospect on seaward & landward. Open sea, & high picturesque defile of valley. Delightful air, clear blue sky, trade wind clouds.

WED. SEP. 28. Call & deliver letters of introduction. King is absent. Trouble about his shooting Mr. [Neilson]⁴⁹. Call on Prince Lot Kamehameha, his brother, who is Minister of Interior, Mr. Wylie, Min. of For. Affairs, Mr. Gregg, Min. of Finance, Mr. Bates, D. Att'y., Ch. Justice Allen, Judge Robertson, R. S. Davis, Rev. Mr. Damon, Seamen's Chaplain, Mr. Smith, Missionary, & some merchants.⁵⁰

⁴⁷The lateen is a triangular sail extended by a long yard, slung to the mast.

⁴⁸The Chinese passengers on the *Mastiff* were returning home with savings earned in America and accused crew members of the *Achilles* of robbing them.

⁴⁹King Kamehameha IV inherited the throne from his father in 1855 and was to rule until 1863. The government was a constitutional monarchy, established by his father in 1840. Mr. Neilson, who was the King's personal secretary, recovered from his wounds. Presumably the shooting took place over a dispute concerning Neilson's secretarial duties.

⁵⁰Two members of this group have been identified. Prince Lot succeeded his brother and reigned as Kamehameha V, 1863–1872. David L. Gregg (d. 1868), former Joliet, Illinois, newspaper editor and state senator, was U. S. Minister to Hawaii, 1853–1858. President Lincoln later made him Receiver of Public Monies in Nevada.

Beautiful evenings, little showers, but not frequent, & otherwise *always* fine weather, except a few S. turns in winter. Thermometer even thro' the year.

Fruits — oranges, bananas, taro, cocoa nuts, breadfruit & guava, potatoes &c. Plenty of trees, flowers & grass. Contrast with S. Francisco.

SUNDY. OCT. 2. Last 4 days busy aiding Capt. Johnson in his business, by friendly advice &c. Time for few calls. Call on Dr. Armstrong, Min. of Instruction,[51] & on the R. Cath. Bishop. He & his clergy live in the Church yard, where all the mission buildings are. Contrast betw. this system, & that of Prot. missionaries in their families, at diff. houses — advantages & disadv. of each. Large R. Cath. Church of stone. Large Native Ch. of stone, abt. same sise. Attend service in Native Ch., Dr. Armstrong preaches in native tongue. Singular congregation. Sixty horses at door. Bonnets of all fashions of 60 years past — curiosity shop — natives awkward in shoes — only wear them Sundays. Look better bareheaded & barefooted, with flowers in hair, as on week days. Several chiefs in Church — but all [wear] the European dress. Women wear usually only one garment, a thin gown, not stiffened.

Week days women (except upper class) wear one gown, no shoes or bonnet, almost always wreaths on head. Men wear jacket & trowsers. Occasionally a man with only a malo round waist. Many young women very pretty. Many, especially older, walk like men.

All native women ride astride, with long flowing robes, & bare heads — look well. Upper class use side saddles. Almost every native seems to have a horse, whether man or woman — average cost of their horses $5. Many houses & walls are of stone — coral. Color of ground is brown, agreeable to the eye — so of the stone — like England. Roads hard, very little dust. Am much interested in the people, like them. Climate perfect, I should judge. Every day been delightful.

Sund. aftern., went to Bethel. Mr. Damon preached on the loss of the Mastiff to a good congregation.

Spent an evening with a female chief, Pauwahe, married to Mr. Bishop, an Am. merchant. She is an interesting, well educated & well bred woman of 27 years.[52]

Called on Judge Borden, U. S. Commissioner.[53] He & the For. Sec.

[51]Richard Armstrong (1805–1860) came from Dickenson College to the Islands as a missionary in 1832. He had been an official of the Hawaiian government since 1847.

[52]Charles Reed Bishop (1822–1915), from Glen Falls, New York, became a successful banker and philanthropist. In 1850 he married Bernice Pauahi Paki (c. 1832–1884), a high chieftess of the royal blood.

[53]James Wallace Borden (1810–1867) was a prominent member of the Indiana Bar, came to the Islands in 1857 and stayed until 1864 as U. S. Minister. He returned to Indiana as a judge of the criminal court.

arranged for me a private interview with the King, for Monday next. The
King has shot a man, his private Sec., not fatally — cause unknown — but
people seem to sympathise with the King, regretting his loss of temper.
The King is considered a man of superior intelligence & of honorable
character.

Rode out to the Pali, a precipice, from wh. Kamehameha I pitched
his enemies.[54] The scenery beautiful & picturesque. About 5 miles from
the town. Deep gorge in the mountains, valley on each end, & blue sea
on each end — the height of the tops of the mountains 1800 & 2000 feet —
very striking.

HONOLULU OCT. 3, 1859.   One ev. last week called on Pauwahe (Mrs.
Bishop) a native female chief — well educated & well mannered &
interesting — as dark as a mulatto. Husband a merchant — rich. She is
treated with reverence by the natives, & even whites treat her with some
deference, in social circles. Entitled to seat in House of Nobles. Her
gr[and] f[ather] was a naked savage. Called on Ch. J. [E. H.] Allen —
laid up of the "Maui fever" or "Boohoo fever" — a kind of short infl.
rheumatic fever, wh. has come in here within 5 or 6 years & attacks
strangers almost always. Not dangerous, but painful & depressing. The
wife [Mrs. Allen[55]] an intelligent young lady fr. Bangor — talk over Prest.
Woods of Bowdoin, & the G. B. Emerson family &c.

Called on Rev. Mr. Smith, an Am. Missionary — very intell. wife. (All
say that the Missiony. wives, as gen. thing, more intellectual than
the men).

Hardly a native man or woman but owns a horse—average cost 4 & $5
each — & are constantly riding. Women bare headed, flowers in hair,
riding astride, with long strips of cloth covering limbs, & coming nearly to
ground.

Last battle ground betw. Kamehameha I & rebels, between the Pali &
the falls — very pretty place.

Water brot in open runs, by road-side, from Nuuanu Valley.

Sunday morning early (Oct. 2) passing by a Missionary's house, heard
the family, at prayers, singing one of the popular hymns of New England,
wh. they introduced here. How it carried me back to the early hist. of the
Am. Missions among these savages, & the changes now — , when Honolulu
is a civilised place.

(In journal sent home)[56] *Sund.* morn. to Native Church. 200 feet

---

[54]Kamehameha I, who reigned from 1795 to 1819, consolidated the Islands under
a single rule and in the process had to subdue a variety of local chiefs.

[55]Formerly, Mary Harrod Hobbs.

[56]For a brief interval at this point the *Journal* contains some repetitive entries, but
there seems to be enough difference between the various versions — some of which
Dana kept with him, some of which he sent home — to justify reproducing all of them.

long (?) stone — full of people — elevated seat for the King, he not there. Curiosity shop of bonnets, — in ev. style of 60 years past. Natives look better bareheaded & barefooted than in shoes & bonnets — especially awkward in shoes. People take no part in the service. Music by small choir, prayers & sermon by preacher (Dr. [Richard] Armstrong) & people sit & stand in prayer, at option, & sit all the rest of time. *Mere listeners.* No outward app[earance] of devotion — think it fault of clergy. As soon as benediction *began,* they begin a rush for doors, & minister turns directly round, & no effort is made to keep up any outward form or show of devotion. Confident that a liturgy & responsive service would take with these people. They must be *actors.*

Bethel — good congr. of leading whites. Wylie, Bates, &c. ([D. L.] Gregg is Catholic) & fair sermon on loss of Mastiff. Large Sunday School — well ordered, & plenty of books.

R. Cath. Cathedral large stone Ch. No seats, with plenty pictures &c. Great many Kanakas stay in the yard — all the recess. Two instructions & confessions in afternoon. Intellig. & respectable German priest, speaking English.

Kanaka women only one garment, often of thin material — must be more fav. to development than our tightened loads of clothing.

The washing is done in open streams, on stones — streams run along the outside of the village — lined with women washing — sometimes scarcely any dress on. Riding out to Pali, saw one woman bathing in a little pool, taking her bath, by road side — held her gown before her as we passed.

The King's schooner came in sight early Frid. morn. (Sep. 30) & he landed under salute & flags raised, but [went] privately to his palace. In retirement on acct. of his shooting Mr. Neilson, his secretary. (Causes not known, but people disposed to uphold the King).

The libel suit by Hart for his salvage on the $83,000.[57] Libel filed Thursd. Answ. filed Frid. morn., hearing Frid., & decision Saturday. Montgomery (Irishman) counsel for Hart, & Blair (½ br. of F. P. B.) for Johnson.[58] Case very imperfectly managed, both on law & facts, by the counsel. Robertson, J[udge], a sensible man, few words, & good kn[owledge] of law; tho' never saw a law book until middle life — & been a

---

[57]Captain Hart of the *Achilles* was suing for salvage rights on the *Mastiff* and her cargo, including the specie, which Dana earlier calculated at $76,000. Largely through Dana's efforts, the claim was reduced by Judge Robertson to one fifth of what was demanded.

[58]Mr. Blair, whose father, James Blair, was Attorney General of Kentucky, 1796–1816, was half-brother to Francis Preston Blair (1791–1876), member of President Jackson's "Kitchen Cabinet" and editor of the Washington *Globe.*

common sailor. Gives ten per-cent for salvage, (Achilles in no *peril,* & no extr. service, & the owners of the money not to pay for the humanity &c.).

MON. OCT. 3. [CONT.] By applic. of Judge Borden, & the intervention of sev. friends in office, King agrees to give me a private audience at 12.30 to-day. Go to palace — dress coat &c. House of Nobles in special session — in uniform, blue riband across breast & some in milit. dress. The Old Governor of Oahu ——, who once was a naked savage — dignified old man — Wylie, [D. L.] Gregg &c. & 3 or 4 Kanaka Chiefs. Hs. is mixed of Native Chiefs & Whites holding by appointment of King. (Bishop & Armstrong were added to the Nobles to-day).

The King, a tall, well made man of abt. 25, good looking, dignified & easy manners, & makes very agreeable impression both as to intellect & character. His friends say he is a true nobleman by nature. Speaks Engl. as native tongue. Interview of ½ hour. All stand when he comes in, & remain so until he asks us to sit. All the etiquette of royalty is observed. Guards at palace door &c. (Queen is at Maui.) Speaks of my book, of his visit to America & Europe, of the friendly aspect of U. S. Govt. &c. (Refers to Noah & Daniel, as the Websters of the anecdote.)

Palace very fair suites of rooms, high & well furnished. Contrast of few lasy Kanakas lying on ground, basking in sun, about the sides of the palace.

"Yankee" sails to-day (Oct. 3), Capt. & Mrs. Johnson & "Watch", & "Billy", kangaroos, the 2 Mates, "Tap" "Joe" &c.

Party this ev. at Mrs. Ch. Brewer's.[59] Musical. Very good playing on piano & violin, & good singing. This musical soiree once a month. Great int. in it. Among performers, one half-caste lady, Mrs. Coady — rich & well educated. Sings well. Mrs. Bishop there. Mrs. Allen, Mrs. Gregg &c. &c.

Call on Lt. Reynolds U. S. N. laid up with bad leg, crutches &c. Here as U. S. Naval Store keeper.[60]

A king is a king. The King here is a *power,* social as well as poli[tica]l. Not only natives but the intell. & wealthy Engl. & Am. whites have an unconsc. loyalty. The *person of a king* is superior. My having a private interv. with him, at this time — when he is in retirement, has made an impression — and almost ev. leading man claims to have been instrumental in bringing it about — & even their wives intimate to me that, "my husband saw the King &c. &c." The King is an interesting spectacle —

[59]Charles Brewer (1804–1885), sea captain and merchant, headed the Honolulu trading firm of C. Brewer and Co. In 1839 he married Martha Turner of Boston.

[60]William Reynolds (1815–1879), Antarctic explorer, had been sent to Honolulu as naval storekeeper in 1857 due to ill-health. He recovered his health, served during the Civil War, and went on to a prosperous administrative career in the Navy.

to any but a low mind, it is affecting & inspiring to see a young man struggling to maintain his Government & the supremacy of his race. It goes to your heart, & has an air of chivalry. Besides, the Govt. is a good one. Order & law are well preserved & administered — nowhere better, & education & charities sustained. Seamen are better regulated & protected ag. landsharks here than in any port in the U. States.

Visited Seaman's Home — Admirable institution. Good rooms, good table, reading room open to all Seamen — boarders or not — Shipping office attached. Stationary &c. furnished *gratis* to all seamen wishing to write home &c.

Pride of India trees planted freely here & grow fast. Tamarind trees, slow growth. Oranges plenty & sweet. Like the *taro* fried or boiled, but not the *poe.*[61] Bananas excellent & wholesome. The Lahala tree with roots from the branches — species of *pandanus.* Dr. Armstrong, Min. of instruction, takes me to see the schools. The "Royal School" for natives, taught by Mr. Morris Beckwith & a Miss Cook. Beckwith is br[other] of the principal of the Puna Ho College, & edd. at a N. E. college. 2 rooms — one for girls & one for boys — all Kanakas [natives]. Recite in geography, grammar, & arithmetic, with free use of black-boards. A girl of 15, half Kanaka & half Chinese is head scholar & assistant, a girl of intelligence & good character, named Rebecca. A very smart boy of 12 or so, full Kanaka, leads the boys class — his answers as quick as thought & face all alive. Kanakas generally find it hard to sit still, & attend — & assume very uncouth positions. Teacher says punctual in attendance.

Another school, in stone building, kept by Ingraham, for half-castes & a few whites. Mr. Armstrong says find it better to separate the full bloods fr. the half castes. Some fair drawings. Kanakas take to geography & drawing. Mimetic powers great. Yet, recitations in analysis of sentences in grammar very good — metaphysical trial.

Puna Ho. School of abt. 80 scholars, 60 or 70 of wh. are boarders, chiefly fr. the other islands. All but 4 are whites, children of missionaries, prof. men, & merchants. Very pretty spot, about 2 miles out of town, low buildings with verandahs, & well planted with trees. Day scholars come on horseback or in wagons. School of high character. About ½ girls. Girls live in building by themselves, but they recite in classes with the boys. Two daughters of [Benjamin W.] Parker, the Missionary, clever girls, are teachers. Men teachers are all graduates of N. E. colleges. Beckwith, the principal, just left, with high reputation & much beloved. The boys are carried as far as the Sophomore studies. Heard a capital recitation in Horace, under Haskell, — the grammatical analysis as good as anywhere.

[61]Here and throughout Dana misspells "poi," a food made from mashed, fermented root of the taro.

Recitation in Greek, read by the printed accent & in Continental sound of vowels. This is a school of high character, & very attractive to the pupils.

Dined with Mr. Armstrong. Fine family of children & nice large house & grounds — all his trees grown in 8 years — as is chiefly the case in Honolulu (his great admiration of Charles Sumner & desire to see him.) Usual dinner hour here is late in afternoon, 4 or 5 o'ck., & the school keeps from 10 to 3 or 3½. So the Courts, from 9 or 10 to 3 or 4.

This ev. (Oct. 4) rode to Waititi, about 6 miles fr. Honolulu, on the beach, near Diamond Head, the site of the old Honolulu, where the first navigators came, & still many native huts there — also cottages occupied by whites for sea-bathing, in mid-summer. Entered sev. huts. Natives very cordial & kindly. Mostly have but one room, & all sleep on mats, some nearly naked & some with blankets, not much better than dogs in a kennel. Yet each hut had a Bible, their only book. These are the lower class, barefooted & bareheaded, but decently clothed by day, & owning horses. Riding by moonlight, under the tall cocoa nut palms, by the sea side of Oahu!

In Honolulu are several rich Chinese, some 15 or 20 who are merchants of high standing & whose word is as good as their bond. They gave a ball to the King & Queen wh. cost $7000.

("Frisco", is the nickname of S. Francisco, among sailors & shipmasters, in the Pacific.)

Visited the prison. It is built of coral rock, well ventilated, & well adapted to the climate. The prisoners work on the public works, the roads, the reef &c. The Warden told me that the Chinese furnish far more than their quota of convicts, the foreigners (chiefly sailors) the next, & natives the least.

Attended Supr. C't. Allen C[hief] J[ustice,] & Robertson sitting, Bates arguing. Jury sit opp. the judges, & counsel sit on opp. sides of the space between.

WED. OCT. 5, 1859. Sailed at 4 P. M. in the little sch. Mary, 80 tons, to visit island of Hawaii. 54 Kanakas on board, men & women, & sev. horses & dogs. Vessel very small & very slow & excess. disagreeable. Only cabin passengers are Capt. Mallett of Waimea (Hawaii), an Englishman, & a lad named Wm. Cornwell. Improve my time in learning Kanaka. Some natives intelligent & communicative. But Kanakas sleep on deck, lie about in heaps, eat poe with fingers fr. calabashes, & seem very much like half civilised Indians. Women like squaws. Yet, no drinking no quarreling. Every evening, just at dark, one makes a prayer, & all give respectful attention.

The mate of the sch. has a Kanaka wife on board, but she sleeps & eats with the other women, & like them, is a mere squaw. The best looking man among them, a young man, I found was of a Chief family — or chief-*ish,* as they use the adjective here.

Go to leeward of Laanai. Long calms, & vessel sails very slow. One blow & heavy sea, & feel seasick, for first time for long while — think it is chiefly the smells. Poe & fish the sole food of natives on board — drink is water.

On Laanai was a settlement of Mormons, nearly opp. Lahaina, but they failed of success & have left.

OCT. 8. SAT. Becalmed all day off Lahaini. Volcanic outlines of mountains behind Lahaina — extinct craters, & broken peaks — very picturesque.

On hill is Lahainaluna, the High School for Educ. of native youths, in Hawaiian. School of high repute, & great utility — furnishes native teachers for native schools in all the islands. Founded by Am. B. C. F. M.[62]

Going into Lahaina are sev. whale ships — & some are lying there.

(Last night dreamed of W. Cedar st., & all day full of strong impressions of my home there.)

OCT. 9. Bay betw. E. & W. Maui, looks like 2 islands. East Maui is very mountainous, & green to summits. Highest is "Hale a ka Lá" — "House of the Sun". McGee's farm, rich, fertile spot. King goes there a great deal. Large extinct crater on Hale a ka Lá — sd. to be 30 miles in circumf.

Capt. Mallett & the mates, who are no friends of religion, admit the civilising influence of the Missionaries, & tell me that Sunday is very strictly observed in the islands — no cargo can be landed or recd. unless live stock, for humanity's sake. Also, the gen. extent of knowledge of reading & writing among the natives.

OCT. 10. MOND. Reach Kawaihae, on N. W. side of Hawaii, early this morning. Last night, saw light of volcano on the side of Mauna Loa, which is running into the sea.

(Spent day at Macy's on shore. Whale Ship Europa of Edgertown, Manter, Master — only 200 bbls., young & excellent fellow, on first voyage as Master, good deal discouraged.)

Temple, or great altar, built to Louó by Kamehameha I, near the landing. Large extent — a great pile of coral stones, terraced down, & large flat area on top. Spent some time there, alone — said the Creed & Te Deum on the spot once consecrated to heathen rites. Sacrifices made here.

[62]American Board of Commissioners for Foreign Missions.

At night, took native canoe, for Kailua, to stop at the outflow of the lava into the sea.

Native canoes, built of one log, outrigger, Kanaka lies out to windward on outrigger. Paddles & sails.

Delightful motion — regulated by outrigger — wh. is a keel, 4 or 5 feet to windward.

3 Kanaka men, one woman & myself. Exquisite moonlight night, steady land breese, bright stars, still water, floating along the coral reef, just clear of the surf, temperature.

About midnight, reach the outflow. The place where the lava flows into the sea, is 40 miles from the crater. The course fr. the crater is now nearly all covered over by crust of cold lava, & the stream runs under it, with here & there a vent. You see no stream of lava, until just before it reaches the sea. Place of outflow is abt. 2 miles wide. Not all flowing at once, but constantly changing. As the red hot lava plunges into the sea, it makes an explosion like a cannon, & a hissing of steam, & roar, as of surf, & clouds of steam rise up fr. the water. The sea is heated to a consid. distance. Felt it warm, to hand, & then hot. When as near as dared to go, found it as hot as cd. bear. Here, a little stream poured steadily in, there a wide thin sheet, then wd. come a large mass, breaking up all before it, & pitching into the sea, with roaring & hissing & clouds of steam. Then the places wd. cool over, the lava turn black, & the fiery mass burst out at another point. Yet the entire space is lava, black or fiery red. These changes added to the interest in watching it.

Natives a little afraid to go near — perhaps remains of superstitions. Peli, their goddess of wrath & vengeance, had her seat on the mountain, & these eruptions were her outbreaks of wrath. *Peli* is now the native word for volcano, & volcanic fires, — as our word comes fr. Vulcan.

After some 2 hours stay, released the natives fr. their unwelcome duty of keeping near the flow, & set sail for Kailua.

(My crackers saturated by smell of oil-skin in the tin boxes, sardines not to be opened by penknife, & tea with no sugar).

Sound sleep in the canoe. Its silence, & steady, quiet motion — air.

TU. OCT. 11. Reach Kailua at about 10 A. M. Large open bay. On left, near the town, are remains of the great fort built by Kamehameha I, with number of cannon still mounted. Fort of coral, & large walls thick.

Small village now — once the residence of the king, & many great chiefs. Still, a large stone house, built by a chief called "Governor Adams", now hired by the King — who sometimes comes here for a few weeks bathing & fishing &c. Two large stone churches, nearly side by side, about same sise, Protestant & Catholic. Rev. Mr. Thurston, the Missionary, has charge, & is the only survivor, with his wife, of the first company of

missionaries that came to the islands, — in 1820.[63] Is the Nestor of the
Missions. Letter to him. Find his house closed — he gone up to a small
grass-house on the hill, where he raises coffee. (Go to the lodging house
of one Travis. Find there Judge ——, circuit judge, just from a circuit
in Kona & Kaú.)

Horse & ride up to Mr. Thurston's grass house, on the hill. Venerable
old man, with long white beard. Mrs. Thurston, strong woman, masculine,
rides astride & wears spurs. Led a life of strange vicissitudes. Found all
savages here, & lived to see Xy. [Christianity] established & reigning, &
to see children & gr. children about them, & all these now left them, &
they alone. Lunched with them in their simple hut. Invited to take tea
with them in their house in the village. From this hut, on hill side, can
see that all between the hills & the beach is a lava formation, & still, in
most places, mere bare lava. On hill sides, the lava is grown over with
bushes, grass & trees, & has become extremely fertile. Chief trees are
bread-fruit, orange, mango, cocoanut, other palms, & the castor oil bush,
wh. is everywhere.

Large number of Kanakas loafing about town, — the King's boatmen &
retainers, waiting his arrival. Stories here not favorable to the King's
temperance & other morals. The Thurstons speak favorably of his natural
qualities, & think the feeling of loyalty is strong towards him — his
intelligence, impulses & manners good.

After noon, under shade of the R. C. Church, saw a priest walking, hot
day, in well worn path. Introduced myself. He speaks only French. Few
minutes, bell tolls for Vespers. Go in. Another priest, in Chancel, saying
the service. From 10 to 15 kanakas, kneeling & singing the responses.
Dim light of the Church — strange remoteness of place — universality of
the worship — effect on the feelings & imagination. After service, walk
with the priests under the shade of the walls. Both are intelligent men,
& apparently good & sincere — at least, their countenances so express.
They live in rear of the Church — what utter loneliness! Two men — no
person for 800 miles knowing their language — only kanakas to talk with.
Both well acqd. with state of the theol. questions in Europe & America.
The church has no seats — but is matted over — people sit on mats, stand
or kneel. Architecture good.

Walk up to Mr. Thurston's. Contrast of two systems. He has 3 grand-
children, walked down fr. their mother's — his daughter — Mrs. Taylor's,
to spend night & next day, bringing fruits & presents — it being the 40th

---

[63] Asa Thurston (1787–1868), Yale, 1816, Andover Theological School, 1819,
sailed for the Islands with his wife in 1819. Resident missionary for forty years, he
translated large portions of the Bible into the Hawaiian language. His wife, Lucy
Goodale Thurston (1795–1876), taught at the Academy in Bradford, Massachusetts,
until her marriage in 1819. Her autobiography was published shortly after her death.

anniversary of the marriage of their gr. parents! Protestant clergy — have families, domestic circles & attachments — duties, pleasures, trials & experiences. Their homes & families are centres & fountains of civilisation to a barbarous neighborhood. Catholic clergy, unmarried, supported on little, free fr. cares of family, able to give all time to Church. Yet without the influences of the family, which meet natives at so many points.

Before going to Mr. T.'s to tea, walked to the fort of Kamehameha, the ruins of his house, & the spot, near the cocoa nut trees, where he died, & bathe in the sea, where he so often bathed, with all his chiefs, giving audience to foreigners, as he came up dripping from the water, with only a malo on.

Is a subterranean passage fr. Mr. Thurston's house to the beach, caused by very ancient volcanic action.

WED. OCT. 12. Started early for Kealakekua. On horse, a Kanaka on foot carrying my luggage across his shoulders on a pole. Took the upper road. Passed Thurston's house, & saw him walking down to an early morning service. Passed Mrs. Taylor's house, in a high place on the hill-side, well wooded & pleasant — too early for a call.

This mountain road fr. Kailua to Kealakekua, is an earthly paradise. Never saw it exceeded. High & airy. Sea on one side. Mauna Loa[64] on the other — rich soils, tropical denseness of foliage, road shaded by trees, air fragrant with flowers, & trees rich with fruit. One wishes to break out in praises to God for his works.

Breakfast at a Capt. Johnson's, an old Californian, who has a farm for sheep & bullocks. House shaded, & plenty of fruits — oranges, bananas, fresh figs, peaches, bread fruit. Also, raises coffee.

Ride on. Spend hour at house of Rev. Mr. Thurston's son — a young man, educated at Wms. College. Married a d. of Judge Andrews of Oahu, in feeble health — rather interesting for his high spirit — doomed to death.

Lunch at house of Mr. Thomas Paris. There meet young Thurston's wife, & her father, Judge Andrews. He (Judge A.) is author of the Hawaiian dictionary & grammar, & is now employed on a larger dictionary.[65]

Little further on, call on Rev. Mr. Paris, brother of Thomas. Fine situation, near brow of the *pali*, a steep hill above Kealakekua. Spend an hour there. Several children — one d. at school at Puna Ho.

---

[64]Here and throughout Dana misspelled "Loa" as "Roa."

[65]Lorrin Andrews (1795–1868) came to the Islands as a missionary and worked there from 1828 to 1841. Before retiring in ill health in 1859 he held important government positions in Hawaii for fifteen years. His published work included *A Vocabulary of Words in the Hawaiian Language* (Lahainaluna, 1836); *A Grammar of the Hawaiian Language* (Honolulu, 1854); *A Dictionary of the Hawaiian Language* (Honolulu, 1865).

Reached top of hill that overlooks the valley of Kealakekua & the sea. Beautiful view. Very rich & green, with stretches of black lava, & Kealakekua, looking more thoroughly Hawaiian than any place I have yet seen. Just as it does in the pictures in Cook's voyages,[66] & there, across the Bay, under the cocoa nut trees, is the place where he fell.

Enter the little village of thatched huts. People look primitive & half barbarous. Yet, a church & school house, & am told a larger proportion can read & write than in the U. States. Men & children tumbling in the surf. Old man, grey hairs, comes dripping out of surf, to look at me, naked all but a little malo. Large proportion wear no trowsers, & some no shirts. Women all have a gown or chemise — barefooted & bareheaded, necklaces of beads or flowers, & garlands of flowers & berries, in hair. Many have very pretty expressions of countenance.

Only one white man here — a Capt. Cummings, a native of N. Hampshire, formerly master of whaler, has a Kanaka wife, & does all the business of the region of 20 miles round — is shop-keeper, collector, harbor master &c. Has good house, shop, wharf & tank. Only drawback here is want of water. None comes fr. above — land being porous & cavernous, fr. volcanic action. Must collect rain water in tanks. Is no trade here now, except occasionally a whaler comes in for potatoes & fresh fruits & water — for wh. C[ummings] has a huge tank & hose.

Bathe in sea. Understand why Kanaka are so good swimmers, temperature of sea so delightful, & same through the year. Shd. live much in sea, if lived here. Amphibious.

Both Johnson & Cummings have native wives. J.'s did not come to table. C.'s did, but sat & ate awkwardly — rather pretty face, & graceful, when not forced into our fashions.

THURSD. OCT. 13. So much pleased with Kealakekua (Ke ala ke Akua, the path of the Spirit) that stay all day. Take canoe & am paddled over by natives to place where Cook was killed. Beach of lava & coral, grove of cocoa-nut trees, close to water, large flat rock, on wh. sea washes a little. Here he fell.[67] There lay his boats, firing on the natives, who used stones & darts. Broke off piece of the rock. Just above the rock, is a stump of a tree, wh. the Br[itish] men of war have covered over with sheets of copper, to preserve it, with inscriptions in commemoration of Cook's death.

In the hill sides are little caves or openings where the natives used to bury their dead. Climbed up, & looked into them — saw skeletons.

Eat bread fruit at dinner. It is not eatable raw, but is boiled or baked.

[66]Editions of the *Voyages* of James Cook (1728–1779), the English explorer, were numerous. First separate publication was in two volumes in 1777. A more complete edition, in three volumes, first appeared in 1784.

[67]James Cook was killed in a petty, pointless brush with natives on February 13, 1779.

Taste is betw. bread & sweet potato. A native climbs up & gets me a cocoa nut. Milk is fresh & slightly tart. Taro is the great vegit. of these islands, for foreigners as well as natives — is to them what the potato is to Ireland. Foreigners use it boiled or baked, as vegetable, with meats. Natives chiefly as poe.

Hire a canoe & three men, to take me to Milorii. Start late in afternoon. Dripping natives, looking on. *Aloha.*

No trade winds felt on this side of the islands — but alternate land & sea breeses.

Grows dark & cloudy & wind ahead & moon not yet up. So natives land & beach the canoe, about 10 P. M., & go to a collection of huts, at a place called Kalaki-ki. People receive us well — gather round a calabash of poe & some fish. I begin to eat. No natives will eat. I ask them to. Look diffident, & one says must say Grace. Mortifies me. One native says grace, & all fall to. Give them my sardines. One very pretty native woman, (Tarahae) takes great pains to correct my pronunciation. Lie down on mats & sleep until moon is up — when take leave & go off in our canoe. (Before lying down kanakas have prayer & hymn to a familiar New England tune.)

In canoe all night. At daybreak, see canoes in groups of 5 to 10 each, fishing — great numbers of them before reach Milorii.

The three natives of the canoe are all religious — & nice fellows, kind & honest, & take pains for me.

At Milorii, are no white men. Go to hut of one Stephen — whom natives call Setepano, the nearest they can get to it. Go to sleep on mat. My natives go back to Kealakekua, in their canoe. Learned my name, & call me *Dena* — (wh. gives our sound), they having no term for Mr. Their highest chiefs have no prefix or affix of honor, either men or women, but are addressed — as Pauwahe, Kaahumanu, &c.

One of them before leaving wakes me up & says — "Dena! Dena! *hen* — you — by & by". "Do you want a hen?" "Aole. Mamuli wahine get hen — oe — oe". That is — I am to have a chicken for breakfast.

Had letter of introduction fr. Rev. Mr. Paris, to Setepano, but he is *máo*, off. A kanaka goes off, & by noon gets me a *hoki* — mule. But *hoki* kicks & won't be mounted. So kanaka goes off for 3 hours more to get a horse. Mean time, I spend the whole day in the hut with the women, except one bath in the sea. Women stringing necklaces of yellow berries of pandanus tree, & sewing & ironing, all seated on mats. Managed to have consid. conv. with them, betw. Hawaiian & signs. Have got a pretty large vocabulary. In course of day other women call in, [to] have a chat, & to see the haole. (One kanaka man's description of one of these women, to her face, in simplicity, in one word.) Probably a fair specimen of the native life & customs.

Just before dark, Kanaka comes with horse. All sit down again to poe & bananas. Am getting expert at eating poe with my fingers.

Kanaka takes my luggage on pole, across his shoulders, & walks off. My horse creeps after, & no whipping can get a trot or fast walk out of him. It grows dark before we get 3 miles, & at abt. 5 miles, we bring up at native house — large thatched hut — with some 20 inmates, sitting or lying on mats around a fire. Are well recd., but they have only poe & bananas. Before lying down, one kanaka says a prayer. (So did my boatman, at the other hut).

SAT. OCT. 15. Slept soundly until dawn. Here dismissed my man, & engaged a new man & horse. Started at dawn, up the lava streams, & across them, for Waiohinu. (The free & gross conv. of some kanaka women, even in the good & well ordered families. The last point that Xn. civilisation has to carry with these people, is that wh. pertains to the relations of the sexes).

At both places, have entertained the natives very much by showing them the inside work of my watch.

Natives pronounce our proper names as near as they can, & in talking with them, we adopt their pronunciation. E. g. *Thurston*, is Kakini, Paris is Pareki, Lyman is Laimani, Stephen is Setepano &c.

From Milorii to Waiohinu, a distance of about forty miles, is a sea of lava. Some of this is smooth, hard lava, called *pahoehoe*, & the rest is rough, loose stones, *aa*. Imagine a blacksmith's heap of some thousand square miles, the shop closed for centuries, & you have it. All this has come from Mauna Loa. Desolation — Desolation.

Within abt. 7 miles of Waiohinu comes vegitation, grass & trees. Gradually the lava is lost — or rather time has grown it over.

Waiohinu is high land, some 1500 f. above the sea, but the sea in sight — long projecting points & the endless breaking of surf on the coral reefs in sight.

Very rich & fertile here. Trade winds are felt — being on the E. side of the island.

Call & deliver letters to Rev. Mr. Shipman. Mrs. S. so ill that refused to stay there, & am introduced to a young man named Gowen, from Maine, with young wife, just built little house here, shop, farm &c. Take my meals there, & sleep at Mr. Shipman's.

Had nothing but bananas for 20 hours. Shipman's a nice house — neatly furnished. Is comfort to undress & sleep betw. sheets — first time for 11 days.

Mr. Shipman & Mr. Gowen are the only white men betw. Hilo & Kealakehua a space of 120 or 150 miles. The physician comes fr. Kealakehua 80 miles, to see Mrs. S., & spends a week there. Also, at the house, a Mr. Frederick S. Lyman, son of Rev. D. B. Lyman of Hilo.[68] He is tax collector for the district, & is on his tour of collection, a young man of about 21.

Dr. Herrick, very homely old man, a *granny,* is nurse & all, & gives emetics &c., in the true old style, to a poor feeble mother.

Gowen & wife, nice people of middle class, intelligent, interested in politics & literature, Republicans — been here little over a year, & married just before leaving home. Take the Weekly Tribune, Independent, & Atlantic Magasine. Have family prayers morning & evening, & are an acquisition to the mission.

OCT. 16. SUNDAY. First rain since came to the Islands. Rained all last night, & most of today. Went to the Native Meeting this morning. Tolerably full & good choir. Mrs. Shipman so ill that Mr. S. not preach. Service is conducted by a Kanaka, & becomingly. Singing good, to familiar old N. England tunes of Hebron, Dedham &c. wh. retain their names here, adapted to native life. Heberona, Dedahamai, &c. Old Hundred, being Haneii &c. The familiar words & tune of

> "The day is past & gone,
> The Evening shades appear;
> Oh may we ever bear in mind,
> The shades of death draw near".[69]

is rendered —

"Ua hala keia la,   *hale,* gone; *keia,* this; *la,* day.
 Ua uhi mai ka po;   *uhi mai,* veils over, *po,* night.
 Pela, e malu kokc mai,   *Pela,* thus. *Malu,* overshadows.
 Ka make o kakou".   *kakou,* us all. *Make,* death.

The hymn sung to Hebron

A kau na la hoano nai;   A *kau,* and. *hoano,* praise & worship.
He maha koe i ke ao,   *nai,* here, below.
He la hoano ano e,   *Maha koe* — to rest; *i ke ao,* as here
He kapu maoli oia mau.   *ano e,* of a different kind.
                        Kapu, sacred, *Maoli,* &c. eternal.

[68]David Belden Lyman (1803–1884), Williams College, 1828, married in 1831 and sailed for the Islands as a missionary, where he worked for fifty-two years without a vacation. His son, Frederick Schwartz Lyman (1837–1918), was a tax collector and land surveyor for the government of Hawaii, 1854–1862. He became wealthy, having installed the first electrical system and the first telephone system on the Islands.

[69]"Hebron," (1707) and "Dedham," (1709), were by Isaac Watts (1674–1748). There were no fewer than five hymns called "Old Hundred," as well as four called "Old Hundredth," but Dana probably referred to a melody adapted to a verse of Psalm 134 in 1551 by Lois Bourgeois. "The day is past" was composed in 1792 by John Leland (1754–1841).

Noticed one man among the natives for his tall figure & dignified air, & learned that he was a chief.

I rode across the country with my California belt with revolver & knife — but told by all that no more need of weapons among these people than among children. All the property of this large district, & all its industry is in native hands, except the Mission & Mr. Gowen's.

Oranges sweet & plenty here. Also bananas.

MOND. OCT. 17.   Mr. Shipman has a native school of about 70 scholars. His head teacher is a native, educated at Lahainluna — an intelligent man. Object is to carry on all the teachings in the native tongue — but desire of some to learn English is so strong that sev[eral] are taught it. Attended the school, & made them an address. Studies are reading, spelling, geography, grammar & arithmetic. Kanakas supple & active, & not like confinement, awkward & uneasy in formal positions, not stand straight or still. Difficulty with our consonants.

Leave of friends here, & start in co. with Mr. Lyman for the old crater of Kilauwea, & Hilo, a kanaka to carry my luggage, & a few pack oxen with Mr. L.'s goods.

Natives treading out wheat   by horses — men & women mounted, & rather furious riding. Stop at chief's house.

Have eaten fresh figs at Waiohinu, & like them.

Journey is over volcanic country, lava fr. Manua Loa, but chiefly very old & well covered with vegitation. Sea is by our side, no harbors, but openings in coral reefs for boats, & little sand beaches, & where these are, you find knots of native houses. Surf breaks off 3 & 4 deep, on account of the steadiness of the trade winds, always in one direction. Here the old style of chiefs used to bathe, on surf-boards.

Spend night at a native house, at a little place called Keáwa, wh. Mr. Fr. Lyman has just bought, & where he intends to have a stock farm. Only natives in the house. Cook us a meat supper — also poe (pó-e, two syllables). Grace before supper, & prayers before turning in, in the native tongue, as matter of course.

TUESD. OCT. 18.   Up at daylight, & off for the crater, first breakfast & prayers. Grace before meat, & some prayer at morning & night are almost universal among the Kanakas — learned it from the Mission. families, who have been there first & often their only patterns of civilisation. While at prayers, felt a slight shock of earthquake.

The road up to the crater is very barren, no water, & chiefly *pahoehoe*. Crater is on a spur of Manua Loa, & abt. 4000 f. above sea. Reach the rim of the crater at noon, go round two sides of it, to an uninhabited hut, where travelers stay. Lunch & start for the bottom of the crater.

Smoke & steam coming up from it. Little openings in the rocks, by the roadside, where steam is coming up. For more than a mile beyond & outside of crater, these openings. Fire is under all the mountain, all about us. In rear of the hut, is a place where sulphur forms. Several small openings or cracks send up a warm steam of a sulphurous smell, & sulphur crystals form on the rocks, in large quantities.

Great Crater of Kilauwéa. Rim is nearly circular, & about ten miles in circumf. From the rim, the walls go down nearly perpendicular to the floor of the crater. The floor of the crater is about 700 f. below the rim This floor has all, at some time been in action, emitting lava. But all except the centre is now hard floor of lava. The outskirts of this floor, near the walls, & especially on one side, are much grown over with fern bushes, & sometimes trees. Ferns grow up in cracks of hard lava. Greater part of floor of crater is lava, mere lava, sometimes *pahoehoe,* sometimes *aa,* generally nearly level. In centre of floor is a lake or pit, a crater within a crater. This is about 100 yards in diameter, nearly circular, & but little lower than the general floor of the crater. (In some parts of the floor, steam comes up through the cracks). Walked to the centre crater. It is all a mass of living lava, & in action. The lava quickly crusts over in cakes. Imagine a space of large cakes of ice, on a pond, with little spaces of water, the water in commotion & the cakes of ice, sometimes uniting & freesing together, & sometimes breaking up & tumbling over. The lava is black, or slate color. Under it is the sea of fire, or of red fiery molten lava. This breaks out, & is thrown up 18 or 20 feet, & breaks up the cakes of lava, & all is fire. Then, the fire subsides, & the black lava crusts over. Sometimes, nearly all the crater is a mass of fiery, boiling red lava, & sometimes it is here, & then there, all in violent action, but changing its place. Heat so that can hardly bear it on our faces. This is one of the mothers of lava wh. cover the country for 1000 sq. miles. *Swelling, throbbing,* & here & there bursting out — is this inner crater.

Return to hut, for night. Kanakas get supper, eat poe with fingers, (one-finger-poe & 2-finger-poe). Old kanaka makes prayer — "Makou, Makou — Akua, &c. pomaissai, pilikia &c.".

Start, by moonlight, at 2.30 A. M. Crater in full blast, & fire reddens the sky over it. Travel by moonlight, over the lava, & down the mountain. Manua Loa, & Manua Kea in full sight. Snow on top of Manua Kea. Manua Loa is abt. 14,000 f. high, twice the height of Mt. Washington.

Daylight. Clear day. Breakfast at native hut. Pretty faces of young native women — necklaces & garlands of berries or roses almost universal.

Some small trees of Sandalwood. The Sandalwood grows slowly, & must be very old before it gives odour. Old trade exhausted all the full grown trees, & is ended. Forests white with kukui trees, like the Amer.

Chestnut in blossom. Guavas, sweet & sour are plenty. Guava tree is like quince tree, & guava like quince in form & color, seeds in middle ditto, tastes betw. insipid & sour. Last 7 miles before Hilo is rich, deeply fertile, luxuriant tropical growth, a *jungle* of flowers & trees, so thick that no animal can go through, (shd. think) except where road cut — yet not unwholesome, no miasma. Guavas, oranges, mangoes, kukui, pandanus, castor oil, bread fruit, banana, cocoa nut, papaia.

Open sea again, coral reefs, ships at anchor within them, & little town of Hilo. Streets straight, houses neat, fences neat, gardens, all shaded so thick that just see the houses. Prettiest town I have seen yet — tho' small.

Mr. Fred. Lyman invites me to his father's. Large, comfortable house, head of street, nice yard, full of flowers, shrubs & trees, like Wethersfield parsonage. Mr. Lyman, grey hairs, between 50 & 60 years, wife good figure & manners, matronly, kind, dignified, intelligent. Came here together in 1832, children all born here. Seen hardships & strange experiences — reared up excellent family. Eldest son, Henry Munson, took first honors at Wms. Coll., 1858, 2d is Fred., an excellent, serious, conscientious man, 3d David B. edd. at Puna Ho, is going to 'States to enter College, 4th, Ellen, at Puna Ho, 5th Rufus Anderson, at home, 6th Frank at Puna Ho, 7th Emma W. a nice girl of 10 years.[70] Well ordered, intell. & well edd. family — all sing, & some play piano. My chamber like front chamber at Wethersfield, very comfortable & homelike. Capt. Brown, of Whaling bark, Belle, & wife are boarding with them.

Mr. Lyman keeps the native school of Hilo. School is boarding-school solely, about 70 scholars, & free, i.e. $5 a year only paid. Is full & more applications than can receive. Is self supporting, scholars working & raising vegetables & fruits. Gives good practical education in arithmetic, grammar, geography, accounts, & music. Nearly all sing, & band of 8 or 10 who play flutes. Education is religious but liberal. All obliged to attend public worship, relig. lectures, catechism &c. Intended to be a Hawaiian language but some classes in English. Attended the school. Pupils live chiefly on poe & vegitables.

Mrs. Lyman taught school for native girls sev. years. At first, having no paper, used plantain leaf & wrote with style of fish-bone.

[70]Mrs. D. B. Lyman was Sarah Joiner (1805–1885) of Royalton, Vermont. She married in 1831. Henry Munson Lyman (b. 1835) took his medical degree at the College of Physicians and Surgeons in New York in 1861, became an Army surgeon during the Civil War, and conducted a successful practice in Chicago after the war. David Brained Lyman (b. 1840), Yale, 1864, Harvard Law School, 1866, practiced law in Chicago until 1895, when he retired to head a title and trust firm. The other children remain unidentified beyond what the context of the *Journal* provides.

OCT. 20. TH[URS]. Rev. Mr. Coan,[71] the clergyman, called & invited me to ride to the falls of Wai anuinui — or "rainbow water". No carriages here of any kind. All ride in saddle. Mrs. Coan went with us. River falls into a large chasm of stone, about 100 f. deep. Pretty scene & effect. Only about one mile from the village.

Returned & took tea at Mr. Coan's. Mrs. Coan is a woman of intellect & culture & very agreeable, & knows the ways of the world. Very large tamarind tree in Mr. Coan's yard, giving large shade.

The shades trees here are the tamarind, Mango, breadfruit & pandanus (puhalla) & papaia, & Pride of India.

FRID. OCT. 21. Called with Mr. Coan on the Governess of the island. She is half sister to the king, & perhaps the best repr[esentative] I cd. see of the old chiefdom. She affects old usages & tries to revive the customs of chiefdom, keeps a large retinue of natives about her, who sit on the floor, or under trees all day, to await her leisure. She is very large, huge, & fat & indolent, but with a proud, domineering look. Her son, a chief of ancient line, with more of the chief blood in him than any one now living, a youth of 19, died a few weeks ago. She keeps his body in a lead coffin, in the large room of her house, behind a curtain, where it lies in State, & in the next room the natives keep up a dirge. It was uninterrupted, all the time of our visit. It sounded not unlike some of the dirges in the R. Cath. Church — low, & monotonous.

In the afternoon, went on a picknick, to a place across the river Wailuku, called Puueo. All mounted — 8 ladies, 9 gentlemen. Pretty spot. View of sea & mountains. (Just behind the town are three extinct craters, close together). Took lunch under pandanus tree — large, wide-spreading, & gives a deep, thick shade, perhaps the most complete I ever saw a tree give. Ladies have each a *re,* (garland of flowers) made up by the native women, who busy themselves at it.

Returning, crossing new chain suspension bridge, across the Wailuku, bridge breaks & falls, & the party are in great peril, thrown into the river, or in the wreck of the bridge, among kicking & struggling horses, & in deep water. Scene of consternation & dismay, for sev. minutes. Natives strip & plunge in — excellent swimmers, & very active in saving lives & extricating the horses. Two of Mr. Lyman's sons, Fredrick & David, distinguished themselves by their swimming, & successful efforts to save life. They swim like natives. Mrs. Henry Burdett, wife of Capt. Burdett of Boston, of ship Raduga, (who is son of H. B. that lived on Dana Hill,

[71]Titus Coan (1801–1882), from Killingsworth, Connecticut, served as a Presbyterian missionary in the Islands, 1834–1882.

Cambridge) was in great peril, & helped out by David Lyman & sustained until natives took her ashore. Fred. Lyman swam with Miss Pratt, sister of Mrs. Ch. Brewer of Honolulu to a point on the bridge where the natives took her. One lady, Mrs. Gulick of Honolulu, held to her horse's mane, until a native took her off. Miss Emma Lyman (10 years) was on a mule, & at the first sound of danger, the mule, with sure instinct, turned round & ran to the land, & carried her off just before the fall, not a second to spare — no horse or man did the like. Mrs. Austin, wife of Judge Austin (Stafford L. Austin of Hilo) was in the water, & helped out by a native, & her husband. None of the rest of the party fell with the bridge, being at the ends — except myself. I fell in the midst, at the worst part, keeping my seat in the saddle, & stirrup was crushed ag. timber & hurt my left foot. Horse involved in the wreck, & I left him & swam to bridge. This place broke down, & I swam to another. Held on upper rail by fingers, Got better hold & went ashore on the rail, hand over hand. Got there too late to do anything but help Mrs. Burdett up the bank, as she could not walk — fr. exhaustion — (but she was in a safe place, & left there by the natives & David, who went back to the wreck). Cd. hardly walk. Bone of little toe broken, & top of foot bruised.

Natives raised a *wail*, as soon as the bridge fell, wh. was heard all over town. The native women wailed over Emma Lyman, until they made her cry. The skill & fidelity & affection of the natives affecting. Kipi, the tax collector, a native, distinguished himself.

Bridge 200 f. long, rested on 2 chains, insufficient — about 8 or 10 f. above water, & water 25f. deep. Broke with a crack & then a tip, crash & fall. The crash was heard all over town, & drew all to the spot. Mrs. Lyman, who had three sons & a daughter in the party, remained in suspense some half hour, & prepared herself to resuscitate drowned persons, got out her book &c.

No one lost, & no one hurt (beyond mere bruises) but me. Wonderful escape. Seemed to me to be certain death to some, & maiming to most. Fall & crash of suspension bridge, 10 f. above deep water, & party of 10 or 12 men & women falling, with their horses!

SUND. OCT. 23. Native worship in A. M. Mr. Coan officiated. Same want of reverence of action & manner. Fault of the *system*. Was no benediction. All sat in prayer & singing, & not even bend the head.

P. M. In the small chapel, service in English — about 50 persons. Returns thanks for the preservation of the party. (This party embraced about half the white residents & visitors in the place). Sermon in revival style, & fluent & rather effective — but too long. Congregational singing.

Little Emma Lyman, whom I like very much, wanted to be excused fr. sweeping out the chapel this morning, because it was so late, & people had [begun] to go in. But it was her task, & she did it — a little natural pride or shame. In the public service, this little child played the piano, (melodaian piano forte) for the singing.

MONDAY OCT. 24. Took tea at Austin's. He is Circ. Judge, & Sec. to the Governess, being, in fact, Governor. Son of a lawyer in Buffalo. Mrs. A. is d. of Rev. Mr. Clark, of Honolulu, & her sister Mrs. Gulick, is with her.

Use arnica on my foot. Swelling goes down. Bone of little toe only, broken. Too small for splints. No pain, but keeps me still. Go out once a day on the horse, walking him. Dr. C. H. Wetmore, a fair physician & surgeon.

Mr. Miller U. S. Consul here.

THURSD. OCT. 27. Spent one ev. at house where Mrs. Burdett & Miss Pratt board. Mrs. B. plays piano very well — in this remote place it seems to me excellent playing. She is just married in Boston, abt. 20 years old, daughter of Tom Comer,[72] an amiable, pretty woman, & very popular. Husband a good fellow, & consid. knowledge of music. His ship is Clipper, in merch. service — wife came out with him, & is good sailor.

Curious feature of life here is the number of whaling masters who bring their wives to the islands & leave them for the seasons, coming back in Spring & Fall. Many in Honolulu, some 40. Here are some 10 or 12. Half the foreign women here are whalers' wives. This is time for their return (October). Every day watching fr. housetops, & as ships come in, watch the whale boats coming ashore, & then the name flies — for no telegraph here. One ship brot news of death of a master whose wife was looking for him — killed by a whale in the Arctic.

Now, all the husbands have arrived but two. All the talk is of ships, the Arctic, the Ockotsk,[73] the no. of barrels. The masters are rather a rough set, tho' two or three of them are well dressed, well bred men. Luck has been bad. Some have nothing, & few have paid their way.

Yesterday afternoon the flute band of native boys fr. the school came down & played for me. Eight flutes — played pretty well. Old fashioned tunes. Taught by a native in the upper class. Flute their favorite, as easy to learn, not get out of order, & can be carried anywhere. This disseminates music among the people.

Music at all fam. prayers here — & so generally, in the island. Custom

---

[72]Thomas Comer (1790–1862), an English entertainer, came to the United States in 1827. He performed in musical comedy in Boston, where he was known especially for his Irish impersonations.

[73]The Sea of Okhotsk, a major whaling ground, is an inlet of the Pacific, west of the Kuril Islands.

to have prayers just after tea, & visitors who happen in, attend them. So, if you go out to tea — at Austin's &c.

Called on Mrs. Coan, spent hour. Also on Mrs. Burdett — plays piano. (The Whaling captains wives sing commonplace songs, negro melodies &c. — but seem to have a notion that Mrs. Burdett's style of music is superior.)

Temperature of Hilo is perfect. Thermometer between 70° at night & 80° at noon. Never intensely hot, & never a chill. Not dry, but always perspiration, if needed. Nights always comfortable, & no mosquitoes — or few. In winter solstice, in worst weather, never below 60° or 50°. No bad weather except in four months. Rest of year, no storms. Only drawback is the frequent showers. In that respect, is like England in May & June. These, however, are weak showers, & keep everything delightfully green.

Century plant runs up a high thin stalk or trunk, to reach the sun. When has reached it, (gone to 40 feet) the plant fades & dies, exhausted.

Sugar cane grows wild & large, & is very sweet. All natives, Hawaiian & white, are fond of it. Two kinds of guavas — little-one, not much larger than plum, very pleasant. Larger, like quince, *ut supra*.

Read Macaulay's article on Wm. Pitt, fr. Encycl. Brittanica.[74] Capital performance, discriminating, &, on the whole, just. Also some of Tennyson's best — his only good things — his earliest.

Kanakas make flutes from bamboo & play tolerably on them.

FRID. OCT. 28. Sailed in whaling bark Favorite, of N. London, Smith, master, for Honolulu. Parting calls on Mr. & Mrs. Austin, Mr. & Mrs. Coan, Dr. & Mrs. Wetmore, & Mrs. Burdett & Miss Pratt. Dr. Wetmore refuses to receive compensation of his prof. services to me. Has visited me to bandage & ex[amine] my broken toe ev. day. Says the bridge accid. was a common calamity, & glad to aid the sufferers.

Left Hilo, good light breese. Fine view fr. the water — the 3 extinct craters behind the town, the sch. hs. & meeting hs., the land marks. North of the river, are the high cliffs, the streams running into the sea, the sugar plantations &c. The only running streams wh. reach the sea in all Hawaii, are the Wailukeu, & the streams betw. that & the N. E. point of the island. (All but one of the sugar estates are Chinese enterprises).

Before leaving Hilo, called on the R. C. priest. A French gentleman, very intelligent, well educated, good books, knows the state of theol. controversy in Europe, the theology of his own Ch., & has good manners.

[74]Published in the *Britannica*, 8th ed. (1853–1860), the article appeared separately in *Biographies by Lord Macaulay Contributed to the Encyclopaedia Britannica* (Edinburgh, 1860).

Very small building, & few disciples — seemed unwilling to tell me the number. Insisted on my accepting fr. him "Bossuet's Exposition de la doctrine Catholique".[75]

The bark Belle, Brown, sails at same time. At night, Brown visits us in his boat. Long pulls of these whalers in boats. Some captains left their ships 20 miles fr. Hilo & pulled in.

Favorite, old bark, strong, fair sailer. Ch. mate, Sherman, good quiet fellow — 14 boys fr. Capt.'s town. Are contented, tho' had bad luck.

In whaler, hours diff. fr. merch. & man of war — 8 bells at 11 o'ck., & so on. Capt., 3 mates, 4 boatsteerers, cooper, blacksmith & some 26 men forward. Not over 300 tons. Ch. M. no watch unless near land or in bad place, or bad weather. Third M. stands his watch. On whaling ground, lie to, & stand in quarter watches, on boats' crews, headed by boatsteerers.

Accomm., cooking, very inferior. Dress of all hands not seamanlike, yet are hardy men, & good sailors, as far as working ship is concerned. Tends to that, yet not to discipline or neatness, — is not a neat calling — oil, grease &c. Men dress & look like a gang of soapboilers.

David Lyman is with me, bound to Honolulu, to fit for voyage to U. States, in the Raduga, where he is to enter college. Capt. Smith has been in the Alert, after she became a whaler. Says her reputation was made in that business by my book — & her captain proud of her as of a toy. Also, the 3d. M., Perkins, has been in her.

SAT. OCT. 29. At noon, are abt. 15 m. fr. Kawaihae, & high M'ts. of Maui in sight. Capt. leaves in boat for Kawaihae, to get potatoes &c. ready for us. All aftern. working in, with light breeses. Manua Loa, & the steam fr. the outflow of lava into sea.

Native pilot comes off. Introduces himself to me. Was a boy on board the Ayacucho, in 1835, 6. I remember him perfectly, & the face of the man of 40, recalls the boy of 16. Goes over the events of those times, for wh. he has a good memory. Says all the Kanakas on the beach are dead or unheard fr. except old "Mr. Bingham", who is at Kawai.[76]

Whalers use boom-lances a great deal — if cannot get near eno' for hand lance. Iron lance about 6 inches long, charged with powder, & fuse abt. 6 inches more. Put in a hand grenade at boat's head. Discharge ingnites the fuse. Lance goes into whale, & explodes in 11 seconds. Mr. Sherman says

[75]Jacques Bénigne Bossuet (1627–1704) published this work in 1671.

[76]The *Ayacucho*, one of the ships Dana saw on the California coast during his *Two Years* voyage, has been mentioned several times before. "Mr. Bingham" was a native mentioned in *Two Years*, named after an Oahu missionary (Hiram Bingham, noted earlier), who worked on the California beaches with Dana in 1835–1836.

are excellent. Complicated outfit of a whale boat — officer, boatsteerer, 5 men, a sail & its rigging & mast, 6 oars, several harpoons & lances, the lines & tubs, 2 brlls. of water, — knives, boom-lances & gun & powder.

Little discipline. Officer of watch lies down on deck & reads, in light weather, or lies down in quarter boat — never obliged to walk deck — & holds long yarns with passengers. Galley is aft, by side of wheel. Crew not kept at work. Lie & stand about decks, & work ship when called upon. Very easy times.[77] Yet, strong, hardy men, & masters & officers are excellent seamen, as to weather, handling a vessel &c., as constant experience, in all weathers & places, more than in merch. service, — often where no pilots or charts.

SUNDAY. OCT. 30. Becalmed all day off E. Maui & Laanai. Deeply-gorged, volcanic outlines & surfaces of Maui. See sketch of Lahainaluna.[78]

The boats are the favorite sitting places. More air & better view than on deck. Capt. & mates sit in the quarter boats, & the boat-steerers in the waist boats. Boat-steerers keep in waist, live in after steerage & eat at 2d table in cabin.

MOND. OCT. 31. Becalmed great deal. Oahu in sight, & a rainbow spanning over it.

Crew sing a great deal, in dog watch. Some good voices among them. Sentimental songs are rather the favorites — one about harp on willow, —
> "If I had loved with a boyish love,
> It would have been better for me".

And one called "The maid of Maui". Poor fellows, been 2 years out, & only 400 bbls., the vessel holding 2500 or 3000!

TUESD. NOV. 1. Off Honolulu at daylight. Several vessels going in, one the Josiah Bradlee, 170 days fr. Boston, the rest are whale ships.

Down boat & pull ashore, some 10 miles.

Honolulu again. Diamond Head, the valley, Waikiki, Punahou, the surf on the reefs, & the inner harbor now full of whale ships, 50 or more.

Am the guest of Mr. Bates, the lawyer — (Ashur D. Bates). He has a large, handsome house, up the valley, with good view of ocean, & well cultivated grounds. Again, the ringing hoofs of the fast riders on the valley road, the native women, riding astride, with long folds of yellow & striped cloth, & a garland on the head, & necklace of flowers or berries. Every person in Honolulu, man or woman, native or foreign, I should think, is on horseback once a day. Their calls are made so. Mr. & Mrs.

---

[77]Dana excised the following line from the text: "Their dress is like that of soap-beaters. Look like a gang of soap-boilers."

[78]Dana's sketch has been lost.

Bishop (Pauwahi) canter up this evening. Judge Robertson &c. Each child in the family has a horse.

Mr. Bates' family is wife (now in U. S.), wife's sister, (who keeps house now), a deformed woman, sister of Dr. Judd,[79] a son, Dudley, 21 yrs., a merchant, 2 boys of 8 or 10, a daughter, Lucilla, 13, & Mary, 6. House handsomely furnished, table well ordered & tended.

Ladies wear garlands of Cape Jessamines. The ginger of commerce bears a large flower, of exquisite fragrance. Mosquitoes so thick that no sleeping without nets. Even in Sailor's Home, have mosquito nets. No mosquitoes in Hilo.

Young Sleeper is dead — son of Sleeper of Roxbury,[80] & brother of Mrs. Austin. He was ass. editor of the chief newspaper here.

No one here (in these islands) says "fine day", "pleasant morning", or the like, for they are matters of course. Only in midwinter is there any unpleasant weather, & not much then.

The Clipper ship Viking of Boston, is expected here from S. Francisco every day, & in her I hope to be able to get passage to China.

THURSD. NOV. 3. Salute fr. battery. King arrived, in his little sch., from Lahaina. Shown my foot to Dr. Ford. Bruise is healed & doing well. The fracture was simple, & cartelage is forming & will soon be strong eno' to admit of walking. At present, keep still, walking only as much as is necessary. Mr. Bates keeps a horse & chaise at my disposal all day.

The Ships are the life of this place, & their only means of communication with the world. Every child in Honolulu knows that the Viking is the next ship expected fr. S. Fr., & that she is going to China, & all watch the harbor for her, & for whalers.

FRID. NOV. 4. Dined at Allen's (Ch. Justice). Present — Allen *et ux.*, Judge Robertson, Harris, Bates, Lt. Reynolds (U. S. N.) et ux. Pleasant time. Like Robertson. Came here before the mast, learned all his law after 30, & is now a very satif. judge — good sense & industry. Knows the Hawaiian language well. Lt. Reynolds is an agreeable man, also. Mrs. Allen is well edd. & good manners. They have an eldest son, baby, whom people call the Prince of Kahoolawe, fr. a poor island the judge has leased.

Am told that the coolies brot here did not exceed 600 or 800, in all the group. They came intelligently & voluntarily, but as bound laborers

---

[79]Gerrit Parmele Judd (1803–1873), from Paris, New York, went to the Islands as a missionary physician in 1827 and became a trusted adviser to the King, whom he served in the highest offices of state from 1842 to 1853.

[80]The dead man's father was John Sherburne Sleeper (1794–1878), long a shipmaster and sailor, newspaper editor in Exeter, Lowell, and Boston, and mayor of Roxbury, Massachusetts, 1856–1858. He wrote many sea stories for children.

for 5 or 8 years — to be used on plantations. Reason was that the natives were lured off to California & wd. not work at home. But coolies not do well under these contracts — as found themselves too valuable. The contracts ran out or were given up or bought out, & all Chinese here now are free laborers, & very good laborers, especially as house servants.

All the gentln. at table agree as to the mildness & gentleness of the natives, & also that they are grateful for what they consider to be real kindnessess — not for mere gifts, perhaps, for they think we have an abundance.

The worst said ag. the natives is that in times of wreck, danger of drowning &c. they wait for offers & insist of high pay before they go off, & stories are told of their letting people drown for want of suff. reward offered. I think these stories — (which are well vouched) are of the regular *beach-combers*, who live by diving & swimming, & not of others.

SUNDAY. NOV. 6.   9.30 A. M. went to a Native Ch. of wh. Rev. Mr. Smith is pastor. Services as usual in congr. societies, & the conduct of the people open to the ordinary objection, coming in at all times, no outward signs of reverence & scarcely of attention, & clergymen apparently indiff. to it. Mr. Smith preached in black sack coat & spurs, — this (spurs) is because all ride here, & he is not attentive eno' to externals to take them off. Yet, he is & has been for 20 years, a faithful laborer & teacher among the natives.

At 11 A. M. went to the R. Cath. Church. Well filled. Few chairs, &, in galleries, seats — but mostly sit down on mats on floor, & kneel. This is agreeable to the natives. Also, the native women here do not wear bonnets as in the Prot. Churches, & look better for it. The sea of bonnets is too ludicrous, in forms & colors. The natives enjoy the music, & many seem very devout in their private prayers & readings. A girl of about 18 was baptised, dressed in white, native sponsors &c.

The words used in all these islands are "Natives" & "foreigners", to distinguish the races. Whites born here are called foreigners. The natives called the first whites "haole" — foreigners, & they too have kept up that term for our race, irrespective of birth. "*Kanaka*" means "man", in their language & is not used except among sailors & by people out of the islands, California, in Atlantic States & in all ships, where it is the only term for the Polynesian race.

No afternoon services in any of the relig. soc. of Honolulu, but one at night. Went to the Fort St. Ch., the principal Ch. of the foreigners. Rev. Mr. Corwin preached. He is of Wms. College, formerly settled in S. José, Cal. — of the New School — H. W. Beecher style, good faculty for public speech, & quick mind. [Here Dana inserted the following vocabulary, with the notation "Words in common use here — for a mem."]

Yes — ai
No — aole
I — Wai
You — oe
He, she — ia
We — makou, kakou
Who? — owai
When? — ahéa
Where? — auhéa
What? — héaha
How much? — héaha ka uku
At what hour? — eka hora ehía
This — keia
That — kela
Here — manéi
There — maláila
Hither — mai
Thither — aku
Towards — ma, i
From (a place) — mai
Distant, away — máo
To-day — keia la
To-morrow — apópo
And — me, ame
But — aká
Be quick! — wiki viki
Done, finished — pau

Verbs

Bring, take — láawi
Bring here — laawi mai
Give — haáwi
Give me — haawi mai
Stop, wait — alía
Come — héle
Come here — hele mai
Go — hele
Go away, go off — hele áku
Talk, speak — olélo
Sleep — kiamoe
Die — make
Eat — ai
Take care — málama

Swim — aau
Pray — bule
Wish — make make
Conciliate, flatter — mavi mavi
Work — hana hana
Kill — hana maki
Make fast — hana pa
Sew — humi humi

Nouns

Water — wai
Wind — makáni!
Sea — kai
Rain — ua
Sun — la
Moon — mahína
Star — ukú
Day — la
Night — po
Week — hepedoma (for.)
Month — mahína, maláma
Year — makahiki
Fire — ahi
Canoe — waa
Boat — waapá
Vessel — moku
Fish — ia
Dog — ilío
Horse — lio
Mule — hoki
Baggage — ukána
Road, path — ala
Male — kane
Female — wahíni
Man — kanáka
Name — inóa
Foreigner, white man — haole
Light, lamp — kukúi
Spirit, God — Akúa
Child, offspring — keike
Father — makúa kane
Mother — makúa wahini

Trouble — pilikía

Church (the institution) — ekelésia (for.)

Church (the building) — hale pule

House — hale

Adjectives

Good — maikai

Bad — aole maikai

Fortunate, blessed — pomaikai

Skillful, clever — akamai

Large — nui

Small — uúku.

Afraid — makau

Ashamed — hila hila

Fast (secure) — pa

Solitary, alone — méha méha

Quick — wiki wiki

All — a páu

Land-ward — mauka

Sea-ward — makai

MOND. NOV. 7. To Punahou, with Mr. Corwin. He teaches Scripture History, but it is only the Old Test., long & diff. researches into obscure parts of Babalonian & Syrian history. They know nothing of the history of Apostolic times except what their own reading may give them. The old Judaising tendencies.

The whole school together. At request of Prof. made a short address to the scholars, wh. was well received, in favor of classical studies & liberal, aesthetic culture.

Lunch at Mr. Corwin's. Nice wife & little children, — come fr. Orange Co. N. Y.

To the monthly musical society, at Dr. Guillon's. The usual company. Playing good — singing not so good as before. A sea captain introduced to me on ground that he was master of the Alert when she was in the whaling trade. Tells me she has always been a lucky ship & a favorite — is known in the whole whaling fleet as Dana's ship Alert.

Anderson, the magician,[81] is here & astonishes the natives a good deal.

Very few birds on these islands — certainly very few in Oahu. Seldom hear a note.

Girls of 12 to 16 years ride on horseback here alone, to go to school, shopping, or to visit friends. Horses so cheap that most families have several, — 4 or 5, & they feed like cows, in the fields.

Spent ev. at house of Mr. Castle,[82] a trader, who came here as the secular, business man of the Mission. Honest & intelligent — but fearfully Yankee-country-deacon*ish*. Cd. not stand him long.

WED. NOV. 9. Called on Dr. Ford. Says the bone has united, & that I shall be able to walk as usual in 2 or 3 days. This is cause of gratitude, indeed.

[81]John Henry Anderson (b. 1810), famous as a magician in Scotland, came to the United States in 1851 for an extended tour.

[82]Samuel Northrup Castle went to the Islands in 1837 as financial agent for the American Board of Commissioners for Foreign Missions, was financial adviser to the king and cofounder of Castle and Cook, an Hawaiian business firm.

Called on Mr. Bishop — out; on the Halls, in; on the Allens, in, — long conv. on theology.

Many native words are in use among foreigners here, as certain French words with us. *Makai* & *mauka,* for landward & seaward, as to the position of houses, streets, lots &c. — *pilikía* for difficulty & trouble, *akamái* for clever, skillful, *pomaikai* for fortunate, *hu hu* for angry, *pau* & *pau voa* for done, ended &c., & the salutation *alóha* is in very general use, written in presentation books, & used in taking leave, it is so pretty.

Went to school of "Les Soeurs des Sacres Coeurs", a diff. order from that of the "Du Sacre Coeur", or a branch, perhaps, of that order. There are six teachers, & a school of 40 girls, all of foreign families — that is — whites. The sisters wear white gowns of some woolen fabrick, & white caps. They have been here only six months, & are all French or German-French.

All speak in high terms of Mr. Damon, the Seaman's Chaplain here. He is the right man in the right place, & has as much as he can do, in the whaling season. He buries all the poor outcast sailors, taking their ship-mates to the grave, in the procession, giving hours to each. Saw him heading one yesterday, mounted, with umbrella, in the sun. He is an honest man & a good one.

THURSDAY. NOV. 10. Calls on a Mr. & Mrs. Bishop, old people, missionaries, whose district is Ewa, beyond the Pali, but who live up the valley. Also on Mrs. Judge Allen, & a Mrs. Patsy, (whose husb. used to command the Don Quixote) — all these calls made with Mrs. Judd, senr., a very old & vigorous woman, a gr. gr. mother.

This evening Mr. Bates took Mr. & Mrs. [C. R.] Bishop, — not the old missionaries, but our friend, the Chief*ess* & her husband — & me to ride, by moonlight, to Waikiki, the sea-bathing place. Bright clear moon, cloudless sky, soft air. We sat an hour or so on the sand-beach; under the cocoa-nut trees. A native walking off into the water, before us, & swimming off out of sight, going to catch fish, just as if he had a boat. Funny notion that Pauwahi (Mrs. Bishop) would throw off her clothes & jump in & swim off to the reefs, into the surf. Her mother, certainly her gr. mother would have done it. She pretends she can't swim.

(Last ev. rode with Harris to the Manóa Valley, near Punahou).

This kingdom, the whole group of the Hawaiian islands, was held by a strictly feudal tenure. All the land belonged to the king. He allotted portions to his chiefs, who held on condition of rendering military service & giving certain returns of fruits &c. The chiefs made subinfeudations to the common people, who were mere tenants at will, also rendering similar services to the feudal lord. The analogy with the feudal style of Europe is exact, only it was not tempered by the aid of the judicial distinctions wh. in Europe created rights in the tenants.

Each district had its name, & so had each subdivision. For instance, Honolulu was the name of a small space, containing about ¼ of the present town. Muuanu was the upper part, Punahou the Eastern &c.

Lately the titles were arranged betw. the king & the chiefs, by a division, or partition, & now the chief holds absolute, allodial [independent] titles. The rights of the common people are secured in the lands they have held a certain number of years. But a great part of the common people are still tenants on chiefs' lands or the king's lands. But the operation of the direct tax system is to compel sales, for it is not income but principal that is taxed. The chiefs are taxed on the market value of their unimproved lands.

The families of chiefs are dying out. They do not increase. So of the common people. This is their own fault, or their misfortune wh. leads to fault. They ruin themselves in early life, & the women do not become mothers, or mothers of many children.

FRID. NOV. 11. Called, with Mrs. Judd senr., on Rev. Mr. Corwin & lady, Mr. Commissn. Borden & lady, a Mrs. Severance,[83] Mrs. Dr. Smith, (née Patsy.)

Went to Punahou again. Heard some declamations, & at req. of teacher, addressed the scholars on subject of reading aloud, declamation, enunciation, pronunciation &c. Spent ev. at home of Mrs. Gulick, a missionary family, with 2 sons & a daughter at the school. Prof. Alexander & Mr. Haskell, a teacher, spent the ev. with us. Several girls of the school came in & spent ev. Their entertainment was to get me to describe persons, places & occurrences I had seen in England & U. States. They seemed interested. Among them were girls of the Hawaii families I had visited, Lyman, Coan & Paris; also a d. of Mr. Parker, the Miss[ionar]y at ─── beyond the Pali, a superior girl, a sister of Prof. Alexander, &c.

Been warm South winds for sev. days, dog-day weather, & people complain, & sickness about. I have not felt it, & few foreigners do at first. All are longing for a return of the trade winds.

SAT. NOV. 12. Rain last night, & this morning the delightful, cool trades are blowing again.

Reading De Tocqueville's U. States.[84] Very able book, especially on the Judiciary, & the *town system* of the North. Entirely wrong on the President's power, ─ a capital mistake, owing to his following the written constitution too much, & underrating the patronage & power over Congress.

---

[83]Presumably this is the widow of Luther Severance (1797–1855), Maine publisher and legislator, who held the post of U. S. Minister to the Sandwich Islands, 1850–1854.
[84]*De la démocratie en Amérique* was first published in 1835.

Took tea at house of Clark, Post Master, son of the pastor of the King's Ch.

SUNDAY. NOV. 13. See that Mr. Bates is sensitive abt. my going to Ch. with his family. So go all day to Fort st. Sermon by Mr. Corwin. Impressive manner direct & earnest.

Pain in limbs all day, head ache & soreness of throat. Symptoms of Maui fever.

WEDNESDAY NOV. 16. Last 3 days a-bed with Maui fever. Called a slight attack, but I think it rather severe, for a mere bilious derangement, tho' not for a fever. Kept abed & still, & obeyed orders. Was blessed by a quiet frame of mind — no glooms or despondencies, or home-sickness. Also, no trouble in my head except the bilious head ache, — I mean, no weight on it, — no congestion.

Last night, Yankee arrived, bringing Mrs. Bates, & a Miss Beals, a niece of the first Mrs. Bates. Mrs. B. has been in the U. States.

No clipper expected to touch here bound to China. Must return to S. Francisco. Great loss of time & money. My first serious disappointment. A vessel sails to-day, but all her berths are taken. Fear I must wait here a week or ten days longer, & then retrace my steps. But, shall I have good & not evil? I must be patient & grateful, for I have had much pleasure & been favored in every way. To-day, am up. No head ache.

Young Mr. Bates writes up that he has got me a passage in the bark Architect, wh. sails to-day for S. Francisco. This is better than nothing. Pack up my clothes, & go down in town. Just learned that a lumberman, bound from Puget Sound to Hong Kong, hove to off the reef for two hours, & landed her captain who goes to S. Fr. I am just too late. She has filled away & gone beyond the Point. Several persons knew this, but none in season to tell me. This confirms me in the opinion that I had better return to S. Fr., for even if a China-bound vessel comes here, she may be off before I can communicate with her. Take the advice of several merchants. All say that no certainty of a vessel for China, at this season. May have to wait here two months. To go to S. Fr. is a certain loss of five weeks, perhaps of more. To stay leaves all uncertain. I may get off in a day. I may not in two months. Determined to go.

Hurried leave of such persons as I meet. Mr. Bates comes to the dock, so Rev. Mr. Corwin, Harris & al. Had promised to speak at the anniversary of the opening of the Sailor's Home. It was due to Mr. Damon, & his excellent house & Mission. My sailing makes this impossible.

WED. NOV. 16. 4 P. M. Sailed out of Honolulu harbor, in the bark Architect, bound to S. Fran. Last view of Muuanu Valley, Punch Bowl Hill, Punahou, & the Diamond Head.

Heavy blow & heavy sea. Double reefed topsails. My bilious derangement at Oahu affects me with sea-sickness, as badly as if it were my first trip at sea. For two days, I have been very sea-sick, or rather very sick, how much is owing to sea, & how much to Maui fever, I don't know; but I have a fair notion of what sea-sickness is, except that the motion is not disagreeable. There is no head-effect. It is merely a sickness of stomach, as one might have on shore. I like the motion, but am miserably weak & bilious — yet glad to find that I have no unpleasant sensations in the head, a proof that my head troubles of last summer are over.

After two days, got over my sickness, & am very well. Sleep & eat well, & keep in good spirits. Yet it is the dullest of voyages. Going right back over my track, & a loss of so much time in getting to China! Nor have I any desire to see Calif. again. Yet, I must have patience. I have had good fortune, & must expect some ill fortune.

Architect a bark of about 400 tons, & 4 years old, been a whaler, & just fr. the Arctic. Fitted up & sent to S. Fr. to be sold. Fish, of N. London, is master, Smith of N. L., Chief Mate, & a queer old duke named Brown, is 2d mate. All are whalemen. For cabin passengers, we have a Mrs. Palmer of N. Bedford, whose husband has just been killed by a whale in the Arctic, leaving her a widow with a boy of 5 years, & an infant of 11 mos., to find her way home. She has her children with her. She is in charge of a Capt. Blackmer, of Fair Haven, an *ex whale-master*, bound home over land. Next is a German, master of the Puget Sound lumberman, (suprá), name is Stege, a dull fellow. Then, two mates of whalemen, bound home overland, Mellen & Sherman & a tall, N. Carolina sand-hiller, who has strangely strayed off whaling, before the mast, had enough of it, & written home for money, got it, procured his discharge & goes home overland. His name is Applewhite. The only one of this co. who is *talkable* is Blackmer. He is an intelligent, well informed man. Fish is a good fellow, & means well, but dull. Rest are nothing. All I can get from them is whaling anecdotes. Have learned a good deal about the Arctic & Ochotsk whaling, among ice & walrus. Hundreds of our ships there from June to Oct. of every year. Whale a good deal in open boats, along the bays, sleeping on shore, & off from the ship for many days together.

Mrs. Palmer seems a worthy woman, & has rather a hard time with her infant & boy, with no servant. The children do not add agreeableness to the passage. Steward an odious man, & a little halfwitted cabin boy, the steward's serf, — the lowest depth to wh. human nature can fall — a cabin-boy in a whaler, under a bad steward. The boy seldom washes, & if he does, whose towel does he use? How idle he is, unless under the steward's eye, & then to hear his half-witted laugh, as he tries to enjoy the steward's talk & doings!

SUNDAY. NOV. 27. Advent Sunday! What thoughts of home, & the church in Boston, & its service to-day, — its 15th anniversary! Went over all the service carefully.

TUESD. NOV. 29. Dull work. Adhere to strict routine, to pass my time. How well Kane[85] learned that & expressed the truth. I must exclude reading, as part of my health regime, — so have little to aid me. Make up fictitious divisions of time. Rise at 6. Toilet of salt & fresh water. On deck, & at unobserved spot, stand & say over the morning service — (all that is appropr. to one person), & a few other prayers, varied by a chant, Te Deum or Gloria in Excelsis, — always beginning so beautifully & appropriately with — "From the rising of the Sun &c.",[86] as it is always sun-rise at the moment. By this time is 7 o'ck. Walk deck until breakfast. After breakfast, walk deck until 10. At 10, read the Morning Lessons & Psalter. Then allow myself to read until 7 bells, 11.30, when go on deck, interest myself in the observations for altitude, & sometimes work up the latitude. Keep on deck until dinner, 1 o'ck. After dinner, allow myself to read or write until 3 o'ck. From 3 to nearly dark, on deck. Interest myself in the altitudes & time taken at 4 o'ck., & get out the chart, & mark our position, & speculate on winds & courses. Before dark, below & read the Ev. lessons & psalter. Walk deck until tea time. After tea, passengers are agreeable a while, if ever. But usually have to rely on walking deck until 8 o'ck. Blackmer often walks with me, & we talk everything threadbare. Sometimes Fish takes a few turns, but after the past, present & future winds are discussed, & the Ochotsk & Arctic are abandoned, he is out — *pau*. Soon after 8 o'ck., alone, on deck, go over the Ev. Service, & then turn in. I rather like this life, for a while. Pleasure in making the most of my resources.

My short reading times are given to Dr. Kane's Arctic Expeditions. This makes me well content in my own situation. An episode of heroism, is Kane's voyage.

(In my Hawaii journal, did I mention the *fleas?* In the native huts, they abound. Was bitten all over, yet can sleep with them — do not affect me badly. Clothes full of them, when got to Hilo.)

The sandhiller is full of dull stories about quarrels, fights & duels in Texas, where he spent two years, yet he is an amiable man, & spends sev. hours ev. day in tending Mrs. P.'s baby.

Head winds all the time. Only 20 h. of fair winds since we left Honolulu, 17 days.

[85]Elisha Kent Kane (1820–1857), pioneer explorer of the American route to the North Pole, was the author of *Arctic Explorations* (New York, 1856).

[86]*Book of Common Prayer,* "The Order for Daily Morning Prayer," Sect. 1.

SAT. DEC. 3. Wh[aling] bark Ripple, in sight. Capt. Fish & Capt. Blackmer go on board to "gam".[87] Nearly calm. Capt. Morgan of the Ripple returns the compliment & stays until 11 P. M., & all but me are drinking in the cabin & making noise, — while we are losing a fair wind, the first for 10 days. Morgan is a "pious" man, speaks at prayer-meetings, & refuses to whale on Sundays, & bores awfully by exhibiting his religion to everyone, even strangers, — full of the conventional cant, — yet he got pretty tight last night. They had a smart lark, (on Blackmer's part) abt. a pig, wh. was carried to & fro in various attempts to get him fr. the Ripple, in wh. our side at last succeeded. Struggle for pig, & he fell down fore hatch.

SUNDAY. DEC. 4. Fine day & good, fresh, fair wind. All in good spirits. Ripple alongside, Capt. Morgan comes on board to dinner, but no delay, as both vessels keep on. I keep clear of Morgan.

Mrs. Palmer improves on acq., & seems to have good plain educ., & good sense & feelings.

WED. DEC. 7. Make the land little below Monterey, some 75 or 80 miles S. of S. Francisco. Bad luck. Calm all day & night.

Calms & head-winds all Wed. Th. Fri. & Sat. Very hard to bear, & our port so near. I could be content no where, in such a case as this, but *at sea.*

Sat. night, strong wind & fair. Good progress.

[87]Gossip.

3. California and to the Orient

SUNDAY. DEC. 11. Arrive at S. Francisco. Pass "heads" at sunrise, beat in ag. strong head winds. Noble bay, & striking points — yet no wish to see it again. Land at noon. Tehama Hs., kept on European plan — more convenient & econom. for me. Comfort of dressing & washing & room eno'. In Architect, had no state-room, but slept in cabin, & no private place at all.

A good dinner, neat funiture, fresh meats & vegit., & excellent cooking, at French Restaurant. No one can conceive of the comfort of it, who has not been through a bad voyage at sea.

Landed too late for the A.M. Service. No aftern. service. At 7 P.M. went to vespers in R. C. Cathedral. Full, but not like the music. An Irish sermon. Said Scripture assures us that ¾ of the seed is lost. The parable says that three of the 4 *parts* are lost — but not wh. was the larger, or that were equal.[88]

MOND. DEC. 12. Ride horse-back to Mission, before breakfast. Horses good & cheap. No vessel up for China. Fear long delay. Glorious weather here — like our warm October weather, & grapes, pears & apples in market, & flowers growing in open air. Dine tete-a-tete with [J. B.] Felton. Introduced to Judge Norton, thought to be the best judge in Cal.[89]

TUESD. DEC. 13. Ride to Cemetery, horse-back. Fine view fr. Cemetery of Pacific Ocean, Bay, City & Golden Gate. Site good, but no trees over 15 feet high — all scrub. Must be so here, I fear.

Dr. Morison, br. of Rev. of Milton, &c. takes me to ride to the beach. By far the grandest surf ever saw. Breakers break 8 or 9 deep, & the outer ones are fearfully high.

Dine with Felton, Abel Guy, the very rich banker, Koopmanschap, a German merchant who is aiding me to go to China, & a Mr. Liés, a lawyer of S. Barbara, French origin educated in Paris, speaks English perfectly, & is very clever, brilliant, drank rather too much & is a mere pleasure seeker. These are F.'s friends, — all too fast & too loose for my tastes. Edward Hoar, brother of Rockwood, left here the reputation of

---

[88] Luke 8:5–13.

[89] John B. Felton is noted earlier. Edward Norton was a judge of the Twelfth District Court in San Francisco in 1859.

brilliant talents & reckless life, — the S[e]argent Prentiss of Young California.[90]

Felton's first introduction to a Judge of the Supreme Court, [Alexander] Wells, a few days after his arrival here, in 1853. Wells was leaning ag. a wall, with a revolver in his hand, & inquiring for "that g — d — s — b — " that had told a story about him — gave his other hand to Felton.

Usual interest here, on good security is 2 percent a month, & that allowed to compound. Principal doubles in betw. 2 & 3 years.

Reasons given are (1) want of any system of credit, by wh. paper doubles & triples the actual specie (2) the risk there is as regards the value of all security, merchandise, fr. fluctuations in market, & real-estate from that cause & the doubts over all titles. Fluctuations in mdse. owing to being no market near here, & all goods sent here must be sold *here* or kept.

WED. DEC. [14.] Yesterday I returned my horse to wrong stable. They took it, thinking I meant to lodge him there. Called at the right stable to-day, & found they had been in alarm. Did not know me, even by name, & the owner had been censuring the hostler for letting a horse to a stranger without getting his name, & the hostler had just said "Well, if I could not trust that man, I could not trust my own father. If a man ever had an honest face, he had. He looked like one of our *first bankers*". I entered, just at the height of it, as they were about sending off for a search, & said — "I'll take that horse again, if he is in".

"He has not been here. He is not returned".

I insisted that I returned him, but on looking further, I saw I had gone to a stable just like it, at the next block, where the horse was quietly breakfasting. They were a good deal relieved.

Rode to a high hill, wh. gave grand view of Bay & entrance & town.

Bark Early Bird is up for Hong Kong — for Jan. 1st. This is probably the earliest vessel. Great loss of time. Yet, consolation is that I am in a healthful, invigorating climate, with nothing to trouble me, & suff. employt. to keep me fr. being dull. Shall employ interval in going to Sacramento, Almeden mines, Navy Yard, &c.

On board the Architect, after finishing Kane, found, in possession of a whaling mate, the fat, one vol. ed. of Byron's life, letters & poems,

[90]Abel Guy was a banker and commission merchant in San Francisco. Eugene Liés, a resident of Santa Barbara, filled a variety of public offices, including district attorney and state representative. Edward Hoar, son of Samuel Hoar, practiced law for a few years in San Francisco and then returned home. Seargent Smith Prentiss (1808–1850) was a lawyer, orator, and U. S. congressman from Mississippi, but was originally from New England. His brief career was presumably cut short by personal excesses.

complete.[91] Dealt out to myself Childe Harold, one canto a day. That done, began the letters. Read about 350 (say ½) of them, when voyage ended. Childe Harold a great production. Spots of highest genius, & nowhere poor, & always an easy mastery of versification. The letters of earlier life, before his return to England — not so good. Vain, egotistical, & not striking. Those written after he left England in 1816, fr. Germany, Switzerland, & Italy, are extremely clever, — witty & often excellent thought as to poetry. He appreciated [George] Crabbe fully. So he did [Edmund] Kean, as an actor, & came to appreciate Coleridge. His mind was less corrupted on the subject of poetry than on any other. It was the last citadel that fell. He was honest there. In a letter to Moore, he rather explains away what he says to [John] Murray about Pope's superiority — yet it is not satisfactory. But what an unhappy wretch! I believe he had a conscience, after all, & that it haunted him & made him desperate at times.

Contrast his lines on his 36th birthday,[92] with the words of St. Paul, — "I am now ready to be offered, & the time of my departure is at hand. I have fought a good fight, I have finished my course, I have kept the faith. Henceforth there is laid up for me &c."[93]

How tired I got of hearing whaling stories. One man kept on, in a dull monotone, long stories, to me alone, the effect of wh. on my mind may be represented thus. "— whale —— the whale —— whales — the whale ——— the whale ——."

Yet, the whaling in the Extreme North is a gallant service. Ev. year ships are lost in the ice, & men killed by whales & by bears. Whaling masters are the best of seamen, as regards working a ship & ground tackle, but not as regards the mechanic art of fitting rigging, & they have much less discipline, order & almost no etiquette. Without these, men alone, out of society & business, as in camp or at sea, soon degenerate & are demoralised. Poor Capt. Fish had none of those. His steward

[91]Probably published in Philadelphia in 1854, with a *Life* by Allen Cunningham.

[92]Byron's "On This Day I Complete My Thirty-Sixth Year" (1824), concludes with the following two stanzas:

> If thou regrett'st thy youth, *why live?*
>   The land of honorable death
> Is here: — up to the field, and give
>   Away thy breath!
>
> Seek out — less often sought than found —
>   A soldier's grave, for thee the best;
> Then look around, and choose thy ground,
>   And take thy rest.

[93]II Timothy 4:6–8.

snubbed him, his cabin boy defied him, men did as they pleased, there were no *stations*, but all went by hap hasard. Whaling crews wear such hats, coats & trowsers as laboring men wear on shore, or loafers — seen them with green plaid pantaloons, Kossuth hats[94] &c. — nothing ship-shape.

Spent ev. at Bishop [W. I.] Kip's. Met a Mr. Olney, a R. I. man, who held high mil. command under the Vig[ilance] Comm[ittee]. Vig. Comm. had determined to destroy the U. S. ship John Adams, if she fired on the town. Olney says most of the naval & mil. officers sympathised with the Vig. Comm.[95]

Meet, in street, Mr. Stien, of Brattleboro' Vt. He has come here to reside. Invited me to call upon his wife, & says her health is much better in California.

THURS. DEC. 15. Rode to Presidio. Troops target shooting. Clipper coming in under her fore & aft sails — pretty sight, hear song of sailors. Fine situation of Presidio.

Breakfast with Gov.-elect Latham, Judge Parsons, Felton, Liés, Hempstead, & Casserly — very pleasant — [96] extravagant breakfast, — given by Parsons. Conv. clever, but on pers. topics, anecdotes &c., only. Stories of fights in Courts. Man drew pistol on Parsons. Two lawyers fought before [John S.] Hagar J[udge], in Court, & he let it go through. In another case, before Hagar J., this conversation took place:

Wilson[97] (counsellor), "I desire a delay on account of absence of my client."

Blake[98] (counsellor) "Of course she is absent. She is on a tour of f —— n through the States".

[94]Evidently Louis Kossuth, noted earlier, set a style in hats when he toured the United States in 1851.

[95]James N. Olney, a stockbroker and member of an old and respected Rhode Island family, was second in command of the great Vigilance Committee of 1856. The *John Adams* was in San Francisco Bay when the Committee was formed, and for a time there was a question as to whether the military would try to disband the Committee and place the town under martial law. The Committee succeeded in keeping control of the city.

[96]Milton S. Latham (1827–1882) came to San Francisco from Ohio in 1850, served as Democratic congressman, 1853–1855, was collector of port, 1855–1857, and was governor of California for six days, January 9-14, 1860, resigning to become U. S. Senator, 1860–1863. Charles H. Hempstead was superintendent of the San Francisco branch of the U. S. Mint. Eugene Casserly (1822–1885), graduate of Georgetown, was a lawyer, editor of a Democratic newspaper, and U. S. Senator, 1869–1873.

[97]This was probably Samuel M. Wilson (1823–1892), who became one of the foremost members of the California Bar.

[98]Maurice C. Blake was a judge of the County Court of Probate and the Court of Sessions in San Francisco in 1859.

Wilson. "You are a liar".

Blake "I claim the protection of the Court".

Hagar J. "I don't see that any injury has been done on either side, yet".

Letters home by overland mail of Dec. 16, to wife, Palfrey, Capt. Davis, & Barnum W. Field, & journal to Dec. 15.

Did I mention supra the anecdote of my returning a horse to the wrong stable, & going for him the next day & the man's trust in my looks?

Walk thro' the narrow alleys betw. Jackson & Pacific st. at night, where the Chinese live, in little rooms. These are coolies, under contracts, & kept at this business by their owners & importers.

FRID. DEC. 16. Visit camp of the "Digger Indians" in outskirts of the city. Several hundreds, captured & transported to a "Reserve" as thievish & predatory. Very ugly & rather squalid.

Call on Mrs. Major [Hiram] Lennard & Mrs. Lawler (Miss Price), & dine with latter. Nice little house, with view of harbor, bay & town, being on top of Telegr. Hill. Frankly says she has been perfectly happy in her marriage, & seems to be so, & Lawler says he shall always keep her so. Pleasant to see line begin in that way. She gave up a great deal for him.

Streets of S. Fr. covered with plank boards, & frequent "man-traps" & "horse-traps" in carriageways & side-walks. All S. Fr. is built on sand, what is not built on water, & hence the planking.

3d Artillery, Col. [Charles S.] Merchant, at the Presidio. Calls fr. Drs. [F. A.] Holman & [S. C.] Hastings, Mr. Fred. Billings (lawyer), [C. R.] Bond, Capt. Thomas of J. Adams &c. &c.[99]

SAT. DEC. 17. Attended Court to hear Judge [Edward] Norton give his weekly batch of opinions. He is said by all classes, parties & callings, to be the best & ablest judge that ever sat in California. The confidence in his integrity & ability is unlimited. His great feat of memory consists in giving opinions in a long list of cases, having before him only the names of parties, referring to names, dates, places, amounts, points taken, cases relied upon, & his own reasons — all *ore tenus* [orally]. It is almost beyond belief. To-day, he gave about 10 or 15 opinions, all in that way. His language is concise & clear, & reasoning good. He decides about 1500 cases a year. In most cases, the parties have a choice of tribunals, among the District Courts, & Norton is such a favorite that the other Court is a sinecure.

Being the Sabbath, went, for the first time in my life, to a Jew.

[99]Frederick Billings (1823–1890), lawyer from Vermont, founded and developed the Northern Pacific Railroad. The town of Billings, Montana, is named after him. Captain Thomas remains unidentified; the rest of the names mentioned here are noted earlier.

Synagogue. Found the clergyman there, Rev. H. A. Henry,[1] before service began, & got information fr. him, & present of a book of his for relig. instrn. of Hebrew youth. In middle is high box, where the clergyman reads & says all the service. Box is large eno' for 3 or 4 persons, cushioned desk for reading &c. At one end, opp. the door, is curtain, which, drawn, shows the 5 books of Moses, written on parchment & rolled on wooden rollers. I was too late for the morning service, & at the ev. service were only some 10 or 12 men & no women. All sit, with hats on, except that stand when curtain drawn & rolls taken out, & ditto when returned. All the service is in Hebrew, (wh. all Jews know, I presume) & all is chanted or intoned, even to the reading of the Scriptures. The parts, as in reading Scripture, the Clergyman reads alone, but the prayers & Psalms are chanted (or intoned) either responsively, or by clergym. & people together. They sit in prayer, with hats on, only occasionally bending heads. They talk in the intervals, & move about, & the whole seemed to me irreverent. A spectator wd. hardly know that it was a relig. service. It might be a school of adults.

Mr. Henry admits that they have lost the distinction of tubes, [?] & the priesthood. The sacrifices are given up for two reasons, (1) because were to be offered only in Judea & (2) no High Priest. They divide the 10 Commandments in a diff. manner fr. both Catholics & Protestants. Their first is the mere declaration, in 20 Exodus 2d.[2] Their second, is verses 3, 4, 5 & 6 united, as the R. Catholics unite them. The others follows as in all churches, to the 10th, which embraces verse 17. Protestants & Catholics do not treat verse 2 as a Commandment, therein differing fr. the Jews. Jews & Catholics agree in making one commandment of verses 3, 4, 5 & 6, therein differing from most Protestants. Jews & Protestants agree in making one commandment of verse 17, wh. Catholics divide into two. Swedenborgians unite verses 3-6, but whether they make their 10th by dividing the 17th or by adopting the 2d, I do not remember. The rabbi told me the Catholics were right in uniting the 3-6 verses, according to the mass. & traditions.

The countenances of the Jews at this service were intensely disagreeable, — indeed, are they not (the men, I mean) almost always so. The clergyman (rabbi?) was not disagreeable in expression, probably from not being in trade. Their worship is dull, formal & unhappy, — the worship of a disheartened people.

Did I mention that, in coming upon the coast, we had a mirage of the Light Hs. on Faroallon? The Light Hs. is a cone. By the mirage [it]

[1]Henry A. Henry (1801–1879), born in England, had had synagogues in Cincinnati and Syracuse before removing to San Francisco, where he conducted a synagogue until his death.

[2]"I *am* the Lord thy God, which have brought thee out of the Land of Egypt, out of the house of bondage." All of the following verse references are also to Exodus.

looked an hour-glass, — two cones, one the actual building, & the other the inverted image, touching it?

To-day, in my morning's ride, saw men ploughing & others hoeing betw. rows of vegitables just coming up (Dec. 17th). There has been no rain for more than two weeks, the finest of our Oct. weather — yet this is the rainy season.

SUNDAY. DEC. 18. Ride to Mission Dolores before breakfast. All building fitted into Chapel, & Mass saying there.

Trinity Church at 11 A.M. Rev. Mr. Thrall[3] preaches. Fair congregation, rather *genteel*, no audible responses, excellent singing & playing, but choice of tunes & chants as bad as can be. No church like the Advent!

3 P. M. to Vespers at Notre Dame des Victoires, the French Church. The contrast betw. that & the Cathedral is that betw. a Paddy Church & a French Church. At Notre Dame des Victoires everything is as neat, clean, & orderly as it is possible to imagine. The vestments of priest & altar boys beautiful & in better taste than I ever saw in a R. Cath. Church, & the music excellent. Chanting, all Gregorian, slow & grave, & several beautiful hymns sung, in one of wh. I found myself shedding tears, mais pourquoi — je ne sais pas. What with the good taste, the neatness, the devout attention of the Congregation, the exquisite music, the odour of the incense, & the slow & reverent steps & genuflections of the priests, — the effect was better than ever saw in a R. Cath. Church. Short, familiar sermon, in French, by the Abbé Blaine.

7.30 P. M., to the Confirmation at Grace Church, with my friend Capt. Blanding, late U. S. Distr. Att., & Capt. in the Palmetto Regt., in the Mex. war, — an excellent fellow. Odd, that the two most religious, moral & gentlemanlike men I have met at the Bar here, should be from S. Carolina, Blanding & Pringle,[4] — both are vestrymen of Grace Church. Church crowded, singing worse than at Trinity, i.e., voices & playing very good, selections of tunes abominable. They know absolutely nothing of the resources of music in the church, by way of chant & hymn, — sounded like second rate opera. Twenty six confirmed, & among them an *ex* M[ember] C[ongress] & leading lawyer, & another lawyer, a reclaimed inebriate. Rest were young. The sermon & address by Bishop Kip.[5]

---

[3]Stephen C. Thrall was rector of Trinity Church in San Francisco.

[4]Lewis and William Blanding were lawyers in partnership in 1859. Edward J. Pringle has been noted earlier.

[5]Dana deleted the following lines from the text: ". . . were nothing — absolutely nothing! Even B[ishop] Eastb[urn]'s stereotype wd. have been a relief. No allusion to anything practical, — duties, reading, self-exn., discipline, habits of prayer, sacraments & preparation for them, public worship &c., — but vague, superficial talk! How *can* a man do so, with such an occasion, & such a company of hearers. B. K. is a gentleman, but a superficial man, in thought & feeling, honorable & kindly but no grasp & no zeal."

Took tea with Blanding, at Martin's. He told me about the battles his regt. was in, from Vera Crus to Mexico [City]. He joined with 1100 men, & brot home 250. At Churubusco, more than half the Regt. on the ground was killed or wounded, including Col., Lt. Col. & Major. Quitman was the best vol. general, after Persifor Smith. Shields, rash & careless of lives, & not trustworthy as to truth, if his own reput. concerned.[6]

MOND. DEC. 19. Ride to Presidio. Warm, June morning & cloudless sky. So far, S. Fr. winter is delightful.

TU. DEC. 20.   Sent journal & letters to wife & Mr. Parker, by steamer. 10 A. M. took steamer for Mare Island (Navy Yard). On board found Mr. Edw. Stanly, late M. C. fr. N. Car., now of Cal., on his way to his ranch, in Napa Valley, Gen. Vallejo (Don Guad. Mariano) & his son-in-law Frisbie, &, above all, old Mr. Yount, the famous pioneer & woodsman, the first white settler in Napa Valley.[7] All invited, & insisted on my going to Napa. Glad to do it — as Napa Valley is the pride of Cal., & the Geysers one of its greatest curiosities, & old Yount is alone worth a journey there. Agreed to meet Stanly at Napa City tomorrow.

Landed at Navy Yard, Mare Island. Spent night at Com. Cunningham's,[8] where met Miss West, fellow-passenger fr. N. York.

The Russian officers, fr. the 2 men-of-war steamers, were spending day there, Com. Popoff, 2 lieuts., & 8 or 10 middies, all young, — all spoke more or less Engl. & French, inquiring & polite. Com. P. & one lieut. were at Sebastopal.

Exd., with them, the docks. Russians lunched, waltsed & took leave early, to go back to S. Fr. (Old Com. C., alone at end of table, oblivious of all guests, barely knowing anything, sticking to his bottle after all left).

[6]John Anthony Quitman (1799–1858) of Mississippi, champion of states rights in the U. S. Congress, served as a brigadier general of his state's militia during the Mexican War. Persifor F. Smith (1798–1858) was a brigade commander during the war, famous for his ability to inspire his men. James Shields (1806–1879) left the bench of the Illinois Supreme Court to serve in the Mexican War, resigned an appointment as governor of Oregon Territory to serve as Democratic senator, 1849–1855. In 1859 he was a U. S. senator from Minnesota. During the Civil War he served as a general in command of volunteers.

[7]Edward Stanly (1810–1872) was congressman from North Carolina, 1837–1843 and 1849–1853, when he moved to California. He practiced law in San Francisco, was defeated in a bid for governor in 1857, and during the Civil War was military governor of Eastern North Carolina. Don Guadalupe Vallejo, mentioned in *Two Years*, is noted earlier. John B. Frisbie (b. 1823), prominent Vallejo business man, married one of Don Guadalupe's daughters. George Concepcion Yount (1794–1865) owned and controlled a large tract of land in the Napa Valley. He was a California pioneer whose career Dana describes in some detail later in the *Journal*.

[8]Robert B. Cunningham was Commandant of the U. S. Navy Yard at Mare Island.

Com. C. takes the Naval Constructor, Hanscomb,[9] & goes all over the new steamer, the Saginaw, with me. Neat boat, side wheel, light draft, first naval vessel built by us in Pacific. Go to Model Loft &c. Yard very large, & on a plan of magnif. proportions, if ever completed. Make acq. of Col. [Daniel] Turner, a Virginian, his wife d. of [Francis Scott] Key, the poet. He is Engineer, & a very kindly, hosp. & honorable man. Wife clever, & good children. Also Capt. McDougal, & Bissell, very civil & attentive, all.[10]

Vessels here are Independence, 50, Receiving Ship, Decatur sloop of war, in ord., Saginaw, & 2 small steamers.

The off[icers] like the position of the Yard — healthy, safe fr. attack, remote fr. city & deep water. Use the native laurel for ship timber. Is very hard, cuts like lead, & fine polish.

WED. DEC. 21. (Mare Island). Up early. Capt. McDougal waits on me, & sends me over to Vallejo in a yawl. At Vallejo, breakfast at Frisbie's, & meet Gen. Vallejo, & his younger d., La Señorita Josita, at school in S. Fr., & wives of Frisbie & his br., both d. of Vallejo. Frijoles for breakfast.

Gen. V. remembers me as a boy in the Alert's boat, in 1836. He repeats some of my conv. with him then. He was Comt. of Presidio.

The Vallejos, Guadaloupe & Salvador, owned nearly all Napa & Sonoma, having princely estates, but have little now, Guad., by bad management, & Salvador by that & gambling. Gen. V. got the capital placed here, on condition of putting up publ. b[uildings] at his own exp. Did so, expended $100,000, but after 2 sessions was moved to S. Jose, & the town fell to pieces, the houses (wood) moved off &c. Within 5 years, has increased to 4 or 500 inh., & is promising. Doubt if V. gains by it, but Frisbie does, who owns most of the land here. All V's d[aughters] are rather handsome, in the Mex. style, & are full blood whites.

Took coach for Napa City, wh. reached at noon. Ride up Napa Valley is beautiful. Never saw so much land under the plough in the same space, except in England. Great fields, level, rich, no undergrowth, fair sprinkling of large trees, & distances so great that the men are ploughing by flagstaffs, as a pilot would steer his ship. Peculiarity of valley is that is enclosed by high hills, river wandering through it, lands nearly level, & small hills, green to top, dotted over the valley, wh. can easily ride round or over — rising like artificial mounds.

[9]Isaiah Hanscomb was chief of construction at the Navy Yard at this time.

[10]David Stockton McDougal (1809–1882), assistant to the Commandant, commanded the *Wyoming* during the Civil War (during which he attacked the entire Japanese fleet at Shimonoseki), and became a rear admiral in 1873. Simon B. Bissell (1808–1883), a commander at this time, became a captain in 1862. He commanded various vessels during the Mexican and Civil wars, and after.

Napa City, small town of say 1000 inhab., Co[urt] Hs., 2 or 3 churches, etc.

[Edward] Stanley there with buggy & pair of mules. He has a ranch just below, sd. to be very valuable, $100,000 or so. Land here varies fr. 50 to $100 per acre. Rich in grains & fruits.

Napa Valley. Reached Yount's towards night. He has a principality here, of some 12000 acres, from mountain to mountain, & running length wise of the valley, the Napa Creek running thro' its centre. He owns a large mill, & has some 100 or so Indians encamped near his house, whom he employs. He lets his land at abt. $5 per acre a year — very much troubled with squatters. Lately married an intelligent middle aged woman, well educated &c., from N. York, who takes care of his affairs, keeps his accts., sees he is not cheated, & pays off his debts, for the old hunter has no business habits or knowledge. He had a former wife, & has children & gr. ch., but all have left him except a gr. d., Lilly Yount,[11] abt. 12 yrs. old, at school at S. Fr., & now at home for Christmas — strong, hardy & fine looking girl. She owns 1000 acres of this land, wh. is a tol. fortune.

Old log house, modernised, one story, huge chimney & large logs & knee timbers burning on the fire. Hearty welcome.

In ev., old man tells us his Indians stories & his life. Born in N. C., Burke Co., in 1794, left home at 15, for Ky. (or Tenn.?), in war of 1812-14, joined mounted rifles & fought the Indians for 2 years, advanced to be lieut., & great reputation for courage & skill in woods & with rifle. After peace, takes to hunting & trapping, & engaged in it until 1843, incessantly, hunting over Arkansas, Texas, New Mexico &c., & trapping the Colorado, Gila &c. Frequent fights with Indians, & bears, panthers &c. Sev. times besieged in camp by Indians, & fights for days. Says, with gr. simplicity, that never killed an Indian for the sport of it, *for game*, but only in fight, when necessary.

He was the first white man that came into Napa Valley. It was then full of Indians & Grissly bears. Built log hut, & fought the Indians for sev. months. Once besieged in his hut for sev. days. Indians had only bows & arrows, & he had rifle & pistol. Usually he had 3 or 4 men, with him, whites or friendly Indians. Where house now stands, scene of sev. fights.

Grissly Bears ("Grisslies") has killed hundreds of. In one day, he & a Spaniard killed eight. Spaniards lasso them, & get a tree betw. them, &

[11]Lilly was Yount's daughter by his first marriage to Eliza C. Wilds, daughter of a Kentucky settler. She had the marriage annulled after she thought him dead, while he was on a long trip, and had remarried.

so the lasso holds the bear at distance, — always mounted. (Story of the Mexican who got lasso round bear's nose, & it came off.)

Yount's famous dream, is told by him to me.

He was living then in the valley, in 1843. He had never been over the mountains, by the N. route, but only by the Southern, & knew nothing of it. Dreamed that walking in strange place, large mountain, a white chalk rock, river & trees, all as plain as if been there, & came on large traveling party, men, women & children, "snowed up", starving to death, eaten their animals & begun to eat their own dead. Awoke, fell asleep, dreamed the same again. Troubled & after lying awake some time, fell asleep & dreamed it all a third time. So much impressed that believed it a Divine Revelation, went off to some hunters who knew this route, told them the dream & described the scene. They said they knew the place from his description. This confirmed him & them, & Yount gave $70, & others contributed, Gen. Vallejo &c., & party went out. At the very spot, as seen by him in his dream, (& they went by that) they found a party, just in that condition, & relieved & brought them in. This is known as the "Donner Party",[12] & their story made a great impression on the public at the time. A large portion of them perished.

All I can say is that Yount believes what he tells, of this dream, thinks it was divinely sent, & the people in the Valley corroborate him so far as came to their kn[owledge], i.e., his telling the dream, with the minute description of the spot, the party going out on the faith of it & finding them there. Gen. Vallejo told me that it was true, so far as he knew of it. Yount is a man of unimpeachable integrity, & moderate & reasonable in his views, & does not exaggerate.

Yount's Ranch is called Caymas, an Indian name.

TH. DEC. 22.   In this latitude, prob. 38° N., breakfasted open door, few remaining strawberries on vines, & some strawberries in blow, grapes still on vines, & fresh flowers in bloom. The creeping vines over the verandah are in luxuriant bloom. Best of weather, wood fires & open doors. This is Cal. winter.

Left for the geysers. Detained until noon by a pompous old half lawyer, Col. Fisher, who is drawing Y.'s Will, & wished Stanly to look at it. Glad he did.

Old man gave us bottle of wine of his own make. I like it. It has no

[12]A party of California emigrants from Illinois, whose nucleus was the Donner and Read families, was snowed in while camping at Truckee Lake in November 1846. Before successive rescue parties from California could bring them in, they were reduce to eating their own dead. From a party of 87, only 47 survived. See George R. Stewart, *Ordeal by Hunger* (New York, 1936).

spirit, but pure juice, pressed by hand. Better so. The skin & seeds of this grape shd. not go in.

Reached McDonald's[13] at night, after delightful ride up valley. Above Yount's, on his land, is a white sulphur warm spring at tem. of 90°. As get higher, land is rougher, stones appear, few stone walls &c. Evergreen oak, & the common deciduous oak droops, almost like willows, with mistletoes & has long pendants of thin hanging grey moss, all among the leaves. Very pretty. Trees are large & come right out of the sod, as in Engl. parks. No clearing to be done, but put plough right in. The Napa Valley is Lake George, dried up, turned to rich soil, level, with little hills sprinkled over the level, & large trees alone & in clumps.

At McDonald's, large wood fire in stone chimney, sticks 4 f. long, & ½ dos. on at time. McD. is away, & his wife & 3 children, a hired man, a Norwegian, called Brady. Mrs. Mc. is neat, pretty & obliging, about 30 years old. Asked her how came to Cal., said, "Over the mountains". "Had hard time, then". She made no reply & did not wish to pursue the topic. Stanly & I both stuck with it, & asked Brady abt. it. Brady[14] told us she was of the Donner Party, that Yount's party rescued. In that dreadful time, she lost father, mother (names were Graves) 2 sisters & br.-in-law, there, & a br. & sister died after [they] got in. She was then a young girl of about 15. The Graves fam. did not eat their dead, but some of the party did so. Her fam. were 11 in all, of whom 5 survived, all now living in Cal. & 2 married near her.

A Methodist Circuit rider spends night here. His first words, in dark, simple reply to Stanley's qu. how far came from to-day, "Well, Sir, from Clear Lake, only" — were uttered in so solemn a tone, as if were last he expected to utter in this life, — a rebuke, a warning, a final testament & benediction — all in one — revealed the Method. preacher.

FRID. DEC. 23. Started on horseback, (Stanly & I) with Brady for guide, for the Geysers. Fine mountain scenery, large trees. Little twinkling leaf of ev[ergreen] oak. Reach Geysers in 4 h. 45 m.

Spend 2½ hours wandering in the cañon & over the little hills. A space of ½ miles square, all devoted to hot springs, sulphur steam, coming fr. ground & rocks, & steam bursting out fr. hill sides, through little fissures, as big as steam boiler pipe, & with all the noise of escape steam in steam boat. Obliged to speak loud, when 200 feet off. Two cauldrons of stuff as black as ink, bubbling at boiling heat. Rest as color

[13]William McDonald came to California in 1846, married Eleanor Graves, a survivor of the Donner party, and lived in Sonoma County, where he was a guide to the geysers.

[14]Brady was a Norwegian hired hand at the McDonald house.

of water, more or less colored by green & yellow of sulphur. One pretty little cool spring of pure water, impregnated with sulphur & soda, pleasant to drink.

One cañon (ravine) is burnt over, & devoted like a Gehenna, to these fires, steam escapes & boiling discolored emissions. Through it all runs a quiet stream of pure water, over the rocks.

House stands prettily, & hot sulphur water conducted to baths in pipes. Scenery in neighb. is pretty, mountainous scenery.

Heavy fog sets in. Rain threatens. Start off at 2.30 P. M., with fear of being caught out in dark & rain. Push on at quick speed. At 5 o'ck., is pitch dark, heavy rain, & can see nothing. Single file, but can see neither Stanly nor his horse, nor can he see the guide or the guide's horse. Call out, at intervals, not to lose each other. Several streams to ford, & occ. a fallen tree. Guide loses the trial, — for we are on an Indian trail. He says he can follow the stream, & knows the hills, — wh. we can see ag. the sky, tho' we can see nothing ag. the ground. Only know we are in water by the splashing of horses' feet. Chance of spending night out in rain, in woods, rather gloomy. Cross stream again. Knows where he is. See light! It is McD.'s. Get lost in the yard, as cannot see fence, or barn or shed.

Glad to get to fire & lights & change of clothes & warm supper. Mrs. Mc. nearly given us up.

Rain hard, all night, pattering on roof. Not cold, not at freesing point, probably.

SAT. DEC. 24. Still heavy rain. Brady reports streams so swollen that cannot get buggy over. May have to stay here sev. days. Dreary prospect. Stanly lately married, sent wife to Sacramento, to spend Christmas with her br. Judge [Joseph G.] Baldwin, & he to meet her there to-day. She not know he has gone to Geysers. Must go on. Walk to house of one Keyes, ½ mile off. He knows of ford, not much over buggy floor. We go over on horses, & he drives over buggy. All right, on other side. But not off before noon. Cannot get to Napa in this state of roads, to-day.

Go on as best we can. Heavy rain, muddy roads & deep streams to ford. At dark, get to little shop, abt. 2 m. fr. Yount's. Must give up Yount's, as too dark, & large stream to cross. Neither of us knowing where. Wagon at door, wh. turns out to be from Yount's, & returning there. God-send. Follow it & get in to Yount's at 7 P. M. Cordial welcome. Mrs. Yount we find to be an intell., well edd. woman, fr. New York, & very useful to Y. Miss Lilly there, too, the old man's favorite. There is a simple, natural courtesy in Y.'s manners, wh. is delightful. The receptions & leave-takings are models. He is a gentleman, roughened by 40 years' hardy adventure, & not a boor half polished.

His story of Glass,[15] the hunter. Wounded by a grissly, shoulder torn, neck open, windpipe open, one flank gone. Major — , Command. of the party, obliged to leave him, pd. man & boy $4.00 to stay with him & bury him when he died. Came in, after 2 days, reported dead & decently buried. Glass ate berries in reach, drank water, killed rattle snake, cut off head & tail, pounded up & ate rest. So, for 2 mos. Crawl a little, walk with cane. At last, got into fort. "How far to fort?" "Well, 200 miles, or so". Man & boy given up to him to punish. "If God forgive them, I will".

Next time, Glass wounded by arrow, companion cuts out the stone by rasor. Got well. Next time, betrayed into Indian Village, guns taken, Glass & six others, run for it. Pursued, 5 killed, "Bill" says last saw Old Glass run round rocks, & Indians soon after walking over 'em. Bill got in, & in few days in comes Glass. Next time, last seen making for thicket pursued by Indians. Gets in, nearly starved. Last of Glass, is that leaves a fort, to camp in open air, & is found on rock, killed by Indians.

All over Calif., the Americans hail from some state. All are emigrants. Men & fam. are described as fr. Va., Carolina, Missouri, Illinois, or from the New England states. State feeling very strong, yet the usual repugnancies of N. Engl. & the North ag. the South, & *vice versa,* are softened by intercourse, intermarriage, & tie of common int. in the new State.

State pride of Californians very strong. Remote. Severed by Ocean & Rocky Mountains fr. rest of world, & have a peculiar climate, & peculiar habits & history.

Pleasant night at Yount's. Still rains. Mrs. Y. just got home fr. below, tired, & no attempt at Xmas Eve.

Old man says "Gentn., I sort of believe in punishment", & goes on to say that some of the Donner Party had left a sick man to his fate — may have been their punishment. Inclined to believe in spiritual manifestations — "cannot limit power of spirit".

SUND. DEC. 25. SUND. & CHRISTMAS. But Stanly must go on to Napa, & telegraph to his wife at Sacramento, or they will be in distress. Been so kind to me, & all on my account that came off here — so I accede to sugg., & our whole Xmas, is spent on a raining, muddy road. Afternoon, too late for Church, arrive at Napa City. Spend aft. & ev. in tavern bar-room, as no fire-place in any other room, where billiards are playing. But Stanly & I have some reas. & agreeable conv. All our journey, have had agreeab. conv. S. has anecdotes of Congr. life, politics &c. He is

---

[15]Hugh Glass (d. 1833), in 1823, while a member of Andrew Henry's expedition to explore Yellowstone, was injured by a bear, in the anecdote that Dana recounts. The two men who left him for dead were one Fitzgerald (the older man) and the famous James Bridger, then a young man. As Dana recounts it, Glass was finally killed by Indians on the upper Yellowstone.

Republican, now, & opposed to ext. of slavery, a Churchman, communicant, Delegate to the late Gen. Conv. at Richmond (1859). He tells me he has seen the letters betw. John Randolph & his cousin Judith, after she had married Gouverneur Morris & had a son, — John writing an infamous letter to Morris, reviving her unf[aithfulness] story. Morris knew it all, shewed her the letter, & she replied. He says if Jack did not bleed & blush, it was because he cd. not. He must have been crasy.[16]

MOND. 26. DEC. Steam Boat at Napa City, 10 A. M., for S. Fr. via Mare Isl., & Vallejo. At Mare Isl., shake hands with Comm. Cunningham, Capt. [D. S.] McDougal &c. on wharf, & Miss West goes to S. Fr., under charge of Com. C.'s son. (Don't like her manners. Attends to nothing but what relates to herself or her friends — so let her alone).

This is surely a grand basin, this bay, or series of bays. There is little Benicia, & now M. I. & V. are hidden. Here is Alcatras, & there the narrow Golden Gate! & there the town — yet a dreary fog lies over all.

Reach my rooms at Tehana Hs. before dark. This trip makes me less regret my revisit to Calif.

TUESD. [27. DEC.] Call on Mrs. Dr. Hastings & lunch there. Dine with B[ishop] Kip, to meet the new Bishop of Br. Columbia,[17] a delightful man, serious, well bred, & well toned, with a peculiarly pleasing voice. He preached at Ch. of Advent, in ev., an excellent sermon, in agreeable, solemn, conv. manner, earnest, simple & cultivated taste &c. — in fact he is worth the B. & all the clergy of Cal. put together.

Ch. of Advent is Low Church, & a McAllister family affair, with great pulpit in middle, no altar to be seen — but beautifully dressed with flowers & evergreens.

TH. DEC. 29. 1859. Rose early. 8 A. M. took stage coach for San José, to visit quicksilver mines &c. Seat with driver. Pass old Mission Dolores & the San Bruno ranch, & go over the new road out into Park by the side of the Bay. Rough country & no trees until come to San Mateo. Here few large [farms] & rich soil. Capt. Macondray's county hs.[18] & farm in pretty place. Public Hs. of San Mateo the best looking edif. out of S. Fr. I have yet seen.

Now, all the way, rich, flat country — a large "land lake" as Dr.

[16]John Randolph's inability to maintain cordial relations with his family — especially the women — was notorious. For a full analysis of the somewhat involved controversy discussed by Dana, see W. C. Bruce, *John Randolph of Roanoke, 1773–1833*, II (New York, 1922), 273–295.

[17]George Hills (b. 1816) was ordained as Anglican Bishop of British Columbia in 1859. For the decade previous he had been Canon of Norwich Cathedral.

[18]Frederick W. Macondray was both a rancher and a merchant in San Francisco.

Bushnell[19] says. After rains is very muddy. Never saw mud before, even in Cambridge — our soil is not deep eno'. Coast Range in sight, with snow on its highest tops, across the Bay.

Redwood City, the Shire town of S. Mateo Co., is mere mud hole, on a slough running up fr. the Bay, & forks there. Trade in redwood timber.

Now comes Santa Clara valley. The live oak abounds here, & the sycamore — the same as our sycamore or plane tree. As far as eye reach, this land lake of rich, alluvial, with no undergrowth, & large trees timbered over it. Ranchos & farms abundant. Some, have pretty houses, & some rather approaching the stately. All ranchos & large farms have names. These often painted on the gate-way. The Spanish are the prettiest names — but the land here is mostly held by Americans & British. One is "Menlo Park".

Three men in field mounted. One rides toward us. "How well that man rides — beautifully!" *Driver.* "Don't he? I'll bet! He is one of the best riders in Cal". *I.* "Who is it?" *Driver.* "Don Secundino Robles.[20] He used to own most of this country here, but has sold or lost most of it, & lives in that little hs.".

This is the way with most of the Old Spaniards.

Now come to pretty little town of Santa Clara, one of the oldest of Missions, estbld. abt. 1770. There is the Mission, its old adobe walls, its gardens & orchards, but in good order & preservation, for it is the seat of the R. Cath. College. Additions have been made to it, & the effect of the whole is pleasing, the venerable & the active & useful. Wish had time & letters of introdn., & wd. stop & see the College.[21] Driver says it is the best College or school in Calif., about 120 pupils. Town grows little, but San José eclipses it, in trade & pop., & is the Co. town of S. Clara Co.

In outskirts of S. Clara are the Agr. Fair Grounds, with Race Course &c. &c., well got up.

This is near head of the Bay. The vessels, steamers &c., stop at Alviso, some 6 miles fr. S. Clara & S. José.

The valley goes on to San Jose. This is a large thriving town. It was the second Puebla estbld. by the Spaniards, Los Angeles being the first. It was known in the North as "the puebla", as Los Angeles was in the South, & they were distinguished as the Upper Puebla & Lower Puebla. The Mission of S. José is some 12 or 14 miles off, on the W. side of the Bay.

[19]Horace Bushnell (1802–1876), a New England Congregationalist minister, went to California in 1856. He published many volumes of addresses and essays, among which is probably the description to which Dana alludes.

[20]Don Secundio Robles (b. 1813) was living at this time on the Rancho Santa Rita in Santa Clara County.

[21]The University of Santa Clara was established by the Jesuit Order in 1777.

The two large buildings in S. Jose are the Church & School. The Church was the old adobe church, wh. looked rather old & crumbling, but was solid, & the Spaniards were not willing to have it pulled down. So brick walls were built outside the adobe walls, a kind of veneering, making them some 7 feet thick, & two wings & a Chancel added, making a very large & fine looking building.

The School is kept by the Sisters of Notre Dame, for girls, & has nearly 200 scholars, & stands very high in public estemn. It is a large brick building, with large grounds enclosed by a wall.

Spent night at a French inn, where cooking was excellent, service as good as in Paris, & prices high. Large wood fire, in bar room, & all the frequenters are French. Great deal of talk round the fire, politics, Napoleon, Austriah, Les Anglais, Moriva, Espagne, Italy &c.

Young gentl. fr. Mr. [Henri] Laurencel, comes over to spend the night & to drive me to the mines tomorrow.

Advertisement of Hamlet, to be played in the little theatre, Mr. & Mrs. W. C. Forbes. Go in & see 2d. & 3d. acts, & can stand no more. Yet interesting to see how this great play interests & affects an audience of farmers & traders & miners & their families, acted as badly as possible. In closet scene, when ghost comes in, Hamlet falls flat on floor, & is picked up by his mother. In the play scene, after hitching himself up to the king, in watching his countenance, fairly staring him out of countenance, when king springs up, & goes off, Hamlet seises him by the shoulders, shakes him, as he would a pickpocket he had detected, — amid great applause.[22] In scene with Horatio, he hugs him in his arms at "as I do thee", — & when he disjoins, he says "Something too much of this"[23] — & so on, & so on. Yet it is an attractive place, in their hands, in S. Fr., & Hamlet called twice before the curtain in one night.

Great French bed, 4 or 5 beds deep, curtains &c. & clean.

FRID. DEC. 30. Up early, & off to the quicksilver mines. Leave the valley, & come to broken, hilly country.

One long vein runs across these hills, sev. miles in length, but held by diff. owners. The oldest & most Southerly mine is called the New Almeden. That is not in operation, being under an injunction, in suit by U. S. for possession, & they do not even permit any one to visit it. Ergo, do not go there, but to Mr. Laurencel's mine, the Enriquéta, named for his daughter. This is the name of the mine, village &c. Mr. L.'s family being in S. Fr., he boards at Enriquéta Hotel, a little place, but kept by Frenchmen, &, of course, well kept. Breakfast there, at 9 o'ck. Two intellig. gentlemen, besides L., speaking Fr. Sp. & Engl. & latter very

[22]III, ii.   [23]III, ii, 79.

fairly. In this little, remote place, we discuss Engl. & Fr. drama, Rachel, &c. They, though French, agree with us about the old Fr. drama.

The Frenchmen can make good bread anywhere, even in Boston. A Yankee can make good bread nowhere.

To the mine. High up the hill. Tunnels cut in, & shafts sunk. This mine only been in operation 6 or 8 mos. One shaft is 60 f. deep. Went down it, by candle lights, ladder, — a small timber, notches cut in it. The quicksilver ore is found only in the vermillion rock. These vermillion streaks run through the other formations. When pieces are broken & brot out to light, picked over by hand, & those that have the red streaks are accepted. These accepted pieces have from six to forty per cent of quicksilver in weight, the average being about 15 per cent.

These pieces are first crushed under stamps, moved by steam, then washed in troughs, shaken by steam, when the ore goes to the bottom & the earth is taken off, — then another washing & shaking, until the ore-bearing earth is pretty well separated. It is then dried, in large pans, & then put into furnaces, & kept in them four hours. In this heating process, the quicksilver evaporates, & ascends into retorts, collected, passed thro' water, in syphons, & then spit out drop by drop, into iron receivers. Then is bottled off in iron flask, with iron stoppers screwed in.

Most of the work men work on contract, by the job, or, as they say, tribute work. All the mines do the working in co[mpanie]s, & are paid by the weight of accepted stone, accounts being kept with each shaft.

Each shaft & tunnel has a name, — usually of a patron saint, & at entrance of it is a framed print of the Infant Jesus.

One year ago, not a house here. Now Enriquéta is a village of 40 or 50 houses, with Post off. &c.

Two or three miles below is another mine, just opened, & worked by a Balt[imore] Co., called Guadaloupe, & a village beginning. If these 3 mines, Almeden, Enriquéta & Guadaloupe, succeed as they promise now, there will be 10,000 people in these hills in a few years.[24]

The quicksilver is carried by mules & wagons to Alviso, the head of the Bay, & shipped for S. Fr. San Jose is the market town of all these miners.

The discovery of the quicksilver mines was fr. inquiries made of the Indians as to where [they] got red paint for their faces &c. & they showed these rocks, with streaks of vermillion.

Lunch, & left my good friends, for San Jose, wh. reached at dark. Dined at my Fr[ench] house. Could not stand another night of the drama, & knowing no one, spent night in the bar-room, at the open fire. I like these French people. They are laborers or journeymen, yet are so

[24]Although the quicksilver mines still exist, the community of Almaden, located eleven miles south of San José, is at present a village of 250 inhabitants.

polite, & more *civilised* than any other people in the same class of life. Drink very little, & smoke & talk.

Amusing, violent, theatr. dispute betw. 2 of them, & appeals to "amour propre" "parole d'houneur" &c. If it had been on stage, wd. have been vehement for Engl. of Am. tastes.

SAT. DEC. 31. Stage coach early, for S. Fr., down the other side, the E. side, of the Bay.

East side of the Bay, San Jose Mission, San Lorenso, San Leandro, & the great grants of the Soto & Castro families, who own some three leagues of land apiece, — forms a glorious agricultural country — great land lake, between the Coast Range of Mountains & the Bay — some 4 to 10 miles wide, a perfect level, except at the foot of the hills, no undergrowth, & trees enough to make shade here & there. Houses well placed under the trees. Fine views of mountains & the great Bay. If the Napa Valley is Lake George, turned to land, this valley, — the Alameda Valley, is Lake Champlain ditto. Napa is more beautiful & picturesque, with better near views. This is on a larger scale with grander distant views. Napa has the great adv. of water, all summer. This is dry in summer, but not so dry as Sa. Clara Valley. The latter, in very dry seasons, loses its crops by drought.

Visit old Mission of San Jose. Church is standing, & in good order & is now in use. The orchard also. But the ruined adobe walls are all that show the rows of Indian huts, wh. the Xd. [Christianized] Indians held under these great mission principalities.

(Old Mr. Yount, by the way, spoke very favorably of the condition of these Missions & of their treatment of the Indians, when he came here first).

Oakland, in Contra Costa Co., is a large town, a populous suburb of S. Fr., & tho' only 6 or 8 miles off, across the Bay, has a diff. climate fr. S. Fr. (See Dr. [Horace] Bushnell's reasonings on those facts). It is not so cold or windy in summer, & trees grow well there. It is, indeed, a grove of live oak, almost hiding the houses. Large steamers go fr. here to S. Fr. ev. few hours.

Reached my hotel, in S. Fr., at dark. Had neither dined, lunched nor breakfasted, — only cup of coffee, with bread dipped in, before left S. Jose.

Dined. Spent ev. at my room, & to bed early — tho' all the city is alive with New Year's Ev., balls, music, street processions, singing &c. Do not feel in humor for it. Feel too serious, away fr. home, end of a year, &c.[25]

[25]Following this sentence, half a page has been cut out of the text. Dana seems to have continued with some personal reflections.

1 8 6 0

[SUNDAY. JAN. 1, 1860.] Auction rooms (night auctions) have drums
& music & buffoons, to draw people in.

Signs here "Ici on parle Francais". "A qui so habla Espagnol" &c.
Cal. phrases.

Spondulics - Cash, ready money.

Dry up - stop, Hold one's tongue.

Gone in. - Dead, Given up.

You bet. - Certainly. Doubtless.

First rate. - used familiarly - for very well.

Ask a girl of 12 or 14 how she is, or how her mother is — she says
"First rate, Sir". No paper money & no copper here. Smallest coin is
½ dime. Small prices go by *bits* i.e. York shillings, or 12½ cents, but a
dime is always taken for a bit.

At restorants, dinner of canvass back duck is 50 cents, & of chicken
is 75 cents, & eggs are 12½ cents apiece.

MONDAY. JAN. 2.   Observed as holiday, for New Year's. Counting rooms
& many other places closed. Calls on friends, as in N. York. All "receive",
unless sickness or calamity, & then place basket on plate at door to
receive cards. Called on *Mesdames,* Kip, Lawler, Blanding, Ewer,
Morrison, Thompson, Hastings, Macondray & Holman.[26]

JAN. 3. TUESD. Took steamer "Queen City", 4 P. M., for Sacramento.
S. is the capital, & the Leg. & Sup. C't. are in session there. Steamer is on
Mississippi style, high pressure, one cabin running the whole length of
the boat, uninterrupted by machinery, & makes great show. Prices are
"high pressure", also. No accoms. for sleeping except state rooms, &
those are $3 apiece, for one night, & not provided with anything but a
bed; & for toilet, you must go to barber's shop & wash *coram omnibus,*
& wipe on a roller. I made some complaint to clerk of boat, for wh. I
suppose he set me down as a "bloated aristocrat".

After leaving the Bay, & getting into Sacramento River, country is
low & level & stream full, as a passenger said, like the Mississippi. The
Sacramento is growing shallow from the immense qu. of dirt thrown into
its waters above by the gigantic hydraulic mining operations, wh. settles
on bars below the city. The Steamers often ground on them, now, when 5
years ago here was water to spare. Marysville, on Feather River, is in
danger of losing all its navigation by that cause.

[26]The only identified person mentioned here who has not been noted earlier is Mrs.
Ferdinand Cartwright Ewer, who married F. C. Ewer (1826–1883) in 1854. She was
Sarah Mandell Congden, daughter of Benjamin Congden of New Bedford. Her
husband was an Episcopalian clergyman and editor.

WED. JAN. 4. 1860. At Sacramento. St. George Hotel, kept by Genl. [C. I.] Hutchinson, who has been Mayor of S., & is Genl. of Militia & vestryman of Grace Ch. &c. Large & first style hotel, excellently kept. Top full of politicians. A *sub.* in the Court Hs., a Mr. Jos. E. Lawrence,[27] came up in boat to promote the int. of the Collector, Mr. Washington, as candidate for U. S. Senate.[28] The election of Senator in [David C.] Broderick's place, is the great thing now, & absorbs all attention. Every promt. man in the state is a candidate, & all are on the spot, making personal canvass, with their retinues. The S. Fr. Bulletin says that the Cust. Hs., Mint, Navy Agency, Post Off. &c. are removed to Sacr., *pro temp.*

No sooner got to hotel than a Boston client salutes me, one Hill, who has come here to dodge an order of Sup. C't. for custody of child. Then, a man comes "Is this Mr. Dana, of Boston]" "Yes, Sir." "You don't remember me. My name is Ryan".[29] Still, I don't recall him. "I repaired your father's house, at Manchester, in 1846". "Oh Yes, you were the carpenter, &c.," & I began to inquire patronisingly after his success here, when he told me he was here as senator from Humboldt County! I had to come down sev. pegs. He was neatly dressed, carried himself erect & straight, & had quite an air, full of tongue, &, I suspect, a thorough going party hack, with none but Cal. scruples. I met him afterwards in the Governor's private rooms, full of importance.

To Supr. C't. room. In lobby, found Chief Just. Field. He is fr. Berkshire, br. of David Dudley F.[30], &c. &c., also [J. G.] Baldwin & Cope J. J., & was introduced to numberless lawyers, who were all either *ex* judges or Cols., or Genls. — Crittenden, Campbell, McDougall, Williams, Hoag, &c.[31] *Baldwin J.* is quick & fertile, but hasty, *Cope* J. is new & slow, but sensible. [S. J.] *Field C. Jus.* is the chief power. The Bench now is honest, learned & independent, &, for the first time, has public

[27]Lawrence was a clerk in the Customs House in San Francisco.

[28]Benjamin F. Washington was Collector of the Port of San Francisco. He was not elected to the Senate.

[29]James T. Ryan served in the state senate from Humboldt and Trinity counties in 1860.

[30]Stephen Johnson Field (1861–1899), Williams, 1837, went to California in 1849. Elected to the state Supreme Court in 1857, he was appointed to the U. S. Circuit Court in 1863 where he remained until retirement in 1897. His brother, David Dudley Field, prominent member of the New York Bar, has been noted earlier.

[31]Warren W. Cope (1824–1903) went to California from Kentucky in 1850, served in the legislature in 1856, and was chief justice of the state Supreme Court, 1863–1864. James Alexander McDougall (1817–1867) was attorney general of Illinois, 1842–1846, went to California in 1849. He served in the U. S. Congress, 1853–1855, and in the Senate, 1861–1867. He retired in 1867, his career cut short by intemperance. Thomas H. Williams worked for the office of the attorney general in 1859.

confidence. *Terry C. Jus.*, was the last of the ruffian & *buyable* order.
Heard two questions argued, one touching the case of Terry, late Ch.
Jus. indicted for killing Broderick.[32]

Only diff. betw. manners of these judges & ours is in their fam[iliar] &
free interc. with the bar, off the bench. At adjt., they come down into
the Bar & talk with the members; & they sit & smoke in the lobby, with
the members. This is wrong, & will die out, as all the tendencies in Cal.
are in a conservative direction. I have been told by Field, Gov. [M.S.]
Latham, the Gov. elect, & sev. leading democratic politicians, that the
sentiment of the state is almost unanimous in favor of removing the
Judiciary fr. polit. infl., of having the judges appointed by the Gov.,
instead of by pop. election, & giving them a life tenure; & that the Dem.
party would take the resp[onsibilit]y of recommending these, if a Convention should be called. Sev. gentl. have told me the people would even
sustain a system of retiring pensions for judges who have served for
long periods.

Field tells me that the Reporter of their decisions makes dreadful
work, being a polit. appointee, & the new Gov. is to recommend to Leg.
to authorise the Court to appoint its own reporter. He thinks the last
few vols. must be re-edited, & says they would give Horace Gray $20,000
to come out here & do it; — for he thinks Gray the model reporter.

A statute, drawn by Field, when he was in the [California] Leg.,
provides that the usages & rules of the miners, in their several localities,
shall be received in evidence, &, when not in conflict with the Const.
& laws, shall govern. This is in lieu of a code of mining laws, & is far
better; for the character of mining in different localities varies so much,
& the needs & interests of the miners, that a gen. code would be
impracticable. This system delights the miners, & the judges say that the
rules & customs wh. have come before them are almost always sensible
& just, though always verging on the severe & summary. When Magistrates
were scarce, & before this statute, the miners in each region had their
organisations, their written laws, their summary tribunals, & banished,
flogged & hanged delinquents, without hesitation or scruple. Without
this, they could not have lived. They still keep up their organisations &
rules, & make prelim. inquiries, like gr. juries, but almost always take the

---

[32]Chief Justice David S. Terry (1823–1889) shot and killed David C. Broderick
(1820–1859) in a duel on September 13, 1859. Broderick had been U. S. senator in
1857 and traded his seat off to William M. Gwin on a promise of political patronage.
The disagreement which led to the duel involved the slavery issue; Broderick was an
antislavery man, while Terry later served in the Confederate Army during the Civil
War. In 1889 Terry was shot to death by a bodyguard of Stephen J. Field after
threatening Field's life when he rendered an adverse decision in a case involving
Terry's client.

delinquent into the nearest magistrate, & don't interfere afterwards, unless they have reason to think the magistr. releases him improperly, — in wh. case they still sometimes take him & try & punish him by their own tribunals, — but a decision of a *Court or jury* they always obey. The Supreme Court is very popular with the miners, as its decisions have sustained their rules, their water rights, & their investments, however rudely cared for by them.

Field tells me he was Alcalde [mayor] of Marysville in 1850, before reg. organisation of counties & courts, had no definition or limit to his authority or jurisdiction, took unlimited jurisdiction over all cases brought before him (short of capital punishment), held the law in his own breast & declared it for each case, *pro re nata,*[33] made novel writs, *in tem* or *in personam,* as he pleased, & the most curious judgments, but such as justice & the state of society required. Having no jails, & no houses but of canvas, & no jailors or sheriffs, no criminal could be confined longer than they could hold him in hand; so he used to order flogging, lashes on bare back, by installments, & where restitution was possible, or some important disclosures desirable, the lashes were to cease, at end of any installment when the required act was done. Under this system, order reigned in Marysville. Subsequently, he got his acts & records recognised by the Legisl., wh. protected him, & on them all the land titles of the town rest. He also told me that from 1849 to 1856, he never went into Court or the Leg. without a pair of Derringers in his pocket & a Bowie knife under his coat, & that he was advised to do so by the judges, who did the same — all men did. If a man was not ready to fight, either on the spot or by duel he could hardly live, certainly not tolerably, in Cal. Now, no man is armed, (except some rowdies who would be so anywhere) & a man may refuse a challenge on grounds of principle, if his life sustains him in the position.

Called on Miss Dana, my fellow-traveler from N. York, at the hs. of her br.-in-law, one Culver. Talked over the "Star of the West" &c. Nice, little helpless, innocent thing. Evg. at Field's rooms — anecdotes of Cal. life 1850-3, — almost incredible. *Inter alia,* he arrived at Marysville with 18 cents, & in 6 mos. made $60,000 by prof. practice & some lots bot on specn. — lost it in suits & pol. contests in a year more, & made another fortune at the bar.

THURSD. JAN. 5. Rain & mud — all day & night.

Called on Rev. Mr. [W. H.] Hill, the Ep. clergyman. He complains of want of relig. interest, & of habits of Ch. — going — indifft., lax &c., but attentive & kind to him personally, & many good traits in the people.

---

[33]"For the existing occasion"; for a special business.

Called on Rev. Mr. Beckwith, late Principal of Punahou School, whose wife is d. of Dr. [Richard] Armstrong, the Missionary at Honolulu. He is in temp'y charge of a Preb. Soc. here. He left Punahou on acct. Mrs. B.'s health. Mrs. B. showed me Daguerrotypes of all the Punahou scholars, wh. were given to them, on their departure. Pleasant to see the faces of the Gulicks, Armstrongs, Parkers, Lymans, &c. &c., — those excellent, intelligent kind young men & young women.

To the Legislature. State Hs. a long, brick building — one story in height. Assembl. & Senate Rooms well eno'. No bus. of conseq.

Long conv. with Don Pablo de la Guerra, who is senator fr. S. Barbara District. He saw S. Fr. twice destroyed by fire, a large city, of shanties & canvas houses chiefly, but large & full of goods & business, in the morning, & nothing standing at night, & rebuilding the next day. Thus, twice. Once, while fire raging, saw an old woman clearing off the coals & hot ashes & putting up a cloth tent with a board & a few bottles. His companion said "We ought to encourage such industry as that — let's take a drink". His anecdotes of early times — & impositions on the old Mex. holders of land — (wh. the judges tell me is true), they paying taxes & all their lands held by squatters whom no law wd. eject. Later decisions are restoring to them their rights. Don Pablo is an intelligent, cultivated man, & is a noble of Spain, by right of birth.

(An ign. judge in S. Fr., on a petn. for Hab. Corp. granted it ag. the petitioner for the amt. he owed the man who was illegally restraining him).

Dined at Gov. Latham's. L. a young man, clever, not more than ordinary in other resp., & a reg. politician. Mrs. L. the best mind of any woman I have met since I left home, & few better have I ever met, if any — ill health, pale, sallow. Is d. of Dr. Birdsall, now or late of the army.[34] She is rich & so is L. *Ex* Lt. Gov. Purdy[35] was present. After gents' left to look after the caucus, had long & intg. conv. with Mrs. L. on thelogical subjects, on wh. she perfectly understands herself.

Introdd. to Livingston, of the Alta, Gen. English ex Treasurer of Cal., &c.[36]

FRIDAY. JAN. 6. Epiphany, &, as I am a man of leisure, feel it my duty to go to Church. Found the only Episc. Ch. in the city locked — evidently the day forgotten or omitted (Mr. Hill complained of want of int., in

[34]Lewis A. Birdsall, residing in San Francisco at this time, had been an assistant surgeon in the Army, 1834–1842.

[35]S. Purdy was lieutenant governor of California in 1853.

[36]Henry B. Livingston was a reporter for the *Daily Alta Californian* in San Francisco. James Lawrence English, a Sacramento lawyer, was treasurer of the state, 1856–1857.

his people). The only other church to keep the day, is, of course, the R. Cath., & I go there, where, in the rain & cold dull day, in a shell of a Church with bare brick walls on inside, mortar standing out, & holes not yet closed in the roof, was a congr. of not less than two hundred; & yet there had been an early service before this. I never saw a more still, attentive & (to all extern. appearance) devout congregation. One priest only, — the only one here. He has a day school for boys under the Church; & seven Sisters of Mercy, recently arrived, have a girls' school of abt. 200 scholars, also under the Ch. in a damp, dreary place, with bare walls. They have bought a lot for a school & convent, & will soon build. At the end of the side aisle was a reprn. of Our Lord, (being X'mas season) lying in the Manger, — a figure of the Virgin of the sise of life, standing before the child wh. is lying on the floor of the small place, & over it is a thatched roof, & grass lying about it, — all actual.

Congr. chiefly Irish, but some others.

To the Legislature. Met Mr. [Frederick] Billings of S. Fr., who introduced me to sev. members & notables. Don Pablo Dela Guerra & Don Andrés Pico[37] are the only men of Sp. descent in a Senate of 40 members, in a country wh. was Mexican 13 years ago! In the Assembly, of 80, there is but one Mexican. Both branches very young men, mostly betw. 23 & 35, few over 35. Ryan sits reading his Newsp. & voting grandly on yeas & nays. My friend Dela Guerra is thot able & intelligent, & has the most of a patrician look of any man here.

Called on Mrs. [J. A.] McDougall. Her husb. is candidate for the U. S. Senate, so he is out. Mrs. McD. is in poor health, reminds me of Miss [Abby] Wheaton, & is an intelligent, well educated woman. Met there the handsomest woman I have seen in Cal., wife of Mr. Stewart, a lawyer & member of Assembly, & d. of *ex* Senator Foote of Mississippi.[38]

Sacramento is on a dead level & low, has been flooded sev. times & twice burned up. Now, a levee of 10 f. high is built round the city, & all the ground in occupation raised to that level, as they are now raising Chicago. It is laid out in regular rectangular blocks, like Philadelphia, the streets being wider. The streets parallel with the river are named by numbers, & the cross streets by letters. In some streets, trees are set out. More brick houses, in propn., than in San Fr., & all wooden houses are

[37]Don Andrés Pico commanded the Mexican force in California at the battle of San Pasqual in 1846.

[38]William Morris Stewart (1827–1909) was a highly successful lawyer in San Francisco, specializing in mining law. He became U. S. senator from Nevada, 1864–1875, and had a distinguished career as a legislator and lawyer. In 1859 he was in partnership with his father-in-law, Henry S. Foote (1804–1880), who served in the Senate from Mississippi, 1847–1852, and was governor of Mississippi, 1852–1854. During the Civil War he served in the Confederate Congress, representing Tennessee.

now prohibited. Awnings of wood, i.e. piassas, are built out to the whole width of the sidewalks, giving protection ag. sun & rain. These are generally made strong eno' for promenading on their tops from the windows of the second stories, wh. are used as parlors. The Episc. & one Presb. Ch. are handsome, of brick, with climbing roses, &c. The R. C. Ch. is a large shell, & there is a huge deformity of a Method. Church.

The statement that the rivers Sacramento, Feather & Yuba are badly filling up by the qu[antity] of earth sent down by the immense hydr. mining operations, is confirmed to me.

The city & Co. of Sacr. built a hall for State Agr. Fairs, in less than 60 days fr. first sod cut — a hall of brick, 140 x 100, the largest hall in U. S. unsupported by pillars. Inaugn. of Gov. Latham & Inaug. Ball to be there. (Obliged to buy a view of Sacr. fr. a young artist — sent it home by mail.)

SAT. JAN. 7. Rode out with two *ex* governors of Cal., Johnson[39] & Purdy, to visit Sutter's Fort.[40] Little of it remains — only the adobe angles & one adobe house.

Rode to house of Col. [J. C.] Zabriskie, f.-in-law of Gov. Johnson, where saw 3 fine looking women, Mrs. Z., & the 2 daughters, Mrs. Johnson, & Miss Annie. They have fine figures & classic features. The Col. a N. Jersey public man, of some note, — now in reduced circumstances. His hs. is on the only rising ground in the neighborhood of Sacramento.

Called on Mrs. [M. S.] Latham & Mrs. [J. A.] McDougall, & Mrs. [W. M.] Stewart. Latter is handsome & bright, but poverty of acquisitions & topics. Mrs. L. admits that the politics of Cal. are & have always been very corrupt, & that most of the votes in the Leg. are purchasable by office if not money — & that arrangements to give offices for votes are not concealed or thought dishonest by the greater number. She says polit. life is closed to any man who does not do such things.

Met two Demt. judges who doubt if the people wd. favor a judiciary for life by Executive appointment, at present; for politics are too corrupt to trust so long terms to the appt. of any governor, or any Convention — yet they think that is the true tenure, & shd. be aimed at. At present, all is too much tentative & fleeting — people, officers & laws.

All praise Don Pablo's[41] speech, in 1855, on the extension of the stat. of limns. as to land titles. It was made in the Senate, in Spanish, & was a

---

[39]James Neely Johnson (c. 1828–1872) was a Know-Nothing governor of California in 1855. He later removed to Nevada where he practiced law and served on the Supreme Court.

[40]Sutter's Fort was the location of the first gold strike, in 1848, that began the California gold rush.

[41]Reference is to Don Pablo de la Guerra.

noble plea for the Old Californians & their rights, & carried the Senate & Legislature, & probably saved the State fr. the disgrace of a great robbery.

Met Major Gillespie,[42] who was in active work here in the war of 1846,7, commanding at Los Angeles. He was beseiged there & capitulated, but with honors of war. He was present at the action of San Pasqual, where Don Andres Pico, with 70 men, defeated Gen. Kearny[43] with sev. hundreds, & at sev. other actions where Pico distinguished himself. He says Pico was as brave as a lion, & the soul of honor. Pico is now in the Senate, sitting by the side of Don Pablo, the only repsves. of the old regime.

SUNDAY. JAN. 8. 1860. To Church. Day reasonably pleasant, yet not above 40 persons in Church, of whom only 8 or 10 were women — very muddy, to be sure, but not raining. Yet a good sised Church, well furnished empty pews, &c. But I fear brother Hill is enough to provoke a good deal of staying at home — , "The bottamless-er-pii-at" (Bottomless pit) &c. *dégoûtant.*

Met Marshal Tukey in street, who saluted me.

Met a lawyer, partner & friend of Gov. Latham, who thinks Latham honest & capable &c., yet he boasted how in the Convention wh. nominated Latham (the contest being betw. him & Weller),[44] he "traded Weller out of his boots", — got [W. W.] Cope, a lawyer fr. the mountains, to run for Supr. C't. judge, to be voted for by L.'s friends, & C's friends to go for L., & so on as to M. C.'s, State offices of all sorts — "Yes, Sir, Weller was 10 ahead on the first ballot, & before next morning Latham was 10 ahead. He worked it round by setting these offices & tickets ag. each other, & traded the Weller people out of their boots before they knew it". This lawyer is a reputable man, & does not think those things dishonest, so no money is paid down as a bribe.

(Telegraph, yesterday, that the "Early Bird" will not sail before Wednesday — so shall stay over the inauguration).

The univ. habit of "drinks" here, tells especially on the politicians. The candidate for Speaker had to be dropped because he got on a spree which lasted over the election day, & there was a drunken row at the

[42]Archibald H. Gillespie (d. 1873) carried dispatches to Frémont in California during the Mexican War and was commandant of Los Angeles. In 1860 he was elected clerk of the state senate.

[43]Stephen W. Kearny (1794–1848) was brigadier general in command of the Army of the West in 1846, and led his forces against the Mexicans in New Mexico and California.

[44]John B. Weller (1812–1875) served in the U. S. Senate from California, 1851–1857, and was governor of the state, 1858–1860. He eventually left California and settled in New Orleans.

Leg. caucus Frid. night. One member drew a knife on another, who drew a pistol, & instantly as many as 20 pistols were cocked. This stopped the fight. It was too serious. (The question is gravely discussed whether A. *did right* in drawing his knife, &c.) The best man among the Sen. candidates is [J. A.] McDougall, — but his habits have been very bad, & his state is now critical, — wh., they say accounts for his wife's ill health. (Intemperance is the worst vice in a husband a woman can suffer from, for it is constant, public, & mortifying). So, the best two orators on the Repub. side, Judge Tracy & Col. Baker[45] are the same way; & ex Gov. [J. N.] Johnson, my entertainer of yesterday, was "as tight as a peep" in the hotel the night before, & not quite straight yesterday, & he told me he was taking care of a young lawyer fr. the mining region, who could not get away unless a friend forced him off before the morning drinks began. While I was calling at Mrs. McD.'s, her husband came in rather boosey.

[Joseph E.] Lawrence, whom I supposed to be a N. York fast man & a mere Co. Hs. dem. politician, turns up a "spiritualist", in the techn. sense. He tells me he was a disbeliever in immortality &, of course, in X'y. [Christianity], & in all spiritual powers, — saw the rappings, mediums &c. (among good private circles at home), was led to think & read, & came to a belief in the immortality of the Soul, its active state after death, spiritual agency of angels & saints, miracles &c., — thinks there shd. be prayers for the dead, invocation of saints &c., making the World of Spirits practical parts of our religion. How little we know of what is going on in men's minds! I had seen him here canvassing for his friend for the senate, & thought him a man that would laugh at the mere mention of a religious subject. So, I find that Mrs. Latham & Mrs. McDougall, in the whirl of bad politics, have given anxious attention & are now giving it, to the highest of subjects, & know their grounds. And *per contra*, how often men of good reputation & high profession have *no* religious or spiritual life or thoughts *whatever*. We are deceived both ways. Spent the ev. in [S. J.] Field's room. His wife has come, — a very pleasant & pretty young woman fr. Virginia, with cordial manners, & knows how to blush, — a lost art in California. They were in Berkshire in Sept. & gave me late news fr. my friends there.

Major [A. H.] Gillespie married a d. of Duane of Phil.,[46] has been unfortunate here, tried to be elected clerk of the Senate, but the Caucus set up another man, who, of course, would be elected, but Gillespie's old

---

[45]Judge T. P. Tracy has not been identified. Edward D. Baker (1811–1861) served with distinction in the Mexican War, was a leading San Francisco lawyer and orator, and U. S. senator from Oregon in 1860. He was killed leading a charge at Ball's Bluff.

[46]Gillespie, noted earlier, may have married a daughter of William John Duane (1780–1865), Philadelphia lawyer, editor, and political leader.

opponent in the war of 1847, Don Andrés Pico, made a speech in his favor, detailing, as a generous foe, his good conduct in the war, & expressing his astonishment that *Americans* shd. refuse to sustain a man who had shed his blood for his country's cause, & spoke so feelingly & well, that Gillespie recd. *every vote*.

There are three great interests in Cal., mining, agriculture & commercial. At present, I think that, in polit, & economical questions, the mining is the most powerful of these, — not in wealth or numbers probably, but by unity of interest. In questions touching their affairs, they are one man. (In this interest is included, of course, those who depend on them, — the mech. & traders in mining regions). Next is the agricultural, the richest & most numerous, but divided into various interests, grain growing, vine growing, cattle raising, &c., & large rancheros & small yeomen. The members of the Legislature are spoken of as from mining districts, or agric. districts. The comm. int. is almost solely San Francisco.

The practice of hailing from the state of previous residence is so general, that the state is put in the City Directory — thus: "Brown, John, druggist, 105 K. st., (Penn.) &c.", & new, permanent residents, are *introduced* as Mr. A. B. from Georgia, or Mass. &c.

Found out the member from Mendocino Co. & inquired about Canning Smith.[47] He says Canning is Clerk of the Co., which is a good office. I inquired how he was succeeding, his character &c., as a relative, — he replied, being a Southern Chivalry man — "Well, Sir, him & me has had a difficulty, & I prefer to say nothing about him,   except that in his office he is thought an efficient man & good clerk".

Inauguration, in large Agr. Hall (120 x 100, instead of *140* x 100 as I said before). Three cos. of Militia. Gov. Weller introdd. Latham, & Latham, & Latham, (previously sworn in, at the Leg. Hall) delivd. his inaug. address. No allusion to Nat. pol. Loud & pretty good voice. Large audience. Not order eno'. Boys making noise. Judges of Supr. C't., *ex* Gov. &c. on platform.

Don Pablo introduces me to Don Andrés Pico, who has old Spanish manners.

A humbug named Warren, editor of a paper here, has just been married, & told Mrs. Field he had married a woman who was "sound on all the progressive principles of the age".

The Chinese Chapel — a small brick building, arranged inside exactly like a Methodist Chapel, open pews, middle aisle, small square pulpit at head of the aisle. A few small tables about the pulpit were piled with pamphlets or unbound sheets, like tracts — in Chinese.

[47]Canning Smith belonged to the Rhode Island Smiths, Dana's mother's family.

Inaug. Ball at the Agr. Hall. Complimentary ticket for me — including carriage. Arrangements of dressing rooms, supper room, &c. excellent. A hall of 120 x 100, no pillars, & very high roof, & the best dancing hall I ever saw. Large assembly, nearly all dance. Many fine looking women, & many very costly dresses. Mixed with them, the common rustics, with ungloved hands. *Ex* Gov. Weller & wife, Gov. Latham & wife, Lt. Gov. Downie[48] & wife (a Mexican, cousin of Mrs. Henry Mellus), Ch. Jus. Field & wife, McDougall & wife, & innumerable ex governors, ex judges, &c. with wives & daughters.

Weller is a coarse, tobacco spitting man, with inattentive manners, & I had but few words with him.

TUESD. JAN. 10. Parting calls, & took boat at 2 P. M. for S. Fr. Beautiful sail down the river. (Better site for city below, & reasons why failed). Felton on board. Tells me the secret that Latham is to be nomd. Senator to-night — all arranged — the word here is "combination", wh. means jobs, trades, &c. L. is as honest as any of them, & more free fr. trammels. Capt. of Steamer tells good stories of early Cal. life, the infamous, murderous *wag*, Ned McGowan[49] &c. (Ned Mc's funny acct. of his man killing the Dutchman — 'the only place he was mortal' &c. his *inf. machine* &c.). (Also, of Ned Marshall, & Senator Foote[50] — "That or *rain*" — fellow with window sash over his neck "running yet" —). The "same old drink".

At *S. Fr.*, 9 P. M., & my hotel & long night's rest.

WED. JAN. 11. The Bark "Early Bird" sails to-night. Call on Mr. & Mrs. [Edward] Stanly — letter fr. Frémont &c. Fine large French ship to sail for Hong Kong in 10 or 12 days. Shd. like to go in her, for advantage of speaking French — & wd. wait that time were I not already out of season in the East. Two weeks may make the diff. of my visiting or not visiting a country, escaping a quarantine or not &c.

To-night, I hope to see my last of California.

[48]John G. Downey (b. 1826) succeeded Latham as governor and served from 1860 to 1862. He was instrumental in swinging California support to the Union cause during the Civil War.

[49]Edward McGowan (1813–1893) was a notorious outlaw arrested by the Vigilance Committee of 1856. He managed to avoid conviction, left the area, and published a memoir of the experience.

[50]Edward Colston Marshall (b. 1820), a Kentuckian cashiered from the Army for dueling during the Mexican War, arrived in California in 1849, served as congressman from the state, 1851–1853, returned to Kentucky in 1856 to win fame as a lawyer and orator, and returned to California in 1878, when he became attorney general. Henry Stuart Foote is noted earlier. Dana is here making notes to remind himself of stories he has heard.

"A few short hours, & we will rise to give the morrow birth,
And I shall hail the main & skies, — but not my Mother Earth".

The Capt. of the steamer came fr. Panama with Edm. D. Otis, & says he was a capital fellow, cheerful & full of fun & courage & the favorite of everybody. So, in S. Fr., but he fell away, & got to driving a job wagon, & was taken home by compassion, & died on the passage. Felton speaks very well of Bruce Upton, & says he was respected & liked here & his failure was owing to overconfidence.

SUNDAY. JAN. 15, 1860.   At sea, on board bark "Early Bird", four days out fr. S. Francisco.

We sailed fr. S. Fr. Wed. night, Jan. 11th, about midnight. As this was my 8th time of passing the Golden Gate, I did not care to see it, & went on board, put state room in order & 'turned in', & waked up next day, (Thursd.) abt. 7 o'ck. with gentle rolling of the ship, to find myself at sea, the Golden Gate in sight, & the hills of the Coast Range. Calm or light winds all day. Next morning, Friday, out of sight of land, & glad am I to see the last of California, & to be on the broad Pacific, ev. hour bringing me nearer to China.

"Early Bird" is a neat, serviceable bark, of 500 tons, & a good sailer. Capt. M. H. Cook, Ch. M[ate] Cook (his brother), 2d. M. Fields.

What passengers are most concerned with, the cook & steward, are both excellent — cooking good, neat & with variety, & steward civil, neat & attentive. Voyage promises well, tho' we had no great expectations fr. it. Cabin small, but neat, no women or children in it, or cabin boy, & our passengers seem to be pleasant & intelligent men. The Capt. & Mate are sons of Cook of Hong Kong, a Highlander, an Engl. by birth, — they born in Delaware. My room-mate is a Mr. Williams, brother of S. Wells Williams of China, the author of The History of China.[51] Another passenger is a young man named Robert Raymer, native of Hamburg, who speaks English perfectly, & French well enough, &, some Spanish. I have a rule with him, that we speak only French together, — for my benefit, as he speaks far better than I do. He has a great deal of information & is clever — going to China, on some mercantile business, — has been all over U. S., & in much of Europe & S. America. Another is Speidon, son of a purser in our Navy. He is Naval Storekeeper at Hong Kong. Another is a Capt. Williams, master of a lumberman trading betw. Puget Sound & China. (Large lumber trade fr. Puget Sound to China,

[51]Samuel Wells Williams (1812–1884) is noted earlier. He was a missionary to China after 1833, interpreter for the 1853–1854 Perry expedition to Japan, and member of the American Legation in China in 1856. Among other works he wrote *The Middle Kingdom*, 2 vols. (1848).

Australia & S. Francisco. Chief export of Cal., is wheat to Australia). Also a Kittredge & Doland.

Nice breese set in Thursd. night & has kept up, to this time, smooth & gentle but fair, & we are making satisf. progress. We follow the Sun in his flight & ev. day lose some 10 or 12 minutes of time.

SUNDAY. JAN. 22.   We are ten days out, in Lat. 24° 56′ Long. 142.24, in the most delightful part of the most beautiful ocean, in the *blessed trade-winds,* — those strange winds that have blown in one direction, perhaps from the Creation, never falling away to a calm & never rising to a furious gale, with blue sea, soft, fleecy clouds, & clear sky. We have been fortunate in our weather, having had only one day or 36 hours of "doldrums" — (variables, just before we reached the trades — say fr. 28° to 32°), & 36 hours of heavy rolling sea & strong wind when we first took the trades — & then the *blessed trades* were a little too rough, & one night pitched us about, broke the furniture & dishes & lamps, & kept us awake.

Modern spiritualism, i.e. rappings & mediums has got among ship-masters. Have heard of several who believe in them. Capt. Randlett, Master of the celebrated clipper Surprise, believes that a woman crossed his deck one night in the China sea. Curious, to see superstitions coming in at the cabin as they are going out of the forecastle!

Omitted to mention that we have two hundred & thirty Chinese passengers in the steerage, fifty more than we had in the Mastiff, a ship a double the sise of this one. We have but one boat to lower on an emergency, & that too small for a high sea, & capable of holding only 4 or 5 persons; & have only two other boats on board, lashed on deck, & no doubt leaky, as they have not been in water for a long time — no long boat or pinnace. In fact, in case of disaster, we have *no resource.* Nor is there a breaker (small cask for water) on board. In case of fire, collision, or springing leak, we have nothing to look to. This is very wrong. Still, we are all in good spirits, & hope the best.

To-day — Jan. 22 — is the Chinese New Year. The Chinese have been firing off crackers, suspended over the water by poles — for safety — , & throwing to the winds bits of gilt paper, as *ching-ching* (offerings) to the *Josh.* They chin-chined the Capt. by a box of stockings. The Chinese passengers always find their own food & cook for themselves, — the ship finding only firewood & water. They stow very close below, & have little ventilation; but are a quiet, peaceable, obedient people, & unquestion-ably intelligent. They have books among them, & read a good deal. Their books are printed on thin soft paper, mere tissue, made of bamboo or rice, & with paper covers. I have never seen one with a stiff cover. For

musical instrument, they have a kind of banjo or guitar, with small body
& very long neck, & three strings.

I have an unaccountable sense of happiness, on this voyage, as I lie
on my berth, in my state-room, looking out on the sea, by moonlight, or
starlight or sun light. It is not because I deserve it, or because my
situation — away from all I love — makes me so, but, I suppose it is that
my health must be good, & the air is pure, & I am free from care, — eating,
wearing care, & have absolute leisure. But I believe that if there is
nothing in one's circumstances to make one peculiarly happy or unhappy,
his state will depend on so material & vulgar a thing as his *stomach*.
Dyspepsia makes gloom. Digestion makes good spirits. No *place* is more
favorable to cheerfulness than lying on a bunk, looking out one's window
on a tropical sea, in fine weather, the ship gently bounding under you. I
wonder at this sense of happiness, — that makes me ready to sing!

Kittredge is a N. H. boy, of good principles, with courteous manners,
going to China, to engage in trade, determined to hold fast to integrity &
temperance. Doland is a mechanic of Hong Kong, young & worldly, but
well read & intelligent. Speidon is gentlemanlike & amiable. Raymer is
engaged to a Miss Gardner of Salem, & is making a third effort to make
money enough to marry, his efforts in the Western states & in S. America
having failed — yet he has youth & spirits.

WED. JAN. 25. Said a little too much about the *blessed trades,* they
have died away & left us in a calm yesterday, & to-day, the wind has
been ahead, all day, & we are obliged to beat to windward. I knew that at
& about the Sandw. Islands, in winter, the trades sometimes intermitted
for a few days, & calms & S. winds set in; but I did not know that this
intermission extended far out to sea. Capt. Williams, an old trader here,
says that fr. Dec. to M'ch., there are intervals when you will sometimes
lose the trades, for a few days, in certain latitudes, & S. & W. winds,
calms & squalls intervene.

Calms & squalls (not heavy) all day & night.

THURSD. JAN. 26. Last night, about midnight, after the winds had
gone round the compass by way of W. & N., the trades set in again, &
nothing can be more beautiful than this day — all sails set & drawing,
studding sails full, freshening sea, clear sky. At noon, the Sand. Isl. abt.
250 miles off. Hope to *sight* them tomorrow.

Strange how I am able to spend my time. No *ennui,* no spare time, no
weariness! Yet, my sanitary rules allow me not over 2 or 3 hours reading
in the day. Called at 6½, washing &c. & on deck soon after 7. Breakfast
at 8. On deck until 10. Reading or writing fr. 10 to 11½. On deck at 11½ &
take observation for meridian altitude & work up the latitude. On deck

12 to 1. Dinner at 1. From dinner to 5 o'ck., talk, read & sleep. On deck 5 to 6. Tea at 6. On deck all the evening, walking or sitting. "Turn in" soon after 9. I suppose I walk deck an average of 5 hours a day. Ship, sea & sky are the same ev. day, & no news fr. without, — yet to me all is interest & variety, & no exhiln. is like a cracking breese & foaming sea. How much better is a sailing vessel than a dull, monotonous, steaming, smoking, greasy, oily steamer!

FRID. JAN. 27.   Fine weather & good winds. Went to topmast cross-trees to look for the islands. Not in sight. Glad to find that I can sit on cross-trees & look down on deck without any dissiness of head, as well as when I was a sailor boy. Am sure I could not have done this any time during the year before I left home. Regard it as proof of improved health.

SAT. JAN. 28.   Day of white chalk! "Land ho!" at day break. The island of Hawaii on our larboard bow. To mast head to look at it with glass. See the point & hill near which lies dear Hilo, &, over all, the summit of Mauna Kea, above the lower clouds, with patches of snow lying about it.

All day is passed delightfully, sailing through the channel betw. Hawaii & Maui, with Kawanawi & Lanai in sight. Could see the gullies & rivulets running to the sea, on Hawaii, & the mission of Rev. Mr. —— , & the point behind wh. lies Kawaihae, & the further point, off wh. I lay in my canoe to look at the out flow of the volcano. On Maui is the mountain, Hale a ka La, the bay where we were becalmed in the little sch. Mary, & the barren island Tahawarawe, where Judge [E. H.] Allen & Mr. Wylie feed their sheep. Can just see the slope, at the foot of wh. lies Lahaina.

The weather is exquisite, neither hot nor cold, sky & sea clear, & a steady trade blowing us rapidly along. How all enjoy it! Even the Chinese fire crackers & beat gongs to chin-chin the Josh for the fair wind. Delightful sunset & clear moonlight on the waters all night.

I do not believe I shall see, in my long journey, a place that will interest & charm me so much as this group of islands. It would delight me to land at Hilo & Honolulu, & spend a few hours, making flying calls among my friends, to see the native sights, & hear the native tongue. *Aloha! Aloha Nui!* Never, in all human probability shall I behold you again! The islands melt away in the golden sunset. As I walk the deck, I parody Byron's Farewell.

> "Adieu, Adieu, my island home
> Fades o'er the waters blue. . ."[52]

---

[52]"Adieu! adieu! my native shore
    Fades o'er the waters blue."
        Childe Harold's Pilgrimage I, 13.

SUND. MORN. JAN. 29. At sunrise, can just distinguish a dim outline of the highest points of Maui, & by noon, these are lost, & we have again an open horison.

Sund. night I always have a memorial of home, in singing to myself, on some spot on deck, alone, the chants & hymns of our Sund. nights at home — Venite, Bendictus, Benedia anima mea, Deus Misereatur, De Profundis & Adeste fideles.

WED. FEB. 1, 1860. We are now well to Westward of the S. Islands, & farther to Westward than I have ever been before, wh. makes me feel that I am at last really on my way to China. But the trades have been very light since we left the islands, sometimes for hours almost a calm, & then rising to a 4 or 5 knot breese. This is discouraging, & deducts fr. my admiration of the trades, yet the winds are always fair, & — what can be more charming than these moonlight nights! Nothing but sea, sky, moon, stars, the deck, & the towering, white, silent sails! The passengers sit on deck, hour after hour, reluctant to go below.

I have a window in my state-room, just beside my berth, so that I can lie in it & look out upon the waves. Every morning, now, betw. 3 o'ck. & sunrise, I see the Southern Cross, gleaming in the Southern horison, just where my eye turns when I wake.

Last night, found a centipede in the cabin, & Raymer killed it. It was six inches long & as thick as my thumb. Mr. Williams, who we all think a little timid & splenetic, was not a little frightened at the thought of such animals being in the ship, & the Cap. & Speidon told him stories of their coming out in ships as you draw into warm weather. No sooner had he got to bed, than he sprang out, hurting his arm in the jump, thinking he felt one crawling over him.

I have adjusted the mate's quadrant successfully, by the rules in Bowditch,[53] & take observations with it daily.

Capt. Cook is a quickwitted, entertaining, good natured, but profane, indolent, improvident, low toned fellow. Mate is better. Passengers hold out well. We are fortunate, on the whole in our chance gathered company of passengers. The ship is poorly provided except as regards the cabin table & the berth furniture, wh. are good. With over 200 Chinese steerage passengers, there is not one ventilator in the ship, nor a force pump, & only one little boat on the davits, & only two other boats, both lashed on deck. In case of necessity, we could not lower these boats in less than a ½ hour, & then they wd. not hold over 15 apiece. To put out a fire, we have only buckets.

[53]Nathaniel Bowditch, noted earlier, won fame for his book, *The New American Practical Navigator*, which appeared in many editions after 1799.

SUND. FEB. 5. We have been disappointed in our trades. They have been very light, sometimes almost a calm, & never above 8 knots, & the last three days the winds have been from S. to S. W. But the weather has been exquisite.

One of the Chinese plays a kind of violin, with three strings, singing at the same time. This he keeps up by the 2 & 3 hours together, without intermission, with a downcast & doleful countenance, though the others seem entertained by it. Surprised to find so much neatness among the Chinese. Most have tooth brushes, & brush their teeth scrupulously, & most seem careful to wash, generally. I think they are neater than the same number of Irish wd. be, of the same class in life. As for myself, in these warm latitudes (18° N.), I take a salt water bath, by bucket & spunge ev. morning.

Have finished Williams' Hist. of China — a careful, elaborate, dull, ungenial book, & written in an inelegant but ambitious style, with prodigiously long & unusual words — "decollated" for "beheaded", "contracted a matrim. engagement" for "married", &c. My kn. of Latin, Greek & Fr. taxed to utmost to get at the meaning of some of his English words — must have a dict. in hand. He is a dry & narrow man, & repeats mere *phrases* about the Bible & Xn. Civilisation. Yet, is a good repository of facts.

Began Huc's Travels in China.[54]

WED. FEB. 8. The steward found two tarantulas, in the cabin — large hairy creatures, wh. disturbed the passengers not a little, but some say they are not poisonous.

The chronometer stopped to-day, the only one, & we are driven to dead reckoning & taking time by Mr. Speidon's watch. Our Chinese passengers play dominoes a great deal. Some play all night, by lanterns, & when the lanterns get dim, they hold the dom. up to them. Gambling & opium smoking are their chief amusements.

FRIDAY. FEB. 10. To-day we perform the strange feat of skipping a day. Yesterday was Wed. Feb. 8th. To-day is Frid. Feb. 10th. Thursd. the 9th has no existence. Going round the globe with the sun, from E. to W., we lose a day. Of course, it makes no difference *where* we skip the day. Only we must do so before we get to port, as we should otherwise find ourselves one day in advance of the world. By this strange law, the indevout astronomers pussled the devout un-astronomers, & showed the Sabbatarians that if two Jews left Judea on their Sabbath, & went round the world different ways, when they met again one would be

---

[54]Evariste R. Huc, *A Journey through the Chinese Empire* (New York, 1855). Huc was a French missionary and traveler.

keeping Friday & the [other] Sunday instead of Saturday. It is a strange feeling — this annihilation of a day, when one comes actually to do it, notwithstanding your reason tells you that [you] have lost no time, but only added a little to each day of your voyage, by following the sun, until you make a total addition of 24 hours & must erase one day from your calendar, to be even with those who have stood still.

The crew would not be cheated of their duff[55] day, so to-day is to be Thursd. in the galley, & the cook skips his Friday.

SUND. FEB. 12. It does seem strange to have Sunday come in six days. Some of the Chinese who had learned in California, to count by our days, were much pussled to find it Sunday.

I am struck with the good temper of these Chinese. They cook for themselves in two galleys on deck, the wood being served out to them by the pound, & they take their turns at the galleys, with their pots & pans, with little sticks of wood under them, over 200 of them, in messes, & yet there is no quarreling or crowding, but quietness & good order. Our women passengers, 5 or 6 in numbers, have very black hair, glossy, done up in our style, with handsome hair pins, & all have bracelets & ear-rings. The bracelets are said to be put on in childhood, & never removed.

Little bull dog pup on board — favorite with me — all yellow but a black face — came on board before his eyes were open.

Been examining Thoms' book on navigation.[56] Think his explanation of the modes of ascertaining latitude & longitude are more intelligible to the unscientific than those of [Nathaniel] Bowditch. His explanations of Zcnith, celestial equator, altitudes, declination, polar distance, mean time & apparent time, dip, asimuth, parallax &c. are excellent.

TUESD. FEB. 14. At 11 A. M., sailing along, in beautiful serene weather, & gentle breese, — "Land ho! Right ahead!" — "Keep her up— Keep her up North West. Brace the yards!" called us all on deck. We were going directly towards a low island, of coral reefs, just emerging above the water, & very near it, too. We could see the surf break upon it. Had we made it last night, we should probably have struck, the land is so low & the reefs extend out so far. Went into main top with glass. Island about 5 miles long, from S. E. to N. W., with heavy breakers on the N. W. end, a few trees & shrubs & grass, in parts. S. E. end has a grove of trees. We are in Lat. 19° 22' N. & our Longitude is supposed to be 166° 28' E., but as our chronometer has stopped we cannot be sure of the

---

[55]A pudding with plums or raisins, served once a week to a ship's crew.

[56]William Thoms, *A New Treatise on the Practice of Navigation at Sea* (New York, n.d.).

latter. Wake's Isl. is in 19° 10′ N. & Long. 166° 30′ E. by the general chart. It is, therefore, no doubt, Wake's Island. We strained our eyes to see if we could discover any signs of habitation, or signals fr. shipwrecked mariners, but could see none. Should have liked much to land on it, & search for fruits & berries & make sure that no one was on it.

WED. FEB. 15. We have now been out 34 days, & have had but 3 rainy or anywise unpleasant days, & taken in the royals only 3 or 4 times, & not reefed topsails once. Thermometer at 70° to 78° all the time, & the temp. of the sea about the same, at noon. No weather can be finer. Trades have been steady for the last week or 10 days, & moderate.

Travelling as I do gives one a strong notion as to the difference of races. The differences seem almost of the essence & ineradicable — Not to speak of the original unity, but of the present state of things. Mixtures of races seem doomed to extinction. There is a Chinese infant on board, born in Cal., but its little eyes are as Chinese, from the moment they were opened as any "oldest inhabitant". I do not believe the Kanakas can either increase & maintain themselves long as an equal race with the whites, or that a mixed race will multiply at all. These facts, & even that most striking one respecting the intermarriage of mulattoes, do not disprove the orig. unity, nor relieve the difficulties in the theory of orig. diversity.

Great disappointment in the steward. He turns out to be far from neat. In dress, habits, ways is rather disgusting — though civil eno' to us. Capt. Cook has no sensibilities, & is so incorrigibly careless & indifferent, that no hope of reformation of steward. Capt. smokes a pipe nearly all the time & drinks whiskey, & has no taste, & would not see it if the steward used a dishcloth for a napkin. We are all in a state of disgust, but there is no help for it. All depends on the Capt., at sea.

FRID. FEB. 17. The water in the new casks is so bad that it made all the passengers sick yesterday. Could not drink it even in Chocolate. Mate ex[amine]d & found all the casks the same. Gross negligence. Fortunately, the water in the tanks will last us in the cabin, & the Chinese boil their water & take it only in tea — rarely if ever drink water.

This is the third Am. ship I have been in since left the Mastiff, & the master of each has been a slovenly, careless man, with no discipline or system, & no care over his steward.

Finished Huc's China, narrative entertaining & descriptions as graphic as ever met with. He makes his reader a spectator & actor with him. His statements as to the religious, civil, social, polit. & econom. condition of China are more to the point & more intelligible than Williams', & in ¼ the space.

Also read Sir John Davis' China.[57] Davis is a pedant & quotes in-
applicable passages from Greek & Latin. Still, it is a fair work, & has
been largely borrowed from by all writers since. Huc has the advantage
of having lived in the interior of China 14 years, speaking the language
&c. It is plain to me from Williams' own statements that the Am. Prot.
Missions have, so far, done *nothing*. They never go into the interior, but
only try to circulate books in the sea ports, & have hardly ten converts to
show. He seems, himself, to be discouraged, & says that the random
distribution of Bibles has been a failure, & worse.

SUNDAY. FEB. 19. This day, 37 days out fr. S. Fr. Last four days very
heavy rolling seas, wh. send sofas, trunks, chairs & dishes, lashed or
unlashed, to & fro, & hardly let us sleep at night. Still, wind is fair & strong,
& we make an average of 200 miles a day. If we had a neat steward, &
a proper Capt. & it were not so late in the winter, (putting me out of
season for India) I shd. be very well content here. As it is, days are
seasons to me, now. Fear I must give up Japan & India.

Attempt at a popular explanation of the mode of finding the latitude,
at sea, — with which I have entertained myself — it is original, & made
without referring to books.

I am at sea, & wish to ascertain how far I am from the Equator, or, my
latitude. Suppose two lines to be drawn from the Earth's centre, the one
to my position, & the other to the Equator at a point nearest to my
position. The angle formed by these lines is my angular distance from
the Equator, or my latitude. I cannot see the Equator, & cannot, therefore, measure this angle directly; but I can see the sun at noon. Suppose,
then, the two lines to be extended. Suppose, for convenience, the Sun to
be exactly on the Equator as it is twice a year. The line from the Earth's
centre through the Equator will touch the Sun's centre, & the direction of
the other, produced into the sky, is my zenith. The Sun's angle with my
zenith is the Equator's angle with my position, or my latitude. I cannot
fix the exact spot of my zenith for the purpose of an ordinary observation,
but I know that my zenith is always 90°, or a quarter of a circle, from my
horison. If, therefore, I measure the angle the Sun makes with my
horison, I can obtain the angle it makes with my zenith. I measure, by a
quadrant or sextant, the angle the Sun makes, at noon, with my horison,
& find it to be, for example, 40°. As my horison & zenith form an angle
of 90°, & the sun is between them, I deduct 40° from 90°, & get the angle
the Sun makes with my zenith which is 50°. As the Sun is supposed to be
on the Equator, this is also the angle the Equator makes with my zenith,

[57]Sir John Francis Davis (1795–1890), British commander-in-chief at Hong Kong,
1844–1848, published various works on China, including *Sketch of China*, 2 vols.
(1841).

or with my position, at its nearest point, which is my latitude. The reason I take the Sun's angle at noon, is that it is then nearest to my zenith, & thus gives the desired angle.

But, suppose the Sun is not on the Equator, but to the North of it. Suppose me to be also to the North of the Equator. I obtain the angle the Sun at noon makes with my zenith, as before. The books give me the angel the Sun makes with the Equator at the time of my observation, which is called its *declination*. As the Sun is between my zenith & the Equator, the angle it makes with my zenith, added to the angle it makes with the Equator, gives the angle my zenith makes with the Equator. In other words, the Sun's zenith distance, added to its declination, gives the latitude. The principle & process are the same, if the sun & the observer are both South of the Equator. If one is North & the other South, then, as the Equator is between the zenith & the sun, I deduct the declination from the angle the Sun makes with my zenith, & obtain the angel of my zenith with the Equator, or my latitude.

This explanation is in general terms, merely to explain the principle. Several corrections must be made in details, for refraction of the atmosphere, the height of the observer above the earth's surface, &c., but the only correction necessary to be explained for a correct understanding of the foregoing, is that which is made for *parallax*. It will be observed that in measuring the angle the Sun makes with my horison, the angle is necessarily formed at my eye, on the Earth's surface, while the angle of the Sun with my zenith, & that of the horison with my zenith as referred to the Earth's centre. I must therefore make that angle equal to what it would have been if observed at the Earth's centre. This correction is given in the books, for every degree of altitude, & is called the correction Parallax.

Popular explanation of mode of ascertaining Longitude at sea. The time the Sun takes to go round the earth (to speak according to appearances), is divided into 24 hours, & the Earth's surface into 360 degrees of longitude. The sun, therefore, makes 15 degrees in an hour, one degree in four minutes & so on. We count our degrees of longitude from Greenwich. If at the ship's position the time differs one hour from the time at Greenwich, the ship is 15 degrees of longitude from Greenwich. If the time at the ship's position is later than that of Greenwich, she is to the Westward, & if earlier, to the Eastward of Greenwich. If, then, I can ascertain the exact time at the ship's position & at Greenwich at the same instant, I can get her longitude. Chronometers are set to Greenwich time, & what with their present accuracy & what with the means of ascertaining & making allowances for rates, the time at Greenwich can be sufficiently well ascertained for practical purposes. It then only remains to ascertain the time at the ship's position. The most convenient way would be to ascertain the exact moment of noon, that is, the moment the Sun passes the meridian of the ship's position, & note the time given by the Chronometer at that instant. But the sun rises & falls so little & so slowly at noon & seems to hang so long at about the same altitude, that no ordinary instruments can ascertain the exact moment of its passing meridian. The most usual method of ascertaining the time is to measure the altitude of the sun when it is rising or falling fast, that is, early in the forenoon or late in the afternoon. Certain formulae in the books enable us to learn, from this altitude, the exact time when the observation was made, as shown by the sun, — that is to say, how long time it was before or after the Sun's crossing the meridian of that place on that day. By noting the time by the Chronometer at the moment of the observation, we get the difference between the time at the ship's position & at Greenwich, and thus the longitude.

This is sufficient to explain the *principle*. An important correction must be made. The sun does not, in fact, go round the Earth in exactly 24 hours; and, consequently the difference between noon of one day & noon of another, as shown by the sun's crossing the meridian, is not exactly 24 hours. It slightly varies from that sum, & this variation is not always the same at all places & times, being sometimes more and sometimes less than 24 hours. Now, watches cannot be made to keep this varying time, so they are constructed upon an allowance of exactly 24 hours to a day, which is the average, or mean, of the Sun's days. The Sun's day, or the exact time as ascertained by the Sun's crossing the meridian at each place, is called the *apparent* time. The watch's day, of 24 hours between noon & noon, is called the *mean* time. The observation above described gives the *apparent* time, or the time as measured by the Sun's progress; while the Chronometer gives the *mean* time. This difference must be reconciled. A formula given in the books & called the Equation of Time, enables us to reduce the apparent time shown by the observation to mean time at that place. Having then the mean time at the ship's position & at Greenwich at the same instant, we obtain the exact difference of time, & thence the longitude.

WED. FEB. 22. This is Ash Wednesday of this year, & Washington's Birth Day, & the birth day of my little daughter.[58] I must try to remember them all. I do love that little baby, & long to see her. As for Washington, the nation can take care of him to-day, & I confess I would rather kiss the baby, of the two, regimentals notwithstanding — "If that is treason, make the most of it." Lent, I shall not attempt to keep, as a bodily fast, at sea, for our meals, at best, are not too good for health & life.

[58]Angela Henrietta Channing Dana, born February 22, 1857.

Still fine weather, day & night, & fair, gentle trades, all the time. Read Hildreth's Japan.[59] A dull & ill jointed arrangement of facts, yet of value, & mostly new to me.

SUND FEB. 26. Forty four days out, & yet 1000 miles to go. The winds have been fair, but very light. Read the condensed narrative of Perry's expid. to Japan[60] — well enough.

Mr. Doland, the sailmaker passenger, is a kind of John Halifax, gentleman.[61] In point of manners, tact & general information, & knowl. of current Engl. literature, he is above the average of men one meets in good society.

Reading life of Charlotte Brontë.[62] Very interesting. The best part is where one Lewis patronises her, & gives her advice as to novel writing, being himself an author, & she *uses him up* so on Miss Austen's novels, & the nature of poetry & sentiment. Emily Brontë's dog is a good point, & so is the end of the Chap. that describes the success of Jane Eyre. I lay in my berth, reading, & my girlish habit of crying at pathos or sentiment came over me. But my tears are few & short. The reservoir is low. It is only books that have that effect — actual cases not, — I think, so far as I recollect — which shows something wrong.

Winds being very light, a Chinese woman is burning four incense sticks & throwing overboard quantities of yellow strips of paper, with pin holes in them, as Chin-Chin. "By & bye catchee wind".

Sleepiness of Ch. mate, & long efforts of Fields to get him out. He is a spoiled child, selfish, indolent, sleeps on his watch, snubs his brother, the Capt., to his face, & it often takes ½ hour to get him out. Then he sits in a chair on deck & smokes a pipe, in his watch, &, if he is merry, dances a negro dance, in sight of the man at the wheel. His discipline is nothing but out breaks, & he always swears at the Chinese. *Per contra,* he read Mr. Everett's Address at founding of Dudley Observatory,[63] was captivated by it, & has been trying to study astronomy ever since.

[59]Richard Hildreth (1807–1865), founder and editor for several years of the *Boston Daily Atlas,* published *Japan As It Was and Is* in 1855.

[60]The full account of Matthew C. Perry's 1853–1855 voyage to Japan was published in 1856 by the U. S. Government, in three large folio volumes: *Narrative of the Expedition of an American Squadron to the China Seas and Japan.*

[61]*John Halifax, Gentleman* was a novel by Dinah Mulock (1826–1887), published in 1857, which told the story of a low-born, but noble-hearted, self-reliant, self-made Englishman.

[62]Elizabeth C. Gaskell (1810–1865), *The Life of Charlotte Brontë,* 2 vols. (New York, 1857).

[63]*Works,* III, "The Uses of Astronomy," 422–465. Edward Everett delivered his lecture at the inauguration of the Dudley Observatory in Albany, New York, August 28, 1856.

WED. FEB. 29. We are near Formosa, & the trades have left us, & the Monsoon not reached us, so we have had three days of nearly entire calm. Hard to retain patience. Shall miss the steamer of M'ch. 5th fr. Hong Kong. Ev. day brings summer nearer, & so cuts me off more & more in my plans of Eastern travel.

Finish life of C. Bronte. Suspect that Mrs. Gaskell suppresses a little, or we shd. hear more of the opinions & thoughts of such a woman on the greatest of all questions. How lightly she takes Miss Martineau's atheism, yet quarrels with her for honestly telling her, when asked her opinion, that she thinks there are indelicacies in Shirley.[64] Such a woman, with such a life & such experiences must have had something strong in the way either of faith or doubts. Where are they? Emily's bull dog is overworked — well the first time, but not bear three productions, — yet I'd rather have seen him than her, I fancy.

Ships with house on deck & lazeretto aft, & houses amidships, are not seamenlike. Were I an underwriter, I would object to them. Our crew might as well be in another ship, a-head, & the man at the wheel in a boat, astern.

FRID. MCH. 2. Six days of calm & light, very light breeses, — about half the time a dead calm, & the rest a 2 or 3 knot breese. Hard to bear. The steamer sails on the 5th & we shall lose it. Patience taxed, but holds out.

Yesterday a Chinaman dropped his wooden pillow on the head of a man below. What a row! Just such as Huc describes, all chattering & sticking out their skinny yellow fingers, & looking as if blows or scratches wd. come next, but no blow struck. *Debated* & settled.

Caught a shark. Great relief to monotony of a long dull day of calm. The 200 & odd Chinese, men & women, all on deck. Amusing to see them throw themselves upon him, knives in hand, when he was left to their mercies, on deck, — & such a chattering, squalling, bawling, & yet, with a dosen knives drawn & all the pushing & crowding, no one hurt. They cut him up for cooking. Our 2d M. got the head away fr. the whole of them.

SAT. MCH. 3. Good breese all night, & steady fair wind all day. Passengers in better spirits. Are now within 600 miles of Hong Kong. But it is not the distance but the calms that trouble us.

Chinese difficulty, characteristic of them. Late in the evening, terrible chattering & yelling & crowding & sticking out of fingers & threatening

---

[64]Harriet Martineau, noted earlier, was critical of Charlotte Brontë's novel *Shirley* (1849). By the "greatest of all questions" Dana may mean theology.

with cleavers. Our men got away from them the man ag[ainst] whom their attacks were directed, but such was the Babel that, what with that, & what with the bad English & bad interpreting, we could not ascertain whether the charge was that he had assaulted a woman "with intent &c.", or whether he had broken her teapot. In this state of things, the hearing was delayed until the next day, & the man stayed aft, sleeping on a settee on deck. Early in the morning there were messages to & fro, & negotiations, & it appeared that these born politicians had formed two parties, 19 in his favor & 190 odd ag. him, but terms were adjusted, & he went forward again. (Chinese are readers, talkers & traders, by habit of 4000 years).

We are now at the antipodes of home. It is noon here, midnight in Boston, day break in London, breakfast time in Calcutta, dinner time at Honolulu, & tea time in S. Francisco.

MOND. MCH. 5.   Sail ho! Larboard bow. Just visible. First sail we have seen since left S. Fr. We gain on her & she gradually drops astern. Never near eno' to see her colors by a glass.

TU. MCH. 6.   Land ho!, at day break. Bashee Islands on our port bow, 4 miles off. Pass to Northward of the group. Small, bold, high, rocky & desolate looking islands. The Southern-most & largest is sd. to be inhabited, by people of Malay race. This is our Last stage. We are now in the Chinese sea, & we have the N. E. monsoons blowing us towards Hong Kong, the "loom of the land"[65] over the S. end of the Island of Formosa.

The f[ore] t[op gallant] yard broke, (for 3 d. time) yard fell & struck man on the t[opsail] rigging, & he fell to deck, distance of 50 or 60 feet — broke leg & badly cut. Great escape that not go overboard. If he had, cd. not have saved him, as high seas & hard blow & no proper boat. Took him to forecastle, where Capt. Williams, a passenger, assisted by Kittredge, whose father is a surgeon, set the leg, made splints & cradle. I helped as much as I could. Capt. Cook did *nothing*, either by word or hand — not even to see that he was taken below. Man's name, George H. Plummer, of Portland Me. — been at sea 11 years, & from home 5 years. Young, intelligent, but a victim of bad habits which will retard his cure. Wonder not kill him. When sat by his berth, in the small, dirty forecastle, where 10 men burrow, hung round with wet clothes, & paved with chests & boots, — recurred to my own lot in my youth. Now I have seen forecastle life & sailor's life *from the cabin*, I begin to wonder how I endured it.

The moment we passed the Bashees, changed to heavy blow fr. N. E. & heavy sea, & 10 & 11 knots an hour.

[65]A nautical expression for the indistinct appearance of land when it is first sighted on the horizon at sea.

Very bad night. Carried away main topgallant mast, — broken short off just above cross-trees, sail being set. All hands all night clearing the wreck. Capt. C. no more use than a child. The 2d mate did all, with the crew, who are excellent seamen — 4 or 5 of them as good as need be for any service. Hard work at mastheads, in heavy blow & sea, clearing rigging & sending down the wreck. In midst of it "Sail ho!", & saw a steamer, under fore & aft sails, beating up to windward, crossed our stern, — probably bound to Japan or North part of China. Crew behaved like men, & after 14 hours' work, when hoisted new topsail, gave us a jolly chorus of "Rando, boys, a-rando". Topsail tie broke again, & yard fell, for the fourth time. No one hurt.

WED. MCH. 7. Strong blow & heavy sea. Expect to make coast of China to-night. Capt. Williams & I visited sick man. W. loosened his bandages — man said all hands been so employed that no one had wet his bandage, & limb inflamed. Capt. C. not been near him, nor, so far as I know, even inquired for him.

4. China

TH. MCH. 8. Made land at midnight last night. At daybreak, are close in shore, just above entrance to Hong Kong. My first view of continent of Asia! Coast is line of bare rocky hills, & deep water. Chinese fishing boats. Excitement of Chinese passengers — some not seen home for 10 or 12 years. Hove-to for pilot. Chinese boat, bamboo sails, sharp bow, broad high stern, 4 men & 2 women & some children on board, — one woman working at ropes with baby strapped to her back. Families live in these pilot boats, having no other home. Managed her well in the sea & wind, though with great deal of noise — "too much bobbery" — (*Bobbery* is Pigeon for all kinds of trouble, row, fright & confusion.)

Pilot speaks no English — gave orders by signs — Hong Kong is an island, at mouth of Canton river, & harbor is the deep, wide passage, between it & the main. Called Limoon Passage. Passage winding — high, rocky hills each side, & bold shore, deep water. One turn more — Hong Kong in sight. Fleet of vessels at anchor, all flags, Engl., Amer., French, Spanish. Chinese junks & boats moving about by oar & sails — with all their families on board, babies strapped to back, little children with floats fastened to them, in case fall overboard, — bamboo sails. Engl., Fr. & Am. flags flying fr. large buildings on shore, Engl. man-of-war steamers, little fiery steam gunboats, & great hulks of superannuated & superceded line-of-battleships, for store ships & hospital ships. Drop anchor safely — & our voyage of 55 days is ended in safety. Reason for gratitude, for *if an exigency had occurred,* were unfit to meet it, — Capt. & mate quarreling, & both unfit, no discipline, no system, useless in an emergency, & no proper provision of boats, or spare spars, & short handed of men — with 220 passengers.

Hong Kong is built on a shelf between the high steep hills, & the sea, not more than wide enough for two parallel streets. Fine stone quay the length of the town, houses & stores large, high, & all of stone or brick, — some creeping up the hills, — hills dotted with evergreen trees, — looking like N. England, rather than tropical scenery. Ashore in Chinese boat, & deliver my letters in person to Russell & Co. — who make me their guest. At Russell & Co.'s, find letters from home, dated in Aug., Sep., Nov. & Dec., latest Dec. 6. Sat down to long enjoyment of them. No bad news, *laus Deo,* except death of Adele.[66]

Also faithful file of Weekly Advertisers.

[66]Adele Watson, noted earlier, wife of Sarah Watson Dana's younger brother William.

Mr. Warren Delano[67] is here, just arrived, to take charge of the house of R. & Co., when Mr. Beckwith goes home.

All the business houses of the merchants here are large, high & stately. Rooms & entries as large as in Court Houses & like public buildings at home — long vistas of rooms & desks, at "magnificent distances". Crowd of coolies at the door, to do errands, & a comprador, in decent long robe of blue, in charge of them. Recd. by Delano & Beckwith with cordiality, & take me home, as guest. Each large merc. house here, Russell & Co., Aug. Hurd & Co. &c. &c. has a large palatial looking house, where the clerks & unmarried partners live. I have a room at Russell & Co.'s. Mr. Delano is there, his wife being at home. All dine together there, at 7 o'clock. Beckwith dines with us. A junior partner, Mr. Tyson, is there, & clerks, Torrey of Roxbury, (nephew of Sam. Torrey), King of Newport R. I., Frank Forbes, &c. &c., eight in all, live here — all New Engl. young men, training to Chinese business.

Handsome dinner, six Chinese servants & a Chinese butler, waiting on table — all so neat & clean. Cooking excellent — nice mutton, duck, rice & curry &c.

After dinner, call on Mrs. Beckwith, next door. Large handsome house. Beckwiths knew Ned in Heidelberg. B. thinks Ned one of the best conversers he ever met.

All houses (foreigners') are brick or stone, thick walls, large deep piassas, with blinds all round, at outside of piassas, making a kind of double house, large doors, windows & halls, & every possible contrivance to secure against heat in summer. This gives the town a look of patrician solidity & dignity.

Streets full of red coats & blue coats — English soldiers & seamen — 1st Royals, 99th, 67th, 3d &c. Regiments, & numerous naval uniforms — & medals & clasps frequent. A sepoy regiment, black straight hair, regular features, jet black skins, mustaches, — as far as possible fr. Negro —, tall, straight & spirited looking fellows. Here & there Malays clothed all in white, with white turbans, & Parsees, in sombre colors, high hat of dark straw, without rim, grave & decorous. Europeans & Americans of all qualities, & all the rest Chinese.

Chinese coolies, or mere manual laborers, wear wide short trowsers, & loose sacks or tunics & barefooted. Superior classes, as traders, compradors, better shopkeepers &c. wear decent, grave long robes of blue or black, stockings & shoes of white or blue, like canoes.

[67]Warren Delano (1809–1898), whose daughter Sara married James Roosevelt, and was the mother of Franklin D. Roosevelt, traveled for Russell and Co. for thirty years, mostly in the Orient. After the Civil War he retired to Newburgh, New York.

What a hive of industry is a Chinese town! No industry is so minute, constant & infinitesimally divided. China is an ant hill. Shops with lacquered fronts are very pretty. What a reading or letter-using people they are! Words printed on every door post, & on masts of every boat or junk, & men reading in the streets & at the shops' counters their thin yellow paper books, with paper covers, wh. they roll up in their hands.

When Chinese build a house, they first erect a staging of bamboo to sustain a roof of straw, with projecting eaves, & under this they do all their work, protected ag. sun & rain.

All the Br. Govt. buildings are large, stately & strong. The streets are paved with stone, & a stone pier or quay runs the length of the town, the vessels lying at anchor in the stream; & only boats lying at the pier. From the pier, at intervals, are iron dants, as from a ship's side, to wh. the private boats of the foreigners are hoisted up.

(Understood, of course, that Hong Kong Island is Br. possession, ceded by treaty of 1843.)[68]

Beckwith & Delano say, & so others have told me, that the peninsula opposite Hong Kong is a far better place for a town than Hong Kong — & they are very desirous that the Am. Govt. shd. get it by treaty. Tried to make Reed secure it, but they speak contemptuously of Reed's course & capacity as a diplomatist.[69] Two objections to Hong Kong. I. The high hills shut off the S. W. monsoons, which blow fr. May to Oct., & the town, at foot of hills, is exposed to a dead, sultry heat, all summer, & is very unhealthy then. II. There is not room enough betw. the hill & the water, for the trade & houses, & hill too steep for convenient use — & further, in typhoons, vessels obliged to go over to opp. shore to be safe. The opp. peninsula, Cowloon [Kowloon], is open to S. W. monsoons, & not so much exposed to typhoons, has hills of moderate height, & un-limited water front &c.

---

[68]As a result of a series of disagreements over the opium traffic, the Emperor of China, in 1840, issued an edict interdicting all trade and intercourse with England forever. Two years of intermittent hostilities ensued, the Chinese suffering consistently heavy military losses. The hostilities concluded with a treaty, signed August 29, 1842, and ratified by Victoria on July 22, 1843, which called for lasting peace and friend-ship between China and Great Britain; payment by China of twenty-one million dollars; a number of key Chinese cities to be thrown open to trade and consulates; and the ceding of Hong Kong in perpetuity to England.

[69]William Bradford Reed, noted earlier, was U. S. Minister to China under Presi-dent Buchanan, 1857–1859. In 1858 he concluded the Treaty of Tsientsin, made at the end of the Anglo-French war with the Chinese. The treaty secured for the United States the same terms as had been afforded the British and French victors in the war, and, in spite of Dana's remarks, would seem to have been a diplomatic accom-plishment of some distinction.

FRID. MCH. 9. Quiet Chinese servant to brush clothes, black boots, &c., but think he meant to pocket a knife I left in pocket — found it when I insisted it was in pocket of coat when he took it.

My room is larger than my parlor at home, & I have a dressing room out of it, with bathing tub, &c., so that need not leave room for any purpose.

Russell & Co. has a breakfast at the business house, at 9 o'ck., where the same company, all the partners & clerks, sit down together. But, when we are called, at 7 o'ck., servant brings cup of excellent tea, with slice of toast. So they have two establishments, breakfast & lunch at the counting room, & dinner at the lodging house — & complete outfit of plate &c. for each. Same servants, I presume, — but very likely not.

Find that the Br. & Fr. embassadors, to whom I have letters, are at Shanghai, & the Bishop of Hong Kong is on a visit North, & Mr. Ward (Am. Min.)[70] is at Canton, & Sir John Bowring[71] has gone home. So my *grand* letters are useless here.

Tailors, shoemakers &c. come to your house, with their patterns &c., & take your orders & measures there. "Pigeon English" — or business English, is the intermediate language. *Walkee,* come, go; *talkee,* tell, say; *topside,* up, above; *downside,* down, below; *piecee,* number, as 2 *piecee man* 2 men — 2 piecee chicken. Screw steamer, is *walkee inside,* & paddle-wheel is *Walkee outside. Pigeon,* is business, duty — "No my pigeon", not my duty.

This afternoon, visit fr. Capt. Wm. Ellery, whose ship, the "Starr King" is here.

Took R. & Co.'s 4 oared boat & rode about the harbor, & visit to the Early Bird. The 120 gun ship Princess Charlotte, a monster, is a hospital ship. So, the Minden, & others, all superceded by steam. Two or three neat Eng. & French steam frigates, & several little Engl. steam gun boats. These steam gun boats thought very serviceable in China. They are propellers, with 2 or 4 very large guns, & usually 3 masts, topsails & topg. sails at the fore, & only fore & aft sails at the missen. They have their numbers painted in huge letters on the quarter, — but have also names, I believe. The only Am. ship of war here, is the great useless Hartford, too big to go into most harbors. No small vessels, to give our

---

[70]John Elliott Ward (1814–1902), whom Dana will see frequently, was U. S. Minister to China, 1859–1860. A Georgia lawyer and legislator, he was an influential leader in the Democratic party. He opposed the secession of Georgia during the Civil War and finally established a law practice in New York.

[71]Sir John Bowring (1792–1872), linguist, writer, and traveler, was governor of Hong Kong in 1854. When Dana arrived he had just left for England.

young officers commands, experience & knowledge of steam, or to protect our interests.

Labor so cheap in China, that each clerk of Russell & Co. keeps a sedan chair & two coolies, & that is not thought extravagant, beside his indoor servant, at his room. Rode home in Young Torrey's chair, wh. two small coolies, one not over 14 years old, bore on their shoulders, up the long hill, at a rapid walk, not stopping for breath. I think the Chinese laborers very strong, even when not large, but very broad shoulders are common.

Coolie, is the name given to the mere manual laborers in the open air, — the porters, errand runners, hod carriers &c. The indoor servants are a step higher. They never go errands out doors, or carry bundles — "not my pigeon". (*Pigeon*, is *business*.) Indoor servants of whatever age, are called "boys".

Indoor servants, like the traders & contracting mechanics, usually wear the long blue robe, stockings & shoes. The coolies & boat men, wear tunic, or sack, short wide trowsers, coming to knee, & are barefooted. They often strip to it, when at hard or hot work, having on only their trowsers.

Nothing can be more decent, neat & convenient than the dress of the women of the lower classes — Women of the upper classes are not seen abroad. Whatever the occupation or character of the women, they wear a loose tunic, reaching below the knee, with long sleeves, high neck, buttoned over the throat, & long loose trowsers. They think the dress of European women indecent. Nothing would induce even a girl from the "flower boats" to be seen abroad with low neck & short sleeves. If their lives are ever so polluted, they are decent & even carefully modest in their dress & manners.

At dinner, had dried lychee fruit. It has a stone, & is in shape & consistency like the prune, & very agreeable, — I think better than either prune or raisin.

SATURDAY MCH. 10. Took steamer Willamette for Canton, at 8 A.M. Commanded by Walcott, late of the Navy, — displaced for intemperance from the Navy, wh. reformed him.

My shipmate, Capt. Williams, on board, going up to join his ship at Whampoa [Huangp'o].[72] Two young British Officers, in scarlet loose sacks, buttons &c., going up to join their regiment, — 3d (Buffs), hoping to go North, into action. Generally understood that a blow will be struck,

[72]Dana spelled most Chinese proper names phonetically, and therefore incorrectly. In this text the correct Chinese spelling, if it is known, is bracketed after Dana's first misspelling, for purposes of identification, but Dana's text is followed thereafter.

North, soon, perhaps at Peiho. Sir Hope Grant is to come fr. India, to command in Chief.[73] They are taking up ships at great prices, to carry troops & ammunition North.[74]

Lower part of the Bay, about Hong Kong, & for sev. miles up is high & rocky & barren. As draw into the river, becomes lower, & richer, & cultivated.

The famous "Bogue forts", & Bocca Tigris & Tigre Island. These forts are large, long & well placed, on each side of the narrows, at the entrance to the river, & if well manned & served, could command it. They are nearly in ruins now from the English guns, & are abandoned. The Allies (Engl. & Fr. are allies in the *present* war) do not occupy them, & the Chinese dare not.

Tigre Island is a peculiar elevation of base granite rock, one looks like a dome. There are fancied resemblances to Tigre & Elephant in the rocks.

[73]Sir James Hope Grant (1808–1875), commander of the British forces in the second Chinese War, 1860–1861, had been very active in earlier Chinese campaigns.

[74]In 1857–1858 the British, with French assistance, had waged a successful war against the Chinese, having broken with the Emperor over the question of his right to search English vessels and seize foreign citizens. The Allies imposed peace terms by the Treaty of Tsientsin (Lord Elgin and Baron Gros negotiating), which opened eleven more ports to trade and foreign residence, and provided protection for foreign nationals traveling and trading throughout all of China. The treaty further stipulated the right of the British and French to diplomatic representation at Peking, toleration for missionaries, and a standardization of tariff practices. Thus the war ended, but the treaty stipulated that ratification by the parties should take place at Peking a year from the date of signing (June 1858). The hostilities which Dana is observing grew out of difficulties arising from this ratification.

Lord Elgin's brother, Frederick Bruce, came out from England in 1859 as Envoy Extraordinary and Minister Plenipotentiary to China, under special instructions to see that the ratification ceremonies took place at Peking. Admiral Hope, commander of the British naval forces in China, was instructed to accompany Bruce to the mouth of the Peiho river (the waterway to Peking), and to provide force, if necessary, to allow Bruce to complete his mission. Bruce evidently mistook Chinese circumlocution for deliberate evasion and ordered Hope to clear a passage past the Chinese Taku forts, which commanded the river. Hope was badly beaten, both in his attempts to outgun the forts from the water and in his subsequent attempt to storm the forts on foot.

Lord Elgin and Baron Gros returned to China while Dana was there, mounted a full-scale military offensive, captured the forts and occupied Peking. During this campaign the Chinese captured a party of French and British under a false flag of truce, and so abused them that thirteen died in prison. When Lord Elgin learned of this treatment he punished the Chinese by destroying the Summer Palace in Peking — a vast storehouse of art treasures set on miles of landscaped grounds. It is the progression of these events that Dana remarks upon during the rest of the time he is in China.

First sight of a pagoda. Some 10 or 12 stories high, octagonal (? polygon, at all events), with shrubs & flowers growing out from the balconies or little verandas that separate each story. Yet these are not planted. They are the growth from chance deposits of seeds & earth. They are striking & handsome objects. They multiply as we go on. Now, there are 3 & 4 in sight at a time. Rice fields, or *paddy* fields, (for it is called paddy until it is shelled) abound, & trees, & little close villages. Fear of robbers & pirates keeps them in close villages, as in the feudal times in Europe.

This river has been a scene of piracy, robbery & violence for years, — chiefly of Chinese on one another, but sometimes on foreigners. The master & mate of this steamer point out to me the spots where the most famous murders & robberies have taken place. They usually murder, if they rob. The steamers, even now, go armed. Two years ago, the Chinese Govt. offered a reward, & a large one, for every head of a foreigner. That is withdrawn, but the effect of it remains among the common people. Since the bombardment of Canton by the English in 1858, nothing but their military occupation keeps the Europeans safe here.

The famed anchorage of Lintin [Lint'an], a high rocky island, far off on the S. side of the Bay.

Wahmpoa — the anchorage of large ships trading at Canton. Large numbers of Am., Engl. & Fr. vessels there, & some men of war. The Hartford lies below Whampoa, to practice at target firing.

Boats, junks, of all kinds become thicker & thicker. How swift they go, by wind & tide, their huge single mat sail, with bamboo horisontal sticks across it! They reef by lowering only. This is quick & simple.

Now, the boat houses, anchored, in wh. thousands of the Cantonese live. The small boats are chiefly managed by women. They row & steer. Girls of 8, 10, & 12 years pull vigorously at the oars, & are very skillful in steering, & skill & quickness are required, in the crowds here. Our steamer goes slowly among them, bobbing them up & down in the heavy swell she makes, the boats just saving themselves fr. her paddles. But, how good natured the girls are! They pull away at the oars, & jump about, & laugh & show their white teeth — though they seem to be just on the point of upsetting, children, household goods & all, into the river. Now, we have passage boats, & cargo boats, & Mandarin boats, & sea-going junks, & river going junks, & anchored house-boats, & flower boats, & moving boats of all kinds, by the thousands, as thick as carriages & foot passengers together in the Strand. Some of the boats are very prettily fitted up, & you see the sacred fire & the incense of their rites, the worship of ancestors. (It is not prayer or invocation, but respectful, religious acts of veneration). Now we are in Canton! There are the ruins of the large stone buildings, & of the walls, in all directions, the effects of 36 hours of pitiless bombardment by the Engl. & Fr., not a shot being returned, & not one in 10,000 of the poor Chinese knowing what it was for.

Just before this, passed the "Barrier Forts" taken by our squadron under Com. Foote,[75] the Portsmouth, Levant &c., & taken by the Eng. twice.

Came to anchor, & boats alongside, for freight & passengers. City on each side the river, wh. seems to me to be nearly as wide as the Thames, — but chief part on North side — small suburb only on South.

Russell & Co.'s Hong is on river bank, on S. side. Their boat comes off & takes me ashore. Mr. Orne, the partner here, receives me kindly, & room & servant assigned me.

The bombardment of 1858 & the occupation of Canton by the Allies since, have depressed trade here, & the burning of the foreign factories (agencies) have left the merchants only temporary places of refuge. Russell & Co. have only one partner & a clerk, (Sheppard, an Englishman) here, yet the house is large & there are some 10 or 12 indoor servants, & as many coolies for the boats & chairs.

How strange everything is! I am in the midst of China & Chinese, & from our windows & the balcony I look out upon this ancient river, literally alive with passing boats & junks, & cries as thick & fast as of birds in a forest!

Mr. Orne takes me out to visit the grounds preparing for the new factories. The site is much better than the old, being opposite the Macao Passage, wh. gives a sweep to the S. W. monsoons in summer. It is chiefly made-land, & will form an island of about 50 acres, separated from the city by a canal. It has a stone wall in building, & the coolies are filling in dirt in baskets, from little boats — 50 acres by basket loads, on men's backs! What wd. the Back Bay Commnrs. say?[76] The site for the new factories is called Shameen.

As we return, it is getting dusk, & the Chinese are lighting the lanterns in their boats. The river looks like a swamp of fire flies. Each boat, however small, has its little shrine, at wh. tapers or incense sticks are burned morning & night.

[75]Andrew Hull Foote (1806–1863), famed as the U. S. naval officer responsible for the abolition of the grog ration in the Navy, commanded the *U.S.S. Portsmouth.* On November 20–22, 1858, in retaliation for "attacks on our flag," he violated U. S. neutrality with China and led a party of 287 American seamen in an attack on the group of Chinese forts that Dana is observing. Though the forts were defended with 176 guns and manned by 5000 defenders, Foote captured and demolished them.

[76]Boston began filling in her Back Bay area in 1856. The project was completed in 1886.

Call on Rev. Mr. Bonney, a Missionary of the Am. B. C. F. M.[77] Mrs. Bonney has a school of Chinese girls — 15 or 20 scholars, who board & lodge with them, & are indented to them for a term of years. They are taught Chinese, & not English. The effect of teaching Engl. to girls is said to be bad. The children said, or rather, *chanted,* the Lord's Prayer and sang a hymn, in Chinese, to an English tune, singing by note — "glory to Thee my God, this night".

Some conv. with Mrs. Bonney. She is daughter of Gen. Solomon V. Rensselaer of Albany, niece of the Patroon, & inquired after Mrs. N. Thayer, & Mrs. John E. Thayer of Boston, knows Mrs. Barnard, the Grangers &c. &c.[78] & knew the Webbs (John & Hy), Mrs. Courtland V. Rensselaer &c. Mr. Bonney was a mechanic, with only a Lowe Sem. education — rather strange match — made by the Board, I fancy! She seems devoted to her work. Mr. Bonney is interpreter to the Am. Consulate, & is much respected here. He reads & speaks Chinese tolerably well. Their house is on the river bank, N. side, & our boat lay at their front door.

Called on Rev. Mr. Preston,[79] missionary of Am. Presbyterian Board. He also lives on river. Wife from E. part of Conn., — well enough — commonplace woman. Both these gent. offer me their services as *cicerones.*

Close by Mr. B.'s house, a fleet of boats is getting ready to sail with Chinese soldiers, up the river, to attack the robbers, who are in great force some 20 or 30 miles off. Robbers have taken sev. towns, & Canton wd. be in danger, but for the Allied occupation. The boats are gaudy with banners & devices & brave mottoes, & the soldiers have "victory" painted on their breasts. They are armed with spears & shields & a few matchlocks. It is said that not one in ten of them reaches the destination — they desert. There was a great beating on drums & gongs, & burning of incense sticks, & throwing to the winds of gilt paper, for a propitious voyage.

Returned, after dark, through this swamp of fire flies & jack o'lanterns, to Russell & Co.'s hong.

[77]American Board of Commissioners for Foreign Missions.

[78]Solomon Van Rensselaer (1774–1852), veteran of the Revolutionary War and the War of 1812, was a U. S. congressman from New York, 1819–1822, and postmaster at Albany, 1822–1839 and 1841–1843. He was a cousin of the patroon, Stephen Van Rensselaer, whose son, Courtland, living at this time, is noted earlier. Nathaniel Thayer (1808–1883) was a Boston financier and philanthropist. John E. Thayer and Mrs. Barnard remain unidentified. The Grangers are probably the family of Francis Granger, noted earlier, of Canandaigua, New York.

[79]Charles Finney Preston (1829–1877), Union College, 1850, was a missionary in China, 1854–1877. He translated the New Testament into Canton vernacular, wrote a Chinese hymnal, and published a great variety of essays.

Dinner at 7 P. M. Mr. Orne & Mr. Sheppard appear in full dress of black dress coats, pantaloons & waistcoats, fresh shirts &c. This is the custom here & at Hong Kong, for dinner, & a good one, has a civilising effect on the young men. Only we three at dinner. Four servants wait at table. Excellent service, still, silent, clean men, & know their duties thoroughly – natural house servants. Orne tells me they are the best in the world, & trustworthy. Cooking excellent, such rice as we never get at home. Rice is steamed, here, dry, & each kernel separate. In-door servants all dress in long blue robes, white stockings & China shoes — heads & faces close shaved.

At night, watch the boats, from the balcony, & listen to the cries, & the broad field of moving & stationary lights.

Large sleeping room, open rafters, & mosquito nets — though cool weather — but heard no mosquito, yet.

When lie down to sleep, in the midst of this strange city, food enough for meditation & cause eno' for gratitude.

SUNDAY. MCH. 11, 1860. Up early. Chinese servant comes, takes away clothes, brushes & cleans them, folds up & places on chair, with boots blacked, as an Engl. servant does, & asks if have tea or fruit. As breakfast is late, take tea & toast, — tea a delight to smell or taste. Walk balcony, over river, until breakfast. See the families cooking, sewing & washing, in their little boats. These boats are covered over in stern & open in front. Here they sleep, cook, eat, wash & work. The girls row & steer, while the men are usually off at work as coolies, on shore, or in vessels. They pick up a living by carrying passengers (for there are no bridges across the river) & goods. Some of these boats are stationary, & only the houses of laboring men, but most are in motion. Such fleets of market garden boats, with meats, fruits & vegitables! Then shop-boats, & mechanic's boats, & large passenger boats going to & from the country (for a boat can go, by canals or rivers, all over China), & soldier-boats, & Mandrin-boats, & cargo boats, & the large, ornamented Hong-boats, the pleasure boats of the merchants.

Breakfast is of made dishes, rice & curry, eggs & omolettes, & fragrant tea. The tea this house uses costs *here* nearly $1 per pound. Tea must *not* be boiled. Pour upon the leaves boiling fresh water, as you need the tea. The water must not be allowed to stand in the kettle, simmering, but should be freshly boiled. Here, you can trust the Chinese to make it, but the merchants say that, at home, it should be made at table, tea in caddy, & water boiling at table.

After breakfast, go, by invitation, to hear (or rather see) Mr. Preston preach to the Chinese, in the open air, at one of their temples. Wonderful change wrought, here, by the Allied occupation. No foreigner has ever[80] been inside the sacred walls of Canton, until now. In 1858, Engl. & Fr. took the city, stationed troops here, & established guard posts, & police & now foreigners can safely, by day, go all over the city. Engl. policemen, with neat blue dress & white band on hat, at corners of streets. In the suburbs, foreigners could hardly go beyond the factories without insult & risk, & the boys & all saluted them with the most odious appellations. Now, all is respect & deference. And so far is it carried, that the missionaries can safely &, even with pleasure, preach in the porches of their temples, while worship is going on within. (The missionaries differ as to the expendiency of this, however, & the Catholics never do it).

Cross the river in the Hong boat of R. & Co. It is a long, wide boat, with a large covered part aft, large eno' for 4 persons to recline at length, furnished with Chinese pillows &c., & blinds — rowed by 5 men. Take two sedan chairs — each carried by 3 coolies, 2 before & 1 behind — Mr. Orne & I.

Now we pass the gate, in the city wall, a Fr. sentry one side & an Engl. the other, & are in the city — where in the world's history, no foreigner has been, with their knowledge, until now.

And, what a strange world, within! This long, narrow, winding alley, — not over 4 feet wide, from house to house, crammed, jammed, brimming, overflowing, shops, shops, shops, men, men, men, — a stream of life drifting up & drifting down, — cries & talking, — now & then a sedan chair, at a slow trot or fast walk, crying out to make way — make way! Little, minutest shops, crammed full of things to sell, & the grave shop-men behind their counters. Little bits of shops, full of little people working at the minutest work, with the minutest instruments! Coolies, in shirt & short trowsers, bare headed & bare footed. A better class, in long robes, skull-caps, shoes & long socks — women, in their sober comely dress of close necked tunic & long trowsers, some stepping free, with feet of natural sise, & some tottling on their little goat's feet, just able to get over the ground, in that mincing, swaying, tottling [gait] which they think so genteel. Close sedans, with ladies, behind closed blinds or curtains, or with a grave mandarin, or Chinese gentleman, — with pre-cursors & post-cursors, crying out to make way — & carrying, one his umbrella, another his fan & another his lantern & another his tablet of rank & office. Through all this, we drift along in our open chairs, at a jog trot, carefully navigating round the corners, &, if 2 chairs come abreast, making a dead stand, & edging sidewise into the shops. At some places, we stop, to see the vases & work. All is done in sight, & much in open air. At each open space, where there is a little more room,

[80]Dana added in a marginal note: "Some have been, a little way, by stealth."

is a barber, with his chair & tools, & a cook with his portable furnace & little table of eatables, & a money changer, or a gambler, or a juggler. The compulsory shaving of the heads of all males, young & old, gives employment of numerous barbers. No Chinese wears hair on his face until he is 45 yrs. old, or is a gr. father, when he wears, or may wear, a moustache & beard or chin, but they never wear whiskers or long beards. The barbers not only shave heads & faces, but clean out the ears, & lifting the eyelids, run a piece of vine across the inside of the upper lid, to clean off the mucus. (This is thought to be one cause of the numerous opthalmic diseases here). There is a man bowing his head to a block, while the barber shaves & washes the crown, & there the barber is picking out an ear with a stick, delicately, & here he is nicely touching an upturned eyelid. In the shops are silk weavers, wood carvers, ivory cutters & carvers, seal cutters, spinners, lacquer workers, — an ant hill of industry! Everything done by hand & nothing by machinery. You might as well introduce steam into an ant-hill as into China. What would become of these 300,000,000 workers, each making the 9th part of the pin, & each getting enough to eat & to clothe himself!

Beside the modesty & neatness of the women's dress, they take nice care of their hair. It is always black, & usually abundant. They dress it in large bunches or ridges behind, with stone or glass ornaments & hair pins. They put no oil upon it, but plaster it with an extract of the slippery elm, which keeps it in place & makes it always look smooth, & yet does not make it greasy. Dishevelled or even rough hair, or curls are never seen. (I speak of the lower & middle classes, who walk the streets. The ladies, I have not yet seen).

Just as we reach the "Temple of 500 idols", we meet Mr. Preston coming away. We are late, & his preaching is over, & his crowd dispersed. He says he had a large & attentive audience, & told them their gods were wood & false, & could not do anything, & they rather assented to it.

Visited this Temple, or Pagoda. It is of the Buddhist (*pronounced* Bood-ist) religion. One large idol of Budda in the centre, & rows of little idols, (see infra, as to whether *idols*)[81] each, however, about the sise of life, sitting, in long lines around the temple, & in the passage ways. These are said to be actually 500. They are of wood, gilded over. The gigantic central figure is Buddha (pronounced Boo-da), & he is of brass — a great, sleepy beast. Before him burn tapers, oil lamps & candles, & incense sticks, wh. consume slowly, without flame, like a slow match. On a large table before him, are offerings of fruits, meats & confectionary. The walls & door posts are covered with inscriptions in Chinese characters. The temple is of stone, with pagoda roof, the floors stone, the

[81]See p. 956.

roofs tile. The grounds are extensive, with trees & grass, & long corridors & cloisters where the priests live; — for it is a Monastery as well as a temple. Sweep away the idols, & it would make a grave & venerable monastery or college of a Greek or R. Catholic Church. The stillness, the trees & the grass, the high roofs & high excluding walls are a relief from the streets (or lanes) of a Chinese city.

Return to lunch. Too late for the service of the Church of England, wh. is held in remote part. (Wherever there is a Br. consul in China, the Br. Govt. agree to give as much to sustain a Chaplain as the foreign residents will raise). Rev. Mr. Gray is Chaplain here, on those terms, $2000 a year in all. All speak well of him. On our way, call at Rev. Mr. Bonney's Chapel, wh. he has opened since the Allied occupation. Small, with seats for about 100, & a pulpit. He has a Chinese Chatachist, who addressed the people. The congr. consisted of Mr. B.'s school, — some 25 boys, & about 30 men — all Chinese. They sang "Jerusalem, My happy home" in Chinese, few joining except Mr. B. & the Chatachist & boys. Then he distributed copies of the Lord's Prayer & of the book of St. Mark. (They find it best to distribute the Bible in parts, a single gospel, they say).

Chinese have no weekly sacred day, but there are two sacred days in a month (lunar), which are somewhat observed as fasts & days of worship, but labor & trades go on.

Visit to the gardens of the great Hong merchant, Howqua. He is son of the great Howqua,[82] who died a few years ago, worth, it is said, 30 millions of dollars. The gardens are his pleasure house & grounds, in the suburbs. Like everywhere else, you go to it by water. Here are some 20 acres of fish ponds, lakes, canals, stone bridges, grottoes, temples, pagoda roofs with stone pillars to shade the sitters at the beautiful tables of marble & ebony, grass plots, terraces, flowers in beds & flowers in pots, trees, shrubs, the lotus & the banyan, urns of flowers, the walks all paved with brick or large flags of stone, lines & lines of walls of open brick work with stone copings, some 2 or 3 feet high, on which rest thousands of flower pots with every kind of flower; & then there are singing birds, cooing turtle doves, & falling gurgling waters. What an enormous outlay of expense! Worthy the Khan of an Oriental Empire!

From this, we go to Puntinqua's gardens — (*pro.* Poon-tín-qua) which are larger & richer than Howqua's. In the midst of these gardens, is a

[82]Howqua was the name by which a family of Chinese merchants were known to Westerners. The "great" Howqua, Wu Ping-chien (Woo Pingkien), is noted earlier. He died in 1843. The Howqua alive at the time of Dana's visit was Wu Ch'ung-yüeh (1810–1863), famed for the philanthropic use of his wealth to underwrite publication of many rare Chinese books. He was the chief negotiator between the Allies and Chinese in the wars of 1858–1860.

private theatre. One house is for the guests, & another, separated from it by a canal of some 12 f. wide, in wh. swim fish & out of wh. grow creepers & shrubs, is for the stage. It is luxury itself. The guests sit at open windows, in large chairs, with tables before them, & look across the water to the stage. Also, there is Puntinqua's summer house, full of rooms, & furnished with chairs, tables, mirrors & bedsteads. The favorite style of Chairs is to let in pieces of polished stone for backs & seats, which have different colors, resembling scenery. Some of the tablets, chairs & tables are extremely costly. Some of the canals are large enough for large pleasure boats, & one, almost dismantled, stands by the theatre.

Since the Br. occupation, these gardens are less cared for by their owners, everything being unsettled in the state of things, & incomes diminished.

The fish-ponds in the temple grounds as well as here, are covered with a little green leaf, not larger than a mosquito, & they tell me a few are thrown on the water, & they multiply & cover its face, & the fish eat it.

Sam-pan is the name for the smaller boat, roofed over at the after part, used to carry passenger short distances. Families live in them. They are very neat. Each sampan has its little shrine, where incense sticks or a taper burn twice a day. The boat-people is the lowest class of Chinese, in morals & intelligence. Yet the boat women are dressed in the same style of neatness & modesty, do up their hair with the same care, & each little boat has its looking glass. The sam-pans are mostly rowed & steered by women, & in the melée of boats, amid all the threatened collisions, & turnings & stoppings to avoid each, they laugh & show their white teeth, & seem perfectly amiable. The babies are strapped to the backs of the mothers, but the smallest children tottle about the little decks, tied by a string to a stancheon or bench, & with little gourds tied to their necks, as floats or buoys in case they fall overboard.

There starts a big passenger boat, for the interior, with some hundreds crowded on board, & tapers burning at the shrine, a gong beating, fireworks letting off, & gilt paper thrown to the winds, for propitiation of the appropriate divinities. There floats a big junk, a sea going junk, with an eye painted on each bow — "S'ppose no got eye, no can see. S'pose no can see, no can sa-vee; s'pose no can sa-vee (from French — *savoir*), no can make walk-ee all same so".

Coin. The Chinese have no coin except a base copper, with hole in middle, to string by, worth about a tenth part of a cent. They use the Sp. & Mex. dollar, ½ doll. & ¼ doll., but for less values they use bits of silver, uncoined, wh. go by weight, altogether. Indeed the Sp. & Mex. coins are taken by weight, so it is usual & as convenient to buy & sell in small sums by these broken bits of silver. For a dollar, you get a handful of them of all shapes & sises. Each shop & house has its scales, & each bit is weighted. The buyer as well as the seller has scales, in shopping & marketing. Almost everything is sold by weight — never I believe by measure, — sometimes by piece. Phrase is — children & chickens sold by the piece, all else by weight. The copper coin is called by Europeans, & in the Pigeon English, *cash* — so many cash, one cash, ten cash. Poor people seldom get silver, but buy & sell by the cash, in small sums. Gold does not pass in China. The great transactions of the foreign merchants are in Sp. dollars. The Chinese are very expert in counting dollars — I mean the bankers, brokers & clerks — weighing each on the finger, passing the good & throwing aside the light for subsequent weighing, & do this as fast as one can take up & drop them.

Great deal of sugar cane eaten. Bits for sale in the streets. Beetle nuts, to chew. Oranges excellent — & supply good, for 9 mos. in the year. Bananas, all the year. Chinese drink no water. Drink is tea, & grown persons occasionally wine, wh. they drink hot as they do tea.

Curious effect, going through the streets, to see a mechanic, in his shop, pegging away at an idol, pinching into his belly & chipping at his cheeks & shoulders.

MARCH 12.   Rev. Mr. Bonney breakfasts with us, & gives me his day. We have an open chair & 3 coolies each, but walk, for convenience & exercise, most of the time, coolies following. He speaks the language & knows the habits of the people — so this is, in fact, my first real visit to the city — for any useful purpose.

We dive into the little streets, with their close jam of shops & people. A street in Canton is like an entry in the upper story & rear of a large country tavern, about as wide — doors as close together. They are all flagged with stone, & perfectly clean, — more easily kept so, as there are no horses or large animals in them. All is *foot work*. These little lanes are very gay, & even gaudy, with decorations, little flags & tablets & strips of cloth & paper, of all colors, with inscriptions in Chinese characters. These almost cover over the street, over head, from side to side. The houses are a story & a half high, the half story above for sleeping.

Each shop has its name, wh. is printed over the door, — indicating some quality claimed or desired. By this name, the shop is known & not by the name of its owner. (Even Howqua, is not the name of the gentleman, but of his hong, (counting-room, store-house); yet foreigners know him by no other name).

What a literary, or lettered people, these Chinese are! Over each door is an inscription, & over each inner door, & over each bench or oven, or anvil, or desk, or whatever place for working.

Meals are two a day, breakfast at 10 A. M., & dinner about 5 P. M. When they rise, they take a little tea or [fruit?].

Went into a shop where [are] made pottery, porcelain cups &c. The master & his long robed workmen were breakfasting at a table in the front room, & the coolies in a back room. Breakfast of Coolies was rice in abundance, tea, a made dish of vegitables, & some little cakes of flour or ground beans fried in oil. The table & plates were clean & neat, & their food well cooked & neatly set out. Their meal was neater & more wholesome than such as the poorer classes of Engl. & Am. get. Think of our grease & fat, & tough meat, bad bread, & worse hot cakes. I have seen something of the cooking of England, France, Sp. America & China, — & believe the worst cooking in the world is that of the middle & poorer classes in America. The Am. & Engl. are not *cooks*. The Fr. & Chinese are, & so are the Sp., to some extent. Think, too, of the great junks & slices of heavy meat we all eat at home! Think of the head of a family, up to his elbows in blood, distributing half raw meat among his children, from fork & knife reeking with blood! Then a few waxy potatoes, clammy bread, & hard thick pie crust!

In this shop wh. is a fair specimen of all, over the front door is the usual inscription — "May rich customers enter here!". Over the steps up, a motto to the effect that all who ascend, shall bear in mind the elevation of virtue. Over the door to the hollow below, — "May all who go down remember humility" &c. So, over the oven, a call for good luck to what comes out, & over the work benches invocations & maxims & proverbs of virtue & industry. In a high place, hung with curtains, is a shrine with an idol, at which a taper is burning. The smaller shops have a little shrine at the door, in a niche. People of the shop very civil to us, rising from table, offering us tea & pipes, & making salutations as we come in & go out. Custom to make salutation when one enters or leaves a shop, — wishing good luck, excusing interruptions &c., in the florid style of Chinese politeness.

They are very fond of proverbs, maxims, mottoes &c. & cover their walls & door posts with them.

Visit Temple of Longevity. This covers large space of ground, in middle of the city, grass plots, trees, ponds of gold fish. The walks flagged with large, wide stones. It is also a monastery, & 200 priests reside here, in long cloistered ranges of one storied rooms. In centre is a large one story, pagoda roofed, temple. At door of temple, on each side, a huge ugly idol. In middle, a great image of Budda asleep. Around, are smaller images. Buddha is brass, rest are gilded. Howqua has ordered a daily service here for the long life of his mother, now 70 years old, for which he pays about $300. It is to last 49 days, & is now about half through. This service consists of prayers twice a day, for ½ hour each, & a perpetual burning of incense sticks & tapers. Before the idols stands a candelabra of 49 lamps, one for each day, & an incense stick before each lamp. Also, a large table on wh. are offered daily fruits, cakes &c. — wh. the priests eat, after they have been there a while. Mr. Bonney says (& so says Huc) that no intelligent Chinese think the God eats these things, or can, but they are offering to show willingness to part with goods &c., — perhaps also, a notion of a *spiritual* partaking by the God, the things themselves, in their materal form, being untouched.

Buddhist priests shave the entire head & wear cap. (Chinese laity, shave only front & top, & leave hair & long tail behind. This was not Chinese custom, but is compelled by the Tartars. Think of compelling 300 millions to shave heads & wear tails!)

A priest recognised Mr. Bonney. He had kept a shop, & Mr. B. had lent him Christian books & been kind to him. "Why become priest?" "Shop burned & all goods in it. No money to set up again. No friends to help. Very poor. Will starve. Now, have place to live & eno' to eat". He proceeded to say that Chr. books very good, & this religion not very good. This was to conciliate Mr. B., or rather a Chinese politeness, possibly he thought. A temple boy that stood by asked Mr. B. why he did not help the man, if he wanted him to be Christian. (This all in Chinese).

Pawn shops, very numerous. Pawn the smallest articles. Shops different times & rules of forfeiture. Went to one pawn shop & saw the system. Books carefully kept, & tickets given to each pawnor, & articles placed in store. The clerk wrote, or rather printed, (for they rather print or paint, than write their characters) very fast & handsomely. A handsome handwriting is highly valued by the Chinese, — & is very common. All writing is like printing of copper plate. They write with a brush of camel's hair, ground to a fine point, using India ink, which is placed on an ink-stone, by the writer's side. The operation is very neat & pretty. The clerk gave a pawn ticket, wh. he wrote out at Mr. B.'s request, for a hat, for 15 cents, (150 cash), with an indorsement in the corner, to show that it is of no value.

Met a detachment of coolies, under a Br. officer, each with a long bamboo pole. They arc employcd by the Br. army as porters & laborers, & are called, familiarly, the "Bamboo Rifles".

Quarters of the Tartar General — Chief of the Military. His old quarters battered by the bombardment & abandoned. Now, in smaller place.

Head quarters of the Allied Army. These are at the Yamún (pro. ya-mooń — once for all, *a* is *ar*, *i* is *ee*, & *u* is *oo*), or palace of the Governor or Chief Magistrate, who is dispos[sess]ed by the Allies. Large & regal place — broad stone walks, high roofed buildings, large grass plots &

numerous trees. Found here Mr. Parkes,[83] now one of the commissioners for China, & formerly Br. Consul at Hong Kong, a man of large experience. Spoke of my book on Cuba, in connexion with the Coolie trade, & said they had got valuable hints from it, in arranging their regulations here. He was in hurry, his wife leaving for England tomorow. Is to see me again on his return fr. Hong Kong.

Buddhist Temple & Pagoda, 1300 years old. Great ugly idols each side door, as usual, great brasen idol of Buddha in centre, & numerous other small idols. The Pagoda is 300 feet high, & more than ten centuries old, & delapidated. One cannot get above the third story, as the balconies (or whatever they are called) have fallen offf.

Nearly all the temples & other large buildings in Canton suffered in the bombardment. One of the priests telling us of this, politely added, — they did not know they were our temples, or they would not have injured them.

Called on Rev. Mr. Graves,[84] missionary of the Southern Bapt. Board. Found him dressed in suit of blue flannel, such as sailors & naval officers now wear. He has a small chapel & school, with a few scholars.

Time for *tiffen,* which is lunch, in all Br. India, China, & Australasia. Go to a China tea shop "True Abundance". Little tables, for 2 & 4 each, as in our eating houses. Place 2 cups on table, with tea leaves in each, turn hot water on them & cover the cups with saucers. Little cups to dip out tea & sip it. Tray, with 15 little plates, each holding diff. kinds of preserves & confection. Little cakes of black beans baked & ground to powder & mixed with little oil & scented, & covered with a crust of baked wheat flour — very good. Little preserved oranges, not larger than olives — excellent. Other confections of nice, quaint contrivance. All Chinese drink tea pure, without either milk or sugar. Milk not to be had. Sugar can be had if ordered. Drank it pure, *a la Chinoise,* & found it refreshing & agreeable. Nice little tiffen. Paid in silver bits, wh. they weighed at the counter, giving us cash for change.

Visit Temple to Confucius. (His Chinese name is Kong-Foo-Tze, which the Jesuits latinised to Con-fu-cius). Large grounds, walled in, silent groves, large trees, broad walks of flag stone, & one large temple, in centre, one story, pagoda roof, high, stone floor. No idol or image in it, but simply a tablet to the honor of Confucius, on a kind of high dais,

[83]Sir Harry Smith Parkes (1828–1885) had begun his diplomatic career in the Orient in 1841, was later to be Minister to Japan and, still later, China. He was one of three commissioners appointed to settle the treaty dispute with China. During the negotiations he was captured, kept at Peking for three weeks, and constantly threatened with death.

[84]Rosewell Hobart Graves (1833–1912) was a Southern Baptist missionary in China 1856–1912.

with an inscription over it "Sacred to the Spirit of Kong-Foo-Tze, the most sacred teacher. None such have been before him, nor since". In another place "the teacher of 1000 generations".

On the sides of the temple are tablets to the great pupils of Confucius, — the chief of whom is Mencius (Men-Tze'). There are no priests or preachers or teachers of the Confucians. He established no religion, no system, no sacrifices, & pretended to no revelation. He was simply a philosopher, teaching only moral philosophy, political economy, the social duties, manners & ceremonies in public & private life, the duties & rites arising out of the social system &c., — with maxims, proverbs, rules & parables. On these his fame is founded. They do not elevate him above a human being, but venerate his memory & pay honors to his spirit, — not by prayers or sacrifices, but by creating temples or monuments, by tablets, & 2 or 3 times a year by a great procession of all the dignitaries, reverential salutations &c. &c. A scholar who resides at the temple — for it is a kind of refuge for poor scholars, told us he had been through five of the annual examinations, but had failed each time. "Why so?" "My poor exercises were not thought good enough". "Shall you try again?" "Yes. I have nothing else to do".

The system of competitive literary examinations has always prevailed in China. All social & official rank (except the military, which [is] rather looked down upon) depends on these examinations. Without a degree, no civil office is open to any one. A second degree, called by foreigners Master of Arts — opens higher offices, & the third degree, the highest of all. The examinations are in writing (chirography, I mean) composition in prose & verse, in the Classics — i.e. Confucius, Mencius &c. &c. The ex. are held in every district, for the first degree, & thousands present themselves, & it lasts sev. weeks. Candidates are locked into little rooms, each day, hardly large eno' to turn round in, with only paper & ink stone. Not over 1 in 10 gets a degree. Those who have a first degree may be afterwards exd. for the 2d, & so on. China is full of poor *plucked* men, whom the dignity of scholars will not allow to labor or trade, & the want of a degree keeps from civil office. They are the copyists, & smaller pedagogues. One rejected friend looked rather weak & simple. I cd. not but pity him.

On our way, dropped into a little school of 12 boys, under one teacher. Mr. Bonney asked him if he had a degree. Not yet. Not able to pass — therefore, he teaches this little school, for very small pay. The boys sit, as Chinese boys probably have for 2000 years, on just such seats & at just such benches as Engl. & Am. boys. They study aloud. When they recite, they turn back to teacher, & rattle off, swaying the body to & fro

They are taught to read & write, & then they commit to memory passages from the Classics, which they do not understand. A bright little boy of 12, stood up, back to teacher & said off his day's lesson, *memoriter,* wh. was a passage from Confucius, of about 12 mo. page, entirely unintelligible to him.

Thence, to the Foundling Hospital — a Chinese institution, but so run down after the Allied occupation that Allies have been obliged to aid it. The Engl. support here 50 nurses, & the French about 20, the rest by Chinese. There are about 100 nurses & 200 foundling infants. Yet the institution will accomodate 1000, if there were nurses eno'. They are all wet nurses, & the children are sent away when weaned. There are some 8 head women, or matrons, all of whom presented themselves to us. Lanes of little rooms, brick walls & earth floors, each with a nurse or 2 & a quota of babies.

Went to top of the city wall, where the Fr. & Engl. garrisons chiefly are. The Engl. are Marines, the 3d Buffs, & 67th. The French are only Marines. But in French navy, there is no difference betw. marines & sailors — all are sailors & all are drilled to the musket & drum. To make them into marines, they tuck their wide bottomed blue trowsers into white gaiters, & strap a belt round them with sword & pistol &c. The rest of their dress is sailor. The Engl. marines are soldiers only, with red coats.

Before leaving the Hospital, we made a call upon the resident physician, a Chinese. He is an M. D., & has two degrees in the public examinations, & wore a gilt button. The general supervising officer, a higher mandarin than he, was paying him a visit. There they sat, these two Chinese gentlemen, in long robes, black skull-caps topped with the button of literary & official rank, each with his long pipe & his tobacco box, with two servants in waiting, having a quiet talk, fanning themselves & looking out on the trees, — wh. I suppose is the sum of the official inspection. Each rose, clasped his hands together & bowed low, in the Chinese fashion, & had seats brought to us, & the servants brot us tea & pipes. Declined the latter but took the tea, — wh., as every where here, is made as you use it, a cup with a great spoonful of leaves, water poured on it, cup covered & left to stand about three minutes. Mr. Bonney had a long talk with them. The Dr. inquired after an Engl. work on anatomy wh. had been translated into Chinese, & Mr. B. gave him a note of introduction to the person who had it for sale. When the note was finished, a Chinese envelope was produced, highly ornamented, open at an end instead of the side as with us. "Then they have envelopes here". "They had them before we had them in Europe".

What did not this wonderful people have before us? Gunpowder, printing, mariners' compass, — & now, *envelopes!*[85] And how exquisite is their politeness! Their motions are slow, their eyes fixed on you with an expression of interest & affection — the hypocrites — not exceeded by that of a young belle seeking to make her first conquest, & if they hand or take anything, it is with a bow & a careful place of the thing in your convenient reach. They are trained, & have been trained in the *rites* since the time of Confucius. When we take leave, they press their hands together & bow low, at the door, follow us to the outer door & repeat the performance there, with a look mingled of delight at having had such a pleasure & pain at losing it so soon.

The next place we visit, is the Hall of Examination. This is a large building where the examiners sit, & around it is a large area of some 6 or 8 acres, with bricked passageways lined with one story sheds or cabins, each large enough for a big Newfoundland dog to kennel in, which are the rooms in wh. the candidates are shut up, each to prepare their writings & theses. There are no less than 7000 of these. Think of 7000 candidates, in one district, & the chance for a degree not more than one in ten! But these buildings suffered so in the bombardment that they have been allowed to go to ruin, & the last two examinations have been held at a large temple in the country.

Here is the parade ground of the Chinese, in the day of power, where the soldiers practiced their gymnastics, for they were little else, & shot their arrows. Now buffaloes are feeding upon it. The buffalo is the principal beef & milk animal here. It is what is called "Water buffalo", & differs from the Am. bison. It is fond of water, & lives in it, in warm weather.

The Br. have a telegraph to & fr. each military station in the city, but it is under ground, as the Chinese would cut it, were it in the air. They have also a post-office & parcels delivery, — but only for the Military. With all the civilisation of the Chinese, they never had a post, for public use, but only Govt. couriers.

The last place of our visit to-day is the "Execution Ground". Here, for centuries, the capital punishments of the city have been inflicted. Here thousands & tens of thousands have been beheaded, & the soil is saturated with human blood. Nor is this all. Tortures the most frightful have been inflicted here, such as it can hardly enter into the mind to conceive, & the air has been rended with shrieks & cries of the ultimate agonies of men.

Yet, the ground is small & obscure, with no indication of its purpose, being merely an open space or yard, behind a row of humble dwelling

[85]Dana adds in a marginal note: "And there lie their visiting cards before them. These, too, they had before paper was known in Europe."

houses, some half acre or more in extent, without any public building, or other mark of a public character to it. Broken pottery lies about it, & people pass & repass over it, & when not in use for executions, it is used as a rubbish yard by the neighborhood. Mr. Bonney told me he saw 15 men beheaded there not long ago. The convicts are tied hand & foot, made to stand in rows, facing all one way, with heads bent over, & 2 or 3 executioners, each with a sharp cleaver, goes along & lops off their [heads], with one blow to each, the head rolls off, the body starts up & falls over, & a very few minutes does the whole work. Sometimes 200 have been beheaded here at a time. Last week two were beheaded. They were to have been flayed alive, wh. is the favorite process, but the **Br.** officers forbade it, & the judicial mandarins had to content themselves with lopping off the heads.

A gentleman, Mr. Owen of the Br. Co. House, told me he was here once at an exn., & saw them begin their cutting up of a live man, but was obliged to leave, it was so dreadful. They began, with their very sharp cleavers, to cut slices off his cheeks & breasts & thighs & to lop off fingers & toes. The decree of the Court orders death by a certain number of cuttings, & the skill of the executioners is shown by getting all his cuts, his 20, 50 or 100, before the man is fully dead. This miserable dirty undesignated back-yard of a place has been for centuries the scene of these horrors.

As we are going home, towards dark, the shops are lighting up their shrines. In the larger shops, large lamps or candles burn before the large idol in his curtained shrine, in the rear, while the bits of shops, mere front counters, have their bits of niches at the door posts, in which the doll idol sits, & before it burns the bit candle. The candles & sticks burn abt. 15 or 30 minutes, for this ev. oblation.

Stop at the door of a large house, of a mandarin whom Mr. B. knows, in hope of seeing the interior. But the very polite door keeper says the owner has taken a wife, & the marriage fête is not concluded, & he has friends at dinner &c. &c. The front door is open, & through it we see a hall brilliantly illuminated with Chinese lanterns, & hurrying servants, & walls tapestried with red paper inscribed all over with characters in honor of the event, the family & the Gods. At the door sit four minstrels, a drummer, a cymbal striker, & 2 guitar players. They play a salute to each guest, when he enters or leaves. I spoke to Mr. B. & pointed to the minstrels, & they, thinking it an order to play, gave us a salute as we left.

Dined at Mr. Bonney's. Mr. & Mrs. B. feel very favorably to the English Army of occupation. They tell me the Eng. officers are very polite to the missionaries, often make contributions, offer them aid & protection in anything they undertake, & absolutely know no difference betw. Am. & English in their attentions & protection. So it is, they tell me, as to all Am. here. They are protected by the Allies equally with the Engl. residents. Mr. B. tells me that the Fr. troops are not so popular with the Chinese as the English. Mr. Preston confirms this statement.

Messers. Russell & Co. sent their great Hong-boat for me, & it was kept waiting from 6 o'ck. to 9. But that was thought nothing of. The coolies *live* in the boat, & may as well be here as at R. & Co.'s wharf.

"Old Head", the boat-master of Russell & Co., is an old Chinaman, known to all Am. who have been in Canton the last 30 & even 40 years. He knew Mr. John P. Cushing[86] & inquired of me about him, & Mr. C. must have left here more than 30 years ago. This nick-name of "Old Head" he is proud of, & the Chinese call him by it. He has charge of all the boats & boat-coolies of the house, & also owns sev. boats on the river. (Funny story of Old Head's being cheated in buying a boy, in the market).

TUESD. MCH. 13. To-day, the Rev. Mr. Preston is to be my guide. Boat down to his house, wh. is on the river side & near the Gate of Eternal Purity. Start off, on foot, at abt. 10 A. M. for a ramble thro' the city.

Small door, curtain before it — "That is an opium shop. Go in!" Went in. Two rows of sleeping tables, with mats & pillows, to hold 2 or 3 persons each — & lamps & opium pipes. Smoker reclines at length, head on the hard pillow, & a servant loads the pipe with opium, puts it to his mouth, & tends it for him. Mode is to put little of the opium, in a soft gum form, into the small hole of the bowl, & put bowl to the lamp & inhale, swallow the smoke into the lungs. This was a low class shop, & poor people attended it. They come in & get a pipe or two & go off. Some, the confirmed topers, smoke until they are stupefied.

To the "Ten Thousand ages Temple", or "Temple of the Emperor" — for "10,000 ages", is a title of the Emperor. This is a large building, standing in an extensive enclose, planted with evergreen trees. It is a mere temple of honor. On the Emperor's birth day, on New Year's days, & on the 1st & 15th of ev. month, there are services here is his honor, burning of incense & lamps, & prostrations of the people before his tablet. I believe they bow the head, touching the forehead to the earth 9 times

Large Mahommedan Mosque, outside the walls, in the Eastern suburb. It is in the Chinese style of architecture, & has no sign of the crescent about it, or anything else to distinguish its religion, except the absence of

---

[86]John Perkins Cushing (1787–1862) was the most highly respected foreign merchant in China, where he made his fortune in the period from 1803 to 1830.

all idols or images of any kind. At middle of one wall, opposite the door, is a recess, with curtains. Over it are Arabic characters, & the posts & columns are lined with Arabic, & there are tablets of the same. The floor is matted all over. There are no seats, & from the ceiling hang Chinese lanterns & European chandeliers, — but these are used for lighting & not for worship.

Temple of the God of War. Walled in, & large yard, grass plots, evergreen trees (chiefly a kind of bastard Banyan), flagged walks, large Chinese building of one story. This temple is confined to rich & superior people, who alone worship there — it being, I believe, their property. Consequently, it is not much frequented. Usually, it is a complete solitude. The idols are as usual, large & small, some of brass & some gilded, some hideous, some merely funny, & some grave & proper. There is one tablet here given by the unfortunate Commissioner Yeh.[87]

A Buddhist Monastery. Quiet enclosed spot of several acres, standing in midst of city. Long rows of rooms for the priests & scholars, with cloisters, like the old monastic institutions of Europe. It has an open temple, in wh. the people go — freely to worship. Several women worshipping there. Before each idol incense sticks as usual & tapers. Each worshipper buys her sticks & tapers at stalls in the temple, also all her other offerings. The temple, like that at Jerusalem, is a place for sale of everything used in the worship, & of refreshments. There are more buyers & sellers than worshippers. One woman touches her forehead to the pavement 9 times, with her open hands reverently placed together, & then throws up two bits of wood & as they come down is good luck or bad luck. She is either seeking a lucky day, or a lucky place for a house or shop, or a lucky name for something or somebody, or a prophecy of good or ill luck on some proposed enterprise. She repeats the operation several times. Another woman, after prayers & prostrations, draws an incense stick from a number, examines its mark & goes to an old priest, who examines his tables & tells her whether it is good or ill luck. Before the great idol, is a large table with offerings of fruits & confectionary. The women also burn gilt paper, & paper-money. This paper money is of slight value, if any, but answers as well as money for the spirit of deity to which it is offered.

Great numbers of book shops & book stalls. Stop at one of the best of the shops. Mr. Preston knows the man, & says he has many valuable books. Showed me some books of Confucius & Mencius, & the four classics. No Chinese book is ever a stiff cover. The books are laid away on shelves as

[87]The Chinese official whose seizure of prisoners from an allegedly British ship in 1856 precipitated the war.

we put away note paper. Printing is on a yellow colored paper with very black ink.

Next visited the Governor's College. This is an institution for the education of youth already advanced in their studies, like the fellowships & scholarships of England.

The Treasury — a truly magnificent building — long vistas of avenues under trees, with broad flagged pavement, & large buildings of Chinese architecture, of stone & brick, with highly ornamented tile roofs — all in the usual gay & gaudy style of Chinese edifices. It is now occupied by the French officials & troops.

Now in the Tartar quarter. All the Tartar women have three earings, while Chinese women have one, & the Tartar women never cramp their feet. The Tartars are the dominant race — that is to say, the imperial fam. is Tartar, & so are the military commanders, (all, or nearly all) & a portion of all civil officers. But here there are Tartars of the lower class. They have taller & larger figures than the Chinese, with a more manly carriage & air, noses larger & more acquiline — the Chinese being usually small & flat —, & eyes more like the European. They wear the shaven front & tail behind. But the Tartar is not suited for the quiet industry of the city. He must be a soldier, or a mountaineer, or herdsman — either the open country, or at least, command & leisure in a city. Consequently, the Tartar quarter contrasts very unfavorably with the Chinese. There is something approaching the city Irish of America about the quarter — though not one half so bad — the women neater & the children neater & better clad, & the men more civilised far, than our city Irish. Still, they are not so neat as the Chinese — there is little trade or business in the quarter, the houses have little furniture & often are dilapidated, & there is a look of impending bankruptcy about the whole region.

Called at French Mission. Delivd. my gen. letters fr. Bhp. Hughes & Fitzpatrick.[88] B'p. of Canton a tall, slender, middle-aged French gentleman of agreeable manners & mild voice. A Fr. priest with him who has suffered fr. imprisonment, want of food & clothing, in the interior, & fears he has consumption — rather an interesting man. Whole number of priests in the diocese, 10, of wh. 2 are Chinese, educated at Macao. No sisters, of any order. Thinks there are 2000 Chinese professed Catholics in the city, including the families of professors. Am to call again to see school. Rooms very plain. Since the Allied occupation, not built or made any permanent arrangements as things uncertain. The European priests no longer wear the Chinese costume & tail &c., while in the city. Did so, in the interior, & do now, wherever for. dress is objectionable.

[88]John Hughes, Archbishop of New York, and John Fitzpatrick, Bishop of Boston, have both been noted earlier.

Saw juggler practicing his tricks in an open square, with crowd round him. No police there, & no disorder. Tricks were of the usual sort that we see at home.

Famous temple known among foreigners as the "Temple of Horrors" — not its Chinese name. Large seated image of God of judgment & punishment — same in each chamber, & 4 or 6 chambers on each side. In each chamber he is represented as sentencing a poor creature to some punishment for his sins in this life, — the dreadful executioners standing round. The figures are about the sise of life. In one, the man is standing upright in a wooden box & two men are sawing him in two, from the head downwards, with a two handled saw. In another, he is lying down & beaten with great bamboo sticks. In another, he is put into a mill, & they are grinding him up. In another, the victim is standing, & the executioners are lowering over him a large red-hot bell.

Amid all these horrors, the people are busily buying & selling, in the Temple Court, & some are worshipping at shrines, & throwing up the bits of wood, to learn the luck. These bits are flat on one side, & convex on the other, & if they fall in diff. ways it is good luck, if alike, bad luck. The luck of every day & place must be ascertained. The advertisements of houses to let, represent them as lucky, built on lucky days &c. One shrine in this temple is for all prayers &c. relating to children, & another for ancestors.

As we pass out, we see a room, near the temple — not of it — where a story teller is entertaining his company. He has a large room, with plain wooden benches, where his audience sit, he sitting on a raised platform. We take our seats, & Mr. Preston interprets the story. It is of a young scholar — scholars are the heroes of Chinese novels & stories, & not soldiers — learned & beautiful. He walks into the open country, & this country is described. Then reaches a mountain, finds a cave in it, enters, goes on, comes to another open, secret place. This he describes minutely — the trees, flowers, birds &c., & an exquisite palace & gardens. At a window of the palace, a beautiful lady, looking into the garden. She sees him, closes ½ the window, looks at him secretly with one eye. He is enchanted, lingers, grows late, a messenger comes fr. her to warn him off, as in danger, he replies how can he leave such a place & such a lady. Messenger says gate will be shut. It grows twilight, she leaves window, & he obliged to return thro' the gate & mountain to the city. Such a simple, harmless story as this holding a chance crowd in a large city! I doubt if N. York or London wd. be content with anything so harmless. The story teller has an animated, but dignified & simple manner, with rather graceful gestures, & Mr. P. says his language is good. His paragraphs are marked by striking on the table a small bit of wood, like a chequer man.

Each auditor contributes a few cash, & there is tobacco for sale, for the smokers. Some idlers spend hours here, smoking & listening. The story teller has no book or notes before him.

A temple to the God of Medicine, with very elaborate figures.

Temple of the "Five Genii", — one of the most famous in the city. It belongs to the sect of the Taope, or Rationalists, a sect founded by Lao-tze, about 600 years B. C. This is the first Taos temple I have seen. It is very large, in the same style with the others, & has numerous images. It has the famous foot of Buddha, a stone which marks its form. (I forget whether it is an image of the foot, or merely its impression, — last or a shoe). The 5 genii sit on 5 thrones, & before each is a little insignificant block of stone. The tradition is that each genius[*sic*] had a ram, & each ram was turned into these very blocks of stone.

Great Temple to Confucius. Like the others I saw, it is a silent solitude in the midst of this great city. The grounds are walled in & embrace some 6 acres or more, with avenues under trees, grass plots, flower bed, flower pots on low brick walls, & several large buildings. In centre is a large tablet to his honor, before wh. the scholars prostrate themselves sev. times a year. The front gate has never been opened, they say, since the tablet was carried thro' it, & Mr. Preston doubts if even the Emperor wd. be thought worthy to have it opened for him. This temple is now chiefly used as the place where the candidates for degrees assemble after their examination is over, to hear the result. The names of the successful candidates are written on large pieces of paper, & pasted to the wall of a certain avenue, at the side. Some parts of the papers are on the wall still. This is the spot of triumph or defeat to thousands every year. In front of the chiefly building, in the Court Yard is an avenue flagged with stones, which crosses a small canal by a handsome stone bridge, arched & on some 20 f. in length. This place is called the "Scholars' Pool" & "Scholars' Bridge", for all scholars cross it to receive their degrees. To cross the Scholars' Pool, is the phrase for obtaining a degree.

Next, we visit a Mahommedan Mosque, in the old city. It is in the Chinese style, & not distinguishable from a college or exn. hall, except by the Arabic Characters upon it. In a little room, in the Purlies of the temple, a poor Chinese scholar, a Mahommedan, has school of some 20 Chinese boys, the children of Chinese Mahommedans, whom he is teaching the Arabic. I presume all the Mahommedans learn it. Whether the Mahommedans here are descendants of the Mongols & others who came to China centuries ago, or of their Chinese converts, I do not know — perhaps they do not. Mahommedanism has always been tolerated in China, but not spread much. We make an appointment to attend worship here Friday at 1 o'ck., — the Mahom. Sabbath.

So ends my second most interesting & instructive day of examination of this strange city & people.

WED. MCH. 14, 1860.   The Chinese watchmen are required to beat on a hollow piece of bamboo, as they walk the streets at night, to show that they are awake. One hears this continual *thung, thung,* every waking hour, & the boatmen's cries on the river never cease.

To-day saw a lorcha. It was a long, sharp three masted schooner-rigged vessel, of about 3 or 400 tons, with duck or cotton sails. At each mast a large fore-&-aft lug sail, (by wh. I mean a sail that goes forward of the mast as well as abaft) & at the main a square topsail & t. g. sail. The junks have also lug sails, very large, of fine matting, with bamboo horisontal sticks each of wh. acts as a boom when the sail is lowered to it. While we sit at breakfast, in the room on the river, a shade passes over us as if the sun were eclipsed, & looking up we see the huge sail of a junk covering up our whole patch of sky.

Went out with Mr. Orne to see the shops for working in lacquer & ivory. The work is exquisitely neat & minute, & all done by hand. Every form & color of the lacquer tables & chairs & stands is the touch of a pencil by hand. A silent company is this little low room full of lacquer workers, each at his seat pencil in hand, & colors at his side. The patterns are on paper, & lie open before the workers. The outline is transferred to the table by pricks of needle points in the paper, thro' wh. a powder is spread.

In the ivory shop, I saw a nest of 21 ivory open-work balls, each so open that could see through the 20 to the little inner ball, not larger than a pea.

The master of the ivory shop has a nephew who is practicing gymnastics to fit himself for a mandarin soldier. There is an exn. for this office, as for the literary degrees, but all that is required for the military art is strength & agility. We went to the little room where the candidate was practicing. He is a small, thin man, with small hands & legs & skinny fingers, but very strong. His feats were equal to the Acrobats. A weight I could scarcely tip on end, he lifted, put on his breast & bending backwards sustained it there for sev. seconds. He is also required to practice with bow & arrow. At the last exn. he passed in the bow & arrow, but failed in the gymnastics. He will try again this year.

To the Honám Temple, at 5 P. M., to see the priests worship. This is by far the largest temple & grounds in Canton. These priest were men of large ideas. The grounds & structures are stately & generous. On entering the gate, a long vista of wide, straight flagged avenue, with tall evergreen trees on each side, terminates at the main temple. But there are numerous smaller temples, & a *town* of cloisters & dormitories, running in even lines, right & left. One could easily be lost in them. Then there are sev. small gardens & grass plots, & one large garden, beautifully laid out comprising sev. acres, reaching out to the suburbs of the city. In this garden is a brick structure where they burn the bones of the deceased priests, another where the ashes are temporarily placed, & a third, a large handsome sarcophagus, wh. is their final resting place, & on wh. appear the inscriptions of their names & with the appropriate mottoes & invocations. The chief trees are banyans & olives — I mean the chief that we recognise. The worship began just at dusk. There was 28 priests, probably the whole number now occupying this once populous monastery. They kneeled on the matted floor, facing one way, towards the shrine of Buddha, joined their hands by touching their fingers together & not by clasping them, & occasionally touched the foreheads 3 times to the floor. These kneelings & prostrations, with the continual repeating in unison, in a sort of droning chant, some sounds of words, once having a signification, in the land this worship came from, centuries ago, but now unknown to the Chinese, — traditionary sounds of more than a thousand years — these constituted the worship. This was continued about half an hour. Then they filed into line, headed by the chief priest, & made the circuit of the temple, inside, three times, their hands reverently meeting before them, & droning over a chant, the words of which were nearly these — Ma Ma Hominy For — Ma Ma Hominy For. Then another prostration, & it ended. All the while tapers & incense sticks are burning before the Chief & the smaller shrines.

I must say that the manner of the priests was grave, slow, reverential & dignified. The old oriental tradition of manner, — & much better than that at the Cathedral at Havannah, wh. it a good deal resembled. If the idols had been removed, & the furniture of the Cathedral put in their place, I could have recommended these boys & men as patterns to the boys & men of the Havana Cathedral. The close resemblance of the Buddhist worship to the R. Cath. has been noticed by all writers & travelers. It is so striking, that some of the early Jesuits in China ascribed it to the work of the Devil, counterfeiting true religion. Some will attribute it to a common element of idolatry & formalism, & others to the common traditions of the Patriarchal ages; — as the temple worship at Jerusalem, with its bloody rites, its altars, its priestly vestments, its images of Cherubim over the Mercy Seat, its brasen oxen, & its memorials of Moses & Aaron, differed not much *to the eye* from that of the surrounding heathen nations. But one was to the Most High, & the others to idols.

Visited the ancestral temple of the Howqua family. It stands by itself, in enclosed grounds, is large & costly, with porcelain tiles in the ceiling,

& the walls covered with tablets in honor of the different ancestors. Before these, incense sticks are continually burning. Wealthy families have the separate temples, for their ancestral halls. Others have a room set apart in their houses, & the poorest have a little shrine with a tablet or two in the corner of the chief room. (See the account of this ancestral worship, its nature, whether idolatrous or not, in Williams' China, Davis' China & Huc).

THURSDAY. MCH. 15, 1860.   Take a coolie & go alone into the city, to call on the R. Cath. bishop & see his institutions. It is a long walk — say 2½ miles from the boat landing. Saw the same priests as before. Showed me an orphan asylum, in wh. are 70 orphan boys. Chinese, with 2 Chinese teachers, priests — educated at Macao. When I go in, each Chinese priest comes forward, stands before me, puts his hands together, bends on knee — not quite to the ground, to make his salutation. I answered it the best I could, by bowing low & taking off my hat. The latter is known to be our usage, but is not that of the Chinese, who keep on the hat, — sitting bare headed being a familiarity. The boys learn Chinese & a little Latin — the latter in the Roman Characters — for it is not possible to write a foreign language in the Characters of an ideographic alphabet.

They have also a small hospital, wh. I did not see. The priest who went with me, a Frenchman, asked me if I was not struck with the resemblance of the Buddhist worship to their own.

Chinese tiffen. Very good — tea pure (without milk or sugar) &, as before, a tray with exactly 15 little plates with two pieces of confectionary or preserve on each. Preserved oranges, about sise of Sp. olive, excellent.

A great city without a sound of carriage wheels or the hoofs of horses! Only the human voice & the human footfall strikes the ear!

Canton seems to be one great one-storied house, with its entries & long passage ways, with doors each side, crammed with people, with an occasional glimpse of sky at openings in the roof, & here & there an open Court Yard. As you go through the streets, the shops seem to have [no] front, but to be open on that side, like a booth, but they have movable shutters wh. they put up at night.

Called on Rev. Mr. Gray, the Br. civil chaplain. He is too ill to go about with me, which he very much regrets. He says the 500 images in the Temple are not of gods or demi-gods, but of sages, the supposed pupils of Buddha, to wh. these honors are paid.

Among the gates of Canton are Eternal Purity, Eternal Joy, Tranquil Sea.

FRID. MCH. 16.   To the Mahomm. Mosque at 1.30 P.M., with Mr. & Mrs. Preston. Called at house of a Chinese Mahommedan. The people in the street saw Mrs. P. get out of her chair at the door, & crowded into the gentleman's house, to inspect a European lady. Mr. P. tells me the people of the street take great liberties in the outer courts of private houses. They thronged round Mrs. P., chiefly children, but as the news spread, some Chinese ladies, of the better class came in. Such a jabber as they kept up! The old Chinese gent. was powerless to get them out.

Went to the Mosque, under his wing, the crowd following. Let in at a side gate &, upon our distinct promise not to step inside the Mosque during worship, (wh. is an abomination unto the Mahommedans), we were led to the open door. The floor of the Mosque is open, covered with matting, & without seats. Only men were present. — men & boys — whole number some 60 or 70. They sat down on the mats, in rows, all facing one way — wh. doubtless was towards Mecca, & in that direction is the pulpit & a niche, like a shrine, but with no image or picture — for the Mahom. allow none. They pray kneeling, & mostly in silence, with hands joined, & occasionally bend forward & touch the forehead to the floor. This motion, though reverential enough, presents a curious spectacle when long rows of men are seen from behind. Some 8 or 10, who seemed to be leaders in the worship, wore white turbans. The rest wore skull caps, going up to a point in the middle, like a minareted dome. The chief officiator, at one point, went into the pulpit & chanted a long piece, whether it was from the Koran, or a sermon I do not know. Each man took off his shoes at the door, & a long line of strange looking shoes was ranged against the wall, inside. From here they took them by hand to the door. They all wore some kind of sock.

Desirous of seeing the interior of a Chinese gentleman's house, we called on a gentleman whose name is spelt by Europeans Hu, but pronounced Huŕ-y. He is a friend of Mr. Preston. He is the head of one of the most wealthy & distinguished families in the province; &, "China fashion", the whole family, brothers, uncles, nephews & first cousins, live under the roof — or rather, in the same enclosure, for there is a little village of houses & court yards & passage ways constituting the establishment. It is said that 2 or 300 persons form the household, including servants. There are no less than three schools for the children of different ages. The ancestral hall is a small temple, standing by itself, with tablets to centuries of ancestors, before wh. lamps continually burn, & [around which] are grouped the standards of the various offices they have held. Room after room, court after court, open ranges of flower pots & bird cages, garden plots, furniture of ebony with variegated polished stone backs, profusions of lanterns, 20 sedan chairs standing in the halls, & the flitting of long-robed upper servants & short-tuniced Coolies indicated the wealth & consequence of our host. The man himself, we found in one of his

smallest & plainest rooms, in a plain dress. He received us with the usual
courtesy of his nation, & made the usual minute inquiries they think so
polite, after our age, our families, our health &c. He is a little over 30, &
has but one wife. He is a scholar, & over his front door is inscribed his
second degree of Master of Arts. We found him engaged with a galvanic
battery, wh. he had imported from New York. He was in the habit of
giving electric shocks to his friends, & offered us one. He had had two
steel plates made in the horse shoe form, & was trying to get them
magnetised, but had not succeeded as yet. Mr. Preston offered to introduce to him the Br. officer of Engineers, who has charge of the underground magn. telegraph betw. the military posts in the city. Mr. P. says
he is a man of intelligence, but, excepting these little curiosity matters,
is wasting his life with opium. He was smoking tobacco from a long water
pipe, wh. a servant ever & anon prepared, put to his mouth & took it
away again. He offered us tea, wh. we accepted — also what he called
wine, wh. I drank fr. curiosity. It was as colorless as water, was made fr.
rice, & was, in fact, not wine but spirit. Going out, we passed under a
gate way the inscription on wh. showed that it was built by one of his
ancestors by special permission of the Emperor.

Our last visit to-day was to a festive temple, a temporary erection of
bamboo poles, covered with richly painted cloth & matting, set up by vol.
contrib. of the neighborhood, in honor of the fact that the city had not
been entirely destroyed by the Allies. Each person in the neighborhood
contributed a sum equal to one month's rent of his place of business. The
interior was very showy with lanterns, & suspended strips of cloth &
paper of brilliant colors, with shrines & idols, & tables of fruits & flowers.
It was to stand but three days. The place was also decorated with furniture, paintings & other works of Chinese art, lent by their owners.
Entrance free to all, & perfect order prevailing. This is, certainly, rather
a liberal contribution for a mere temp. & occas. offering of thanks. The
presiding deity of the Temple is called the Queen of Heaven.

This evening, went to visit the famous Flower Boats. For safety, & to
prevent all misconstruction as to purposes, took Mr. Orne & Mr. Sheppard,
"Old Head" & an escort of Coolies with lanterns. It seems the custom is to
let a boat for the night, with its contents & appurtenances, & the Chinese
invite their friends to dine with them there. One cannot see them, as a
mere visitor, without intruding upon [some one's] party. Still, as the
doors & windows are wide open, it is not unusual or unexpected. We
selected one wh. seemed a good specimen, & introduced ourselves, in
Pigeon English, to the man who was giving the entertainment. He
received us politely, & offered us tea & pipes. His company consisted of
three friends. A Chinese dinner was about being served to them, on

separate stands, in their little saucers, & all were smoking. Four young girls, with hair most extravagantly extended behind & dressed with flowers, with faces conspicuously rouged, but modest in dress & manners, denisens of the boat, were of their company, & there were two musicians & several waiters. Mr. Orne told our host that I was a foreign gentleman, that I had never smoked an opium pipe, & was desirous to do so. He courteously ordered a servant to prepare one, & directed me how to lie down & take the pipe to my mouth — for they always smoke opium reclining. The servant loaded the pipe, & I drew the smoke, swallowed as much as I could into my lungs, puffed out the rest, & got a good notion of the taste, though not enough, of course (I was not willing to risk it) to get the effect of a sleep, or indeed any effect on the consciousness. The taste is acrid & not pleasant. It remained in my mouth all night. We asked for music & the grave gentleman placed a stand between his legs, with a box upon it covered with hide, on which he beat with two sticks, while the two musicians played on their stringed instruments, — one like a guitar & one like a banjo, a kind of music between that of the bagpipes & the banjo, to a monotonous song like the genuine negro plantation chants. I cannot see in their music, so far, the signs of a tolerable civilisation, — to be sure, I have heard only that of the lower classes.

Our whole stay was only about 15 m. & we were bowed out of the boat, our host glad eno' to be rid of us, & left the gaudy, illuminated flower-boat, for a pull back, against the tide, on the dark river, glittering but not lighted by its fire-fly boat lights.

All our passing about involves boats, as we are on the Honan side of the river; & Russell & Co.'s hong, has its retinue of boats & boatmen, as well as of other coolies. I have become so much at home here, that I take no coxwain, but steer the gig among the junks & boats, by day or by night. But the sampans & the hong-boats provide their helms*man*, who is usually a woman. Most large vessels are propelled in part, by a long large scull at the stern, formed of two pieces of timber lashed together, which requires 2, 4 & sometimes 6 persons to work. It is surprising to see with what ease & grace a woman will manage the sculling oar of her boat, often with one hand. It is rather a graceful motion, in their easy dress.

SATURDAY. MCH. 17. This day, by Mr. Bonney's kindness, is given to an expedition to the White Cloud Mountain. This is a hill, about the height, I judge, of Blue Hill, Milton, lying about six miles to the N. E. of the N. E. gate of the city. We hired two chairs, with 3 coolies to each, to carry us there & back, to the summit if we required it, for two dollars in all — one dollar for a chair & 3 bearers for all day! As we went thro' the city, Mr. B. pointed out certain places for my observation. Several small academies, for the instruction of advanced scholars. These, he says, are very common, &, before the capture of the city, were very well attended. One large place enclosed by a high wall of open brick work, through wh. we could see the grass & trees & a large building — that is the ancestral hall of a clan or tribe; for the Chinese keep up their clans like the Highlanders, & the ancestral hall for the common ancestors binds the clans together. Over the entrance to one, are five papers, for the Five Filicities.

As we go out, beyond the walls, we come upon a party of the Buffs & 67th, target shooting, with English rifles, at 600 yards.

We leave behind us the venerable walls of the city — more than 800 years old, grass grown, shrub grown & even tree grown, on their perpendicular sides. They are perpendicular faces of brick, outside, & sloping earth mounds inside.

As we get out into the country, we see something of Chinese horticulture & agriculture. Large paddy fields, low & wet, where the rice is sown & nursed, & from which, when it has reached a height [of] 6 inches, it is taken up & set out by hand in open rows, in wider spaces, in the drier fields. Next are tea fields, where the tea shrub, with dark green leaves, & looking like a close clipped hawthorne hedge, is growing. Then there are sweet potato fields, & olive fields, where the tall, thin olive tree grows, with dark green leaves.

Now we leave the low country & ascend the hills. These hills are rocky & entirely barren of trees & vegetation, except in the little valleys or cañons, where the water flows over rocky bottoms in the wet season, edging them with rich green grass & shrubs & trees. But these barren hills are cities of the dead! Not one hill, or one field, but every hill, every high field is a cemetary, a necropolis. The tombs of the wealthier classes are large & stately, not high, never towering into obelisks or arches, but far extended curves of ornamental walls within walls, centering & culminating in the portal of the tomb, over which is the inscription of the name, age & office of the deceased. Sometimes these costly structures are tombs for a family, sometimes sacred to the remains of one person. The tombs & graves of the less wealthy, have simple head stones, as with us, with the name & date of birth & death of the occupant. Indeed, a Chinese cemetary differs not from one of our own except in the style of the more costly structures, &, (as to this region at least) in that they are not enclosed spaces, like Mt. Auburn & Greenwood, but the entire region of barren hills, for miles, without enclosure or landmark, are given up to them.

This is possible in a country like China, for here people cannot live sparsely about the country. It is not safe. As soon as you have passed the walls, & the close suburbs nestling under them, you see no houses; but only towns or villages, built as close as the centre of Canton, where the people herd, even if they have no walls, for the advantage of common vigilance & strength. Some of these tombs were built, as their inscriptions indicate, more than a thousand years ago.

In a charming green valley, amid olive trees & banyan trees & running water, with a view over the city & river & country below, secluded yet commanding a beautiful prospect, beautiful to look at & to look from, lies a Buddhist monastery. It is new, — that is, not more than 50 or 60 years old. It is built of dark bricks, with tiled roofs, in several buildings separated by ports & cloistered passages. It is out of our way, & as there are several more to be seen, we do not stop.

Here is a little close village, stifling & stinking with its narrows streets — less clean than Canton.

Now, out on the open hill our path leads directly through the open Court Yard of another monastery. It is silent, our knockings at the great door meet with no response. The monks — there are but 2 or 3 here now — are out either begging or buying at the village or the city.

The tombs & graves follow us all the way up to the very summit of the White Cloud Mountain, & the finest sites, commanding the nobler views, but always on high & dry ground, the tombs are built. And every step of the ascent, from the first leaving of the low ground to the top of the mountain, the broad walk is paved with wide flag stones, &, in the ascents, these stones are laid in stairs. The expense of this may be estimated when it is remembered that these stones are carried by men, slung from their shoulders, two by two, & that the stones for the tombs are also mostly brought far by wind & tide.

Now we are nearly at the top, & here, in one of the most delightful spots conceivable, stands, or rather lies, & nestles, the monastery of the White Cloud. It is built in a little valley wh. opens wide at the lower end, disclosing a view of the river, city & distant country, while the site has the advantage of perfect quietness, seclusion, a look of entire repose, the shades of trees & rocks & hill sides, the fall of water & the singing of birds. And how exquisite is the note of that bird, in that deep green tree just over the farther roof! We stand & listen, & catch it again & again. It is a new note to me. As liquid as falling water — & so rich & soft in melody.

Our chairs & coolies we leave at the monastery, & climb to the top of the hill, but the cloud is too thick to give us the full view. Our chairs, by the way, we got out of, as soon as we began the ascent, not only fr. regard to the coolies, but because we preferred the walk.

Above the monastery, at the top, or very near the top of the hill, is a large tomb, erected by a pious son & gr. son to their mother, who was buried there. Their name is Fang. It is a costly structure, every stone brought from a distance to Canton, & carried up the hill by hand. It has 2 lions, of the sise of life, & 2 high stone columns. Over the numerous ravines, thro' which, in the rainy season the water pours, handsome stone bridges are built, with a perfect arch span, & stone railings on either side, as good as any in England. Yet they are very old. The arch is no special tradition or local invention, but something to which all cultivated knowledge & experience would lead.

Return to the monastery. Its architecture is as noble as its situation. How lofty, how spacious, how airy, how strong, is everything! A noble stone bridge, a noble platform of stone — such spacious halls & passages & courts, — & all so solid & so ancient! To be purified from its Buddhist idols, & transformed to a Christian College, school, or monastery, is all that it needs. How I would delight to come here, in the heat of summer & spend a few weeks of leisure, with books & nature!

The old abbot (if one may so call him) held a long conference with Mr. B., over our lunch, in wh. he could not be persuaded to join, but wh. he had set out for us in his best hall. He says the monastery is now poor — very poor, & one of the brothers who has an ulcer, cannot get money enough to put himself under the charge of Dr. Kerr,[89] in Canton.

In a lower court is a stone well, of the sweetest & purest & softest of water. People send all the way from Canton for it. The abbot offered Mr. B. leave to send for it at all time (it would take a coolie all day to get 2 buckets full). The well is not deep, — about 10 f., full nearly to the top, clear bottom, & always the water running in & out. It is, indeed, a stone pool, in a running underground stream. Over it grows a large olive tree.

The chief idol in this monastery is the Water Dragon King. But Buddha is its divinity. In one shrine, are tablets on wh. are engraved the names of the founders & chief benefactors of the monastery, & before the tablets tapers & incense are always burning.

Take our leave of the courteous solitaries; & resume our walk down the stone steps, & down the miles of nicely laid flag-stones, towards the level country. About ½ way down — another road from the one we came up — we stop at a very pretty monastery, prettily situated. It, is of the Taos, or Rationalist religion. We find only one priest there. He is alone, in a small room, reading, in Chinese, an English tract against the use of opium. He receives us politely, & praises the tract. Mr. B. gave him a copy of the Gospel of St. Mark. How dull & lonely this place & this life is! The Taos

[89]John Glasgow Kerr (1824–1901) went to China as an American missionary physician in 1854, and for forty years was head of the famous hospital of the Medical Missionary Society in Canton.

priests wear the long queu wh. the Buddhists do not. This Taos priest is from the upper provinces, & talks what is called the Mandarin dialect (Anglicé for Mandarin is not a Chinese word).

Between the White Cloud Monastery & the city, by this route, are 3 monasteries, 2 Taos & 1 Buddhist. We stopped a while at each. At the Buddhist, is a large image of Buddha, wh. represents him as a fat, jolly god, with a huge paunch, & fat laughing eyes. "Yes", said the priest, "he does not trouble himself about anything. He is always happy & easy. Your God does concern himself with everything — Buddha does not. But, you see he is happy to see you". "Yes", said I "& equally so to see us go away". "Yes, Yes, he cares for nothing". How much of this is sincere confession, & how much is Chinese politeness?

How scarce fuel must be in Canton! Here are poor people about among the hills scratching up dried grass to burn under their pots.

Between the city walls & the top of Mt. White Cloud are nothing but monasteries, close villages & tombs. There is a party of 3 Chinese, of good condition, selecting a spot for a tomb. Yet, little doubt, they will, sensible as they are, consult the luck sticks or some other device, in the Temple.

On the ground, at intervals, are bits of paper cut in curious forms, dropped as they go by funeral processions.

The last thing on our way in, is the village devoted to the lepers, — the Leper Village. What associations of ancient story does the very name recall! We turn aside & enter it. I may well say enter it, for it [is] as close & compact as a fortress, though without a wall. And how filthy it is! The main street is straight, & flagged, about 10 f. wide. From this the side streets run off at right angles, mere dirty passage ways betw. houses, & not over four feet wide.

A respectable looking man, the best dressed, comes forward, & offers to be our guide. He is not a leper. He says he is of a younger branch of the Howqua family. He lives here because his wife is a leper. Not one in ten of the people we see, including children, are lepers. They are the children of parents, one or both of whom may be lepers, or they are husbands or near relatives of lepers sent here, whom they have faithfully followed. Some, not lepers, remain here, because they were born & have always lived here, & have property here. They do not seem to think leprosy contagious or infectious. The lepers are not white, as I supposed. On the contrary, their skin is red & blotched & swelled, like a spot just recovering from being frosen, &, in some cases, the hands & feet dwindle away & fall off. Even here, the all pervading Chinese literature extends itself. Here, at the end of a dirty passage, is a school, of some 20 boys. Not one of the boys is a leper. Perhaps the leper boys are kept apart, — though in the streets & at the little temple they all sit & walk together & in the temple porch we saw four men playing cards, 2 of whom were lepers & 2 not. In one corner of the school room, in a square part set off to him, was a pig! He was clean enough to be sure, but a pig in a stye, & close against him, not 4 feet off, sat a boy of ten studying Confucius! (The smallest boys that can read, read the great classics & commit them to memory, without understanding more than a few words).

The whole population of this village is about one thousand. A little temple & god & shrine & lepers, of course, at the head of the main street. It is a dreadful, piteous little den. The people, young & old, come out to see us. I suppose a foreign visitor is a very rare thing among them.

Now, to the walls again, into our chairs, through the gates, along the narrow, close, gaily decorated, intensely alive & industrious streets, two or three miles, & then the river, the sampan girls crying out recommendations of their respective boats & smiling at us, showing their white teeth — we select one that has a little earnest boy of 8 or 10, clamoring for us, — & are landed at the Russell & Co.'s. Hong — wh. the boat-people call "Lussel-y Hong", as near as they can get to it — at exactly 5 P. M., in time to get ready for our dinner at the house of Yung Ting, the nephew of the great Howqua. There [are] four visiting cards from Yung Ting, on our table, one for each of his expected guests. These cards are pieces of red paper, about 4 in. by 2, with the name written on them. These visiting cards they had, too, in China before Europe learned to write.

Reach the house at 6 o'ck. Received at the door by an upper servant. Yung Ting soon appears, — a man of about 35, dressed in plain grey silk high necked long robe, with black skull-cap. None of the Chinese show or wear any white linen or cotton. We are led to an open room, opening into a Court, & take seats. Yung Ting inquires with anxious solicitude the name & age & residence of each guest, & seems struggling to keep all in mind. (The guests, are Mr. [Warren] Delano, Mr. Orne, Rev. Mr. [C. F.] Preston, who is also interpreter, & myself). Tea is brot as soon as we are seated. When he is called out by his steward for an instant, he apologises all around & places his little boy, who is formally introduced to each of us, a boy not over ten years old, in his chair, to do the honors in his absence, — tho' it is but for a moment. The little boy looks as composed & grave as a mandarin, with no boyish awkwardness. Then Yung Ting re-appears, dinner is announced, & we are led to another room. Here is a table for six, for the boy sits at the foot, grave & silent for 3 hours, eating little, but never faltering or moving fr. his upright, respectful position, & never speaking.

The room is brilliantly lighted with Chinese lanterns & European chandeliers. There are some six or eight servants waiting on the table. It is set with fruits & flowers, & some 10 or 12 dishes of preserves, but the preserves are no more offered to us to eat than the flowers. Our seats have no backs, which is tiring to us, unused to that since school days. There is European wine & Chinese. Which will we have. Of course, we choose the Chinese. This is always served hot, from little china tea-pots, in very small porcelain cups, not over 2 thimble-fulls to a cup, but when your host drinks with you, you must exhaust the cup & turn it upside down, in proof [of] your fidelity to the *rites*.

Now begins the series of courses. I did not count them, I am sorry I did not. We agreed that they must have been between 20 & 30. And such strange compositions, fins of sharks, sinews of dolphins, berries of the lotus, the most recherché & improbable things are the most prised. He told us fairly that many of them had no other merit, & were made eatable by condiments only. I ate too much of the first courses, not expecting so many, & the courses began to pall. But, I did not like to refuse. I *tasted* of each, & our host required ever so many little bumpers of us all, & I feared we were all over-charged with food & liquid — not that the wine was at all intoxicating, for it is weak, & we did not take enough for that, but it is sweet & palls on the taste.

A course consists of one dish, & that is given to each guest. There is no helping from large plates to small, but to each guest is brought a large tea-cup or deep saucer full of what he is to eat, seasoned & mixed with its vegitables & sauce, & covered to keep it hot. Sometimes there is a second dish, for the sauce or seasoning. Chop sticks, of ivory! It is my first attempt, but I resolve to do or starve & after frequent failures get the nack of them pretty well. For the liquids, — for some courses are soups — we have porcelain spoons. The last course is tea, wh. is always a signal to go. Our dinner took about three & a half hours — & all devoted to the courses, with little intervals. This style is very favorable to conversation, as there is no helping & offering or requesting of things to eat, — the bane of an ill-served dinner at home.

But, how exquisite is the politeness of Yung Ting. He exhausts inge-nuity in framing inquiries to show his unspeakable interest in each of us — our ages, if married, how many children, & of what sex & ages, how came here, if had pleasant passage, how many days, was the boat crowded, was the weather good, — & at each question he bends his eyes on you anxious for your answer, & if your ship was crowded or the weather bad he is distressed, & if it was good he is relieved & delighted. Then, when you speak to him or answer his questions, he never allows himself an abstracted look, but fixes his eyes on you, & gives frequent emissions of guttural sounds, to denote his attention & interest & varying emotions. Indeed, he knows nothing but the pleasure of his guests. To that every-thing bends. Now, all this is from the books of rites, which educated

Chinese study from early boyhood, — books written 2000 years before Chesterfield was born!

From dinner, we adjourn to another room, where tea is offered again. (I forgot to name, as an instance of the freaks of fashion, that the dishes he took most pride in placing before us were European porcelain, when many of his plates & cups would be worth their weight in gold in Paris or London, among connoiseurs). Now he invites us to walk round his house, & we are shown through a series of rooms for sitting & rooms for sleeping — no women's apartments, however are ever shown to men, nor can Madame Howqua or Yung Ting be seen on any terms — & a library, wh., being of unbound books, looks like a paper shop, &c. &c., & one shrine, with tapers & incense sticks. His ancestral hall is, I suppose, that of the Howquas. (By the way, How-qua, is the personal name, & not the family name, nor, as I have said *ante*, the hong name of the great merchant of world wide renown. But it is given as a family name by foreigners, and the son & successor of the great Howqua, is known as Howqua by all foreigners & in all his relations with the allies).

When we rise to depart, our host says he has chairs for each of us. He bows low & takes impressive leave of each of us at the door, & again at outer door, & we go home, through the narrow streets, a flashing train of lanterns, — Chinese lanterns — 2 or 3 hung to each chair, & lantern bearers before & behind our train.

So ends my first Chinese dinner.

SUNDAY. M'CH. 18, 1860. Rise early, & after a cup of tea & slice of toast in my room, go, with my coolie guide — whom the Russell hong call "Chesterfield", from his politeness, to the 7 o'ck. Mass of the French mission. It is a long walk, of 2 or 2½ miles, thro' the heart of the city. There were about 200 Chinese, at the mass, all sitting on the matted floor & kneeling. They had mass-books in Chinese, & seemed to enter intelligently into the service. The chief portions usually sung by choirs, were chanted by the Chinese, — the Lord's Prayer, Creed, Confiteor &c. in the Chinese. They do much better with chants than with metrical hymns. There were two Chinese priests in the Chancel, with two Europeans, & six Chinese altar boys, dressed in Chinese costume (as, indeed, the Chinese priests were) with red skull-caps.

Returned to breakfast, walking back. At 11 A.M. went to the English Consular Chapel, where we had the English service, with a congregation of about fifty English & Americans, with a very fair choir. I was very grateful to take part in this service after more than two months deprivation of it. Mrs. Bonney was there. The American Prot. Missionaries have no service in English on Sunday, only a kind of Sunday ev. Prayer

Meeting at one of their houses. (I suspect that the Bonneys both rather incline towards our church).

Called on Mr. [H. S.] Parkes, this afternoon, taking a third long walk. Staid at home, read & wrote.

MONDAY. M'CH. 19. What with the Chinese dinner, & what with the three long walks — but I admit it was the 20 or 30 courses — I had a tossing feverish night, with extravagant & erring dreams. To-day, better, but rather tender, & keep at home, in order to be well eno' to dine with Parkes this evening. Parkes promised to send an Orderly sarjeant & chair for me, as the gates would be closed at 6½ P.M.

Find myself feeling pretty well at night, & having had no tenderness about the head, which is good sign. At about 6½, coolies comes to door — "One piece-y Sojer-man downside talky you", & there is the striped Orderly with band on hat & military salute, to conduct me to Mr. Parkes. Boat to the Allies' Landing, where a chair waits. The great gate is closed, but opens its ponderous & *iron* jaws[90] to the potency of the Commissioner's pass, & I am taken to the Yamun. Had hoped to see Parkes alone, to get his views of the Engl. side of all these questions, as he knows the history better than any official now here. But there was company — for Sir Hope Grant, the new Commander in Chief for China arrived in the city this evening, &, among others, one of his staff, Major Taylor, is staying with Parkes. Major Taylor was at the 2d relief of Lucknow by Sir C. Campbell,[91] & in the war since, seen service, has clasps & medals — a young man, with a soft voice & gentle manner, but with a long head. There is something taking in this life of the officer in an army like the British, now a few years in India, under the eye of the world, & now in China, in great operations, — epoch of history, & such opportunities for learning human nature & the ways of the world. This young man had been preparing himself, by reading Huc, &c. He tells me that the Highlanders, in the Indian campaigns, fought in the bonnet & kilt, in full costume.

At 11 o'ck., took leave, & headed by the Orderly, my little procession of lantern bearers & sedan bearers traversed the dark narrow streets. Few were abroad except the watchmen, each with his lantern & two bits of bamboo, wh. he beats together. These gay shops have their fronts closed in by shutters. At the great gate of the Wall, the guard are turned out to

[90]Why, the sepulchre, Wherein we saw thee quietly inurn'd,
Hath oped his ponderous and marble jaws.
Hamlet, I, iv, 50.

[91]Major Taylor remains unidentified. Sir Colin Campbell (1792–1863), British field marshal, led the relief of the Indian city of Lucknow in November 1857 when the city was beseiged by Indian revolutionaries.

unlock it, & the chains grate & bars fall, & the lanterns shine on the red coats of these foreigns possessors — a strange & unwelcome sight to the poor Chinese, who thought themselves lords of the tributary earth. So, each street is closed & locked, at its end, & at each we make a few minutes stop. The water side is reached, I dismiss my orderly & suite, & take a sampan for the hong. A whole sleeping family are turned out from the little covered cuddy to make room for me & row me up to my place — Lussel-y Hong.

(At Parkes', one waiter at table was a thin, tall black, silent sepoy, dressed in white from head to foot, turban robe & all. The rest were Chinese. Have I mentioned, too, that there is a regiment of sepoys in the city. How England has subdued nations & races to her use! The Scotch & Irish fight the E. Indians in the Oudh, & the Sikhs & Sepoys are carried to China to fight the Chinese!)

Parkes says that Howqua is squeesed by the Chinese Government, on every pretext. It is thought that he lately was obliged to make a *donation* of $50,000.

TUESD. MCH. 20. Dinner, or rather *tiffen,* at Howqua's at 2 P.M. Mr. Delano, Orne & myself. His house in the old city, within the walls. Howqua, who is son & representative of the great Hong merchant sev. years dead, is about 50 years old, pale & thin, dressed in blue robe, black quilted silk tunic over it, edged with blue collar, & skull-cap. He has bot the right to wear red button, & is of the highest attainable rank.[92]

First, sit few minutes at round table & take tea. Then dinner announced. Dinner much as at Yung Ting's, except that D. & O. say was better cooked. Sit on stools without backs, & each guest has, on floor, by his side, a china jar to put anything in off his plate. Wine both European & Chinese. The plate, of the richest & most exquisite old china make, very rare. Table set with 16 kinds of preserve & confectionary, & fruits & flowers — all untouched. Twelve courses, first being the celebrated Bird's Nest, & the 2d, Shark's fins, & the 3d lotus berries &c. &c., the Key Lung's eggs, (a fruit) &c. Then 14 dishes of more solid *food,* handed round in order to each guest, — making, in fact 26 courses, only that the last 14 are handed for a choice. Now we rise & retire to the reception room, for an interval, with the intimation that dinner is not done. Quarter hour in *this* room, walking & talking, dinner announced again, & we return to a table with 6 kinds of confectionary, & 12 of cakes, all at our choice. After these, tea, wh. is a signal of end. Then to the reception room again, where the little round table is set with tea again, wh. we only play with. Then take

[92]The red coral button was the highest possible award for a man who did not hold an official public office.

leave. Howqua is a grave, polite man, & kept up the same course of inquiries, polite listenings for answers, & apparent devotion to our happiness as his nephew. At the latter part of dinner, his son joins us, — a man of 22 or 23, who has recd. a second degree — pale, sallow, physically feeble, as nearly all Chinese of the upper, unlaboring classes seem to be — for they take no exercise, not even walking if they can be carried. The Chinaman does not live who has ever taken a constitutional walk. Mr. Preston was again a guest, & interpreter. Howqua is well informed as to position & gen. character of Engl. Fr. & America, our rail roads, telegraphs, commerce, &c.

To-night sit on piassa, over river, looking at the flitting boat-lights, & listening to the strained cries of the Chinese boat-people — those who had something to sell, on the water to be heard more than a mile up the river.

("Mak-y-larn-boy" — make-learn-boy, a boy who lives at a hong, without wages, to learn English &c. "Nias-kee" never mind, no matter. "Man-man", stop, wait. "Go up stairs & show this gentleman my two guns". "Walk-y topside, make see this gentleman two piece-y my gun". &c. Pigeon English).

WEDNESDAY, AFTERNOON, M'CH. 21. At Macao. Talk of palaces — I have never seen in any Engl. gentl. or noblemen's house such chambers as there are in this house, where I am lodged, the guest of Mr. Ward, our Minister![93] My chamber is 19 paces long & 12 paces wide, & about 20 feet high. The walls are 2½ f. thick. It is a palace. It was built by one of the wealthy old Portuguese families, & bought by Augustine Heard & Co., who still own it. As they live & do all their business in Hong Kong, they use it only as an occasional place of resort for a pleasure trip. Yet, this gives an idea of the style of these Anglo-Chinese merchants, that they maintain such a palace, for old associations sake, & a little present convenience. Heard & Co. put the house at the disposal of Mr. Ward, during his sojourn in Macao, & he invites me to be his guest. Mr. John Heard, of the firm, is also here for a day or two. And we three gentlemen, each living *en garcon,* wander about these huge lofty rooms, with their echoing bare floors, & under the shaded piassas. In one side of my room is a bed, a portion of which I occupy with sheets & blankets of the usual width, leaving several feet of waste land on each side. One gets exercise enough in walking from the toilet table to the wash stand, — a chamber of magnificent distances.

But, how came I here? I left Canton at 7.30 A.M., in the little steamer Spark, taking grateful leave of Delano, Orne & Sheppard, & "Old Head" (who desired his remembrances to Mr. J. P. Cushing, Messrs. [Robert B.

[93]John Elliott Ward, noted earlier, author of the controversial treaty, was American Minister to China, 1859–1860. Macao was a Portuguese possession.

and John M.] Forbes &c.) & steamed down among the tossing & tumbling sampans & hong boats, banging ag. each other under our paddle-surf, but the laughing girls never losing their temper, & men reaching poles on board with letters attached at the last moment, after we are under way, — & we pass the now familiar grounds of the Old Factories & the Dutch Folly, & pass the great junks with their preposterously gaudy banners & red scarfs tied to the mussle of each gun, — & now the ruins of the Barrier Forts, & now the tall pagoda on the hill top, & are clear of the city & down in the wide Estuary. There lies the Fr. steam frigate, & there the Br. Admiral's tender, the Coromandel, & there the Br. gun-boat "89", & here is steaming slowly up with a leadsman in the chains, gunboat "87", both "walk-y insides" & rigged with 3 masts, with fore & aft sails & a square topsail at the fore.

At Whampoa are some 30 merchant vessels at anchor, not counting the junks & schooners. Here, too, is a stone dry-dock, for vessels of the largest class, & 2 or 3 mud docks. Rice fields, Pagodas on hills, a few close villages, like sections taken from the centre of a city, & now the Bogue Forts, & the widening estuary, & the low fields rise in high picturesque hills, & the country becomes rough & granity. The outline of country on all sides of the great opening, between Macao & Hong Kong, below, & the Bogue Forts above, is picturesque with high receding distant hills, & impending cliffs.

There lies Macao, open to the sea, its half moon beach, its stone sea-wall, its broad flagged sea-walk, & its old, very old Portuguese forts & churches & convents, & its palatial private houses & gardens. And such crowds of little boats, hurrying off to us, & the chattering, crowding, struggling boats & boat-men & boat-women, urging their boats under our very wheels, to secure the first passengers. Land, & Mr. Heard sends my luggage to his house.

Mr. Ward (his Excellency, John E. Ward, Min. &c.) is here, & a very pleasant, manly, intelligent person, he seems to be, & so all report him. He is of Savannah Geo., but educated in N. Engl., — 2 years at Cambr. Law School, 1836,7, & married Olivia Sullivan. Unfortunately, Mrs. Ward is not here, but in Europe, with her children.

Dine with Mr. Nye, at 7 o'ck. Present, Nye, Ward, Heard, Capt. Devens, (Charlestown), & Mr. —— Gassett, of Boston.[94] Nye was a dashing merchant, failed for 2½ millions, paying 5 per cent, & now lives in retirement at Macao, but in a palace of a house, with suites of elegantly furnished rooms. Says he was introduced to my father in New York, heard his lectures there, & my father went to his house to see his picture gallery. Gassett talks of my father's tales & poems, & has a favorite copy

[94]With the exception of Ward, none of these men has been identified.

here with him. Devens is the deft. in the suit that [B. F.] Butler of Lowell tried so often. Gassett has been a R. Catholic, became so at Singapore years ago, but has renounced that Church. Tells me he has the highest admiration for the self devotion of the clergy in this part of the world, — that there is nothing beyond it in history, & respects the piety & faith of the devout members of the Church, — but his difficult[y] was in the necessity of surrendering private judgement entirely, not only as to the great doctrines, — wh. was not a serious difficulty with him — but as to the conduct of life. He says it is an iron system, & the devout man (& such he says he was for some years, following all the discipline) is required to follow his spiritual director in all things of a moral or religious character, as the voice of God. This he could not do. He reviewed the grounds, & renounced the Church. But he says he sees no middle ground. Without the authority of the Church, there is no revelation, & with the Church falls the "mythology" of Christianity. He is a Theodore Parker man, now.

THURSDAY. M'CH. 22. Walk with Mr. Heard & Mr. Nye to the Peña, a hill on wh. a building, formerly a convent, stands. Here is a beautiful view. The stiuation of Macao is almost without an equal. Before it is the open sea, with the distant mountains across the wide expanse, the surf breaking on the half-moon beach, close to wh. the solid yellow stones houses stand. Behind the town, is a large but land-locked bay, called the Inner Harbor. Between them is a second passage to the China Sea, & beyond these a fourth bay. Macao is a peninsula, with two passages to the sea, & two large bays. The peninsula is diversified, in a picturesque manner, with hills, & every wind has a fair sweep, making this the most salubrious place in China. Were it not that a bar keeps all vessels drawing over 16 feet out in the open roads, 4 or 6 miles off, — it would be the favorite business place also. As it is, betw. this disadvantage & the disadvantage of Portuguese rule, it is chiefly a pleasure & health resort. Rents are low, & labor very cheap. (Washing & ironing of the nicest kind is $2 for 100 pieces). Its history is most interesting, going back to the heroic age of navigators & missionaries.

Called, with Mr. Ward, on the Governor of Macao. Dom Isadoro Guimaiaes. He is a perfectly well bred man, of the simple but high manner, speaks English pretty well, & is thought a man of entire honor & more than usual capacity. What a beautiful foot he has! He is recently married. La Senora is a native, Portuguese, very large, very dark, very sallow, & rather stately, — love affair.

Called, with Ward, on Mrs. Endicott, wife of Mr. Jas. P. Endicott (Salem) our consul here. An incredibly spacious house, with a street of piassa lined with flower pots, & open to the sea. Mrs. E. rather a pretty English woman. Afterwards, to a place Mr. E. has bought, intending to build on it. It is one of the noblest sites possible, commanding the 4 bays & town.

Mr. Hunter calls. Go with him (Ward & I) to Camoens' garden & grotto. The garden is the private property of a wealthy & ancient Portug. family, who have owned it over 200 years. It is the garden of their house, & under lock & key, but is opened to all who send in their cards. I think it is the most beautiful garden I ever saw. Excellent taste has been shown in dealing with nature, for the garden is a rocky, broken ground, with boulders & large trees, yet interspersed with the nicest arrangements of horticulture. At the top of one of the hills, commanding the full sea-view, is the grotto, where Camoens used to sit to read & to compose his Lusiad.[95] And how it is honored! A kind of temple built over it, & a pedestal surmounted by a terra cotta head of Camoens, & several tablets erected by the voluntary gift of admirers. Next this garden, is the Protestant burying ground, a beautiful spot, filled with graves, the stones & monuments over wh. are in the highest degree creditable to the liberality of the Engl. & Am. residents here, as well as to the piety of the friends of the dead. One is of Dr. Morrison,[96] & there are others of his family. Several to Engl. & Am. naval officers, among others to Mr. Waldron, Lt. Brooke, &c., Ld. H. Churchill, &c. &c.

This ground is full & closed. But a new one, almost, but not quite as beautiful is opened. Mr. Hunter tells me that the Portuguese authorities & people are liberal & kind, in the highest degree, to foreigners & Protestants. He thinks there is no place on earth where there is less bigotry of religion & nation.

To the Temple of Wanghia (*pro.* Wong-yor), where the first treaty betw. America & China was signed, that of Mr. Cushing, in 1844.[97] (By the way, all persons, merchants, diplomatists, & residents of leisure — all

[95]Luis de Camoens (1524–1580), most famous of Portuguese poets, published his epic poem *The Lusiad* in 1572.

[96]Robert Morrison (1782–1834), English missionary, published a dictionary of the Chinese language (1815–1823) and translated the Bible into Chinese. He died in Macao. His son, John Robert Morrison (1814–1843), colonial secretary at Hong Kong, was even more celebrated, and a monument to him might well be in the Protestant burying ground at Macao, where he was born.

[97]Caleb Cushing (1800–1879), conservative Massachusetts Whig, was U. S. Commissioner to China in 1844 and on July 3 of that year concluded the Treaty of Wang Hiya, which opened diplomatic relations between the United States and China. The treaty won for the United States the same terms as the British received as a result of the "Opium War" treaty of 1842–1843. These treaties introduced the principle of extraterritoriality into Chinese-Western relation: that is, Westerners accused of crimes in China were to be tried by the consuls and laws of their own countries, not by Chinese courts and laws. By the time of Dana's writing, Cushing had become an antislavery Democrat and was to join forces with Lincoln and the Republicans during the Civil War.

agree that that was a most excellent treaty, — perhaps the best ever made by any body with China, & much better than Reed's.[98] They only wish Reed had let it alone. We lost by the change. Poor Reed! Nobody speaks well of him. The — yes, contempt — felt for him by *all* Americans in China — I have seen no exception, is sad to think of. They say he was a quiddling Philad. lawyer, a mere toady, to Lord Elgin, thinking only of the honor of his position, the passage out in a frigate, & the passage home thro' Europe. *Here,* he did nothing, or worse. I can't find a man to speak patiently of him. All agree that Elgin is a man of extraordinary sagacity, firmness, perseverance & pluck.)

Extraordinary & anomalous state of things betw. Engl. & China. At Canton Engl. & Chinese officers meet & dine together & inquire the news from the North. Whether there has been a battle, & which got the victory, — & the Br. fleet & army are going up to fight, & a battle was fought at the Peiho, — yet all the time, the Br. are collecting the Custom House duties for the Chinese Govt., in all the free ports, as the agents of that Government, & paying the money over to the Chinese treasury!

Pigeon. In America there are a great many ships. "America-side, too much piecey ship, have got".

Went to Nye's to see his pictures — one ¾ length of William 1st, Pr. of Orange. The face is very like it in Motley's book,[99] wh. tends confirm the correctness of both. Also one of Chinnery portraits, Sir Andrew Ljungstedt.[1] Went to Temple of Ama Kok, dedicated by some survivors of a wrecked junk, centuries ago. Curious scene of a quarrel betw. two women, each [on] her knees, knocking her forehead on the pave, before the idol, each telling Josh the story, interrupting each other, & the men of the two families standing by the side & backing the women — precisely as if they were before a Justice of the Peace, all jabbering fiercely. I doubt if the poor Josh could have understood it, if he had had ears. Offerings of fans & a pair of boots made to the God, or to some spirit.

Visit to Ap-pong, one of the wealthiest Chinese here. House very large, with sev. foreign pictures & engravings. Conversation with him in Pigeon English.

Visit to house of Wo Lung, another leading merchant. His is a new house & very beautifully furnished, with European pictures, & a piano.

[98]William Bradford Reed, noted earlier, was U. S. Minister to China, 1857–1859. His treaty of Tsientsin very much resembled the Treaty of Wang Hiya in that it acquired for the United States the same rights that the British received as a result of *their* treaty of Tsientsin, negotiated at Peking in June 1858.

[99]John Lothrop Motley, fellow member with Dana of the Saturday Club, published his *Rise of the Dutch Republic* in 1856.

[1]George Chinnery (d. 1852) was a portrait and landscape painter who traveled and painted much in the Orient. He died at Macao.

IIis son, a nice looking youth of 14, received us. This family are Christians, & it was a comfort to see a house without the idols & Josh sticks. In place of them, was a handsome private Chapel. The lad speaks Spanish, being educated in Manilla. He told me there were about 500 Chinese Christians — all Catholics — in Macao.

(Go-down, a corruption of some E. Indian word, is the universal Engl. word in the Eastern world for a store-house).

Spent the ev. at a party at the Governor's. Present, his lady, & his sister Mrs. Cate, Hunter, the Endicotts, Count Klyskowski, the Fr. Sec. of Legation in China, Mr. Ward, & the Capt. of a Portug. man-of-war, who is here. The ladies all speak English.

Pop. of Macao is about 60,000, of wh. 50,000 are Chinese, & the rest chiefly a mixed race of Portuguese with the people fr. Malabar.[2] There is consid. mixed Portug. & Chinese blood, but the mixture is chiefly the former.

SATURDAY. MCH. 24. Pick-nick at Pak Shan temple, a place some 10 miles fr. Macao; one of those exquisite spots, like the White Cloud Monastery, wh. the Buddhist priest here selected with so much taste. It is on high ground, yet sheltered, with evergreen pines about it, & pure mountain water, with a view over Macao Bay terminating in the high hills of pale stone. Our party was Ward, Hunter, Nye, Mr. & Mrs. Endicott, Count Klyskowski, Ch. Sec. of the Fr. Legation, & 2 or 3 others. Mrs. E. was the moving spirit. We had a train of 10 sedans & about 40 servants. An excellent lunch. At the Temple, some of the servants laid out their "cash" in buying tapers & incense sticks & after due worship tried their luck with the Josh sticks. They shake them up, & the one that falls out is their luck. This has a number, wh. is compared or professed to be compared, with printed paper. Mrs. E. & some of our party prevailed on the men to try luck for them. The answers are vague, general & written in characters capable of different interpretations. Yet this consultation of the oracles is the prevalent custom of China — but so it was of Rome & Athens, in their best days.

The buffalo, as it is called, is the ox & cow of China. There is two kinds. One is more like our bison, has a short sharp horn & a large hump. The other, the water-buffalo, has horns turned back upon the head, *a La 'Imperatrice*,[3] & its skin has a good deal the look of [an] aquatic animal.

There are large coolie barracoons in Macao, one of wh. we saw fr. the Camoens garden.

---

[2]Malabar is a region in southwest India.
[3]Like the crown of an empress?

SUNDAY MORN. MCH. 25. The U. S. frigate Hartford has come over from Hong Kong & I am invited, by Mr. Ward, to return to Hong Kong in her. Would like it much, — but fear that must go over to-day, to be in season for the mail steamer up the coast. No service in the Engl. Chapel, so went to High Mass at the Cathedral, but could not understand or follow it at all, so left early. Walk round the pits &c. with Mr. Ward. Crowds of Parsees, Chinese, Portuguese, mixed races, & some Engl. & Americans in streets.

Cathedral is large, & open floor, but tawdry & not rich — imitations, all.

The village of Pak Shan, wh. we visited yesterday, is composed entirely of people of one clan or family, by whom it was settled 700 years ago. The men marry without, but no man is allowed to settle there from without. The population is now about 4000.

Parting calls, this evening, on Governor & lady, the Endicotts, Hunter, Case & lady & Gassett.

MOND. MCH. 26. Hartford too late for us. Obliged, after all, to take the mail steamer Feima, & reach Hong Kong at 11 A.M. Steamers for North sail this afternoon & tomorrow.

Recd. a kind letter from Jona. Russell, at Manilla, inviting me there. By this learn the death of Mrs. Russell.[4]

This place is full English soldiers & sailors, ships of war & troop-ships, bound up the coast, to strike a blow if terms are not made with the Chinese. I fear these poor Chinese are more sinned against than sinning. And if they err through ignorance or wilfulness, yet they are visited with terrible punishments for small mistakes or misconduct. A young officer came over with us from Macao who had the Victoria Cross, & medals for Sevastopol, Delhi, Lucknow &c. &c. — yet he cannot be more than 25 years old.

Walking thro' the streets of Hong Kong with Mr. Delano yesterday, a Chinaman came up to me, with beaming countenance, & with that practical equality wh. marks their common society, said "Ah! How you do? My glad see you!" & held out his hand. I shook hands with him, but could not remember him, as all Chinese look alike, at first. "My in ship, burn up. You savee — you have got". "Oh yes. The Mastiff". "Yes. Very good — very good". And he told me he came in the Elisa & Ella from Oahu to H. Kong. The good fellow seemed truly glad to see me.

TUESD. MCH. 27. Sailed in P. & O. steamer Pekin, for Shanghai, 9.30 A.M. Left the shelf on the hill-side on wh. Hong Kong stands, — its flying

[4]Dana's correspondent here was informing him of the death of Mrs. Lydia Russell, mentioned so frequently earlier in the *Journal*. She was first cousin to Dana's mother and died at Milton on December 20, 1859 (see Genealogy).

flags of all nations afloat & ashore, its men-of-war & its merchantmen, & steamed thro' the high hills & bold shores, & frequent islands, steep & bold, into the open sea. Opposite to Hong Kong, on the peninsula of Kowloon, are the tents of the 44th Reg., which has taken possession of it, — a most important movement in the history of China, for if the Br. hold it, it will probably surpass Hong Kong.[5]

Passage fr. H. K. to Shanghai, a sail of 4 or 5 days, is $95 dollars. The P. & O. Co. keep up the unjust custom of making all pay for the liquors drank.

FRID. M'CH. 30. Yesterday we were off Amoy, to-day we are off Fu-Chau. No incidents. Few passengers, large vessel, plenty of room, large state room to myself, & good table. Chief interest in the vessel is as an exponent to Br. power & the Br. system in the East.

This ship is built by Br. art & capital at home, owned by Br. capital, & officered by Br. subjects, engaged in the trade of the East, & manned by the practically subjected nations of Asia. The captain & mates, the engineer & his assistants, the purser, Steward & under steward are English. All the rest are Asiatics, six Secunneys are the helmsmen, three mixed Portuguese & Malays are quarter-masters, a surang (boatswain), two tindals (boatswain's mates) & 40 Lascars, are the sailors. There is a boat's crew of 6 Chinese. A Harildan (corporal) & three Sepoys in red coats do soldier's duty on the quarter-deck, some 20 Lascars & Malays & Chinese work under the engineers, & the cabin servants are turbaned Bengalese & Malays. How thin & black they are! And that Bengalese, in the maroon colored long robe, when he is sea-sick, vomits a dark yellow bile drawn fr. 4000 years of tropical life. The British is the dominating race of the Oriental world. They have eclipsed us in steam, far more decidedly than we have them in canvass. Our merchant sailing-vessels are faster & finer than theirs, but in both navy & merchant service, & in all their numerous steam Co. services, they have left all the world behind them in steam.

It is a comfort to exchange the disorder, negligence & close quarters of the Early Bird, for the strict, almost military discipline & etiquette, the neatness & thoroughness of this ship, — where every man has his place & his uniform or badge of office, where the officer of the deck is not allowed to speak to a passenger or to sit down or lean ag. anything, & where there is always a quarter-master at the Conn [helm].

The Chinese are as industrious on the sea, as on the land. For 10 & 20 miles off all the great ports, Canton, Macao, H. Kong, Amoy, &c. the

[5]The British held this peninsula opposite Hong Kong and it became a part of that colony.

fishing boats are to be counted not by scores but by hundreds. They go out from 2 & 3 to 10 & 15 miles fr. shore, & cast drag nets, two vessels to a net, & lie, as if at anchor, moored to their drifting nets, tossing about in the heavy sea, some of them with families of women & children on board. There could not have been less than 500 in sight at one time yesterday morning.

(By the way, Dominick Lynch, Adele's brother,[6] though something of a brag, has a high reputation here for pluck & seamanship. He has conducted enterprises ag. pirates, rather desperate in their character, with success, & recd. large compensation for them). Last night, in the crowd of fishing boats, we unfortunately ran over one. The companion boat went to its help, & there was great halloing, & we hope no one was killed or drowned. They were all either drowned or saved before we cd. have got back to them.

SUNDAY. APRIL 1, 1860. For two days we have had weather very rough, cold & rainy. To-day, we had snow & sleet. Three days before, in H. Kong, prudent people were walking under double umbrellas, to keep off the sun. It is piteous to see the lascars & Bengalese shivering in their cottons & linens, for this boat does not belong to this line, but to that betw. H. Kong & Bombay, & is here, for the *nonce,* & the poor fellows are unprovided. Capt. Brooks does his best for them.

As an off-set to running over a boat to-day we rescued a boat full. It was a little open boat with 22 men in it, whose junk had sunk in the gale, & who had been drifting about helpless for two days. They were very grateful, & chin-chinned, & kow-towed at a great rate, especially when the kind hearted Capt. sent them two great pots of hot tea & some rice. Chinese like, they squatted down on deck, & patiently kept their places all day & night, & were covered over in line, at night, by a strip of canvas.

Our pasengers are Count Klyskowski, the Fr. Chief Sec. of Legation, a Russian naval captain going to join his ship in Japan, a Master in the Br. navy, a stupid Belgian-French-Pole coming to China for a civil office, & a few Engl. travelling & mercantile snobs.

The peculiarity of the Br. marine system is the great number of steam companies it has all over the world, Atlantic, Baltic, E. Indies, W. Indies, S. America, Australia, India, & Africa. These are now chiefly screws, with full sails, like their men of war. They are officered by a class of men betw. the commissioned officers of the Navy & the common merchantmen, — the same class that make the masters & master's mates in the Navy, — like those of the old E. India Co.

[6]Adele Lynch Watson, recently deceased wife of Dana's brother-in-law, William Watson, evidently had an adventurer for a brother, but no clear identity has been established for him.

In the thick mist & snow we see a Chinese boat with bamboo sails, & pilots flag, & she comes alongside, & a smart unmistakable Yankee pilot springs on board. Sev. of the pilots of the Yang Tse Kiang are Yankee, & they use Chinese boats of choice. This pilot tells me they are the best.

All the afternoon we are at the mouth of the great Yang Tze Kiang, the great river of China. It is here about 20 miles wide. The Br. steam corvette Furious has lately ascended it 800 miles.

MONDAY. APRIL. 2. At anchor at Woon Sung, to discharge opium, & we go up to Shanghai in small boats, I in one of Jardine & Co.'s. At Woon Sung lie the opium receiving ships, stored with this curse of China. They are very large ships, well armed & manned.

Shanghai lies on a river, or arm of the sea, that makes up from the Yang Tze Kiang. The country around is flat, liable to inundation & protected by a levee, called Bund, wh. extends hundreds of miles. The city is only on one side of the river, so there is none of that *boat life* you see in Canton. The Bund lines the river, being here some 50 or 60 feet wide, & is the pier for commerce. The vessels lie at anchor in the stream, opposite the Bund, & boats carry to & fro mdse. & people. On the Bund, at the E. end, are the great Commercial houses, the Consulates, the Legations, & the residences of the chief foreigners, wh. are stately solid buildings. That of Russell & Co., their lodging house, is said to be the best private house this side the Cape of Good Hope. Then there are Heard & Co., Jardine, Watteson & Co., Dent & Co., &c. &c., and the "flags of all nations" from Consulates, & those of the "Treaty Powers" from the Legations. The Br. men of war, the noble frigate Imperiuse, the beautiful corvette Cruiser, & the Furious & Roebuck, & a few gun boats, (all steamers), lie among the shipping close to the Bund.

Installed at Russell & Co.'s, with two rooms & a coal fire, a servant &c., & Mr. Walsh (the partner) very attentive. Breakfast at 11. (You call for tea & toast in your room when you please, before that). Another guest is the French Col. of the Commissariat, a monster, with grey hair & beard & three decorations & blood-red trowsers — name is Du But.

Called on Hon. Mr. [Robert] Bruce, the Br. Minister. He looks something between his brother Ld. Elgin & Thackeray. Talk about coolie trade here, & in Cuba. He has quoted my book in his despatches. Dine with him tomorrow. Call on Heard & Co., & M. de Bourbulon the Fr. Minister. Spend the evening at the latter. M. de B. speaks English perfectly & was Sec. of Leg. at Washington several years. Mde. de B. is Miss Kate McLeod, niece of those Inglis-McLeods that used to be in Boston, Mde. Calderon &c.,[7] & looks like them. Am to dine there Wed., if do not sooner sail for Japan.

[7]This family has not been identified.

Walked about the city this afternoon, — the European part, or Concessions, as they are called. This part is level, regularly laid out, & built with large, solid houses. Shanghai is to be the great port of China. It is the centre of the Silk trade & has as good & perhaps even a better chance for the tea trade than Canton.

Coolies here are larger & fuller in face than those of Southern China. As they trot along under their burdens, they keep up an unvarying grunt or cry, at every step, so that the crowd of them in the close streets, sounds like a drove of cattle going through our streets to Brighton fair. What a caprice is custom! There is none of this sound in Canton, & here it is universal, & yet they are the same people, doing the same work, in the same manner.

Visited the mud dock for ships. It is like our stone dry docks, only the walls are mud, kept back by piles, — needing constant repair. The ground does not admit of stone, they say.

I believe I omitted to speak of the climate, in Southern China. At H. Kong, Canton & Macao, when the wind was Northerly, it was cool & good out-door weather, & if there was also rain, a coal fire was agreeable. When the wind was Southerly, or calm, it was warm & rather close, & the direct rays of the sun it was best to avoid. Umbrellas & pith hats were then worn, or common hats with folds of crape, turban-wise, on the outside. This was fr. M'ch. 8 to 27th. Here it is cool, & fires are used. But warm weather is expected.

TUESD. APRIL 3. Called on Bishop Boone.[8] He has a promising institution conducted in proper style. He is its head & all the clergy & teachers, men & women, are working under him; — they all live together, the unmarried in his house, & the married in houses adjoining, & the Chapel & schools are in the grounds. Conv. with him about the diff. missionary plans & theories. After long experience here, he has come to the conclusion, & acts upon it, that a random distribution of the Scriptures or of parts of them, does more harm than good. As to mere preaching, without more, — it is useful only as a mode of inviting the Chinese to come & learn. He has no confidence in any mode but that of thorough *instruction, ab origine.* He begins with the Creed, & instructs them in it, article at a time, requiring them to commit it to memory as they go on. For instance, the first article "God the Father, Almighty" is an unknown idea to them, & must be thoroughly instilled first. Then, the second — respecting Our Saviour, & so on. After they are taught, & as they can understand it, Scripture is given to them to read, in selected parts, & some to commit to

---

[8]William Jones Boone (1811–1864), an Episcopal priest of South Carolina, came to China as a missionary in 1837. He became Bishop of China in 1844.

memory, & then they are taught the Liturgy, the greater part of wh. they come to know by heart, by reason of the wonderful Chinese power of memory. He has sev. blind Chinese, who know almost the entire liturgy, especially the Communion Office. They also learn the Canticles, & chant them. He spoke of the notion some have that putting the Scriptures into the hand of an intelligent heathen is a promised means of grace, as bibliolotry. Every Chinese is treated as a Catechumen, & the Creed is taught *as truth*. His Government also is thoroughly Episcopal. He is head & ruler. Nothing is submitted to vote. He confers & consults with his clergy, but he says they do not believe, nor does he, that a *majority* is "set over them as the Lord". His corps consists as follows — 4 American presbyters, 2 Chinese deacons, 3 Chinese candidates for orders, studying in his house, 3 Chinese male teachers, 4 American ladies (unmarried) teachers, & 2 American men with their wives, training as teachers. There are 2 boarding schools, one for boys & one for girls, each limited to 40, & always full, & with innumerable applicants. No scholars is recd. as boarders unless the parents bind them, as apprentices are bound, by indentures to the Bishop for ten years, — anything less than that is not worth while.

Mrs. Boone is a sister of Bishop Elliott, of Georgia.[9] Took the address of the R. Cath. Bishop's residence, wh. is at the other end of the city, & with a chair & 4 coolies, started to make it a visit. It seems there are two R. C. institutions, one at Ton Ka Du, wh. is the Catherdral, & another at Tse Ka Wae, wh. is a college, & is some 6 or 8 miles in the country. By some mistake of mine, or in the direction given me, my coolie started off for Tse Ka Wae. I knew the Cathedral was in the city, & I found they were taking me into the country, among rice fields & peasants' cabins, & along the tow-paths, of canals & creeks, with a pagoda in the distance. But explanation was out of the question, as none of them could speak a word even of pigeon English. I made up my mind to let them go on until 5 o'ck., & then if they came to no stop to make them turn back. At this moment, I saw four men coming along the tow-path, in full Chinese costume, tails & all, dressed after the decent manner of Chinese scholars, when, just as they passed me, I caught a word of French. I stopped & spoke, & they answered in French, & fortunately they proved to be four Jesuit scholars, & said they had been at Tse Ka Wae, & were returning to Ton Ka Du; so I got out & walked with them, after a hubbub of explanation among the coolies. These were Frenchmen, young, candidates for orders, & are here, dressing eating & talking & reading as

[9]Stephen Elliott (1806–1866), Harvard, 1824, was chosen first Episcopal bishop of Georgia in 1840. In 1844 he was made provisional bishop of Florida. He rose to the highest councils of his church. Dana spelled the name "Elliot."

Chinese, as do all the R. C. priests in this part of China. (I was some four miles out of my way).

Ton Ka Du is a large collection of buildings, of wh. the cathedral is the chief, on the water's edge, composed of schools & lodging rooms for priests & scholars. Delivered my letters to the Bishop, M. de Bornier, who, with his vicar, received me with true Fr. politeness, & showed me the Church, dedicated to St. Francis Xavier, the largest in China, with a portrait of St. Francis over the altar, & the school &c. In the school, the pupils (Chinese) are taught latin. The statistics he gave me are as follows — 1 Bishop, 29 European priests, 10 Chinese priests, 270 scholars in the college at Tse Ka Wae, & 480 Chinese girls in the girls school. In the entire province, the pop. of wh. is abt. 10 millions, they reckon 75000 Catholic Chinese, & 5000 scholars in all the Catholic Schools. Return thro' the city, at candle lighting. Difficult to realise that I am in the centre of a strange Chinese city, — I a Boston lawyer, with large family & clients!

Dinner at Mr. Bruce's. Present, Admiral Jones, R. N., Capt. Jones R. N., Mr. Parkes, Br. Commr. at Canton, Dent, the merchant &c. &c. A young nob named Wyndham, who talked in the extreme style of Punch's Engl. fash. youth — *aw-fellaw-clevaw* &c. Bruce has humor & more than ever reminds me of Thackeray. He spoke with earnestness & even with emotion of Commodore Tattnall, his aide at the Peiho, & especially his despatch to the U. S. Govt., wh. Bruce thinks so magnanimous, & so modest. Tattnall went thro' the thickest fire to visit Adm. Hope, when he heard he was wounded, & his coxwain was killed by his side.[10]

WED. APR. 4. Spent morning at Bishop Boone's. Ex[amine]d his schools. The 40 boys are taught by 3 Chinese men & one Am. lady, Miss Fay. Miss F. is great admirer of father's poetry & prose, & quoted it to me & has his 2 vols. A class of boys demonstrated difficult problems in spherical geometry, respecting sections of pyramids. They read fr. Mencius & Confucius, as well as fr. Engl. books translated into Chinese. The girls have two Am. ladies, (one a d. of Gen. Walter Jones[11] of Wash. D. C.) & one Chinese man, for teachers. They chaunted the *Venite* in

[10]Josiah Tattnall (1795–1871), U. S. naval officer, was appointed in 1857 to command of the East India station. When Robert Bruce and Admiral Sir James Hope (1808–1881), British Naval commander, were defeated at the Taku forts in 1859, Tattnall, in command of the U. S. naval forces in Chinese waters, intervened to aid the British. He explained this breach of neutrality in a dispatch to Washington which quoted the adage "blood is thicker than water."

[11]Walter Jones (1776–1861), distinguished lawyer of Washington, D. C., was a founder of the American Colonization Society. He was a powerful opponent of secession in the years before the Civil War.

Chinese, to our familiar chant. Neither boys nor girls are taught English, except in special cases, where the Bishop feels entire confidence in their religious character. The effect is always bad, on the poorer classes. Good judgement is shown, in making no attempt to change their customs. The girls are dressed in the comely & modest Chinese costume, & the boys have the tail & tonsure, & all the native dress. They eat with chopsticks, & use only Chinese cookery. The girls are all employed in housework & sewing &c. in turn, to fit them for humble spheres of life, & even the cramped feet are allowed to go on, if the parents insist upon it, — for it affects their social position, chance of marriage &c. The girls looked fat & happy. Here, as elsewhere, I see the difference betw. the N. & S. of China. Here there is more flesh & color, — a kind of brunette.

At 2 P. M., Rev. Mr. Lyles, one of the longest resident here of B[ishop] Boone's clergy, called, to take me to see the city. He speaks Chinese well & is very kind, as well as duly inquisitive into everything Chinese. Rev. Mr. Smith, a new comer, accompanied him. We gave five hours to a very interesting exn. of the city.

Shanghai has about 500,000 inhab., ⅔ of whom live within the walls. The streets are as narrow as those of Canton, & here, as there, there are no horses or carriages, & only human foot-falls. There is less wealth & style here, & the people do not seem so neat, & the city arrangements are not so good. The temples, ancestral halls, yamuns &c. bear no comparison with those of Canton. It is like comparing Limerick with Dublin.

We were fortunate in our day. It was a Sacred day, the Spring Festival of Tzing Ning, 14th day of 3d mo., & the tutelary-gods were carried about in processions, in large sedan chairs, looking like so many gaudy Mandarins, with long lines of men bearing umbrellas, lanterns, boards with inscriptions, & great beatings of gongs. People who have been sick & made vows in their sickness, & recover, pay their vows on this day. These devotees are dressed in Scarlet & were frequent. Some very small children were dressed out in red, babies, whose parents had vowed for them. Some of the vows are explained to Mr. Lyles by the parties; were of rather a trifling character, — as, to wear a kind of wooden manacle all day, — while some were painful.

This is also one of the days of ancestral worship, & the streets were crowded with people bearing strings of silver paper money, — this is a cheap silver-foiled paper, made in form of dollars, several hundreds of wh. can be bought for a cent. The poorest burn a string of these, & the rich burn incredible quantities of the foolish stuff. We passed coolies bearing large basket loads of it. It is sold in the shops, hung out in strings like onions at a green grocers. The are thought, when burned at the shrines, to be worth their *face*, their nominal amount, in the Spirit Land.

Baptist Chapel, with a high tower fr. wh. is best view of the city. For 90 miles in all directions is dead level. For 3 or 4 miles, a level of tile roofs & beyond that a level of rice fields, & vegitable fields, intersected by dull canals. Interior of Bapt. Chapel is plain, & like their Chapels at home. Built by Engl. Baptists.

Calendering [pressing] of cloth done by rolling a huge stone over it, to & fro, weighing 1000 lbs., & moved by men's feet.

Just in time to see the return of an idol to his temple, fr. his procession thro' the city. Great crowd before the temple door, but no confusion or violence, — an orderly, self-regulating populace. Long procession, on a fast trot, as draw near the temple, & the great sedan chair is hurried into the temple, with its upright sitting figure of an idol. Then the chief men in the processions, make circuits thro' the crowd, coming back to the front, &, as soon as they come in sight of the idol, they are supposed to be so inspired that they break into a run, & trot in a quick run to the idol, & prostrate themselves before him. Yet it is to be observed that in none of their rites is there anything bloody or obscene, — the purest & simplest of idolatries the world has ever seen. After the procession was dismissed, we went into the temple, & poked about into all the secret places, even to the *sanctum sanctorum* — where the idol is enshrined. There it was, rather oppressive, with close air, burning incense, dark & damp passages, with grim effigies of attendant deities, & the bedisened idol himself. It is to be noticed that the utmost freedom is allowed, not only to Chinese, but to foreigners, to go into all parts of the temple, & without fee; & so I have found it everywhere in China.

Coming out, we found a Missionary of the London Miss. Soc., addressing a crowd of auditors, on the folly & wickedness of their idolatry, & the necessity of worshipping the one true God. He had a considerable audience, & there was no sign of opposition or dislike. They are eminently a reasoning people, & think ev. man entitled to a hearing.

Went to a tea-shop, in wh. some 500 Chinese, men, women & children, were taking their public evening meal of tea with a few cakes, vegetables & confections. We had cups of *red tea*, with pea nuts to eat. This is their best tea here, & is very good. This, too, is an orderly & quiet multitude — yet it is a great fête day. A man must have sharp sight & a knowing turn, who can see any external signs of vice in a Chinese city. I have not yet seen even a drunken man.

Here is a juggler, naked to the waist, with a crowd about him, swallowing swords & stones, & doing very strange things, with extraordinary ingenuity, — more surprising from his being without sleeves or any places of concealment, & no trap-doors, or accomplices, — a half naked man, in the open air, with a crowd pressing upon him. And here is a fortune teller, at his tables, & there is a man throwing bubbles from a stick, in the most incomprehensible way, — filling the air with them. At this shop, I bought a Chinese pencil, ink, ink stone, & paper, the sacred articles, which by their liberal system, pass all custom houses & excises duty free. Gamblers & gambling shops are frequent — but there is no violence or anything to shock one, & the risks are not large. But the taste for gambling is universal. A boy, who wishes to buy a cake with 6 cash, will put down 3, & by the turn of the die, get the cake for ½ price, or lose his money. Opium shops, too, with their close drawn curtains over the front door, are in every street. We go into one. There are 6 or 8 men lying at length on the mats, each with his pillow & pipe, — & seedy, jaundiced, weak eyed looking wretches they are. One told Mr. Lyles he had a trouble in his bowels, & took opium for it. "Yes", said Mr. L., "that is always the story — medical advice. It relieves the difficulty the first time, but when it comes again, there is no strength to meet it with, & the habit has become too strong". There was one dreadfully haggard looking woman, but whether a customer or an attendant, I could not tell.

Now to the Chapel, in the city. It is a respectable building, is of brick, rather of the Gothic type, but without tower or spire, & capable of seating 3 or 400 people. It was built at the expense of Mr. William Appleton of Boston, costing $5000. A[12] creditable building. It is used chiefly as a preaching place. It is in a public street, in the centre of population, & here, every afternoon, one of Bishop Boone's clergy comes, & the doors are opened & people invited to come in. He preaches to them, addressing them on any subject he pleases, calculated to draw them from their idols, & interest them in the Christian religion, & after the address, he asks them to stand reverently, while he prays to God for them, & then he offers a prayer, in their behalf. Then he invites any who are interested & desire to know more of the matter, to remain & see him in the vestry. There the clergy talk with them, take their names & address (to guard against impositions) give a few tracts, & engage them to come again. In this way out of hundreds & thousands, they occasionally get a catechumen or a child out of a family for a school. They have to guard especially ag. their coming under pretence of learning in order to get assistance. Their charities are very sparing & cautious, on that account — yet without charity to the distressed, they will not be respected.

The catechumens are taught in the way I have stated, by instruction founded on the Creed, & the Creed committed to memory, as they go on, & Scripture deal[t] out, as they can understand it, the Ten Commandments & the chief parts of the service gradually learned — baptism administered when they have come to a reasonable understanding of the

[12]Here Dana excised the word "very".

faith & desire to obey the law. Then Confirmation & Communion, as they are fitted. Of course, no attempt is made to perform the Church Service regularly at the preaching places in the city, as our Service is intended for the common worship of a company of Christians. There is, however, a day school at the Chapel, & occasionally, I believe ev. Sunday, the Service is performed there in the morning, to the Christians. The offices for Communion, Baptism & Confirmation, & the morning & evening prayer are translated & taught, & lately the Litany. They agree that the Liturgy is invaluable, with these converts. Their interest in it & knowledge of it grows daily, — & it is a rock of defense & support.

This evening, dined at French Legation, with M. & Mde. de Bourbulon. *Present*, a Fr. Admiral & Colonel, Count Klyskowski, & a few others. Service handsome, & cooking good, being French. After dinner, Mde. de B. sang some Fr. songs. Can anything be more meagre than a Fr. song? & then two Spanish songs — & what a contrast! A grace, a charm, a spirit indeed! The Sp. song of Maria Dolores — the "Mulatto, — Mulattito" song, was fascinating — guitars & troubadors & contradansas combined!

THURSD. APRIL 5. Spent two hours on board H. B. M. steam frigate Furious, by invitation of Capt. Jones. Capt. J., a post-captain, is not much over 40, his first lieut. is about 24, & his second lieut. only 19. In our Navy they would all be midshipmen except Capt. J., & he a lieut., with chance of being Commander at 50, & post captain at 60. Saw them furl sails. The whole crew are Britons, & a fine manly, seamanlike set of fellows they are — the boatswain & his mates, & the quartermasters &c., especially. Now, seamen are degraded to 2d class for gross & frequent misconduct, & only 2d class men can be flogged, & that only by the Capt., after inquiry & exn. of witnesses, & an interval of 24 hours for *cooling time*.

All agree, here, American, Fr. & Br., that the Br. Navy on the coast of China, is in fine condition. The officers are all on the start for work & adventure, like the Greek athlete; — for promotion & decorations follow every act of distinguished good conduct, & their fleet of small vessels gives junior officers chances for command, experience & distinction. Our poor Navy is in a deplorable state, — no chance for young officers, no promotion or orders or decorations for good conduct, & a deadness over all, — minds becoming inane over ward-room gossip.

Called on Rev. Dr. Bridgman, A.B.C.F.M.[13] Large house & comfortable, but in the room, three women & a baby that they all *mam maed* to, & one man in [a] white chokey [cravat] that they all *wived* to, & things were

---

[13]Elijah Coleman Bridgman (1801–1861) was a missionary to China for the American Board of Commissioners for Foreign Missions, 1830–1861. He edited the *Chinese Depository*, 1832–1847.

so muxy & uninteresting that I soon left them. Dr. B. seemed rather an old granny.

Called on the Bishop of Victoria, the Br. Bishop who has jurisdiction over all Br. Church people in China.[14] He is rather ditto to Dr. [E.C.] Bridgman, & his talk was of externals, & not deep in them.

Called on Dent & Co., A. Heard & Co., & a Russian Commodore who is staying with Heard & Co. The Dents have a palace. It is sumptuous. In their grounds are a small pack of Chinese & Japanese deer, an aviary of tropical birds, &c. &c. Among the birds, the Japanese pheasant exceeds in grace of action & richness of colors any bird I ever saw. The Russian Commodore speaks English very well, cannot be more than 30 years of age, had read my Two Years &c., & has soft, pleasant manners. Visit Russell & Co.'s *go-downs*, — large store houses, lighted by clerestories, & looking like our rail-road depots, & full of teas & silks.

Walsh (Russell & Co.) gave me a dinner party. Company were Meadows, author of a big work on China, Wade, formerly Capt. in Br. Army & now Chinese Sec. to the Br. Legation, Major Fisher of the R. Engineers, Davis, a Br. Magistrate & barrister &c. Wade & Meadows are thought to be the best Chinese scholars in the country.[15] Davis is a man of various information, & an A. M. of Cambridge, Eng. Wade told some excellent stories about Sir John Browning, Chisholm Austey & the H. Kong Bar. Wade & Meadows both oppose & discourage the plan of putting Chinese in Roman letters, wh. Bishop Boone has adopted.

To-day great pleasure & advantage of an offer of a passage to Japan, in Dent & Co.'s steamer Yiang Tze, in wh. Mr. Dent is to make an excursion to Japan, on a partly business & partly pleasure trip. He has invited, besides me, the B. of Victoria, & Mr. Parkes. It is a great opportunity. But for this, I should have to wait here indefinitely, perhaps 2 or 3 weeks. They sail Saturday, 7th. Sorry for that, as Sunday is Easter.

FRID. APRIL 6. GOOD FRIDAY.   At 9 A. M. went to the Chinese Service, at Bishop Boone's Chapel. This is a simple building, in the Gothic style, with a tower in the middle of the front, & well proportioned, & in every way Ecclesiastical in its style. Surprised to find a full company, of some 200 Chinese, men & women, including the 80 children of the school.

---

[14]George Smith (1815–1871), a British missionary to China since 1844, was consecrated bishop of Victoria in 1847. He published at least six volumes dealing with the Orient.

[15]Thomas Francis Wade (1818–1895) began his diplomatic career in the Orient in 1841. He continued as a British diplomat and linguist until 1888, when he returned to England to a professorship of Chinese at Cambridge. He published a great many papers on China and the Chinese language. Thomas Taylor Meadows was a British linguist and scholar who wrote several books on China, the best known of which was *The Chinese and Their Rebellions* (1856).

These are nearly all communicants or catechumen, or, at least, advanced enough to take part in the service. The singing, responses, Creed &c. were joined in very generally & heartily. Having an Engl. Prayer Book, I could follow the services perfectly well, not knowing a word of Chinese, & say the same things in Engl. that these poor converts or half converts said in Chinese. A Chinese clergyman, in full canonicals, distinguished only by his tonsure, tail & skull-cap, officiated with B. Boone.

At 11 A. M. Litany & Communion, in English. Company of about 20 persons, — chiefly the mission family. The Br. & Am. *public,* who go to church at all Good Friday, go to the large Engl. Church, near the middle of the Br. Concession. This is only a mission & school Chapel. But very interesting to join with these earnest people, in their little chapel, in our bond of Common Service, in wh. this day millions in all parts of the world are uniting. And beyond the Engl. & American communities, — all, R. Catholic, Greek, American, the Eastern Christians, Lutherans — all commemorate the Central Fact of the Christian Faith, — & the Jews, the world over, on this day keep their Passover.

This afternoon Dr. [E. C.] Bridgman called. He appeared better. Says there are only two missionaries of the A.B.C.F.M. in Shanghai, & Mrs. B. is the only Am. teacher. There is one boarding school of 22 scholars, & 2 or 3 day schools, wh. Mrs. B. visits & supervises, taught by older Chinese pupils. They also make no attempt to interfere with the dress or mode of eating of the pupils. Dr. B. confines his labors to a translation of the Scriptures, wh. has been on for sev. years. Spend rest of day quietly, at home. Weather cool & bracing.

5. Japan

SATURD. APR. 7. Steamer Yang Tse, for Japan. It is a large Am. built steamer, commanded & officered by Americans. Parkes does not go. So our company consists of Ld. Bishop of Victoria & myself, as guests, Mr. Dent, his partner, Mr. Webb, Mr. Ashton, a merchant, & a small staff of clerks & interpreters. Get underway at noon. Pass the Fr. frigate Forban, the Eng. men of war Furious, Roebuck & Nimrod, & the fleet of merchantmen, & the great transport wh. last night brot up Sir Hope Grant & staff, & the fleet of junks, with their great eyes & gaudily painted sides & scarfed cannon & are out in the great river. The Yang Tse Kiang, tho' so large, is shallow in parts, with shoals & banks, & is very difficult of navigation. Toward the mouth of the river, we pass the Pei Ho, going up, having on board the Fr. Gen. Montauban & his staff.[16] (The Fr. Govt. bot this steamer of Russell & Co. for $200,000, cash).

SUND. APR. 8. EASTER. The bishop is sea-sick, & keeps his bed; — so we have no service. It is a dull, rainy, rolling & pitching day, — as dull an Easter as I had Christmas in the Nappa hotel.

The commander of this boat is a Capt. Dearborn, a N. H. man, who commanded Boston ships for sev. years on this coast, & Forbes' brig, the Antelope, for sev. years, & has commanded this boat for three years. He is a man of character & experience. Conversed with him about our navy. He is a patriot, but says our navy on this coast is, & has always been, in a deplorable state. The officers idle & often scandalously dissipated, & their minds set on trading in *curios* & on getting home. The discipline slack, & no spirit or energy. He named two or three ships wh. were exceptions to this; but it is the rule. He says the British navy is, & for years has been, in the highest practicable condition, full of work, energy & emulation, young officers employed & encouraged, promotion, prise-money & honors accessible to all, the mess expenses low, & dissipation among officers rare, & gross cases rendering them liable to public disgrace & suspension fr. command. He thinks them far before the Fr., as seamen.

Capt. Dearborn mentioning the "Mary Ellen", I inquired & he told me he commanded her when she was lost, & remembered Chantrand (See

[16]Charles Antoine Cousin-Montauban (1796–1876) was Commander-in-Chief of the French forces allied with the English against the Chinese.

"Cuba & back"),[17] & says C. was very intelligent & active, & that his quickness in learning words of the Malay language, & the favor he got into with Malay families, were the chief causes of their getting along as well as they did.

(Did I mention that Mde. de Bourbulon smokes a genuine cigar, after dinner — no cigarrito, but a full Manilla cigar? She reminds me of Mrs. S. G. Ward, & affects to speak Engl. with a foreign accent).[18]

MONDAY. APR. 9. Land of Japan in sight. Cape Gotto, some 80 miles fr. Nagasaki. Run close in. Land is bold & rocky, but with more trees than that of the Southern coast of China, — evergreens, pines &c., — & patches of rich green. There is no sandy & flat spots. All is bold, hilly, rocky, & well sprinkled with trees. My first view of Japan!

We are heading, the Capt. tells us, for the entrance to Nagasaki, but it cannot be seen. There is no sign of an opening of a harbor, but only bold hills, with green valleys. Vessels have been known to cruise here 2 & 3 days without finding it. Round a little point we go, & behind an island, where there seems no room, & we open a narrow, deep channel. Here is a fort, & there a few houses; — & how very prettily that little village lies on the slope! There is a Japanese boat, with a dark blue jib & a white mainsail. Now, as we pass rapidly along the shore, cultivated spots, groups of houses increase. The distribution of hills & valleys, trees, rocks, green spots & houses is beautiful, & the bay is completely land-locked. Here, on the left, as we enter, is the famous Mount of Martyrs, where the early Missionaries & Japanese Christians were martyred. Here, in 1597, 26 Franciscans & Jesuits were crucified. And, for nearly a century afterwards, the executions of persistent Christians, foreign & Japanese, took place, until it became a place of terror at times, & at times a place of pious pilgrimage by Christians, & gained its name of Holy Mount, or Mount of Martyrs.

Now we open the shipping. There are 8 or 10 ships, chiefly Am. whalemen, lying at anchor, & beyond, a fleet of Japanese junks. There, in that boat that is coming off to us, is my first sight of a Japanese. Three

[17]In *To Cuba and Back* Dana tells of visiting the plantation of a young man named Chantrand and his father. The younger man had been wrecked in the Boston ship *Mary Ellen* on a coral reef in the India seas, had been taken captive by Malayans, and finally been returned to Boston in a rescue ship (see *To Cuba and Back*, p. 151).

[18]Madame de Bourbulon, mentioned earlier as the wife of the French Minister to Shanghai, was Kate McLeod of Boston. Samuel Gray Ward, a member of the Saturday Club and a prosperous Massachusetts banker, is noted earlier. He married Miss Anna Barker, daughter of a New Orleans merchant and one of the brilliant Concord circle that included Margaret Fuller.

men row the boat. They are strong, large men, darker & less yellow than the Chinese, more silent & less decently clad. They scull the boats, both at the sides & stern, & never pull the oars, as we do.

How beautifully the town lies, at the foot of the many topped gently sloping hills! And the harbor is landlocked, like an interior lake, more so even that Acapulco. And how pretty are these numerous little bays, or havens, that make up on all sides, with the cluster of houses at the head of each. There is an appearance of considerable cultivation, on shore, & trees are frequent, shading the outlying groups of houses. We come to anchor, near the shore, among the ships, one of wh. is a Dutch man-of-war.

And this is Nagasaki, famous in the history of the long attempted contact of East with West. Three hundred years ago, Nagasaki was solely a Christian city, its prince, its nobles, its people were all professed Catholics, & no other places of worhip existed here. Here the Catholics had churches & colleges, & this was the seat of the Chief Labors of Fathcr Valignano,[19] not the first but the most distinguished & longest resident of the missionaries. This was made the centre of the persecutions, until, after a struggle of a century, & after the endurance of incredible trials & tortures, the Catholic religion was exterminated, & at the beginning of the 18th century not a church nor college nor even the ruins of one could be seen, & even the graves & tombs of the Christians were dug up & their bones scattered, so that not a sign of them remained. Along with this, came the ignominious career of the Dutch merchants, who were tolerated on the understanding of their not being Christians, & who, it is even said, conformed to the ceremony of trampling on the Cross, required of all resident foreigners & all suspected Chinese, & made the most debasing concessions to retain the trade, & lost it after all. There is the little peninsula of Desima, in the centre of the city, to wh. the Dutch were so long limited. For 150 years, no Christian, known to be such, has been allowed to live here. But, now, under the late treaties,[20] they can live here, & may hire houses, but cannot own land or build. There fly the consular flags of Gr. Britain, the U. States, France & Holland, & now, some 10 or 20 merchants, chiefly Engl., American, & Dutch reside here, attempting to open a trade, & there is one missionary, & only one, a Mr.

[19]Alessandro Valignano (1539–1606) participated in the great Catholic conversion of Japan. He died in Macao some seven years before the outburst of persecution began in Japan.

[20]Commodore M. C. Perry, whose voyage to Japan has been noted earlier, signed a treaty of commercial alliance with Japan on March 31, 1854. The following October the British signed a similar treaty with Japan, and in 1858 Russia and England signed further treaties.

Williams,[21] one of B. Boone's clergy. The B. of Victoria goes ashore, to be his guest. Boats come off to us, bringing all the Europeans of the place, for letters & news. Among them are agents of Dent & Co., Jardine & Co., Mr. Walsh, who I suppose acts for Russell & Co., & some small traders, Jews & Parsees. But it is late in the afternoon & we dine, & put off our visit on shore until tomorrow. While we are at dinner, a company of Japanese officials enter the cabin, each with his two swords, to make official inquiries & to get some cognac or Curacoa to drink. But we put them off, as we are dining, & they quietly go ashore, — rather a sign, I think, of their declining power, in competition with the advancing European race.

TUESD. APR. 10.   Beautiful morning, & nothing can be more lovely than the scene fr. the deck of our steamer. There are patches of granite rock, with evergreen shrubs & trees about them, as on the coast off Beverly & Manchester, & patches of cultivated land. Above Nagasaki, the land is terraced, on the hill sides by walls of stone, & well cultivated, & among the stones & over the walls is a thick growth of creepers, like the Engl. ivy & lichen.

Go ashore. Call on Am. Consul, Mr. Walsh, br. of Walsh of Shanghai, & get my permit to change money. For foreigners can only change a limited quantity of money into Japanese coin, & that only on a consular permit. A passenger is allowed to change $3 a day, wh. he must do at the Custom House, & have each entered on his permit. For each dollar, I got 3 itsbus, (or inchebus), a oblong square silver coin, very prettily devised. For an itsbu, you get four itsus, silver of same shape of the itsbu, but smaller, or 2 nitsus, wh. are itsus, a little gilded. The Co. Hs. officers were squatting on mats, each wearing two swords, one with a book & writing materials, & one with the counting board of China on wh. they count by balls on wires, on the decimal principle.

Met the Bishop of Victoria, with Rev. Mr. [C. M.] Williams, & went with them to call on the Br. Consul, who is a son of the celebrated [John R.] Morrison, & a gentlemanlike man. Thence walked thro' the city, to Mr. Williams' hs., where I staid & lunched. It is a Japanese house of dark wood, with sliding screen doors everywhere, by wh. rooms may always be thrown into one. Mr. Williams tells me there is only one clergyman here besides himself, a Mr. Verbeck,[22] of the Dutch Refd. Ch.; but

[21]Channing Moore Williams (1829–1910) arrived in Japan as an Episcopal missionary in 1859. He returned to the United States in 1866 to be consecrated Bishop of China, with jurisdiction in Japan. Later he became Bishop of Japan.

[22]Guido Herman Verbeck (1830–1898), born in the Netherlands, took orders in the United States in 1859 in the Dutch Reformed Church, married, and went out to Japan. With the exception of a few trips back to the United States he spent his life in Japan.

neither of them is permitted to preach or teach in the Japanese, & they are consequently mere students of Japanese. There are no Cath. Missionaries, & it is said none will be sent until they are permitted to act as Missionaries. Called on Rev. Mr. Verbeck, who offers to go about with me tomorrow & show me the curiosities of the town, — Mr. Wms. being engaged with the Bishop.

After this, finding it almost impossible to lose my way, betw. the hills & the harbor, I wandered about by myself, for 3 or 4 hours. Among other places, I got to a theatre, where a play was going on, before a very large audience, promiscuous, of men women & children, crowded, jammed in together, under a roof of bamboo & grass. The play consisted, as in our lowest style of farces, of practical jokes of falling & pushing & striking with fans & brushes, & high sharp unnatural tones of voice. At the side of the stage, was seated on a mat, a man who seemed to me to act a chorus, occasionally speaking & singing. The singing, like that I have heard in the streets, is deeper toned than the Chinese, &, even with the women, a kind of unnatural barytone seems to be the fashion.

The streets are wider than those of Chinese cities, full twice as wide, & well flagged with broad stones, & neater than the Chinese. Here, also, there are no carriages, — only human foot-falls — & curious foot-falls they are. For all wear the sandal, the heel of wh. is not tied up, but flaps at every step, slip-slap, slip-slap, so that there is a perpetual clatter of heels in the streets, — indeed, the only sound to be heard, but those of human voices. I am told that only persons of high rank are permitted to ride on horseback, & they seldom do it. Occasionally a bullock is used as a beast of burden, in the streets, but loads are carried by coolies (Japanese) with sticks, as in China, & they usually grunt & chant as they go along, like those of Shanghai.

Walking at random thro' the streets, thro' an open window I saw one of those public warm baths, of wh. so much has been written, & wh. tell the tale of Japanese life so fully. They were open to sight of all who chose to stop & look at them, & the bathers seemed shameless. A woman sat on a platform, by the window, mending the clothes she was going to put on, heedless of the passers by. In the bath were some 8 or 10 men & women, as close as they could well stow, while others were wiping themselves on the platform, in a condition tolerable only before the Fall. Yet, there was nothing improper in their *conduct.* For aught one could guess, the secret might be that they knew no evil; but the fact is known to be that they know more evil than any other people. All foreigners here agree in their testimony, that, in one respect, the Japanese are the most shamelessly immoral people on earth.

A large tract, on the water, has been allotted to foreigners here, & is in process of filling up, like that at Canton, & the work is done by the basket full, on the shoulders of coolies. Yet there are some thousands of them, & the work goes on pretty well. Near the ground, saw a large house of thatch & bamboo, where were tables set for some 1000 coolies, a tea cup & plate to each.

Dined with Mr. Walsh. He has a wife, who is a Canadian lady of the name of Church. She & Mrs. Verbeck, are the only foreign women in this part of Japan, & are very lonely. Especially good fish at dinner, & Japanese oranges. (Excellent fish market, & this morn. Capt. Dearborn went ashore early & bot fish eno' for 70 persons — all hands — for one dollar).

Walsh & his br. in law, Church, speak well of the Japanese in some respects. They say they are full as intelligent as the Chinese, & more manly. It seems to me they are less civilised, more of the savage in their dress, or want of dress, stronger, more willful, & not so excessively rooted, in their ways & opinions, to antiquity. But one day is little ground for a generalisation.

Passed the night on board the Yang Tse.

WED. AP. 11. The steamer Aroff is in, fr. Kenagawa, bound to Shanghai. As we leave for Kenagawa tomorrow morning, I close this journal, to send by the Aroff. She brings such news of civil war in Yeddo[23] as makes my chance of visiting it very slight.

The Japanese have less of the pale yellow complexion than the Chinese, & are both darker & fairer, some a clear dark, & some a brunette. The little children are often fair brunettes, & so are many of the grown women. But the women rouge a great deal. The married women, & unmarried women who has reached middle life color their teeth black. This is considered an elegance, & girls are eager for the time when they can do it. The men shave the front of the head & bring the hair up to the top, in a small cue, of 4 or 5 inches long. The women draw their hair to the top where it is kept in place by gilt or silvered pins & combs, & by a thin paste or glue. The men wear a loose robe, wh. opens in front, tied at the waist by a belt, & the lower classes wear nothing else. The better dressed wear trowsers. The women wear robes, less careful & proper than the Chinese,—and indeed, those are not national ideas. No attempts

[23]The commercial treaties between Japan and various foreign nations had aroused great internal dissent in the country. Perry's expedition had been a show of force to coerce the Japanese into cooperation, but there was much opposition among the feudal lords in Japan to the trade agreements. The news Dana received was premature, but the following year, and for four years after that, sporadic military attempts to void the treaties and drive out the foreigners took place. The attempts were costly and unsuccessful.

to Christianise the Japanese have been made for 150 years, since the Catholics were exterminated, & none are making, or permitted, now.

WED. APR. 11. [CONT.] Nagasaki, Japan. (Sent journal to Apr. 11, fr. Nagasaki, by steamer Aroff for Shanghai.) This is a great relig. festival day, among the people. The temples are thronged, the women & children are dressed in their best, simple arches of bamboo dressed with leaves are thrown across the chief streets, lanterns are suspended fr. every available place, & transparencies prepared for the evening. Rev. Mr. Verbeck's to dine, at 1 o'ck. Mrs. V. is from Troy N. Y. a pleasant & rather pretty young woman, with exact manners. A Japanese pheasant, roasted, tastes like our partridge. After dinner, Mr. V. & I make an excursion thro' the city, on foot. There are no sedan chairs in Japan, the only conveyance being a close box, fitted with complicated slides, on the floor of wh. you have to sit. These are rare. I have seen but one in the city.

Our first visit is to a Temple, the principal one. It is on the hillside, with broad flights of stone steps leading up to it, &, at the foot, on the street, two large columns of copper, supporting a cornice of the same. The Temple itself is plainer than those in China, but in good condition. The site is one of the best in the city, commanding a noble view of the city, harbor & hills beyond. Next we went to a temple where worship was going on. This was Buddhist, & like the worship in China. The entire floor of the temple was filled with sitting & kneeling persons, chiefly women. The interior is gaudy with gilding & lacquer work, the shrine is overloaded with ornaments, tapers burn & incense smokes before it, long robed & shaven priests kneel, & a choir sing a long hymn, accompanied by an instrument that sounds like a comb & paper, — the singing being in a thin, high, sharp key. Saw some persons at the door, who could not get in, throwing little pieces of copper at persons who were kneeling, hitting them in the neck & on the head. At first, we thought this was sport, & irreverent, but we noticed that they looked grave in doing it, & those whom the pieces hit took it gravely & picked them up, not intermitting their prayers. Mr. Verbeck suggested that the pieces thrown were a substitute for the presence of those who could not get in, — a vicarious or symbolical attendance. This is a mere guess, but it receives confirmation from the fact that absent people send their cards to the temple, by servants, who paste them on a table before the shrine. We saw a girl bring her mistress' card & paste it there, where there were already some hundreds. The only difference I could notice in the worship fr. that of China, is that in prayer the people rub the palms of their hands slowly together. Rosaries are in use among them. The priests file in before the altar, kneel, prostrate themselves, &, at the end of the service, file out at a side door, as in the R. Cath. worship. Indeed, there is no striking difference betw. the Buddhist & R. Cath. worship, in the externals.

To another temple of the ancient religion of Japan [Shintoism], wh. prevailed before the introduction of Buddhism. (Mr. V. thinks this has assimilated itself to the Buddhist. There is no conflict between the two sects). This temple was chiefly frequented by children, who played freely about its most sacred places, & over its nicely matted floors, but without undue noise or any rudeness.

There is a street in Nagasaki known as the Street of Temples. One side of it is occupied by the grounds of various temples, extending fr. ½ a mile to a mile in length. These grounds are all on the hill-side, with flights of stone steps & terraced grounds. The beggars are innumerable, importunate & sometimes offensive. Probably these are more numerous to-day, it being a festival. Some are begging monks or friars, & are respectfully treated. They are known by their dress & a little bell they beat, hung at their stomachs. Some seemed well & hearty, & must be begging by some heridiary or official right. The children of the poorer class often hold out their hands for coin.

The Japanese children are very pretty & engaging. They look happy, as if they were well treated & well fed. I am told that the parental rule is gentle. I think in two days, I have not seen or heard a crying child. They have very bright eyes, white teeth, & clear brown complexions. The young girls, too, are pretty. Low broad foreheads, of the Greek type, thick black hair, white teeth & intelligent ardent eyes are common. But as soon as they come to the age of blackened teeth, they are hideous. They keep their mouths open, to exhibit these black teeth, surrounded by highly rouged lips, wh. gives them a look of toothless fatuity, as if of extreme old age. Beside the rouge, wh. is so common on the lips & cheeks, they often whiten the rest of the face & the neck, to the hue of the palest Northern complexion. A Japanese married woman is this — black teeth, rouged lips & cheeks, neck & rest of the face whitened, & black hair dressed on the top of the head with ornamented combs & pins & stiffened by a wash of thin paste. The dress of all women is a wrapper, gathered by a belt at the waist. Of wrappers, they wear one, two, three, or more, according to their taste & wealth, & the state of the weather. In cold weather, one will be quilted. The poor usually wear but one. But whatever the number of garments, they are all wrappers. The under wrappers are of rich silk. The men also wear wrappers, but trowsers are also worn by a portion of the men. The babies seem to live out of doors, being carried everywhere by the women, sometimes on the back, as in China, but usually in front, lodged in the loose folds of the wrapper above the girdle. (The women nurse their babies, in the most open manner, in the streets, theatres, temples & all public places, & often go with entire open fronts, the whole field of the infant's labors being open to view. This, however, is nothing. For, when it is warm, the women of the lower classes leave off all clothing above the waist, & the men have nothing either above the waist or below it).

This day, we were told, was for the worship of the middle & poorer classes. The upper classes have a separate day. Here, as in China, the names of benefactors to a temple or shrine, are engraved on tablets & conspicuously placed. The Japanese bell is of copper, struck with a heavy stick of soft wood, wh. is swung by machinery, & strikes at the end, giving a soft deep tone. The bells do not bulge or flare out at the bottom, like ours, but are shaped like a thimble.

The hills wh. surround the city are covered with tombs. The city of the dead is above, & the city of the living is below. The tombs are in the Chinese style, surrounded by low walls, terraced, & some 2 or 3 feet high, wh. go about the tomb a little after the manner of the child's "Walls of Troy". The stone used here is a kind of dark granite, a good color.

The combined moisture & warmth of the climate of Japan, give rise to a growth of creeping plants, with tiny leaves, like the clover, but of a thick, evergreen texture, like the ivy. The [plant] grows out of the joints of stone walls, & even from the tiled roofs of old houses, & so dense is it, that some times you can hardly tell whether the structure before you is a stone wall or a bank. This gives great beauty to the terrace walls, the temples & large stone enclosures, public & private.

Mr. Verbeck (whose initials are G. F.) took me to pay a visit to a Japanese gentleman of the middle class, a two sworded man. He has a house on the hill-side, commanding a fine view. The temple grounds, — the range of them, lie beneath him. He received us courteously. The Japanese salute is to join your hands before you, & bow profoundly once or twice. The only diff. in the Chinese is that they shake their joined hands, as if they were shaking props.[24] The Japanese gentleman gave us tea & some nice spunge cake, just such as Mrs. Nichols makes. He sat on his mat, & the servant brought him the teapot, hot water, portable fire apparatus, tea cups & tea caddy, & he made the tea himself. I noticed that he heated the cups with water first, à la R. H. Dana Senr. The tea was ground fine as flour, & of a bronse color. This he said was rare & nice. He also made us some from the leaf, wh. I like better. The Japanese tea is not prepared, like most of the Chinese, for a long sea voyage. The leaf seems to be simply dried. It is soft & tender, & the

[24]Dana may be referring to the prophetic sticks which the Chinese used to cast before their idols in an effort to foretell the future.

beverage has a taste of weak green tea. (*Mem.* the professed tea-tasters in China, who buy for the merchants, rub the tea in the hand, blow upon it, & put it to the nose. If it stands this test, it is afterwards subjected to boiling water).

Our host inquired whether the Japanese embassy had reached the United States.[25] Mr. V. says he understood the difference between America, & the great nations of Europe.

The Japanese wear handsome colors of silks. It seems to me they have more varieties of colors & more taste in them than the Chinese. The Chinese wear chiefly blue, white, black & brown. Here they have beautiful tints of purple & lilac, & a kind of checked grey, or grey & lilac, wh. is very pretty.

On our way down fr. the old gentleman's house, we passed a tree, — a small tree or large shrub — covered & filled deep with beautiful pink flowers, small & close together. Laid upon the ground, it would have made "a bed of heaped Elysian flowers".[26] Mr. V. did not know its name. I believe I have mentioned the double flowering cherry tree, wh. has no fruit, & the Camelias Japonicas, single & double, wh. are so rich & so common.

The manners of all the people, young & old, are civil. The little children are becoming accustomed to foreigners, & at every step meet us with the pretty salutation — Ohio — pronounced exactly as we pronounce the name of the State. The chief amusement here, of young & old, now, is the flying of kites. They are of all shapes, & beautifully colored & figured. An amusement & mischief is to cut the string of another kite by drawing across it. To do this, they put upon a portion of the string fine particles of glass, by a kind of glue or paste.

Currency. As well as I can make it out, the chief silver coin is properly called a *bu* (pronounced *boo*), worth about 35 cents, an oblong square of silver. *Ichi* is Japanese for *one*, & one of these is called ichibu, whence the name for the coin among foreigners has become *ichibu,* & we speak of 2 & 3 ichibus. The *shu* is a silver coin of the same shape, worth about eight cents. One of these is called an *ishu,* wh. is a contraction for ichi shu. Whence foreigners call this coin also the *ishu.* The *ishu* gilded, or of nikle, doubles its value, & is called a *nishu,* wh. means two *shus.* Then they have a copper coin, flat, of an oval shape, as large as the longitudinal section of an egg, with a square hole in the middle. This is the *tempo,* sixteen *tempo* go to the *ichibu,* which makes it about two cents. They have also the little copper *seni,* or *kas* or *kash,* of China, getting out of

[25]A Japanese embassy of good will visited the United States May 14 to June 30, 1860.

[26]Milton's *L'Allegro,* line 147.

circulation, & worth about 2 or 3/10 of a cent. Of all these, I have specimens. The gold, I have not yet learned. The *tael,* like the English pound, is not coined. It is the sum by wh. all reckonings are made, & represents here, as in China, about $1.30. The iron *zeni* is worth about 1/50 of a cent!

There are two little mountain streams that run thro' Nagasaki, crossed by high arched bridges of dark granite. On one of these I saw a water wheel, of full sise, in operation. Mr. Verbeck gives me a Japanese map of Nagasaki.

On board again, at night, as we start for Kenagawa at day-break. Take my leave of Nagasaki by its bright lights seen from the steamer's deck.

THURSD. APRIL 12. At sea, again, going round the South coast of Japan, bound to Kenagawa. Mr. Dent tells me that about one & a half million of dollars worth of silk has been exported fr. Japan in the last nine months, wh. is pretty well for the beginning of a trade. Also, considerable vegitable wax, sapan wood, for a die. The tea has not yet been prepared for a sea voyage, & its adaptation to the European market is not settled. The trade to Japan is something, especially in edeble seaweed. But the Japanese take nothing in return. They have never either imported or exported anything! They have produced & consumed, by themselves, independently of the rest of the world.

Mr. Dent also tells me that the Russians are introducing their woolens into China, by overland trade, & undersell the English & Americans, who are limited to cottons.

Mr. Verbeck tells me the best he can learn as to the women of Japan, is this. The virtue of the wife is strictly guarded, & a failure punished severely. So, of the unmarried daughters of men of the upperclasses. Men seem to be under no particular control in that respect, more than is the case of drinking, — excess or publicity is to be avoided. The licensed public brothels, are the peculiarity of Japan. The daughters of the poorer classes are placed there, freely, & indented to the keepers. In them, they get a better education than they can get at home. The mistress is bound to teach them reading & writing, music, manners & accomplishments. From these places they marry, & often marry well. It seems to be con-sidered an advance in the condition of a poor girl, but would be a disgrace to one of the upper classes. To carry out the anomaly, the master of one of these houses, though recognised by law, loses caste, & however rich, is regarded a little as the Southern planter regards the slave-dealer. He thinks the concubines are mostly serfs & vassals, — for, all know that the feudal system prevails in full vigor in Japan. The concubine is protected & has rights, for herself & her children, but is not a wife. There is but one *wife*, which is substantially the law of China.

FRID. APR. 13. Very heavy sea all last night, & all to-day. None but a strong vessel could stand it, Capt. Dearborn, who has been 30 years at sea, & is a moderate talker, tells me it is the most dangerous sea he ever saw. It comes fr. all directions. It stove in our larboard box & swamped a boat wh. was above the hurricane deck. All-day 8 men are employed driving the water off decks. It comes pouring over all parts of the ship. The Capt. thought at one time it would carry off everything. The seas off Japan have the reputation of being the worst in the world. The Chinese servants were all fastened below, under battened hatches, all sea-sick. There was something bewildering in the effect of the seas, as they tossed about, & broke over us, & we tore through them with the power of our great engines. It is a wonder to me that the complicated machinery of steamboats holds out so well.

Yesterday was a calm, beautiful day, & the picturesque coast of Japan, blue in the distance, passed by our sides, mountains, hills & vales. At night, it was so dark that, on deck, I could not see the passage down, & had to grope, like a blind man, & the sea was all alive with phospherescent light. I thought something was going to [happen]. Roll, pitch, plunge, bang, splash, swash — all day long, — a dreary time. I read Oliphant's China & Japan,[27] but not with pleasure, & those who are not sea sick [are] rather grouty.

SAT. APR. 14. All cleared off. Fine day, & sea almost smooth. All hands bright again, & the Canary birds are singing.

MONDAY. APR. 16. At Yokahama, the sea port of Yeddo, in the centre of the kingdom of Japan! On shore, at the house of a kind friend, walking in the country among groves & plantations & temples & the huts of the poor, by hill sides & rivulets, & examining the rich trees & foliage & flowers of this wonderful country. Have I not every reason to be thankful for the success that attends my steps?

But, to go back to my voyage here. All day Saturday, we were out of sight of land, & at sundown none was to be seen, but no sooner was it dark than first one volcano, then another, & at length four were to be seen, now fading almost out of sight, & now brightening up into a steady glare, through the darkness. They must have [been] very distant. Coming among islands, our Capt. whose charts, the best to be had here, were 30 miles out of the way here, putting us at noon some 20 miles in the country, on a mountain, — hove us to under short head of steam until daylight of Sunday, & all Sunday morning we were on deck, watching with delight these beautiful shores, as we passed up the great bay of Yeddo. The shores are as beautiful as the Isle of Wight, the best points

[27]Laurence Oliphant (1829–1888), *Narrative of a Mission to China and Japan in 1857–8–9* (London, 1859).

of Staten Island, or of the North of England. No sand, no flats, no rugged bare hills, nor merely a rolling country, — but such a disposition of hills, valleys, slopes, small plains, occasional rocks, half concealed by evergreens, & the whole sprinkled over with trees, sometimes sparse & sometimes in groves, & signs of the most elaborate cultivation, terraced gardens, the deep green of the rice fields & the brilliant yellow of the rape seed. Then this magnificent bay, as open as the sea, 20 & 30 miles across, seems all alive with boats fishing for the great market of Yeddo, & the daily wants of the dwellers on its shores. To count these boats is out of the question. They dot the horison as thick as an artist could put them on his canvas. I have no doubt that 2000 could be seen from our decks. Meat is scarce with these people. Fish & rice are their subsistence.

While we are looking at the shores, through our glasses, I see a large cloud, close to the horison, singularly regular in its shape. It is broad at the base, very high, & cut sharp off at the top. "Do you see Fusiama?" "No". "There, just where you are looking". "That. No. Impossible, that is a cloud – all snow white — too high for a mountain". Is it a cloud or a mountain? That is the question. John Bull proposes to take a bet on it. As we draw nearer, spots, then strips of dark green are disclosed on its sides, low down, but all its upper half, at least, is pure white, the white of snow, — for the great mountain, volcano, of Fusiama, it certainly is.

Now comes in sight the shipping at anchor, in front of the double town of Yokahama & Kenagawa, H. B. M. brig Camilla, a raking bark from the Sandwich Islands, the Zoe, a pretty little herm[aphrodite] brig fr. S. Francisco, the Ida Rogers, & a bit of a topsail sch. from S. Fr., the Page, & Dent & Co.'s great receiving ship loading a ship alongside of her, & a Dutch bark, & a Br. ship, & there, up the bay, out of sight, lies the mysterious inapproachable city of Yeddo. We are soon at anchor, & boarded. Three Custom Hs. officers, each with two swords, go into the cabin & take notes in strange characters of the Capt.'s report & drink their Curacoa, & a midshipman from the Camilla, for letters & news-papers, & some half dosen Am. & Engl. come in sampans. Among them is Dr. Bates, son of my kind host at Honolulu, established here as a physician, & soon Dr. Hall comes on board, to whom I have letters, & invites me ashore to be his guest.

Dr. Hall, (George R.) is a Mass. man, married a d. of Mr. Beal of Kingston, knows the Severs, Lt. James Dana, & our Plymouth friends, especially [B.] Marston Watson.[28] He has been in China sev. years, & in Japan six mos., in mercantile pursuits, partner of Walsh & Co. He has

[28]George R. Hall remains unidentified. He probably married a daughter of Thomas Prince Beal, of Kingston, who was the father of Joseph S. Beal, noted earlier as a classmate of Dana's at Harvard. William Russell Sever of Plymouth has been noted earlier, as have James Dana and Benjamin Marston Watson.

just finished a plain house of wood, but well furnished, & installs me in a good room, with many of the comforts of life. He has begun a little plantation of shrubs & trees about his house, wh. I examine with him. Here are camelia Japonicas, white & red, single & double, double flowering cherry & peach, & evergreens of the most beautiful varieties, some closely resembling our hemlock & cedar, yet with differences. One with very graceful weeping branches, called the weeping pine, for it is a white pine. The yew grows to great height here, & bears its red berries. There is also the ground pine, the savin, the juniper, the pitch pine & the English holly. Then there is the Cryptomeria Japonica, a celebrated evergreen among Naturalists. Of all these, he has small growing specimens, while they are in sight, in full growth, on the neighboring hills. The privet, used here for hedges, is in abundance. Probably Japan is the best country in the world for varieties of evergreens.

By the Treaties, the 3 ports opened to foreigners, are Nagasaki, Kenagawa & Hakodadi. But the Japanese insisted that Yokahama, adjoining Kenagawa, should be the place for the residence of foreigners. As it is more convenient for commerce, having deeper water, the foreigners have gladly accepted it, but the foreign officials, to preserve the treaty, enter their protest, & fix the Consulates at Kenagawa. They are about three miles apart, but Yokahama will be the place of foreign trade & residence. A large, liberal allotment, or concession of land has been made for the foreign settlement, with the waterfront of about five thousand feet, & embracing, in all, some one hundred acres. Here are to be the houses, offices & "go-downs" of the foreign residents. This allotment was made only a little over a year ago. Twelve months ago, there was not a house upon it. Now, houses & offices & godowns are going up in all directions. Heard & Co.'s is nearly done, Dent & Co.'s in progress, Walsh & Co.'s nearly done, & numerous others, just completed, in progress or planned out, for the various Dutch, British, American & Russian merchants who have flocked here, among whom is the usual proportion of Jews. The foreign Concession is regularly laid out in wide streets & enclosed within a stockade, at the gates of which the Japanese military keep guard, not to shut in the foreigners, for the treaties give them a range of about 20 miles into the country, in one direction, & seven in the direction of Yeddo, but to guard them against robbers & assasins. This is not unneeded. Not long ago, (about 6 mos.) a Russian officer & two seamen were attacked & butchered, just at dusk, in the open streets of the Concession, & only 3 or 4 weeks ago, two masters of Dutch merchant vessels, said to be steady & respectable men, were set upon & cut to pieces, at about the same hour & place. Since the last event, the foreign consuls have issued an order, advising all foreigners to go armed, & not be out unnecessarily after dark, & the Japanese guards are strictly kept. No clue can be found to either of the murders. The common report among the Japanese is that they were done by retainers of some great neighboring princes, known to be hostile to foreigners & to the powers at Yeddo. My California belt comes into play now, & is a convenience.

In the afternoon, Dr. Hall takes me a delightful walk into the country, for a mile or so. I cannot cease admiring the picturesque beauty of the disposition — the *lay* — of the land, in this world of Japan. The hills are just high enough, they are of every shape & form, the valleys & levels lie delightfully among them, & the trees shade everything, & every wall, every stone, every big trunk of a tree has its "garniture & screen" of ivy & other creeping vine. The ivy is that of England, without poison & an evergreen hue. There are sturdy oaks, too, for it to grow upon.

The hill sides are always terraced, where they are cultivated at all. This, Dr. Hall tells me, is to prevent the washing down of the soil. Acres & acres are laid down to paddy fields, from wh. they are now just beginning to draw off & pump off the water. Rice is the staff of life here, & its exportation is prohibited.

The houses are tiled on the roofs, & to resist the force of the typhoons, & to give tenacity to the roof, there is a plantation of the *fleurs de lis* at the ridge of every roof. This produced a singular, but pleasing effect. The yards are lined, & the walks are lined with hedges, close cut, as in England, — their own invention, centuries old. These hedges are of privet, & various evergreen thorn bushes, & of the yew. The rasberry abounds here, & is in full blow, now, & the little, simple violet, "wee, modest",[29] but world known, violet, sprinkles over all the warm banks.

Before an old temple, wh. we visit, stands an ancient oak, an old gingo tree, & several of the Cryptomeria Japanica; and in the court of a Jap. gentleman's house, is the curiosity of a pitch pine tree, — or, what ought to have been a tree — 150 years old, grown to the height of about four feet, & then spread out over a flat surface, 15 feet square, supported by a trellis. The Japanese, like the Chinese, delight in torturing trees into grotesque shape, imitations of birds & beasts. In that respect they have not much more taste than a Dutchman. We made a call upon a dignitary, who was holding a court of conciliation, at which sat, or squatted, some half dosen litigants & witnesses, & there was ever so much writing, in big books. They gave us cups of hot saki, a wine made of rice, the chief drink of the country, & a pleasant confection of bean. (You cannot call on a Chinese or Japanese, without an offer of tea, or wine, & tobacco, & some little cake or confection).

---

[29]Burns, "To a Mountain Daisy," (1786): "Wee, modest, crimson-tipped flow'r. . ."

Returning through the Japanese village, we saw one of those institutions of the country, the public bath, where, as at Nagasaki, men & women were bathing & making their toilets. These are as open to the street as a barber's shop. Dr. Hall thinks the water is not changed all day, & that the better class bathe early. At the Guard House were a file of Japanese soldiers, squatting on mats. Behind them was a row of musquets, with percussion caps & bayonets, made by native workmen. The Japanese make minie rifles & Colt's pistols. They have none of the obstinate Chinese nonsense of matchlocks & bows & arrows. Saw some exquisite red porcelain cups. Dr. Hall says their colors, in their silks, are not fast, tho' pretty.

Calls & returns from Habersham (formerly Lieut. in U. S. Navy, author &c.) Stearns, Brower, & Knight, merchants here, & Dorr, the U. S. Consul.[30]

Went with Dr. Bates, in his boat, to Kenagawa. It is about 3 miles across. (Dr. Bates hires four boatmen, to be always by the boat, & to find themselves, & gives for the four $12 a month. Manual labor is worth about 50 or 60 cents a week). Kenagawa is a village, lying along the Imperial high road, Tekaido, wh. runs through the realm to & fr. Yeddo, & wh. skirts between the hill & the water. Called on Rev. Mr. Brown, Missionary of A.B.C.F.M., but he & all his family, & Dr. Hepburn, the Miss. phys., were gone on a day's excursion.[31] These families occupy a temple, & live among the idols. How did they get it?

Speaking of missionaries, Mr. [C. M.] Williams, at Nagasaki, [said] that when he gave a Chinese Bible to a native, it was sent back the next day, with a message fr. the Governor, that if it was done again, it would bring both parties into trouble. And Mr. Verbeck told me that a Japanese, who had bought a translation of an Engl. work on history, came to him for an explanation of the words "God" & "Jesus Christ", & that he felt obliged to decline his request. The consequence to the Missionary, might be banishment or such restrictions & annoyances as would make his life there useless, & to the native might be very serious if not fatal. This can hardly be called Missionary work! In truth, the few Missionaries in Japan are simply what the Chinese call "Makeelarn boys", — learning the language & customs.

[30]The only member of this group who has been identified is Alexander W. Habersham (1826–1883), son of James Habersham, who resigned his commission in the U. S. Navy to become a tea and coffee merchant in the Orient. He published a number of articles on China and Japan.

[31]Samuel Robbins Brown (1810–1880) was a missionary to Japan and China from Connecticut. He was not sent by the American Board of Commissioners for Foreign Missions, but by the Dutch Reformed Church Board. James C. Hepburn (1815–1911), Presbyterian missionary and doctor (M.D., University of Pennsylvania, 1836), came to Japan in 1859 and stayed until 1892.

Called on Mr. Dorr, the U. S. Consul. He lives in a temple, on the high ground above the village, fr. wh. flies the Am. ensign. This is a large & beautiful temple, with grounds laid out in the usual taste of the Bonses (Buddhist priests). The gods are screened off, by a paper wall, but all the rest of the temple is for his use, assigned to him as the official residence. He tells me it is the best residence that any foreigner has in Japan, better than the foreign ministers have at Yeddo. Dorr, (E. W.) is a Boston [man], & is said to be a generous fellow. He presses on me an invitation to visit him at his temple, wh. I shall accept. Yesterday, he sent to Mr. Harris, our Minister, at Yeddo,[32] my application for permsision to go to Yeddo. By the treaty it is not to be opened to Americans or any foreigners until 1862, except those connected with the Embassy. But he thinks I can go, notwithstanding. In his grounds are Camelia Japanicas (or, is it *Camilla?*) fifty feet high, with deep crimson flowers to their very tops. The haliards that hoist the Am. ensign on the flag staff are made fast round the chin of an idol! The oddity of this is extreme, & perhaps it is a portent. In part of his grounds are the tombs of the priests, & in another, the place where the dead are burned. This latter is still in use. Dorr tells me that they only burn off the flesh, & bury the skeleton entire.

Mr. Dorr tells me that the report of the assassination of the Prince Regent by emissaries of the Prince of Mito, is true,[33] (The Emperor is a boy of 16). The Prince of Mito is a great feudal chief, who is bitterly opposed to the foreigners, to the treaties recently made, & to the party in power, which is supposed to favor foreigners. Immediately on the assassination, the Prince of Mito withdrew to his country, in the mountains, & has been levying a large force. Civil war is apprehended. The Japanese authorities have told Mr. Dorr that they cannot protect him in Kenagawa, if the Prince of Mito comes this way, & advise him to withdraw to Yokahama, but he refuses, believing it to be a dodge to remove the Consulate.

The view of the Bay, from the terrace of Mr. Dorr's temple, he compared to views on the Isle of Wight. The same thing struck me.

[32]Townsend Harris (1804–1878), merchant, politician, and diplomat, was appointed Consul-General to Japan in 1855 and Minister Resident four years later. He is credited with the U. S.–Japanese treaties of 1857–1858. Despite Dana's feelings about him, Harris was very highly regarded for his diplomatic skill. He resigned his post in 1860.

[33]Naosuke II (1815–1860), Minister of the Shogunate and principal figure in the formulation of commercial treaties with the United States, alienated large parts of the feudal Japanese establishment by his diplomatic activities and responded to opposition by wholesale arrests and assassination of his critics. He himself was assassinated on March 3, 1860, by agents of Mariaki Tukugawa (1800–1860) 9th Lord of the Mito Clan. Prince Mito had been a leading opponent of the treaties from the start, advocating instead the development of strong coastal fortifications for Japan.

Returned to Yokahama. (I believe the Japanese authorities, contend, under the treaty, that Yokahama is part of Kenagawa). Dorr opened his collection of ancient Japanese coins, & gave me several. One, a *koban*, gold, some 200 years old, worth, intrinsicaly about $4.85. Another, a gold *ichibu*, of the value of $2, & one of the old silver ichibus. He says that the unit of their coinage is the *zene*, (Chinese *kas* or kash), a small iron coin, with square hole in middle. Of these, there are about 1600 to an ichibu. The smallest silver coin is the *ishu*, equal to 400 zene, or ¼ ichibu. The *ishu* made of nikle, wh. is called the *nishu*, is worth two *ishu*, or 800 zene. The large, oval copper piece, with the hole in it, is the tempo & is worth 100 zene, or ¼ *ishu*. Small transactions are measured by *ichibu* & *tempo*.

This afternoon, went with Dr. Hall to inspect the Gankero. There is a large section of ground set apart especially for this purpose by the government. It is separated by a creek & bridge fr. the rest of the town. Licenses are given to persons to build houses & maintain them there, for the purpose of prostitution, on the Japanese system, of wh. I have spoken. A year ago there was not a foreigner here, & no trade & few inhabitants. It was opened to foreigners & trade on 4 July last, & now it has grown so, chiefly in Japanese, of course, that the place, the Gankero, has sprung up as in a night. Most of the houses now are but partly built, & the utmost industry prevails, — carpenters, painters, tilers &c. The chief establishment looked like a temple, it is so large & handsome. Within are parlors, reception rooms, dining rooms, a dancing hall, a theatre, &c. &c. The chief rooms were beautfiully carved & elaborately painted. The chief artists of Yeddo contributed each a panel, for the walls & ceiling. Lacquered furniture & screens abound, & great neatness everywhere. It is not yet occupied, being in the finishers' hands. It has a court yard, planted with trees & shrubs, where is to be a fountain.

Next we visited some of the other establishments, a specimen of each class. Those of the 2d & 3d class were large houses, well ventilated, with bathing rooms & kitchens & sleeping rooms, & each a large reception room. These were occupied & in full operation. The women, being all unmarried, have white teeth, are painted white & red, especially the lips, & have their hair dressed in the most elaborate style, with large puffs, hair pins & combs, stiffened by thin glue; & some of them wore huge head dresses of cheap finery. These girls belong to the establishment, almost like slaves. They are sold, or apprenticed by their parents. They are usually taken very young & are taught. We saw some practicing instrumental music & singing. One girl Dr. Hall thought could not be over 10 or 12 years old. One was a new comer, & was in the hands of the barber, a woman, who was dressing her hair in the most artistic manner, with brushes in the glue or paste, combs, pins &c., decking the poor

victim. The lowest class of houses were what the foreigners call the
stalls. Here are rows of stalls, each about 8 feet by 4, with a sliding door
in front, & each occupied by a woman. We passed through them. In
some, the women were asleep, in others they stood at their doors to
entice the passers by. We had to dodge, to avoid being seised by them.
This was the lowest & most distressing view of all. I cannot think the
whole number of public courtesans in the entire Gankero, can be less
than a thousand. Yet the entire population of the town does not exceed
3 or 4000. But the town is a place of constant resort for traders, travellers
& sight-seers from the interior, as well as of sailors fr. the ships. The Govt.
undertakes the police regulation of the Gankero, & Dr. Hall thinks there
are Japanese physicians employed there. But venereal disease is almost
universal. Not one in ten is clear of it. Mr. Habersham dined with us — a
man of good manners, but ill reported of in the Navy.

TUESD. APR. 17. Go again to Kenagawa. Short call on Dorr. Call on
the Browns. Rev. is off with the Consul, but see Mrs. Brown. Who should
she turn up to be but a daughter of Rev. Shubael Bartlett of E. Windsor,
Conn.[34] She & Mr. B. were 8 years in China, left on account of her health,
spent 12 years at home, & have been in Japan some 6 or 8 mos. They have
handsome quarters, in the Jobúchichi temple.

All the Protestant Missionaries I have seen, whether in China, Japan or
the S[andwich] Islands, live in respectable, comfortable quarters, with
servants, on equal social relations with the wealthy classes, & are able to
give time & attention to visitors. Their position is an advance in social
position & comforts of life to many of them. They do not live as well, with
as much leisure and as many servants in the grade of life many of them
come from. They live better than the families of the poorer country
clergymen at home. If this is known & understood, it is not to be complained of. It is their policy to present themselves to the natives as well
ordered, dignified Christian families. Many have ridiculed them &
sneered at them for their sedans, & coolies & cooks &c. But the poorest
foreigners keep servants, & labor is cheap, while labor might be injurious
to their health & position. Their position is that of fairly salaried Congregational clergymen's families in our larger New Engl. towns. If they claim
to be making sacrifices, beyond such as are implied in a residence in
such places, they claim too much. Beyond what is necessarily implied in
residing in such places, a Missionary life in S. Islands, China & Japan is
no sacrifice to any but a person coming from the "upper 10,000" of society.
I speak of the missionaries of the Am. Board, the Ep. Ch., Presb. & Dutch
Refd. Churches.

[34]Samuel Robbins Brown has been noted earlier.

Met a funeral procession, with drums, gongs & all sorts of banners & devices, & four women in white, either mourners or Buddhist nuns. Streets are full of Major Fonblanque's horses, he has been buying for the Engl. army.

Went on board the Japanese hulk. It is a ship of 6 or 800 tons, built entirely by the Japanese, some 30 years ago, unfortunately from the model of a very old Dutch ship. She is laid up useless, in the present state of naval architecture. It is creditable to them, still. Now they have 5 steamers, all commanded & engineered by themselves.

The Japanese language has more vowels than the Chinese. It has, occasionally a little of the sound of the rougher Spanish. Instead of the Hwangs, Kongs, Chungs of China, they have Kenagáwa, Yokoháma,[35] Yeddo, Meto &c., & the pretty salutation of *Ohio,* & the *alingáto* for thank you.

They have the lotus here, in abundance, & the Oleander all the year. The wheat gives a deep green to the fields.

Young Talbot, of Olyphant & Co. is here.[36] Oliphant & Co. are one of the great Am. Merc. houses of China, next after Russells and Heards.[37]

The proper spelling of the city is *Yedo,* with one *d.* The Japanese scarcely sound the Y; & the d goes with the last syllable, Yé-do. The volcano is Fusi Yama, Matchless Mountain.

THURSD. APR. 19. Called on M. de Bellecour, the Fr. Consul Gen. He is a most elab. polite man. Dined & spent the ev. with Mr. Brown the Missionary. He is of the D[utch] Refd. Board, & not the A. B. C. F. M. Great variety of evergreens in their yard & garden. They call the Temple "The Evergreens", — the Japanese name is *Yobúchichi.* They have pitch pine, white pine, cedars of various kinds, ground pine, a delicate weeping pine, something resembling the hemlock, the arbor

[35]In the spelling of place names Dana often changed abruptly from phonetic to conventional spellings, presumably when he discovered the correct forms. He changes the spelling of Yokohama and Kanagawa in this fashion, though he seems not to have discovered his error in spelling Hakodati "Hakodadi."

[36]Here Dana noted: "Closed Ap. 17, to send by the Sch. Page, to S. Francisco."

[37]Here Dana inserted the following catalog of words into the text.

Japanese Words

So, yes	*San ny,* three
Ny, no	*Sii my,* four
Ohio, good day	*Go my,* five
Arlingato, thank you	*Rook my,* six
Yuroski, very well	*Stii my,* seven
Ichi, one	*Hachi my,* eight
Nii my, two	*Ku my,* nine
	To, ten

vita, the yew, the holly, juniper, savin, & the box tree, wh. grows to the
full height of a tree, with leaves like our low box. The box is used here for
hedges, & makes a thick hedge of full height. Mr. B. is a man of learning
& good sense. He is studying the Japanese, under a native teacher. Gave
me his views as to the Chinese & Jap. languages & characters. Thinks the
Chinese characters were made for the purpose of representing the word
or sound attached by usage to the thing, & that the ideographic or figura-
tive character was adopted for its fitness, convenience & ease in being
remembered. These characters being established, the *sound* of each must
be taught by tradition. Abstract ideas were represented by characters
somewhat arbitrary, & therefore purest phonetic, in principle, but often
in fact also, & somewhat ideographic, on principles of mnemonics. The
characters have now come to be substantially phonetic, & differ from
our system in this, that each character represents an entire word. The
fact that diff. provinces will recognise a character & its *idea,* & give it
diff. words & the same meaning, (as the Eur. nations will the sign V, for
five, or cinq, or fünf) is historical merely — that is, the sounds have
changed, or, the character has been taught, under a sound, like V, X, &c.
in numerals. He thinks the Japanese had no writing, until taught by the
Chinese. The Chinese teachers used their own characters for their
appropriate meanings, & taught them to the Japanese, who gave them the
Japanese sound, as the Am. missionary teaches the Kanaka to use the sign
V, & tells him he must call it *alima,* while we call it *five.* The Japanese
afterward constructed a system of letters or characters, more on the
principle of an alphabet, i.e., or rather, *syllabarium,* phonetic purely.
They adopted the basis of Chinese characters, but used only a few of
them. This is the running hand of Japan, & resembles our written style.
Then they adopted another alphabet of square characters. The former is
in chief use. The latter is used for annotations chiefly. They also use the
Chinese characters sometimes alone, & oftener interspersed with their
own. Consequently, a Japanese scholar must know three systems of
writing. A great many Chinese words are introduced, modified by the
Japanese tongue, wh. requires more vowels. They count in two sets of
words, the pure Japanese, & the Chino — Japanese. I rarely saw a Japanese
writing that was not sprinkled with Chinese characters.

The [S. R.] Browns have a piano, probably the only one in Japan. Miss
Julia Brown, the d. has pressed some leaves & flowers for Mrs. Dana, in a
book. There is a newly arrived Baptist missionary here, Goble & wife. He
was a marine in one of our vessels, & seems a dull, unlearned & unteach-
able man. He speaks Engl. so indistinctly that I cannot always understand him, & has no breeding — one of those to whom it is a social

advance to be a Missionary, & have a servant, & do no labor, & be called *Rabbi, Rabbi.* There are 2 Miss[ionar]y phys. here, with their wives — Dr. Simmons & [J. C.] Hepburn — just saw the latter a moment.

Did I mention that Wednesday, I moved over fr. Yokoháma to Kanagáwa, & am the guest of Mr. Dorr, at the Consulate, the Temple Hŏngáskugŕ? Here is a Mr. Henderson, of N. Y., who assists Dorr, & Davenport, son of Rev. Mr. D., once an Ep. clergyman, & now Irvingite,[38] — used to visit at our house. Young D. came here before the mast, & was wrecked on the coast of Japan, in the bark Nymph. He tells me the Japanese were very kind to them, treated them hospitably, sent them to Kanagawa in a junk, & stole nothing. The Jap. authorities made an inventory of everything saved fr. the vessel, even to old paint-brushes, & insisted on restoring everything acc. to the inventory, & wd. not allow them to give away, or even throw away anything — from fear of suspicions or other trouble. D. thinks it was not so much superior honesty in the common people, as fear of the Government's thoroughness & severity.

This (Th. 19th) afternoon, storm of wind & rain — very heavy. Some vessels drag at their anchors. I staid at Mr. Brown's until late. He offered me a lantern & a soldier to light & guard me home. But as I could see my way, & had my revolver & bowie knife on an outside belt, I declined both, & went to the Consulate alone. It was rather dark, & a few men were in the street. I kept the middle, with hand on pistol. When got in, both Dorr & Henderson said it was too great a risk. Dorr intended to send a guard for me. It seems the Jap. authorities have advised foreigners not to go out after dark unless with guards, armed, & with lanterns. I did not know *so* much danger was attached to it, or I should have accepted the guard. What a *bore* it must be to the Japanese, who have got on well enough by themselves for 20 centuries, to have us come in here, & be obliged to find us guards at our houses, & in the streets, & give us privileges, & yield up their customs to us!

But, how it did blow through the great trees around the Temple, to-night! Then, too, the officials came round & doubled the guard; for there were reports that a gang of bad fellows were in the neighborhood. Beside the gen. risk of robbers, it is generally believed or feared, that there are emissaries about of those princes who are hostile to foreigners, sent to make trouble with us, if they can. It is the gen. opinion that the murders of foreigners that have taken place, were by these last. Some, however, think these fears & notions groundless.

FRID. APR. 20. Beautiful, still day, warm — hot, — the bay stilled down like a lake. Very hot at noon. Japanese boys running stark naked down

[38]The unofficial name for the Catholic Apostolic Church, named after Edward Irving (1792–1834).

The last page of the last volume of the *Journal* manuscript. On September 27, 1860, Dana completed both the *Journal* and "the circumnavigation of the globe" (p. 1138).

Dana in 1879, nineteen years after the *Journal*'s completion.

Sarah Watson Dana, from a portrait painted in 1876.

"Just before sundown, reached the high rocks that overhang the Yosemite Valley — 'Inspiration Rock' &c. View of Valley beneath & Bride Veil Falls. Rocks over 2000 f. of perpend. height — bold, clear of trees, rising right from Valley" (p. 853).

"The dock into which we drew, and the streets about it, were densely crowded with express wagons and handcarts to take luggage, coaches and cabs for passengers, and with men . . . agents of the press, and a greater multitude eager for newspapers and verbal intelligence from the great Atlantic and European world. Through the crowd I made my way" (*Two Years*, "Twenty Four Years After," pp. 464–465).

John C. Frémont. "Chief topic in Mariposa Co. is 'The Col.' The Col.'s mines, & the Col.'s mill, & the Col.'s struggles the Merced Co. Half the personable men are colonels, but 'the Col.', fr. Stockton to the Sierra Nevada, is Frémont" (pp. 850–851).

Bernice Pauahi Bishop, 27 years old when Dana met her, pictured here in later life. In 1859, on a moonlit Hawaiian beach, Dana sat with the Bishops and recorded: "Funny notion that Pauwahi (Mrs. Bishop) would throw off her clothes & jump in & swim off to the reefs, into the surf. Her mother, certainly her gr. mother would have done it. She pretends she can't swim" (p. 889).

King Kamehameha IV and his Queen, Emma, about as they were during Dana's 1859 visit to the Hawaiian Islands. "The King, a tall, well made man of abt. 25, good looking, dignified & easy manners. . . . His friends say he is a true noble-man by nature" (p. 865).

The three Richard Henry Danas. "May there ever be a Richard Henry to stand before the Lord!" (p. 410).

Hilo, Hawaii. "Little town of Hilo. Streets straight, houses neat, fences neat, gardens, all shaded so thick that just see the houses. Prettiest town I have seen yet — tho' small" (p. 878).

The foreign "factories" or agencies at Canton, each flying its merchant company flag, depicted in an 1855 painting by a Chinese artist. Dana lived amidst the ruins of these agencies, which were burned in 1858 (see p. 947), at the Russell and Co. "Hong."

COMMODORE TATTNALL VISITING THE BRITISH ADMIRAL IN THE MIDDLE OF THE ACTION.—[FROM A SKETCH BY OUR OWN CORRESPONDENT.]

Josiah Tattnall (whose name is misspelled in the *Harper's* caption) "went thro' the thickest fire to visit Adm. Hope, when he heard he was wounded, & his coxwain was killed by his side" (p. 994).

Chinese cartoon depicting Western missionaries, who often adopted native costume, preaching in the streets. "We found a Missionary of the London Miss. Soc., addressing a crowd of auditors, on the folly & wickedness of their idolatry, & the necessity of worshipping the one true God. He had a considerable audience, & there was no sign of opposition or dislike" (p. 996).

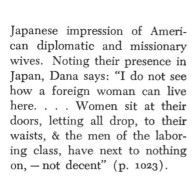

Japanese impression of American diplomatic and missionary wives. Noting their presence in Japan, Dana says: "I do not see how a foreign woman can live here. . . . Women sit at their doors, letting all drop, to their waists, & the men of the laboring class, have next to nothing on, — not decent" (p. 1023).

Sarah Watson Dana in old age, with two of her daughters, Elizabeth Ellery Dana (left) and Angela Henrietta Channing Dana.

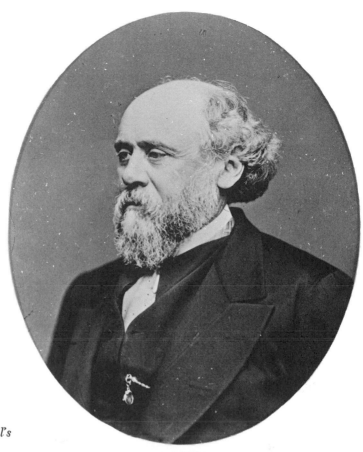

Two views of the *Journal's* author in later life.

TWO YEARS

BEFORE THE MAST.

A

PERSONAL NARRATIVE OF

LIFE AT SEA.

——— Crowded in the rank and narrow ship,—
Housed on the wild sea with wild usages,—
Whate'er in the inland dales the land conceals
Of fair and exquisite, O! nothing, nothing,
Do we behold of that in our rude voyage.
COLERIDGE'S WALLENSTEIN.

NEW-YORK:

HARPER & BROTHERS—82 CLIFF-STREET.

1840.

Title page of first edition of *Two Years Before the Mast.* "My life has been a failure compared with what I might and ought to have done. My great success — my book — was a boy's work, done before I came to the Bar" (p. *xxxii*).

the Tokaido, from their swimming — leaving their clothes at home. Women sit at their doors, letting all drop, to their waists, & the men of the laboring class, have next to nothing on, — not decent. I do not see how a foreign woman can live here. The men of the better class — soldiers, officials — wear trowsers, shoes & tunics.

The chief object of my visit here, has been to go to Yedo. It seems, Mr. Harris, our Minister, puts a strict construction upon the treaty, — that no Am. can go to Yedo unless he has business with the Embassy that cannot be conveniently transacted elsewhere. Had I known this, I could have obtained some official rank or business to bring me within the rule. As it was, I sent him my letter from Mr. [J. E.] Ward, & my request for permit to visit the city. He replied, in complimentary terms, — would make an exception in my case if he could in any, &c. &c., but must stand to his rule or admit all who applied, — wh. wd. be a violation of the treaty.

At the same time, the Br. Minister, who takes a more liberal view of the treaty, invited Messers. Dent & Webb; & the latter went to Yedo. On Harris' asking expln. fr. the Br. Minister, Alcock,[39] he said that Dent was an official at H. Kong, & Webb a Portug. Consul at Shanghai. But as neither of these offices gave them any relations or business with the Embassy, it amounts to this, — Harris admits none unless on necess. official business at Yedo, while Alcock exercises a discretion, according to the pers. claims of the applicant. The Fr. Minister does the same. Mr. H. may be right & they wrong in the course, but it places Americans at a disadvantage. I own it was rather provoking to see a mere Br. merch. going to Yedo, & an Am. gentleman, travelling for information, shut out, when that merchant at home could no more approach the Society I visit in England than he could read Greek. The Fr. Minister, Bellecour, to whom I bore a despatch fr. the Fr. Legation, was unfortunately at Kanagawa, & I did not feel at liberty to keep it back until he should go to Yedo. M. de Bellecour deprecated Harris' construction, & said if I were not a citisen of a country wh. had an embassador at Yedo, he would give me a permit. To wh. I replied that this was the first time I had ever felt inconvenience fr. being an Am. citisen. The Americans here seemed mortified at the result, & Dorr talked large & did nothing.

Crossed to Yokohama, to do [a] little shopping. Young man, named Richards, fr. Roxbury, Mass., who speaks Jap. a little & knows the habits of the people & the value of their goods, went round with me. The shops are neatness itself, the floors covered with white mats, & every

[39]Sir Rutherford Alcock (1808–1897), British diplomat, went to the Orient in 1844. He was appointed first Consul-General to Japan in 1858. He was Minister Plenipotentiary at Peking, 1865–1871.

table & shelf looking as if it were lacquered or veneered. The Jap. take off their sandals at the doors of their houses. At shops, there is usually a row of sandals at the door, standing like carriages at a fash. shop in London. Bought a small cabinet of rattan inlaid & silver, lacquered, — intended as a present to Miss Porter, — ½ dos. vermillion tea cups & saucers, & a piece of silk for a thin coat, & a *puckeny-Japonica,* as I call it, — a hat turban for hot weather. Dr. Hall made me several presents, — wh. I value highly — a Japanese official sword, with its little *hari kari* dagger attached, & a Jap. dagger with white shark's skin handle, two inlaid card cases (one for Mrs. Dana) & ½ dos. vermillion tea cups & saucers of child's sise, for one of my daughters. Mr. Dorr was profuse in his presents, so that I had to stop him. He has given me a gold *koban,* about 200 years old, of an intrinsic value of about $4.85, 2 gold *ichibus,* worth about $2 apiece, 3 or 4 little pieces of carved figures, — the Dragon of Japan &c. &c., & 2 crystals, & one large piece of unwrought crystal, & a gold charm (essence bottle), & a beaten out koban, for a clasp. Mr. Dent has given me — very old ⅓ koban, gold.

While shopping, saw the Governor of Yokohama go by, in his box. He was preceeded & followed by guards with lances & swords, & all the people dropped on their knees & bowed their foreheads to the ground, as he passed. This is always done for great officials. For the lesser, the people bow low as they walk. Henderson tells me he saw the Prince of Satsuma go thro' Kanagáwa, on his way to Yedo, with a train of fr. 4 to 6000 persons, soldiers, civil & mil. officers, & servants. This is the usual retinue of the daimios, or great princes, when they travel in state.

The Jap. have built 2 moles in the harbor, for the accomn. of the foreign commerce, entirely of their own engineering, wh. look well, & are said to be very strong.

The horses are usually shod with shoes of straw. The people, — especially women, in wet weather, wear clogs — pieces of board, raised 2 or 3 inches by blocks, & fastened round the naked foot by straw thongs. On these, they get over the ground fast. Sometimes I have turned round thinking a horse was coming upon me, & found it a girl on a fast run. The upper classes have ornamented clogs. Before the mole, the Jap. have driven piles, to keep off the heavy seas, but it is said that the worms eat up a pile in a year. This is a pity, as this port, Yokohama-Kanagawa, is a mere open roadstead, & the mole exposed to typhoons.

Tho' the Japanese have a literature, & a large proportion of the people know how to read, yet they are by no means as literary as the Chinese. I saw few or no mottoes, proverbs & quotations, inscribed on their doors & walls.

By the rule, foreigners change dollars here daily at the Co. Hs. into ichibus, fr. 10 to $15 a day. This gives a profit to the changer of 20%.

My host made about $3 a day on my name, as I did not use the ichibus. This is a gratifn. to a visitor, to be sure that he costs nothing.

Dined with Dorr. Thunder storm. Cleared up by 10 o'ck. P.M., & as we start at 4 A.M., must go on board to-night. We went down in a grand procession, 2 large Jap. lanterns in front, & 2 behind, each painted with the stars & stripes, & ½ dos. soldiers with 2 swords each, & Dorr & I, arm in arm, & 2 more Americans, all with revolvers, — thro' the great st., to the Consular boat, & off in the boat with our lanterns & men, to the steamer.

SATURDAY. APR. 21. Steamer Yang Tse, at sea, off entrance of Yedo Bay. Fusi Yama (Matchless, Mountain) in plain sight, early this morning, — its huge cone of snow piercing the sky. The coast to the N. of Yedo Bay is rather more rugged than at the Southland, yet it is green, among the hills. The countless boats! And we are 10 to 20 miles fr. the coast!

SUND. AP. 22. Capt. Dearborn says the Engl. chart is as bad to the Nd. as to Sd. of Yedo. A large bay is omitted, & a headland is 30 miles too far out at sea. Last night, at 2 A. M., Capt. D. saw a ledge of rocks, with breakers, nearly a-head, abt. ½ m. off, we being 50 miles from the land. This is down on no chart. Perry's Chart, true as far as it goes, is professedly imperfect & partial. No regular survey has ever been made of the coast.

Mem. The Jap. officers on guard at the Am. Consul's temple, take down a note of ev. person who goes in or out.

Sin Syn is the ancient Jap. faith, & *sintoo* is the name given to the believers. The spiritual emperor, the Mikado, is believed to be of divine descent. The temporal Emperor, Tycoon, was first a civil & mil. chief under the Mikado, but is now the real head of affairs.[40]

The Fr. priest at Yedo is not, as I said, a bishop, but only an abbe. The dogs are numerous in Jap. villages, with wolf heads, bark much, cowardly, sometimes bite the heels, — Oliphant thinks them handsome — I do not. The Japanese build fire-proof houses of a kind of clay, wh. they lay on the walls to the thickness of 2 & 3 feet, the walls being furred out, interlaced with lines of rope. This process requires long time for hardening, but answers its purpose. The Europeans have their store-houses built in this way. Country too volcanic, too much danger of earthquake for brick or stone.

On board the Yang Tse, the officers give orders in Malay — as all the crew are Malays, & the Europ. & Am. officers here soon learn it. It seems full of r's & vowels.

[40]Dana has misspelled "Shinto" here. Indeed, a great many of his spellings in this section are phonetic, but they have been changed only where the original might be misleading. In Japanese, *taikun* literally means "great lord." Tycoon was an incorrect title applied to the shogun of Japan to impress foreigners.

MOND. AP. 23, 1860. Made the mouth of the Straits of Sangar, wh. lie betw. Nipon & Yeso, & in the ev. are at anchor in Hakodadi. The hills are covered with snow at the tops, & patches of snow lie about them, almost to the foot. It is weather for over-coats & thick gloves. No small change in 3 days!

Hakodadi lies on a peninsula, & has a good, landlocked harbor, but so wide as to give great range to the Northerly winds, making holding a little insecure. The peninsula is hilly, one peak being about 1000 f. high. There are small groves of firs & pines, but trees are scarce, — cut down, I fancy, for firewood, as coal is scarce, & the weather cold. The town lies at the foot & on the lower slope of the hills.

Three Jap. officials come off, two-sworded men, & sit in the cabin & take notes of name & tonnage of the steamer, departure, objects &c. Polite in their manner. One speaks Engl. intelligibly. Drink a good deal of Curacoa. Leave an inf[erior] officer on board, who first makes an effort to get quarters in the cabin, but subsides into the steerage, & then diplomatises for a seat at our table, but acquieces in his fate.

TUESD. AP. 24. Landed. The town is like Kanagawa. Streets of fair width, clear eno', & pretty well watered, — wh. is done by pails & dippers. Great many shops. I believe everybody in China & Japan keeps a shop, & they live by buying fr. each other. Lacquers, carvings, & other *curios* for sale, but inferior. Small sweet oranges, with loose skins, large acid oranges, large tasteless pears, dried persimmons, & all kinds of confectionary & cakes, but rather for poorer people.

Called on the Am. Consul, a huge man, named Rice, 6 f. 5 & covered with hair, a loud talker. Has no salary, & not much in fees, & is also a merchant. This is wrong in our Govt. A Consul shd. never be a merchant, for 2 reasons — 1st he becomes often a party in questions submitted to him, & 2d he has advantages over other merchants, by knowl. of their affairs officially derived. In Japan, there is a 3d reason, — that merchants are looked down upon, as an inferior class.

Call on Capt. Fletcher, I believe the only other Am. here. His wife is here, an intelligent English woman. F. is a merchant here. Mrs. F. likes the Japanese — says she has some most faithful & intellig. servants fr. among them. (Her story of her servant who took a wife on trial, in case *Mrs. F.* liked her, — otherwise to be returned). Met there, a Mrs. Grinnell, wife of a whaling Capt., a delicate, pleasant woman, who has been two Arctic seasons in the ship, & is going a third. She had met some of the whaling madams who were at Hilo, & heard of our Bridge accident.[41]

[41]Mrs. Grinnell was probably married to a younger son of the well-known New Bedford whaling family of Cornelius G. and Henry G. Grinnell. She is recalling the accident at Hilo, detailed in the *Journal*, when a suspension bridge collapsed while Dana and a party of friends were crossing it.

She had spent a season at Hilo, knew the [D. B.] Lymans, [Titus] Coans, Austins, &c. At the Am. Consuls', met some ½ dos. whaling masters, all of whom knew of my having been at the Islands, the Mastiff, & bridge accidents &c., & were very attentive to me, & desirous to talk & make my acquaintance.

There are, in port, 8 Am. whaleships, 1 Am. merchant ship, 1 Russian war steamer, 2 Japanese war schooners, & the Yang Tse. The schooners were built by the Japanese, & are well modelled, well looking vessels, like our Baltimore Clippers.

Called on the Abbé Mermet, the only R. Cath. missionary in Japan, except the Abbé Girard at Yedo. He is a young man, with intellig. countenance & very agreeable manners — thoroughly polite. Tells me he is not allowed to preach or teach. His mission is to learn the language, history, religions &c. of Japan, & to make acquaintances & remove prejudices. He is very popular with the natives as well as foreigners, & is thought to have influence with the authorities. His quarters are very plain & poor, — bitter cold, he says, in winter, but how the presence of one man of intellect, culture & high breeding, illumines a humble room! He is of the Mission Etrangère, a French order. He tells me there are no memorials or relics of the ancient Christians in Japan — utter extinction of everything, not even a sign to denote a sacred spot. Hakodadi was never a seat of missions. This island, Yeso, is a conquest of the Japanese (Niponese), from the Ainoes, or wild hairy men, — a few of whom still live in the remote parts, tributaries, — whom the Japanese, in their pictures, represent as being as hairy as baboons. Mermet tells me that the bridge wh. connected the Decima with the city of Nagasaki had the cross inlaid in it, & the Dutch were obliged to step upon the Cross whenever they passed, & when the later Europeans came, & went round it, the Jap. said — "See, they are not Dutch" — ("Hollander" is the Jap. word). By the way, everywhere in Japan they distinguish Am. fr. Engl., & as soon as they hear us speak, even in the little shops, they ask if "Americani" or "Ingelesi". Our flag is the favorite in Japan.

At Mermet's met a young Japanese, who is son of one of the physicians of the Tycoon. He speaks English well, & French pretty well. His uncle & brother are in the Embassy to America. It is hard to conceive of a gentleman without linen — but all the Japanese, of whatever rank, wear the cotton or dark silk wrappers about their bodies, with open necks, & no relief. The Chinese wear no linen or cotton, but have a kind of collar of blue silk, that is some relief. Imagine a swarthy man, just coming fr. a bath, with only pantaloons & a dark cotton wrapper, & you have the middle class of Japanese. Ditto, without the pantaloons, is the laboring man, in cool weather; & with neither, is the laborer in hot weather.

Heard the dull, stern beating of a gong, & followed it into a small temple. The priest on his knees, before the shrine, is beating the gong & chanting the same 3 or 4 words, over & over, & the worshipper, a woman, who has paid for the performance, is kneeling there too, rubbing the palms of her hands together, swaying her body a little, occasionally touches her forehead to the floor, & telling the beads on her rosary, a bead at each repitition of the words by the priest, who is tired, & looks out the corner of his eye to see if she is near the end of her string. Mrs. Fletcher tells me that the Jap. women are frequent & regular in their attendance at the temples, at the morning service, which is soon after dawn. Little idols & rosaries & incense sticks are for sale in the shops, — the rosaries of stone, crystal or carved wood. There are no signs of decay, neglect or disorder in the Japanese temples.

The Jap. Govt. is building a fort here. The masonry is very well done, to my eye, & so say others. They are their own engineers. (The war steamer they have sent to California is navigated by themselves).

Where we landed, this morning, at the Custom Hs., in a small enclosure, was an affecting sight. The little enclosure was fairly floored over with the bodies of supplicants, on their knees, with foreheads to the earth, before the Magistrate, who sat within the door, waiting their turn to be examined & receive permits, either to journey or to sojourn here, I forget which. But the bending attitude before the Magistrate is not so significant here as it would at first seem, for polite men bend to each other, almost to the ground, in meeting in the street, & quite so in their houses. And all servants & laboring men do so, in coming into the houses of their employers.

WED. APR. 25. Ashore at 6 A. M. Called on Mermet. He has finished his private mass & prayers, in his little chapel — (open to foreigners on Sundays) & is ready to see me. I told him how Bishop Boone proceeded, & he says that is the way the Catholics have always done, on principle; & intimated that B. Boone's course was a violation of the Prot. principle. Take tea & toast with him.

Worshippers coming fr. the temples, & sound of dull gongs. After a breakfast on board, walk, alone, to the summit of the Peak. Enjoyment of a lonely walk in the country, to a man who has been long on ship board! Always found it so, in Cal. & elsewhere. View good — rather desolate, the foggy ocean & the rugged peninsula. On the way up & down the Peak, in little hollows, & where the paths meet, are little shrines, with carved figures, on slabs of stone, — as in the times of the "Ages of Faith" in Europe, & they are as well covered with inscriptions & votive offerings. Beside the Shrines, there are sev. little temples, wh. have signs of being in use. One seemed to be for mariners, as it was plastered with pictures of ships in various conditions of peril. I wanted to take one away, but thought some poor devil might miss his offering & think himself coming to grief. Stopped & ate snow, in the hollows. Counted the vessels at anchor in the Bay — 180 junks, 10 Am. Ships, 1 Am. steamer, 1 Russian war steamer, & 2 Jap. war schooners.

On the side of the hill are superficial quarries of rock, wh. they are getting out to build the fort. Stopped & talked with the laborers — or rather tried signs with them — with more or less success. They all seemed polite & pleasant. Even these common laborers could read & write, & one got out his paper (wh. ev. man seems to carry in his bosom) & wished me to write my name on it. Pipe & pouch, paper, pen & ink stone, almost ev. man carries on his person.

At the foot of the hill, is the Russian Consul's new house, built of the mud walls, in the native fashion, colored on the surface. It is a large & handsome house, designed by the Russians, but built by Japanese.

Walking thro' the streets, heard noise of children in school, followed the sound, & came to a humble little house, in the porch of wh. was a collection of sandals, straw & wood, & inside some 40 boys, fr. 6 to 10 years of age, sitting on benches at little tables, each with a book before him, swaying their bodies to & fro, & all reading or repeating at the very top of their voices, making a horrid din, in this little, dark low-roofed room. The grave old teacher sat in the midst, keeping a good eye over them. Here, as in China, the boys study aloud, & the reason is said to be that the teacher may hear the sounds they give to the characters, — for a character does not indicate its sound, but the sound must be taught. As the teacher & I had no language in common, I learned nothing fr. him. The boys looked very lively & happy — a contrast with the stupor of an 8 year old school, when I was of that age.

I fully agree with the Japanese travellers in their opinion of the cheerfulness & happiness of the children. It is obvious. They sing as they go along in the streets, sometimes 3 or 4 hand in hand, & the discipline seems easy. Parents seem to be affectionate & equable with them, & so their elder sisters, who lug them on their backs. Saw two little girls, some 5 years old, sitting on a bench, before a door — & singing & beating sticks in time. They looked so pretty & good that I gave them a silver ishu, (worth about 8 cents) — a fortune to them. They bowed their little foreheads to the bench, in adoration, & would not raise them up until I was out of sight.

The roofs are mostly covered with stones, to keep them steady in the high winds. Mr. Rice, the Consul, gave me 2 silver coins, which will soon be rare. They were issued by the Jap. Govt. 8 July 1859, to pass for a half dollar each, being actually of that weight. They were stamped with characters signifying that they were for use in dealings betw. foreigners & natives. The Am. & Br. Ministers repudiated them, & the coinage is stopped. It was called 2 ishu, or ½ itsibu.

THURSD. APR. 26.   Sailed fr. Hakodadi, at day-break, through the Straits of Sangar, & at 8 o'ck. were out in the Japan sea. So we shall circumnavigate Nipon.

We take on board a new passenger, a Dr. Lindau, a Prussian, by birth, & a Swiss Comm. envoy who has been sev. months in Japan, & collected a good deal of information.[42] His great treasure is a duplicate of the colored drawings of the birds, reptiles, insects & flowers of Japan, made by the celebrated Japanese savant, Dr. Kusimoto Tzuiken, the chief physician to the Tycoon. This morning, he exhibited them to us, on the cabin table. I was amased. They are as good as Audubon, possibly better. I do not see how they could be exceeded. They are all done by hand, & copied. Kusimoto Tzuiken has let Dr. Lindau have them for the purpose of getting them published in Europe, under his name, for the honor he expects to gain by it.[43] Dr. L. is to have the credit of the scientific arrangement, wh. the Jap. Dr. cannot make. The attitudes of the birds are full of spirit, & every *hair* is painted. The silver hues are so well given that they seem to quiver in the air. The insects are done with exquisite taste & finish. The pencil is as fine as the cobweb. They interested & pleased me more than anything of the kind I ever saw before. These people are not to be treated as uncivilised, when, unknown to the world, unaided, uninfluenced fr. abroad, they produce such works.

Dr. L. says the college at Yedo has faculties of med. & belles lettres, & gives degrees, as in China, & that a kn. of reading & writing is almost universal.

At Hakodadi there are several jorogas, as at the other places we have visited, but having seen fair specimens at the Gangero of Yokohama, I did not care to enter them. They looked neat without, & one was the largest & best looking private house in the town. This is said to be a Govt. affair, & the Am. Consul told me that one of the Govt. officials came to him to ask him to remove the prohibition upon Am. seamen coming on shore after dark, as it diminished the receipts of the joroga.

In sev. houses in Hakodadi I noticed that certain places wh. with us are in the rear are here at the front door, just inside, & open.

Great complaints are made here & at Kanagawa of the conduct of the officers of the Mississippi & Powhatan, in trading & taking adv. of their position to speculate in itsebus. It is said that they took up itsebus, under

[42]Rudolph Lindau, diplomat and writer, traveled in the Orient and America, 1860–1870.

[43]The drawings seem never to have been published.

the Cu. Hs. privilege, so largely that the merchants could not get enough for their purposes. They took them up by the thousands, & some officers are said to have made sev. thousands of dollars by it. They also bought up large quantities of articles, as mdse., to sell in China, turning the ships into mere traders, & having no freight, duties or commissions to pay, could undersell the merchants.

The Japanese use wood cuts, & it is said, have begun to engrave on copper plates.

SAT. AP. 29. Last night, being 30 miles off by our reckoning, came near running upon an island of the Oke group, a current having set us 30 miles to the S. E., in 15 hours. The bright look out always kept here, saved us. Capt. D[earborn] had been told that the current here was the other way. Perhaps it is changeable.

> I'm on the sea. I'm on the Sea,
> I am where I would ever be![44]

No quite so — but the abundance of fresh air & exercise, the regularity of hours, the simplicity of food, the abundance of sleep, & the freedom from cares & duties have great value & charm.

[44]Lines from "The Sea," by Bryan Waller Procter (1787–1874).

6. China Again

MOND. AP. 30. Coast of China in sight, off mouth of Yang Tse Kiang. Shall be in Shanghai to-night. Had a most delightful voyage, successful throughout — & seen all in an unprecedentedly short time. Mr. Dent refuses all compensation. It is his party of pleasure — I mean Dent & Co.'s.

(Contrast betw. the steamers that steer forward & those that steer aft. The quiet, order & watchfulness of this vessel. Excellent sea-boat. Excellent qualities of Capt. Dearborn.)

Yellow water of the Yang Tse' Kiang, far out at sea. Light ship. At Woonsung, the French fleet. The Renommée, Vice Admiral's, & a rear admiral, & the Entreprenante, 80 guns, full of troops, la vivandière, looking over the rail. At anchor, in Shanghai, before dark. Mr. Grew kindly comes on board, to see me ashore. All inquire for news. The *ultimatum* of the Allies is refused, & preparations for an attack at the Peiho. The Br. have taken possession of Chusan, & all their troops & ships (except the Furious) are there. Lord Elgin & Baron Gros are to come out by next steamer. Yet, so anomalous is this war, that whole regiments of coolies are hired as laborers, & on the other side, Br. & Fr. ships pay duties here, & they are still collected by the Treaty Powers, on the Emperor's acct.

Here I am, again, in my sumptuous rooms, at Russell & Co.'s, with all my luggage safe & in its old places, my bed, my books, a good fire (for it is cool at night) & a file of Boston papers, & tea, & so many kind & attentive friends, & myself brot back in life & health, after a delightful & instructive voyage to a new Empire! If one has not a heart of stone, here is a time & place for gratitude! And, I felt it, when I sat down in my chair, & looked about me & reflected.

WED. MAY 2. Called on Bruce. He has very handsome eyes. Professes to think his brother's superceding him is good policy.[45] Then, to M. & Mde. de Bourbulon. M. is evidently annoyed by being superceded by Baron Gros. Met there Genl. [C. A.] Montauban, Com. in Chief of the Fr. army in China. (Conversation about the horses the Fr. have imported fr.

[45]The Honorable Robert Bruce had been replaced by his brother, Lord Elgin, as the British official empowered to ratify the treaty of 1858. As noted earlier, Bruce had bungled the job of ratification, and Lord Elgin and Baron Gros were in China to force the ratification through. The remarks that Dana makes about the progress of their efforts, which in fact were a military advance upon Peking, refer to the systematic encircling of the Chinese forces and the eventual capitulation of the Emperor to the Allied demands.

Japan, & the General's curious question thro' M. de B.). Then, called on [T. T.] Meadows & [T. F.] Wade, the Chinese scholars, & on Dent & Dearborn & Webb & Ashton. (Gilman & Co. is *Tay Ping*, or Lasting Peace. Russell & Co. is *Ki Chong*, or Long Flag).

THURSD. MAY. 3. Mr. Grew drove me to the Races. Horses all owned & ridden by the Engl. here, & no jockeys allowed. One good run betw. Cammabert & Cheerful. The white top boots & small clothes are a becoming dress — manly.

Tea with Rev. Mr. Lyle, Smith & wife, Dr. & Mrs. ——. Most of them been in Boston, & had good Boston talk, for a change.

FRID. MAY. 4. Dined with Bishop Boone. He says Chinese eating rats is very rare, & denied by them. He never, in 17 years, known a case. The man in the street, with rats on his pole, & bell, is not selling them, but they are his sign as a *rat-killer*. This has misled foreigners. So, as to dogs. Very rare. Doubts Cushing's "bow-wow" story. Severe on Bayard Taylor's book on China.[46] Thinks him prejudiced & ignorant of the subject — *full* of mistakes.

SAT. MAY. 5. Walk to Ti Ka Wei, about 6 miles out. Priest receives us kindly, on my letter of introduction. Here are 94 pupils, boys, all Chinese, & children of Xn. [Christian] parents. There are three priests now, 2 French & 1 Italian, & several Chinese teachers. One room for drawing, painting & sculpture, & sev. youths at work. Another for music. In that was a choir of a piano, violin, base viol, clarionet, 2 flutes & nine voices — performing a Kyrie Eleison, & very creditably. Rooms neat. Gardens & play-grounds. Boys are taught Chinese literature, with our sciences, history &c. No attempt to Europeanise them, but to be educated as *Chinese* Christians. The priests dress in Chinese costume. Gave us (Grew was my companion) a tiffin of cake, dried fruit & claret wine. Large chapel, dressed with flowers, for May, in honor of La Sainte Vierge. Return thro' the city.

Dinner at Ashton's. Present, Dr. Lindau, Meadows, Compton (Ed. of North China Herald) & al. All in best style. Each guest, as it is raining, comes in his sedan, & all the coolies wait at the house until we are ready to return, — 3 or 4 hours — & take us home with lanterns.

Omitted to mention that on our way fr. Ti Ka Wei, we stopped at a small obelisk, wh. is called the "Baby Tower" by foreigners. Said that

[46]Bayard Taylor, as Dana has mentioned earlier, accompanied M. C. Perry on his voyage to Japan in 1853–1854, which originally established the treaty with Japan. Taylor recorded his experiences in *A Visit to India, China, and Japan, in the Year 1853* (New York, 1855). The "bow-wow" story, presumably told by Caleb Cushing, probably concerns the popular belief that the Chinese ate dog meat.

Chinese throw into it their living female infants, when they want to be rid of them. *Quien Sabe?*

SUND. MAY 6. At the Fr[ench] Chapel at 9 A. M. Fr. & Engl. soldiers & Chinese. Mass for Br[itish] at 9 & for Fr. at 10. Genl. Montauban & brilliant staff present. Sermon to the Br. soldiers. At 11, to the Engl. Church, where we had sermon & Communion. Start to-night for Suchau [Suchow].

Having a few hours of leisure before dark, strolled off into the city, alone. Enjoyed my stroll, stopping at shops, buying a few cakes &c. to taste their street cookery. Passed Gen. Montauban & his 2d in command, also on a stroll. Passed near a temple, & hearing a noise & seeing a crowd, went in. A play going on. Dense crowd in the area, & 2 galleries, one for men & one for women — so different from the indiscriminate Japanese huddle. Wished to get into the gallery, wh. seemed to be reserved for select persons, & went into rear of the temple, behind the idol, to a side door. Keeper, an old bonze, shut it against me, but opening it to let out a person, I went in, & he consented to show me up — all this by signs. So, I got a front seat in the gallery.

Actors all men, & mostly bonzes. Two dressed as women — for women never play in public here. Of the characters, one seemed to be an absurd pompous magistrate, & one was the fun-maker, who made dum show to the audience, ridiculing the others. After the play was over, I went to the door leading behind the scenes, &, by quiet perseverance & bowing, succeeded in getting in, & saw the actors undress, & wash off paint. They were civil & amused.

The audience never clap or stamp or cheer. Nor did I hear them cry out at all. Except by laughing, they give no audible approval.

Trip to Suchau.[47] Started from Shanghai this ev., May 6th, on an expedition, by boat, to Suchau, — the famous city — the "Paris of China". Doubtful if any foreigners will be admitted now, as late visitors have been refused; but, if not, the trip will show me the interior of China. We have three boats, one for cooks & chow-chow, & 2 for passengers. Mr. Walsh & Dr. Lindau in one, Rev. Messers. Lyle & Smith & I in the other. And a beautiful start off we have! Full moon, fair tide, clear sky & exquisite weather. The river, the bridges, the gliding boats give it a fairy-like air.

At the first bridge is a gate, & there was a characteristic row of Chinese officials, wh. ended in our giving a few cash for leave to pass. Stay up until 11 o'ck., delighted with our voyaging.

[47]Dana prepared this section of the *Journal* — the excursion on the canal — for publication. It appeared posthumously as "A Voyage on the Grand Canal of China," *Atlantic Monthly*, 67: 482–496 (May, 1891).

Our boats have settees, on wh. we sleep, & tables, book-racks & other conveniences, & we are entirely comfortable. Each boat has a crew of six boat-men, a boy to wait on each of us, & a cook & butler.

MAY 7TH. Settled our regime — to rise early & take tea & toast, & walk until breakfast, wh. is to be at 9. Dinner at 4. Betw. br. & dinner, keep under cover. Walk again towards evening. The walk this morning was very interesting, along the track path, through little villages, stopping at temples, under groves of trees, & amid the fields of wheat, rice & vegetables wh. mark the endless industry of this people. Verily, there is no end to it. Every square foot is under cultivation, & laborers are everywhere. How the manuring is attended to! They dig up the mud & other sediment fr. the rivers, place it in pits, add all they can get to it, to make a compost, & cover their lands, wh. in this way give two crops a year, one of wheat & one of rice. They fish the mud up fr. the river by a machine wh. one man works, on the principle of a pair of snuffers.

At almost every house people are weaving cotton cloth, sometimes indoors, by a small loom, & sometimes in the open air, on warps nearly as long as a rope walk. Numerous little pits, in wh. they make indigo. The frequent little tributaries compel us to walk back into the country, to find bridges, wh. we always find not far off — & always of stone, neatly arched. All the bridges across the Suchau Creek are of stone, neatly built, high & arched. That at Wang Du, is the largest we have yet seen. A few pagodas in sight, & groups of small gates or arches, to the honor of persons who have been noted for virtue, especially to young widows who have refused remarriage.

Pass the bridge of the "Literary Star". Most of these bridges are segments of circles, say 220 degrees. No windmills in China, so far as I can learn.

Hill & city of Ksohun San. Passed the city & hill of Khsoun San. Pagoda on hill, in centre of city.

TUESD. MAY 8. Early this morning, reached the city of Su Chau [Suchow]. For sev. hours, we passed along the suburbs, & halted at the great gate, & made the boats fast, & had our conference as to how we should assault the city. One plan was to take chairs, close them up, & go by the gate unseen. Another was, to try to take our boats thro' the water-gate, keeping in the cabins. But came to conclusion to try the open course of presenting ourselves at the gate. At the gate Zi Mung, 2 or 3 mandarins came out & we were stopped, & a crowd soon gathered. Mr. Lyle, who is interpreter & cicerone, got into a conference with the head officer, wh. resulted in our being invited into the office. Here we were ceremoniously seated, & general conversation began. The chief politely, with smiles & bows, inquires the ages, names & occupations of each, & writes them down. How Chinese was the scene! As ceremonious & dignified as the Chinese officials are, yet the people crowd in & take part in everything. We had some friends among them. The official said — "No. Very sorry. Fixed rule. No foreigners could be admitted". Mr. Lyle knew eno', & we had read eno', of Chinese character, to be quiet & persevering. We kept our seats, talked, spoke of the great reputation of the city, our desire to see it, our disappointment &c., & at last the official confers, & says the rule is strict, but admits of one exception. If a *few* foreigners, 5 or 6, come *early in the morning*, before great crowd assembles, the officer has a discretion to let them in. We say we will take a soldier, who can keep us out of trouble &c., & pay for him. "Oh, No. You are welcome to two soldiers, & no pay". So, two rather forlorn soldiers, with white badges on their breast, go, one before & one behind us, instructed to show the great places to the distinguished foreigners, & we take a ceremonious leave, with great bowings & tsing-tsingings, & go on our way.

Su Chau is much like the cleaner parts of Canton & Shanghai. We were early, & the streets were not so thronged as I have usually seen them in those cities. Our first visit is to an old, dim, smoky pagoda-built temple, dedicated to Sau Tsing, the Three Pure Ones. It is 4 or 5 stories in height, each with its idols, shrines & tapers. One great idol has the name of Shang Ti, wh. Mr. Lyle tells me the first Protestant translations of the Scriptures unfortunately adopted for God, very much as if the Evangelists had taken Zeus (Jupiter), from the Greeks.

Next visit is to the famous Nine Storied Pagoda. All the way, we are followed by a crowd of hundreds of men & boys, & as we go thro' the narrow streets, all come to their windows & doors to stare at us. A foreigner is a rare sight in Su Chau, most of the people have never seen one, & now, foreigners have no right here, & are only admitted by special courtesy. But at the Pagoda, the crowd must stop; for we pay $2 for our admission, & we do not choose to invite the crowd. (But, in the Temple, there is no exclusion, & they pressed on our heels even up to the feet of the idols, & saw our familiar way of tapping them with our canes, without objection. Indeed, the crowd, tho' intensely curious, was civil & well deported).

The pagoda is in good repair. Each story has its gallery entire, on wh. we can walk, & wooden stairs lead fr. story to story, inside. The upper story gives us the view of the great city & suburbs. Su Chau is said to contain two millions of people. The suburbs are very large, & the walls on one side enclose large spaces of unoccupied land, some of wh. is used for wheat, & none of it arranged for pleasure grounds or walks for the people, — mere wastes. On the walls, — wh. are high, in good repair &

moated, & in places ivy grown, are numerous banners & a few soldiers. Name of Pagoda is Vok Tss' Tah, — (*tah* is pagoda, *Vok,* divining, &c., *Tss'* monastery).

The Chinese are not free fr. our vanity of writing names on walls, & the stories of the pagoda are covered over with names & sentiments. Visit the institution for the poor. It is not a house, but streets of small houses, all within a wall, & all under rule. There are 900 paupers here. They live 4, 8 or 10 in each small house. It is a public charity. Not clean, bad smells, no drainage, & very little care. The paupers seem to take care of their own houses. Saw among them sev. cases of ophthalmia & elephantiasis.

Return to our boats to breakfast. We pay our guides a reasonable sum, & immediately the officer appears, looking very grave & distressed, & asks how we could think of giving them money, & begs us to take it back, — but Mr. L. thinks it will do if we apologise & leave it with them, wh. we do, & then come the bowings, & smiles & wishes for good voyage.

After breakfast, walk thro' the great Northern suburb, built on the Grand Canal of China. This is beautiful. The canal is wide, lined with trees, good houses, pretty shops, & open spaces behind walls, indicating residences of wealthy people. The bridges are stately, & always of stone, usually with arches, most of wh. are more than half circles, & canals run across the main canal, making a Chinese Venice of this city. A long line of people follow us along the bank, as we drop down the canal, exhibiting ourselves sitting in chairs on the front of our boats, the Am. ensign floating fr. the masthead, & each bridge is covered with gasers.

Now we get out & walk among the shops. A crowd presses on us all the time, but almost always civil. A few cases of bad words to us, but when Mr. L. turns & rebukes them gently, the crowd takes his part. We do some shopping, & I buy a box of Japanese dominoes for 80 cash, — 8 cents. The most attractive are the flower shops wh. are very numerous, & filled with beautif. flowers in pots, & dwarfed trees. In most cases, we are invited to the gardens in the rear, where these flowers are growing. Graffing is in high fashion. We buy some flowers, cheap eno', — I mean plants in pots, to ornament our boat. The great number of these flower shops indicates a good taste among the people.

Lastly we visit the celebrated pagoda & pleasure grounds of Hu Chau Tah. (*Hu Chau,* is Tiger district, & *tah* is pagoda). The Pagoda is on a hill, & the grounds are made up of artificial piles of rocks, groves & lines of trees, plateaus of smooth rocks, stairs in rocks, roofs for shade, groups of flowers &c., &, at frequent intervals, houses for refreshment. In one of these, wh. looks out over the whole city of Su Chau & the country for miles about it, we took a refreshment of tea, cakes & confectionary, &

bought out a confectioners' entire waiter full for .75 cents, & distributed it among the boys that had followed us.

These grounds are the favorite resort, day & night, of the people of leisure in Su Chau, & Su Chau is said to have more such people than any city of China.

In the pagoda, in a dim room, among grim idols, was a school of some 30 or 40 boys, reading at the tops of their voices, under the usual half starved, disappointed looking teacher, — the disappointee of a dosen examinations for degrees.

Returned to our boats to late dinner, after a day of great interest & pleasure, — with the triumph of entering Su Chau, fr. wh. nearly all foreigners are excluded, & into which none entered before 1857.

After dinner, we sit out on the deck, in chairs, smoking & talking, & looking at the never ending varieties of boats, bridges, towns, gasing people, evening lanterns, & lighted houses.

At about 9 o'ck., we reach a gate wh. shuts across the Grand Canal, & blocks all progress after dark. Here is another case for diplomacy. Mr. Lyle & I go ashore, & seek out the Custom House, presenting ourselves, on our way, before the astonished eyes of the *sanctum sanctorum* Chinamen, at the counters of their quiet shops, at this late hour, in a central city of China. Here, at the Custom Hs. we meet the chief official, who has charge of the gate, & assures us that no boats can pass after it is closed for the night. There is something interesting in the appearance of this gentleman, for *gentleman* he was, if ever there was one. He is young, say 2 or 3 & 20, with a countenance of great intelligence, frankness & gentleness, with every appearance of integrity, & a charm of manner, wh. wd. have carried off the prise in a competitive exn. of manners, I doubt not.

The refusal being positive, there is nothing to do but to sit down quietly, & wait for a change of policy. So, we seated ourselves, & Mr. Lyle had a gen. convn. on topics of interest, & our friend inquired about Dr. Hobson's work on anatomy,[48] wh. has been translated into Chinese, & for other books of history & geography, some of wh. he possessed. He had spent sev. dollars in buying our books, & Mr. Lyle offered to get him others. We then invited him on board our boat, & as he accepted the invitation, we had hopes. In our little cabin we offered him cigars & wine. He tasted the wine, but politely intimated that he was not strong eno' to drink such wine, & smoked only a part of the cigar. At length, signs of concession appeared, & soon the order was given to open the gate. Mr. Lyle asked him to distribute some money among the men who had been set to work at this unusual hour, — wh. was as near to an offer of money

[48]The reference could be to Hugh Lenox Hobson (1796–1873), who wrote several works on anatomy.

as Mr. L. liked to go. His refusal was a master-piece. It could not have been better done. It was deprecatory. It seemed to say, — *how could you think of money?* He looked hurt, yet superior, & waved it off, & gently placed his hand on Mr. Lyle's shoulder to seat him again, & passed directly to another subject, as you would hurry by a bad smell in the street. Nor was it acting. He was in earnest. Mr. Lyle gave him a translation of St. Luke's Gospel, a brief catechism, & 2 or 3 other small tracts, & a lead pencil (always acceptable to Chinese, who have only ink) & as it rained, we insisted on his taking an umbrella, wh. we wd. not hear of his returning. Indeed, he became such a favorite, that we should soon have given him half we had. He remained on board until we reached the end of the city, & then took his leave with many professions of esteem of each side. I never saw, in any country, or society, better manners, — self-possessed, gentle, dignified, & giving the impression of a single eye to the pleasure & convenience of others. By his kindness we saved an entire day, in one town; for thus, by traveling all night, we reached our next place of visit at early morning, instead of late in the afternoon.

(Our friend's name is *Oo* or *U*).

WED. MAY. 9. Our next point is the city of Pu Si'. This is a large city, on the Grand Canal, surrounded by very high, moated & ivy grown walls, with populous suburbs. We stopped our boats, & walked to the gate, &, as usual, were refused admittance. Here was another sit down, another long talk, another most gracious & special yielding, & a walk through the town under guidance of a soldier. This is a poor town, — at least the parts we went thro', — except that the Yamun, (the seat of the city Government) is the largest & finest official building I have seen since leaving Canton. It is stately, with spacious grounds, walks, trees &c. But near the gate, on a stone platform, under a little roof of tiles, at a kind of Market Cross, lay 3 or 4 beggars, in their rags, piteous objects, one *dead*. He had died in the night, & no one had yet removed him.

Boats & late breakfast, & stop at the village at the foot of the Wei San, the famous range of hills, the highest in this region. *San* is hill, & *Tsung* is village. The village, Wei San Tsung, is beautiful. It has a sheet of water, an artificial basin, lined with trees, covered with lotus leaves, & ending in a stone coping fr. wh. pours a stream of pure water.

From the village, we ascended the series of hills, each (except the highest) having its temple. At the highest we stop, & spend an hour or two in delighted viewing of the broad landscape. The cities of the great plain, lie beneath us. A boundless plain it is, appearing to us perfectly level, & so green with fields of wheat & rice, & cultivated every-where. No fences. No roads. No feeding cattle. But rivers, canals, bridges,

& endless, endless fields of grain, & mites of men at work, & mites of boats floating up & down, & the whole studded over with hamlets of 3 & 4, or 20 & 30 houses each, standing under groups of trees, & looking like islands in the green sea. The industry, & the populousness of China! It has not been overrated. Large cities, of 20, 50 & 100,000 inhabitants, occur at not long intervals, & villages like ant hills, while the country is alive with laborers, tracking boats, dredging for the muck heaps, fishing, sowing, transplanting, & digging & spinning in the open air. The Grand Canal, in a long silver thread runs thro' the plain, to the Northward, & there, just seen in the horison, is the broader sheet of the Great River. And in that direction, not in sight, but not far off, lies the former capital of China, the Southern Capital, Nan King, — now in possession of the rebels — the long haired men. That collection of white tents, at the foot of our hill, is the Imperialist camp, for the protection of this region. Bounding the whole Western horison, filling up a quarter of the circle, is the Great Lake, Ta Hu, looking like the sea coast, with no land visible across its waters. The air is so pure, the day so fine, the view so limitless, that we can hardly leave it in time for our descent. The laboriousness of the Chinese has furnished a brick & stone walk, from the highest temple quite to the low land, sometimes in steps, sometimes on a slanting plane. On an inclined plane, they lay each brick with narrow side up, & horisontal, so as to form ridges. This prevents slipping.

In all this interior of China, where foreigners are everywhere rarely, & in some places never, seen, — we cannot move without a retinue of boys & men, some of them well dressed & decent persons. We left the village with 100 or more, wh. fell off at every stage of ascent, leaving us alone on the highest hill. Now, as we descend, they join us again, & we troop thro' the village & the rooms of the temple, & to the tea garden. The latter is the usual rockery, with water covered with lotus leaves, & deep shades of trees, & rows of flower pots on low brick walls, & climbing roses, & ivy grown walls, & little grottoes, & little roofed polygons, in wh. are polished tables, & solemn Chinese with pipes & tea cups.

On the whole, this village, Wei San Tsung, is a choice place, — a place of retreat for people in good circumstances, & adorned & kept in order accordingly. One private estate has large rich gardens, & several ancestral halls dignify the suburbs.

After dinner, drop down to visit the Camp. Just before we reach it, at a handsome polygonal building with pagoda roof, our boat is stopped — & our boatmen report that "No can", & a prodigious hubbub of voices ashore, & an over seeing military Mandarin, with pale yellow button & peacock's tail, comes to know *how we could possibly think of going to the camp.* So, Mr. Lyle comes into requisition again, & we ask leave at least to pay our respects to the Chief, in the big house. This is right, & we go ashore & enter the great hall, & the chief receives us at the door, most graciously, & begs us to be seated; & tea is brought, & he has a long conversation with Mr. Lyle. Here, again, is this singular development of Chinese life. Awful as the great Mandarin is, the common crowd come into the room, filling up all but the little space about the chairs, listening to all that is said, & signifying their interest, or approval of each thing by unmistakable signs. The officer thinks it quite eno', if the crowd gives us space about the chairs. Mr. Lyle says that most of this Mandarin's talk was to exhibit his importance & knowledge to the crowd, — his acquaintance with foreign affairs & great people, & to magnify his condescension in allowing us to enter the camp, — wh. of course he eventually did, giving us two officers to guide us.

The military are not distinguishable by their clothes, which are those of civil life. This Mandarin had three plumes, one a peacock's tail & the others of fox' fur, hanging behind his hat from the button. The officers had the fur plumes without the peacock's tail, & the common soldiers had only a piece of white cotton on the breast of their tunics, on wh. is inscribed the name of their corps, with a character signifying "brave", or "valiant".

But, the poor camp! The miserable camp, that looked so gay at a distance, with white tents & numberless banners of every hue! It is a mud hole, in low ground, hardly drained at all, enclosed by a breast-work, on which is one gingall,[49] & from wh. flutter the gayest banners, I should think one to each man, almost — while 2 or 300 miserable lowest caste men, unarmed & undisciplined, lie about in the tents, or stroll over the ground. I did not see a pistol or gun, & only 2 or 3 swords, & not a spear in the entire camp. It looked as if the troops were away, & the loafers had taken possession. We asked to see a lance exercise, but the lances were on board the junks. The crowd of common soldiers followed us & crowded about the officers, & got up on the platform with them, without any appearance of discipline or etiquette. Still, the tents were new, clean & white, & the first thing that my eye fell upon, on entering the camp, was the words "Lowell, Massachusetts", "Amoskeag N. H." on the white surface of the tents. They were all of Massachusetts drillings. The floors, too, were matted, & clean, & so far as the tents & their *con-tents* were concerned, the Government had made good provision, but there seems to be an entire ignorance of what a camp should be, either in a military or a sanitary point of view. These were, however, the Militia, & no Tartars among them.

[49] The gingall, or jingal, was a rude canon, fired from a rest, used in Central Asia.

Did I mention that Mr. Lyle put his melodeon (?) wind-piano, on board? We have music every evening. He & Dr. Lindau, both play, & decent singing is got up among us. Lindau has a large répertoire of German songs — among wh. we have Lützow, Mide ven vege ne jag', Das leben lange Tag, gaudeamus igitur, Edete bibite, Vedrai Casino, & passages fr. operas, waltses & a few religious pieces, & Mr. Lyle has Moore, & Scotch ballads &c. We spend the early ev. very pleasantly in this way. Indeed, our life in the boats is delightful — all agree that it is so. We go ashore & walk when we please, in town or country, stop & go on as we please. We have books & music, conversation, an excellent table, good servants & plenty of them, convenient places to sleep, wash, read or write, fine weather, neither hot nor cold, & new objects of interest every day, — & we are free from the noise & dust of a road, the steam, smoke, & oil & din of a steamer, & the rolling & pitching of the sea. We are floating, on even keel, through towns, between fields, & past temples, pagodas & hamlets.

On one Chinese boat, as we pass, in the dusk of the evening, a woman is on the roof, crying out, with strange cries. "What is it, Mr. Lyle?" Mr. Lyle listens. She is calling home the spirit of her child. The child is in the boat below, unconscious, or delirious. The spirit of the child has wandered off, & the mother goes on the roof & cries out to call it home. Now the attendant below says it is right, the child is itself again, the spirit has found its way back, & the mother comes down. In another boat is a wail for the dead, whose coffin is borne along in it.

It is funny to see our cook take his charcoal out of the barrel with chopsticks; yet it is a clean way of doing it. All his cooking is done with bits of charcoal, in small pots, yet we have soup, rice & curry, fish, meat, vegetables, & pudding ev. day.

THURSDAY. MAY 10. Walk for 1½ hour, along the canal, before breakfast. After breakfast, pass the town of Mok Tok, the Bridge of the Winds, & towards noon, reach the point of our destination in this direction, — the beautiful hill, Ling Nga, San. We mount the hill & from the temple at the top, (the *Tsung Pau*) have the most exquisite view any of us have seen in China. It is not so high, & therefore the view not quite so extensive as that from Wei San, but it has more variety, & more striking points, & the great city of Su Chau with its tall pagoda lies beneath us, while the close view, the scene where we stand, is exquisite — a grove of evergreens, ivy grown walls, a half ruined Seven Storied pagoda, a venerable temple full of courts & passage-ways & cloisters, once an imperial residence, enough for a monastery & college of hundreds of pupils, — all but entirely deserted, & terraces with walls of brick & stone, grown over with creepers, overlooking precipices at the foot of wh. lie the immense plains, teeming with people, boats, & hamlets, & covered with the verdure of increasing cultivation. This is the sea mark of our utmost sail, & we are satisfied! It is enough.

As we go slowly down the hill, we see a wall, & two men beckoning to us from it, & pointing to a ladder they have placed against it. Behind the wall are roofs of a group of buildings, all lying nestling in a most romantic spot. No one but Mr. Smith is with me, & the rest of our party have gone round the hill. I am for following the signal, & Mr. Smith agrees to it, so we go up the ladder, where two Chinamen on the wall help us down, & we find ourselves in a most romantic spot, grottoes, deep shades, terraces, opening vistas, & a group of handsome buildings in the best repair; &, as we follow our guides, we come to an open court, roofed over, where, at little tables, some dosen or more Chinese, well dressed men, of the upper class, are taking tea & pipes & sweetmeats. They rise & with the urbanity of 30 centuries request us to join them, & our tea & sweetmeats are brought us, but not a word can we say. In a few minutes a man comes in & makes signs to us that there are three men on the path, & to know if they belong to our party. We make signs that they do, & we should like to have them join us; so they are sent for, & are soon brought in, astonished at the discovery of this enchanted scene, — Arabian Nights, Aladdin — Open Sesame, & what not. Mr. Lyle gets into conversation with the elder & apparently chief man of the party, whose long silk robe, of beautiful purple hue & graceful shape, & rich lining, fascinates us all, & learns that this place is the ancestral hall of the Tsiang family, who allow it to be used as a summer resort for people from the town below, & an old dependent of the family makes a penny by supplying tea & cakes. An hour more must be spent in rambling about the delightful spot, where Chinese taste has fallen in with & not interfered with the natural beauties.

We invited the chief man of the company, the fascinating silk robe, to visit us in our boat, & he spent a half hour with us, Mr. Lyle playing for him on the melodion & giving him some tracts & St. Luke's gospel. He was a little senile & dull, but we respected his exterior.

(*San,* hill; *Ta'h,* pagoda; *Miau,* temple; *Yuen,* garden; *ka,* family; *Sz',* monastery; *Nan,* South; *Pe,* North; *King,* capital.)

FRID. MAY 11. Another walk before breakfast, of an hour or so. At noon, reach the city of Khwun San. It is celebrated as having a high hill & pagoda on its top enclosed within the compass of its walls. We find the city rather a mean one, with few objects of interest. From the hill top, we see that the walls enclose a space entirely unused, equal in extent to the whole city. Either the city has fallen away to ½ its original sise, or it was walled in on a notion of increase that has not been answered.

The silence of a Chinese city is surprising. Two cities we have passed, under the walls, just after night-fall, & they were as silent as cities of the dead. So is it, even with this city, at high noon. No wheels, & no shod hoofs, & the city gives out no sound. In the town, we saw a man standing at the temple gate, in a *cangue*. His offense was that he had concealed his property from arrest. He seemed quiet & content eno', & could walk about. The cangue is only a square piece of board, perhaps 3 f. sq., with a hole for the neck. Inside the Yamun, we saw some boxes, like cattle racks, in wh. men are placed standing, & left to die of starvation & fatigue. Behind the temple were tea gardens, of the usual pattern, lakes & lotus flowers, grottoes, trees, benches, roofed courts, tables, & a few tea-sipping & pipe-puffing, contemplative, *farniente* Chinese.

Late dinner, conversation, music & bed.

SATURDAY. MAY 12. Early up — tea & toast, walk along the banks, & through the town of Wong Du, where we examined an oil factory, — pressing of oil from the bean, commonly called the Shanten bean. This is a great article of trade, in the Province, the oil being used for cooking & lights. Mr. Walsh says the trade in it is enormous. We sit on a high stone bridge & await our boats, with a crowd about us. This is our last landing. At 2 P. M., within 12 miles of Shanghai, get aground in narrow bend, & cannot move until full tide. Heavy rain & mud, so cannot walk home. Spend afternoon & night pleasantly on board, in conversation, reading & music, &, starting at daybreak, reach Shanghai Sund. morning at 9½ o'ck., & am again in my quarters at Russell & Co.'s. No news, but the arrival of U. S. steam gun-boat Saganaw from S. Francisco, via Honolulu & H. Kong. Mail fr. home not arrived.

So ends a delightful & instructive trip into interior of China.

[THURSDAY. MAY 17.]⁵⁰ Through the kindness of my friend Capt. Oliver J. Jones, of the Furious, I recd. an invitation from Capt. Francis Marten, of the Roebuck, to make a passage with him to Chusan. Dr. Lindau is also of the party. The Roebuck sailed Tuesd. ev. May 15th. I first called on Mr. Bruce, who gave me a letter of introduction to Mr. Hughes, the British Commissioner at Chusan, & Count Klyskowski gave me one to De Meritens, the Fr. Commissioner. It seems Chusan is taken possn. of by the Allies, jointly, & a Commn. appointed, as in Canton, for reg[ulatio]n of all civil affairs.⁵¹

⁵⁰Here Dana added the marginal note: "Sent Journals to May 14th, from Shanghai."
⁵¹The Allies were formally occupying China and setting up military governments in the political centers. Later that year Peking fell, and the treaty was finally ratified.

The Roebuck is a screw sloop-of-war, used now as a Despatch boat, & is going to Chusan with the mail for the Allies, & despatches. Our quarters in the small cabin, where we all (Capt., Lindau & I) sleep in cots or on the lockers, & have one place for washing. The fleet here is so short of officers that the 1st lieut. is a mate, acting as lieut., a youth of 20, & the only other officer is a midshipman of 17, Ellis, who acts as a lieut., & keeps a watch & commands a division. There is also a Master, a man of experience, — but in the Br. Navy the masters are not in the line of promotion. Marten, however, does all his own work, & is 1st lieut., master & all, — on deck nearly all the time, & giving orders directly to the men.

Fine looking crew. No better looking men than the petty officers — qu. masters, b[oatswain]'s mates, gunner's mates, Capts. of tops &c. Some of these men were with Sir Wm. Peel at Lucknow &c.[52]

Anchored Tu. night near Wosung. All Wed. were steaming down the Yang Tse', & across to Chusan, & Wed. night anchored off the group, & Thursd. morn came in sight of Chusan. The Corvette, Scout, lay off, & signalled us to the Admiral, & in an hour more we were at anchor at Ting Hae — the port of Chusan. Here lie the Imperieuse, Admiral Jones' flag ship, Capt. Maguire, 51 guns, the corvette Pearl, 21, Capt. Borlase, two gun boats, a French gunboat, & outside, the corvette Scout, 21. Ashore, the two flags are flying on the Fort, & red coats & red trowsers fill the streets.

I like Marten much. He is a handsome, spirited, gallant fellow, and an excellent seaman. Want of interest at home has kept him back fr. a post capt's. commission, & he feels it, but loves the service, & wd. not leave it, tho' younger men go over his head ev. day, without merit or service. Yet, in the Am. Navy a man of 46 would hardly think himself slighted that he had not been a post captain sev. years. The Midshipman, Ellis, is an Hon., a son of Lord Howard de Walden, & gr. son of the Duke of Portland.[53] It is interesting to see his soft, delicate manners, blushing face, & drawing-room voice, giving orders to the great rough seamen. I spent an hour in the ward-room, & I thought the seniors, — the lieut., Master, Surgeon &c., were too rough & hard upon him, & certainly his birth & connexions are entirely disregarded there. The engineer, who is merely a mechanic, ranks above him, & Ellis has to defer to him, — but Ellis is the only *gentleman* in the ward-room, — the others are roughs.

[52]Sir William Peel (1824–1855), son of Sir Robert Peel, distinguished for his bravery at Sebastopol during the Crimean War, led a naval brigade in the relief of Lucknow during the Indian Mutiny in 1855. He was severely wounded and succumbed to an attack of small pox shortly thereafter.

[53]Lucy Cavendish-Bentinck Henry, daughter of the 4th Duke of Portland, married Charles August Ellis, 6th Baron Howard De Walden (1799–1868), British diplomat. Dana's young Ellis was one of six sons born of the marriage.

Chusan is an archepelago, a group of almost innumerable islands, if we include the rocks. The chief island, commonly called Chusan, has a small but safe harbor, Ting Hae [Tinghai]. Here is a town of about 20,000 inhabitants, with walls, a high fort, gates &c. It surrendered, without attempt at resistance, a month ago, & is now garrisoned by some 2000 Engl. & 200 French. The Engl. have the 99th & 67th, Marines & Artillery.

Delivered my letter to Mr. Hughes & am invited to stay at his Yamun. The Commissioners have a large Yamun, & subdivide it, the Br. one end, & the French the other. Call on Meritens, the Fr. Commn.

Ting Hae is walled, & has a citadel, called, sometimes the Fort of Horrors, because of some little figures representing the punishments of the wicked, but on small scale, making the name ridiculous. Walked there with Mr. Hughes. Outside are the graves of the soldiers who died here during the Br. occupation in 1843 (?),[54] in such numbers. It was then very sickly.

Mr. Hughes takes me to two tea gardens, one a private residence. As usual, rock-work, flowers, trees, water, bridges, & roofed seats. Called on the Chief Mandarin of Chusan, the military commander, a red button, but sadly shorn of his beams, as the Br. garrison has taken possessn. of his Yamun, leaving him only a few rooms. Yet his manner is stately, & his politeness unabated.

A police of Br. & Fr. soldiers, acting under the Allied Commissnrs., control the city, & Martial law reigns. There have been many outrages by the Br. soldiers, mostly when drunk, for wh. they are severely punished. Of 50 cases brot before the Court, all were British, & none French, — so the Fr. Commn. told Lindau.

The Br. commander, Col. Reeves, of the 99th, is an old ass, — almost brainless — an amiable man, but tiresome, loud-laughing, & unamenable to logic. Spent a half hour with him.

In our walk, met a Chinese albino.

Did I mention, in my trip to Su Chau, the boats with the fishing cormorants, 6 or 4 on each side, trained to catch fish? *Vide* Huc.

This ev. (Thursday) dined with Admiral Jones, on board the Imperieuse. Present, Lady & Adm. Jones, Capt. Maguire, Capt. John Borlase, of the Pearl, Capt. Marten of the Roebuck, Lts. Jones & Robertson, & Dr. Lindau. Band to play, for an hour or so. Noble ship, 51 guns, & large quarters. Singing & guitar in the ward-room. Marten gave me his gig to go ashore, & as it was dark, & I had never seen the harbor by night, & the men mistook the outer hill for the citadel, we pulled half round it before

[54]The "Opium War" hostilities ceased in 1842, but the British occupation continued until July 1843. The British lost far more troops through sickness than in combat.

was found the landing. Walked to Yamun, challenged by sentries &c., all in due style.

FRIDAY. MAY 18. To the French Mission. It is at Uku San, about 2 miles out of town. Here is one European priest, Père Montagneux, a Lasarist.[55] He has 2 Chinese priests with him, & 6 Chinese lads who are Seminarists, to become priests. He has a small school, of 20 boys or so, & there is another for orphans in the city. This is a recent institution, not over 6 years old. The Chapel is proper, & of good sise. The père is polite & ready to inform me. His Chinese priests speak Latin, but neither Fr. nor Engl. It was curious to hear them talking in Latin about sending a Coolie to find Père Montagneux.

At the citadel, found a genuine young Irish officer, of the Charles Lever novels stamp,[56] from Galway — sweet voiced, warm hearted, careless, dashing fellow, lacking in that controlling self respect & propriety that marks the English; — but you pity & like him.

No one could point out the Cameronian Hill, so called from the great number of the Cameronians, 36th, that are buried there.[57]

The Commissioners hope to make Chusan more healthy, by regulations, than it was in 1843, but the stagnant water of the paddy fields must be hasardous, always in summer, — & a Chinese city is always nasty & full of smells, & nuisances.

Ting Hae is overrun with camp followers, who have opened shops & put up signs here, to attract the foreigners. These are both Chinese & foreigners. Tailors advertise themselves as fr. Paris & London, & confectioners, & even take great London & Paris shop names, in their wretched little hovels — "Stults, tailor, fr. London".

Major Gen. Sir Robert Napier[58] arrived unexpectedly, in the Granada, to take command of Chusan. He came to our Yamun, with his staff, a set of showy, handsome youngs dogs, in their scarlet & gold & clattering swords. Napier is a tall, handsome man of about 5 & 40.

Dined with the Commissioners, vis: Mr. Hughes, Capt. Gibson & Baron Meritens, & the chief of police, a young Capt. Clayton, & a Fr. Capt. Dabry, a very pleasant man, said to be of note in literature & science.

<hr>

[55]The Congregation of Lazaristes, or Prêtres de la Mission, was founded by Vincent de Paul in 1625.

[56]Charles James Lever (1806–1872), an Irish novelist, wrote a number of novels featuring the dashing, reckless type of which Dana speaks.

[57]The Cameronians suffered greatly in the sickness of 1843, which Dana has mentioned earlier.

[58]Sir Robert John M. Napier, 9th Baron Napier of Merchistown (1818–1894), seems not to have been related to the Napiers Dana knew in England in 1856.

My lodgings are in the room once sacred to various idols, & passing along the passage, by night, with a single candle, I light up a part of the dim temple, revealing huge threatening & smiling idols, of colossal forms. But one gets used to gods in this part of the world, & sleeps & eats & reads among them without thought.

SATURDAY. MAY 19. Dr. Lindau & I sailed this morning, in a Chinese junk, for Ning Po. The passage lies through the Chusan Archipelago, famous for pirates, who infest it now even more than formerly, for they are driven from other places. "Flapped in the bay the pirate's sheet". Recently, one of their leaders, an Englishman named Ferguson, was killed by some of his gang. The Dr. & I had our revolvers, & a good supply of powder & ball, & if our men were not treacherous, could probably drive them off, — as they do not like to fight foreigners. No other course is open to us, as no men of war are bound that way, nor foreign vessels.

We make ourselves comfortable in our junk, by mats & blankets, wh. we take with us, & enjoy highly the delightful scenery of the archipelago. Dr. L. says it is like a Swiss Lake. We are, all the while, among islands, some rocky & high, & some undulating & cultivated to the tops, & all green with vegetation. The sea has the yellow muddy color of all the seas near the great river, wh. mars the beauty of the scene. Otherwise, it might be a lake of Switzerland or Northern Italy. Fleets of junks, by scores at a time, pass & repass, bound to & from the Continent, chiefly Ning Po. There are so many that an attack by pirates by day would be impossible, if they had any courage. These junks are loaded, chiefly with stone, & the industrious Chinese are cutting the stones on the passage. Our junk is light & outsails all. She has a head man (lauder) & six men, large cotton sails on bamboos, in the junk style. The Chinese sing at the ropes & windlass, a word or two & chorus, as our sailors do, but more often & more generally.

We are fortunate in our day & wind & weather. Fair, strong breese, smooth sea, & rapid sailing, & favorable tide for six hours, & reach the entrance to Ching Hae, by the middle of the afternoon, pass the high citadel of Shing Hae, & long before dark are at anchor at Ning Po, where lies one of those ubiquitous English gunboats, & by 5 o'ck., I am at the house of Dr. C. W. Bradley,[59] the Am. Consul, his guest, in a nice room, filled with books, on open shelves, with that delightful library smell that open shelves give one, & windows looking out on the ivy grown walls of Ning Po, said to be 700 years old, wh. form the limit of Dr. Bradley's garden.

[59]Charles William Bradley (1807–1865), from New Haven, Connecticut, was an Episcopal clergyman, sinologist, and U. S. Consul in Malaya and China, 1849–1860.

Walk in the garden. Varieties of flowers & shrubs. Handsome house, & full of books. Dr. Bradley very kind & attentive. In the vol. of poets of America, find my father's face, & spend some time over it. Dr. B. offers to cut it out & give me, — but must decline it. It is the best face in the volume, though I say it &c.

Dr. B. says there are no antiquities in China, — scarcely anything over 6 or 800 years. Their buildings are not durable. The walls of Ning Po are said to be 700 years old. The oldest monument in China is Christian, — thot to be of the Nestorians.[60] Dr. B. is hardly over an attack of fever & ague, the 3d he has had in 6 mos. He says they are very subject to it in Ning Po. (Have I mentioned that at Shanghai? There is a great deal of it there. Several persons had it while I was there).

SUNDAY. MAY 20. Although there are 4 clergymen of the Ch. of Engl. here, there is no service. They are all very low churchmen, &, on Sundays join with the Presb. & Baptists for an Engl. service, — a unity in wh. they yield all. An Am. or Engl. layman cannot have his service, tho' there are 4 clergymen here, — even on Easter or Whitsunday. This is wrong. They can be *compelled* to give the service.

Went with Dr. B[radley], (who is a Churchman, & dislikes this course) to the Presb. Chapel. Sermon in wh. the preacher, a Baptist, named Lord, gave up the whole doctrine of death as a consequence of the fall, to what he called the results of Modern Science. Called at house of Mr. Rankin, a Presb. Missionary, & then to the Chinese Chapel of the Presbyterians. They have about 150 in attendance, men & women. The Missionary said it was hard to teach the Chinese to sit still & listen for a long time. A quiet, still meeting was unnatural to them. This is a proof in favor of liturigical worship. All the singing is of metrical hymns, wh. is also unnatural to the Chinese. They know only melody, & sing chants naturally. They would sing well in unison. I believe their women never sing in meetings.

There are 3 missions here — Ch. of England, Am. Presb. (Old School) & Baptist. The Presbyterians live together, on the river bank, outside the city, in a very pretty place, good houses. The others are scattered. Saw houses of two Ch. missionaries, Gough & Russell,[61] in the city, large handsome houses.

[60]The Nestorians were an early (450–1400) Christian sect, heretical to the main body of the Church, which was virtually destroyed in China under the persecutions of Tamerlane.

[61]The Reverend Gough remains unidentified. William Armstrong Russell (1821–1879), educated at Trinity College, Dublin, in 1872, was to become the first missionary bishop of North China. He published treatises on the Chinese language and translated portions of the Scriptures and the Book of Common Prayer into Chinese.

Church Missionaries.		Gough, Russell, Mole.
Presbyterian	" .	Rankin, Nevius,[62] & Dr. McCarty.
Baptist	" .	Lord, Knowlton.[63]

Talked with Dr. Bradley about China. He says [S. W.] Williams had not seen the N. of China, nor even the city of Canton, when he wrote his Middle Kingdom, & that his generalisations are often wrong, but thinks it the best treasury. Dr. Morrison had no ear for sounds, & made great mistakes, in consequence, so that his translation of the Bible is worse than useless, & is abandoned — also he translated phrases directly, making unintelligible stuff.[64] A new translation is now going forward, on wh. there has been a long continued & rather bitter feud, as to the word to be used for God. Some contend for *Shang Ti*, & others for *Shin*, or *Sin*. Each party thinks the other fatally wrong, & wd. suffer martyrdom rather than use their word. The translation leaves it blank, & there are two sets printed, one by each party, or rather by the Boards. Each makes it a conscience not to use the other. Bishop Boone is of the Sin party, — wh. the other side call the *sinners*. The Engl. Ch. Miss. are Shang Ti men, & the Presb. are divided.

Dr. B[radley] says that the deaths among the Miss[ionary] women, here, in China, especially in child-bed, are frequent, & they fail under the climate. They are obstructions to work, & do very little themselves. The Chinese, also, are offended by much publicity in the action of women. He thinks the Miss. should not marry.

I think, myself, that these missions are temptations to second rate young men & to women who have little chance of marriage. They can not only marry, but have a relay of wives, & live pretty well, keep servants, & become gentlemen. I have seen no Miss. yet in China, except B. Boone, who has not bettered his condition by coming here. They are in many cases inferior men. Some of the women are ladies, & have made sacrifices in coming — Mrs. B[oone] is sister of Bishop [Stephen] Elliott, Mrs. Smith is d. of Dr. Sparrow,[65] Miss Jones is d. of Gen. [Walter] Jones of Wash., & Mrs. Gough is a lady of fortune, & so with Mrs. Bonney at Canton. But the men are mostly of a lower type, & would do little at

[62]John Livingston Nevius (1829–1893), Union College, 1848, was a Presbyterian missionary in China, 1853–1893.

[63]Miles Justine Knowlton (1825–1874) came to the Orient from New York in 1854. He became celebrated as an authority on Chinese missionary work, publishing considerably, and periodically returning to the United States for lecture tours.

[64]Robert Morrison, noted earlier when Dana visited the site of his grave, published his *Dictionary of the Chinese Language*, 1815–1823.

[65]Dana may be here referring to Patrick J. Sparrow (1802–1867), president of Hampden-Sidney College, 1844–1846.

home. All persons I have seen here, of all nations & religions & of no religions, — if disconnected fr. the Missions — speak with more respect of the R. Cath. than of the Prot. Missions.

Bayard Taylor is spoken very lightly of here. His China[66] is said to be a sham. — Rev. Mr. Gough & wife, of the Eng. Ch. Miss., are persons of independent fortune, & spend all their income on the Mission — much respected.

MONDAY. MAY 21. Called on Rev. Messers. [W. A.] Russell & Gough of the Ch. of Engl. mission, & on Bishop Delaplasse, the R. Cath. bishop. The R. Cath. have 2 schools, 1 of boys & 1 of girls, of about 100 scholars each, — the latter under charge of Sisters of Charity. There are 11 Sisters here, 3 died last year, of cholera, & 6 are coming out. They have a small hospital & a pharmacy, fr. wh. they dispense med. to the poor daily. Four of the Sisters came in & shewed us their chief rooms — of course as neat as possible. Boys' dormitories, Chapel, apothecary room &c. Bishop have 6 or 8 Chinese youth preparing for orders. He & his clergy dress in Chinese costume.

Visited the Pagoda. Seven stories. The galleries are gone, but the stairs, inside, are entire. View of city & suburbs. Ning Po is walled, uniformly, & with some 6 or 8 gates. Walls about 40 f. high, & thus[67] — — thro' the whole length — so are all city walls I have seen, — & with moats. Population about 350,000.

Great number of beggars at the city gates, — dreadful objects, some very sick, & all ragged & lousy. Chief temple seems to be used as a furniture shop. They are very liberal in allowing selling, gambling & working at trades in & about the temples. Here was also a play going on, in the usual artificial falsetto voice, with the usual preposterous dresses & coarse painting of faces. Actors are outcasts. For 5 generations their descendants cannot become scholars, — so of barbers.

Those innumerable little huts we saw, coming up the river, with thatched roofs, are ice-houses. The Chinese use ice to preserve meat & fish, & not for drinking. Dr. B[radley] tells me there are 5000 ice houses in this district.

The U. States Govt. furnish to the Consulates here no jails nor jailors nor Marshal. By the treaty[68] the jur. to punish Am. citisens is surrendered by China to our Consuls. Having none of these means, our Consuls can neither arrest, detain nor coerce. In short, Am. offenders go unpunished, unless we borrow, as sometimes we do, the Engl. jails. The Chinese

[66]Bayard Taylor and his book on China have been noted earlier.

[67]Here Dana drew a sketch of a crenelated wall.

[68]The treaty referred to is the one over which the allied military action is being conducted.

complain, our Consuls admit the justice of the complaint, write despatches home, but nothing is done.

This ev. (Mond. 21 May) we start on an excursion to the Snowy Valley, Siueh Tau. Our party is Dr. [C. W.] Bradley, Rev. Mr. Nevius & myself, with 3 house servants, the chief of whom is Filial Piety. We have two Chinese boats, one for cooking & servants, & one for ourselves, & take cots, bedding, food &c. Start at 7 o'ck., & glide along the canal, under the wall of the silent city, for 2 hours, the canal crowded with boats, & the suburb lighting up its shops & houses.

Now comes the open country. By the side of the canal is a river, into wh., in due time, we slide, by what is called the Mud Slide, — where boats are pulled up an inclined plane of slimy mud by capstans, & slide down into the river. The jam of boats at these slides is great, & we buy off our predecessors by a few *kas*. Now, in the river, retire to our cots. Here, as on our Su Chau expedition, we have service in our boats.

TUESD. MAY 22. Wake up. Boat still & fast. Daybreak. At a village, Su Fau, tau, where we leave the boats. Crowd gathers, & large concourse of spectators to see us wash, & free criticisms of our combs, brushes, towels &c.

Here hire 3 chairs, & 6 bearers, & 10 burden carriers, & start for the mountain. Ride on the plain, & walk up the ascent. Very hot, but have umbrellas & pith hats, & the free perspiration is the safest thing in such climates — only keep off the direct rays of the sun, & you do well eno' — wearing flannel.

The endless cultivation! Rice fields everywhere. Water is raised by the endless chain pump, — a Chinese invention, small ones worked by hand, & large ones by cattle, — buffaloes & bullocks. These rice fields, or rice *ponds,* one might call them, go to the very mountain tops, & into the deepest ravines, always on a plumb level, & terraced. On a sharp hill they look like low fortifications. The wheat is nearly ripe, & its yellow alternates with the green of the rice. This is the time of transplanting the rice — & the paddy fields are full of laborers, picking up, putting in baskets, setting out, & raising water. Every hill top discloses miles of industry. From them, the paddy fields look like vats of all colors of water, placed side by side all over the country.

The camphor trees are in flower, & have much the effect of the Chestnut trees in an Am. forest. And we have evergreens of the cedar sort, the weeping cypress, the Sihu willow, daphne odora, camellia Japonica &c., & all kinds of creepers & climbers, many in full blow. One old tree has its trunk covered with roses.

Reach the monastery, Siueh Tau S'z', Snowy Valley Monastery, by 11 o'ck., when Mr. Bradley, who has hardly got over his fever, is too weak to go to the falls, & here we leave out chairs, luggage & coolies, & Mr. Nevius & I go on. We mount to the top & view the falls fr. above, & force our way, where no path is, thro' thickets & over rocks, to the foot. This celebrated fall, She Hu Gau, is in a chasm formed by flat perpend. rocks, of not less than 400 feet in height, opening like a half opened book, the fall coming down at the angle. Below, the valley opens into the plain & discloses a noble landscape. The falls are one sheet, small & broken into silvered drops, falling in a basin, — a direct fall of at least 400 feet, & plenty of trees, shrubs & grass & creepers.

Wound up the rocks on the other side, & stopped a while at a wood-cutter's hut, & reached the monastery, the Siueh Tau Sz', just before dark. On our return, passed another fall, smaller, with less extensive views, but dark, deep & romantic, Lung Yin Tan (Dragon's Shady Dell).

At the monastery, the monks give us house room, tables, chairs & bedsteads, fuel & use of kitchen, — but we find victuals, cooks, table furniture, & bed furniture. We have good dinner, prepared by our cook, with wine, tea & all the usual luxuries, & a good night's sleep, after a walk of not less than 8 hours, mostly up & down steep hills.

The idols in this temple are gigantic, & look rather fearful in the large dingy rooms, by the flicker of candles, & there is a huge new drum, the recent gift of some votaries, whose names are inscribed on a tablet, & a large bell, struck, as usual, by a wooden hammer, on the outside, the end of a stick suspended in air. While we are at dinner, the drum, the bell & the gong are all at work for the ev. service. But all is decay & neglect. Except the votive drum, nothing is repaired or supplied. The priests are mere ignorant drones. In China, there are three unlearned professions, — or rather, the priests & physicians are illiterate, & lawyers or jurists there are not.

WED. MAY 23D. Rise early, walk about the monastery, the lower courts of wh. are filled by our servants, & then breakfast, & take an early start, sending the burden bearers off to their village, & our servants to the boat, all but Filial Piety, who, true to his name, gets leave to go & visit his parents in a neighboring village.

To-day we visit the falls of Tsien Chang Gau (the chasm of 10,000 feet) wh. is an exaggeration, it being about 500 feet, but a romantic scene, perpendicular rocks, a deep ravine, a broken fall of about 500 feet, & a closed-in view.

All our way down to the boats is this endless succession of rice fields & grain fields, & here & there tea fields, & some tea picking I saw. At noon, passing thro' a village, being hungry & thirsty, & our provisions gone on, stopped at Chinese shop & had eggs boiled & some tea, wh. we found or thought excellent, & wh. we drank in the sight of as large a crowd as could get into the two rooms, leaving us elbow room, — Mr. Nevius making a short sermon, in wh. he had to encounter a quick witted scoffer, & Dr. Bradley refusing to eat or drink anything fr. the unclean kitchen of the Chinese.

Here we left our chairs, & sent the bearers to the boats, & got the variety of a passage down the river on a raft. These rafts are of bamboos lashed together, bent up for a prow before, loaded, & drawing not over 6 inches, the river being very shallow here. This is a pleasant mode of travelling, in fine weather. It is noiseless, gentle & with variety of river scenery. These rafts carry a large commerce down to the head of boat navigation. We placed our chairs on the rafts, spread our umbrellas, & enjoyed a drift of 2 or 3 hours very much, wh. took us to our boats at Sa Fau Tau, & there we begin our course down the river, homeward. Stopped, however, just at night-fall, at a pagoda on a hill that overlooks the village of Kiang Kau fr. wh. there is a good view, tho' we were a little too late for it.

(Mr. Bradley's excited state. Not over his fever, talking in sleep for hours, but he is a generous, hospitable man. Nevius tells me B.'s story, his marriage, separation, insanity, recovery, holy orders, scholarship &c. N. is an ordinary man, of no philosophy or theology.)

THURSD. MAY 24. Reached the crenalated walls of Ning Po, at day-break, drop down the canal, under the walls for 2 hours, amid a throng & jam of early boats, & reach home in the early morning.

Rev. Mr. [M.] J. Knowlton, Baptist Missionary, calls. Gives me statistics &c. The Southern Baptists have missions at Canton & Shanghai. The Am. Bapt. Board, here & at Hong Kong. There are three clergymen, 28 Chinese Christians, all told, & one native Assistant. They have 2 day schools of about 45 pupils in all. He tells me that all the Prot. Missions pay the girls to come to school, for the parents do not care to have girls taught, & their time at home is of some value. The R. C. bishop had told me this, but I thought him mistaken. Mr. K. says it is necessary to do so. Mr. K. is a dull man, imperfectly educated.

Being the Queen's Birth Day, Mr. Bradley & I, dressed in our best, he in consular gold lace, & I in dress coat & kids, under a hot sun, & called in the Br. Consul. The gun boat Restive fired salutes.

Walked round the city, on the walls, with Mr. B. Very pretty views. A river & a canal nearly surround the city, under the walls. The walls are wide & furnish a pleasant walk, but the beggars, in filth & rags, lying at the Gate houses, are a distress & disgust. The city abounds with little stone, close houses for burying babies. The babies are not killed, as many supposed, but no baby is *buried* in China, but merely wrapped in matting & thrown away. These tombs have small holes in the tops, just big eno' to admit a little body, & the people tumble them in until they are full to the top, & then new ones are built. Mr. B. pointed out one, now full & overflowing, wh. had not been built 3 mos., & yet there were 4 built at that time.

Rev. Mr. Rankin calls. He is of the Presb. Mission, & was once settled in Rochester N. Y., & knows Mr. [O. E.] Daggett well, & talked of Canandaigua.

The complication of Prot. Missionaries here is increased by a New Engl. Society, called the Soc. for Evangel[izing] China, wh. has sent two open Communion Baptists here. Tried to learn the mystery of the Prot. translations of Scriptures. There are so many, & none are confided in, & then there is the Shang Ti & Shin controversy, & the Baotigio controversy,[69] & all seems a chaos. I wonder they have *one* convert. The Presbyterians are doing pretty well, & have some 75 or 100 communicants, & 2 boarding schools, boys & girls, of about 30 each, & sev. day schools.

This ev. Rev. Mr. [W. A.] Russell, of the Engl. Ch. Miss. Soc., called & spent an hour or so. He is an Irishman, of the Univ. of Dublin, & a very polite man, faithful, & of good sense, — a very, very low churchman. Yet I found him decided in favor of the superiority, indeed almost necessity, of a liturgy for the Chinese. The Ch. of Engl. Mission at Ning Po was established in 1848. There are now 4 missionaries & their wives, & (including the out-lying station of San Pâ) 160 baptised Chinese, 100 adult communicants, & 3 schools for boys & 3 for girls, in all about 60 scholars of each sex.

He entirely denies the *extension* of learning among the Chinese. He says thus — The Chinese written language is so difficult that only scholars can read it to any advantage, & it is forgotten if not constantly kept up. The common people know only a few characters, for necessary purposes, & do not read at all. In Ning Po, of 350,000 people, & one of the best cities of China, there are only 4 small book-shops, & in the entire district, in all the 15 or 20 towns, of from 5 to 50,000 inhab. each, there are no book-shops, & no peddlers of books. The poor have no books in their houses, not a new book is produced in this province in 20 years. Literature is *deified* in China, because it is so difficult & rare. The Chinese character has no sound known to the spoken dialect. The *sounds* attached to the characters give no idea to the hearer. Reading aloud is never done, & wd. be useless. It is the eye only that gives the idea, & the characters are by myriads. They must be translated into the spoken dialects, as we

---

[69]The "Baotigio" controversy, like that concerning the proper translation of the word "God," must have had to do with scriptural translation, although the precise term in this case is unknown. Dana's spelling here, as so frequently with Oriental words, is probably phonetic.

would translate Cicero, & this can only be done *orally*, for the spoken dialects have no characters to represent their sounds. It is like latin books among a people who have no written language, but learned scholars who can read latin. Now, the object of the Roman letters is to make the spoken dialects written languages. This they cannot be, by using the Chinese characters, & the making of new Chinese characters, added to the myriads, would be worse than useless. They translate foreign books into the dialects, & print them with the Roman letters, on the phonetic principle, — just as if the Chinese had only unwritten dialects. As to the book language, the — , that is to stand. All Christian Chinese are to learn that also, if they wish, & to read the classics in those characters. It is hardly practicable to translate the Classics into the dialects, & the prejudices of centuries must be respected. (Qu. If the prevalence of the Roman letters, & the making the dialects written, will not result in burying the ancient literature of China?) A Chinese can learn to read by Roman letters, any book, quite as quick as our boys at home, — while to read the character requires a teacher for every word & sound, years of study, & then an imperfect result.

FRIDAY. MAY 25. Called on Rev. Russell. Saw there a blind Chinese girl, a foundling, who had been made blind to use her as a beggar, — no unusual thing, & saved by Dr. Gützlaff,[70] sent to England when very young, carefully educated there by a benev. Engl. lady, & now lives with the Engl. Ch. Missionaries here, & teaches the Chinese girls orally. She reads English, on raised type, beautifully. She read to us a passage fr. St. John's Gospel, with a justness of emphasis & delicacy of intonation I have rarely known equalled, & with no sign of foreign accent. She also played to us pieces from Handel, — on a very disagreeable melodeon, but well.

Mrs. Russell has a school of 7 blind Chinese girls, who plait straw, & are taught orally, chiefly by this girl, Agnes.

Called on Mr. & Mrs. Nevius, Mr. & Mrs. Rankin, Dr. & Mrs. McCarty, of the Presb. Mission, & Mr. Knowlton of the Bapt. Mission, & exd. the printing press of the Pr. Mission. They print the Chinese character fr. types, & the number of characters being thousands, setting up is slow work.

Take leave of my kind host, Mr. Bradley, & go on board the lorcha Rosina, to sail to-night for Shanghai. Bradley loads a basket of prog [food] for me, & seems really sorry to have me leave him.

Our boat I call a lorcha, for she is as much that as anything, of about 50 tons burden, commanded by an Englishman with a crew of 8 Chinese sailors & 3 Manilla men. The latter, one of whom is the gunner, live

[70]Karl F. A. Gützlaff (1803–1851) was a German missionary who died in Hong Kong after a career of over twenty years in the Orient. His *Journals* of the period are well known.

apart fr. the Chinese, & are the guard, as well as sailors, & are relied upon to do the fighting, in case of an attack by pirates, for the Chinese will not risk their lives to defend foreign property ag. Chinese. We have two long six pounders, & a quantity of rifles, musketoons & pistols, and are in good order, for the pirates have been bold of late, & the news has just come of the capture of a Ning Po boat by them & the murder of all hands, — one Smith, a European residing in Ning Po, being master. Dr. Lindau is with me, & so we muster 3 foreigners & 3 Manilla men, but the captain says the pirates have never, of late years, attacked a boat belonging to one of the greal Engl. houses, (the Rosina is Dent & Co.'s) although they know how much opium & treasure they carry as well as the owners themselves, for fear of the consequences, — the gunboats being sent to break them all up.

Decent cabin, Chinese cook & steward, & fair living.

SAT. MAY 26. At day light are going down the river, passing Ching Hae, & the junks, & the citadel, & with a leading wind & fine weather are just able to stand our course. Dr. L. & I lounge & read & sleep & talk, in our small quarters, or sit on deck with the crew. Afternoon & ev. rainy & thick. The Chinese are good pilots & go on, see or no see.

Late in P.M., make the Rugged Islands, & at midnight then make Gutslaff, & then the Light Ship, as true as the needle. Weather rough, & seas come on board, & crew bailing a little. Racing with the Heather Bell, wh. sailed at same time. She outsails us.

SUND. MAY 27. In the Yang Ts' Kiang, & reached Wosung by 8 A.M., & obliged to lie there at anchor nearly all day, until 2 P. M., within 8 m. of Shanghai, wind & tide adverse, & see the steamers Yang Tse & Aden, former with the mails fr. Europe, go up. At turn of tide, in heavy rain, with thunder & lightening & close hot air, we scull up to the anchorage, & in a few minutes I am, for the fourth time, instated at Russell & Co.'s, in my old quarters, where a bath & change are agreeable. My China boy seems pleased to see me, tho' they say the Chinese have no emotion or attachments. (Mr. Nevius denies this, & thinks they have gratitude & affection, but are not treated by most Europeans in a way to draw them out).

Gordon Dexter is here, also a guest of Russell & Co. He has been at Manila, since Japan. He says that Commodore Tattnall & the Capt. of the Powhatan traded in itsebus & purchase of kobans, as well as the junior officers.[71] The Am. merchants in China sent great quantities of

---

[71]Josiah Tattnall, noted earlier as the American naval officer who aided Robert Bruce at the Pei Ho Forts battle, joined the Confederate navy in 1861. Here he is being implicated in the Japanese currency black market which Dana earlier deplored as a vice indulged in by American officers.

specie to Japan in the Powhatan, on freight, wh. freight goes to the Com. & Capt., & with this & borrowed money they bought kobans. The junior officers bought with money borrowed of the Am. & Engl. merchants. Only 2 officers were clear of it. This was when the Jap. Govt. had forbidden the exp. of kobans, — & the Naval officers were exempt fr. Cu. Hs. examination.

MOND. MAY 28. The Yang Tse is chartered to take down the Chinese Gov. Gen. to Fu Chau, who seems to be flying from the rebels, so I cannot go in her. The rebels are making head again, after their success at Hang Chau, & have greatly alarmed our good friends at Su Chau, & its neighborhood. I wonder how our magnificent Mandarin with the 3 plumes feels about it?

Called on Mr. [John E.] Ward, who arrived Sat. last in the Hartford. He is justly angry with Ld. Palmerston for his reference to him in his speech of M'ch. last, & has written to Sir M. Seymour to thank him for his correction of Ld. P. on that head, & a full expln. to Mr. Cass.[72] Ward also thinks Harris did very shabbily not to invite me to Yedo, & wishes to resent it.

Marten, in the Roebuck, has been here & gone again to Chusan. The Hartford & Saganaw lie opp. us here, & the river is full of ships of war, transports & despatch boats.

(Read Seward's Speech, at Ning Po. Admirable!)[73]

This afternoon walked into the city with Mr. Lyle. The alarm at Su Chau has spread here, & numerous fugitives are on their way. The Govt. have yesterday beheaded some 20 as deserters. The deserters fr. the Imp. Army are feared as robbers, & usually executed when caught. Bruce & de Bourbulon have posted proclamations, in Chinese, all about the city, assuring the people that the foreign forces will protect them. This satisfies many, but the panic exists, increased by the recollection of the

[72]It has been noted earlier that the troubles of the Allies in China stemmed from the failure of Robert Bruce and Baron Gros to effect the ratification of the 1858 treaty with the Chinese at Peking. Dana's reference is to a March 1860 parliamentary debate over the British defeat. Lord Palmerston defended Mr. Bruce's decision to proceed up the river to Peking rather than take an alternate land route, and claimed that John E. Ward, the American minister, had suffered severe loss of face by submitting to such an alternative (though Ward, unlike Bruce, had succeeded in getting the United States' version of the treaty ratified in Peking). Sir Michael Seymour (1802–1887) rose in debate to reply to Palmerston, quoting a private letter to the effect that Palmerston's story was untrue. See *Hansard's Parliamentary Debates*, CLVII (March 16, 1860, 806; March 20, 1860, 925).

[73]Dana is probably referring to the speech entitled "The State of the Country," delivered by the New York senator in February 1860 and printed in William H. Seward, *Works*, IV, 619–643. In his address Seward argued for the admission of Kansas to the Union on a free soil basis.

horrors of the rebel occupation of Shanghai 5 years ago,[74] & there is a steady exodus of the people, all day, through the N. & E. gates, with their little stocks of furniture & household goods & gods, hurrying out into the distant villages. They have a proverb to the effect that "in little troubles, go to the city; in great troubles, go to the country". But one cannot wonder. What must a panic be in a city of sev. hundr. thous. inhab., with streets so narrow & choked that no communication can be had betw. diff. parts by the officers, & where the houses are so frail & consumable! As I walked the streets, I cd. not but think what suicides by scores — nay, by hundreds — what famine, plunder, distress wd. be enacted here, if the rebels shd. reach the walls.

Went with Mr. L. to his house for the blind. Here are about 60 blind people, mostly women, adults, who are employed all day in braiding straw, & get the diff. betw. the cost of the straw & the price of the rope or twist. It keeps them in food & clothing. The land & house are held by Mr. L. in trust, & the foreign merch. contribute about $1000 annually for it. (Mr. L. says the for. merch. here are truly liberal in all cases of charity well approved to them). Of the 60, over 20 are Christians.

To the chapel, where Mr. L. got a collection of 20 persons, talked a while, & distributed books.

At an open door, heard music & went in. Had been a marriage three days before, & the wedding feast was still going on. It usually lasts 3 to 7 days, & often involves the party in burdensome expenses. This is a house of mod. pretensions, but there are 8 pieces of music, mostly played by children, & tables are standing, set out with confectionary, cakes, tea & sugar-water, & some 6 or 8 solemn guests are tasting & smoking. The bridegroom, who has a broad piece of gold leaf on his breast, comes forward, & receives us politely, though strangers & intruders, makes us sit down, sits with us, devotes himself to conv. with us, & has sweetmeats & sugar-water served. He thinks little of the rebels, & sees only happiness & security before him. Of course, the wife is out of sight, in some hidden room within.

Per contra, Mr. L. takes me to a small hut of a poor Chinese Xtian, — a blind old crone, who has 2 blind old crones visiting her. L. says she is a model woman, for sense & kindness. One story is that these people cry themselves blind, by immod. weeping.

To a vapor-bath, or sweating house. The Chinese do not use much water, but here the poor go into a steam room, & sweat themselves & wipe off, & then take tea & a pipe. The cost of the bath, towel, tea & pipe is, in all, only about four cents!

[74]In addition to her difficulties with Europe and America, China had been torn by a civil war which began in 1850 and would continue until 1864.

TUESD. MAY [29.] Visit on board the Hartford, to Commodore Stribling. Then to Capt. Lowndes, & then to the wardroom.[75] Fine looking ship. Ward room very large — steerage too small, Com.'s cabin small. Stribling says the ship was an outrageously costly job, among politicians in Yard, & so was the little Saganaw. Jobs to keep voters in pay. All the officers, in cabin & ward-room alike, deplore the condit. of our Navy — the political jobbing, the negl. & indif. of Toucey (Sec. of Navy)[76] to the interests of the Navy, & number of incompetent officers, & the slowness of promotion. Lowndes is a white haired old man. 1st. lieut. is Barnet. A midsh. named Greene is neph. of Gen. Dana of Charlestown.[77]

Dined with Webb, present, Hon. Col. Foley, of Br. army, Capt. Barnard of the P. & O. steamer Aden (a grad. of Cambr. Univ.) who talks of latin & German authors, Dr. Lindau & myself. Col. F. thinks I *can* do India in July. Lindau thinks the Chinese character, as used by the Japanese, does *not* give the image or idea it does in Chinese, but is used only to express a sound, & that sound diff. fr. its Chinese sound. (Qu.?)

The Chinese are beginning to believe that they can have junks without eyes painted on the bows. They see foreign ships make long voyages safely without them, & are slowly beginning to be willing to sail in small vessels without them.

WED. MAY 30.   Called on the Capt. Schenck of the Saganaw.[78] Pleasant man. His 1st lieut., —— , is almost imbecile in mind & body. The 2d & 3d, Wardell & Campbell, are excellent men, — the latter a scholarly man. But absurd to have 3 lieuts., & a Master, to so small a craft. She is a success, as a steamer, excellent machinery, steams fast, — but cost 3 times her value.

[75]Cornelius K. Stribling (1796–1880) joined the American Navy in 1812, a career that was to continue until 1872. He became a rear admiral in 1866. Charles Lowndes (1798–1885) had been a captain since 1855. After two years of commanding the steam sloop *Hartford* he was abruptly placed upon the retirement list, perhaps because of suspicion that he was in sympathy with the Confederacy.

[76]Isaac Toucey (1792–1869) was Secretary of the Navy, 1857–1861. A prominent Democrat with Confederate leanings, his record in the office showed efficiency and economy.

[77]Edward A. Barnet (d. 1864) had been in the Navy since 1837. A lieutenant since 1850, he was to reach the rank of commander in 1862. General Napoleon T. J. Dana, a brigadier general in the Minnesota Militia, 1857–1861, has been noted earlier. Samuel Dana Greene (1840–1884) later served as executive and gunnery officer on the *Monitor* in her fight with the *Merrimac*.

[78]James Findlay Schenck (1807–1882), in the Navy since 1825, saw action in California in 1846, later commanded a division during the Civil War, and retired as a rear admiral in 1869. His brother, coincidentally, Robert C. Schenck (1809–1890), served as Minister to England after the war, was forced to resign in 1876 because of ill-conduct, and Dana was named to replace him. The Senate, as the editor's Introduction explains, refused to confirm Dana's appointment.

Thence to my friend Jones, of the Furious, who is receiving Com. Stribling, manning yards for him, &c. Pleasant call. He thinks highly of Marten, & that he will get promotion soon. Introduced to Capt. Windgard, of the Nimrod, a twin of the Roebuck.

This ev. Mr. Ward called & spent an hour or so.

THURSDAY. MAY 31. Last day at Shanghai. Take leave early, & at 8 A.M. am under way for Hong Kong, in the P. & O. steamer Aden, Barnard, master. At Wosung, a fleet of Fr. men of war & transports full of troops, ready to start for the North. Boat fr. Fr. Adm[iral], comes alongside & puts letters on board. The Hartford does not look so well head on. Rises too much.

SAT. JUNE 2. At sea. How marvelous content I am at sea! Believe I was intended for a sailor. State-room to myself, usual routine of hours & duties. Discipline the same here as in the Peking. But this is a screw, & what a terrible noise, what beating & thumping of the ship's bottom a screw makes. It seems to be breaking thro' keel, keelson, floor & all. I wonder that delicate passengers can endure it. It would drive crasy some persons I know.

A little boy passenger about 7 years old, looks & acts so much like little Dick [Dana], that can't keep away fr. him. Has his figure, complexion, lay of hair & eyes. Find him to be Robert Olyphant, son of Mr. O. the China merchant. His parents on board.[79] Make acq. of Mr. O., Mrs. O. seasick. Mr. O. is a strong Presbyterian, lives in Shanghai, & tells me that the Presb. Mission there is large & successful — regrets I did not make acq. of its clergy. Also, the Ch. Miss. Soc. (Engl.) has 2 missionaries there. He thinks very highly of Bishop B[oone]'s mission. Says there have been 2 "Seventh Day Baptists" missionaries in Shanghai — who are returning there, to complicate matters & confound the Chinese. They make it a principle to work on Sunday.

Another passenger is a Mr. F. D. Williams, formerly of Boston, now of Wetmore & Co. He has large B[oston] acq. — rather of the Cadet & fast order, I think.

Mr. Cheney, who knew Ned slightly in Heidelberg. Campbell, agt. of Oriental B'k. Cheney is a silk merchant, nephew of Seth & John Cheney, & acts as agt. for his br. & uncle who are silk manuf. in Manchester, Conn. Mrs. Olyphant is a d. of Mr. Wm. Vernon, of Newport R. I., & talked with me about the Newport people, Aunt Phily, Hasards, Perrys, Vernons &

[79]Robert Morrison Olyphant (1824–1918), son of David W. C. Olyphant (noted earlier), engaged in the China trade, 1844–1873. He was president of the Delaware and Hudson Co., 1884–1903. He married Anna Vernon of Rhode Island after his first wife, her sister Sophia, had died.

Ellerys.[80] Master Bob [Olyphant] is like Dick in his manners, also. Olyphant tells me that sev. of the Miss[ionaries] at Shanghai whom I did not see, are able men, who gave up high situations at home, & are here at a sacrifice, — some of the Presb. B'd., & one of the Engl. Ch. Miss. Soc., & that the Presb. have 3 chapels in Shanghai & suburbs.

Rainy & windy, rolling sea & ports shut down.

SUND. JUNE 3.   At anchor, in [Hong Kong], at 7 A. M. Ashore at Russell & Co.'s, at breakfast. Mr. [Warren] Delano not returned. Mr. Beckwith at Canton. Most news is that no letters have come for me fr. Calcutta.

To the Engl. Church at 11 o'ck. Large, handsome church, well filled, good share of red coats. No singing, in this great & rich congregation! The preacher a puppy! Sorry to say so — but no other phrase meets his case.

A Mr. Ellis calls, who is friend of C. F. Adams, Fr. [W.] Palfrey &c. &c.

Flowers, trees & shrubs in Bradley's garden, at Ning Po — Pride of China, Woodbine, Maiden's bower, honeysuckle, yellow jasmine, chrys-anthimum, spirla, tree peony, hyperacum, banana, rhododendron max., Camellia Japonica, althea, magnolia, weeping cypress, sika willow, daphne ordora, camphor tree, China astor, tree hybiscus, moutan, & 15 kinds of roses.

MOND. JUNE 4.   Call on Mr. & Mrs. Olyphant, Mr. Heard, Mr. Dent, & on Père Libois, the director of those R. C. missionaries in China who are supported by the Fr. Soc. des Missions étrangères. He has an intellectual head. Tells me there are 8 bishops & 56 European missionaries of his Society, in China, & about 40 native priests. This is excl. of the Jesuits, & the missionaries of the Propaganda. At Hong Kong is the Head Quarters, station house & bureau of the Two Societies, the Miss. Etrang. & the Propaganda. The Propaganda directs ultimately all the Missions, but some miss. go directly fr. it, supported by it. Père Ambrosi, an Italian, represents the Propaganda here.

Grand looking fellows, the Sihks. Proud of step, flashing eye, reg. features, but black as black can be. Look at the Sepoy soldiers, in black glased hats, without front-pieces, looking into the glaring, burning sun

---

[80]Dana met Frank Woodbridge Cheney (1832–1909), who toured the Orient during 1859–1861 buying raw silk. Cheney's father, Charles, and his uncles Fred, Ward, Frank, and Rush were owners of a successful silk mill in Manchester. But the two uncles that Dana mentions, Seth Wells Cheney (1810–1856) and John Cheney (1801–1885), were both artists and engravers, and not active in conducting the family business. Aunt Phily was probably a Smith, Dana's mother's family. There were several prominent Hazard families in Rhode Island. The family of Oliver Hazard and Matthew Calbraith Perry, both noted earlier, was from Newport, as were the descendants of Dana's great grandfather, William Ellery.

without blinking! How picturesque, too, is the white turban, with the dangling white robe & half bare legs & dainty step!

TUESD. JUNE 5. Last night, dined at Heard's, with Mr. Greene of Manilla, (Russell Sturgis & Co.).

To-day, called on Gen. Keenan, the Am. Consul, a tall, well made, rather Westernish man, illiterate, pleasant & natural. Then, on Sir Hercules Robinson,[81] the Gov. of H. K. Sir H. is a thoroughly well bred man, intelligent & young looking for his post — an Irishman. Then, on the Sisters of St. Paul de Chartres. The Superior is very ill, & affairs not in so good order as usual, as there is only one sister for all the establishment, in wh. there are a great number of children, all orphans or children abandoned by their parents. It is called La Sainte Enfance & is a charity, very highly spoken of. Then called on Speidon, at the U. S. Naval Store Hs., where met Rev. Mr. Johnson, Bapt. Missionary, & wife. J. says no *mission* strictly here, & are going to Swatow. Thinks they have 30 Chinese here, whom they can rely upon as converts, & from 4 to 6 native preachers.

Letter from Mr. Nye, at Macao, respecting the portrait he is to send me, probably by the ship Judge Shaw. Spent ev. at Mrs. Beckwith's; — sister of P. S. & Rev. Dr. Forbes.

WED. JUNE 6. Call on Father Ambrosi. His title is Procurator of the Propaganda Fide in China, & Prefect Apostolic of Hong Kong. He is repr. & ag't. of that Soc. & head of its missionaries here. The missionaries of the Fr. Soc. des M. Etrangères are under a head at Paris, who is under the Progaganda at Rome. The Prop. Soc. has in China 5 bishops, 36 Europ. missionaries, & 40 native missionaries. The Lasarists have bishops & clergy. In all, — Jesuits, Prop. Lasarists & Miss. Etrangeres, are abt. 20 bishops & 120 Europ. priests. Each b. has his province.

He tells me that the sisters I saw yesterday are to go to Macao, & that an Italian order of Daughters of Charity, is to come here & have a convent, school, hospital &c.

The Cath. clergy originally adopted the "Shang Ti", for God, but after long & patient investig. (so says Père Ambrosi) they discarded it. The objection was that it signified Supreme Governor, & is applied by the Chinese to the Emperor & to powers supreme in part. They then, 200 years ago, adopted T'ien Chu, wh. means *Coali Dominus*, Heavenly Lord, & have been united on that ever since. The first Protestants took Shang Ti. They later discarded it for S'in. On this is the Prott. controversy.

[81]Sir Hercules Robinson, 1st Baron Rosmead (1824–1897), Governor of Hong Kong, 1859–1865, had a long and distinguished diplomatic career. He was raised to the peerage in 1896.

The Bishop of Victoria has adopted the Cath. word "T'ien Chu", & it is placed on the Br. Ch. College in H. Kong.

Spent all day, after 11 o'ck., alone, in this great house, no one but Chinese servants near, & a hot Chinese sun out of doors, & Chinese locusts murmuring, & I reading Webster's correspondence.[82] Read the 2d vol. He does not put his *mind* into *these* letters. Has not Mr. Everett weeded out the strength of them, or left out the strongest?

[82]*The Works of Daniel Webster,* in six volumes, had been edited by Edward Everett in 1851.

7. The Voyage Back

SATURDAY. JUNE 9. Westward & Homeward, at last! Left Hong Kong, Th. 7th, at 2 P.M. in the P. & O. steamer "Madras". She is a large screw steamer, one of the best of the line. The last three days in H. Kong were hot, — the regular summer heat, & we dined under punkahs [fans], wh. are worked by men out of sight, the lines going thro' the walls, so that the luxurious diners need not be heated by seeing the labor of others. But I have liked this heat, so far. I like the clean white clothes one wears, the slow gait, & the gentle perspiration, & the indolence. Pith hats abound, & other hats & caps with all sorts of puckenys [pugrees?]. How cool are the naked feet, the loose dangling white robes & the gause turbans of the E. Indian races! One meets 6 or 7 races, in a walk up the street of H. Kong — Chinese, Europeans, Parsees, Malays, Hindoos, Negroes &c. &c. & ev. subdivision of those.

Mr. Greene (of Russell Sturgis & Co. of Manilla) has been extremely kind — done more than all the rest, as a mere volunteer.

When I told Beckwith I wanted an introduction to the Capt. & purser, as my comfort depended on it, — he gave a long dissertation on steamers, & sneered at all officers thereof, & all arrangements, — but Greene quietly wrote to the captain, whom he knows well, & got a Director of the company to speak to the purser for me, & thus I got a stateroom to myself, & a seat at the head of the table, & all proper attentions.

Just as we steamed out of H. Kong, Jardine's steamer fr. Calcutta steamed in, — I fear, having my letters on board.

The expenses of exchange & of getting money available among the Chinese are so great, that one gets just about 65 cents for every dollar he draws for. My total expenses in China have been about $300, of wh. $200 are for steamer passages. For this $300, I have been obliged to draw on London for nearly 100 £. At Shanghai, I had to pay 26½ per cent for money. Including my passage home in the P. & O. steamers, I shall lose on exchange about $500!! This is hard to bear. It wd. have been cheaper to pay full board for 6 mos. than to pay exchange.

Still, China & Japan have been a great experience, & a constant pleasure, & I must not grumble!

So far, I have liked the universally abused P. & O. steamers. There is most excellent discipline on deck, & cleanliness, & I have found only civility among the officers. Hours are regular, & cooking, so far, good. The heat does not trouble me. I rather like the tropical routine. Perhaps I shall feel it more in time.

Routine. Made interest & got my steward to spread my mat on the transom in the large cabin, at 10 o'ck. ev. night, & there I lie down in pajamas, with head on a hard China pillow & sleep comfortably. At abt. 5.30, stewards begin to move. Turn out & get a salt-water bath, in a comfortable bathing room. At 6, stewards serve tea or coffee to those who wish it. Gentlemen lounge about in pajamas & China slippers & take coffee, until about 8 o'ck. I take fruit, instead, so long as it lasts. (Delicious fruit is the lychee of China!). At 8, or 8½, go to state room & dress — slippers, loose clothes & straw hat all morning. Breakfast at 9 o'ck. Lunch at 12. Dinner at 4. Tea at 7. In hot weather, at sea, best rule is to take a little at each meal. Never be hungry at sea, or in the tropics, & never be full!

Dress a little for dinner, — a waistcoat, new-collar, &c., & shoes. After tea, I walk deck for 2 hours or more. I believe in exercise in the tropics. It makes perspiration. How wretched are the hours at H. Kong & Shanghai! Dinner under hot lamps at 8 o'clk., & no exercise. The young men say it is hurtful, — & they all drink too much, & of too many kinds. The steamer hours are better.

(Beckwith tells me that the silk trade of China is rapidly increasing, & is now greater than the tea trade, & that much of the raw silk goes to France, but it goes via England. If France took home her silk in her own vessels, & pd. by drafts on Paris, there wd. be a large Fr. commerce, but London does all).

No distinguished passengers. Three or four invalided young officers, going home — rather ordinary persons. Two Sp. gentl. fr. Manila, one a Lt. Col. of the Sp. army, — the other has wife & 2 children, & none of them speak a word of Eng. or French, & have great difficulty. El Señor sits next me, & I help him all I can, — but my stock is small. Still, I gain in Spanish, daily.

Punkahs over all the tables, & swarthy boys in turbans to pull them, — *punkah-wallahs.* Our punkah-wallah has large languid eyes, turban, fes & cap — picturesque!

Last night, heard a song so much like some of our genuine negro songs, that I went forward to see if it was possible that lascars or Malays had learned the negro minstrel melodies. But the song came from the gang of Abysinnian negroes, who are the stokers of the ship, — and it was one of their native melodies. Singular that it should so resemble the melody of the N. Am. negroes that I should mistake it! Proof of unity of negro race. Capt. B. tells me these Abys. negroes are always singing at their work, & are light hearted, — while the Malays & Lascars never sing. The language of the Lascars is all ábrakadábraka, Káraktaŕaktarak.

SUND. JUNE 10. Coast of Cochin China in sight all day. High, with some mountains. At 10 A.M., crew mustered, in neat dresses. Officers & stewards, engineers & petty officers Europeans. Seamen are Lascars & Malays. Firemen & stokers are Abysinnian negroes — "sidis". Some are Mahommedan, with turbans, feses & sashes. Officers have blue coats, uniform caps & buttons, & the Europ. petty officers have white trowsers & frocks — all very neat.

At 10.30, the Church service, read by the Captain, at the capstan. Officers, the Engl. part of the crew, & most of the passengers present. How respectable & proper is this usage of all the ships of the Engl. companies, the world over!

Dead calm, & sun very hot. Even under the awning, it is hardly safe to sit uncovered. An officer told me his head was a little affected, being uncovered. Hence the Eastern custom of covering the head — necessity.

Reading Sir J. Bowring's Philippine Islands.[83] In this, he says that China now clothes her 300 millions with cotton of her own production.

Delightful nights! Great Bear & North Star, in the North, & Southern Cross in the South, both visible together here, in Northern Tropics.

THURSD. [JUNE] 14. Islands off the Coast of Malacca in sight all day. Towards night, saw the P. & O. steamer Peking, bound to China. She has the Eng. & Fr. ensigns set. Ld. Elgin & Baron Gros must be on board. Hove to. Boat comes alongside. Crowd gathers round the officer. The "Malabar" was lost in Point de Galle harbour, having Ld. E. & Baron G. on board, all lives saved, but all or nearly all luggage, & all cargo lost. After delay of 2 weeks, the passengers come on in the Peking. Govt. had great amt. of money on board the M[alabar]. Ld. E. & Baron G. are on board.

Arrive at Singapore at 10 P. M., & can only see a few lights on shore, some elevated, — said to be on the Government Hill. Gun & rocket.

FRID. JUNE 15. At daylight, on deck, & Singapore lies about us. Land is level, but not low, with one or two eminences, & rising into undulating country in rear of the town. Large Govt. establishments & Br. flag waving fr. them. Good deal of shipping in port, of all nations, & numerous Malay, Chinese & Siamese junks. Malay boats come off — long, sharp bows. Malays have broad faces, broad & flat noses, & expression not kindly, nor particularly intelligent. boat loads of pine-apples going by.

Steam up, & go to the new harbor, where P. & O. Co. has a coaling yard, & we all go ashore, with liberty to 2 P.M. of Sat.

To Hotel de l'Esperance, & — first thing in a tropical voyage — , get washing taken, on promise to return tomorrow at 10 o'ck. This hotel is on the Esplanade, — an open ground, with walks & trees, on the sea shore,

[83]Sir John Bowring (noted earlier), *A Visit to the Philippine Islands* (London, 1859).

pretty & cool — open sea, sea-breese, & needed, as this is almost directly under the Equator.

Town is English, in plan & construction, — large buildings of stone & brick, wide, straight streets. ⅔ of the people you meet are Chinese. Shops, shops, shops, & all kinds of work, by the endless industry of these strange people. They come here without women, by the thousands, have children of Malay & Madras mothers, grow rich, & absorb the business & merch. trades. Next to the Chinese, are the "Klings", or Madras men. They are nearly black, but with reg. features — blacker than most negroes. They, too, supersede the Malays, where the Chinese do not, & the Malays, go to the wall, & diminish in numbers.

Sun hot, of course, but air agreeable, & effect of all you see & feel is pleasing. Plenty of trees & shade, & open country abt. the town is rich with grass & trees — palms of all sorts, mango, nutmeg, cocoa nut tree, & bamboo groves & hedges. Pine apples, oranges & bananas in abundance, & the celebrated mangosteen is in its finest condition.

Get carriage — no one walks, as too hot, at noon — & drive to Boustead & Co. to see if my letters have been sent here fr. Calcutta, as I directed. The junior partner says "No" positively. Great disappointment. Let out some of my grief & surprise to the Senior, who sends for the file, looks it over & finds a complete budget for me, fr. Calcutta, & I sit right down & read them all — dates are fr. Dec. to Feb. & fr. all the family, & all are alive & safe. Three letters fr. Dick, — dear little fellow. [A torn corner of the manuscript breaks text here.] Write & spell them correctly. [Mr. Brown invites me to dine. Meet Mr.] . . . O'Sullivan. He invites me, also, but too late — sorry — think shd. have preferred him & his wife, who is sd. to be a pretty Wallachian woman.

At Hodgdon's, Hasen's partner. He was out. At the R. Cath. Convent, to see Miss Spooner. Sister Joseph, I think is her name — came in with the Lady Superior. She is thin & rather pale, & was moved at seeing me & speaking of her Boston friends. Asked her to write to Charlotte, & offered to call for the letter tomorrow. "May I write to Miss Dana?" "Oh yes, certainly", says the Superior. This is a Convent & School. Here are about 60 scholars, girls, & of all races & mixtures of races, educated here at exp. of parents or friends if rich, otherwise *gratis*. Grounds handsome, & houses large & airy. Miss Spooner says she likes the climate, has perfect health, & is happy. Is also a day-school connected with the institution.

In Singapore, is the large & handsome Engl. church, not yet finished, & one R. Cath., & one American. The American was closed, or I shd. have entered it. It is in handsome style, & has a cross on the spire.

The variety of races is greater here than in China, if possible. Europeans, of all races, Chinese, Malays, Parsees, Hindoos, Klings &c. &c. Chinese keep to their costume, & the E. Indians wear turbans of all colors, with white dangling robes. The drivers running beside their horses when in full trot. The Klings "fr. Madras" are well formed, active men, & run beautifully, — thin arms & legs, but very straight, & well set about the hips.

Anderson, to whom Greene gave me a letter, comes in & invites me to breakfast. Just before dark, Brown drives me to his "box" in the country, 3 miles or so out of town. Ground rises, & fine views of the ocean. Delightful ev. breese. House large, rooms lofty, beds large & stately, with rich mosquito nets, — baths & all appliances, large piassas, grass lawn in front, & palm trees, bananas, orange trees, nutmeg, &c. &c.

Company all Scotch. One lady, a Mrs. Davidson — & we have Scotch [political] talk, Scotch landscapes &c. They are all Jacobites. [Arise] at day-break, & enjoy cool morning mist. [Anderson sends] buggy to drive me to his house to breakfast. It is some 3 miles off. Thence, to the river, to see a Malay river. Water dark & deep, & shores lined with jungle. Jungle by the road side, & stories of tigers. Sometimes, the tigers come in towards the settlements, & an average of a man a week is taken off by them.

Surface undulating, & scenery tropical. Pepper fields, on all sides. Pepper grows like hops, on poles, & looks like it. Pineapples grow in ridges, on low bushes.

Anderson has a huge house, with plenty of ventilation & distant views. In the goodness of his heart, he took pains to get me an American breakfast, with salt mackerel, balls of salt cod fish, & such things, when I wished only to eat the products of the place. But he ended with some excellent mangos from Bombay — much better than the mango of Singapore. Taste is something betw. a peach & a muskmellon. The mangosteen has a thick dark red rind, within wh. is a small fruit as white as milk, which melts on your mouth & is delicious, tho' not piquant. Hardly know wh. to prefer the mangosteen, or the lychee of China. They are the most etherial of fruits.

Passed a rajah's house, built in Europ. style, large & sumptuous.

Lucky in getting my washing back safe & in season — wh. all steamer passengers do not. To the Convent, to get Miss Spooner's letter. She says — "tell my friends I am happy here, much engaged in teaching, like the climate better than ours at home, & am in good health" — & desired me to call on her mother, & to remember her to our family, Metcalfs, Judge Bigelow, Sister Jane &c.[84] Leave to shake hands with her. Happening to turn back, saw tears & a h'd'kf., — but not much.

[84]Miss Spooner, obviously a Boston friend of Dana's sister Charlotte, has not been identified. Her other Boston friends were the families of Judge Thernon Metcalf and Judge George Tyler Bigelow (1810–1878), chief justice of the Massachusetts Supreme Court, 1840–1844, and state senator, 1847–1848.

Anderson drives me to the boat, & gives me loaf of cake, & letters of introdn. to Bombay. Going out, drift into the big steamer Coromandel troop ship, — no damage & Capt. not blamed, as pilot directing. On the whole, much pleased with Singapore. Tell me climate healthy, temperature uniform, always hot, — but tolerable, & showers & rains, but no dangerous blows. Harbor open, but safe, for the season of no storms. Is the greatest *place of call* in the East, & has consid. trade of its own, in pepper fr. the Main, & tea fr. China &c., spices, &c.

SUND. JUNE 17.　At sea again, & in the good routine. Glad to find that I can bear the heat as well as others, & better than many, & can sleep when m[ost must sit up in] chairs, for want of air. Again, the good res[ponses in the service,] as general & loud as in the best churches. My home letters give me constant pleasure. Having no letters of introdn. to E. India fr. England settle the little doubt I had about going there — added to expense, loss of time & midsummer heat.

A passenger, bound to Siam, named Allen. Intoduces himself to me as a Mass. man, knowing the Salters, under obligations to them for much kindness in Boston. He is in business in the capital of Siam.

MONDAY. JUNE 18TH.　*Penang* is the most beautiful place I have seen in the East. It is a large island separated by a wide still bay from the main land of Malacca, — the town level, dry & not low, & hills immediately behind it, sloping gradually up, & rising to small mountains, with a waterfall & picturesque scenery. The town is healthy, free fr. malaria, though hot, the temperature & weather being the same through the year. The only bad effect is debility & lassitude. Those who can afford it live part of the time on the hills, in bungalows. The streets are straight & wide, & the whole town is under shade, — the shade of cocoa nut trees, (fr. wh. the name comes), with an interspersing of other palms, of Pride of India & Weeping Cypress. The houses are large, airy & with large yards. How very hot the sun is at noon! — for as we stay here but 6 hours, I must be about at noon, if at all. A double umbrella, linen over silk, & a pith hat covered, hardly defend one. Yet the air is pure, & a gentle sea breese blows all the time, & the sensations are delightful. The Eng. Ep. Ch., & the Presb. are large & handsome, & stand in large yards, under trees.

The mixed races who do the labor here, are very slightly clad, merely white long cloths thrown over the shoulders, & the hard workers not that. The E. Indians, the turban. The drivers of [carriages run by] the side of their horses. Mine ran so all the morning. Cook, acting Am. Consul, head of Currier & Co. He [is generally said] to be accomplished, but as ev. man in Penang is writing letters for the mail, I cannot ask him or any one else to do more than direct me.

Remembered that this was the place where George Channing died & was buried.[85] Mr. Cook thot was a grave stone to a Mr. Channing, but not sure. Drove to the cemetery. In outskirts of town, in good condition, handsome monuments, shaded with trees. In the multitude of tombs hardly expected to find what I sought, when saw a small foot-stone, with letters G. E. C. At the other end of the grave was the head stone, of marble, in good condition, on wh. was the perfectly legible inscription —

> George E. Channing.
> born in Boston,
> United States of America,
> August 10, 1815,
> Died in Penang,
> July 20, 1837,
> from a fever contracted
> on the West Coast of Sumatra.

This was, perhaps, the most interesting incident of my travels in the East, — the more so from its being unexpected. George Channing, & our youth, our College days, our separation to go East & West in 1834, & his coming down to the ship to meet me on my return from California, — these have been in my mind all day. I hope, too, it will gratify his family, & I plucked some grass & leaves wh. were growing on the grave, to take home to them, — & a piece of brick wh. had crumbled off the arch wh. lies over the grave. I am glad, too, to get rid of the associations I had had with Penang, — of deadly fevers, miasmas, Malays & low damp soil, & to see his grave amid so much beauty of nature & so much care of art.

No Am. missionaries here. Called on the rector of the Engl. Church. He lives at a beaut. spot, a mile out of town, high one story house, roomy, airy, blinds, punkahs, verandahs, trees, & the garden running to the bay, with view of the sky-piercing mountain tops of Queda, across the still blue bay. He has gone to town with his letters, but his wife receives me. His name is McKay, a Scotchman, was sev. years assistant to Dr. Harry Croswell of N. Haven,[86] then in Scotland, then chaplain in India, now has this desirable post — wh. is, in fact, a Br. Govt. Chaplaincy.

The chief institutions here are the R. C. College for education of Chinese, & the Convent & School for girls. Called at the Convent. Lady Superior gave me a few minutes. Same order with that of Miss Spooner

[85]George Edward Channing, noted earlier, was Dana's boyhood friend. Both left Harvard to go to sea, and Channing, sailing under Dana's old superior, Captain Thompson of the *Pilgrim*, died of a fever in Penang.

[86]Harry Croswell was the father of Dana's friend William Croswell, rector of Boston's Church of the Advent.

at Singapore, — "Saint Enfant Jesus". There are 8 sister, & 240 scholars, all girls, few of rich parents, who pay, but chiefly foundlings, orphans or abandoned by parents, & of all those mixtures of races wh. the Oriental life of Europeans results in. Buildings, & grounds large & handsome. Lady Superior a bright Fr. woman, & praises Penang, except for debility & lassitude from heat. "Have you no bungalow, on the hills?" "Oh no. Expense of two establishments too great".

Disappointed by not seeing the Chinese College. The Bishop was away, & the priest in charge evidently busy, & I did not wait for the B., as his return was uncertain. The priest told me they had about 120 Chinese, all studying for Holy Orders. Prefer this place for ed. of Chinese, as safe, & remote fr. unfav. influences.

Did I not eat, here, on my way back to the boat, thirsty & hot, the most delicious of pine-apples! It needed no chewing, but melted in the mouth, — completely ripened in the tropical sun.

On board again at 1 o'ck., as we sail at 2. Find the cabin table set out with the fruits of Penang, — Mangosteens, pine apples, mangoes, lychees, oranges, custard apples & bananas. Those called lychees are not the same, nor so good as those of China, — they have prickers on the rind, like a chestnut. Custard apple is pleasant, but insipid. The pine apple can be *imagined* by one who has eaten them at home. Mangosteen is a little pearl of a fruit.

Punctual in starting at 2 P.M. Take lesson fr. the engineer on the action of the screw, in going forward & backing. Backing, turns the vessel round rapidly. Capt. much prefers screw to paddles for working ship.

Leave the little, shady silent town, behind. But the well wooded hills, wooded to their tops, are still in sight, & across the bay, the mountains of Queda, the highest, a slanting wedge, piercing the deep, deep blue of the tropical sky! I cannot [take] my eyes off from it. What stupidity called it Elephant Mountain? It is like Chocorua Peak in N. H., seen fr. Conway, only a sharper wedge, & more slanting.

TU. JUNE 19. High lands of Sumatra in sight. We are steering now due West, for Ceylon, & soon shall be in the Bay of Bengal.

Capt. Brown of P. & O. S. N. Co's ship Madras, pronounces, from the head of his table, that Poe is worth all the Lake Poets put together, ten times over!

We have one Musselman passenger, who has his separate cooking stove, poultry, cook & table, eats by himself, & his cook kills all his poultry. He is a dignified man with long gray silk dress & white turban.

SAT. JUNE 23. Very heavy seas the last 3 days, with squalls. Carried away foretopmast. Most passengers sea-sick. S. W. Monsoons, wh. are light in the China Sea, are very heavy in Bay of Bengal.

MOND. AFTERNOON, JUNE 25, 1860.   The island of Ceylon, — that dream of the poet, — that isle of romance, of aromatic perfumes, in sight all day. Indeed it is very beautiful. There are high mountains in the interior, & undulations of hills & valleys all along the coast, & a dense vegitation of trees. The trees come to the water's edge, as in a lake, but the white surf that lines the shore, & the small rim of beach show it is no lock or mere, but the great ocean that surrounds it. There are few breaks to this close approach of trees & salt sea, — here & there, at long distances, a broken gravelly side of a hill. With our glasses we see a few houses wh. look large & well built, as if of Europeans, standing among the trees. This is the S. Eastern coast we see, between Trincomalee & Galle. We shall be at an anchor in Galle before dark.

Came to anchor at Point de Galle,[87] Island of Ceylon, at about 4 o'ck. this afternoon. A water-spout follows us for a while, outside, in the dim half rainy sky, but soon dissipates. This place is at the S. end of Ceylon, an open harbor, with a surf always rolling, & merely a little sheltered spot for boats to land, under the lee of the fort. The fort is large, of dingy yellow, with high parapets & numerous bastions, over wh. sweeps whatever of sea breese may be blowing, & within its limits are the light house, the churches, & most of the houses of the foreign residents. The view in all directions is delightful, — truly & thoroughly tropical. Nine trees in ten are cocoa nuts, — tall, gaunt, perverse & whimsical in the course their trunks take, with the large tuft at the top of long leaves or branches, swaying about in fantastic directions in the wind, rustling like so many silk banners, & the little knots of fruit, lying half hid at the top of the trunk. There are also the other tropical trees, plaintain, breadfruit, mango & soursop, but the cocoa nut is the feature. The land is high enough, undulating, rising into high hills, & then into mountains, in the interior, & everywhere wooded, — covered with verdure. Hardly anywhere on the globe will you see so much verdure at one glance, — one *circumspection* — as in Ceylon, & it is high, healthful & not low, dank, pestilential luxuriance.

The native boats that come alongside, & the pilot boat that boarded us, are canoes with outriggers, like those in wh. I skirted Hawaii by moonlight. The native boatmen are naked, except a cloth wrapped about the waist, & wear semi-circular combs to keep back their hair, like our school girls.

Landed, & went to Lorette's hotel, where is large piassa, opening on a large yard full of cocoa nut trees, swaying in the cool afternoon breese. It

[87]Dana added the marginal note: "Sent journal to June 25th, from Point de Galle."

is delightful. We are nearly under the Equator & the direct ray of the sun is severely hot, but there is a delicious airy balminess, with a gentle roll of surf, & the rustling of the long palm leaves, — & I am on the Island of Ceylon! It feels like it! All looks like it, as I lie for an hour or more, languidly, at length on a couch, in the piassa.

Call on Mr. John Black, to whose wife I have a letter of introduction with a parcel of Japanese charms from Greene of Manilla, — the universal favorite Greene, to whom every one seems to be under obligations. Black is a Scotchman, acting Am. Consul, & a merchant, & most Americans of note visit him *en route* to & fr. India & China. Mrs. B. is English, well educated, agreeable & lively. Family of 3 small children, — betw. 12 & 5 yrs. old, — all born in Ceylon.

Surprised to hear them talk of *telegrams!* "Is it possible?" "Yes. We have a telegraph direct to Madras, where it goes to Bombay & Calcutta". The communication to those places is immediate, & to England only 6 or 7 days. The island is close to the main. Plenty of Engl. & European news here, but scanty, jumbled & hardly intelligible accounts of Am. politics, — the two Nat. Conventions.[88] The "Overland Mail" & "Home News" gives as much space to America as to Hessi Casel,[89] & what they give is often unimportant & untrue & sometimes unintelligible. Tea at the Blacks. "Assam" tea, a product of Bengal, very strong, goes twice as far as Chinese tea (*on dit*) & bears high price in England. Like it very well. Conversation about Ceylon & its people. B[lack] been here 20 & Mrs. B. 10 years. They say the natvies are gentle, amiable, reasonably intelligent, but inefficient. They have no power of organisation, & no civilisation or social order except what the Europeans put over them. All authority & organisation & learning is exotic, — British. The natives are merely individual subjects, & take what is given them. Offices are open to them, but few rise above the laborer, servant, small trader or small yeoman. The Br. Govt. maintains excellent native schools, in wh. Engl. & Ceylonese are taught, & the people learn generally & readily up to the point of ord.

[88]It would have been difficult to get clear reports on American political conventions, the arrangements for which were in fact jumbled and unintelligible. Dana had probably read reports of the split conventions held in Baltimore, just the week before, by opposing factions of the Democratic party (their first convention, in Charleston, South Carolina, in April, having adjourned with no nominations). John C. Breckinridge of Kentucky and Joseph Lane of Oregon were nominated by the southern faction; Stephen A. Douglas of Illinois headed the other ticket. The Constitutional Union party nominated John Bell for president and got his name on the ballot. Lincoln and Hamlin had been nominated by the Republicans in Chicago in May.

[89]Dana's spelling is unclear, but he may be referring to Hesse Cassel, or *Hessen Kassel,* the name of the eldest in the line of the House of Hesse, the royal house of Prussia. The name would have been in the news because the current ruler, Frederich William IV, had recently been deposed, because of a mental disorder, by his brother and successor, William I.

school edn. A few have risen to be magistrates, & one, who I believe, however, is a half-caste, is a judge of the Supreme Court. You may travel through the interior of Ceylon, in all directions, without weapons. The natives are as inoffensive as women. (They call themselves & are called, — not Ceylonese, but Cingalese, tho' they call the island Ceylon).

They learn to speak English easily & well. All the servants, the laborers, the men one meets in the streets speak English, much more correctly & intelligibly than the natives of most countries under English control. The clerks at the hotels & shops, — who are usually natives, speak it as a mother tongue.

The climate is uniform, — always hot, never cold enough for a change or recruiting of the system, yet agreeable & free from malaria; but the effect on the Northern constitution is debilitating. The women fade & the men run down. The mountain climate is bracing, & has not its superior in the world. There is no special rainy or dry season.

Fruits are oranges, limes, pómiloses, mangoes, breadfruit, plantain & banana, cocoa nut, pine apple, custard apple &c. &c. Pómilo has a rind like a lemon, is about twice the sise of the largest oranges, divided & formed inside precisely like the orange, but with tougher & stronger pulp, & the juice is in little red vessels. It must be torn open & not cut, & the pulp not swallowed. Taste is pleasant, slightly acid, like Deacon Brown's "Good family oranges" — & healthful. Natives live mostly on breadfruit & yams, with a little rice. The rice is more cultivated of late, since the volunteer E. I. coolie emigration of coffee planters. Coffee is a large article of growth. These coolies come overland, & on their own hook.

Invited to take an early drive into the country, before sun well up. Mr. & Mrs. B. cannot go, & their eldest child, Miss Lissy, a girl of about Rosamund's age, is to be my guide.

TUESD. JUNE 26. Rise at day-break, bath, coffee, & at Black's door in good season, where the carriage & Miss Lissy are ready. We drive along the esplanade, through the gates (by the way, the usual tantanana of trumpets of a garrison town is going on here all the time) & into the country. Lissy knows everything, & talks like a book, — is very clever & observing & self-possessed. She could not do better at fifty. She tells me the names & history of everything; & I tell her she may travel the world over (she has never been out of Ceylon) & never see a richer landscape than she showed me from the mount we drove to, about 5 miles out of town. The Serpentine river winds for miles, the green hills & green vales are everywhere, the high mountains in the distance, the soft tropical clouds, that always seem to be ready to drop water, floating over all, & the waving palms & rich scents & perfumes! But the citronella is a little two strong in its perfume. It almost stifles one to ride past it, after it is bruised & crushed to be made into oil. At the Mount is a house, occupied only by servants, who get us fresh cocoa nuts, to drink the milk, & mangoes. Lissy tells me they never drink the cocoa nut milk after the sun is well up, of choice, as it is then a little rank.

I am struck with the excellence of the roads. They are as good as in the suburbs of Boston or London. Lissy says they were made under direction of an engineer, & are kept in good repair by the Govt., & that the road to Columbo is the same, all the way, — some 60 miles, — & that Sir Henry Ward, the Governor, is to be transferred to Madras, & that Sir Ch. Trevelyan[90] is recalled, & much other news & information for a girl of ten, — & that the natives' jewelry wh. they try to sell me at every stop is "glass & brass".

The native life here seems to me to be more truly that of the tropical aborigines, than I have yet seen anywhere, as I see the simple Ceylonese in their open-thatched huts, under the groves of cocoa-nut trees, in their scanty clothing, with their simple inoffensive, gentle manners & expression of countenance.

The girls tie their hair in behind, but the men wear it short, kept back by combs. The usual dress is white, tho' there are some gay colors, — a dangling robe, sometimes drawn over the shoulders, but oftener merely tied about the waist, the women always (I speak only, of course, of the neighborhood of the Engl. settlement) with a decent jacket or short tunic of white.

We see several trees about the sise & shape of an American walnut tree, covered all over with the most brilliant scarlet flowers, as thick as leaves. Indeed, they obscure & eclipse the leaves, & you see only their flaming mass. Unfortunately my Lissy-peadia balked only at that, — she could not recall the name, nor could her mother, — tho' they know it. The sensitive plant grows along the road side as common as grass. A touch shuts it up for the day.

Along these excellent roads, the Govt. has considerately built, at intervals, "Rest Houses", decent covered buildings, with seats. These the Chinese have had fr. time immemorial.

Parrots & paroquets abound in Ceylon, & so do pearls & many kinds of precious stones.

Returned to Black's to breakfast, at 9 o'ck. Call on a Mr. Toppan, agt. for Mr. Tudor's ice business,[91] & get some odd numbers of the D.

[90]Sir Henry George Ward (1797–1860), after a long and distinguished diplomatic career, was Governor of Ceylon 1855–1860. He transferred to Madras in June 1860 and died there. Sir Charles Edward Trevelyan (1807–1886) had just been recalled from the office of Governor of Madras.

[91]Frederic Tudor (1783–1864), brother of William Tudor, had been exporting ice from Boston to the tropics since 1806. The trade was marked by business tactics of great ingenuity and ruthlessness.

Advertiser. Visited two Govt. schools. The buildings are large & airy, & the boys are not compelled to sit confined to benches, as in China & Japan, but, with books in hand, walk up & down the piassas studying aloud. The boys look, ordinarily, intelligent, but effeminate. They are to be the gentle inefficient men their ancestors have been. The teachers were all natives, full blood or half-caste, speaking Engl. perfectly well. In these schools the boys were decently dressed from the shoulders.

A tolerable library of periodicals & books, to wh. I was admitted by Mr. Black, maintained by subscribers.

Sailed at 5 P. M., for Bombay, leaving all our passengers behind, to take the expected boat fr. Calcutta to Aden. We have the boat almost to ourselves, the officers & the Musselman & myself, with Capt. King & the officers of the P. & O. steamer Oriental, condemned.

At Galle, saw the wreck of the Malabar. Ld. Elgin is said to have shown great self possession & coolness in the danger, when many were rushing from the ship.

Long lingering last looks at this beautiful island, as it recedes, in the fading sun of the late afternoon, its deep green hills & vales growing dim, & the white surf that rolls all around its shores less & less audible. Good Night!

Rather a rough & disagreeable passage of six days, from Galle to Bombay, rolling sea, rain & head winds all the way. The last day, Sunday, I was thrown violently, by the pitching of the vessel, & over a wet deck, against a stancheon, receiving a very heavy blow on the ribs that knocked me down & took the breath from my body, leaving it doubtful for some seconds whether I ever breathed again. I fainted dead away for a minute or two, & could not breathe freely for a long time. I struck the right side. Nearly at the same time the Second Steward was thrown down & dislocated his shoulder bone.

It is interesting, Sundays, to see the crew drawn up, for quarters — the Engl. stewards & waiters, in their neat white trowsers & blue jackets, the Engl. seamen, who are all petty officers, in neat white trowsers & white shirts with blue collars, & then the Abysiannian negroes, & the Lascars, — Bengales, Hindoos & of all classes, with robes & turbans, & to hear them answer to their names — the British John Brown, Tom Adams, William Jones, & the Oriental Ismad Mahommed, Ali Abdullah, Mahommed Ali, Daused Sulimanji, Hoosenboy Hoosenji, &c.

Of a rainy night, when the decks are wet & dreary, & the passengers have left the cabin for their berths, how cheerful it looks to go into the engine room, & see the engine working away briskly, the fires gleaming & the oil lamps burning bright. It reminds one of boyhood, when you come home & find the parlor deserted & cold, & take refuge in the kitchen, where there is a cheerful fire, & the preparations for tea, & the smell of newly ironed clothes, & the sight of busy people.

MONDAY. JULY 2, 1860.   Early to-day we make Bombay, but I see nothing of the passage, being laid up in my state-room by my hurt of yesterday. I only hear the jabber of strange voices alongside, & see the red masts of the pilot's boat through my port.

When I am up, it is so rainy & cloudy that I see but little. We are at anchor opposite the company's dock, about 3 miles beyond the city, & the decks are half full of P. & O. officers & clerks, — for Bombay is the seat of the P. & O. power.

The surgeon is very kind, & sees me safe ashore, & goes with me to my hotel, the Adelphi, kept by a Parsee, named Palanjee. I have a nice room in a bungalow, in the yard, opening out towards the sea. Too stiff & painful from my injury to enjoy much. But I am in Br. India, & the servants call me *Sahib*, & say "Salaam" & touch their turbans. My room is long & bare, but with good ventilation, & I have a servant to stay in the room all the time, or about the door. This is the Indian custom.

One of the firm of Dossabhoy Merwanjee & Co., a Parsee house, calls on me, with offers of civilities, in conseq. of letters from Anderson in Singapore. He sits an hour or so, in his cherry colored silk trowsers, white robe & Parsee hat, & declines an invitation to dine, alleging that Parsees never dine with strangers, as cannot eat our meats, beef & pork. Letter fr. Mr. Stearns, an Am. merchant, inviting me to his house.[92]

It rains all the time, being the S. W. Monsoon, wh. is the rainy season, & is rather dreary. Proof that my health must be good, that I can be so cheerful in solitude & dull weather, confined to my room by a hurt.

TUESD. JULY 3.   In my room all day, finishing "Friends in Council",[93] & reading the Am. newspapers my friends the Parsees have sent me. My heart sinks at the nomination of "Abe" Lincoln & Hannibal Hamlin, instead of Seward.

At 4 o'ck., Mr. Stearns comes for me, in carriage. He turns out to be son of Prest. Stearns of Amherst College, & his wife is a niece of Kittredge of Roxbury. Very kind of him. Request him to call in a good surgeon, & sends for Dr. Meade, Surgeon of the Gen. Hosp. to meet me at his house. Ride in the rain through Bombay. See but little. Much is European, or European modified by tropical necessities, & some is native. Here are

[92]William French Stearns (1834–1874), son of William Augustus Stearns, president of Amherst College, was for some years head of the Bombay house of Stearns, Hobart and Company. He returned to New York and is noted for having sponsored the last expedition in search of Dr. David Livingston.

[93]Sir Arthur Helps (1813–1875), *Friends in Council, A Series of Readings and Discourse Thereon* (London, 1847).

tanks, where the water is collected in the rainy season, & women carrying pitchers on their heads, & oxen drawing water fr. the tanks. What strikes me most is the free, graceful, queenly carriage of the women, — even the poor women that carry water on their heads. It is a delight to see them move. A white robe drawn over the shoulder hangs gracefully about them, allowing perfect freedom of motion, & showing the shape & movements, while they step off with a proud, dainty step, each a duchess, — but no duchess that I ever saw walked so well. [Duchess of] Sutherland is a waddle to them.

This place has the greatest conglomeration of races, sects & castes, of perhaps any place in the world, — everything that Africa, Europe & Asia, & all their intermixtures, can produce.

Stearns has a pretty bungalow on Malabar Hill, some 2 or 3 miles fr. the fort. Here most Europeans live. There is a view of the sea, wh. opens at the foot of the hill, & we can both see & hear the breakers. The house is one story, with piassas all round, & long projecting thatched roof, like all bungalows, & is airy & shady, with large, high rooms. I have three rooms *en suite*, a sleeping, sitting & bathing room assigned me, & a native servant. This is very agreeable, & a most pleasant change fr. my hotel. Mrs. Stearns is a pleasing woman, in appearance & manners, with good sense, apparently. They are young, married at home last year, & have their first child, only 6 weeks old, — a boy.

Accident no. 3! Dr. Meade comes & makes a thorough examination, & discovers that I have broken a rib. It is a small rib, & a simple transverse fracture, with no unpleasant attendant circumstances. The break is just over the liver, on the right side, & if I had not been strong in the chest might have given me trouble through the liver, sickness, fever, cough &c. But I am very well, good appetite, no fever & he says I have nothing to fear. Indeed, I can go on in the "Madras" next Sat., if I must, but he rather recommends my staying over one steamer, until I can move about freely, without bandage. Now, he has girded me up as they do a poor saddle horse. But I am allowed to walk about the house & yard, sit at table &c. I take no medicine & not diet.

A good Providence has decreed me an accident, but mercifully made it light, & all its circumstances as favorable as possible, a pleasant home & kind friends, a good surgeon, & above all the good health that gives good spirits & sleep.

In this connexion, Friends in Council quotes fr. Nat. Hist. of Enthousiasm,[94] — to the effect that "the world of nature affords no instances of complicated & exact contrivances comparable to that wh. so arranges the vast chaos of contingencies as to produce, with unerring

[94]Isaac Taylor (1787–1865), *Natural History of Enthusiasm* (London, 1830).

precision, a special order of events as adapted to the character of every individual of the human family. Amid the whirl of myriads of fortuities, the means are selected & combined for constructing as many independent machineries of moral discipline as there are moral agents in the world; & each apparatus is at once complete in itself, & complete as part of a universal movement".

JULY 4, 1860 WED.   Early this morning, my Parsee friend, Dossabhoy Merwanjee, sends me, after the pretty Eastern fashion, a basket of fruit & flowers, in commemoration of our American holiday, with an invitation to dine to meet some Am. residents. The latter I must decline, with thanks for the former. The dinner is to be at the house of Bomanjee Tramjee Camajee! This afternoon, Mr. —— calls, & brings his Hindoo friend, Dr. Bhow Dajee, a scholar & physician, who offers to be my cicerone as soon as I get out. There they sit talking with me, the best of friends, but they cannot eat together! They would loose caste forever. Ask Dr. Bhow Dajee if he was going to Europe. He said it was difficult for a Hindoo to travel out of India, for if he ate with one not a Hindoo, even at a public table, under any circumstances, even of necessity, he was no longer a Hindoo, & could have no dealings with his race & family as an equal ever after. He kindly brought me some photographs of scenes & persons in India, to examine. He inquired about Prof. Dana, the great chemist & geologist, & said his book was thought here to be the best treatise on chemistry extant.[95] How glad I am these people keep to their costumes, — their robes & turbans, while they speak Engl. & read our books! A barber shaves me every morning, dressed in a maroon turban & white robe, & my servant wears a red turban.

All parties, races & persons in India agree in giving Sir Ch. Trevelyan the credit of being the ablest civil ruler India has seen in this generation, however much they differ about his course in publishing his minutes.[96] For insight into the native character, energy & administrative genius, & influence over the natives, he has had no equal.

JULY 5.   Dr. Meade says I am doing very well. Think of that stupid, negligent surgeon of the Madras, having me two days in charge, & not

[95]James Dwight Dana, noted earlier, was a famous geologist but he did not write a book on chemistry. Dana's companion may have confused Professor Dana with James Freeman Dana (1793–1827), whose *Epitome of Chymical Philosophy* (1825) had wide circulation. Both men were distant cousins of R. H. D.

[96]Sir Charles E. Trevelyan had recently been recalled by the British Government from the position of Governor of Madras. The cause of his reprimand was a minute, or memorandum, which he "leaked" to the press concerning a dispute he was having with some administrators in the Legislative Council of India. The minute was thought to undermine the current British effort at presenting a unified front against the Indian rebels.

discovering that I had a broken rib, but setting a man to rub me, — to *knead* me, for a bruise! I wonder the fellow did not break it in, or effect a displacement, at least, — right over the liver, too! Dr. Meade is an attentive careful man, & says I have been fortunate both in the nature of the orig. injury, & in escaping the effects of bad treatment. The fact is that throughout the East, I have experienced the benefits of two good habits, *first,* that I have not, in my youth, " 'plied hot & rebellious liquors to my blood"[97] — & second, that I have the habit, of years, of drinking nothing, not even water, between meals. In the steamers & hotels, & private houses, when almost every one is contriving cooling drinks, & some take soda bottles to bed with them, I drink nothing & have no thirst. And I have the inestimable advantage of a body untouched by anything injurious, blood & marrow as pure as in boyhood.

FR. JULY 6.   As it is now the 5th day since my accident, & I am in excellent health, & sleep soundly all night, I may congratulate myself; &, now, I have no pain in my side. Dr. M. thinks I had better not go on in the boat tomorrow, as the weather is rough in this monsoon, & to be obliged to keep still & watch ev. step & roll is not agreeable. I agree to this, fully. Beside, it would be absurd to leave here without seeing anything of Br. India except from this bungalow. This next boat is the 23d July. This [loses] me two weeks, but patience, amid so many blessings, is not great virtue.

SUNDAY. JULY 15.[98]   I have now been in the house for 14 days; — well all the time, & in good spirits, but advised to be careful about moving suddenly, lest rib be displaced. To-day, Dr. Meade says rib has closed well, & may be risked. Ride to Church this P. M. with Mr. & Mrs. Stearns, & get my (really) first view & notion of Bombay. It is a picturesque & interesting spectacle — that of the E. Indian races, in their marked costumes — Hindoos, Musselmans & Parsees, & here & there an Arab or Persian or negro, each cognisable by his dress, — all, or nearly all with turbans, — but differing in form & color, as much as a 'prentice cap differs from a grenadier's hat. Then, too, of the Hindoos, the divisions of race & region, the Mahrattas, the Gussarattas, the occasional mountaineer from the Scinda & Rohilla country, — & then the marks of caste in the forehead, the caballistic dots & streaks of white or red or yellow; for wh. they will give up their lives — at any time, — that caste wh. will not let a Brahmin beggar take a cup of water from a king of the second caste, — wh. keeps ev. man & woman in India in relations with 9 in every 10, not indeed of hostility, but of separation & abomination.

[97]*As You Like It,* II, iii, 49.
[98]Dana added the marginal note: "Sent journal from Bombay, to July 6th by boat of July 7th."

It is the middle of the "Rains", — the S. W. Monsoon, & everything is green, & rich, & dank & mouldy. The mould affects all the houses, making them look as dull & dingy as St. Paul's. Our woolen clothes, books, shoes, gloves — all are mouldy, & servants are employed in wiping & drying, day after day. This is not the most unhealthy season, tho' it is so damp & warm. There is but little cholera, & not a great deal of dysentery. My phys[ician] is down with dysentery & fever, & about half the Europeans you hear of are sick, in one way or another, — yet there is no epidemic.

The tanks are pretty places. They are of all sises, — some as large as the Brooklyn Reservoir, others as the Frog Pond, & so down to the sise of dry docks & small basins. They are little lakes or reservoirs, open, edged with stone or grass, & in them the water is collected during the rains, for all the year. They are built by benevolent persons, & usually bear their names. They are free to all, to "come & draw freely, without money or price".[99] Now, I see the force of the Scripture figure, — in these dry hot lands. And there are the poor, drawing water freely! & by the banks they wash. And how graceful are these water bearers, — the women, I mean! Here are a thousand swarthy Dianas, Hebes & [Charites]. I cannot keep my eyes from them — there is such grace, freedom & ease in their movements & attitudes. No credit to the Greek sculptors, for their female figures, if they had such before them. These women wear a short, low-necked, short sleeved waistcoat or boddice, just eno' to cover the chest, & then fold about them a piece of cloth, usually of a gay color, wh. falls to the figure, & is gathered up at the knee or thigh, like the pictures of Diana. When they stand to rest or talk, they fall into the attitudes of the antique Greek statues.

The Church we go to is called the Byculla, — fr. the quarter of the town in wh. it stands, — an Engl. Ch. It is curious to see it fitted with punkahs, 6 on each side & one over the Chancel, & an Engl. Congr. inside, & the poor heathen, to whom the Gospel is sent, standing outside pulling the punkahs. As it is dark before the service ends, each pew has a light, at the corner, a candle in a glass globe, & all are lighted, — but the waving punkahs keep us cool. Then, almost ev. one rides to church, & the garra-wallahs & drivers, hang round outside. I fear the congr. of heathen servants outside is greater than that of Europeans inside.

On our way, passed a group of Bedouin Arabs. The heathen might as well be outside. The stupid Chaplain had such a thick, lolloping tongue & bad elocution, that I could not tell what he was reading about, in the lessons, & the sermon, scarcely more articulate, had nothing to do with the text, & the parts of the sermon no connexion with each other. The Stearnses say the Engl. chaplains & preachers here are intolerably dull.

[99]Isaiah 55:1.

While I was laid up, my friends Dr. Bhawoo Dajee, the learned Hindo, & Dhunjeebhoy Merwanjee, the Parsee merchant, called & offered services, brot books &c. I delivered no Engl. letters & made no calls, — as I had little time, & preferred to give what I had to natives.

MOND. JULY 16TH. Rode to town, & called on Merwanjee & Co. & Dr. Bhawoo Dajee. The streets in the "Fort", where all the business is done, & where most of the natives live, are very narrow, with high walls, 5 & 6 stories high, & crowded with passers, & hot & close. How can these people live there, day & night, for years! No wonder they are so yellow & bloodless. Passed the Basaar at wh. the stock brokers congregate, all in white robes, & white or red turbans.

Bombay is built on an island, or series of islands, connected by causeways. The harbor lies betw. these & the Main. On the rear, & open to the sea, is Malabar Hill, where the bungalows are, in wh. the Europeans live who can afford it. The Parsees own the hill, or rather hire of the Govt., & no bungalows can be got but fr. them, & rents are very high. The next best section is Byculla, but it is low, & the next is Colába. In the centre is the Fort & esplanade. The Fort has walls & gates & a ditch, & is guarded; but within its straightened limits is all the business of Bombay, wh. is now or soon is to be, the largest in India.

At Bhawoo Dajee's, introduced to sev. venerable old Brahmins, & at Merwanjee's to some Persians, with long beards & long white robes.

Dined with us to-day Rev. Mr. Harding, Miss. of Am. Board, & his wife, & Rev. Mr. Bowen. H. is rather a flat, — no match for a Hindoo. Mr. Bowen is a character. Was a rich, fashionable New Yorker, of liberal education, European travel &c., love affair, death, change of life, Missionary, renounces all "Boards" & denominations, supports himself, lives among the natives, in their closest streets & among their meanest houses. Yet, when he does go out among the Europeans, he is prised above all men for his convers. powers & manners.[1]

Bowen tells me there are as many as 100 castes now, & that they have little power in regulating the callings & occupations, little being left but their exclusiveness, wh. continues unabated.

TUESD. JULY 17TH. Call on Bhawoo Dajee, by appointment. Shows me his library & cabinet &c. he took the prises at Elphinstone College, & studied 6 years at the Grant Med. College, in all branches of Nat. science, & was distinguished. He has large practice & consid. influence, both with natives & Europeans. Shows me a Ms. on palm leaves, 500 years old, &

[1]George Bowen (1816–1888) preached in Bombay for forty years before his death. A Methodist after 1873, he edited the *Bombay Guardian*, 1854–1888.

the title deeds to an estate engraved on plates of copper, bound together by chain & key.

B. D. took me to Sir Jamsetjee's Hospital. This was founded by Sir Jamsetjee Jijibhai, the Parsee merchant.[2] He gave a lac of rupees (100,000) & the Govt. as much more. Much has been added since & its entire cost, to this time, has been about 700,000 rupees. Large stone building, long & low, in large yard, & well ventilated. Wards for leprosy & small pox. Prevalent diseases (chronic) are elephantiasis, opthalmia, leprosy & dysentery, & (acute) small pox & cholera. Next, went to the Grant Med. College, an admirable institution, where all the nat. sciences are taught, with good apparatus, museum of comp. anat., cabinets of minerals &c. Rather an imposing building. Then, saw outsides of the Elphinstone College & the Byaulla School, & Sir Jamsetjee's Charity School. (Sir J. was made a baronet, in 1858, & died soon after). His son, Sir Custeebjee, is now in Engl. Sir J. is said to have given away 100,000£ sterling.

To the Bot. Garden. Saw there a strychnine tree, every leaf a deadly poison, sev. banyan trees, & the cinnamon, frankinsense, tamarind, nutmeg & teak. The common laboring coolie, half naked (& more) who followed us to climb the trees & cut flowers, knew the names of all the rare trees & shrubs.

On our way, stopped at the cottage of a laboring Parsee, to taste the toddy, made from the wild date tree. A naked coolie went up the tree, like a monkey, with a hoop of pliable bamboo round his waist & round the tree, to keep him to it, & then bore off by his feet — hatchet & pitcher in hand, — tapped the tree & brot down the pitcher full of juice. When allowed to ferment, it becomes intoxicating, & is the *arrak*. But when fresh, it is pleasant & healthful, slightly acid.

B. D. takes me to the house of a wealthy Hindoo, perhaps the wealthiest in Bombay. His son is in, & does the honors, — a most sensual & gorged looking chap, of about five & twenty, turning into an animal, fast, as in the fable. His house is very large, halls & rooms large & high, & a great deal of the black-wood furniture, for wh. Bombay is celebrated. But this is a waste of taste or experience, for cheap & commonplace Europ. prints, plaster casts & furniture are mixed with it. Gardens large, level, exqui-

[2]Sir Jamsetjee (or Jamsetji) Jijibhai (1783–1859), whose name Dana misspelled "Jejeebhoy," was a highly successful Bombay merchant who had specialized in catering to foreign customers. Knighted in 1842, he was widely known as a philanthropist. In 1855 he was presented with the "freedom of the city of London," in 1856 was honored with a statue in the Bombay Town Hall, and in 1858 was created a baronet, the highest honor ever given to a native Indian. His son, mentioned later, seems not to have extended his father's holdings, and public records make remarkably little mention of him.

sitely neat & carefully attended. Low, open-work walls of porcelain, on each side of the walks. Servants in troops, 4 or 5 dusting one room. Sepoys at the door. Sepoys in mil. dress are the Suiss, the door keepers, of the great houses in India.

In a carriage saw a man having a full sised crown [on] his head, with high points, gold or gilded. Bhawoo Dajee tells me he is one of the lineal descendants of Mahommed, who are known by that crown, everywhere, & are treated with honor or worship — descendants of his daughter. His sons died without children. It is worth coming to Bombay, to see a lineal descendant of Mahommed!

Bhawoo Dajee rejects Hindooism, & abhors the system of castes, & receives all the moral teachings of X'tianity, but has doubts abt. the X'n Revelation. In this state, he conforms outwardly to Hindooism, wears the caste mark on his forehead &c., but is doing all he can indirectly by aiding the dissemn. of knowledge & education among Hindoos & intercourse with Europeans, to break in on the system.

WED. JULY 18. Called, by appointement, on Merwanjee & Co., who have promised to show me the ladies of their households, in full dress. In the third story of their house, is a large drawing room, with richly carved blackwood furniture. Here the ladies & children were seated. The women were most richly dressed. Short low tunics, & long robes, of bright colors, & jeweled rings in the ears, at top & bottom, in one nostril, on neck & wrists & fingers & ankles & toes, barefooted, of course, except that they have ornamented slippers, into wh. they sometimes thrust their feet. Hair black, eyes black or dark, complexions — the best a fair olive, but ordinarily yellow, noses aquiline & sharp, & a kind of Jewess look, — usually very thin, — tho' I have seen fat Parsee women. None of them spoke Engl., & I believe none of them can read or write. A Parsee has but one wife, but divorce is allowed in case of having no child. The Parsees are the Jews of India, excluded fr. other occupations, have taken to trade & become very rich. They live by themselves, never eat or marry with others. No Parsee woman in Bombay ever became a public woman. Their rigid system prevents it. When I rose to leave, they gave me a bouquet & showered me with rosewater, from a silver censer, & brot me paun soparees on a waiter, — these are little mixtures of spicery rolled up in a betel leaf, wh. the natives are fond of chewing. They are agreeable. I have become fond of them. Betel nut is an ingredient & alspice, cloves &c.

Nearly all the men of this large family were present. The family name is Lowjee, but that is not in use ordinarily. They use two names, as Dossabhoy Merwanjee, Dhunjeebhoy Merwanjee, Cursetjee Dhurjeebohy &c.

This ev. at abt. 8 o'ck., set off, with Mr. Stearns, for Poonah, in the Deccan, the ancient capital of the Mahratta Empire, the headquarters of the Brahmin power in S. India. The great enterprise of the rail road has brot Poonah within attainable distance, & only the Ghats Mts.[3] are to be crossed on foot. Went up by night, because Mr. S. cd. only give two whole days.

Rail road carriages large & commodious & as it was dark & raining, had only to lie down on the benches & sleep. At stopping places, heard jackals, close to the cars, & occasional other distant cries, wh. *may* have been tigers.

About midnight, reached Kampoolie, where the road stops, at the foot of the Ghats, & we take palkees (palanquins), to ascend the Ghats by torch light. It is dark & rainy, & we see nothing but high hills ag. the sky, & the flash of torches, along the steep winding ascent. I get a palkee, a kind of palanquin, in wh. one lies nearly at length, — not high eno' for sitting up, with sliding doors on each side, borne on men's shoulders, 2 before & 2 behind. I have seen no sedans in India, & saw no palanquins in China. My palanquin had 10 men, & I suppose each had the same, 4 bearers, 4 reliefs, & 2 torch bearers. The carriage of all the passengers & freight up the Ghats, by night, in this style, makes an array — but the freight, I believe, is carried in gharreys, or bullock carts.

I dosed away most of my time, & about 3 o'ck. in the morning we reached Khandála, whence the rail road begins again, & half sleeping, half awake, were precipitated along to Poonah, wh. we reached just at dawn. I believe the distance is 130 miles fr. Bombay.

Look out of our carriage just eno' to see that Poonah is on a wide spread of high table land, with mountains in the distance, & are driven to a hotel, called the Queen's, owned by Parsees, kept by a Hindoo, where we have a bed-room & washing room a piece, & after washing & a cup of tea, & ordering breakfast at 9 o'ck., Stearns & I walk out to get our first fair view of Poonah.

THURSDAY. JULY 19TH. The ancient city of Poonah is about a mile below us, the Br. garrison about 2 m. off, on the high plain. All the space abt. the garrison & betw. that & the city is called the Camp. We walked thro' the Camp Basaar, wh. is a town of natives, laid out by the Br. in reg. streets & built mostly of native houses. Here are the Fish Basaar, the Meat Basaar, the Fruit Basaar, & the Vegit. Basaar, & the usual varieties of mango, pineapple, pómelo, pomegranite, banana, custard apple &c. &c., & the usual sprinkling of Parsees & Mussulmans among the Hindoos. Out of the basaars, the streets are wide & straight, & lined with bungalows of

[3]Dana misspelled this as "Ghauts."

Europeans, each having the occupant's name on a sign at the gate —
"Capt. Barker, 19th N. I.", "Lt. Jones, 4 E. Cavalry" &c. These bungalows
are pretty, with grass & trees. The roads are hard & well kept, & the
horses & carriages in good Europ. style.

All the ground betw. the city & garrison, or nearly all, is occupied by
Europeans. Soldiers abound. Red coats & topees (pith hats) & pugrees &
Sepoys in the half Europ. uniform.

After breakfast, called on Rev. Mr. Gell, Army Chaplain, to whom Mr.
Bowen gave me a letter, & Stearns called on a Mr. Mitchell,[4] a Presb.
Miss., whom he knew. No tropical vegitation visible on the high plain of
Poona, — that is, no palms, cocoas, or palms of any kind. It might be
England, or N. England. Yet many of the trees are tropical & aromatic,
like the mango, nutmeg &c., but do not look peculiar to the tropics.

It rains ev. hour or two. Gells have a pretty house. Mrs. G. is young &
pretty, & Mr. G. has the University Gentleman look. But they are going
out on a visit to sick friends, & I beg not to detain them. While they
are gone, Stearns comes in with an invitation fr. Mr. Mitchell to go in his
carriage to see the famous old Hindoo temples on Parvutti Hill. Leave note
for the Gells, & go to Mitchell's. M. & wife, & a Rev. Robertson & wife, all
invalids, & all drinking ale or wine, at tiffin, under advice of physicians.
Mrs. R. too ill to come to table. The heats of May & June, wh. are terrible
on this plain, have done them all up. Both R. & M. are scholars, & talk
of Greek & Modern Greek &c.

After tiffin, ride to Parvutti Hill. Get out at foot, & walk up. Broad
stone steps all the way up, 20 f. wide or more. Temples & fort in one.
Well fortified, for old times. Temples in the Saracenic style, with numerous little domes & minarets, richly colored. Not permitted to enter —
profanation. Several Brahmins to wh. Mitchell talks freely ag. their idols.
They say they do not worship the idol, but only reverence the representation of a Divine Power or agency. They are all beggars & stipendiaries,
& the British Government pays an annual sum for the maintenance of this
Heathen Temple! The defence is that they succeed to the custom of the
Hindoo Govt. they subverted, & policy requires its support. The temple
is decaying & the Brahmins diminished in number, & but for the Govt.
support, I think the whole wd. fall to the ground.

(Parvutti is a daughter of Vishnu.) From the battlements of the
temple, fine view of the great plain & distant empire. There lies the

[4]John Murray Mitchell (1815–1904), Presbyterian missionary and Orientalist, arrived
in Bombay from Scotland in 1838. Making many converts, he established the Free
Church Mission at Poona in 1843. A writer on theological subjects, he was later at
Simla, Bengal, and still later at Nice. Shortly before his death he returned to
Edinburgh.

ancient city of Poona, the capital of the Mahratta Empire. Hyder Ali took it once, Wellington was here, but not as conqueror, I believe, & there, only 3 or 4 miles fr. the city, just below where the two rivers join, is Kirkee, where the battle was fought, in 1817, that ended the power of the [Peshwar], & placed Poona in the hands of the English. Mountstuart Elphinstone was residing near there, the "Resident" at the court of Poona, & the Peshwar went out to take him prisoner by subtlety, but E. got notice, swam the river on his horse, reached the Engl. camp at Kirkee, & the Br. sallied out, & the battle ended the Mahratta Empire.[5]

Returned slowly through the ancient city. The great palace is converted into a jail & hospital. Several of the old palaces frown upon the streets, looking like store houses, four storied, mouldy stone buildings, in plain style. The streets are narrow, & so crowded, so dense with people, who all look so hot, & sweaty & bilious, as if they never breathed fresh air. Here, too, are some very pretty tanks, & women bearing water on their heads, & bullock with leathern panniers filled with water, & monetary looking Parsees, with long receding hats, & Hindoos with the patch of "caste" on the forehead, & the grave Mussulman, & turbans of red & yellow & white & green, & dangling robes of all colors, & the common people naked to a mere hand breadth, — making the greater number of all you meet. Naked men lie on the floor & ag. the sides of houses, & all wear as little as possible, & of a form to drop off as easily as possible. Here, too, the common women are bangled & spangled & ringed like the richest Hindoo matron, the only difference being that the one wear real gold & jewels, & the other glass & brass; but, at a distance, the common woman is the counterpart, with her nose rings, & ear rings, necklaces & bracelets, finger rings, anklets & rings on her toes. How proudly & daintily she steps off, barefooted, bare headed & bare armed, with the water vessel on her head, & her glitter & jangle of glass & brass!

Spent the night quietly at the inn, where were a party of three commonplace Englishmen, who had been drunk all day, & were sick, & one thought he had cholera, & made a sad scene of it. The next day they looked wretched eno'. The wonder is that they stand these excesses in such a climate as long as they do.

[5]Poona (Poonah, Puna) was the capital of the Mahratta realm of the Peshwa. Hyder Ali defeated a Mahratta–British alliance against him when he was Maharaja of Mysore. The British sued for peace terms in 1769. In 1817 the new Peshwa, having been released from custody in the form of official British protection, attacked the British at Kirkee. Mountstuart Elphinstone (1779–1859), British Resident at Poona, 1810–1816, participated in the repulse of Mahratta troops. The Peshwa's kingdom was taken away upon his defeat, and Poona was annexed to the British Empire. Elphinstone was governor of Bombay, 1819–1827, and upon retiring published a *History of England* and, posthumously, *The Rise of British Power in the East*.

FRIDAY. JULY 20TH. Took rail-road at 9.45 A.M. for Bombay. Stopped at Kirkee, wh. is a cavalry station, & where there are red coats & spurs & pugrees on the platform; & then at Campowlee, where we took palkees (palenquins) to descend the Ghats.

This descent, wh. occupies about 2½ hours, is glorious! The road, cut by the native princes, centuries ago, to connect the upper Deccan with the sea coast, winds down the mountains, as steep as men or bullocks can safely walk, while above, below & around are the high tops, the deep ravines & gorges, & the opening, far stretching plains; & now, in the midsts of the rains, the mountain sides are alive with cascades. Water falls fr. all points, & in all forms & quantities. The bearers sing all the way, a rude line with a short chorus of 2 or 3 words.

Khandala. Tiffin at the "Victoria Hotel", a hut of 2 rooms & no furniture but chairs & plain tables. Still, got a decent lunch, for the natives can cook, — all people can cook but the Yankee & Englishman. Reached Bombay at dark, where Stearns' faithful garra wallahs & coach were waiting for us.

It rained nearly all the way after we left the Ghats. The laborers in the field wear a curious rain coat, a mat with a top like a hood, partly surrounding them. They put it on & stand with the back to the rain, as if they were looking out of a mat cabin that had no door. Most of the laborers in the fields are men. The women, if they work at all, do light work. In the heavy rain, & up to their ankles in mud & water, the natives are ploughing & weeding. The plough is the scratch plough, wh. goes lightly over, & the animals are the Indian bullock, wh. has a high hump ag. wh. the yoke rests, or the water buffalo, an animal as common here as in China, & always rolling in the water or sand when it can.

(On our way down, stopped at Tannah, wh. was a Portuguese fort & settlement. Some Portuguese are there still). (At Poonah, saw great abnormal, towering awkward camels, with riders, passing through the streets).

SATURDAY. JULY 21. An Anglo Indian household has a great many servants. The native servants do but one thing each. One sweeps, one cleans furniture, one takes care of the lamps, another waits on table, & in the stables no man takes care of more than one horse. Their pay is very small & they find themselves — food, lodging & clothing. The rules of their religions & the rules of caste keep them from the food of Europeans & often fr. the tables of each other. They sleep on mats under the verandahs, or, if they have families, in huts of their own in the compound (yard). Some have as little as $2 a month, feeding themselves. Mr. Stearns has a reasonable establishment for a successful young merchant with only a wife & child; yet he has, in all, 17 servants. The butler is the chief officer of every household, a kind of steward & housekeeper. He presides over the servants, & all complaints on discipline are thro' him. Mr. S.'s butler has $7 a month. The other servants are bobajee (cook), cook's coolie, 2 table boys, musaul (lamps), hamaul (furniture cleaner), 3 gorawallahs (grooms), shobee (laundry man), parree wallah (water carrier), dirsee (tailor & seamstress), sweeper, gardener, watchman, & coolie. These are men. Then there is the ayah (child's nurse), Mrs. S. is thot very self denying not to have an amah, or waiting woman for herself, & when the pair of horses is out in the carriage, one of the gora wallahs is coachman, wh. is an economy. Each gora wallah sticks to his horse, & either drives him or sits behind or runs by his side. No coach goes without at least one footman, & often two. They run before, when coming to a corner, to warn & give notice, & stand by the horse's head when the coach stops.

Mr. Stearns' broker is a liberal Hindoo, a disbeliever in Hindooism, & inclined to X'tianity, a very clever young man named Kársandros Madhavadras. Knowing that I wished to see Hindoo ladies, he prevailed on a friend to have his wife dressed in her full dress, & sent his own wife & sister to join them, at a certain hour, when I was to be introduced, secretly, for, if known, they would be considered as polluted. We drove to the house, & after a while I was presented to the ladies. They were richly decked. Rings in ears & noses, on fingers & toes, & necklaces, bracelets & anklets. Their dress was a small tunic just eno' to cover the breast, feet, arms & neck bare, & a mantle of silk or cotton wrapped about the figure, coming down to the knee & looped up. It is very graceful, & very cool. They are of sallow complexions, & without the sharp features of the Parsee women. They sat on sofas, & gathered their feet up, or one foot, & bent the knee, as small children would do. They spoke no English. Karsandros' wife was fat, — the others lean & sickly.

Thence to Bhawoo Dajee's. My good friend has taken great pains to entertain me. Several Hindoo friends of rank come in & are presented. The first entertainment is a juggler. He sits on the floor of the verandah, & we sit in chairs directly before him, & he has no table or accomplice, or long sleeves, or any means of concealment, except a small coarse bag wh. lay by him. He is a Mahommedan & has grave & decorious manners, salaaming to us before & after each trick. He produced a small mango tree with flowers from nothing, & brought sev. cooing doves from nowhere, & burned out the insides of his mouth, & performed inexplicable tricks with cups & balls. B. D. apologised for not getting a snake-charmer. They are not here in "the rains". Next came a man with two bears, who performed creditable tricks, salaamed, wrestled, were thrown &c. Then came a man with monkeys & goats, who acted little farces, taking parts of soldiers, old women &c., he singing all the time, & shaking a little drum wh. was thus beaten by two balls on the ends of strings.

Now we adjourned to the parlor, & minstrels came. One played an instrument like a guitar with a bow. The other played a lute & sang. The songs were in Hindostanee, Mahratta, Gussaratta & Persians. The singer is said to be the best in Bombay. I liked the Persian songs best. They had more air & the words were more articulate. They were like Spanish airs. Next a boy of 14 or 15 sang, the most celebrated boy singer in Bombay. B. D. says the Hindoos have little notion of harmony, & make no direct attempts at it; but he thinks the Hindoo music fully equal to the European in melody. In his *omnifacent* way, he is arranging some Hindoo airs with the harmonies.

The next & last entertainment was a mimic. He gave imitations of Brahmin pundits disputing on a nice point of metaphysics, of Parsees chanting their prayers, & of a Brahmin reading passages of Sanscrit & expounding them. The latter caused great merriment among our grave friends, for B. D. says the Sanscrit was mere sound & the interpretation mere jumbles of great words. Then he imitated Arabs singing, in deep, hoarse voices, ending almost in a bray, & the sharp, high-voiced people of the Carnatic.[6] I called for an imitation of English. They declined, but when I insisted, he gave one, but seemed embarrassed & drew it mildly. But I could get their notion of us. He rubbed his chin, rubbed his knees, worked his face, turned his head on one side & the other, talked in a thick voice, often too low to be heard, & as it were by jerks, with awkward attitudes & motions. It is evident that the native notion of the Englishman is not of a lion or tiger, but of a wild boar.

After this very agreeable entertainment, we drove out. Drove to a beautif. Mahomn. mosque, very large, of white stone, with numerous domes. Then to the chief Parsee Fire Temple. This is a clean, quiet house, in a clean quiet yard, with a verandah at each end, & rooms with books & pictures, & a few white robed Parsees lounging there to read or pray. In the centre, where I cannot enter, is a room with a kind of altar on wh. burns the perpetual fire. It is a clear hot afternoon, & from the walk we see the broad Back Bay, & the Parsees making their evening worship to the sea. Bhawoo Dajee gives me his expln. of what we call worship of sun & sea. He says the Oriental habit is reverential & worshipful. They bow down before parents, elders & benefactors & they honor by outward reverence all great manifestations of goodness & power. In theory, the sea & sun have no being, no soul, no power to will or do, & are not treated as persons, but the people declare & speak out, by outward reverence, their admiration of the greatness & benefits of the Sun & Sea.

[6]The Carnatic (or Karnatic) region is in southeastern India.

Stopped at place where four streets met, & sat in our carriage while B. D. pointed out to me the races, castes, nationalities & occupations of the thronged passers by. He knew them all — by dress & feature — Mahommedan, Parsee, Hindoo, Persian, Arab, Nubian, & the Mahrattas, Gussarattas, [Sihks], Bengales, Rohilla &c. Among them were devotees, fakihrs, one who lived under a log by the wayside, & wore his hair to the waist uncombed, & lived on charity. He was a traveling fakihr, & had seen all parts of India, going fr. temple to temple.

Then to the dense basaars, — where one can hardly breathe from the closeness. At an ivory carver's shop, he selected an ivory music box, & insisted on making it a present to my wife in America, & added to it two carved paper folders of sandal wood. A Mahommedan beggar stands in the middle of the street, with a fan, & gives a single stroke of the fan toward each passer by. B. D. says the theory is that every benefit, however slight, calls for a return, & a whiff of a fan in the heat, is a benefit, & he is to be compensated. But very few seemed to notice him.

My friend B. D. had got me an invitation to a party at the house of a Parsee millionaire, one Byranjee Hormuejee Camagee,[7] said to be worth 25 laco, & head of the house of Cama & Co. of Bombay, having a branch in London. At 10.30 P.M., B. D. came for me in his brougham, for, as an M.D. he drives in a brougham; but, *mem.* that the natives all keep to their costumes. It was a dark rainy night, & the monsoon blew half a gale, but all houses here have a vestibule to drive under, a protector ag. sun & rain. Here were numbers of servants & lights, & going up the broad steps, we came into the hall. We were very late, & the guests were just going into supper. I was duly presented to Byranjee, & recd. with elaborate but kindly politeness, & placed near him at the table. In the supper room, a long table is set, with fruits, flowers & cakes, — no meats or fish — & an abundance of wine. Byranjee took the head of the table, & all the Europeans sat down, but no Hindoo sat at the table, or ate anything, for that is an abomination to the Hindoos. The Parsees, too, ate nothing, but took wine. The party was given to a Mr. Fleming, an Engl. merchant, who takes leave of India on Monday, having made a consid. fortune, & is much respected. Byranjee, in a simple, straightforward speech, in good English, proposed Mr. F.'s health, spoke of his kind & just conduct toward the natives, & their respect for him & regret at parting with him, & added a few proper words about the amity &

[7]This is probably Pestonji Hormusji Cama (1805–1893). Cama and his brothers established the first native Indian house of business, for trade, in London in 1855. Known as a philanthropist, Cama was awarded the title of Companion of the Indian Empire in 1887. The man Dana met might also have been one of the other Cama brothers.

intercourse of the races in India. This was done in a diffident but dignified & graceful way. Thereupon the English drank Mr. F.'s health, standing, with hip, hip, hurrah & 3 cheers. Mr. F. made a few remarks in reply, with good feeling, & propriety, but not so well as the Parsee. Then followed a long awkward silence. I spoke to my neighbor & asked if no one was to propose the health of our host. I suspect all the company were merchants & traders, & not used to such occasions, for no one spoke, & my neighbor was a nobody. At length poor Byranjee rose, & begged his European friends to excuse him if he omitted anything that became a host, as he was unacquainted with our usages, & proposed the health of all his guests. His guests drank their own healths, & then came another silence. I was strongly tempted to get up & thank & compliment our host, & lead the way, — but I was an entire stranger, & it might be thot an Am. interference, besides, I expected some one to rise ev. moment & do the proper thing. But no, — all rose & left the table, without a word. Byranjee seemed to think it all right, & they thanked him privately for his hospitality &c. — but how stupid it was! So some of them admitted after it was too late.

From the dining room, we went into the large saloon, where seats are ranged against the wall, on three sides, the outer doors being the fourth side. At the head of the room are the seats of honor, & there the guests shaded down to those of the lower degrees near the doors. There were occasional pressures to "go up higher", (see Scripture),[8] & having taking a low seat, not intentionally, but in ignorance of the order & to be nearer the musicians & dancers, I was eventually carried up.

The entertainment consisted of music & dancing by Nautch girls. This is the usual entertainment at Parsee & Hindoo parties, for their own ladies never are present, & they never dance themselves, — neither men nor women, — the accomplishment being confined to girls who live by it & by its usual accessories. The guests sit round the 3 sides of the square, the Parsees in high receding hats, red loose trowsers & white cassocks, & the Hindoos in turbans of all shapes & colors, tunics & togas wrapped or draped about them, & all without stockings, & some without shoes, & conforming to the European custom of sitting in chairs, they still ease themselves occasionally by gathering up one or both legs.

At the other end, by a pile of shawls & cushions, on the floor, sit two Nautch girls, & two grave musicians, playing on stringed instruments.

The gravity & even sadness of the countenances of these girls was most striking. It fascinated you. What can it mean? What hidden grief? What concealed sickness?

[8]Luke 19:10.

Presently the elder, who is perhaps 18 or 20, rises & begins the dance. She is dressed as a Persian, in a rich gown, coming to the knees, with pantaloons below. It is not so graceful a dress as the Hindoo, but it is perfectly proper & decent. The dance is as slow & dull & meaningless as I have seen it described, — more like a funeral solemnity than a social entertainment. She is a Mahratta girl, of that warlike race that so long ruled the Carnatic & the Deccan, & gave so much trouble to the English, a race of natural politicians & soldiers, as the Gujaratas are natural traders. She is very, very, thin, very, very, sallow, with damp black hair parted & drawn back from her ears, & deep, deep dark eyes. How fixed, sad, serious is their look! Is this all mere color, or is it character?

Now the girls retire, & come in again in their native Hindoo dress. The graceful mantle, or wrapper, gathered across the shoulders & falling as drapery to the figure. She looks larger, & less thin in this, & the yellow hue suits her face better. But her features are irregular, & she has no beauty, — yet there is a charm in the gravity & seriousness of mien & the *capabilities* of that eye. Now the girls sit & only sing. The other girl is only 12 or 13, & does not dance at all, & only sings to accompany the elder. The songs, wh. B. D. translates to me, are all light, fanciful love songs, & here — as I believe almost always in E. Indian love songs, the woman is the lover, the adorer & the sufferer. One song was that calling on her dear rajah to take her to Calcutta. Marajah.

Fleming & his friends having taken leave, & it being late, I followed, leaving the Nautch girls & some 20 or 30 Parsees & Hindoos still there. I am told that the dancing is often more animated at the small hours, if the host encourages it. Before leaving we had bouquets, paun soparees (spices, & betel nuts in a soparee leaf) & were sprinkled with rose water.

SUNDAY. JULY 22.　To the Engl. Church at Colába. It is a truly beautiful church, large, cruciform, of yellow stone, with clerestory & very deep Chancel. Large part of the congr. were soldiers & officers & red-coats prevailed. The high roof & open windows make the church a resort for sparrows, who twitter distractingly all the time, &, though the parson is, no doubt, of more value than many sparrows, he did not make as much noise, & we could hardly distinguish what he read or said. Besides, he kept his voice up at the same key with the twitter. If he had pitched it as low as possible he would have been heard.

Rode home fr. church over Malabar Hill from the Back Bay, a picturesque scene, of high rocks, deep dells, & a climbing carriage way. All along this hill, across it & on the W. slope are the bungalows of all who can afford to live out of the town, — that is, afford the necess. horses, carriages & servants.

Spent the ev. quietly with my kind host & hostess, for tomorrow I leave India.

S[tearns] is a true N. Engl. youth, alert, quick, fond of trade & enterprising, with respect for learning & talents, moral, supposes himself Orthodox, & attached to his wife, to whom he was engaged before he came here. Came to India as an adventurer, with nothing but a good merc. education at Weld & Co.'s Boston, & good letters. In less than 3 years, he was able to go home & marry & bring his wife to a handsome home & a position of respectability. Mrs. S. was edd. at the High School at Cambr., & has excellent sense, self respect & an unaffected taste for good reading & for the best of culture, — & natural kind manners. Stearns is lucky in his wife, — who is his superior in all the essentials. They have been extremely kind to me, & my visit has been made very agreeable to me.

MOND. JULY 23. Dr. Meade's bill is 100 rupees, more than S. thot. This & other inev. exp. of a 3 weeks delay, cut in on me again.

Take leave. Ride to town. Send notes of thanks & farewell to Merwanjee & Co., & to Bhawoo Dajee, — as no time to call, & go on board the steamer China, a screw of 2000 tons, P. & O. line, bound to Aden & Sues. Stearns goes with me to the pier, over wh. the monsoon is pitching the waves in wild confusion, & going off is no little trouble. Merwanjee & Co. send me off a letter of intense politeness, & a present of an E. I. inkstand of papier machee.

At 5 P.M. steam out of the bay, — wh. is a truly noble harbor, of vast dimensions, yet safe, & in the dim cloudy monsoon, leave the far outreaching reefs, over wh. the seas are tossing, behind us, — & steam directly out into the dull, leaden ocean, & dull leaden evening sky, the tossing sea, & whistling monsoon.

WED. AUG. 1. My birth day [forty-fifth]. Nine days out. Passed Socotra Island. It is high, with sand beach for its shore. The W. end breaks off in a precipice, called Ras Kattanie, 1455 f. of nearly perp. height, — one of the most striking points of sea scenery I have ever met with.

I have a state room to myself, & am entirely comfortable on board. My rib & trunk get better daily. I can now lie on my side, & have no pain except a little, in particular *junctures,* as Prest. Benson of Liberia would say.[9] Company better than in the Madras. Henry, the commander, an Irishman, — with the goods & ills of a Hibernian, — the former predominating. A Mr. Pollock, a solicitor of Bombay, who goes home at 45 with an impaired consitution & a handsome property — a nephew of Sir Fred. & Sir Geo. Pollock, & son of Sir David, late Ch. J. of Bombay. He is rather

---

[9]Stephen Allen Benson was president of the Republic of Liberia.

of the fast & superficial order.[10] Mrs. P. is pleasant & well mannered, my chief friend on board. Mr. Fleming (supra). He has made a plum, & goes home to be head of the Engl. branch of his house. He is sensible & upright, & well informed, — but no more. Mrs. F. is young & pretty. Col. Brown, of the Royal Artillery, I am inclined to like the best of the men. Lt. Col. Cleaveland, ditto, is amiable, but a flat. Then there are some 8 or 10 returning lieuts. & ensigns, mostly on sick leave, — some on duty. There are 60 soldiers forward, all going home at the expiration of their terms. One is dying of dysentery, & must be left at Aden, if he lives to get there. Capt. Miller of the Boston ice ship Squantum, wrecked, is on board, 2d class, with his wife. I have been kind to him, & Capt. Henry & I have waited upon Mrs. M. to a seat on the qu. deck, wh. she now uses, & wh. has made their lives on board much more tolerable. M. felt bound to save expense.

At Bombay, read Mill's India,[11] the dullest book on the most interesting of subjects — a sister piece with [S. W.] Williams' china.

SATURDAY. AUG. 4. At daylight, the high, dry, treeless, verdureless mountains of the peninsula of Aden are in sight, & the low sandy waste of the isthmus that connects it with the main land of Arabia. Soon we can see lines of fortifications curving along over the rocks, & then a telegraph station & small houses. We wind round the rock, & see masts of ships, & then come to anchor, in the harbor, where are two P. & O. steamers, a sch[ooner] of the E. I. Navy, & some merchantmen.

After breakfast, go on shore. Capt. Trumbull, agent for the Salem merchants, (who have the Am. trade here in their hands) to whom Stearns gave me a letter, has gone home very ill, & his successor, a Mr. Webb, died a few days ago, so there is no Am. merch. or consul here. Threw myself on the kindness of a Parsee, who got me a covered chaise & negro driver, wh. was an accommodation, for, being the Sabbath, the Jews, who own nearly all the carriages, will let none. My turn-out & driver were $2 for the day. It is scorching hot. Many of the passengers are afraid to tempt the shore. But I am armed, as to the head, in a double ventilating felt helmet, over wh. are a ½ dos. folds of a Japanese pugree, & I have a double umbrella, when in the sun, & my carriage has a white

[10]Mr. Pollock was one of seven sons of Sir David Pollock (1780–1847), chief justice of the Supreme Court of Bombay, 1846–1847. His uncles were Sir Jonathan Frederick Pollock, 1st Baronet, (1783–1870), Attorney General of England, 1834–1835 and 1841–1844, and Sir George Pollock (1786–1872), field marshall in the British Army, celebrated for his brilliant command in the Indian wars of 1842.

[11]James Mill (1773–1836), British philosopher, published his *History of India* in three volumes in 1817. By 1858 the work had grown to ten volumes "with continuation by H. H. Wilson."

cotton cover over the leather. There is a good breese. It is only the sun & rocks that give the trouble.

My driver speaks English. He is a negro from the African coast of Sobaya (?). He tells me there is no water, wood or grass in Aden, & no vegitable or fruit grown there. All are brought on camels from the Arabian shore, across the isthmus; & we are passing streams of the strange creatures, bearing leather bags of water, large piles of fuel, & fodder, & baskets of vegitables. A camel's load of water sells for from 1½ to 3 rupees. It rains here about once in two years, [or] 18 mos., & then usually in torrents, for a few hours, making cataracts fr. the mountains. If the time goes by without the rain, they may have to wait 18 mos. more. Lately some very ancient tanks were discovered, filled with rubbish, wh. indicate that there must have been a consid. city here centuries ago. The Br. Govt. are digging these out, & find the cement unbroken, in sev. of them. To these they have added two, & now there is, or soon will be, a series of tanks, as large as dry docks. It is thot that one of these bi-ennial torrents will fill them, with, as a Br. officer told me, 80,000 rupees worth of water.

Passed the village of straw & mud huts, where the Africans live, along the shore, along costly cause ways, thro' gates guarded by Sepoys, to the Turkish Wall, as it is called, wh. extends across the isthmus, & guards the landward side of the Peninsula. There are two high hills, of volcanic stone, rising fr. the water on each side, & betw. them is the passage. The hills & the passage are alike fortified, & guns mounted. A seige of Aden must be a short matter, for no army can subsist before it long. It wd. be capture or retreat very soon. All the peninsula is volcanic stone, & mountainous, with valleys & little plains, lying like little ovens betw. the broken sides of the hot rocks; & this volcanic rock gives no water, at any attainable depth, except brackish water fr. the sea, nor does it admit of vegitation. Nothing can be more dreary, or, as an officer said to me — heart breaking. It is perhaps the most undesired station in the Br. dominions. It is, moreover, often unhealthy, with fevers & dysentery, & the usual chances of cholera, while opthalmic disorders are almost inevitable, from the fine dust as well as the reflected sun.

Called at the Guard House, on the Isthmus, & sent in my card. The officer in charge is Lt. Wm. Melville Lane, 29th B. N. Inf., & he has two juniors, lieuts. of the 4th, King's Own. They receive me kindly, explain the works in sight, & Lane offers to take me to the camp & tanks, & to tiffin at the Mess. Lane has been here nearly 3 years, & expects to be relieved in 4 mos. The others are new comers, & have a long term in expectn.

We drive along the ramparts, thro' a very long dark tunnel, & emerge into the town & camp. This is in the extinct crater of a volcano, with dry crumbly, pummice stone, hot, hot hot hills, on all sides, & rising almost perp. fr. the outer edges of the volcanic crater.

The town is larger than I expected to find it. They say there are 20,000 Arabs, with a sprinkling of Parsees & Jews, & sev. thousand Africans, who live in the village outside the walls. No Europ. who can escape, live in the town, & the officers have bungalows high up the hills, outside, where they go for a week or two, on furloughs. I think this camp at Aden is the hottest place I have ever seen, & the fine dust is extremely annoying. The Sepoys do the exposed duty: the Africans the servile labor, & the Europ. are kept in the shade as much as possible. The drills & parades are fr. 5 to 6 A.M.

Lane said I must see the tanks & if I wd. risk the sun, he wd. go with me. It was just noon, but we went. We rode to the foot, in my chaise, & then walked up. They are a series of dry docks, in the hills (if those can be called hills, on wh. there is not a spade full of earth), cemented, with stairs leading into them to the bottom. The ancient tanks, recently excavated, are in whimsical forms, like some intricate sea shells, & the lining is as white as marble, in this dry hot climate.

They are well worth seeing. The last rain, some 14 mos. ago, tho' it lasted but 6 hours, was such a terrific torrent that it bore along rocks, broke the walls of the tanks, & let out the water, 80,000 rupees' worth. Now the engineers have guarded ag. the recurrence, as they hope.

Returned to the Mess Room of the 29th, very hot, & glad to wash, & sit in the high room, where the mats keep the heat fr. the doors, & windows, & the punkahs give free air. There I find one Engl. weekly paper, of July 18, wh. gives the arrival of the Gr. Eastern at N. York, & the nomn. of Douglas.[12]

Absences at sanitariums, returns to Engl. on "sick leave", or absence on staff duty, have thinned the Mess down to 5. They tell me that 2 years at Aden makes almost entire changes in the Mess. The officers seem well mannered, intelligent men, of good connexions at home, tho' their talk is almost exclusively of the service. Yet, to me, the anecdotes of the late mutiny are as interesting as any thing of the sort can be.[13] With these gentlemen, Sir Jas. Outram is the favorite of living officers. Of the dead,

[12]The steamship *Great Eastern* completed the first laying of the Atlantic Cable in 1858. When Stephen A. Douglas received the Democratic nomination for president, the southern faction withdrew and chose John C. Breckinridge as their candidate. The rift contributed to the election of Lincoln.

[13]In May 1857 the native Indian regiments of the British Army in India began a series of bloody mutinies which were not completely quelled until 1860.

Havelock, the Lawrences, Nicholson & Wheeler. Rose, Grant & Mansfield are thot the ablest of the Gen. officers.[14]

After a long rest & a very good dinner under the name of tiffin, where our soda (*cum* claret) was cooled by saltpetre, we drove back to the point, in what is called the "cool" of the evening — when the therm. is perhaps at 94°.

Certainly this Aden is a place to be seen. But great exigencies only will warrant a man's living here. Some of the fortifications are as high as the eagle flies, & one covered way is at a dissy height.

Walk round to the Point, where the houses of the chief officers, & the retiring places of others are perched on rocks to get the sea breeses. There are the grave yards, & an Engl. & a R. C. chapel.

Returned on board at 7 o'ck., & Lane came & took tea with me.

At 9 P. M., steamed off fr. Aden, leaving the dull hot rocks in their picturesque outlines, broken, jagged, sharp, standing dry & stiff in the moonlight.

SUND. AUG. 5. At 8.30 A.M. passed the straights of Babel Mandeb, & are in the Red Sea, Arabia on our right, & the mountains of Africa on our left. My first view of the Continent of Africa. At the straights is the Island of Perrin, wh. the Br. have occupied, & on wh. there is a light hs. & a few simple works. It has no water, nor a blade of grass.

Met two large ships, coming down Sues or Medina, with returning pilgrims fr. Mecca, bound to India. Sev. ship loads go in this way ev. year.

---

[14]Sir James Outram (1803–1863), from 1819 with the British Army in India, engaged in frequent diplomatic missions and during the Indian mutinies commanded two Bengal divisions. Sir Henry Havelock (1795–1857) went to India as a regimental officer in 1823, was a major general by the time of the 1857 mutinies. He led a series of dashing victories over the rebels until the second relief of Lucknow where he succumbed to intestinal disorders and died on the day the garrison withdrew. John Nicholson (1821–1857) went out to the Bengal Infantry in 1839, built up a glittering record of military distinctions during the Indian uprising in 1848–1849. During the mutinies of 1857 he outdid his earlier accomplishments in the field. He was mortally wounded storming the fortifications at Delhi, September 14, 1857. Sir Hugh Massy Wheeler (1789–1857), after a successful military career, was in command of the British garrison at Cawnpore, India, in 1857. Failing to appreciate the gravity of the Indian uprising and to make sufficient preparations for defense of European noncombatants, he capitulated after a brave defense. He was murdered in the first of a series of massacres. Hugh Henry Rose (1801–1885) served in the Near and Far East until 1860, distinguishing himself in the Indian uprisings. Sir James Hope Grant, commanding British forces in China at this time, has been noted earlier. Sir William Rose Mansfield (1819–1876) was Chief of Staff to Sir Colin Campbell during the Indian mutiny. Sir Henry Montgomery Lawrence (1806–1857), a brigadier general, died in action in the Indian mutinies. Sir George St. Patrick Lawrence (1804–1884), his brother, served as a colonel during the mutinies and survived.

(The people at Aden see rain storms pass over the Arabian coast, a few miles fr. them, frequently, but they never come to them).

FRIDAY. AUG. 10.   This is the 6th day fr. Aden, & we expect to reach Sues by mid-night. Our fears of extreme heat have not been entirely met. The passage up the Red Sea in mid summer, in a steamer, is commonly thot to be the extreme limit of human endurance. Feeble persons die of mere heat, sometimes. For three days it was intensely hot. The scene was this, & no more nor less — a burning sun, a smooth sea, a dead calm or very light breese, & a hot hase lying over the African or Arabian mountains. We sleep on deck, wherever we can lay a mat & pillow, for the cabins are too hot. The thick awning of sailcloth is but little defense ag. the sun, & under it we are obliged to wear pugrees & double hats as if we were in open air, & fr. 10 to 4 it is cooler in the saloon, under deck, the punkahs waving. I live light & am perfectly well. But there is great deal of drinking, — the thirst tempting so much. There is much sickness, — tho' none dangerous, & only among persons who have had disease before, — the victims of E. I. fevers & dysenteries. My friend Col. Brown has been very ill, of return of jungle fever, but is better to-day. The sick soldier died before getting to Aden, & was buried at sea. He had served 20 years, had 3 good service marks, & was going home with his discharge & a pension. My steward was sun struck yesterday, by standing in sun without cap a few minutes — brot to by throwing buckets of cold water over his head, & putting feet in cold water. He is at work to-day — stroke must have been slight. Cold water on his head is the E. I. remedy now, & no bleeding.

Yesterday was a little more comfortable, & to-day is delightful. We are betw. the Egypt. & Arab. mountains, in a smooth sea, with fresh breese. How aerial those mountains do look — how barren, hot & deserted! On the Arabian coast we see the range that lies about Sinai, & is called after it, & some say that solitary peak is Sinai itself, but no one seems sure. It begins to become exciting as we draw near these ancient long honored scenes of the world's history, Egypt, Sinai!

SATURD. AUG. 11.   Last night we came to anchor at Sues, & this morning we are lying in the narrow top of the Red Sea, with a sand plain on one side & barren hills on the other. The sunset last night, disclosed the *beauty of desolation.* I can now believe that the hues in Hunt's picture of the Scape Goat may be in nature.[15] The sands are not white but reddish brown, & so are the hills, & the flush of sunset makes them

---

[15]Holman Hunt's "The Scapegoat" has been described earlier by Dana. It depicted a forlorn sacrificial goat, almost dead from exhaustion at the edge of the Dead Sea, with the purple mountains of Edom in the distance.

red. The hills are not hills, but the ruins of hills. They have been *pared*, below the roots of all vegitation, & then sliced off, leaving bare the gravel & stones, & then gouged & hacked & sliced, after every wild fashion. They are not only irregular in outline at the tops, but in the sides & at the bases. They have as little shape as a boy's lump of crystal. I attribute this — being no naturalist — to the entire absence of rain & all water-shed, to smooth things off.

Landed at Sues, at 10 o'ck. I remained until the 3 P.M. train. Got lunch & cup of Turkish coffee, full of grounds & no milk. It is too hot to go about, so I lounge in the inn. While I am at the Transit Co.'s office, the clerk, an Englishman, has occasion to speak, & does so, with apparent fluency, Greek, Italian, & Arabic. My trunks are exd. by an Egyptian Custom Hs. officer, dressed just like the pictures of Joseph & his brethern.

Took train at 3 P.M. for Cairo. Have a car (carriage) to myself. Our course lies thro' the desert, — & it *is* a desert, — miles & miles of mere sand, but not white, a kind of brown or yellow sand, & those strange, shapeless, verdureless hills! No one can live on them. I should think no one could climb them. They must exist for some meteriological purpose. The poorer Egyptians live in mere pens on pounds, — enclosures of mud or stone, with little or no roof, & that flat, mere covers of straw, & open holes for doors or windows. They look like little cattle pens. Here & there are tents, & men & women standing at the tent doors, at close of day.

I am now in Africa, have set foot on all the continents, unless Australia be one, wh. I will not admit; — this is old Egypt, & hereabouts the children of Jacob came to buy corn, & hereabouts they passed out of Egypt, a disenthralled multitude! But what a country to dwell in & to travel in, — so hot, & no rain ever! There is not a tree or blade of grass betw. Sues & Cairo!

The sun goes down, in a hot flush, & the stars come out, & soon there are distant lights, & now a row of trees & houses, & then close streets, & a great "Station", & we come to a stand. It is nearly 9 o'ck., there is no light in the station, but a small fire of faggots burning at the end of a long stick, & not a European in the station,[16] but a crowd of howling Arabs. It is with great difficulty I secure two carriers, & have to wait for the men to beat off the cleats from the baggage crates by bits of soft stone, & can find no carriage — as my train was not expected, & start off into an unknown city, in the dark, with two Arabs. But we find the hotel, at last, & after bath & dinner, I am at home in my room, with my red striped luggage about me, — nothing lost.

[16]To say that Dana was going inland at an off season would be putting the case mildly. Europeans almost never ran the risks of climate at this time of year, and Dana's unexpected, brisk appearances must have caused general astonishment.

SUND. AUG. 12TH. Took donkey & guide & rode to find the British Consul. This is the oddest place I have seen yet — more picturesque than a Chinese city, or even than Bombay or Poonah. In the old parts of the town, the streets are as narrow as in Canton, & the houses are of stone, with thick walls & 3 stories high. To see a street roofed over some 40 or 50 f. above the ground, with great rafters & occasional open spaces, has something of the fearful. It is a city of back entries. This cannot be a street. It must be a paved back passage of a house. But here & there are open spaces & gardens kept alive by artificial irrigation.

Donkeys, donkeys everywhere, & camels! There are Joseph's brethren, ambling down the street, each riding his ass, & the asses bearing provender & corn; & there are the Midianites with their camels, bearing spicery.

The Br. Consul, Mr. Calvert, is also acting Am. Consul, & promises to send off my letters this afternoon, to Alex[andria].

The Engl. service is given up, in the midsummer heat, & so is that of the Am. Presb. missionaries.

Called on Rev. Wm. Barnett, of Am. Pr. Board, with letter of introdn. from Mr. Prime. He has had an Arab class, but says there is no Engl. Prot. service, & I am too late for the Coptic service, & the Greek Ch., both [of] wh. I should much like to have seen. The Copts are the descendants of the early Egyptian Christians, converted in the Apostles' times, & soon after, Mr. Barnett says, and have kept aloof fr. all European X'tians, whether Greek Ch., R. Cath. or Protestant. Their faith & forms of worship closely resemble the R. Catholic. The Coptic language has become a dead language, & is not even understood, when read, by one in a thousand. All Egyptians speak Arabic, & all but the Copts became Mahommedans. The religions here are Mahommedan, & Coptic, Greek & R. C. Christians. Mr. Barnett has been very kind in instructing my dragoman (guide, valet & interpreter) as to my desires in the way of Pyramids, Sphynxes &c., & I am to start off tomorrow morning, at 3 o'ck., by moonlight, for Memphis, to see the upper pyramids, a two days' journey, on donkeys, with my dragoman, one Mahmond ——, to return by Old Cairo & Persepolis, & Thursday, 16th, I expect to go to Alexandria, & hope to sail for Trieste on the 17th or 18th.[17]

MONDAY, AUG. 13TH. This Cairo is a grand, ponderous, solemn old city. It is as far before the E. Indian cities in romantic interest, as they are before the Chinese. There is something great as well as old & quaint about it. And now, by moonlight, of this Monday morning, Aug. 13th, I am traversing its great shadows, & threading my way, donkey-back, among its narrow streets, betw. its high, thick prison looking walls, on my march

[17]Dana added the marginal note: "Sent journal & letter fr. Cairo, Aug. 12th, 1860."

out to Memphis, — every now & then in danger of treading on some
sleeper; — for in this dry, hot climate, they sleep out of doors all night.
We pass by high walls of gardens & high walls of palaces, &, to ev.
inquiry, my dragoman says the garden, the palace of Achmet Pacha, or
Ibrahim Pacha's sons, or Seid Pacha's daughter, or Suliman Pacha, or the
hareem of the Pacha. These few Pachas, of the reigning family, descendants of Mohammed Ali,[18] seem to own everything in the grasp of their
sensual despotism. At last, we are in the open fields, & can see the stars,
in their last glimmer.

To Old Cairo, where we take a boat & cross the Nile by sails. It is here
& now a turbid & rapid river, but the all in all of Egypt! They drink the
Nile, cook with the Nile, wash in the Nile, give the Nile to their cattle to
drink, & where the Nile does not go they carry it, by canal & aqueducts.

Pass Roda Island, in the Nile, where is the Nilometer, & the Palace &
hareem of Seid Pacha, & one of Ibrahim Pacha's sons, & in the open
country, in the grey of the morning, miles & miles off, we see the great
Pyramids!

Stop under a grove of date-tree palms & get breakfast. This sounds
very fine, but a grove of dates, at early day, gives as much shade as a
grove of liberty-poles.

My dragoman is Mohammed Hossayn. He has taken many parties to
Upper Egypt & Syria, & has their certificates; — among others, last year,
Lord Dufferin.[19] He charges me 4 shillings a day, & does everything as a
bodyservant as well as interpreter & guide. He makes good Turkish
coffee.

Our first visit is to the ruins of Memphis.

The sand of the desert has covered all. Only where this is dug off &
down is anything reached. (Metrahineh is the present name). Visited
the recumbent statue, some 40 f. long, all fr. one block of stone, & then
the bits & reliques wh. have been gathered in the tents of the excavators,
who are acting under the Pacha.

Then to Sakkára, where is an underground temple, the walls of
alabaster & black granite, & the inscriptions on them as plain as if written
yesterday. There are remains of vermillion paintings on the figures. It is
called El Biar.

[18]Mohammed Ali (1769–1849), progenitor of the group that Dana catalogues
here, was an Albanian officer of militia who was sent to Egypt in 1798 with a Turkish-
Albanian unit as a part of a French invasion force. Active in political insurrection
after the departure of the French, by 1805 he had become Viceroy of Egypt. Annex-
ing Nubia in 1820, he built defenses against the Greeks and began the conquest of
Syria. In 1848 he was replaced by Ibrahim Pasha (1789–1848), who ruled for only
two months before dying. The family continued in control of the country at the time
of Dana's visit.

[19]The 1st Marquess of Dufferin (1826–1902) was a well known diplomat.

It is now about 11 o'ck., & the sun, on this sand plain, in August, intensely hot, & notwithstanding my double helmet & pugree, I am relieved to reach the tombs of Serapion, where the sarcophagi of the bulls were kept, & to get under ground. Here we were, under ground, myself, 3 Arabs & 3 donkeys, & here we rested. They spread my mat, & lay themselves on the sand, — & we rested, with a lunch of meat & wine & water, until 4 o'ck., when we explored the tombs. They are vast & deep, & doubtless built to hold the stone coffins of the Sacred Bulls. These sarcophagi are enormous, all but the cover being of one piece of stone, & that as big as it would seem possible to get to its place. The tombs are in high galleries, & each sarcophagus has its tomb at the side.

Thence to Kanéseh, where is a newly discovered temple, in wh. the paintings are still bright. Rev. Mr. Barnett says Kanéseh will serve as a substitute for going to Upper Egypt.

The afternoon sun is still hot, & the breese from the desert still warm, when we issue from our subterranean cavern, & a ride of two hours (have I said we were on donkeys? The *sina qua non* of Egyptian life, & neither obstinate nor sure footed) brings us to the great Pyramids of Gezeh, & the Pyramid of Cheops, & the Sphynx. All the way they loom before us, sharp, high & wide, looking about as large 15 miles off as close by.

Here (at Gezeh) 3 pyramids stand near together, 2 large & 1 small. Of the large, Cheops is the larger, & the only one that can be entered. But these have been too minutely described & too often! I need only say that they are built of large blocks of stone, of diff. sises, & irregular, but resulting in rows, each receeding, so as to form something like stairs, fr. top to bottom. By climbing & a little aid from lifting by others, any person of ord. strength of body & steadiness of head can go to the top. Perpend. height, little less than 500 f., about double Bunker Hill M't. The stones are not white, grey or black, but of a yellow color. Some of the blocks are huge, so that it excites your wonder how they got there. The dreary look of all around the pyramids & sphynx is first to be noted. The sands of the desert have blown over & submerged temples, palaces, tombs, — all but pyramids. Imagine a long Northern snowstorm, of yellow snow, only rock-tops peering above, & the open channels & lagoons of the great river.

The Sphynx disappoints — being in a scooped out hollow, & dwarfed by the pyramid. You have to stimulate your wonder by remembering that it is one block of stone, & was once a kind of face.

Before dark, we entered the tomb discovd. by Col. Vyse,[20] & the temple under ground, or under sand. The latter is in good order, with no

[20]Richard W. H. Vyse (1784–1835), British general, explored the Pyramids, 1835–1837.

arches, but only the Egyptian upright pillars & flat top stone — but very large & heavy.

It is now sundown, & here, in this dreary magnificent spot, I am to pass the night. My dragoman makes me up a bed of blankets & my mat on the hard stone forming the lower range of the pyramid, & with moon & stars bright overhead, in this clear dry sky, with a congregation of a dosen Arabs, disputing & howling & praying towards Mecca, kneeling on carpets, & as many donkeys eating out of bags, myself trying to look up & realise the place & the scene, I dropped asleep, having been up since 4 o'ck. & much of the time on the road. The great dispute was betw. my dragoman & a huge Arab, who insisted on letting himself to us as guard for the night, & I dropped off when it was at the highest.

Once in the night, I awoke. Stars & moon bright, — sky cloudless, & the Arabs lying in the sand, but the pyramid receedes too fast for me to see the top, where I lie.

TUESD. 14TH. AUG. Dragoman calls me at 4 o'ck. Coffee & bread, & my 3 Arab guides take me inside the Pyramid, entering a small door, up several ranges of stones, insignificant, — the door, I mean, showing that the pyramids were never built for *use*, & following low passages, often bending to the ground, visit the well known & often described recesses & chambers. Then, just at clear day dawn, begin the ascent outside. It is not extremely difficult, & I reach the summit a few minutes before sunrise, & have the great gratifn. of seeing, from the top of the highest pyramid, the blood red African sun rise over this vast expanse, — this expanse now of sand & water, of scattered villages, the illimitable Lybian desert on the West, & glittering in the East the citadel of Cairo.

The Nile spreads itself & winds itself everywhere, in branches & off shoots, in lagoons & pools, in parallel streams & artificial canals, & the agriculture of Egypt is exactly coextensive with the Nile & its influences.

The Second Pyramid has a part of its casing of hewn smooth stone still at the top, & all antiquarians agree that the great pyramid had also once a similar casing, wh. has been removed for use in building the palaces of Cairo. If so, it was not intended to be ascended without, any more than within.

Descent, & take our asses for Old Cairo, following the dikes all the way, as the Nile has begun to rise. This more than doubles the journey, but we reach the river by 9 o'ck., & crossing close by the island of Roda, where are the palace & hareem of a great pacha, are in Old Cairo.

Irrigation is the great subject, in lower Egypt. Canals, sluices, dikes, culverts & tide gates, give the people the control of the waters of the Nile, — & this is their all.

The Citadel of Cairo is a grand object, for miles around — one of the grandest imaginable; — dominating as it does over all the region about, high, dome-filled, & glittering, mosque, palace & fortress in one.

In Old Cairo, after breakfast of bread, grapes & coffee, went to an ancient Coptic Church. It is thro' a close alley, thro' a deep gate way, up flights of stairs, & in the 3d story of a house are the several rooms, separated by wooden screens, dark, dingy, dusty, ratty, mousy, wormy, — old — very old — making the place of worship of the Copts. The walls are lined with very old & quaint pictures of saints, with extraord. legends attached. There is a Chancel, altar, candles, & the Chancel is separated so as to let people only look in, or peep in, as at the small door of a stage. They have a few books, as I understood, in Coptic, now a dead language. All Egyptians having adopted the Arabic of their conquerors. They seemed very poor. Mr. Barnett tells me the R. Cath. have drawn many of them into union, & the Gr[eek] Ch. press them, & Prot. have little sympathy with them, so they seem destined to extinction. Yet they are the successors & representatives of the Christians of Egypt in the Apostles' days, when St. Mark planted X'tianity there.

Visited also a Greek Ch. An intelligent priest showed me the building, wh. is also, I believe, a monastery, but as he spoke no Engl. or French or Sp., we could get on only by writing Greek, — for the pronunciation of Mod. Greek is unintelligible to me —, & by guessing at Italian. This Church is rather full of paintings & seems prepared for a good deal of ceremony.

To the Mosque of Amer [Emir], said to be the oldest in Egypt. This is built round four sides of a square, the enclosed square being open to the sky & paved with flat stone, & capable of holding an immense multitude. There is no central dome. The four sides are high roofed, with rows of pillars to sustain the roofs. At one end is the tomb of Amer. While I was there, two women were admitted to kiss it. They embraced & kissed, with a loud smack & unction each corner of the tomb, & really seemed to enjoy the process. I thought the younger one looked at us rather wilfully — as much as to say — what would you give?

Next, to the grand Mosque or whatever it may be called, built to contain the tombs of the descendants of Mohammed Ali. It is stately & sumptuous. Over each tomb is a dome, & the various rooms in wh. the tombs lie, open into each other. The light is dim & from above, & the entire flooring of all is covered with rich Turkey carpets. The faithful come & go freely, & the rooms seem to be used as resting, sleeping, reading & smoking places for whomever chooses & is decently dressed. All that was required of us was to put on slippers. The tombs are large costly structures, of marble, inlaid with gold, & in much better taste than the costlier monumental architecture with us — no effigies, all images being prohibited by the Mahom. faith. Lying about, on the carpeted floors, were lasy Turks, sleeping & smoking, & avoiding the heat of the outer sun.

The tombs of the Mamelukes, was the last place we visited to-day, — & it was now nearly noon, & the sun intensely hot. I was glad to get back to my hotel, & have a warm bath & change of linen, & lie down to rest. I had done & seen a good deal since 4 A.M. of Monday.

Rev. Mr. Barnett, & Mr. Calvert, the Br. Consul, called. Barnett is of the Scotch Presb. Ch. of the U. S. (Rev. Blaikie's connexion[21]), a well meaning man, but dull & half taught, & I suspect the Mission is feebleness itself. His associate, Mr. Mc — , goes home in feeble health.

The great Square of Cairo is very gay at night. Cafés & other places of entertainment are open, & bands of music play in the open air, & it is in open air that all sit & take refreshments. One band was fr. Damascus, playing on Damascene instruments, among wh. were 2 or 3 harps with some 50 strings each, running across a nearly flat board. The musicians sang a good deal with their playing. The Turkish bands used European (as we now call them, at least) instruments.

The system of polygamy & concubinage does not prevent tho' it may diminish public harlotry. I saw sev. Egyptian harlots, most sumptuously decked & perfumed, in the square, & had the offers of services of sev. men in Italian & French, to act as brokers. It seems this is the usage, & direct address is not the custom; & so a worthy class of men get a pittance in this way & are encouraged. Mr. Barnett told me that the public women are numerous & have sections of the city where they are known to be. They were all banished by the late pacha, but have been silently tolerated by the present pacha. It may be that they get their support from foreigners, — not Mahommedans.

I am, to-day, the only guest at Shepherd's enormous hotel. In midsummer, Egypt is deserted by travelers, & the transit passengers, to & fr. India, are much fewer in summer.

WED. AUG. 15. Off early, on donkeys, to see the remaining sights. The sight to-day, & the great sight of Cairo, is the Citadel. It is the highest point, dominating over all the city & country round, & a splendid group of buildings, — castle, palace & mosque, together! The color of the stone is beautiful, a reddish brown. The great building is the Mosque of Mohammed Ali. Here is something that may truly be called magnificent!—

---

[21]William Garden Blaikie (1820–1899), Scottish divine, was at this time editor of the *North British Review.* He was an extremely active figure in the Scottish Presbyterian Church.

I mean one of the magnificencies of the world. I think, for gorgeousness, it surpasses all I have ever seen. The marble court is surmounted by a dome, from wh. comes the most delicious light, fr. the stained glasses. Marble, alabaster, polished stone, stained glass & gold, above, below & on all sides, & smaller domes, rising from the sides, each beautiful & rich.

The view fr. the Citadel is noble. Cairo is a city of domes & minarets & towers, & the great Nile, with its canals, lakes, lagoons, ditches, & its separating channels, lies before us, & the steep Citadel-hill, & the boundless Lybian desert stretching westward, & the lonely pyramids, rising out of the desolation of sand. The whole presents a scene wh. no where else I think can be matched, for interest. The Pacha being away, at Alexandria, with all his hareem, & officers, the palace was open to me. I made the circuit of all but the hareem, wh., tho' unoccupied, is closed. The palace is very costly & sumptuous — marble, gold, alabaster & precious stones. The great halls of reception & audience are very large & imposing, & the luxury of the old wretch's couches, divans, beds, baths & smoking rooms, is unspeakable. He is so large that it is diff. for him to mount, so he has a dumb waiter, by wh. he ascends & descends. It has a very mysterious & treacherous look, in a dungeon-like closet. Mohammed Ali is the favorite of the common Egyptian. Everything great is attributed to his times. My dragoman's eyes glisten as he tells stories of the power & splendor & great doings of Mohammed Ali, & if anything is in a bad state now, it has become so since Mohammed Ali's time.

One of the most extraordinary things in the Citadel, &, indeed, in Egypt, is the Great Well, called Joseph's Well, — said to have been built (tho' that is doubted) by the Soldan Josef, known to us as Saladin, the Conqueror. It is an enormous work. Not a mere well, but a stone room, some 20 or 30 feet square, descending more than 200 f. into the ground, to water, wh. is drawn up by the perpetual chain & buckets, worked by oxen. (The oxen of Egypt are chiefly the water bison, as in India & China). There is access nearly to the foot of the well, outside the wall, down a wet, spiral passage of mud, perfectly dark, along wh. guides take you with torches.

The Mosque of Sultan Hassan is the next sight in order, — a large, plain, grave structure, in extreme contrast with that of Mohammed Ali, & with the Sit Teinab, a light, modern, showy mosque, from wh. the worshippers were pouring in a throng as I went by. Then, too, I went to the Tayloon, — but, for the life of me, cannot recall it, or how it differed from the Mosque of Sultan Hassan.

This ended my early morning excursion. Returned to late breakfast — & at 10.30, am to go, in a carriage, with Mr. Barnett, to visit Shubra palace & gardens, — the sumptuous pleasure grounds of the Haleem Pacha.

There is a straight avenue to Shubra, lined on each side with trees, affording a good shade, & kept watered. The trees are pine, cedar, acasia, & sycamore, — Mr. B. says the sycamore of Scripture.

At the gate of the Shubra gardens is a new palace, now finished. It is of blue, with cornice & outworks of white. Mr. Barnett said, well, that it was like coming upon a cloud in the sky — the blue & white. The gardens occupy about 100 acres, & all under full cultivation. The gardens seemed to me as costly as any I saw in India or China, & in better taste. Shade is appreciated, & all the walks & avenues are well lined with trees, among wh. the pines & cedars abound, — with sycamores. The flowers & shrubs I cannot specify, except that they took pains to show me the sensitive plant.

In the gardens, is a second palace, or pleasure house. It encloses an open space wh. is filled artificially with water & lined with marble, & a marble island in the middle. The palace runs round the four sides of this small lake, consisting of broad marble walks, beautifully roofed & supported by pillars, with here & there rooms, — & at each corner a suite of rooms. These rooms are furnished in the most costly style of the Eastern & Western luxury — as Burke says — "uniting the vivid satisfactions of Europe, with the torpid blandishments of Asia" — such divans, such carpets, such couches, such gilding & precious stones, such mirrors & such Cashmere coverings! An evening party, a ball, given here, with a band of music on the island, would be unsurpassed. But, poor creatures, what is all their style, without women! A few prisoners in the hareem, & all this show & style is for the heavy men alone.

THURSD. AUG. 16. Took train at 8.30 for Alexandria. The officers of the road seem to be natives, but it is said that the chief engineers are Fr. or Engl.

The Delta of the Nile seems very fertile. So far as the fertilising effects of the overflow goes, there seems to be abundant productiveness. For sev. miles the scene reminded me of the bottom lands of the Connecticut, trees, rich fields, — only the cuts & canals for irrigation, & the constant occurrence of wheels to raise water, were Egyptian. But lower down, towards Alexandria, sandy plains occur again. The common people live in mere cots, or pens of mud, while here & there are great houses of big men, usually of yellow stone, but sometimes plastered & painted blue & white. Now, the country is perfectly flat, & there — that long, low blue ridge is the Mediterranean, — my first sight of the Mediterranean! & houses thicken, streets show themselves, & we are in Alexandria.

Alexandria is a Europeanised city. The streets are wide & straight (mostly) & the houses of white stone. Seen from an eminence, it is a city of white stone — solely. The signs are in Italian, Greek, French, Arabic

& English. European women, in crinoline & retreating bonnets are frequent in the streets, & all mixtures of costumes, from the pure Turk to the pure Frank, abound.

Took lodgings at the Hotel Abbot, where we sat at table, — Turk, French, Greek, Italian, I the only Anglo Saxon.

FRID. AUG. 17.   Gave the day to sight seeing, — that is the morning & ev., for it is here the noon in wh. no man can labor. Pompey's Pillar — (nothing to do with Pompey, more than Cleopatra's Needle has to do with Cleopatra). All know its form. Its material is brown stone & one piece. Cleopatra's Needle, of wh. only one is standing, is of darker stone.

Visited a Synagogue, built of white stone, handsome & in good repair, a handsome Jew girl showing it to me, & taking her fee — the eternal *backshish [baksheesh]*, the one word of Egypt. Then a Coptic Church, in wh. service was going on, — a baptismal service. The Chancel is screened off entirely, & the child is handed in to the priest, as at a parcel's delivery office. The women were behind another screen, making almost a separate room. Four or five men were standing & chanting, & the congregation, beside the invisible women, consisted of some dosen men & boys. Three children were baptised. They seemed to me to use chrysm as well as water. The boys demanded bakshish of me, after the service, & they & the older girls, now emerged, scrambled for what my dragoman threw to them, on the church floor.

There is a handsome Engl. Ch. of white stone, & sev. R. Cath. & Greek churches.

The Syrian massacres excite great interest among the foreigners here.[22] Many X'tian refugees are here, at the house of the Lasarists.

At 5 P.M. took a Turkish bath. Rooms with marble floor, vapor, so that [one] can hardly breathe, wrapped in dry clothes, rubbed, put into warm bath, rubbed & kneaded, cooler water poured on, soaped & washed again, slowly dried, let into a breathable air, dried more, laid down on couch. Pipe (water) & coffee, & bakshish & Adieu.

Rode down to the point between the two harbors, & visited the Pacha's palace. It is very large, & finely situated, with one sea front, & one on each harbor. I was not admitted. The soldiers on guard seemed careless, & sat at their posts, & an air of languor & disorder was spread about the palace.

Strange there should be so few objects of historical interest in so ancient & distinguished a city — but so it is. It is probably the most cosmopolitan city in the world, — having little character of its own, but made up of all nations, races, religions & languages. The French influence

---

[22]At Damascus, Syria, on July 9-11, 1860, there took place a wholesale massacre of Christians.

seems to prevail. They furnish more high officers in the Pacha's service than any nation. (By the way, Mr. Fleming told me that the Engl. merchants & others in Bombay, leased the stations & built the buildings for the land route between Sues & Alexandria, & when the rail road superceded the stations, instead of surrendering them to the Egyptian Govt., these merchants made them over to the British Govt., & they are now maintained by the Foreign Office).

SAT. 18. AUG.   9 A.M., took Austrian Lloyd's steamer "Bombay" for Trieste. Mr. & Mrs. Pollock, Major & Mrs. Russell, & Mr. Kenshaw, of the "China", are on board. Alexandria looks well in going out. It is low & level, but the buildings are striking, the palaces, mosques, minarets, domes, & towers. A great many vessels of all flags, in the harbor. Long rows of windmills! City of white stone!

Now, we are out on the blue Mediterranean — my first experience of it, & it is not long before the low shores of Africa are out of sight, & we are at sea. It is smooth, & very pleasant, & a gentle breese. In the afternoon, the ladies say it is really cool & they send below for shawls. One of us has the curiosity to look at the thermometer. It is at 84°! Such is the effect of India & the Red Sea on the blood. But there is a difference in the *sun*. Even at 84°, it is cooler than in Asia or Africa, for the sun has not that peculiar power. We sit under the awning at noon, without feeling the sun striking through it & our hats too.

SUNDAY. AUG. 19.   4 P.M., made island of Candia. Weather comfortable, & a change at night, tho' still very hot. Plenty of fruit on board, — grapes, melons, peaches & figs, — & variety of vegitables.

MOND. AUG. 20.   The Peloponnesus! Made the S. W. end of the Morea, & all day are coasting the Morea, close on board, & going between it & the islands. Here is Navarino Bay! The captain points out the place where the Turkish fleet lay at anchor, & where the allied squadrons came in. There is a fortified town just at the mouth of the Straits, above Navarino, now abandoned.

How deeply interesting is the sight of Greece, — the Peloponessus, — tho' it be of a part little known to fame! Yet it is Greece! And these are the

> Isles of Greece — the Isles of Greece
> Where burning Sappho loved & sung,
> Where grew the arts of war & peace.[23]

and we are to see Ithica, the isle of Ulysses! And worthy of Greece is the outline & figure of the land & the islands as seen from the sea! There are no flat marshes or sand wastes. Everywhere the hills & mountains come

---

[23]Byron, *Don Juan*, canto III, stanza 86.

to the water's edge, the hills crowned with forests, & breaking into dells & glens & ravines, & small plains. It is picturesque, everywhere. Nowhere strikingly rich or fertile, in appearance, but a land of diversity & interest, hill, mountain, grove, valley, shore. We are all enthousiastic Greeks, & wish to wander about the shores. We pass the entrance to the Gulf of Corinth by night.

TUESD. AUG. 21. Pass between the main land of Albania, & the islands of Zante, Cephalonia, & Corfu, & at 10 A. M. are at anchor in the beautiful harbor of Corfu. What a romantic & beautiful spot! Those who have seen Malta put this far before it. The rocks run up to sharp points, overlooking all, & crowned with forts, & the tall houses, all of white stone, & some of 3 & 4 & 5 stories in height, seen like watch towers & fortresses. And how beautifully the blue sea lies all about the islands, & away up in the little bays!

We are ashore, amid Greek signs, & Greek faces & Greek speech! How odd to see the language of your school & college, your Homer & New Testament, on placards & signs, & applied to modern things. I buy a daily paper, "Συνοπσίσ Είδησεων" 'Εν Κερκυρα τη 9[21] Αυγουττου 1860, (Πωλείται 'οβολούση),with news of the Αποβασισ Γαραβαλδη, ending in Τηλεγράφημα. [24]

It struck me that in this hot climate, there should be no verandahs, piassa or porticos. The houses have flat fronts, with wooden shutters. Drove to the town palace & the country palace of the Br. Governor. Large & sufficiently stately buildings. The country about is beautifully diversified with hill & dale, & all has a healthful, variegated, romantic air. How much of this is fancy? But who can resist it, in the isles of Greece, amid olive trees & vineyards, & where the Greek of the world's poetry, eloquence, philosophy & art is domesticated. We fancy, too, that the women have a *castey* look. See the low forehead, full temple, straight nose, & chiseled lip! And the men, — how keen they look, & active! Certainly, they are neither a dull nor an oppressed people. They look independent & clever. Among these faces, is a sprinkling of what must be Austrian, sunburnt yellow complexions, large foreheads & brown hair. The red coats of the Engl. *protectorate* soldiery, are the only signs of a present subjection, mild as it is, & the Venetian lion, carved on the gateways, tells of that of years gone by.[25]

[24]Here Dana gives the name of the newspaper, roughly "Daily Gazette," the fact that it is from Corcyra, that it is dated 9th of August, that it sells for 3 obols, and contains news of Garibaldi's invasion of Sicily, transmitted by telegraph.

[25]In May 1854 the British and French sent troops into Greece to force a change of ministry and to ensure that the king remain neutral in the matter of Turkey's internal affairs. In 1466 and again in 1687, portions of Greece were held by the Venetians.

What delicious grapes are these purple grapes of the open vineyards! And these fresh figs, so cooling & soft! And how full are the basaars of melons, peaches & all manner of vegitables!

Went into the Church of San Spiridion, sumptuous & burning with candles, — the body of the Saint being on exhibition, & paying one shilling I get a sight of it. The face is entire, in a glass case, while the legs are exhibited & open to the touch, but cased in painted cloth. A Greek girl, a cripple, sits by it, with a truly beautif. & classic face, & fair complexion.

(It must not be supposed that Greek is the only language. On the contrary, Italian is perhaps even oftener met with on the signs. French & Engl. are occasionally seen, & a good deal of Engl. is spoken, on acct. of the Engl. protectorate & commerce).

But our 2½ hours' leave is up, & we must take our feet from off the classic soil, to the sooty deck of the steamer, — newly coaled & well stored with fruits & vegitables. We are all on deck, & delighting ourselves with the views as we steam out of the harbor. What a place for yatching! What drives & walks! What shooting [mountains] opposite, & so near! We are so glad we [avoided] commonplace routes by Marseilles or Southampton. We turn the corner, & the castle, forts, palace, towers, & towering stone houses are hidden, & Adieu to Corfu!

All the afternoon we are skirting the Albanian shores, often within a mile of the beach. Here again, thro' its whole length, there are no reaches of sand, or of low marsh, but always a bold shore, & hills & mountains, with opening valleys, & the blue sea washing their feet.

All day Wed. (22d) the coast in sight on the right hand, — the coast of Dalmatia & the Austrian-Turkish provinces. Delightful sailing.

THURSDAY. AUG. 23RD. The entrance to Trieste in sight, early this morning, & at 8 A.M., we are at anchor in the port, the slopes of the hills, well dotted with pleasure houses, villages & churches, & the close built city before us. Custom Hs. officers easy & civil, & by 9 o'ck., I am in my room at my hotel — Hotel de la Villa, — & all my luggage safe, & my sea-voyage ended.

I am in Europe! It is an exciting thought, & one calling for gratitude. I have been carried across the Pacific, through all the seas, & inland journeys & changes of climate, & heats & dangers, of China & Japan, & of the Eastern seas, & British India, & Egypt, — without so much as a hair of my head injured. I am, & have been, in perfect health, & have apparently escaped every danger & ev. inconvenience of the hot climates, in midsummer, & am now on European soil. I feel almost as if my journey were ended, & these European customs seem so homelike, — no more

Chinese, Hindoos or Arabs. How much I [have seen] & how constantly I have enjoyed! Can I expect the [same in Europe]? Yet, why not? *Nec temere, nec timide.*[26]

Venice! Venice! Venice! All my resolutions broke down, & my principles gave way! I left Trieste with a virtuous resolve to spend one day only in Venice. But it was impossible. I can allow for anything a man may do in Venice. It took me as much by surprise as if I had never heard of it. I did not really believe that things were as I had read. People may be divided into two classes, those who have seen Venice & can believe in the actualising of the imagination, & those who have not seen it, & may not so believe.

And how strange it all is! Here, in the midst of the banks & shoals of the Adriatic, not only off the land, but *out of sight of* hard ground, — where only coral insects would think of beginning, they build a magnificent, sumptuous city, — a city of marble & gold & precious stones, of palaces, churches, monasteries, courts, bridges, columns, arsenals, & prisons, — where every stone had to be brought from a distant *terra firma*, & gardens, where every morsel of earth was imported; and there they led about the sea, in canals, as they wished for it, & excluded it, by breakwaters, where they did not desire it; and on the weakest foundations of mud & sand, they built the heaviest & loftiest structures, & undertook to rule the Mediterranean world. The wonders of the place, the never ceasing charm of canal & gondola, front-door steps washed by the tide, & overlooking balconies, & noiseless motion, of a city without wheel or shod hoof, — so seised on me, that after going all Friday to sights, & finding them not half finished, I gave way, & sacrificed another day, — wh., indeed involved a third, for that was Sunday, & I did not wish to travel all that day, as I must — if I did not stay over.

I shall not attempt to *describe.* I will only *catalogue.*

But, first, have I said that we arrived in Trieste, Thursd. morning, Aug. 23d, & spent the day there? Trieste is beautifully situated, on the gentle slope of hills that run to the Adriatic; with every variety of inclination, & is well built of white stone, the houses large, streets generally wide, & a good deal given up to public uses, squares, promenades, drives &c. Left at midnight for Venice, in a A. L. steamer. Waked up at day-light, about an hour fr. Venice, & came into the city, or *among* the city, at sunrise, — & could not have had a more beautiful entrance. Passed the Lido, where Byron used to ride, & the open port where the

---

[26]Dana added the marginal note: "Sent journal fr. Trieste, to Aug. 23." The brackets suggest Dana's meaning where the manuscript is mutilated. The Latin means "neither rashly nor timidly."

Doges wedded the sea, & came to anchor nearly opp. the piassa de San Marco — (the Square of St. Mark).

Stopped at the hotel Danieli, wh. was a palace, & has 2 doors on canals, & balconies, & marble floors & marble halls, & the arms of the old family cut into the walls.

The first day, I saw the Piassa de San Marco, with its campanile, its clock tower, the 2 marble columns, one surmounted by the winged lion, the facade of San Marco, & the ducal Palace. I ascended the Campanile, & got a gen. view of the city, — all white houses & brown roofs, with towers & domes, canals & bridges.

Next, the Palace of the Doges, the giant stair case, standing on the spot, at its head, where Marino Faliero was beheaded, — the hall of the Senate, the hall of the Council of forty, & the hall of the terrible Council of Ten, & the Sentence room, where the 3 masked Senators, unknown to each other & to the accused, gave sentence, — & saw the Lion's Mouths, where anonymous accusations were furtively dropped, &

> "I stood in Venice, in the Bridge of Sighs,
> A palace & a prison on each hand"[27]

& saw the statues & the pictures, — the Titians, & Tintorettos, & P. Veroneses, &c. &c. & got a notion no book can give of the splendor, the taste, the grandeur of idea, the luxury, of this remorseless, despotic oligarchy.

Next, the Church of St. John & St. Paul. (S. S. Giovanni & Paulo), — splended, vast, gorgeous! "The Venetian pantheon" — full of chapels, altars, monuments, tombs, statues & pictures, & frescoed from floor to dome, & Titian's Martyrdom of St. Peter, the Dominican, & Paul Veronica's Adoration of the Shepherds &c. &c.

Next, the S. Maria die Frari, (commonly called the Frari, to distinguish it fr. the other Marias) where is the tomb of Titian, & pictures & statues by all the great Venetian artists, & altars & chapels, & tombs & fresco & mosaics.

And, last, the Academy of Fine Arts, (Academia di Belli Arti), where I spent hours, in the various halls of this wonderful collection, & could well have spent days.

An hour of rest, a late dinner in the Square of St. Marc, & an evening of strolling about the Square, in the clear Italian summer moonlight, & hanging over the railing of the bridges, & walking under the shadows of the columns & porticoes, & listening to the music of violins & guitars & voices, of wh. the Square was full, — & so ends my first day in Venice! — &

[27]Byron, *Childe Harold,* canto IV, stanza 1.

I lie with my window opening on a canal, & hear an occasional cry of a gondolier, & can hardly sleep fr. the fascinating music of a violin & guitar from across the water.

My second day in Venice (Sat. Aug. 25th — wh. I also observed as my wedding day). Breakfast in Sq. of S. Mark, wh. is lined with the best of restorants & cafés, where people eat & read, at tables, in the open air, — where fruits are abundant & cheap — grapes, peaches, figs & melons.

Order of Sights.

1. San Biagio, a Mariner's Church.

2. The Arsenal, — full of trophies of the Venetian Republic, & curious models of galleys & of armor. Among other trophies is the Turkish Admiral's flag taken at Lepanto. Model of the Bucentaur, &c.

3. The Jesuati Church (Real name is S. Maria del Rosario).

4. The Palace of the Giovanelli family, said to be as good a specimen as Venice affords. (Family now on *Terra Firma*, — wh. is the natural phrase here for going into the country). And exquisite, — exquisite, it is, in every part! No people ever equalled the Italians for maintaining exquisite taste & refinement in their pomps, pleasures, luxuries & pride. With them "vice lost all its grossness",[28] & pride & pomp seemed elevated to an angelic state. Our vulgar modern shoes are unfit to tread these marble floors, & our mean French costumes make us look fit only to be the servitors of a race who planned & lived up to such refined splendor.

Passed the Palace that Byron occupied, on the Grand Canal, the palaces now owned by the Duchess de Beni, her son, the Count de Chanbourg, the Duchess of Parma, of the (late) Taglioni, & the ancestral palaces of those great Venetian names, Fóscari, Faliéro, Contárni, Cappello, Donato, Rimini, Giustiniani, &c. &c. — all splendid monuments of those high, wide, refined minds that gave Italy its place at the head of art. Each palace fronts on a canal, & each has a back or side door on a canal. The sea washes the marble steps, & the balconies overlook the sea. And it seems a city of palaces. Were there any poor? Where did they live? But, on what terrible terms, of a secret, oligarchal despotism, they held their lives & fortunes!

5. Church degle Scabze, (S. Maria in Nasaret), not one of the largest or most costly, yet it cost 1,200,000 francs, & one Chapel alone, of the Giovanelli family, cost 18000 ducats.

6. Church of San Rocco, one of the finest in the world, & full of the works of Titian, Tintoretto & Michael Angelo, & lined by chapels of great Venetian families.

---

[28]"Vice itself lost half its evil by losing all its grossness." Edmund Burke, "Reflection on the Revolution in France," *Works,* III, 323.

7. The Rialto (Ponte de Rialto). How much more real & natural are the characters of Shakespeare, than the shadowy, *masky* characters wh. historians give us! "On the Rialto" one looks to see where Shylock trod, & watched & bargained, & where Antonio "rated" him, about his "monies & his usanses".[29] It is larger & wider than I supposed — has three passages along & one across, & shops — little brokers' dens, & notaries', between. The Exchange is now removed to the floor of the Ducal Palace, & the Rialto is becoming a market.

8. Church of the Redentore, erected by the State, in pursuance of a vow, at the termination of the Plague, in 1577. It is immensely costly, with fine pictures, statues, bas reliefs, frescoes & mosaics, — & all a public gift.

9. Church of San Giorgio Maggiore — also large & costly, but situated on a small island, remote, & deserted, & service in it only kept up by 2 or 3 Benedictines (?). But all the world visits it.

10. Last of all — the Basilica of St. Mark! Here I saw all that is to be seen of this wonder of the world, built over the body of St. Mark, the Evangelist, who lies under its High Altar. I cannot recall one thing in ten, except a shoe of St. Charles Boromeo [Carlo Borromeo]. But the wonder is that a church of five domes, all the walls & ceilings alive with scenes & figures, & yet not a touch of a pencil — all is *Mosaic!* One can hardly believe it! Those pictures, of all forms & colors, — all made by bits of colored marble! And then the bronses, the bas reliefs, the marble statues, monuments & columns, the gorgeousness of all! It cannot be exaggerated.

After dinner, joined my friends, the Pollocks, (who have just arrived fr. Trieste) in an evening row about the city, by moonlight, in a gondola. We passed thro' the Grand Canal, under the Rialto, & by the famous palaces, — whole streets (or canals) of fronts equal to Whitehall, & many superior, — & ended in seats in the Square of St. Mark's, with passing crowds, moonlight & music.

SUNDAY. AUG. 26. Church at St. Marc's. Succession of masses, from 9 A.M. to 12 M. & Vespers beginning at 2½ P.M. I spent some 3 hours in the basilica, dreaming, looking about on the crowds at the different altars, & hearing the music, & understanding next to nothing of the Services.

Kept quiet the rest of the day, writing this, in my room, dropping bits of paper into the canal. Every moment I have been in Italy has been exquisite weather, — neither hot nor cool, — that is, not hot, to an escaped

---

[29]*Merchant of Venice*, I, iii, 108.

E. Indian, — & clear & pure, & I have seen few mosquitos & meet few bad smells, wh. we were told would plague our lives.

Tomorrow morning, I leave for Milan. People here are excited & uneasy. All minds are turned towards Garibaldi.[30] The city is full of Austrian soldiers, & said to be full of spies, 10,000 Austrian regulars — ft. & cannon planted so as to command the square & great avenues. The soldiers on guard & post are behind railings, caged in.

Another moonlight evening, & music in St. Mark's Place, by a mil. band of 36 instruments. Pretty to watch the parties coming to the stairs, in their gondolas, so still, so swift, so dream like!

MOND. AUG. 27. Took leave of Venice by early morning, going to the R. R. Station, in a gondola, under the Bridge of Sighs, by the Rialto, & passed the palaces on the Grand Canal, — &, Adieu to the most interesting & incredible creation of men's hands in the form of town or city on the Earth's surface!

All day on the R. R. fr. Venice to Milan; — a delightful day it has been — finest of weather, few clouds, clear sun, & this peculiar Italian scenery. The peculiarity, I think, is that the hills have the characteristics of mountains, — the breaks, the peaks, the irregular & picturesque outlines. The country is under high cultivation, every foot of it, as in England, & the roads & bridges are admirable, & the fields are separated by rows of trees or high shrubbery, or hedges, & almost every road, lane or foot-path has its double border of trees or high shrubbery. Then, there are so many churches, & relig. buildings of other sorts, castles, towers, watch-towers, bell towers, fortresses, & so many of these buildings are on the summits of the hills. In the ext. face of the country there is no sign of poverty or oppression. The *gravamen* is the subjugation of Italians to Austrians, & necessarily severe, often cruel, & always harassing & irritating regulations, enforced by soldiers, who are *everywhere*.

Passed thro' Padua, Vicensa, Verona, Peschiera, Desensano, Brescia, Bergamo & Treviglio, — "names that bear a perfume in the mention" — & along the beautiful Largo di Garda, wh. looked, all the afternoon, as if it were lying there waiting to be sketched by Claude. These towns all look

[30]In 1859 Italy was divided into provinces, with no effective unifying agency. The Austrians, who already occupied Lombardy, formed an alliance with France in 1859 and marched on Sardinia. Giuseppe Garibaldi (1807–1882) took the opportunity to try to unite Italy under King Victor Emmanuel. When his public appeal failed he made a military landing on Neapolitan-occupied Sicily, proclaimed himself dictator, and drove the Neapolitans out. Subsequently he effected the entrance of the king into Naples, as recognized ruler, and two days later, on November 9, 1860, Garibaldi resigned his dictatorship and retired — if only temporarily. The king created a parliamentary monarchy, a process complicated by a war with Austria which lasted until 1866. Dana was observing the beginnings of these events.

historical, & like collegiate or ecclesiastical cities, adorned by the residence also of a peaceful & cultivated nobility.

We find the usual delays for exn. of passports & luggage, & fee-ing of officials, & — did any one *ever* see a polite German? — except as you may see a blossom on a graffed limb. Their language, by the side of the Italian, sounds Hyrcinian & hirsute. If I were an Italian, I would conspire to cut their throats over tubs, as Leonard did his hogs.

Reached Milan at 10 o'ck. P.M. In the dominions of Victor Emmanuel, regenerated Northern Italy; & ancient Milan, — the Milan of Attila & Charles V, of St. Ambrose, St. Augustin & St. Ch. Borromeo, of the Iron Crown of the Lombards! Hotel de la Villa, my window opens on a huge dome, — at least it looks so against the stars, — the Church of St. Charles Borromeo. A warm bath & bottle of German ale, — having had no dinner, & too late now, & bed, & waked up at 9.30 A.M. of —

TUESDAY. AUG. 28TH, to the beautiful light of another day, & to hear a party of English women, at breakfast, making themselves wretched about beds & coffee & inns, in such a "glorious birth"[31] as this country is to a newly arrived person of any reading or thought or feeling!

To-day, I devoted chiefly to the Cathedral. One should not begin too strong to talk of Italy. I called St. Mark's a wonder of the world. So it is. But what is the Cathedral at Milan? No words are adequate for the dedication of such a structure but *Gloria in excelsis Deo*. It is overpowering. I really believe that if a sensitive & imaginative person, who had seen nothing but N. England (say Miss Lydia Marsh[32]) were transported into the interior of that church the effect might be too great for the brain to bear. And the prodigality of riches in the architecture & sculpture without! It is endless. The marble (white) keeps its color so beautifully in this climate. Most parts, — the upper especially are snow white, & the slight yellow tint the ceilings get, in the interior, is beautiful, & gives the fine work of the marble ceilings the look of old lace. One feeling, & a constant one is — is it possible? Is this the work of men's hands? I can imagine an excitable person, if out of sight, doing anything — rolling on the pavement, jumping up into the air & yelling, gasping for breath, or clapping hands to head & running until out of sight.

I mounted to the top, passing lines, — crowds — of statues, all the way, — for the ascent is over the exterior, in a way only a view can explain.

Milan lies in the great plain of Lombardy, wh. looks as green with grass & trees as the richest valleys. The charm of an Italian city is that

[31]"The sunshine is a glorious birth," is a line from Wordsworth's "Intimations Ode."
[32]Lydia Marsh was a sister of Dana's mother-in-law, noted earlier.

it is *finished*. There are no vacant lots, no prepared streets unbuilt on, no pulling down & altering. Centuries have done the work, & the present accepts it. From the top of the Cathedral is a sea of brown roofs & white stone houses, avenues & patches of deep green, for gardens & public grounds, within the city, & a flat circumference of deep green extending to the distant hills. Not England is greener.

From the top to the crypt. Down to the tomb of St. Charles Borromeo. This is in a small chapel, where light always burns, & the sacrifice of the Mass is daily offered, the altar being over the tomb. This is the richest tomb in Christendom. Everything about it seems to have cost hundreds of thousands, & all gifts. The cross of emeralds, the gift of Maria Theresa, is the richest & most beautiful I ever saw. The affect. devotion to the mem. of this man is unlimited. I was pleased to see that the priest, when he opens the tomb, puts on a surplice. The golden side of the tomb is lowered by machinery, & the interior is disclosed, thro' pure & genuine crystal — all the side is crystal. There is his body, in robes of office, but the face is open to view, being enclosed in hermetically sealed crystal.

Lingered about the Cathedral until I had barely time to go to the incredibly ancient Ch. of St. Ambrose. Some service or other seems to be going on nearly all the time, in the Cathedral, & there are always people sitting or kneeling, reading or praying, somewhere.

Ch. of St. Ambrose. A curiosity. His body is there, under the altar, & there is the verit. pulpit in which he & St. Augustin preached, & the altar where St. Aug. renounced his errors. — (But, see Murray for dates).[33] It is a quaint old place, & must not be suffered to decay.

Milan is very military — not only the regular army, but the Nat. Guard, the Militia, is in constant training, & nearly half the men one meets are in uniform. They mean to be prepared for Austria, if necessary. All the talk is "Garibaldi". I cannot understand them, but his name is in all mouths, & the speech is apparently always earnestly in his favor.

I like the open-air habits of the Italians, in the evenings. Walked about Milan from 9 to 10 P.M. — a well ordered, quiet, sober decent people, & no external signs of vice. In Venice, there were a few signs, as in Boston, — but Milan is better.

WED. 29, AUG. Left Milan for Arona, by rail. On our way out, saw handsome boulevards & walks, & numerous large public buildings.

Train passes thro' Magenta, the scene of the dreadful battle of 1859.[34] They say that hardly a house is without shot marks; for the latter part of the battle was fought in the streets.

[33]St. Augustine was baptized by St. Ambrose in Milan in 387. His "Retractions" were published in 428. Dana refers to the standard tourist guidebooks published by John Murray.

[34]On June 4, 1859, the Austrians were defeated at Magenta by the Sardinian army.

To Arona, at foot of Largo Maggiori, is about 4 hours. We stopped a half hour at Novara, & I walked about the town, to its cathedral & market &c. I like very much these middle sised Italian towns. They look solid, finished, ancient & tasteful, & the niches, oratories, frescoes out of doors, give an air of art to them.

(Selfish, hard headed, wiley priest, maneuvering to keep a double seat. Three Franciscans, in full garb, in my carriage).

At Arona, took steamer, on Largo Maggiori, for Farioli. Sail up the lake is one of those scenes to be remembered for life, especially the Isola Bella, & the other islands of the Borromeo family; & there, at Arona, in full view, out "in the open", overlooking the lake, is the colossal bronse statue of St. Charles Borromeo, erected by the city of Milan.

At Farioli, took diligence for Domo D' Ossola, where passed the night. The way was directly up the Alps, & I had an outside seat, with the driver, & commanded the whole view. It was the height of harvest, & laborers were out in all the valleys & green spots — & the laborers were mostly the women & girls, carrying heavy loads of grass & wheat on their backs, & often no hats or bonnets, & the sun very hot. The verdure is intense, as great as in England, in the valleys & slopes, & vines, fruit trees & cultivated grounds are everywhere. The mountains are tipped with perpet. snow, & snow & glaciers go far down their sides, & in great prairies across & between them. Nothing in America is to be compared with the Alps. All the mountains in N. H. might be taken fr. a single range of the Alps & not missed. And, besides being double their height & more, the Alps have wild, broken, surprising outlines, — wh. our mountains have not. Then, in the midst of this prodigality of grandeur, there are the sweetest scenes of quiet industry & peaceful life, for the valleys & nooks & slopes, wh. with us are unoccupied, here centuries of labor & civilisation have peopled & cultivated, & spotted with Chapels, towers, quaint churches, & hospices or monasteries. The road over the Simplon (Bonaparte's work) is solid & smooth as any road about London, & the walls that support it as good as any of Ben. Bussey's.[35] It is a miracle of human skill & labor.

Now, imagine the roads & viaducts of Ancient Rome, & the cultivation of the best counties in England, & the architecture of Tuscany, spread among & over the wildest parts of the Himalayas & Andes, & you can get some notion of the Alps. But you must add that water is everywhere, cascades & rushing streams, wh. the everlasting snows never permit to fail. In one place the Simplon road passes under the sheet of a torrent.

---

[35]Benjamin Bussey (1757–1842) made a fortune in trade in Boston after 1782. A noted philanthropist, he built many roads, as well as endowing Harvard's agriculture, law, and divinity schools.

(Have I remarked the prevalence of blue eyes, yellow or flaxen hair, & red hair, in Northern Italy? In Venetia, & Lombardy, very generally, & in Piedmont more. The blonds & auburns & light brunettes almost equal the dark hair & eyes, in numbers, on the plains, & exceed them as you ascend the mountains).

This diligence traveling is delightful, if you are outside — air, view, & sight of all the people, on the road, & in the street of the little hamlets.

Night at Domo D'Osola, window looking out on the snow covered mountains, & sleeping by the sound of the rushing water.

THURSD. 30TH. AUG. From Domo D'Ossola, over the summit of the Simplon Pass, to Brienz for the night. At the summit, stopped at the Hospice, where were four monks of the St. Bernard Monastery, in charge, with some noble dogs, of the true breed, dark brown color with white spots. The monks gave us wine & bread, & we put a gift in the box in the Chapel. (The St. Bernard monks are all of the Augustine order, & not of the order of St. Bernard, — if there be such).

At the Swiss border, stopped at a little, humble inn, kept by a Swiss woman, who had five daughters, from 4 to 12 years old, all healthy, pretty, well behaved children, & where we got good bread & wine. (Good bread everywhere but in America).

This has been a glorious day — a day for a life time — a succession of wonders & delights. How the Himalayas or Andes compare with the Alps I know not, but it is certain they have not the presence of ruined castles, towers & hospices, still-used hospices & churches, villages & vineyards, close in upon the snows. The constant presence of water is a great feature. Think of poor, dry volcanic Mauna Loa, without a drop of water fr. summit to base!

FRID. 31. AUG. Diligence (outside, always) fr. Brienz to Sion, rail road from Sion to St. Maurice. Diligence from St. Maurice to Bex. Rail Road from Bex to Villeneuve, on the banks of the Lake of Geneva — Lake Leman, — which we reached at night, & saw the moon shine over the "pure, placid Leman".[36] The road all day has been by the side of the rushing Rhone, & through the valley of the Rhone, — a stupendous valley, or chain of valleys, & everywhere the Rhone a torrent of clay colored water. Between Martiguy & Bex is a famous cascade, the —— . Everything is dwarfed & ordinary in comparison with the Alps & their peaks & vale & torrents. Europe is *the continent*, after all.

SAT. SEP. 1. Steamer from Villeneuve to Geneva. This is the charm of charms! First the dull white, sullen walls of Chillon, foundations sunk

[36]Byron, *Childe Harold*, canto III, stanza 55.

in the lake, & then Vevey, Lausanne, Nyon, Coppet, &c., & the succession, all the way to Geneva, of castles, towers, villas, simple country houses, churches, chapels, cities, towns, hamlets, washed by the Lake, or lying on its slopes, & in the distance, the towering Alps, & Jura in its "misty shroud".[37] I should think that no small portion of the world had country seats upon the Lake of Geneva. And, now, we approach the high walls of Old Geneva. Here the narrow, rushing Rhone divides the city, bridged across by many bridges, but no longer of a clay color, but of a beautiful light green, as it hurries past the arches & along the walls.

Sat. afternoon, I am sitting at the window of my chamber in the hotel, looking out upon the Rhone, the island with Rousseau's statue, & the great bridges & opposite streets, & towers of the cathedral. This may be called a stage in my progress round the world.[38]

SUNDAY. SEP. 2, 1860. At Geneva went first to the old cathedral, & saw the pulpit in wh. John Calvin preached. The Church is still used by a Calvinistic society, filled with pews, & no altar. Next went to morning service at the Engl. Church. Stone, good sise, well designed, built & supported by vol. contributions. One of the best, — perhaps the best, congregation I ever saw, in quality, — picked people — Engl. & Am. travellers, decent eno' to stay over Sunday & go to service, — or with means & taste eno' to have permanent residences here. So many healthy sensible looking Engl. girls, & mothers & fathers. Church crowded — seats in the aisles. The Am. Consul (one Giles, of Md., son of Dist. judge, a flat) tells me there are 200 Am. boys at school within a day's journey of Geneva. So many Americans attend the Eng. Ch. here, that they add a prayer for the Prest. of U. S. to that for the Queen, in the Liturgy.

In afternoon, walked with Giles & Mr. Peters, son of Peters the U. S. Reporter,[39] to the confluence of the Rhone & Arve, — beautiful spot. Rhone is dark green, & Arve is muddy. At sundown walked, alone, on the high grounds of Geneva, & saw clouds & openings here & there, where Mt. Blanc lies, but not sure whether got a glimpse of the Mt. or no. It is seen plainly in clear weather. The rushing of the Rhone past the bridges, at night, is fearful. It is a torrent, & by day, of a dark emerald color.

Swiss troops are mustering & drilling everywhere, to preserve the integrity & neutrality of the poor little republic.[40]

---

[37]*Ibid.,* stanza 92.

[38]Dana added the marginal note: "Sent journal from Geneva, to Sep. 2 1860."

[39]Richard Peters is noted earlier as the successor of Wheaton as Reporter of the U. S. Supreme Court.

[40]The Swiss were attempting, successfully as it turned out, to remain neutral with respect to the wars in Italy.

Geneva is a large place now, & growing, — a centre of travel & pleasure residence. Population abt. equally Cath. & Prot. Houses built of light colored stone, & high, 5 & 6 stories, & let by stories, as in Paris. Adds to style of place.

MONDAY. SEP. 3. Rail Road, along the Lake of Geneva, towards Neufchatel. Skirted the pretty Lake of Neufchatel, had a good view of the town, where we stopped a few minutes, & then across country, to Landeron at the foot of Lake Biel (Fr., *Bienne*), & there took steamer through the length of the lake, to the town of Biel (Bienne), & thence, by rail again, through Solence, Aarburg, Hertogenbuchsee, & Olen, to Basle, where passed the night. At Basle, first view of the Rhine, wh. is here a broad, shallow, rapid, turbid river. Reached Basle in season to visit the cathedral before dark. It is a large, respectable looking edifice, of red sandstone, with roof of colored tiles. In it is the tomb & monument of Erasmus. I had the satisfaction of reading the latin epitaph in the manner he succeeded in banishing from England, but wh. is now regaining its place among English & Am. scholars. Here is a nemesis for you, after centuries, — to have an Am. standing over his ashes & reading his epitaph in the Roman manner![41] In the Chapter House, is the desk or chest used by Erasmus, — also a chest (very old) wh. contained the records of the Chapter before the Reformation. In the rear of the church, is a platform wh. overlooks the Rhine & all the town, planted with trees & grass. Here I walked, in the beautiful twilight & moonlight, for an hour or more.

As one comes North, from the Oriental, tropical regions, — the gradual changes are curious. First, in Switzerland & Upper Germany, began to notice the blowing of noses, coughing, sneesing, spitting, & other signs of regions of phlegm & saliva. Then, the increasing fairness of skin, prevalence of blue & grey eyes & fair hair — increasing breadth of jaw, thickness of lips, bigness of head; &, in Germany, a cowlike heaviness of tread & width of foot. The gradual mixture of French with Italian, in Piedmont, French with German, in Switzerland, & the ceasing of French in Germany. In nature, you notice the length of twilight, the coming in of turf, grass plots, thick shade trees & hedges.

TUESDAY MORNING, SEP. 4. Rail fr. Basle to Heidelberg, by the Black Forest. Next me, in the car, made an acquaintance in young James M. Crafts, gr. son of Jeremiah Mason,[42] a capital fellow, good looking, strong,

---

[41]Erasmus employed what classicists regarded as a colloquial or vernacular form of Latin expression. His "method" had a great influence during the Renaissance.

[42]James Mason Crafts (1839–1917), after study at Heidelberg and Paris, in 1868 became professor of chemistry at Cornell, later taught at M.I.T., and did extensive

intelligent, manly, — been on a tramp over Tyrol, & bound to Heidelberg, where he is to study chemistry & geology.

Reached Heidelberg by 1 P.M., & gave the afternoon to the Castle, with young Crafts. Went all over it. It is a noble — not quite *ruin*, but memorial or monument of feudal & chivalric times, & the grounds & walks about it are more varied & beautif. than I have seen connected with any such place. View of Neckar, & distant white stripe of the Rhine, & the level Palatenate, is grand. Heidelberg stands just where the hills cease.

In ev., walked about the town, to do honor to memories of Ned's eight year residence.[43] Called at Wittermaden's — but he was *ex re,* & it is vacation. Looked at the University, Museum, bridge over Neckar & chief churches. It is a nice quiet, old town, & with its numerous shady hill-side walks, well adapted for resid. of people who love such things.

Lodged at the "Prins Karl".

WED. SEP. 5. Heidelberg, by rail, to Mayence, & there took steamer down the Rhine, to Cologne. Passed, by rail, through Darmstadt, where large body of Hessian troops were parading, to receive the King of the Belgians.

Will not describe Rhine. Trite. Was not disappointed. Scenery is not (& I did not expect to find it) on a gigantic scale, like the Saguenay, or Yosemete, — nor impending & perpendicular, but often very high, sharp, ragged & wild, & interspersed among exquisite beauties, & everywhere the imagn. & feelings are touched by the ruins of successive ages — Roman, Dark Ages, feudal, ages of chivalry, Religious wars of Reformation, & abbeys, convents & churches, among the castles & towns. Passed & saw the usual most marked objects — Johannisberg, Rüdesheim, Bingen, Rheinstein (a rebuilt castle, occupied by Princc Fr. of Prussia) the island rock of Pfalz, The Seven Maidens, St. Goar, Boppard, Stolzenfels, Coblens, Ehrenbreitstein (wh. is not, as I expected, a castle, but a great series of towers & walls, making a long & very extensive fortification, on the high hill-top, with a noble position, & almost unrivalled *outlook*), Rheineck castle, Drachenfels, & Bonn.

As far as Coblens, we had beautif. weather. From Cleins to Cologne rain, & chilly weather. This cold rain is new to me, & rather gloomy, but the scene & sights interest me eno' to keep off dullness.

Yankee face, gold specs, — Yankee voice, — loud, *platform* conversation — "Professor in a college — New England — knew Wayland,[44] of course, — He was my chief. Yes Sir, Frank Wayland & I ... Shoulder to

research abroad. He established a distinguished international reputation. His grandfather, Jeremiah, lawyer and New Hampshire legislator, has been noted earlier.

[43]Edmund T. Dana, his younger brother, who took a doctorate in law at Heidelberg.

[44]Francis Wayland, noted earlier, was president of Brown University, 1827–1855.

Shoulder. Yes, Sir — shoulder to shoulder, 30 years — all the influences — Abolition — Now, there, Sir . . . Brown Univ. . . . Minister of the Gospel. Baptist. So offended that made acq. of no Baptist clergyman in England. Know was wrong, &c. &c.". He saw none of the scenery. When could not get an auditor, sat with back to the house, eyes shut, meditating more talk. Could it be Gammell?[45] He had a wife with him, — been pretty. "When other boys playing, I was digging into hard theol. controversy".

Reached Cologne in dark rainy, chilly night. Hotel Hollande. With my topee & red stripes on luggage, was taken for a returning E. Indian officer, & got the best rooms.

(Noticed the entire absence of *animal* life in Germany. No cattle in the fields, — neither sheep, nor cows, nor oxen. High cultivation, but all inanimate nature).

THURSDAY. SEP. 6. At Cologne. Spent the morning at the Cathedral. It is a stupendous structure, even now, & when completed, will be, probably, the largest cathedral in Christendom. But it is not interesting or agreeable now; for the work going on interferes with the effects. False roofs, low & plain, destroy the chief effect of a cathedral — height & elegance of roof, & vistas are cut off. Moreover, it must be said that the German Prot. Church can do nothing with a cathedral. As well might the Temple in Jerusalem, after it had [been] consecrated by Solomon, have been handed over to the Moravians. All looks cheerless & unused & misapplied & merely a show. There is R. Cath. worship held in some side chapels, & in one aisle, & was going on, at the time, — but it filled little space. I went to the top, & got lost in coming down, & wandered among dark passages ending in closed doors, & went up & down, for about a half an hour, until a workman coming along gave me a clue. I had taken no guide, I hate them so, in a Cathedral. The day was beautiful, & the view of Cologne & the Rhine, well repays the labor of ascent. Absurd bank of *Sunflowers*, around the Chancel, outside.

Geo. F. Hoar. "Why do men hate Geo. T. Curtis so?"

Mr. Choate. "Why, Mr. Hoar, some men we hate for cause, but him we hate peremptorily".

In the afternoon, took the train for Antwerp. A beautiful journey this — fr. Cologne to Antwerp! It is lower Prussia from Cologne to Aix La Chapelle, (or, more strictly, Verviers) & thence it is Belgium. I am charmed with Belgium. Here is a sight that comes home, — cattle grasing in the fields, under the trees, — cows, oxen, sheep, — everywhere, — & English hedges, & shrubbery, & thick trees, & groves, & such nice

[45]William Gammell (1812–1889) was a professor of theology at Brown until 1864. He published widely on theological subjects.

houses, — all so neat & tasteful — a good medium between the Dutch & French.

All the way, I should say, from Cologne to Antwerp, the rail road is lined, on each side, by a hedge. The towns & villages are delightful. The better classes speak French, the lower, Flemish, — & tho' the German is a far greater language than the French, for poetry, theology, oratory & metaphysics, — yet, after the popularly spoken German, it is a pleasure to hear the French again, — so *genteel* & facile a language, — so civilised, urbane & complaisant.

(The train starts by a trumpet, instead of a bell, at each station).

Liège (French, & in 2 syllables — the German being Lüttich) is a beautiful town, & the watering-place of Chaudefontaine, as pretty as need be. From Cologne to Liège the country is hilly, well diversified, & picturesque & abounding in water, as well as rich & populous & highly cultivated. After Liège, comes the "Low Country", — Netherlands, — of the Flemings & Netherlanders proper. No longer picturesque, but as pretty as art & industry can make a level country.

At Malines (Mecklin) trams separate, to Brussels & Antwerp. Reached Antwerp at 10 P. M., — so the last three hours, we saw nothing. Lodged at a capital hotel, the Hotel St. Antoine, — such beds & sheets & pillows & curtains!

FRIDAY. SEP. 7. Took guide, this time, & made a pretty active campaign, from 8.30 A. M. until 12 M. *Cathedral.* Large, high rich & especially rich in Rubens' pictures. Such is genius — Rubens is a revenue to the Cathedral. All the world pays to see his pictures. They are the Descent from the Cross, the Elevation of the Cross, the Resurrection & the Assumption. My remark is that the pictures seemed alive, — full of work. The way they are shown, by drawing up a curtain & keeping it up a few minutes, for each set of comers, at so much a head, is not agreeable. While the beadle was drawing the curtain over the Assumption, & I was contemplating it, he breaks in, to a man before me, — "that is not 5 shillings, only 4 s. & 6 d". "That is the Virgin Mary", said he, to a common-place, diffident English woman — "Who is that *other lady?*" said she.

Went to the top of the spire, 466 feet high. Can see Bergen op Zoom, & the spires of a town in Holland, at the North, & the spires of Ghent, in the South. Perfectly level country, thickly populated & richly cultivated, & no signs of poverty or neglect anywhere, in city or country.

Next, to Church of Saint Jacques (St. James). This is more curious & extraordinary than the Cathedral, tho' smaller — also richer & more beautiful. There are no less than 22 chapels, each of marble. The whole church seems inlaid with beautif. stones, — roofs, floor & walls. One chapel of the Rubens family, with marble groups & effigies. Both here & in the cathedral a great deal of exquisite oak carving. (Omitted to mention the picture of St. Francis, by Murillo, in the Cathedral, wh. struck me very much).

Church of St. Paul's — also large & rich, full of marble & oak & gold, with a renowned picture of the Scourging of Jesus, by Rubens, & of the bearing of the Cross, by Van Dyke, — the latter in bad light at this hour. In the close of this church is a famous representation of the garden, Mt. Calvary, & Purgatory, in the grotto form. My guide explained the figures to me, & as he turned to go out, I asked "What are all those other figures?". "Oh, only Twelve Apostles, four Evangelists, & Angels, — that's all".

Visited a private collection of the late Mr. Nuyts — who died 2 years ago, & gave the collection for the benefit of the poor. It is in excellent order, & each visitor pays a small fee, for the good object. Here are master pieces of Van Dyck, Teniers, Rubens, Jordaens, Guido & Murillo, &, I believe, one of Claude. Murillo's (?) St. Anthony, looks like Father.

All the great churches here — Cathedral, St. Paul's, & St. James, are Catholic, & worship was going on, & people reading & praying, in the usual manner, & at some altars lights burning, & the smell of incense, & the sounds of voices. To my surprise, my guide told me that Antwerp was entirely a Catholic city, & that there were no Protestant churches, except of foreigners.

Took leave of this clean, orderly, wealthy, respectable city, with regret, — & took steamer, at 1 P.M., for London, & took my latest step on the *Continent* of Europe. Passage down the Scheldt, by the neatest little villages, with red roofs, & by night were out at sea, — on the German Ocean. So natural is it now to me, to be on the deck of a ship! I am at home, at once.

SATURDAY. SEP. 8. Here I am, in dear old London, again! At the house of the Bithneys, too, — tho' they have moved fr. 19 Regent st., to 7 Bury st. St. James. They received me most cordially, — & in half an hour, my trunks were unpacked, my clothes sorted in drawers & shelves, & I sat down to read my letters from home, (wh. I got at the Barings) — not having heard from home, a word — for six months, — and when I found all well, — all living, — it seemed that my cup of blessing was full. Here, in England, in perfectly good health, in vigor of health — with no loss even of an umbrella, from my luggage, — escaped all dangers of sea & land, of violence & sickness, — in all climates & countries. If I am not grateful, it is because gratitude is not in me.

[Russell] Sturgis was very cordial & kind, & got me the last berth to be had in the Persia, on the 15th, & sent a line to F. E. Parker, by extra mail, *via* Cork, to notify my arrival. Mr. Baring, also, interested & cordial.[46]

None of my great friends are in town, — my friends of 1856, — as all the world that can leave London has gone. Called at houses (or clubs) of Parkes, Senior, Sir Wm. Heathcote, Mr. Gladstone, &c. & left cards or notes, — & the papers announced that the Duke of Argyll, the Sutherlands, Lord Lansdowne, Ld. Campbell, Ld. Cranworth, &c. are in the country. Better so, — for I have no clothes to make visits in. Have seen no washerwoman since Cairo, & Mrs. Bithney has a large bag to deal with, — & tho' I have a superabundance of tropical clothing, have hardly a decent suit for Engl. cilmate. Turn up Henry T. Parker, who is full of kindness & introduces me to a proper tailor, who is to get me in order before I sail.

How pleasant are the old London sights! And the parks — Hyde, Green, St. James', — are more beautiful, after all I have seen elsewhere, than my recollection held them.

SUNDAY, SEP. 9. What could I do but go to the Abbey, to the early Communion Service, at 8 o'ck.? How still! How solemn! The high roof, the dim sunset colored stone, — so much more agreeable to the eye than the white & red of most of the Continental churches — & the still statues of the great dead, — statesmen, orators, soldiers, poets, scholars. In this early service there is no music, & the whole company — in deserted West End — did not exceed twenty.

After breakfast H. T. P. called & took me to the morning service at the church of All Saints, Margaret st. This is the most perfectly finished, rich & exquisite religious structure, for its sise, — it is not large, in England, — & probably not exceeded in Europe. Beresford Hope[47] gave 10,000£. towards it, & a London banker gave 30,000 £., & it cost much more. The outside is of dark red & black brick. The interior is a masterpiece of color & arrangement. Yet not a touch of paint, or stucco, — all is marble & stone, inlaid! It is a wonder of skill & beauty. Yet, this exquisite Church — not for the rich & fashionable, but a Free Church, — open to all, — a *gift* to the public, & in a poor neighborhood, & its congregations made up much of the poor. It has a rector & four curates, who all live in

---

[46]Thomas Baring (1799–1873) was grandson of Sir Francis Baring (1740–1810), founder of the great banking house of Baring Brothers. Dana sometimes misspelled the name "Barring."

[47]Alexander James Beresford Hope (1820–1887), prominent parliamentarian, inherited Lord Beresford's English estates in 1854, founded the *Saturday Review* in 1855, and engaged in a wide variety of philanthropic enterprises.

the Church Yard, & its services, schools, charities &c. are constant. The order of services is this —

Every day in the week.

Holy Communion at 7 A.M.
Morning Prayer at 8 A.M.
Evening Prayer at 5 P.M.

Sundays

Holy Communion at 7 A.M.
Morning Prayer Sermon & Communion at 11 A.M.
Litany 12 M.
Evening Prayer 5 P.M.
Evening Prayer & Sermon 7 P.M.

Other Holy Days

Holy Communion 7 A.M.
Morning Prayer, Sermon & Commn. 11 A.M.
Evening Prayer 5 P.M.

And the Church is always open for persons to sit & read, or meditate or for private devotions. And this has been entirely successful. The clergy & active parishoners are even overworked. The church, this morning, was so full we could scarcely get a seat, & many could not sit. The service was choral, throughout. When the Communion office begins, they light the candles on the altar, as in the Eastern Greek & Roman Churches, — & I think, too, but am not sure — the Lutheran.

Went to [H. T.] Parker's to dine (3 Ladbroke Gardens, Kensington Park, Notting Hill). Mrs. P. & children well, & nice house with good country view.

At 6½ P.M., went to Ev. Service at a nice, half rural, half city church of St. Stephen's, Notting Hill, — where the service was choral, half the seats free, & — tho' a beautif. Sunday twilight, — the church was crowded. Respectable sermon. To-day, all the clergy preach on the Harvest, & have prayers, — at request of Bishop of London, — as has been danger of losing it. The Harvest & Garibaldi, are the two topics, in all men's mouths, Parliament being adjourned.

MONDAY. SEP. 10. In my rooms, writing & reading, all A.M. by a sea-coal fire. Memories of Egypt & Aden & Red Sea!

Parker calls & takes me to the British Museum, to see the Reading Room, wh. has been built since 1856. It is the room where students & readers have their desks, & consult the text books, cyclopaedias, catalogues &c., & from wh. they send orders for books to the Library, — the Library not being visited, at all, for study. There is no such room as this in Europe. It is a circle, with dome, lighted from above, & its diameter is 4 feet greater than that of the dome of St. Paul's.

The autographs are now open to view of all, spread out in glass cases, — as well as many other lit. curiosities. This is the grandest Literary & Scientific institution (not for instruction) in the world. The Reading Room, I told Parker, was a temple to the deification of Bibliology.

In the ev., called on Mrs. Leslie, (widow of C. R. Leslie, the artist, who was so attentive to me in 1856, — the friend of my father & Mr. Allston) at 2 Abercom Pl. — far out. She was evidently touched by my attention, & I was glad to pay it. Her son-in-law Fletcher, was there — daughters in Scotland. She gave me a photograph of a portrait of Leslie by himself in early life.

TUESD. SEP. 11. Kind letter fr. Sir Wm. Heathcote, inviting me to Hursley. Cannot go, — as no clothes fit. *Au lieu,* shall go to York, Boston &c., to pass the time until Friday, when pack up & go to Liverpool.

Weather has been clear & fine, now, for four days — good for me, — but almost a salvation of the harvest.[48]

From Trieste to Antwerp, inclusive — Austrian Italy, *Italian* Italy, Piedmont, Lombardy, Switzerland, Southern Germany, Prussia, Northern-Germany, and Belgium — have seen no signs of poverty, pauperism, beggary, idleness, drunkenness, obtrusive vice, decay or wanting. The signs of industry, prosperity, advance, growth, progress, content, are as general as with us. I saw, in no city, anything so bad as New York & Boston & London present, — (& N. York worst of all) in the regions of the abject poor, & the abandoned vicious. Other travelers tell me that those things not only are not seen, but are not. External, offensive vice & pauperism are suppressed & controlled.

But *industry* & *decent provision for life,* — are general, — as in New England, — & more than in many parts of Old England, Scotland, — far before Ireland — & more than in California, & many parts of middle & Western America. Doubtless, *change of condition* is rare, the ruts are deep, & routine governs, — but order, industry, sobriety, outward decency prevail also on the Continent of Europe as I saw it.[49]

TUESDAY. SEP. 11. Drove to Barings & settled accts. Spent morning in Chamber, before sea-coal fire, writing journal & letters.

[48]Dana added the marginal note: "This to go by Adriatic of Sep. 12th & I to follow in Persia of 15th. Send no letter, as I come so soon."
[49]Dana added the marginal note: "Sent journal from London, to Sep. 11. 1860."

At 5 P.M. took train for York, at King's Cross station. (I have traveled 2d class throughout the continent of Europe & in England. On the continent, the 2d class are generally excellent, — as good as our cars at home, but in England they are not quite good eno' for a long journey, — stiff, straight backs. The company is mixed, — sometimes the best of people, that is, scholars, professional men, &c., & with them a good many lower & disagreeable persons, but the chance for view is about as good as fr. the first class).

Stopped 5 minutes at Peterboro', & got a view of the outside of the cathedral, but over the tops of low houses, &, of course, not satisfactory.

The long rains have kept everything green, & now the clear, fine weather, wh. has relieved the mind of the whole kingdom fr. fear of an entire loss of harvest, seems to take everybody out of doors. The number of boys playing cricket in the green fields, as we hurry by (for it is vacation, now, at the schools) would surprise one. They seemed to have been arranged for a show, — & the girls are walking about & looking on, & women sitting under the trees, sewing or reading, or tending babies, — & all the working people are at the harvest, — cutting, gathering, binding or "carrying". After all the world seen, — there is no land like England, for a home!

After Peterboro', it is too dark to see, & we are thundered through Grantham, Dorcester, in the dark, &c. &c., & reach York at a little after 10 P.M., & I am soon in a comfortable chamber, in this most ancient of towns, — the scene of great events in British history.

WED. SEP. 12. Rose early, & walked the circuit of the walls, round the half of the city on the S. side of the river. The walls are in excellent preservation, & a walk of about 6 f. in width is carried along them, bringing the parapet breast high. This preservation of the walls of the old walled towns has the advantage, not only of antiquarian interest, & effect on the imagn., but it gives an open space for healthful air & exercise, & if the towns grow, they can build outside the walls as well as inside. At York, the gates are preserved, & have a heavy, sombre, feudal look about them, & the chief streets are named from the gates, which are called "bars", as well, or in addition — as in Petergate Bar, Micklegate Bar, Bootharn Bar, Monk Bar &c.

The river Ouse divides the town, & over it is one stone bridge & two ferries. Spent the chief part of the morning at the "Minster" — (no one calls it the "Cathedral"). It is very grand & large. The stone is not so dark & agreeable to my eye as Westmin. Abbey, but more so than the chief cathedrals on the continent. The interior has a hollow & deserted look. There are no frescoes, no paintings, & the choir is shut off by screens & organ, so that the vista is interrupted. The chapter-house is handsome & in good order. On the whole, I am not disappointed in York Minster as regards sise, & grandeur, but it does not *interest* me; & in mere sise, & especially in height of roof, it is entirely eclipsed by Milan. No cathedral that I have seen, anywhere, approaches Milan for effect of height & vistas, & then it is warmed & alive with color & paintings, burning candle, praying people, moving priests, & the smell of incense. The few marble monuments & effigies, in York Minster, have a peculiarly cold & desolate look.

Walked round the castle, wh., like most of the castles in the English country towns, is used as a prison, & in good repair, & visited the ruins of St. Mary's Abbey, & the Manor House, & looked at some of the quaint old churches, St. Helen's, St. Sampson's (*what* St. Sampson, for the δγουιστ was an evil liver,)[50] & went into one — St. Mary's something, — and an odd old place eno' it was, — everything where you did not expect to find it, & black with time, & rather damp for comfort, I should say. Attended morning service at the Minster. Choral, with two choirs, & pretty well done.

After lunch, took train for Doncaster, learning that I have just time to see the Doncaster races, — the great race of the St. Leger, — wh. ranks next to the Derby, — &, as I have never seen a race in England, I am fortunate to catch this, unexpectedly.

Reach Doncaster at 2 P.M. Great crowds, pouring out to "The Leger". Thicken as we go on. Great open fields, roofs of the few houses abt. it covered with people, — & there is the "Grand Stand", a large house, with piassas &c. A guinea admits to the Grand Stand & Betting Ring, — but I do not afford it, & take my chance in the crowd. The horses that are to run, — some 15, are walking & prancing & running about, in the course, — & their riders in gay dresses, marked on the cards wh. nearly all spectators carry.

1. Lord A.'s ch. m. Firefly, red coat & black cap.
2. Col. B.'s b. h. Swiftrune, blue coat & red cap.
3. Mr. C.'s b. s. Onward. Yellow coat & black sash. &c. &c.

The most observed among the horses are the winner of the Derby of this year, "Thormanby", the American horse "Umpire", and one named "Wisard". It was a pretty sight, & the horses seemed to me to be brought to the pitch of the combination of strength & fleetness.

They made several false starts, until people got tired & vexed, & one of the Stewards, Lord Coventry, came down & took part in getting them off. It was said that the false starts among the horses, especially if they

---

[50]Dana refers to the biblical Samson of Milton's "Samson Agonistes." Since there was no St. Sampson, the church Dana saw was probably named after St. Samson (d. 565).

get far off &c., & are obliged to come back, as was the case with "Wisard" [are harmful]. They came in at a lightning pace. The pictures do not exagg. the appearance of speed & effort in the horses. To the surprise of nearly all, the race is won by St. Albans, a horse that was not a favorite, & the favorite, "Thormanby", came in 4th, & "Umpire" 5th & "Wisard" 3d, & the 2d being "High Treason", not highly betted on.

There were 2 more races, a Sweepstakes & a handicap, & beautifully run, but the intense interest died out with the "Leger".

The crowd seemed to me decent & orderly, — much more so than wd. have been one near either N. York or Philad., & the desperate rowdies of our large crowd, — the fighters, do not exist, or appear. About ¼ of the crowd were women, & apparently, the greater part, even in the open ground, decent people, the d. & wives of yeomen & laborers. The upper classes are in carriages or in the stands. Lord Derby ran a horse, but, as usual, failed to win. A man I met in the evening at the inn, said the reason Ld. Derby does not win is that he will not cheat, or combine to defraud, & the others oust him. This man thought nearly all the races were frauds. Others, however, tell me they are generally fair. (A man who has once failed to pay a lost bet is not admitted within the betting ring. In some cases, like insolvency, where the man has retrieved himself & paid up in full, he has been restored).

Great crowds at the station, bound up to London, & to all quarters of the kingdom. But good order preserved. I take train for Boston. As go out, get good view of the tower & spire of the large church of Doncaster, — said to be one of the best in the North of England. Reach Boston at about 10 P.M., & "put up" at the Peacock Inn.

THURSDAY. SEP. 13. In Old Boston, — (St. Botolf's town), — & a nice old town it is — not walled, nor with a castle, or a cathedral, — yet an old & important place, — the 2d town in dignity in Lincolnshire, & quite equal to Lincoln in trade & population. All abt. Boston the country is flat, — a dead level — the Fens of Lincolnshire. Yet, it *is* rich, highly cultivated, thickly settled, well wooded & well watered. The Chirwall [Cherwell], a small, slow stream divides Boston nearly equally, & handsome stone bridges span it, & barges, luggers, & even vessels of consid. burden lie in its channel. Boston is closely built, of brick, with red tiled roofs, — the streets irregular but clean & paved, & lighted with gas. (I walked abt. a little, before going to bed, & heard a man & woman sing Byron's "Maid of Cadis",[51] at an inn door, for sixpences, — or rather, pennies & ha'pennies). The only thing to be seen here is the great church of St. Botolf. In this, there is no disappointment. It is not a cathedral, nor an

[51]"The Girl of Cadiz," (1809).

abbey or collegiate church, — but simply a parish church, of the largest sise & highest style. The tower is its chief beauty, & how could a tower be more beautiful? You can stand & look at it for hours. It has *parts*, that interest & please you, as well as its whole. It is at once simple & rich. And high too, for its height is —— feet, half as high again as Bunker Hill Mon't. It is the largest church in England without a transept. I ascended to the top, & got a fine view of Lincolnshire. Col. Sibthorp's house, & Mr. Humphrey Sibthorp's hospital are the chief objects in the neighborhood.[52] The town looks very pretty beneath, & the rooks fly & bother about the coins & buttresses, & in & out of the open work of the upper tower & lantern.

The interior is plain, & without color or ornament, except some oak carving & stained glass. It had been grossly out of repair, utterly neglected, but was restored by subscription & reopened some 7 years ago. It holds conveniently 3000 persons, &, being a great favorite, is often full, or nearly so. A marriage service took place, while I was here, & I attended & took part, so as to be able to say & feel that I had worshipped in the old parent church.

The Chancel is very large. Within the choir sit the Mayor & town corporation on one side, & the singers on the other, each Alderman & Councilman having his stall & his worshipful seat & worshipful stamped book.

The Cotton Chapel, which was restored by subscriptions among the descendants of John Cotton in Boston,[53] U. S., is used to keep the records & for a vestry. They think a good deal of the fact here, & were quite pleased by the attention & interest. The tablet in latin (Mr. Everett's composition), is of brass & makes a good show.

At noon, took the train for Lincoln, which I reached at a little after 1 P.M. & after lunch, walked out to the cathedral.

The chief object of interest betw. Boston & Lincoln is Tattershall Castle, a ruin, but one or two towers of full height. It now belongs to the Earl Fortescue.

Was surprised to find Lincoln standing on elevated ground, a good deal of a hill, & the cathedral really on the top of a hill of some pretensions, & seen at a great distance over the level country of Lincolnshire. It has the highest site & most commanding of any cathedral in England, — unless it be Durham, — which I have not seen & cannot compare with it.

Macaulay was right. He told me, in 1856, to see Lincoln. The question

---

[52]Charles de L. W. Sibthorp (1783–1855), politician and colonel of South Lincoln militia, had been active in Parliament. Humphrey Sibthorp remains unidentified.

[53]John Cotton (1584–1652) of Massachusetts Bay Colony, had been vicar of St. Botolph's Church, 1612–1632.

was to wh. cathedrals I should go, having then seen none but St. Paul's & the Abbey. Some said Salisbury, some York & some Canterbury &c. &c. but Macaulay said — "Lincoln, Lincoln. See Lincoln. That is the best of all". I attributed this to some accidental prejudice, & did not go, but I sympathise with him. If I must choose among all, — taking inside & outside, form & color, beauty, sise & interest, — all into account — give me Lincoln. (*Mem.* that I have not seen Canterbury, Durham & Gloucester & Exeter). For interest in the interior, I will not yield the Abbey, nor for beauty of color & form in the exterior, Salisbury; but the interior of Salisbury is nothing & less than nothing. In exterior, Lincoln has an agreeable color, — not the exquisite touch of the russet of Salisbury, but still, satisfactory, & with its nave, choir, chancel, double transepts, aisles, chapter house, & towers, it has the look of a town of buildings. The color of the interior is beautiful, — a dark buff, — & there is a great deal of black oak, richly carved. There is a look of warmth & richness, in strong contrast with the cold, deserted look of York minster. The evening service began soon after I entered, & I remained through it. The afternoon sun on the "storied windows, richly dight",[54] the charm of the color of the ancient stone, relieved by dark oak, the frequent monuments, the resounding organ & the full voiced choir, made it just what an evening in a rural cathedral should be. I ascended the tower, — the central tower, & stood up inside the "Great Tom of Lincoln" whose tongue is six feet long. The view from the top gives you the hill country of Rutland & Leicestershire, close by, & the fens — the level of Lincolnshire, stretching to the sea. Belvoir Castle can be seen, of a clear day.

In the Close, is a piece of Roman pavement, wh. is housed over & carefully protected.

The ruins of the Bishop's Palace, destroyed by Cromwell, but with much remaining, & venerable with ivy, are among the best pieces of ruins I have seen. They are in the Close, concealed by a high wall, from the casual passer, & hard by the cathedral. The houses of the Dean, Subdean, &c. in the Close, are in the usual cathedral style of beauty, exquisite order, & repose. The description of the Deanery, in the "Angel in the House" (?)[55] applies to almost all of them.

The town of Lincoln, too, I like well. It has diversity of service, hollow, hillside & hill top, irreg. streets, but neat, a river to cross by stone bridges, ancient gateways, cathedral & castle. The castle is large, & now altered for a county prison.

[54]Milton, *Il Penseroso*, line 159.

[55]*Angel in the House* is the composite title of a four-part, unfinished narrative poem by Coventry Patmore (1823–1896), three parts of which had been published at the time of Dana's writing.

Left at about 6 P.M. & reached London at 10.30, & drove, for the last time, along the miles of streets by flaming gas light, Bloomsbury Sq., Russell Sq., & the wide, straight well built streets that fashion has deserted, into the crowd of Regent st., & home to my quiet little room at Bithney's.

FRIDAY. SEP. 14. H. T. P. called, & we went out for a short walk. He took me to two objects of interest I had never seen before, tho' near, — the house of Sir Isaac Newton, in St. Martin's st., & that of Sir Joshua Reynolds, 47 Leicester Sq. Newton's house has still the observatory on its roof, wh. he put there & used. Then we walked down Parliament st., through Whitehall Gardens, past the house of Peel, into St. James' Park, & took our seats in the mall, with a view of the towers of the Abbey just over the trees, — as rural a view as you would get in the Midland Counties.

Rest of the noon in packing, or superintending Bithney in so doing, (except a call on Hon. A[rthur] Kinnaird, who came to town this morning, who, by the way, is now heir presumptive to the title & estates, — his brother's only son, the "Master of Kinnaird", being dead) — & took train for Liverpool at 5 P.M. Short stops at Rugby, Stafford & Warrington, — mostly after dark, & reached Adelphi Hotel, Liverpool at 9.45 P. M.

SATURDAY. SEP. 15. Took steamer Persia, for N. York, wh. got under way at 9 o'ck. The old views of the fortress-like docks, the low shores of Lancashire, & the high coast of Cheshire & Wales, — the light at Holyhead, & then the open sea. Some 180 passengers. Know no one on board.

SUNDAY. SEP. 16. Service, well attended, & singing. [Capt.] Judkins is famed for his good reading. Reads better than almost any Engl. clergy-man I have heard. At about noon, make the harbor of Queenstown, (Cove of Cork) & come to anchor in the Cove. This is an admirable harbor, — perhaps the best I ever saw. Easy of access, landlocked, & large eno' for the ships of the world — one would say. Went ashore, in order to say & feel that I have stood upon the shores of Ireland. Town of Queenstown is small, — all the merchants residing at Cork, 7 miles above, & the population eminently Irish, in look & manner, — the better classes pretty (women, I mean) & all healthy looking, & many barefooted, & some begging, & numerous gin shops, & a look of untidiness & unthrift everywhere. I was surprised to find that of the three churches, one is Ch. of England & large, & another Scotch Presb. (tho' small) & only one — tho' the largest, R. Catholic. Still, nearly all the pop. must be R. Cath.

Harbor is well fortified, & the country about richly green, with plenty of hedges & shrubbery, & few trees. Sailed, again, with mails, at about 5 P.M.

Passage across, is about as usual. 180 passengers, chiefly very commonplace persons. Large proportion of Germans trading in U. S., & cotton dealers fr. the Southern states. About half way across, find out a young Parkman, from Savannah, who was at Cambridge 3 or 4 years ago. The last day but two, Eustis, late M. C. from New Orleans, introduces himself, & I make acquaintance of his wife, d. of Corcoran of Washington, the banker. Eustis is son of late Ch. J. of Louisiana. And the last day, make acq. of Bancroft Davis (formerly I knew him at Cambr.) son of "Honest John", late Sec. of Legation at London, now lawyer in N. York, & his wife, a d. of James Gore King, & a cousin, a d. of John A. King.[56] These were pleasant people. But, as no list of passengers published, & many were sea-sick the first half of the passage, strangers who ought to know one another, do not find one another out.

No incidents. Weather pretty good. But the Atlantic is heavy & dull after the Pacific & the Oriental seas.

Reached Fire Island & Neversink after 10 P.M. & went up N. Y. harbor by moonlight, & anchored at 1 A.M.

THURSDAY. SEP. 27. This day opens in America — home. Been absent 433 days, of wh. spent about 233 on the water & 200 on land. New York completes the circumnavigation of the globe!

[56]George R. Eustis, Jr. (1828–1872) was U. S. congressman from Louisiana, 1855–1859, and was secretary of the Confederate Mission at Paris. His father was George Eustis (1796–1858), chief justice of the Louisiana Supreme Court, 1846–1852. Mrs. Eustis was the daughter of William Wilson Corcoran (1798–1888), banker and philanthropist, who began construction of the Corcoran Gallery of Art in 1859 in Washington, D. C. John Chandler Bancroft Davis (1822–1907), a nephew of George Bancroft, was assistant secretary of state, 1871–1872. His father was John Davis, noted earlier, twice governor of Massachusetts. Mrs. Davis was a daughter of James Gore King (1791–1853), New York banker and railroad president. John Alsop King (1788–1867), brother of James Gore King, was Republican governor of New York, 1857–1859.

GENEALOGIES • INDEX

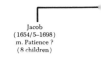

Jacob
(1654/5–1698)
m. Patience ?
(8 children)

Th…
(1693/
m. Mar…

Thomas   Daniel   Ri…

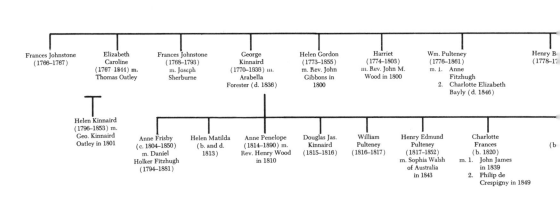

Frances Johnstone
(1766–1767)

Elizabeth
Caroline
(1767–1844) m.
Thomas Oatley

Frances Johnstone
(1768–1793)
m. Joseph
Sherburne

George
Kinnaird
(1770–1838) m.
Arabella
Forester (d. 1836)

Helen Gordon
(1773–1855)
m. Rev. John
Gibbons in
1800

Harriet
(1774–1803)
m. Rev. John M.
Wood in 1800

Wm. Pulteney
(1776–1861)
m. 1.   Anne
        Fitzhugh
     2.   Charlotte Elizabeth
        Bayly (d. 1846)

Henry B.
(1778–1…

Helen Kinnaird
(1796–1853) m.
Geo. Kinnaird
Oatley in 1801

Anne Frisby
(c. 1804–1850)
m. Daniel
Holker Fitzhugh
(1794–1881)

Helen Matilda
(b. and d.
1813)

Anne Penelope
(1814–1890) m.
Rev. Henry Wood
in 1810

Douglas Jas.
Kinnaird
(1815–1816)

William
Pulteney
(1816–1817)

Henry Edmund
Pulteney
(1817–1852)
m. Sophia Walsh
of Australia
in 1843

Charlotte
Frances
(b. 1820)
m. 1.   John James
        in 1839
     2.   Philip de
        Crespigny in 1849

(b

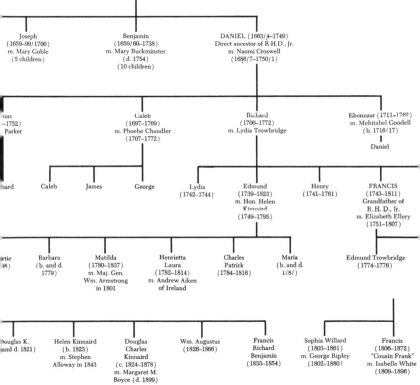

Dana Family

RICHARD DANA m. ANNE BULLARD
(c. 1617–1690)

Joseph
(1659–99/1700)
m. Mary Goble
(5 children)

Benjamin
(1659/60–1738)
m. Mary Buckminster
(d. 1754)
(10 children)

DANIEL (1663/4–1749)
Direct ancestor of R.H.D., Jr.
m. Naomi Croswell
(1686/7–1750/1)

...mas
...1752)
...Parker

Caleb
(1697–1769)
m. Phoebe Chandler
(1707–1772)

Richard
(1700–1772)
m. Lydia Trowbridge

Ebenezer (1711–176?)
m. Mehitabel Goodell
(b. 1716/17)

Daniel

...hard

Caleb

James

George

Lydia
(1742–1744)

Edmund
(1739–1823)
m. Hon. Helen
Kinnaird
(1749–1795)

Henry
(1741–1761)

FRANCIS
(1743–1811)
Grandfather of
R. H. D., Jr.
m. Elizabeth Ellery
(1751–1807)

...rtie
...98)

Barbara
(b. and d.
1779)

Matilda
(1780–1837)
m. Maj. Gen.
Wm. Armstrong
in 1801

Henrietta
Laura
(1782–1814)
m. Andrew Aiken
of Ireland

Charles
Patrick
(1784–1816)

Maria
(b. and d.
1787)

Edmund Trowbridge
(1774–1776)

...Douglas K.
...and d. 1821)

Helen Kinnaird
(b. 1823)
m. Stephen
Alloway in 1843

Douglas
Charles
Kinnaird
(c. 1824–1878)
m. Margaret M.
Boyce (d. 1899)

Wm. Augustus
(1826–1866)

Francis
Richard
Benjamin
(1833–1854)

Sophia Willard
(1803–1861)
m. George Ripley
(1802–1880)

Francis
(1806–1872)
"Cousin Frank"
m. Isabelle White
(1809–1896)

Sarah Watso...
(1842–1902...
m. Walter Sc...
Swayne (d. 19...

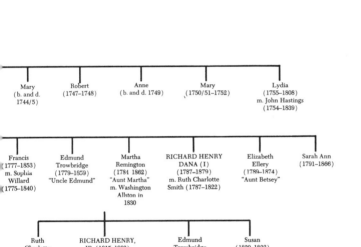

| Mary (b. and d. 1744/5) | Robert (1747–1748) | Anne (b. and d. 1749) | Mary (1750/51–1752) | Lydia (1755–1808) m. John Hastings (1754–1839) |

| Francis (1777–1853) m. Sophia Willard (1775–1840) | Edmund Trowbridge (1779–1859) "Uncle Edmund" | Martha Remington (1781–1862) "Aunt Martha" m. Washington Allston in 1830 | RICHARD HENRY DANA (I) (1787–1879) m. Ruth Charlotte Smith (1787–1822) | Elizabeth Ellery (1789–1874) "Aunt Betsey" | Sarah Ann (1791–1866) |

| Ruth Charlotte (1814–1901) | RICHARD HENRY, JR. (1815–1882) Author of the *Journal* m. Sarah Watson (1814–1907) | Edmund Trowbridge (1818–1869) "Ned" of the *Journal* | Susan (1820–1822) |

| | Ruth Charlotte (1844–1903) m. Francis Ogden Lyman (1846–1915) | Elizabeth Ellery (1846–1939) | Mary Rosamund (1848–1937) m. Henry F. Weld (d. 1909) | Richard Henry (1851–1931) m. 1. Edith Long-fellow (1853–1915) 2. Helen Sherwood (Ford) Mumford (1865–1934) | Angela Henrietta Channing (1857–1928) m. Henry W. Skinner (1852–1916) |

Marsh-Watson Family

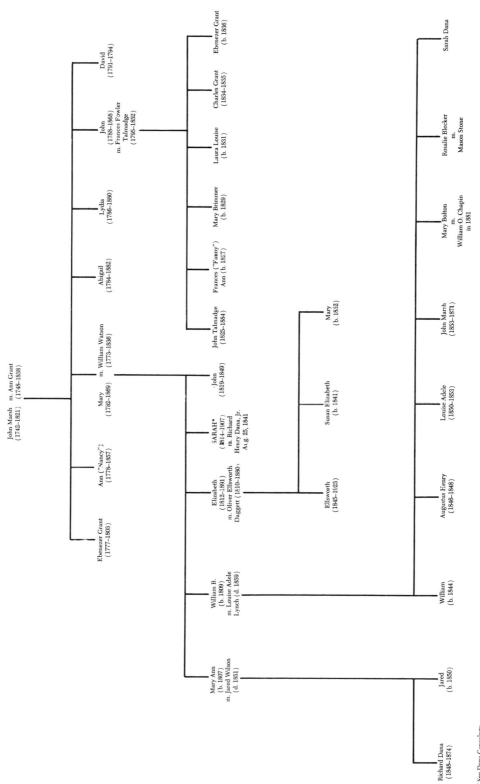

* See Dana Genealogy.

Channing Family

John Channing   m.   Mary Antram
(1683–1731)   (c. 1681–1741)

James (b. 1713)
d. in infancy

John (1714–1771)
m. Mrs. Mary (Chaloner)
Robinson (c. 1721–1790)

Mary (1717–1762)
m. Eleazer Trevett
in 1752

Ann (1719–1801)

Antram (b. and d. 1722)

Antram (b. and d. 1723)

Elizabeth (b. and d. 1724)

Mary (1747–1824)
m. George Gibbs
in 1768

John (b. 1749)
m. Abigail Hazard

William (1751–1793)
m. Lucy Ellery
(1752–1834)

Ann (1753–1809)
m. William Wood-
bridge

Elizabeth
(1755–1820)

Walter (1757–1827)
m. Hannah Smith in
1798

Henry (1760–1840)
m. Sarah McCurdy
in 1787

James Robinson
(1761–1763)

Ruth (1778–1870)
m. William Ellery
Channing

John
(d. young)

Francis Dana
(1775–1810)
m. Susan Cleveland
Higginson (1788–
1865)

William Ellery
(1780–1842)
m. Ruth Gibbs

Ann (1778–1815)
1st wife of
Washington Allston

Mary (1782–
1843) m.
Robert Rogers
in 1821

Henry
(1784–1843)

Walter (1786–1876)
m. 1   Barbara Higgin-
son Perkins
(1795–1822)
2.   Eliza (beth)
Wainwright
(c. 1795–1834)

Lucy (1787–1847)
m. Wm. Washington
Russell of N. Y.
in 1813

George Gibbs
(1789–1881)
m. Elizabeth Parsons
Sigourney (1794–
1870)

Edward Tyrell
(1790–1856)
"Dr. Channing" of the
Journal
m. Henrietta A. S. Ellery
(c. 1802–1888)

A daughter who
died young

Mary Ruth
(1818–1891)
m. Frederic
Augustus Eustis
(1816–1871)

William Francis
(1820–1901) m.
1.   Susan E. Burdick
(1823–1894)
2.   Mary Jane Tarr
c. 1857

William Henry
(1810–1884)
m. Julia Allen
(d. 1889)

Lucy Ellery
(1809–1877)

Susan Cleveland
(left no record)

George Gibbs
(d. young)

Barbara Higginson
(1816–1880)

William Ellery
(1818–1901) n.
Ellen Kilshaw Fuller
(1820–1856)

Mary Elizabeth
m. Thomas Wentworth
Higginson (1823–1911)

Lucy Bradstreet
(d. young)

Wm. Channing Russell

Anna Allston
Russell

Francis Channing
Russell

Elizabeth
B. Russell
(d. young)

George Edward
(1815–1837)
d. in Sumatra

Charles Sigourney
(d. young)

Eliz. Parsons
(1818–1906)

Mary Sigourney
(1819–1842)

Chas. Sigourney
(1821–1892)

Anna Rollins
(c. 1824–1900)

Ellen
(1825–1915)

Susan Frances
"Fanny"
(c. 1830–1916)

Fitzhugh Family

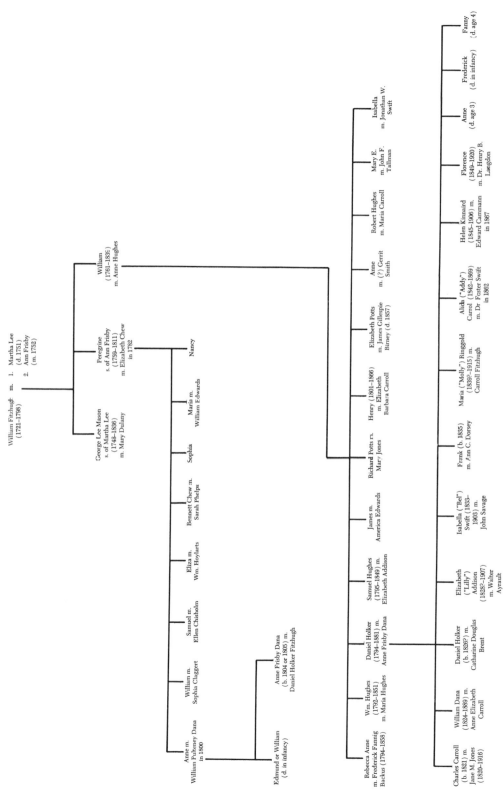

Minot Family

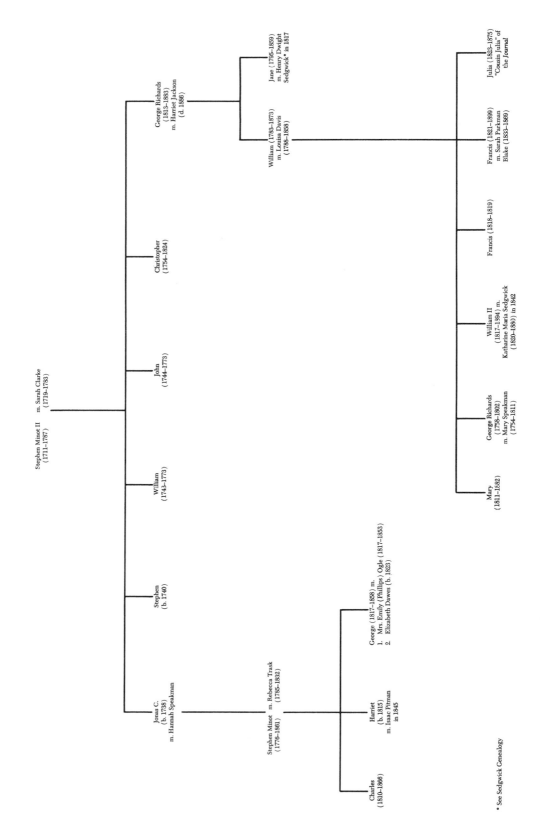

Stephen Minot II   m. Sarah Clarke
(1711–1787)   (1719–1783)

William   Stephen   John   Christopher   George Richards
(1743–1773)   (b. 1740)   (1744–1773) (1754–1824)   (1813–1883)
                                                              m. Harriet Jackson
                                                              (d. 1886)

Jonas C.   Jane (1795–1859)
(b. 1738)   m. Henry Dwight
m. Hannah Speakman   Sedgwick* in 1817

                                     William (1783–1873)
                                     m. Louisa Davis
                                     (1788–1858)

Stephen Minot   m. Rebecca Trask
(1776–1861)   (1785–1852)

George (1817–1858) m.
1. Mrs. Emily (Phillips) Ogle (1817–1853)
2. Elizabeth Dawes (b. 1823)

Harriet
(b. 1815)
m. Isaac Pitman
in 1845

Charles
(1810–1866)

Mary   George Richards   William II   Francis   Francis (1821–1899)   Julia (1823–1875)
(1811–1882) (1756–1802)   (1817–1894) m.   (1818–1819)   m. Sarah Parkman   "Cousin Julia" of
            m. Mary Speakman   Katharine Maria   Blake (1833–1869)   the *Journal*
            (1754–1811)   Sedgwick
                               (1820–1880) in 1842

* See Sedgwick Genealogy

Russell Family

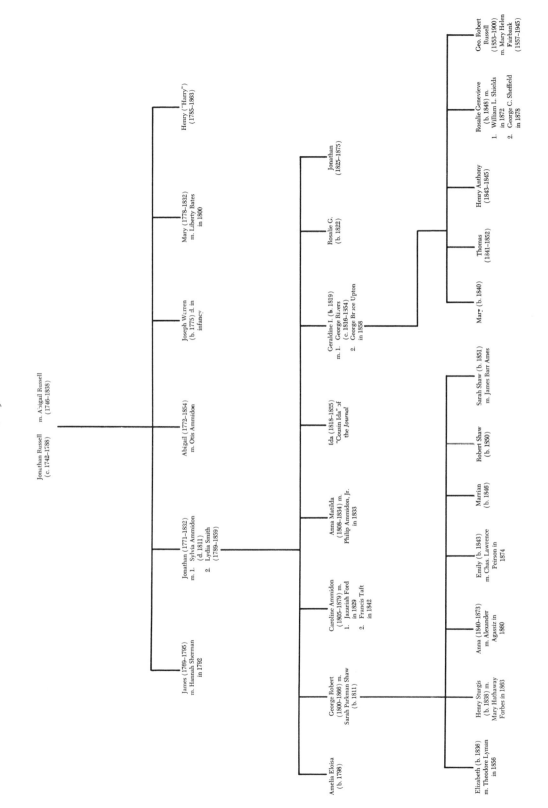

Sedgwick Family

Benjamin Sedgwick   m. Ann Thompson before 1742

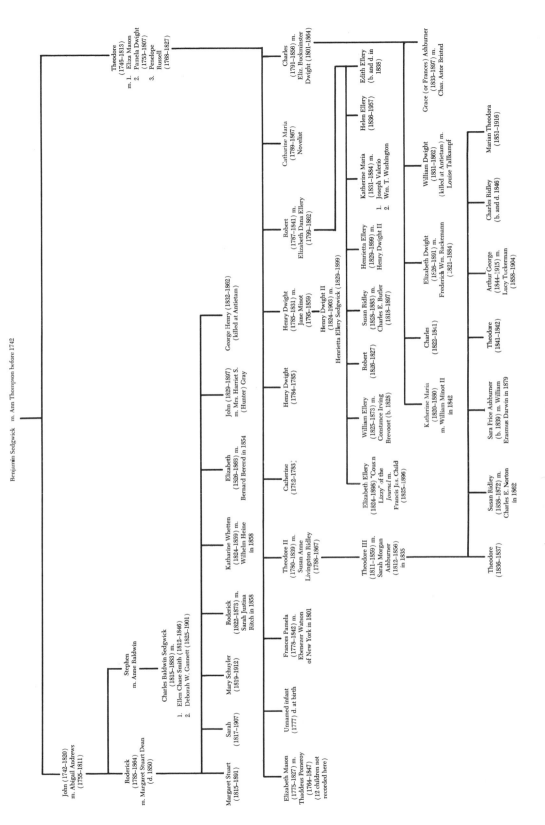

Index

Abbotsford: Sir Walter Scott's home, 57
Abbott, Charles, 1st Baron of Tentereden, 473
Abbott, George J., 90
Abbott, John, 653
Abbott, Josiah Gardner: Free Soil politics, 355; in Constitutional Convention, 558, 560-562, 568-569
Aberdeen Correspondence, 149
Aberdeen, 4th Earl of, 726
Abingdon, Lord, 779
Abingdon, Reverend, 779
Achmet, Pacha, 1103
Acton, Lord John, 553
Actress of Padua, The, 480
Adams, Lieutenant, 706, 708
Adams, Miss, 337
Adams, Mr., 73-74
Adams, Charles Francis, Sr. (1807–1886), xxiii-xxiv, xxix-xxx, xl, 63, 167, 516, 1062; at Buffalo Convention, 349, 351-354; at Quincy, 389, 525, 599; at Free Soil Convention of 1850, 395, 406; at Free Soil Convention of 1845, 396-397; Sims Case, 424; Sumner election, 426; at Homer dinner, 471; Ratification invitation, 502; on Palfrey candidacy, 506; education of, 526; Minister to England, 533; at Hale dinner, 545; opposes Constitution, 602; disagreement with Sumner, 603; and Free Soil meeting, 618; Loring removal, 672; Fusion meeting, 677; Dana's guest, 829; U. S. House, 832
Adams, Charles Francis, Jr. (1835–1915), xxx, 36, 525, 820, 830-831
Adams, Henry, xxx-xxxi
Adams, John, 131, 135-136, 164, 389
Adams, Mrs. John, 786
Adams, John Clark, 429, 619
Adams, John Couch, 739
Adams, John Quincy, 108; at Massachusetts Historical Society, 160; on Francis Dana, 196; in Congress, 241, 243, 245; Dana meets, 254-255; at Phi Beta Kappa dinner, 320; mourned, 352-353; death of, 485; quarrel with Jonathan Russell, 601; oration by, 606
Adams, Mrs. John Quincy, 485-486
Adams, Louisa, 525

Adams, Nehemiah, 31, 844
Adams, Samuel, 844
Adams, Samuel P., 457
Adams, Shubael Pratt, 560
Adams, William, 433
Addington, Henry, 1st Viscount Sidmouth, 472
Aden, 1096-1099
Adirondack Mountains, 360-375
Adirondack; or Life in the Woods, The (J. T. Headley), 371
Adolphus, John Leycester, 749, 771-772
Adrienne Lecouvreur: Rachel's performance in, 681
Advent, Church of the, xxxi, 285, 298, 304, 538
Afghanistan, 109
Agassiz, Jean Louis Rodolphe, 464, 481, 686, 689, 830, 834
Aids to Reflection (Coleridge), 30
Aiken, Charles Patrick, 419
Aiken, Mrs. Charles Patrick, 419
Aiken, Henrietta, 419
Aikens, Asa, 363
Aikens, Villeroy S., 363-364, 368-374
Akers, Benjamin P., 432
Albert, Prince, 762-763, 800
Albro, John A., 173, 175, 181-182, 522-523
Alcock, Sir Rutherford, 1023
Alcott, Bronson, xvii, 666-667
Alderson, Sir Edward Hall, 733
Aldis, Asa O., 101, 225
Aldrich, Peleg Emory, 677-679
Alemany, Archbishop Josè Sadoc, 845
Alert (ship), 68, 111, 153-155, 159, 264, 525
Alexander II of Russia, 700
Alexander, Francis, 55, 57, 59
Alexander, Sir James, 578-580
Alexander, John, 264-265
Alexander, Professor, 890
Alexander's Feast (Dryden), 265
Ali, Hyder, 1088
Ali, Mohammed, 1103, 1106-1108
Allen, Mr. (of Siam), 1070
Allen, Judge Charles: Texas free soil meeting, 395-396; attacks Webster, 419; election of, 419-420, 424; at Constitutional Convention, 550, 561-562,

566; at Worcester, 614-615; on Webster, 676; Fusion meeting, 677-679
Allen, Judge E. H. (Hawaii), 861, 863, 867, 885, 928
Allen, Mrs. E. H. (Hawaii), 863, 865, 885, 889
Allen, Joseph H., 606
Alley, John Bassett, 355, 406, 534, 556, 613
Alloway, Stephen, 418
Alloway, Mrs. Stephen, 418
Allston (Sweetser), 187
Allston, John E., 8
Allston, Joseph, 399
Allston, Mrs. Joseph, 399-400
Allston, Robert F. W., 219, 340
Allston, Washington, xvii, 8, 9, 29, 44, 88, 107, 112, 145, 165, 1131; at Dickens dinner, 59; Harvard oration, 90; appearance and opinions of, 149; on Longfellow's marriage, 159; death of, 170-176; newspaper controversy over, 186-188; paintings by, 213, 214, 226, 230, 265, 265-266, 268, 326, 328, 511, 721, 744; his coffin, 215; Weir on, 219; Jarvis on, 224-225; genius described, 272; talent praised, 340; house burns, 500-501; recalled by Dana, 501; and Horatio Greenough, 523-524; and E. T. Dana, 835-836. *See also* "Belshazzar's Feast"
Allston, Mrs. Washington (Martha Remington Dana), 29, 88, 112, 145, 149, 165, 168, 170, 173-177, 189, 195, 196, 212-213, 218, 223-224, 230, 265, 286, 319, 346, 387, 391-392, 407, 427, 471, 478, 483, 500, 503, 511, 526, 544, 599, 608-609, 658, 685
Allston, William A., 182
Allston, William Moore, 8
Almon, Mr., 479, 489, 619, 635
Almon, Mrs., 619
Althorp, Lord (John P. Spencer), 829-830
Altwood, Mr., 829
Alvord, Daniel Wells, 348, 562, 568
Ambrosi, Father, 1062-1063
America, (ship), 696
American First Class Book, The, 11
American Notes (Dickens), 101-103, 149
American Seaman's Friend Society, 47
American Whig, The, 123
Ames, Mr., 428
Ames, Fisher, 25, 164
Ames, Joseph Alexander, 431, 432
Ames, Mrs. Joseph Alexander, 432, 437, 463

Ames, Samuel, 109
Amistad Negroes, case of, 63-64
Amory, Mr., 292-293
Amy Warwick, case of, xxxix
Andersen, Hans Christian, 693
Anderson, Lieutenant, 311
Anderson, Mr. (Singapore), 1069-1070
Anderson, John Henry, 888
Anderson, Rufus, 163, 221
Andrew, John A., 426
Andrews, Mr., 630
Andrews, Lorrin, 871
Angel in the House (Patmore), 1136
Angus, Mr., 443
Animal caravan, 169
Anstiss, Joe, 449
Anthony, Henry Bowen, 464
Anti-Slavery Convention, (1843),161-162
"Apostate, The" (W. W. Story), 512
Appleton, Miss, 277
Appleton, Benjamin Barnard, 319
Appleton, Edward, 90, 319
Appleton, Frances Elizabeth ("Fanny"), 49, 59, 128-129, 131, 159, 169. *See also* Longfellow, Mrs. Henry Wadsworth
Appleton, John, 606, 649-650
Appleton, Nathan, 131, 229, 291, 396
Appleton, Robert, 222, 292, 296-297
Appleton, Thomas Gold, 49, 55; on Dickens, 57; on Allston, 266; at Longfellow's, 432; in Boston, 463, 478; at children's party, 493; on Alexander Bliss, 577; as conversationalist, 615; on Atlantic crossing (1856), 693-695, 697-698, 700, 703, 704-705, 707-709; in England (1856), 711, 805
Appleton, W. C., 400
Appleton, William, 222, 294, 296, 997
Applewhite, Mr., 892
Ap-pong, 986
Apthorp, Robert E., 526
Archbishop of Quebec. *See* Turgeon, Pierre Flavian
Architect (ship), 891-895
Arctic Explorations (Kane), 893
Argonti, Felix, 74
Argüello, Don Santiago, 848
Argyll, Duke of (George Douglas Campbell), 727, 731-733, 742-745, 749-751, 815, 831, 1129
Argyll, Duchess of, 731-733, 744, 749
Arkenburgh, Mr., 433, 476
Armfield, Mr., 252
Armistead, Lewis A., 849
Armstrong, Mrs., 418
Armstrong, George Whipple, 319

Armstrong, Dr. Richard (Hawaii), 862, 864-867, 918
Armstrong, Samuel T., 88, 106
Arnold, Benedict, 261
Arnold, James, 158, 305, 397, 437
Arnold, Mrs. James, 70-71, 159, 397, 603
Arnold, Matthew, 713, 777
Arts, Mr., 94
As You Like It, 126
Ashburton, Lord, 91-92, 736
Ashley, Mr., 746
Ashley, Mrs., 748
Ashman, George A., 379
Ashmun, George, 462
Ashton, Mr., 1001, 1033
Aspinwall, William, 135, 439, 561
Aspinwall, William H., 841
Astley's (London), 140
Aston, Helen, 418-419. *See also* Mrs John Oatley
Astor, John J., 241, 841
Atkins, Mrs. (Dana landlady, Roxbury), 64, 88, 96, 101, 163-164, 220, 266
Atlantic Monthly, The, 432, 507
Atlas, Boston, 90
Attorney General v. the Proprietors of the Meeting House in Federal Street, 665-666. *See also* Federal Street Church, case of
Atwell, Samuel Y., 109
Audubon, John James, 382, 1030
Augira, Mrs., 336
Austen, Jane, 936
Austey, Chisholm, 999
Austin, Arthur W., 238
Austin, Samuel, Jr., 229
Austin, Stafford L. (Hawaii), 880-882, 1027
Austin, Mrs. Stafford L. (Hawaii), 880-882, 885
Autocrat of the Breakfast Table (Holmes), 830
Avonmore, Lord (Barry John Yelverton), 769

Bache, Alexander Dallas, 338, 658
Bache, Mrs. Alexander Dallas, 658
Bachman, John, 382
Bachman, Wilson, 382
Backus, E. Frederick, 260-261
Backus, Mrs. E. Frederick, 261
Backus, Dr., 311
Backus, Mrs. (Dr.), 264, 311, 325
Bacon, Leonard P., 95, 683
Bacon, Mrs. Leonard P., 683

Badger, George E., 540
Bagley, Lucy, 167, 191, 528, 603, 609
Bailey, Chief Mate, 857-859
Bailey, Mr. (of Philadelphia), 270
Bailey v. Damon, 616
Baker, Charles T., 402-404
Baker, D. D., 209-210
Baker, Edward D., 922
Baker, George William, 259
Baldwin, Henry, 241
Baldwin, James F., 492
Baldwin, Joseph, 106
Baldwin, Mrs. Joseph, 106, 193
Baldwin, Judge Joseph Glover, 855, 907, 915
Baldwin, Loammi, 492, 682, 836
Baldwin, Roger Sherman, 487, 538
Baldwin, Sidney, 524
Balfour, Captain, 141
Ballou, Mr., 162
Baltimore, Baron, 258
Baltimore, trip to, 236-238
Bancroft, Miss, 573
Bancroft, George, 59, 67, 90, 124, 391, 577, 822, 1138
Bancroft, Mrs. George, 107, 334, 577
Bancroft, George, Jr., 577
Bancroft, John Chandler, 577
Bandini, Don Juan, 154, 848
Bandini, Donña Refugio, 848
Bangs, Benjamin, 332
Bangs, Edward, 464
Banks, Nathaniel P., Jr., 511, 563-564, 672, 685
Banning, Phineas T., 847-849
Bannister family, 191
Banyer, Mrs., 119
Barber, Dr., 573
Barber, the Misses, 573
Barber, Mrs., 573
Barca, Calderon de la, 102, 139
Barclay, Dr., 571
Barclay, Miss, 337
Barclay, Mr., 598
Barclay, Anthony, 337
Bareuil, Count, 75-76
Baring, House of, 717-718
Baring, Thomas, 1129
Bark Missouri, case of, 666
Barnaby Rudge (Dickens), 58
Barnard, Captain, 1060-1061
Barnard, Mrs., 948
Barnet, Edward A., 1060
Barnett, Mr., 468

Barnett, Rev. William, 1102, 1104, 1106-1109

Barrett, George H., 480

Barrett, Mrs. George H., 480

Barrett, Samuel, 7

Barrow, Mr., 457

Barrows, Mr., 449

Barry, Mr., 693

Barstow, Simon F., 101

Bartlett, John Russell, 609

Bartlett, Robert, 146

Bartlett, Shubael, 1019

Bartlett, Sidney, xxvii; Wyman trial, 202; death of Webster, 513; Dartmouth College case, 518; at Dedham, 537; Constitutional Convention, 538, 569; Greenleaf memorial, 600; Federal St. Church case, 619, 665-666; *Younger v. Gloucester*, 668

Barton, William P. C., 323

Bascombe, Mr., 746

Batchelder, Mr., 628

Bates, Dr. (Japan), 1013, 1016

Bates, Ashur D. (Hawaii), 861, 864, 867, 884-885, 889-891

Bates, Mrs. Ashur D., 885, 891

Bates, Dudley, 885

Bates, Joshua, 718

Bates, Lucilla, 885

Bates, Mary, 859

Bates, Moses, 557, 570

Bathurst, Miss, 114

Bathurst, Matthew, 114

"Battle Hymn of the Republic" (Julia Ward Howe), 118

Battle of Lake Erie, The (Cooper), 163

Baxter family, 818

Bayard, James, 260-262, 325

Bayard, Mrs. James, 260-261, 264

Bayley, Mrs., 443-444

Bayly, Thomas Henry, 505

Beach, Erasmus D., 570

Beadle, Mr., 646

Beadle, Mrs., 646

Beal, Joseph Sampson, 531, 1013

Beal, Thomas Prince, 1013

Beals, Miss, 891

Beauchampe (Simms), 213

Beauplaud, M., 571

Beck, Dr. Charles, 286-287, 474, 477

Beck, Mrs. Charles, 286, 477

Beckwith, Mr., 941-942, 1062, 1065

Beckwith, Mrs., 941, 1063

Beckwith, Reverend, (Hawaii), 918

Beckwith, Mrs. (Hawaii), 918

Beckwith, Morris, 866

Bedini, Cajetan, (Papal Nuncio), 584, 600

Beecher, Catherine E., 518-519, 539-540

Beecher, Charles, 519

Beecher, Edward, 519, 539

Beecher, Harriet, 518-519. *See also* Harriet Beecher Stowe

Beecher, Henry Ward, 519, 886

Beecher, Lyman, 163, 433, 518-519

Beecher, Thomas Kinnicut, 519

Behurd, Mrs., 818

Belcher, John, 213

Belden, Miss, 95

Belden, Mrs. (of Hartford), 95

Belden, Mrs. (at Niagara Falls), 312-313

Bell, Mr., 446

Bell, Alexander Graham, 479

Bell, Charles, 225

Bell, John, 504, 1074

Bell, Mrs. John, 504-505

Bellecour, M. de David Every, 1020, 1023

Bellows, Henry Whitney, 409

"Belshazzar's Feast" (Allston), 176-184, 213, 219, 226, 265, 328-329

Bemis, Charles V., 90, 319, 337, 379, 383, 607

Bemis, George, 39, 90, 319, 337

Beni, Duchess de, 1116

Benjamin v. Hastings, 147-148

Benjamin, Asher, 164

Bennett, Mr., 754

Benson, Stephen Allen (Liberia), 1095

Bentley, Mr., 818

Benton, Thomas Hart, 243, 667, 851

Bethell, Richard, 725

Bethune, George A., 92, 228, 262, 325

Betts, Samuel Rossiter, 475

Bevan, Mr., 765

Bickford, Lieutenant, 441

Biddle, Nicholas, 169

Biddles, Miss (Atlantic crossing, 1856), 693-694, 699, 700, 703-704, 707-709, 795

Bigelow v. Wood, 536-537

Bigelow, Colonel, 165

Bigelow, Judge George Tyler, 619, 689, 1069

Bigelow, Horatio, 758

Bigelow, John, 390, 392, 409

Bigelow Papers, 432

Billings, Frederick, 439, 899, 919

Billy Budd (Melville), 112

Bingham, Mr., 155

Bingham, Hiram, 123, 883

Binney, Miss, 320

Binney, Bishop Hibbert, 442

Binney, Horace, 320

Binney, William, 325

Binton, Dr., 318
Biographical Notices of Distinguished Men in New England (Bradford), 146
Bird, Francis W., 563, 617
Birdsall, Lewis A., 918
Bishop, Mr. (Hawaiian missionary), 889
Bishop, Mrs. (Hawaiian missionary), 889
Bishop, Charles Reed, 862-863, 865, 889
Bishop, Mrs. Charles Reed (Pauahi), 862, 865, 885, 889
Bishop, Judge Henry W., 557, 569, 631
Bissell, Simon B., 903
Bithney, Mr., 787-788, 815, 1128, 1137
Bithney, Mrs., 787-788, 1128, 1129
Black, Henry, 574-578, 581, 592
Black, John (Ceylon), 1074-1077
Black, Mrs. John (Ceylon), 1074-1076
Black, Elizabeth (Ceylon), 1075-1076
Blackmer, Captain, 892-894
Blaikie, William Garden, 1107
Blaine, Abbé, 901
Blair, Mr., 864
Blair, Francis Preston, 864
Blair, James, 864
Blake, Edward, 332
Blake, Harrison Gray Otis, 319, 337, 471
Blake, Maurice C., 898-899
Blandford, Marquis of, 726, 745
Blanding, Mrs., 914
Blanding, Lewis, 845, 901-902
Blanding, William, 845, 901-902
Blantyre, Lady, 749
Bleeker, Harmanus, 223
Bleeker, Mrs. Harmanus, 223
Bliss, Alexander, 577
Bliss, Mrs. Elizabeth D., 107
Bliss, William Wallace Smith, 342-344, 656-657
Blood v. Soule, 99
Blood, Dr. D., 58
Blunt, Mr., 281
Boggs, Biddle, 851-852
Bolingbroke, Henry, 244
Bolles, John Augustus, 99-100, 511
Bolton, William Compton, 390
Bolton, Mrs. William Compton, 390
Bonaparte. *See* Napoleon
Bonaparte, Jerome N., 337
Bonaparte, Pauline, 757
Bond, Miss, 385
Bond, Charles R., 230, 846, 899
Bond, George Philips, 739
Bond, William C., 494, 739, 829
Bonney, Rev. Charles F., 948, 952-962, 972-975
Bonney, Mrs. Charles F., 948, 961, 979-980, 1059

Boone, Bishop William Jones, 992-997, 999-1000, 1028, 1033, 1050, 1061
Boone, Mrs. William Jones, 993, 1050
Boot, Mrs., 362
Booth, Junius Brutus, 340
Borden, James Wallace, 862-863, 865, 890
Borlase, John, 1045-1046
Bornier, Bishop de (Shanghai), 994
Bossuet, Jacques Bènigne, 883
Boston, floods in, 426
Boston Harbor, 230
Boston Post Society, 62
Boswell's Life of Johnson, 718
Boswell, James, xv, 53, 392
Bourbulon, M. de, 991, 998, 1058, 1032-1033
Bourbulon, Mme. de, 991, 998, 1002, 1032. *See also* McLeod, Kate
Boutwell, George S.: Dana interviews, 479, 486-487; at Constitutional Convention, 551, 553, 557, 559, 562-563, 565, 567; Dana's guest, 617, 620-621
Bouverie, Philip, 765-766
Bowditch, Henry Ingersoll, 27, 358
Bowditch, Henry Pickering, 27
Bowditch, Jonathan Ingersoll, 27
Bowditch, Nathaniel, 27, 929, 931
Bowdoin, Mr., 138, 312, 313
Bowen, Mr., 584
Bowen, Charles J., 584
Bowen, Rev. George, 1083, 1087
"Bowery Boys", 823
Bowles, Samuel, 677-679
Bowring, Sir John, 943, 1067
Boyd, James McHenry, 259
Boyd, Joseph Franks, 635
Boylston, Ward Nicholas, 90, 319
Brackett, Edward A., 173-174, 176
Brackett, Walter M., 594
Bradbury, James W., 504, 604
Brandenbaugh, Charles, 214, 236
Bradford, Mr., 156
Bradford, Alden, 146
Bradford, John, 122
Bradlee, Mr., 109
Bradley, Charles William, 1048-1054, 1056
Bradley, William Czar, 598
Bradshaw, (play), 480
Brady, Mr., 906-907
Bragg, Braxton, 342, 657
Braham, John, 54
Brainard, Mr., 269
Brainard, Mrs., 269-270
Bramin's, 196, 386
Bramwell, Baron, 733

Brandon v. Brandon, 770-771
Brattle House, 427
Breckinridge, John C., 821, 1074, 1098
Breed, Hiram N., 560
Bremer, Fredrika, 164-165, 390
Brent, Mr., 631, 633
Brewer, Captain, 146-147
Brewer, Charles, 865
Brewer, Mrs. Charles, 865, 880
Brewer, Gardner, 471
Brewer, Thomas Mayo, 90, 187-188, 319
Brewster, Mr., 373-374
Bridger, James, 908
Bridget, 305, 356
Bridgham family, 399
Bridgman, Elijah Coleman, 99⁰-1000
Bridgman, Laura, 489
Briggs, Dr., 93-94
Briggs, Mrs. (Lucia Russell), 428, 530
Briggs, Reverend, 385
Briggs, George N., 229, 556, 563-564, 568-569, 690
Briggs, John P., 93-94, 99, 103-104
Brigham, E. P., 675
Brimmer, Miss, 146
Brimmer, Martin, 110, 128, 146, 160, 166, 223
Brinkerhoff, Mr., 306, 317
Bristol, Marquis of, 830
British Critic, The, 146, 159
British Museum, 752
Broad Stone of Honour, The (K. H. Digby), 315
Brock, Sir Isaac, 314
Broderick, David C., 915-916
Bronks and Tuthill Hubbard, case of, 517
Brontë, Charlotte, 936-937
Brontë, Emily, 936-937
Brook Farm, 9
Brooke, Lieutenant, 985
Brooke, Rajah, Sir James, 442
Brooks, Captain, 990
Brooks, Charles T., 320
Brooks, Edward, 351
Brooks, John, 577
Brooks, Peter B., 337
Brooks, Peter C., 351
Brooks, Preston S., 773
Brooks, Sidney, 525
Brooks, Mrs. Sidney, 409, 525
Brougham, Lord, 50, 735, 746, 831
Brower, Mr., 1016
Brown et al., case of, 338-339
Brown v. Gordon, 489
Brown, Captain (Hawaii), 879, 883; and wife of, 883

Brown, Captain (of ship *Madras*), 1096, 1100
Brown, Colonel (of Royal Artillery), 1096, 1100
Brown, Mr. (Boston), 619; and wife, 619
Brown, Mr. (Cadet), 441
Brown, Mr. ("colorman"), 268
Brown, Mr. (Singapore), 1068-1069
Brown, David Paul, 325
Brown, George M., 480-481, 483, 490
Brown, George William, 257
Brown, Mrs. George William, 257
Brown, John, 364, 366, 373-375
Brown, Mrs. John, 364
Brown, Julia, 1021
Brown, Ruth, 364, 373
Brown, Samuel G., 137
Brown, Rev. Samuel Robbins, 1016, 1019-1022
Brown, Mrs. Samuel Robbins, 1019
Brown, Walter, 606
Brown, Mrs. Walter, 606
Browne, Henry, 799
Browne, Joseph, 799
Brownell, T. C., 231
Browning, Captain, 141
Browning, Sir John, 999
Brownson, Orestes A., 822
Bruce, Sir Knight, 770
Bruce, Hon. Robert, 578-579, 736, 945, 991, 994, 1032, 1044, 1057-1058
Brudenell, James Thomas. *See* Cardigan, Lord
Bruen, Mrs., 135, 137-138
Brune family, 285
Brune, Clara, 257
Brune, Frederick, 237, 257, 259, 285, 320
Brune, John Christian, 257
Bryant, Frances, 119
Bryant, J., 106-107
Bryant, William Cullen, 213; Dana's sponsor, xvii, 44-45; described, 116-117, 119; Dana's host, 231-234; in New York, 409; W. W. Story's publisher, 512; *Poems,* 526, 607; on Hillard, 554; Choate on, 686
Bryant, Mrs. William Cullen, 119
Buccleuch, Duke of (Walter Francis Scott), 742
Buchanan, President James, 256, 503, 758, 821, 844
Buck, Daniel, 95, 354
Buck, Ephriam, 646
Buckingham, Joseph T., 220-221, 540
Buckingham, Mrs. Joseph T., 508

Buckler, Elizabeth, 114, 258
Buckler, Mary Theresa, 114, 258
Buckler, Thomas H., 114
Buckminster, Joseph Stevens, 682
Buckminster, William J., 90, 319
Buffalo Free Soil Convention, 348-354
Bull, Mr. and Mrs. (English trip),
   695-696, 698, 700, 703, 705
Bull, Ole, 266, 491
Bulloch, James Dunwody, 834, 841
Bulwer-Lytton, Edward George, xvi, 35,
   50, 682
Bunker Hill, xxi, 12-13, 166-168, 1135
Bunyan, John, 609
Burdett, Capt. Henry, 879, 881
Burdett, Mrs. Henry, 879-882
Burgess, Bishop George, 652
Burke, Edmund: "A Letter to a Noble
   Lord," 43, 376-377; describes Car-
   natic, 85; "Reflections on the Revolu-
   tion in France," 250; use of Latin,
   526; oratory, 530; Dana's opinion of,
   617; Westminster Hall, 715; London
   house of, 775-776; Dana quotes, 1109,
   1116; Dana lectures on, 522, 524,
   526, 601, 603-608, 613, 683
Burlingame, Anson, 491, 540, 545; at
   Constitutional Convention, 552, 557,
   560, 567; and Burns case, 636-638;
   election of, 821
Burnett, Joseph, 542-543
Burney, Francis (Fanny), 143
Burns, Dr., 67
Burns, Anthony: case of, xxviii-xxix, 522,
   625-627, 630-638, 643, 671; rescue
   attempt, 628-629; freed, 672-673
Burns, Robert, 446, 526, 729
Burr, Aaron, 528-529
Burritt, Elihu, 470
Burrough, Mr., 312
Bush, Mr., 292, 294
Bushnell, Horace, 909-910, 913
Bussey, Benjamin, 1121
Butler v. Hancock, 137-138
Butler, Andrew P., 505
Butler, Benjamin F. (1795-1858), 350-
   351, 475
Butler, Benjamin F. (1818-1893), 984;
   Dana's enemy, xxvii, xxxix-xl; at Con-
   stitutional Convention, 548, 550,
   554-555, 557, 559-560, 567-568
Butler, Charles E., 39
Butler, Eliza, 137-138
Butler, Pierce, 829
Butman, Mr., 421-422
Byington, Mr., 128
Byington, Horatio, 533, 535

Byrnes, Mr., 414, 634
Byron, Lord, xvi, 70, 686, 782, 896-897,
   928, 1111, 1114-1116, 1134

Cahawba (ship), 834
Calderon, Mme., 991
Caledonia (ship), 71
Calhoun, John C., 203, 660
California: Dana in (1834-1836), xv;
   recalled (1843), 153-155; Dana in
   (1859-1860), 841-856, 895-925
Calvert, Mr., 258
Calvert, Mr. (Cairo), 1102, 1107
Calvert, Charles Alexander, 704
Calvert, Frederick, 258
Cama, Pestonji Hormusji, 1092-1094
Camajee, Bomanjee Tramjee, 1090
Cambridge Chronicle, 511
Cambridge, Duke of, 762-763
Cameron, Malcolm, 818-819
Cameron, Simon, xl
Camoens, Luis de, 985
Campbell, Major, 592
Campbell, Miss, 492
Campbell, Mr., 127-128
Campbell, Mr. (American Consul, Lon-
   don), 761
Campbell, Mr. (California), 915
Campbell, Mr. (China), 1060-1061
Campbell, Mr. (England), 736
Campbell, Lord Archibald, 732
Campbell, Sir Colin, 980, 1099
Campbell, Lady Edith, 732
Campbell, George Douglas. *See* Argyll,
   Duke of
Campbell, Lord John, 694; his *Lives of
   the Chief Justices,* 472, 508; in Eng-
   land, 720, 733, 737-741, 831, 1129
Campbell, John Douglas Sutherland
   (Marquis of Lorn), 732
Campbell, Mary, 166-167
Campbell, Lt. Morris Robinson, 588
Campbell, Thomas, 291, 686
Campbell, Lord Walter, 732
Campbell, William Frederick, 741
Canada, vacation in, 572-592
Canda, Charlotte, 432-435
Canning, George, 115, 139-140, 472-473,
   723, 773, 788
Canova, Antonio, 474
Capitol, The (Washington, D.C.), 240
Cardigan, Lord (James Thomas Brud-
   enell), 584, 727, 761-762
Cardwell, Edward, 745
Carey, Matthew, 326
Carlisle, Lord, 721, 737, 749

Carlyle, Thomas, 25, 394, 686
Carpenter, Thomas G., 438
Carr, John, 319
Carr, Laura. *See* Cranworth, Lady
Carrere, John, 259
Carroll, Charles, 310
Carter, Robert, 508-509, 534, 629
Carterley v. Gracin, 112
Casault, Abbé L. J., 581-582, 584-588, 592
Case, Mr., and Mrs., 988
Cass, Lewis (1782–1866), 503, 654, 1058
Cass, Lewis, Jr. (b. 1810), 653-654
Cassel, Hesse, 1074
Casserly, Eugene, 898
Castle, Samuel Northrup, 888
Castlereagh, Lord Robert S., 70, 723, 788
Caswell, Joseph, 198, 206-207, 209
Caswell, Lemuel, 224
Catalini, Angelica, 669
Cate, Mrs., 987
"Catharina" (Cowper), 41
Catron, John, 241, 256
Cavendish, Lord Frederick, 833-834
Cavendish, George S. *See* Devonshire, Duke of
Cecil, Richard, 122
Cecil, Robert Arthur Talbot Gascoyne. *See* Salisbury, Marquis of
Cenas, H. Breton, 337
Chamberlain, John Curtis, 598
Chambers, Mr., 447-448
Chambert, M., 589
Champney, Benjamin, 594-595
Chanbourg, Count de, 1116
Chandler, Amariah, 551, 570
Chandler, Joseph R., 325
Chandler, Peleg Whitman, 321-322, 638
Chantrand, Mr., 1001-1002
Channing, Ann, 143
Channing, Barbara, 684
Channing, Edward Tyrell, 24, 36, 88, 93, 136, 148-149, 215, 224, 286-287, 333, 336, 338, 429, 549; and Allston's death, 171-172, 174, 176, 182; Dana visits, 196; on drama, 287-289, 291; resigns Harvard chair, 415; quarrel with Dana's father, 416-417; death of, 684-685; Dana's obituary, 685
Channing, Mrs. Edward Tyrell, 196, 218, 286-287, 429, 436, 479, 485, 600, 609, 619, 658, 684-685, 822
Channing, Elizabeth, 143
Channing, Elizabeth (d. 1768), 778
Channing family (Brattleboro), 175, 545, 551

Channing, Mrs. Francis Dana, 361
Channing, George, 174, 684-685
Channing, George Edward, 29, 1071
Channing, Mary, 143
Channing, Dr. Walter, 166, 174; Allston obituary, 182, 188; attends Mrs. Dana, 355-356; on Europe, 509-510; Dana's guest, 519; death of E. T. Channing, 684-685
Channing, William Ellery (1780–1842), 24, 97-98, 260, 665
Channing, William Ellery (1818–1901), 685
Channing, William Francis, 222, 260, 263, 595; and Buffalo Convention, 348-349; at Kossuth party, 488; death of E. T. Channing, 685
Channing, William H., 97, 162
Chapin, Miss, 308
Chapin, Alonzo B., 217
Chapin, Henry, 569
Chapman v. Hastings, 60
Chapman, D. B., 558
Chase, Mr., 226
Chase, Salmon P., 350-351, 503, 505
Chauncy, Charles, 260-262
Chauncy, Mrs. Charles, 260-261
Chauncy, Nathaniel, 261, 264, 325
Chauncy, Mrs. Nathaniel, 261, 326
Cheever, Mr., 200-207, 220-221
Cheever, Mrs., 202
Cheney, Charles, 1062
Cheney, Frank, 1062
Cheney, Frank Woodbridge, 1061-1062
Cheney, Fred, 1062
Cheney, John (silk merchant), 1061-1062
Cheney, John (woodsman), 368
Cheney, Rush, 1062
Cheney, Seth Wells, 1061-1062
Cheney, Ward, 1062
Chesapeake, U.S.S., 391, 621
Chester family, 360
Chester, Miss, 305
Chester, Mrs., 346, 354, 527
Chester, Betsey, 95, 193
Chester, Elizabeth, 831
Chester, Hannah, 193, 260-261, 346, 831
Chester, Henry, 261
Chester, Sally, 260-261
Chester, Stephen, 831
Chester, Mrs. Stephen, 95, 193
Chester, Mrs. Thomas, 55, 95, 96
Chickering, John, 126
Child, Francis James, 116, 474, 478-479, 485, 492-493, 533, 619
Childe Harold's Pilgrimage (Byron), 928, 1115, 1122-1123

Childers, John Walbank, 743, 753

Childs, Mrs., 95, 538

Chinese and Their Rebellions, The (Meadows), 999

"Chink and Church", 329-330

Chinnery, George, 986

Choate, Rufus, xxvii-xxviii, 144, 160, 225, 538, 620, 1126; in U.S. Senate, 93; trial technique, 105-106; Wyman trial, 202; in U. S. Supreme Court, 241, 244; in Washington, D. C., 245-256; at Macready benefit, 291; Sims case, 422; Story Association oration, 438; on Europe, 506-507; on George Lunt, 509; Webster's death, 513-514; anecdotes from, 517-518; Dartmouth College case, 517-518; Federal St. Church case, 517-518, 619, 665-666; Kossuth address, 521; on C. M. Ellis, 522; political beliefs, 528-529; on Burke, 530; Webster politics, 535; at Dedham, 537; at Constitutional Convention, 548, 551, 556-557, 563, 565; in Boston, 600; anecdote of, 607; Dempster trial, 613; Dana's opponent, 616; illness of, 621-622; Burns case, 628; *Bark Missouri* case, 666; *White v. Braintree,* 671, 685-686; on Pitt, 682-683; on Judge Davis, 687; oratory of, 689; reputation in England, 831; *Russell v. Russell,* 832; death of, 836

Choate, Sarah Blake, 622

Cholera, 384, 386

Cholmondeley, Mr., 666

Christian Witness, 483

Christie, Mr., 286

Chronological History of Plants (Anderson), 221

Church, Mr., 1006

Circus, 141

City of London, case of, 663

Churchill, Lord H., 985

Clarendon, Lord, 721, 742

Clark, Mr. (California), 852-853

Clark, Mr. (Hawaii), 891

Clark, Rev. Mr. (Hawaii), 881

Clark, Abby, 598

Clark, John M., 680

Clark, Louis, 630

Clarke, Sir James Ferdandez, 831

Clay, Cassius M., 545, 547-549

Clay, Henry (1777–1852), xxv-xxvi, 203, 295, 394

Clay, Henry (1811–1847), 343

Clay, Sir William, 510

Clay, William D., 510

Clayton, Mr., 1047

Cleaveland, Rev. E. L., 123, 315

Cleveland, Duke of, 786

Cleveland, Henry, 682

Cleveland, Richard J., 126, 135

Clevline, Mr., 277

Clifford, George, 857

Clifford, John Henry, 428, 534-535, 857

Clifford, Nathan, 630

Clinch, Joseph, 87-88, 480

Clough, Arthur Hugh, xvii, 526, 529, 760

Clover, Mr., 434

Coady, Mr., 865

Coale, Dr., 135, 230, 330, 667, 675

Coan, Titus, 879-880, 1027

Coan, Mrs. Titus, 879, 882, 890

Coast Pilot (Blunt), 281

Cobb, Miss, 399

Cobb, Mrs., 307

Cobden, Richard, 394, 725

Coburn, Mr., 425, 685

Cockburn, Sir Alexander, 758

Codman, Charles, 110

Codman, Henry, 74, 76, 82

Codman, John, 135, 188

Coe, Mr., 280

Coffin, Dr., 58

Coffin, Gardner, 428

Cogdell, John S., 182, 214

Coggin, Jacob, 521

Coggs v. Barnard, 663

Cogswell, Catherine, 193

Colby, Mr., 428

Cole, Jonathan, 13

Coleridge family, 748

Coleridge, Derwent, 446, 735-736

Coleridge, Hartley, 446, 478

Coleridge, Henry N., 733, 741

Coleridge, John D., 733

Coleridge, Sir John Taylor, 733, 737-741, 777, 792

Coleridge, Samuel Taylor, xvi, 30, 607, 686, 733, 741, 813, 835, 897

Coleridge, Sara, 741

Collingwood, Cuthbert, 766

Collins, Miss, 397

Collins, Mary, 854

Colton, George H., 123

Columbia (frigate), 61, 210

Combe, George, 831

Comer, Thomas, 881

Comet of 1843, 141

Commonwealth v. Horace Jones, 676

Commonwealth v. McKie, 538

Companion for the Festivals and Feasts of the Protestant Episcopal Church, The (Hobart), 308
"Composition, Reception, Reputation and Influence of *Two Years Before the Mast*" (Lucid), 28
Compromise of 1850, 618-619
Compton, Mr., 1033
Confessions of St. Augustine, 127
Congden, Benjamin, 914
Congdon, James Bunker, 639
Congress, U. S., 240-241
Conscience Whigs, xxiii, xxviii
Conspiracy of Pontiac (Parkman), 758
Constitution, Massachusetts: election concerning, 602
Constitution, U.S.S., 118, 391, 621-622
Constitutional Convention of Massachusetts: (1780), 542; (1820), xxvii, 542-543; (1853), xxvii, 535-536, 545, 549-570
Constitutional History of England (Hallam), 338-339
Conthany, Mr., 661-662
Conthoy, Captain, 686
Convent v. Harding, 61
Cook, Miss, 866
Cook, Mr. (*Early Bird*), 925, 936
Cook, Mr. (Penang), 1071
Cook, Mrs., 218
Cook, Capt. James, 872
Cook, Capt. M. H., 925, 929, 936, 938-939
Coolidge, Joseph I., 174, 685, 833
Coolidge, Mrs. Joseph I., 174
Coombs, Leslie, 547
Cooper, James Fenimore, 168-169, 265
Cooper, Samuel, 426
Cope, Mr. and Mrs., 402
Cope, Warren W., 915, 921
Corbyn, Rev. Mr., 500
Corcoran, William Wilson, 1138
Cordillo, Donna Noregio, 847
Cornwall, Barry (B. W. Procter), 755
Cornwallis, Gen. Charles, 310
Cornwell, William, 867
Cort, Mrs., 138
Corwin, Rev. Mr., 886, 888, 890-891
Corwin, Mrs., 890-891
Cotton, John, 1135
Cotton Whigs, xxiii-xxiv, xxviii
Cousin-Montauban, Charles A., 1001
Coventry, Lord, 1133-1134
Cowper, Earl, 756-757
Cowper, William, 41, 227, 686, 723
Cowper, William Francis, 757
Cox, Samuel H., 47

Coxe, Rev. Arthur C., 228, 231, 304-305
Coxe, Henry Octavius, 778-779
Crabbe, George, 897
Craft, Mr., 340
Crafts, Mr., 139
Crafts, Ellen, 413
Crafts, James Mason, 1124-1125
Crafts, William, 413
Crampton, John F. T., 580
Crane, Mrs., 360
Crane, Ichabod B., 209-210, 216
Craney, William, 150-152, 228
Cranworth, Lord (Robert M. Rolfe), 720, 724, 726-727, 746-747, 748, 770-773, 775, 815, 831, 1129
Cranworth, Lady (Laura Carr), 746-748, 772, 775
Cravens, James H., 353
Crawford, Abel, xxii, 272-275, 378-383, 594-596, 644
Crawford, Thomas, 305, 340
Crawford, Thomas J., 274, 378-383
Creighton, Captain, 313
Critical and Historical Essays (Macaulay), 143
Crittenden, Mr., 915
Crittenden, John J., 93, 241, 244
Croker, John Wilson, 25
Croswell, Harry, 298, 471-472, 1071
Croswell, William, 474, 1071; and Church of the Advent, 292, 298, 305, 318; religious instruction, 303; officiates at Hare wedding, 319-320; visits Dana, 322; dispute with bishop, 328; baptizes E. E. Dana, 329; baptizes R. H. Dana, III, 410; death of, 467-469; memorial sermon on, 471-472; Prescott trial, 481; bust of, 607
Cuba, vacation in, 834-835
Culver, Mr., 917
Cumberland, H.B.M., 68, 440-441, 804
Cummings, Captain, 872
Cummings, Dr., 359
Cummings, Rev. Jeremiah W., 834
Cummings, Moses, 349
Cummins, David, 517-518
Cunningham, Allen, 897
Cunningham, Francis, 594
Cunningham, Robert B., 902-903, 909
Curson, Samuel, 126
Curtis, Mr. (of Louisiana), 551, 598
Curtis, Mrs. (Mary Channing), 174
Curtis, Mrs. (nurse), 410
Curtis, Judge Benjamin R., 102, 139, 148, 225; Harvard oration, 90; Harvard, 319; Sims case, 422; charge to Grand Jury, 465; rescue trials, 466,

469, 511-512, 514; *Webb v. Peirce,*
484; at Webster service, 514; *Quiner
v. Gregory,* 541; U. S. Court, 549;
death of Francis Dana, 609
Curtis, Charles P., 57-58, 110, 225, 674
Curtis, Daniel S., 539
Curtis, George Ticknor, 225; Shadrack
case, 410, 412, 415; Sims case, 420,
423; death of Webster, 513-514, 644;
satirized, 639; anecdote of, 1126
Curtis, George William, 464, 615, 638-639
Curtis, Judge (of Louisiana), 551, 598
Curtis, Thomas B., 55
Cushing, Caleb, 602, 985-986, 1033
Cushing, John P., 962, 982
Cushing, Thomas, 90, 319
Cushman, Charlotte, 290
Cushman, Henry Wyles, 570
Custer family (Troy, N. Y.), 400
Custis family, 337
Custis, Major, 253
Custis, Mary Randolph, 253
Cutting, Guy, 362
Cutting, Judge, 649
Cutts, Mr., 209
Cyane (ship), 118
Cymbeline, 129

Dabry, Captain, 1047
Dade, Francis Langhorn, 404
Daggett, Judge David, 46-47, 123-124,
227, 308, 313
Daggett, Ellsworth, 307, 496, 829
Daggett, Rev. Oliver E., 46-48, 89,
95-96, 101, 106, 124, 130, 163, 165,
168, 181, 192, 194, 216, 228, 1055;
in Canandaigua, 307-308; preaches,
315-316; prays for Mrs. Dana, 356;
at Hartford, 388, 407
Daggett, Mrs. Oliver E. (Elizabeth
Watson), 47, 95, 101-103, 124, 130,
163-165, 168, 192-194, 216, 387-388,
507; with child, 54; in Hartford, 228;
in Boston, 264; in Canandaigua, 307,
349; visits Danas, 416; Dana's hostess,
496; in Wethersfield, 555, 829; at
funeral of Nancy Marsh, 831
Daggett, Susan, 124, 192, 264, 496, 831
Dagle, Richard, 749
Daily Alta Californian, 860, 918
Dajee, Bhawoo, 1080, 1083-1085, 1090-
1095
Dale, S. H., 605-606
Dale, William J., 230
Dallas, George M., 720-721
Dallas, James, 117-118

Dalton divorce case, 833
Dalton, Miss, 252
Dalton, Mr., 685
Damon, Reverend, 861-862, 889, 891
Dana v. Valentine, 56
Dana family: English branch, 417-419,
757, 784-787
Dana, Miss (Oswego, N. Y.), 841, 917
Dana, Alexander H., 841
Dana, Angela Henrietta Channing, 821,
935
Dana, Charles A., 408
Dana, Rev. Charles B., 97, 214, 246-
253, 337
Dana, Douglass Charles Kinnaird, 418
Dana, Rev. Edmund (1739–1823), 392,
418, 426, 583, 757, 784-787
Dana, Mrs. (Rev.) Edmund (Hon.
Helen Kinnaird), 417, 766, 786
Dana, Edmund (1774–1776), 215
Dana, Edmund Trowbridge (1779–1859),
4, 29, 156, 682; on Washington Allston,
171, 174-180, 184-185, 188-189; appearance, 456; meets Mrs. Dana, 185;
reminisces, 392, 472-473, 497-498; at
funeral of Lewis Gray, 511; and death
of Horatio Greenough, 523-524; on
Burke, 530; Dana's host, 603; at funeral of Francis Dana, 609; on George
Washington, 615-616; with Ashur
Ware, 681-682; death of, 835-836
Dana, Edmund ("Ned") Trowbridge
(1818–1869), xxxvi, 36, 48, 71, 88-89,
99, 102, 104, 112, 127-128, 135, 139,
156, 165, 168-169, 190, 195-198, 212,
215, 217-218, 222-225, 281; at college,
30; partnership with brother, 97; on
Allston, 170, 174-175, 181, 188; dines
with brother, 225, 229; legal work,
283; on Choate, 286-287; on theater,
288-290; at Manchester, 318, 336; at
funeral of William E. Dana, 329; to
Europe, 342; on Mary Rosamund
Dana, 358; college days, 376; absence
lamented, 385; correspondence of, 388,
391, 427, 432, 480, 516, 606; Archbishop Hughes on, 435; brother's affection for, 464; in Europe, 469-470;
recalled, 474; on Beecher family,
518-519; with Mr. Ramsay, 653; sister's affection for, 668; in England,
719, 776, 815-816; fortunes of, 832;
death of Uncle Edmund, 835; in
Heidelberg, 941, 1061, 1125
Dana, Elizabeth Ellery (1789–1874),
29, 48, 89, 106, 135, 165, 170, 173-175,

185, 212, 218, 221, 267, 336, 356-357, 484, 511, 526, 528, 619, 835

Dana, Elizabeth Ellery, daughter (1846–1939): birth of, 328-329; mother's illness, 356; at party, 478; at new house, 483; rides, 499; at Manchester, 502; Christmas, 526; picture of, 543; at Hartford, 546, 599; scarlet fever, 554-555; father writes to, 592; with father, 618; death of Nancy Marsh, 831

Dana, Francis (1743–1811), xxxvii, 26, 36, 119, 129, 146, 417; funeral of, 135; described, 138, 604-605; generation discussed, 164; reputation of, 266; family of, 346; letter to Franklin, 426-427; Uncle Edmund on, 497-498; with Lewis Gray, 511; on Burke, 530; death of son, 608; coffin of, 609; on U. S. Constitution, 652; and his brother Edmund, 785

Dana, Francis (1777–1853), 9, 26, 28-29, 98, 169; and Allston's death, 174-175; described, 346; his generation, 835; death of, 608-609

Dana, Mrs. Francis (Sophia Willard), 185, 209, 215, 609

Dana, Francis (1806–1872), 135, 144, 213, 471; meets *Alert*, 28-29; son's death, 156-157; Allston's death, 174; family tomb, 185, 215; at Rockport, 210-211; Dana's guest, 229; niece's baptism, 285; at St. Paul's, 292, 294; death of son, 329; and ether controversy, 332; at funeral of Lewis Gray, 511; death of father, 608; in New York, 692; death of Uncle Edmund, 835

Dana, Mrs. Francis (Isabella Hazen), 28, 174; at Rockport, 210-211; described, 213; niece's baptism, 285; death of son, 329; at Thanksgiving dinner, 471, 519; at funeral of Lewis Gray, 511

Dana, Francis (1835–1843), 156-158, 185, 215

Dana, Francis Richard, 418

Dana, George Hazen, 471, 519, 609

Dana, George Kinnaird, 418, 786

Dana, Mrs. George Kinnaird, 418

Dana, Henry Edmund Pulteney, 418

Dana, Lt. James, 1013

Dana, James B., 123

Dana, James Dwight, 683-684, 1080

Dana, James Freeman, 1080

Dana, Martha Remington. *See* Allston, Mrs. Washington

Dana, Mary Elizabeth, 48, 174, 176, 287, 356, 511, 609

Dana, Mary Rosamund, 499-500, 658; birth of, 355-358; described, 387; new house, 483; birthday, 502-503; picture of, 543; at Brattleboro, 544-545, 551, 572; compared to orphan, 587; in Cambridge, 601

Dana, Napoleon Tecumseh Jackson, 341-342, 1060

Dana, Mrs. Napoleon Tecumseh Jackson, 341

Dana, Richard, 164, 186

Dana, Richard Henry, father (1787–1879), xxxvi, 4, 10, 15, 36, 44-45, 48, 57, 88, 92, 97, 101-102, 107, 109, 112, 127, 135, 139, 168-169, 185, 191, 195-196, 210-211, 213, 223-225, 267, 385, 391, 393, 528, 546, 549, 615, 620, 661, 692, 1009; death of, xli; mourns wife, 6; with son, 11; on Harvard revolt, 21; advises son, 26; welcomes son, 29; marriage of, 134; confirmation of, 159; Allston's death, 171-173, 188-190; illness, 222, 225; on "Belshazzar's Feast," 226; with grandchild, 285; on vacation, 286, 433; with bishop, 297-298; at Manchester, 304, 318, 499, 552, 571, 598, 681, 832-833; in New Bedford, 305, 437; quarrel with E. E. Dana, 336; at Hanover, N.H., 347; Boston, 385, 391; edition of his work, 388; in Vermont, 406; at grandson's baptism, 410; quarrel with E. T. Channing, 416-417; Sumner election, 427; 4th of July, 436; on Robert Wheaton, 464; Christmas, 476; son's guest, 479, 484, 489, 490, 494, 519, 603, 607, 617, 638; at Ole Bull concert, 491; in *Homes of American Authors*, 502; religious activity, 518; on Constitutional Convention of 1820, 543; at theater, 543-544; illness of, 609; on Choate, 613; Burns case, 629; daughter's accident, 668; on George III, 682; on T. D. Woolsey, 683; on E. T. Channing, 685; Choate on, 686; in England, 739; death of Uncle Edmund, 835; his verse, 994; reputation in China, 983-984; and C. R. Leslie, 1131

Dana, Mrs. Richard Henry (Ruth Charlotte Smith), 5-7, 11, 19, 107, 134, 285

Dana, Mrs. Richard Henry, Jr. (Sarah Watson), xvii, xxxix, xli, 46, 48-49, 54-55, 62, 70-71, 74, 82, 88-90, 92,

94-97, 101-102, 104-108, 117, 124, 127-128, 135, 137, 139, 141, 143-144, 146, 148-149, 153, 157-159, 163-171, 196, 198-199, 210-212, 218-220, 224, 228, 230, 255, 264, 281, 285, 287, 319, 328, 336, 341, 375, 380, 388, 392, 406-407, 409, 437, 463, 519, 637, 692; courtship days, 42-43; first child, 68-69; present to husband, 114; Allston's death, 171, 174, 181, 184; meets Uncle Edmund, 185; ill health of, 190, 516, 675, 681, 832; visits mother, 191-194; husband's love for, 194, 214-217, 334; at embarkation party, 221; at Bunker Hill, 223; in Hartford, 227; in Wethersfield, 231, 318, 360-361; in Philadelphia, 260; second child, 266-267; religious attitude of, 268, 271; at *Hamlet*, 288-289; at Ticknor's, 290; Holy Week observance, 303-304; vacation, 306-315, 823, 828-829; at Skaneateles, 315-316; with children, 317; at Hare wedding, 320; confirmed, 322-323; daughter baptised, 329; at Mary Watson's wedding, 332; censors *Journal*, 333; at Manchester, 338, 501-502; with husband, 345-346, 384, 499; quarrel with husband, 346-347; for Free Soil, 354; danger with fourth child, 355-357; death of brother, 359-360; old friends of, 376; correspondence with husband, 386, 592, 899, 902; in New York, 391; Parkman murder, 393; at Saratoga, 397-406; son's baptism, 410; at Longfellow's, 428, 432; at E. T. Channing's, 429; husband's illness, 436; in Cambridge, 465, 467, 473-474, 477-478; at theater, 480; at new house, 482-484; meets Kossuth, 488; hears Ole Bull, 491; visits Russells, 502-503; at funeral of Lewis Gray, 511; sees Albani, 512; and death of Webster, 514; entertains L. L. Murad, 520; observes Christmas, 526-527; at Church of the Advent, 526, 538; attends Thackeray lecture, 527; and death of Mrs. Eustis, 529; in Plymouth, 530; Brattleboro cure, 544-545, 551, 570-571, 572, 597-598, 601-602; visits Farmington, 555; visits Ida Russell, 603; at funeral of Francis Dana, 609; entertains Fitzhughs, 619; at White Hills, 641-648; fears husband's revolver, 644; at Canandiagua, 658; hears *Norma*, 669; and death of E. T. Channing, 684-685; **husband's** gifts to, 815, 1021, 1024; bears sixth

child, 821-822; hostess, 829-830; and death of Nancy Marsh, 831

Dana, Richard Henry, III (1851-1931), xxxii, xxxviii, xli, 37, 409, 497, 499-500, 572, 601, 658; marriage of, 56; marginal note by, 219, 333; birth, 407; baptism, 410; at Thanksgiving dinner, 471; birthday, 478; at new house, 483; picture of, 543; at Brattleboro, 544-545, 551; at Manchester, 661, 681; in accident, 676; similarity to Robert Olyphant, 1061-1062; letter to father, 1068

Dana, Ruth Charlotte (1814-1901), xxxvi, 4-5, 29-30, 34, 48, 88, 97, 102, 104, 106-107, 110, 124, 128-129, 134-135, 139, 143, 145, 158, 165, 169, 190, 195, 222, 224-225, 235, 328, 380, 385, 388, 391, 406, 436, 526, 528, 555; and death of Allston, 170-171, 174-175; at Rockport, 210-211; in New York, 231-233, 264, 327-328; namesake's godmother, 285; at Beverly, 286; at theater, 289; at Church of the Advent, 298, 304; at Manchester, 318, 501, 516, 572; eye trouble, 323; at funeral of William Ellery Dana, 329; at Hanover, N.H., 347; and Mary Rosamund Dana, 356-358; at nephew's baptism, 410; at New Year's party, 478; brother's guest, 484, 490, 509; hears Ole Bull, 491; conducts Roman Catholic prayers, 500; and Archbishop Hughes, 585; letter from brother, 588; and death of Uncle Francis, 608-609; injured, 667-668; hears *Norma*, 669-670; Miss Spooner's letter to, 1068-1069

Dana, Ruth Charlotte, daughter (1844-1903), 268, 305, 317-318, 393, 436, 437, 544; birth, 266-267; baptism, 285; at New Year's party, 478; at new house, 483; at Manchester, 502, 658; at Wethersfield, 507-508; picture taken, 543; at Miss Porter's School, 546, 548, 554-555, 571, 598-599; birthday, 641; and death of Uncle Edmund, 835

Dana, Samuel Whittlesey, 317-318, 346

Dana, Sarah Ann (1791-1866), 29, 48, 112, 135, 170, 175, 212, 356, 526, 685, 835

Dana, Sarah Watson, daughter (1843-1902), 88-90, 94, 101, 104-106, 124, 132, 136, 153, 159, 184, 191-192, 214, 227-228, 305, 406, 436, 499; birth, 69; vaccination, 112; reunion with mother, 158-159; birthday, 163-

164; visits Uncle Edmund, 185; praised, 196; illnesses, 212, 226, 264; at Wethersfield, 216, 317-318; with servants, 231; birthday, 266; with father, 285; at brother's baptism, 410; at New Year's party, 478; at new house, 483; with Aunt Martha, 500, 544; at Milton, 502-503; father's present, 526; picture of, 543; at Miss Porter's School, 546, 548, 571, 598-599; sister's birthday, 555; at Manchester, 658

Dana, Sophia Willard. See Ripley, Mrs. George

Dana, Susan (1820–1822), 5, 107, 157, 185-186, 215

Dana, Susan C. See Lawrence, Mrs. William Richard

Dana, Theodora. See Willard, Mrs. Sidney

Dana, William Augustus P., 418

Dana, William Ellery, 329

Dana, William P. P., 770

Dana, William Pulteney, 148, 152, 417-419, 784

Dane, Nathan, 439

Daniel, Peter V., 241

Danne, Mr., 598

Dartmouth College v. Woodward, 517-518

Daveis, Charles S., 126, 284

Daveis, Edward H., 126, 283-284

Daveis, Gilman, 126

Daveis, John T., 284

Davenport, Mr., 1022

Davenport, Rev. Mr., 1022

David Copperfield, 433

Davidson, Mrs., 1069

Davis, Mr. (China), 999

Davis, Mr. (innkeeper), 644-645

Davis, Mrs., 379, 386, 530, 596, 644-645

Davis, Charles G., 410, 413-415, 559

Davis, Charles Henry, 218, 417, 430, 474, 899

Davis, George T., 128-129, 827

Davis, Helen, 128

Davis, Isaac P., 183

Davis, Jefferson, 39, 343-344

Davis, Mrs. Joanna, 428

Davis, John (1761–1843), 90

Davis, John (1787–1854), 52, 90, 321, 505, 544, 675, 1138

Davis, John Chandler Bancroft, 1138

Davis, Mrs. John Chandler Bancroft, 1138

Davis, Sir John Francis, 933, 964

Davis, R. S., 861

Davis, Thomas, 457

Davis, William, 40

Davis, Judge Woodbury, 687

Davis, Mrs. Woodbury, 645

Day, Mr. (of Georgia), 402

Day, Mrs. (of Georgia), 402

Day, Catherine (Mrs. S. I. Andrews), 191, 193, 228

Day, Henriette (Mrs. J. P. Putnam), 95-96

Day, Henry, 338

Day, Sarah, 220, 346

Day, Thomas M., 96, 135

Dayton, William L., 245

"Dead Rabbitts" gang, 823

Dearborn, Captain (in Japan), 1001-1002, 1006, 1012, 1025, 1031-1033

Decatur, Stephen, 127, 223, 240

DeCressiguy, Mr. (De Crespigny, see *Genealogy*), 418

DeForge, Mr., 331

DeGraux, Mrs., 596

Dehon, William (1810–1875), 44, 107, 166

Dehon, William Jr., 409

De la Démocratie en Amérique (De Tocqueville), 890

De Lancy, William H., 113

Delano, Sara, 941

Delano, Warren, 941-942, 977, 981-982, 988, 1062

Delano, Mrs. Warren, 941

Delaplasse, Bishop, 1051

Delavan, Henry, 217

Democratic Convention (1852), 491

Democratic Party of Massachusetts, 622-623

Dempster, David, 613

Denman, Lord Thomas, 742-743

Dennett, Mr., 768

Dent, Mr. (in China), 994, 999, 1001, 1011, 1023-1024, 1032-1033, 1062

De Quincey, Thomas, 463, 507

Derby, George, 675

Derby, Lord, 727, 742, 774, 1134

Derby, Mrs. Henney, 479

Devens, Captain, 983-984

Devereux, Mr., 528

Devonshire, Duke of, 115

De Vries, Mr., 442

Dewey, Charles A., 398-399

DeWitt, Alexander, 348

Dexter, Miss, 841

Dexter, Franklin, 71, 82, 144-145, 164; Allston death and work, 174, 176, 179-181, 183-184, 188-190, 226; at theater, 287; Dana visits, 340; Sims case, 420; on French character, 488; at

Norma, 669; and Loring removal, 671, 673
Dexter, George M., 323
Dexter, Gordon, 1057
Dexter, Samuel, 146, 485
Dial, The, 13
Diary and Letters of Madame d'Arblay (Fanny Burney), 143
Dickens, Charles: visit to Boston, xvi-xvii, xxviii, 50-61; *The Old Curiosity Shop*, 64; *American Notes*, 101-103, 149; *Nicholas Nickleby*, 204; *David Copperfield*, 433
Dickens, Mrs. Charles, 59, 61
Different Systems of Penal Codes in Europe, The (Sandford), 670
"Difficulty on Realizing Sacred Privileges" (Newman), 287
Digby, Kenelm Henry, 315
Disraeli, Benjamin, 394, 725-726, 751
Dix, William G., 152-153
Dixey, Mr., 666
Dixon, Mr., 478
Dixon, James, 96, 485
Dixon, Mrs. James (Elizabeth Cogswell), 95-96
Doane, Bishop George W., 333, 474
Dodge, Henry, 505
Dodworth, Thomas, 651
Doland, Mr., 926-927, 936
Donahue v. Richards, 648-650, 659
Don Giovanni (Mozart), 482
Donizetti, Gaetano, 409
Don Juan (Byron), 1111
Donnell, Mrs., 400
Donner Party, 905-906, 908
Dorr, E. W., 1016-1018, 1022, 1024-1025
Dorr, Theodore Haskell, 90, 319
Dorr, Thomas William: "rebellion," 67, 109-110, 260, 561
Double Witness of the Church, The (W. I. Kip), 231
Douglas, Stephen A., xxviii, 503, 1074, 1098
Douglass, Frederick, 161
Downes, John, 600
Downey, John G., 924
Downing, Jack (Seba Smith), 54
Doyle, Manville, 849
Dred Scott decision, 90, 465
Drierback, Herr, 457-458
Drummond, Henry, 394
Drummond, Lewis T., 574, 582, 592
Drummond, Thomas, 245
Drury, Mr., 432, 496
Drury, Mrs., 432, 496

Drury-Lowe, Maj. William, 584
Dryden, John, 265, 291
Duane, William John, 922
Du But, M., 991
Dudley Observatory, 936
Duer, William, 844-845
Dufferin, 1st Marquis of, 1103
Dulany, Major, 630
Dulany, Daniel, Jr., 247
Dulany, Rebecca Ann, 247
Dunbar, Mr., 630-631
Duncan family (of Providence, R.I.), 818
Duncan, Miss (of Alabama), 551
Duncan, Mr. (of New Orleans), 313, 319, 340
Duncan, Mr. (of Boston), 678
Duncan, Samuel W. (of Cleveland, Ohio), 109
Dunmore, Lord, 309
Dunn, Mr., 591
Dunnell, Joseph, 109
Durham, Lord, 579, 588, 775
Durkin, Mr., 573, 592
Durkin, Mrs., 573
Durkin, Matilda, 573
Dutton, Warren: on Allston's painting, 179-181, 183-184, 190, 226; at Constitutional Convention of 1820, 542
Dwight, Miss, 430
Dwight, the Misses, 290
Dwight, Edmund (1780–1849), 101, 131, 291
Dwight, Mrs. Edmund, 131, 291
Dwight, Edmund, Jr., 464
Dwight, John Sullivan, 686, 689, 830
Dwight, Mrs. John, 595
Dwight, Mary, 128
Dwight, William, 606

Earl, Betsy (Mrs. Cook), 218
Earle, John M., 406, 563
Early Bird (ship), 924-940
Eastburn, Bishop Manton, 113, 134; confirms Dana's father, 159; and Church controversy, 296; confirms Mrs. Dana, 322; on William Croswell, 328; and Prescott heresy case, 437, 482-483, 490-491, 493-494, 499; preaching, 901
Eaton, Rev. Homer, 822
Eaton, W. O., 499
Eckley, David, 71, 82
Eclipse (bark), 210
Eddy, Samuel, 109
Edinburgh Review, 736
Edmands, Gen. Benjamin, 632, 635, 638

Edwards, Henry, 153
Edwards, Munroe, 92-93
Egypt: Dana's trip to, 1100-1111
Elegy in a Country Churchyard (Gray), 199
Elgin, Lord (James Bruce), 462-463; in Quebec (1853), 576-581, 589; in England (1856), 731-732, 736, 742, 746, 752; Orient (1860), 945, 986, 991, 1032, 1067, 1077
Elgin, Lady, 579-581, 588
Eliot, Charles, 682
Eliot, Thomas D., 428
Eliot, Samuel A., 52, 131, 168; attends theater, 287; Macready benefit, 291; ostracizes Sumner, 408; attacks Dana, 427; in White Mountains, 595
Ellenborough, Lord, 715, 727, 743
Ellery, William (1727–1820), 240, 389, 685, 1062
Ellery, Capt. William (of *Starr King*), 943
Ellery, William (Dana's guest, 1843), 224
Elles, Mrs., 233
Elliot, William, 314
Elliott, Jesse Duncan, 326
Elliott, Bishop Stephen, 993, 1050
Ellis, Mr. (of Boston), 379, 383, 447, 452-455
Ellis, Mr. (in China, 1860), 1045, 1062
Ellis, Charles Mayo, 522, 627, 629
Ellis, John (of Kineo, Maine), 449
Ellis, "Old Man" (of Kineo, Maine), 448-449, 456-457
Ellsler, Fanny, 71, 80
Ellsworth, William W., 192-193, 313
Ellsworth, Mrs. William W., 55
Elphinstone, Mountstuart, 1088
Elwood, Dr., 379
Elwyn, Alfred Langdon, 829
Elwyn, Mrs. Alfred Langdon, 829
"Embarkation of the Pilgrims" (Weir), 218
Embury, Emma Catherine, 403
Emerson, Mr., 848-849
Emerson, George B., 320, 482, 848, 863
Emerson, Mrs. George B. (Mrs. Fleming), 320, 323, 482
Emerson, Ralph Waldo, xxi, xxvi, 41; Dana's teacher, 13; Dana's host, 394; at Concord, 607; Saturday Club, 666-667, 669, 689, 830; on Stonehenge, 686; and Shakespeare's house, 782
Emerson, William, 13
Emmanuel, King Victor, 1118-1119
Emory (bootblack), 548-549
Emory, Harriet Bowen (Mrs Robert Ives), 110

Encyclopedia Brittanica, 882
Endecott, John, 534
Endicott, Mr., 987-988
Endicott, James P., 984, 987-988
Endicott, Mrs. James P., 984, 987-988
Endicott, William, 534
English, James Lawrence, 918
English Traits (Emerson), 686
Eothen (Kinglake), 758
Episcopal Convention, Boston (1847), 332; (1852), 489-490
Epitome of Chymical Philosophy (Dana), 1080
Eresby, Lord Willoughby de, 750
Errors of the Times (Brownell), 231
Essay on Man, An (Pope), 244
Estes, D. G., 304
Estudillo, Mr., 848
Ether controversy, 304, 345, 358-359, 519
Ethnography and Philology (Hale), 68
Eugene Aram (Bulwer-Lytton), 35
Eustis, Frederic A., 222, 685
Eustis, George, 1138
Eustis, George R., Jr., 1138
Eustis, Professor H. L., 529
Eustis, Mrs. H. L., 529
Euthanasy (Mountford), 539
Evans, Captain, 635
Evans, George, 245
Evarts, William M., 39-40, 116-117, 127, 390, 476; Secretary of State, xl; case of Munroe Edwards, 93; character evaluated, 104; in New York, 327, 332, 408-409, 834; at Delmonico's, 409; Kossuth reception, 475; law practice, 825-826; known in California, 844; on the "Social Compact," 606
Evelath, John, 447
Everett, Mr., 153
Everett, Alexander H., 138
Everett, Edward, 527, 568; "Progress of Literature," 12; Concord oration, 11-12, 620; Harvard president, 337; Harvard address, 497; on Webster, 530; charade of, 624-625; in U. S. Senate, 670; on George Washington, 686, 689; on Bishop of Oxford, 727; "Uses of Astronomy," 936; Webster's editor, 1064; Cotten Chapel, 1135
Everett, Mrs. Edward (Charlotte Gray Brooks), 337
Ewer, Ferdinand Cartwright, 914
Ewer, Mrs. Ferdinand Cartwright (Sarah Mandell Congden), 914
Ewing, Thomas, 245, 256
"Eyewitness of Eight Months Before the Mast, An" (Hart), 848

Fabens, Francis A., 90, 319, 337, 844
Fable for Critics (Lowell), 432
Fabyan's (in White Mountains), 275, 277, 379, 381
Fairfax, Bryan, 246-247
Fairfax, Thomas, 246-247
Fairmont Waterworks, Philadelphia, 261
Falkland, Lord, 75
Fang (*Oliver Twist*), 57
Fanville, O., 277
Farley, Mr., 513
Farmer, Moses G., 222
Farnum, Mr., 319
Farrar, Mrs., 337, 459, 474, 497, 526, 721, 756, 772
Farrell (ship), case of, 125
Farwell case, 148
Faucon, Edward H., 111
Fay, Miss, 619, 994
Federal Street Church, case of, 517, 619, 665-666, 688-689
Felix, Elizabeth Rachel (Rachel), 669
Felton, Cornelius C., 88, 102, 135, 149, 266, 539; and Allston's death, 174; at Channing party, 286; Macready's benefit, 291; at Robert Wheaton's funeral, 464; Dana's guest, 489, 821, 829; at Parker dinner, 674-675; at Saturday Club, 830; brother, 844
Felton, Mrs. Cornelius C., 149
Felton, John B., 539; at Robert Wheaton's funeral, 464; Dana's guest, 485, 492; at Lowell dinner, 529; and Prescott trial, 481; in California, 844-846, 855, 895-896, 898, 925
Ferdinand and Isabella (Prescott), 57, 102, 131, 229
Ferguson, Mr., 1048
Fernald, Judge Charles, 847, 849
Fiedler, Ernest, 332, 407-408
Field, Barnum W., 899
Field, David Dudley, 354-355, 915
Field, Hixon W., 817
Field, Mrs. Hixon W., 818
Field, Stephen Johnson, 915-917, 922, 924
Field, Mrs. Stephen Johnson, 922-924
Fields, Mr. (mate on *Early Bird*), 925, 936, 939
Fields, James Thomas, 507, 521, 529, 541, 543, 675
Fillmore, President Millard, xxvi, 415, 462-463, 493
Finch, Mr., 319
Finch, William B., 390. *See* Bolton, William Compton

Fish, Captain (of *Architect*), 892-894, 897-898
Fish, Hamilton, xl, 503
Fisher, Colonel, 905
Fisher, Major, 999
Fisher, Rufus, 135
Fitch, Mr., 849
Fitch, Henry, 154
Fitzgerald, Mr., 908
Fitzhugh, Mrs. (of Virginia), 252-253
Fitzhugh, Alida ("Addy"), 309
Fitzhugh, Charles, 309
Fitzhugh, Daniel Holker (1794–1881), 148, 253, 308-311, 379, 619
Fitzhugh, Mrs. Daniel Holker, 276, 309-310
Fitzhugh, Daniel Holker, Jr., 148, 152, 224, 309, 311
Fitzhugh, Elizabeth ("Lilly"), 309, 326
Fitzhugh, Francis ("Frank"), 309
Fitzhugh, Helen Kinnaird, 309
Fitzhugh, Isabella ("Bel"), 309, 619
Fitzhugh, Maria ("Molly"), 309
Fitzhugh, Peregrine, 309-310
Fitzhugh, Richard, 310
Fitzhugh, William A., 310
Fitzhugh, William P., 309
Fitzpatrick, Bishop John B., 336-337, 600, 964
Five Points, New York City, 119-122, 232-233
Flagg, George W., 122-123, 175, 227
Flagg, Henry C., 175
Flagg, Mrs. Henry C., 227
Flagg, Jared, 175, 182, 187
Flagg, Mrs. Jared, 95
Flagg, Montague, 95
Flagg, William J., 175
Flahault, August de la Billarderie, 757
Flahault, Georgianna Gabrielle, 757
Fleatcher, Richard, 56
Fleming, Mr., 1092-1096, 1111
Fleming, Mrs., 1096
Fleming, Caroline (Mrs. Robert Hare), 319-320
Fletcher, Captain, 1026
Fletcher, Mrs., 1028
Fletcher, Mr., 1131
Fletcher, Richard, 600, 628, 653
Flogging, abolition of, 541
Florida (ship), 111
Flush Times of Alabama and Mississippi, The (Baldwin), 855
Foley, Colonel, 1060
Follen, Charles, 25
Folsom, George, 817
Folsom, Mrs. George, 817

Foot, Solomon, 505
Foote, Andrew Hill, 947
Foote, Henry S., 919, 924
Forbes, Miss, 399
Forbes, Reverend, 1063
Forbes, Darius, 377
Forbes, Frank, 941
Forbes, John Murray, 128, 982-983
Forbes, Mrs. John Murray, 336
Forbes, P. S., 1063
Forbes, Ralph B., 128
Forbes, Robert B., 110, 128, 229, 336,
    557, 982-983
Forbes, Mr. Seaman, 398-399
Forbes, Mrs. Seaman, 398-399
Forbes, Mr. W. C., 911
Forbes, Mrs. W. C., 911
Ford v. King, 408, 489
Ford, Dr., 885, 888
Ford, Mr., 363
Ford, Professor, 91
Forrester, Lord, 418
Forsyth, Reverend, 619
Fortescue, Earl of, 757-758, 1135
Foss v. Richardson, 833
Foster, Dwight, 538, 615, 676
Foster, Mrs. Dwight, 615
Foster, Nathaniel Green, 677-679
Foster, Stephen S., 161
Four Georges (Thackeray), 682
Fowler, Miss, 376
Fowler, Jeremiah, 130
Fox, Mr. (caretaker), 195
Fox, Mrs. (caretaker), 196, 212, 215,
    217, 318, 356
Fox, Charles James, xxi, 107, 115, 472,
    603, 682, 723, 746, 788, 835
Fox, Thomas, 126
Francis, Convers, 91
Francis I (Kemble), 389
Franconia, trips to, 277-278, 376-384
Franklin, Benjamin, 136-137, 426
Franklin, William Buel, 654-658
Frederich, William IV of Prussia, 1074
Free Soil Party, meetings of: (1848),
    xxiv, xxvii, 347-354; (1850), 406;
    (1852), 502, 505-506, 508; (1854),
    617-618; (1855), 677-680
Freeman, Marshal, 626-627, 629-631,
    634-636
Freme, Martha A., 360-361
Frémont, Dr., 592
Frémont, Charles E., 851, 924
Frémont, Francis (Frank), 851
Frémont, John C., 759, 821, 851-855, 921
Frémont, Mrs. John C., 851-855
Frémont, Lilly, 851-852, 855

French John, 111
French, Luther, 480
French, Mrs. Luther (Sally White), 480
Frick, Elizabeth, 114
Frick, Henry, 254, 256
Frick, William F., 237, 259, 320
Friends in Council (Helps), 1078-1079
Frisbie, Mr., 903
Frisbie, John B., 902-903
Frisbie, Mrs. John B., 903
Frisbie, Levi, 524, 682
Frost, Barzillei, 338; 607
Frost, John, 9
Frothingham, Octavious Brooks, 525
Fuller, Elisha, 615
Fuller, Margaret, 1002

Gage, Nathaniel, 9
Gair, Mr., 361
Gallacar, Mr., 509
Gallatin, Albert, 389
Gallaudet, Mr., 96
Gammell, William, 1126
Gannett, Reverend, 41, 181
Gannett, Ezra Styles, 97, 665
Gansevoort, Guert, 112, 399
Gardell, Mrs., 520
Gardiner, David, 242-243, 254
Gardiner, Julia, 243, 254
Gardiner, Robert Hallowell, 135, 653
Gardiner, S. P., 180
Gardiner, William, 191
Gardner, Miss, 135, 927
Gardner, Henry J., 672
Gardner, Johnson, 569
Garibaldi, Guiseppe, 1118, 1130
Garnham, Captain, 400
Garrick, David, 716
Garrison, William L., 161-162
Gaskell, Elizabeth C., 936-937
Gassett, Mr., 983-984, 988
Gastner, Mrs., 841
Gates, Dan, 366-371
Gavazzi, Father, 572
Gay, John, 527
Gay, Winckworth Allan, 594-595
Gell, Rev. Mr., 1087
Gell, Mrs. (Rev.), 1087
Geneva: 1871 treaty conference in, xl
Germantown, U.S.S., 601
Gerrish v. Emeleth, 103
Geyle, Baron, 73
Ghent, Treaty of, 601
Gibb, Mr., 576
Gibbon, Miss (Mrs. T. P. Presland), 418

Gibbon, Mrs., 418
Gibbon, William Henry, 418
Gibbons v. Ogden, 517
Gibbs family (at Skaneateles), 316
Gibbs, Miss, 174
Gibbs, Mr., 594, 596-597
Gibbs, George (1815–1873), 97, 222-223
Gibbs, Mrs. George (Laura Wolcott), 119
Gibbs, George, Jr., 119
Gibbs, Oliver W., 119
Gibley, Mark, 308
Gibson, Captain, 1047
Gibson, Mrs. C. D., 174, 230
Giddings, Joshua Reed, 351
Gilbert, Timothy, 347
Giles, Mr., 1123
Giles, Joel, 570
Gillespie, Archibald H., 921-923
Gillespie, Mrs. Archibald H., 922
Gilmer, Thomas W., 242-244, 254
Gilmore, Robert, 236
Girard, Ábbe, 1027
Girard College, 261
"Girl of Cadiz, The" (Byron), 1134
Gladstone, William E.: Emerson on, 394;
    political school, 510; college days, 579;
    in House of Commons, 725, 745; calls
    on Dana, 763; invitation to Dana,
    815; Sumner on, 831; in London, 1129
Glass, Hugh, 908
Glazier, William B., 605
Glover, Mr., 408
Goble, Rev. Mr., 1021-1022
Goddard, Mr. (of Cincinnati), 666, 669
Goddard, Prof. William Giles, 110
Goddard, Mrs. William Giles (Miss
    Ives), 110
Goderich, Lord Frederick (John Rob-
    inson), 726
Godley, John Robert, 98
Godwin, Parke, 119, 234
Godwin, Mrs. Parke, 119
Gohian, Mr., 103
Goldsborough, Mrs. (Miss Wirt), 517
Goldsborough, Charles, 252
Goldsmith, Oliver, 530
Gooch, Major (Atlantic crossing), 696,
    699-700, 706, 708-709
Gooch, Mr., 359
Goodrich, James L., 90, 319
Goodwin, Captain, 446
Goodwin, Mrs., 492
Goodwin, Daniel Raynes, 652
Goodwin, Orion, 446
Gorden, Mr., 600
Gordon, Mr. (church delegate), 304
Gordon, Arthur Hamilton, 726

Gore, Christopher, 164, 598
Gorham, Benjamin, 180, 747
Gorham, David Wood, 645
Gorham, Mrs. N., 307-308
Gorham, Mrs. W., 308
Gough, Mr., 1049-1051
Gould, Benjamin Apthorp, 830
Gowen, Mr., 874-876
Gowen, Mrs., 874-876
Graham, Isaac, 155
Graham, Sir James, 725, 745
Granger, Gideon, 308
Granger, Mrs. Gideon, Sr., 308, 315
Granger, Gen. Gideon, 308
Granger, Mrs. (Gen.) Gideon, 308, 496
Granger, Francis, 307-308, 948
Grant, Sir James Hope, 945, 980, 1001,
    1099
Grant, S. B., 92, 96
Grant, Mrs. S. B. (Woodbridge), Caroline
    95-96
Grant, Ulysses S., xl, 39, 503
Granville, Lord, 750
Grattan, Henry, 723
Grattan, Thomas Colley, 56, 59-60
Graves, Eleanor, 906
Graves, John G., 58
Graves, John Thomas, 774
Graves, Rosewell Hobart, 957
Gray, the Misses, 609
Gray, Reverend, 952, 969
Gray, Alfred G., 841-842
Gray, Francis C., 52, 55, 57-59, 102, 110
Gray, Frederick Turell, 331, 345
Gray, Sir George, 725, 745
Gray, Henry P., 143, 169
Gray, Mrs. Henry P., 169
Gray, Horace, 464, 481, 526, 636, 689,
    916
Gray, John, 55
Gray, John C., 338, 570
Gray, Lewis, 511
Gray, Thomas, 199, 729-731
Great Eastern (ship), 1098
"Great Gravitation Meeting, The," 407
"Great Stone Face, The," (Hawthorne),
    278
Greeley, Horace, 408, 852
Greene, Mr. (England), 223
Greene, Mr. (of Manila), 1063, 1065,
    1069, 1074
Greene, Albert C., 109
Greene, Albert G., 109
Greene, Benjamin, 174
Greene, Samuel Dana, 1060
Greenleaf, Mr., 449
Greenleaf, Caroline, 280

Greenleaf, James, 280

Greenleaf, Mrs. James, 280

Greenleaf, Rev. Patrick Henry, 490

Greenleaf, Simon, 37, 280, 490, 526; Harvard Oration, 90; his *Evidence*, 136; Story oration, 321; Prescott case, 483; Webster's death, 513-514; Constitutional Convention, 557, 567; death of, 600

Greenough, Henry, 523, 807

Greenough, Horatio, 102, 527, 807; in Europe, 340; described, 481; death of, 523-524, 528, 530; his work, 524; friend of E. T. Dana, 835-836

Greenough, John, 176, 178, 180-181, 189, 524

Greenough, Richard, 807-808

Greenough, William Whitwell, 675

Greenwood Cemetery, 434-435

Gregg, David L., 861, 864-865

Gregg, Mrs. David L., 865

Greig, John, 308, 496

Greig, Mrs. John, 308, 315, 496

Grew, Mr., 1032-1033

Griffin, 239

Griffin, Ebenezer, 266

Grimes, Leonard A., 626-627, 630, 633-635, 672, 674

Grinnell, Mrs., 1026

Grinnell, Cornelius G., 1026

Grinnell, Henry G., 1026

Grinnell, Joseph, 243-245, 256

Grip: in *Barnaby Rudge*, 58

Grisi (Madam Girard de Melcy), 669-670

Griswold, Bishop Alexander V., 113, 134-135

Griswold, Mrs. John, 409

Griswold, Rufus G., 241-242

Griswold, Rufus W., 169, 260, 262, 325-326

Griswold, Whiting, 562, 566

Gros, Baron, 945, 1032, 1058, 1067

Grote, George, 735, 743

Grote, Mrs. George, 743

Grund, Francis J., 654

Guerra, José de la, 847

Guerra, Pablo de la, 847, 918-921, 923

Guerriere, H.B.M., 391, 621-622

Guesses at Truth (Hare), 64, 108

Guild, Benjamin, 58, 102, 131, 290

Guild, Mrs. Benjamin, 265

Guild, Elizabeth, 286

Guild, Samuel, 314

Guild, Samuel E., 314

Guimaiaes, Dom Isadoro, 984, 987-988

Guimaiaes, Senora Isadoro, 984, 987-988

Gulick, Mrs., 880-881, 890, 918

Gullion, Dr., 888

Gützlaff, Karl F. A., 1056

Guy, Abel, 895-896

Gwin, McKendree, 852

Gwin, William M., 916

Habersham, Alexander W., 1016, 1019

Habersham, James, 1016

Habersham, William Neyle, 320

Habicht, Mrs., 235

Hackley, Charles William, 403-404

Hackman, Reverend, 744

Hadduck, Mr., 127

Hagar, John S., 844, 898-899

Hale, Rev. Dr., 222

Hale, Reverend, 204

Hale, Horatio E., 68

Hale, John P.: Buffalo convention (1848), 350-354; Shadrack case, 429; rescue cases, 432; presidential candidate (1852), 502; on Sumner, 503, 505; Dana's guest, 526; on Congress, 539; honored, 540-541, 543-546, 601; in Kentucky, 548

Hale, Mrs. John P., 429

Hale, Mary Ann, 207

Hale, Nathan, 338, 425-426

Haley, Mr., 208

Halifax: trips to, 71, 439-446

Halifax Fishery Arbitrations, xl

Hall, Mr., 501

Hall, Mrs. ("Aunt", Brooklyn), 306, 327, 402

Hall, Mr. and Mrs. (Mt. Washington), 646

Hall, Rev. George R., 1013, 1015-1016, 1018-1019, 1024

Hallam, Henry, 338-339, 478, 788

Hallam, Rev. Robert Alexander, 480

Hallett, Mr., 623

Hallett, Benjamin F., 67, 674; escape cases, 414-415; Sims case, 421, 425-426; at Dedham, 537; Constitutional Convention, 548, 557, 560-562, 566-567; Dana on, 623; Burns case, 638; anecdote of, 822

Hamilton, Lady, 769

Hamilton, Alexander, 253, 318, 528-529

Hamilton, Capt. Augustus Terrick, 576, 578, 585, 588-589, 592

Hamilton, James, Jr., 187

Hamilton, Paul, 622

Hamlet, 287-288, 387, 501

Hamlin, Hannibal, 1074, 1078

Hammersley, Mr. and Mrs., 818

Hammond, Mr., 341

Hammond, Mr. (Oxford University), 777

Hampden, Renn Dickson, 777
Hancock, John, 137, 498
Hancock, Franklin, 137-138
Hancock Free Bridge Corporation, 340-341
Hancock, Winfield Scott, 849
Hanscomb, Isaiah, 903
Hansen, 272
Harbord, Ensign Ralph, 588-589
Harding, Mr., 383
Harding, Reverend, 1083
Harding, Chester, 226, 379
Hardy, Mr., 769, 804
Hare, Augustus W., 64
Hare, George Harrison, 320
Hare, John I. Clark, 264, 320-325
Hare, Mrs. John I. Clark, 320
Hare, Julius Charles, 64
Hare, Dr. Robert, 260, 263, 319-320, 325
Hare, Mrs. Dr. Robert, 263
Hare, Robert H., 319-320, 323, 482
Hare, Mrs. Robert H. (Carolyn Fleming), 319-320, 323, 482
Harewell, Mr., 511, 607
Harley, Mr., 860
Harney, William Selby, 341
Harper, Emily, 257-259
Harper's Ferry: Brown raid, 364
Harper (publishing house), xvii, xxxv, 44-46, 298-299, 334-336
Harper, Robert G., 257
Harriet, (schooner): case of, 98
Harris, Benjamin W., 529
Harris, Judge Charles C., 857, 861, 885, 891
Harris, Townsend, 1017, 1023, 1058
Harrison, Mr., 495
Harrison, President William Henry, 93, 203, 254
Harrowby, Lord, 727, 743
Hart v. Hart, 407
Hart, Captain, 864, 859-861
Hart, James D., 848
Harte, Bret, 540
Hartwell, Mr., 154
Harvard College: student revolt of 1832, 20
Harvard Library Bulletin, 28
Harvard Observatory, 494-495
Harvey, Peter, 415
Haseltine, Mrs., 277
Haseltine, Miss, 277
Haskell, Mr., 890
Haskins, D. Green, 126
Hastings, Mr. (Dana relative), 417-419, 426-427, 543, 609
Hastings, Mr. (ether controversy), 359

Hastings, Mrs. E. T., 459
Hastings, Edmond, 459
Hastings, Dr. John, 311
Hastings, Mr. & Mrs. John, 499, 619
Hastings, Mrs. Lydia Dana, 174-175, 185, 215
Hastings, Dr. Serranus C., 844-845, 899
Hastings, Mrs. Serranus C., 909, 914
Hastings, Warren, 143, 715, 723, 776
Hatch, Mrs., 499, 619
Hathaway, Elnathan P., 566, 569
Hathaway, Joshua Warren, 649
Hauteville, Mme. de, 111, 229
Havelock, Sir Henry, 1099
Haven, Franklin, 428-429
Hawadji in Syria, The (Curtis), 615
Hawaiian Islands: British occupation of, 163
Hawes, Rev. Joel, 55, 96, 106, 193, 217, 221, 346
Hawes, Mary (Mrs. Henry J. Van Lennep), 217
Hawthorne, Nathaniel, xvi, 116, 278
Haxton, Mrs., 402
Hay, Mr., 441
Hay, Lord John, 91-92
Hayden v. Gracin, 112
Hayden, Grenville G., 332
Hayden, Lewis, 431-432
Haydon, Benjamin Robert, 615
Hayes, Rutherford B., xl
Hayne, Mr., 658
Hayne, Robert Young, 658
Hays, Mr., 330-331
Hayward, Mrs., 385
Hayward, Dr. George, 110, 188
Haywood, William H., Jr., 240
Hazard v. N. E. Ins. Co., 660-661
Hazard family, 1061-1062
Hazlitt, William, 827
Head, Mrs. George E., 165
Headley, Joel Tyler, 370-371
Healy, George P. A., 462, 465, 822
Heard, Mr., 983-984, 1062-1063
Heath, Upton S., 257
Heath, William, 12
Heathcote, Mr., 440
Heathcote, Sir William: Dana's host in England (1856), 720, 725, 745, 748, 750, 788-797, 799, 815; London (1860), 1129, 1131
Heathcote, Lady, 790-797, 802
Hedge, Miss, 592
Hefferd, Mr., 655
Heir of Redclyffe, The (Yonge), 663-664, 795
Helps, Sir Arthur, 1078

Hemphill, Col. Andrew T., 572
Hempstead, Charles H., 898
Henderson, Mr. (Adirondacks), 368-369
Henderson, Mr. (Japan), 1022
Henry, Captain, 1095-1096
Henry, Andrew, 908
Henry, Rev. C. S., 306
Henry, Fanny, 192
Henry the 4th, Part 2nd, 291
Henry, Rev. H. A., 900
Henry, Joseph, 320, 327
Henry, Lucy Cavendish-Bentinck, 1045
Henry, Dr. Walter, 75
Hepburn, James C., 1016, 1022
Herbert, George, 661
Herbert, Sir Percy Egerton, 757-758
Herbert, Sidney, 799-800
Herbert, Mrs. Sidney, 800
Herrick, Dr., 875
Herries, Lord, 72
Herrin, Mr., 573
Hervey, Lord, 829-830
Hewett, Mr., 143-144
Higginson, Captain, 141
Higginson, Anna, 361, 571
Higginson, Louisa, 361, 571
Higginson, Dr. Stephen, Sr., 361, 545, 551, 572
Higginson, Mrs. Stephen, Sr., 361
Higginson, Thomas Wentworth, xxviii, 629, 676
Higginson, Waldo, 28, 347
Hildreth, Mr., 304
Hildreth, Richard, 674, 841, 936
Hill, Mr., 915
Hill, Rev. W. H., 917-919, 921
Hillard, Mr., 265
Hillard, George S., xxvii-xxviii, 90, 93, 102, 114, 131, 135, 169, 215, 219, 229; Dickens dinner, 59; Allston's death, 176; Macready benefit, 291; attacks Dana, 437-438; Boston, 463; defends Dana, 472; Kossuth party, 488; Parker party, 510, 541, 674-675; Webster's death, 513, 521; Constitutional Convention, 551-556, 558, 560-561, 564, 567; attacks Dana, 552-556, 558; Federal Street Church case, 619, 665-666, 688
Hillard, Mrs. George S., 488
Hillhouse, Miss, 137-138
Hilliard, Henry Washington, 505
Hills, Bishop George, 909
Hillyar, Sir James, 439
Hines, "Elder", 115
Hiss, Mr., 674

History of Greece, The (Mitford), 127, 136
History of India (Mills), 1096
History of the Navy (Cooper), 168
Hitchcock, Lieutenant, 191
Hitchcock, Roswell Dwight, 652-653
Hoag, Mr., 915
Hoar, Judge Ebenezer Rockwood, 39, 90, 93, 406; anecdotes of, 474, 681, 832; Dana discusses, 487; Supreme Court, 535; Concord, 607; charges to Grand Jury, 643, 653; Saturday Club, 830; brother Edward, 895-896
Hoar, Edward, 895-896
Hoar, George F., 406, 1126
Hoar, Samuel, 395, 406, 438, 602, 607, 896
Hobart, John Henry (1775-1830), 308
Hobart, John Henry (b. 1817), 234
Hobhouse, Edmund, 777
Hobson, Hugh Lenox, 1038
Hodge, James Thacher, 19, 35, 92, 147, 218, 339, 385, 834
Hodge, Mrs. James Thacher, 165, 385, 492
Hodge, John, 841
Hodge, Russell, 834
Hoffman, Charles W., 117
Hoffman, David B., 849
Hoffman, Ogden, 117-118
Hogarth, Col. George, 572
Hogarth, William, 805
Holland, Sir Henry, 758, 773, 775-776
Holland, Lady, 775
Hollins, George Nichols, 658-659
Hollis Professorship of Divinity: Harvard, 689
Hollis, Thomas, 689
Holman, Dr. Francis A., 844-845, 899
Holman, Mrs. Francis A., 914
Holmes, Mr., 852
Holmes, Christopher C., 127
Holmes, Oliver Wendell, 68, 543, 830
Holt, Lord John, 508, 663
Holy Eucharist, The (Pusey), 194
Holy Living and Dying (Taylor), 127
Homans, Mr., 492
Homer, Peter B., 471
Homer, Sidney, 347, 471
Homes of American Authors, 502
Hong Kong: Dana's arrival at, 940
Hood, George, 557
Hooker, John, 223
Hooper, Mrs., 459
Hooper, Foster, 556-557, 569
Hooper, Sam, 526
"Hope" (*Two Years*), 68

Hope, Alexander James Beresford, 1129
Hope, Admiral Sir James, 945, 994
Hope, Sir John, 588
Hope, Capt. William, 588-590
Hopeton, Lord John, 588
Hopkins, Mr., 395
Hopkins, John Henry, 377
Hopkins, Thomas J., 464
Hopkinson, Mr., 568
Hoppin, Reverend, 624
Hornet, U.S.S., 622
Horsford, E. B., 600
Horsford, Eben Norton, 835
Hosher, John, 139
Hosmer, Ebenezer Mason, 419
Hosmer, Z., 393
Hotchkiss, Captain: case of, 616
Hough, Benjamin K., 295
Howard, Benjamin C., 236
Howard, Joseph, 270, 649-650, 653
Howard, William George, 749
Howe, Mr. (Canandaigua, N.Y.), 307-308
Howe, Mr. (Portland, Me.), 87
Howe, Rev. A. D., 64, 98
Howe, Estes, 391
Howe, George, 761
Howe, Josiah, 117
Howe, Samuel Gridley, 93, 118, 131,
    149; political views, 391; Dana's host,
    463; at Homer party, 471; Dana's
    guest, 479; Kossuth party, 488-489;
    Murray dinner, 540; anecdote of, 601;
    Burns rescue attempt, 629; Saturday
    Club, 669; Fusion meeting, 677
Howe, Mrs. Samuel Gridley (Julia
    (Ward), 118, 149, 463, 479, 488
Howell, Judge, 308
Howell, Alexander, 308
Howell, Thomas, 308
Howell, Mrs. Thomas, 315
Howqua (d. 1843), 229, 952
Howqua (1810–1863), 952, 954, 968,
    976-979, 981-982
Howsey, Miss, 258
Hoxse, Elizabeth, 126
Hoyt, Mr. (artist), 107, 272-274
Hu, Mr., 970-971
Hubbard, Gardiner G., 478
Hubbard, Judge Samuel, 88, 106, 659
Hubbard, William J., 138-139, 616
Hubbell, Mr., 275, 307-308
Hubbell, Walter, 275-277, 308
Hubert, Mr., 402
Huc, Evariste R., 930, 932-933, 969,
    1046
Hudson, Henry Norman, 298, 327, 476,
    675

Hughes v. Thompson, 397
Hughes, Mr., 1044-1047
Hughes, Archbishop John Joseph, 435,
    584-585, 964
Hugo, Victor, 480
Hull, Isaac, 621-622
"Human Life" (Rogers), 716
Humboldt, Friedrich H. A., 852
Hume, David, 784
Hume, Joseph, 753
Hume, Joseph Burnley, 753
Hungerford and McCurdy v. Perkins, 96
Hunt, William Holman, 752-753, 1100
Hunter, Lieutenant, 160
Hunter, Mr. (Adirondacks), 362-363,
    375
Hunter, Mrs., 375
Hunter, Mr. (China), 985, 987, 988
Huntington, Mr., 568
Huntington, Charles P., 559-561, 568
Hurlbert, William Henry, 736
Hussy family, 818
Hutchins, Mr., 258
Hutchinson, C. I., 915
Hutchinson, Mrs. Corrine Elliott, 25-26,
    385
Huxford, Mr. (Oxford), 638
Hyslop, Miss, 399

Iago, 340
Ibrahim, Pacha, 1103-1104
Idle Man, The (Dana), 11
Il Penseroso (Milton), 1136
Inches, the Misses, 223
Inches, Miss, 166
Inches, Henderson B., Jr., 165-166, 223,
    591
Independence (ship), 122
India: native rebellion in (1857),
    1098-1099
Ingersoll, Charles Jared, 487
Ingersoll, Joseph R., 256
Ingham, Charles C., 129
Ingham, Robert, 719, 725, 745
Ingraham, Mr., 866
Irvine, Col. John George, 576, 578
Irving, Mr., 308
Irving, Edward, 1022
Irving, Washington, 110, 308, 782
Island City Salvage case, 833
Isle of Shoals, 197-210
Israel, Mr., 240
Ives, Mrs. (Canandaigua, N.Y.), 308
Ives, Mrs. Robert H. (Providence), 110

Jackson, Mr., 198
Jackson, Professor Abner, 96, 192
Jackson, Mrs. Abner, 95, 192
Jackson, Andrew, 186-187, 203, 241
Jackson, Catherine, 232
Jackson, Charles, 542
Jackson, Dr. Charles T., 330-331, 345, 358
Jackson, Francis (Frank), 192, 362-363, 366, 375
Jackson, Mrs. Francis, 362-363
Jackson, Capt. Francis H., 28
Jackson, Joseph, 542
Jackson, Patrick, 183
Jackson, Mrs. Patrick, Jr., 146
Jackson, Patrick T., 323
Jackson, William, 395, 406
James, Charles Tillinghast, 544
James, Mrs. Charlotte Dana, 418
James, Robert, 399
Jane Eyre (Brontë), 936
Januarius, Saint, miracle of, 522
Japan As It Was and Is (Hildreth), 936
Jarvis, Mr., 860
Jarvis, Elizabeth, 399
Jarvis, Hetty, 399
Jarvis, Com. Joseph R. (U.S.N.), 571, 598
Jarvis, Leonard, 224-225
Jay, Miss, 119
Jay, John, 119, 161, 253, 409, 818
Jay, William, 161
Jefferson, Thomas, 203, 250, 260, 389
Jeffrey, Dr., 292-297
Jeffrey, Mr. and Mrs., 308
Jeffrey, Francis, 394
Jenkins, Miss, 252
Jenkins, Fred (Shadrack), 410-411, 413-414
Jennison, Dr., 213
Jermyn, Earl, 830
Jewett, George Kimball, 605-606
Jewett, Mrs. George Kimball, 606
Jijibhai, Sir Custeebjee, 1084
Jijibhai, Sir Jamestjee, 1084
Jimeno, Angustias, 847
Jimeno, Manuel, 847
John Adams, U.S.S., 210, 898
John Halifax, Gentleman (Mulock), 936
Johnson, Captain, 871-872
Johnson, Miss (of Buffalo), 354
Johnson, Mr. (mate on *Mastiff*), 857-858
Johnson, Reverend (St. John's church, New York), 306
Johnson, Reverend (China), 1063
Johnson, Alfred, 348

Johnson, Andrew, 39
Johnson, James Neely, 920, 922
Johnson, Mrs. James Neely, 920
Johnson, Reverdy, 236, 544
Johnson, Dr. Samuel, 25, 53, 715, 718
Johnson, Capt. William O., 857-862, 864-865
Johnson, Mrs. William O., 857-861
Johnson, Mrs. William S., 117, 264, 390
Johnston, James William, 440
Johnston, S. H. F., 572
Johnstone family (of Armendale), 152
Johnstone, Lockhart, 392
Johnstone, Sir W., 392
Jones, Admiral (China), 994, 1045-1046
Jones, Captain, 49-50, 92
Jones, Miss, 1050
Jones, Mr. (chaplain of *Columbia*), 61
Jones, Lieutenant (China), 1046
Jones, Frederick, 90
Jones, Jacob, 118
Jones, John W., 240-241
Jones, Capt. Oliver J., 998, 1044, 1061
Jones, Samuel, 475-476
Jones, Thomas Ap, 155
Jones, General Walter, 994, 1050
Jordan, Captain, 465
"Journal of a Voyage to the North West Coast, 1798-99" (Curson), 126
Journey Through the Chinese Empire, A (Huc), 930
Joy, Miss, 491
Judd, Gerrit Parmele, 885
Judd, Mrs. Gerrit Parmele, 889-890
Judicial Tenure: debate on, 556-560
Judkins, Captain, 55, 816-817, **1137**
Judon, Cuthbert C., 116
Judson, Andrew T., 487
Julian, George Washington, 548

Kalafsa's riding school, 549
Kalloch, Rev. Isaac S., 833
Kamehameha, I, 863, 868
Kamehameha, III, 163
Kamehameha, IV, 861, 863-865, 867
Kamehameha, V (Prince Lot), 861
Kane, Elisha Kent, 893, 896
Kansas Nebraska Act, xxviii, 618
Kasson, Newton, 348, 354
Kean, Charles John, 288, 463, 705, 731
Kean, Mrs. Charles John, 463, 731
Kean, Edmund, 340, 705, 897
Kearny, Stephen W., 921
Keats, John, xli

Keble, John, 777, 791-793
Keefe, David, 107
Keenan, General, 1063
Kellogg, Mr., 570
Kemble, Fanny, 290, 381, 826-827
Kemble, John H., 845
Kemble, John Philip, 835
Kendall, Mr., 229
Kendall, Dr. Pierson Thurston, 385-386, 428, 530
Kenetry, Mr., 707
Kenilworth (Scott), 784
Kennedy, John P., 244-245, 256
Kennedy, Mrs. John P., 245
Kennon, Beverly, 242-244
Kenshaw, Mr., 1111
Kent, Duke of, 443
Kent, Edward, 649-650, 687
Kent, William, 408
Kenyon, John, 49
Kerr, John Glasgow, 975
Keyes, Edward L., 540, 545, 555-556, 568
Kildare, Marquis of, 749
Kildare, Marchioness of, 749
Kilham, Mrs., 305
Killam, Mr., 227
Killam, Mary, 231
Killan, Miss, 360
Killean, Mrs., 95
King, Captain, 1077
King, Mr. (China), 941
King, James Gore, 1138
King, John Alsop, 1138
King, Rufus, 164
King, Mrs. Taunton, 399
King, Thomas Starr, 540, 675
King, Samuel W., 67
Kinglake, Alexander, 758
King's College, 443
Kingsley, Mrs., 393
Kingsley, James L., 91
Kinnaird, the Misses, 583
Kinnaird, Lord Arthur, 757, 765-766, 1137
Kinnaird, Lord Charles, 152, 392, 417, 583, 757
Kinnaird, Hon. Helen, 757
Kip, Bishop William I., 231, 844-845, 898, 901, 909
Kip, Mrs. William I., 914
Kirk, Rev. Edward N., 108, 127, 163
Kirkland, John Thornton, 524, 682
Kittredge, Mr., 926-927, 938
Kittredge, Mr., 1078
Klyskowski, Count, 987, 990, 998, 1044

Knapp, Mr., 524
Knight, Mr. (Japan), 1016
Knights, Mr., 822
Knopf, Mr., 56
Know Nothing party, xxix, 665
Knowles, Mr., 110
Knowlton, John S. C., 558-559, 569
Knowlton, Miles Justine, 1052, 1054, 1056
Knowlton Mill case, 833
Koopmanschapp, Mr., 895
Kosciuszko, Tadeuz, 404
Kossuth, Louis, xviii, 474-476, 488-489, 520-521, 652, 898
Kossuth, Mme. Louis, 488-489
Krapp, Mr., 174
Kuhn, Miss, 459

Labouchere, Henry (Baron Taunton), 730, 742, 749
Labouchere, Lady Mary, 749
LaCreevy, Miss: in *Nicholas Nickleby*, 59
Ladd, George W., 605-606
Lafayette, Marquis de, 12
La Favorita (Donizetti), 409
LaGranger, Mr., 705
Laighton, Thomas B., 200, 201-202, 220
Laighton's Hotel, 209
Lake, Sir Henry Atwell, 731-732
Lamartine, Alphonse D., 525
Lamb, Mrs., Philadelphia school of, 326
Lamb, Charles, 446, 717
Lambton, Miss, 773, 775
Lambton, Mr., 773
Lambton, Ensign Frederick W., 588, 775
Lambton, John George, 773
Lambton, William Henry, 773
Landseer, Edwin Henry, 749, 768-770
Landseer, John, 749
Lane, George Martin, 619, 653
Lane, Joseph, 1074
Lane, Lt. William Melville, 1097-1099
Langdon, Mrs., 596
Langdon, Woodbury, 399
Langdon, Mrs. Woodbury, 399
Langdon, Woodbury G., 399
Langton, Mr., 718
Lanklaen, Mr. and Mrs., 828-829
Lannean, Reverend, 98
Lansdale, Lord, 742-743
Lansdowne, Marquis of, 727, 742-743, 746-748, 757-759, 788, 815, 831, 1129
Lapham, John, 581

Lardner, Dr., 58
Latham, Mr., 428
Latham, Gov. Milton S., 898, 916, 918, 920-924
Latham, Mrs. Milton S., 918, 920, 922, 924
Laughlan, Father, 78, 82
Laurencel, Henri, 911
Laurie, Thomas, 65
Lawler, Mr., 841, 899
Lawler, Mrs. (Miss Price), 899, 914
Lawrence, Abbott, 52, 54, 129, 141, 291, 396, 470-471
Lawrence, Mrs. Abbott, 52, 138
Lawrence, Amos A., 52, 297, 319, 593, 628
Lawrence, Anna, 315
Lawrence, Sir George St. Patrick, 1099
Lawrence, Sir Henry Montgomery, 1099
Lawrence, James, 621
Lawrence, Joseph E., 915, 922
Lawrence, William Beach, xxxix, xl
Lawrence, William Richard, 592-593
Lawrence, Mrs. William Richard (Susan C. Dana), 592-593
Leary, Captain, 705
Leavett, William P., 358-359
Leavitt, Joshua, 352-353, 355
Lectures on Art and Poetry by Washington Allston, 187
Lectures on the Works and Genius of Washington Allston (Ware), 187
Lee family of Virginia, xxiii, 214, 337
Lee, Captain, 62-63
Lee, Ann Harriette, 253
Lee, Charles Carter, 337-338
Lee, Francis, 363, 375, 501
Lee, Mrs. Francis, 371
Lee, Henry ("Light Horse Harry"), 252-253
Lee, Henry, 375, 501, 833
Lee, Robert E., 252-253, 337, 364
Lee, Mrs. Robert E., 253
Lee, Mrs. Thomas, 609
Lee, Zaccheus Collins, 257
Legare, Hugh S., 254
Legouve, Ernest, 681
LeGrand, Mr., 842
Leland, John, 875
Lemmon, Jonathan, 825
Lemmon slave case, 825
Leonard, Major Hiram, 841
Leonard, Mrs. Hiram, 899
Leslie, Charles Robert, 268, 720-721, 749, 1131
Leslie, Mrs. Charles Robert, 1131
Leslie, Eliza, 129, 138

"Letter to a Noble Lord, A" (Burke), 43
Letters from England (Mrs. Bancroft), 107
Levant (ship), 118
Lever, Charles James, 1047
Leveson-Gower, Granville (Marquis of Stafford), 186
Lewis, Mr., 936
Lewis, Sir George, 721
Lewis, Samuel, 352
Lexington (ship), 25
Lhomond, Francois, 19
Libby, Joseph E., 220
Liberator, The, 337
Libois, Pere, 1062
Lieber, Francis, 93, 474, 665
Lies, Mr., 155
Liés, Eugene, 895-896, 898
Life and Letters of Joseph Story (Story), 427
Life and Letters of Washington Allston, The (Flagg), 187
Life and Times of Frederick Douglass, 161
Life in California (Robinson), 847
Life of Charlotte Brontë, The (Gaskell), 936-937
Lightbody v. DeCamp, 92
Lilly, Chris, 105
Lilon, Mr., 99
Limelight (lamp), 245
Lincoln, Abraham, xv, xxx, xxxix, 491, 861, 985, 1074, 1078
Lincoln, George, 343-344, 656
Lincoln, Levi, 543, 690
Lincoln, Rodney G., 642
Lind, Jenny, 743
Lindau, Rudolph, 1030, 1033-1046, 1048, 1057, 1060
Lindsay v. Delano, 158
Lingard, John, 784
Little, Charles Coffin, 615, 619
Little, Mrs. Charles Coffin (Abby Wheaton), 615, 619, 822, 829
Little Henry and His Bearer (Sherwood), 31
Livermore, Isaac, 341, 567
Liverpool, Lord, 788
Lives of the Chief Justices (Campbell), 472, 508
Livingston, Dr. David, 1078
Livingston, Henry B., 918
Ljungstedt, Sir Andrew, 986
Lloyd, the Misses, 253
Lloyd, John, 253
Locke, Mr., 841
Lockhart, Mr., 507

Lockhart, John G., 507
Loco-Focoism, 73
Lodge, Mr., 598
Logan, Mr., 639
Lombard, Mr., 736
Long, Henry, 413
Longfellow, Charles, 491
Longfellow, Edith, xli, 56
Longfellow, Henry Wadsworth, xvii, xli, 49, 102, 126, 129, 139, 169, 507, 543, 619; with Dickens, 56; *Poems on Slavery*, 107; engagement of, 159; Macready's benefit, 291; Dana's host, 305; Sarah visits, 428; gives party, 432; Dana's neighbor, 437; Robert Wheaton's funeral, 464; at Norton's, 476; Scherb lecture, 478; at opera, 482; Dana's guest, 484, 489, 503, 526, 539, 540, 833; Kossuth party, 488; children's party, 492-493; his children, 526; Lowell dinner, 529; Dana's host, 615, 820; Choate on, 686; autograph of, 705; poems in ballad book, 724; Saturday Club, 830
Longfellow, Mrs. Henry Wadsworth, 305, 476, 482, 488, 492-493, 526. *See also* Appleton, Frances E.
Longfellow, Samuel, 126
Loomis v. Newhall, 538
Lord, Reverend (Boston), 124
Lord, Reverend (China), 1049-1050
"Lord Acton's American Diaries," 553
Lord Chancellor of England (Baron Turno), 470
Lord, Daniel, Jr., 92, 119, 241, 244, 255-256, 327, 338, 390, 408
Lord, George E., 531
Lord, H. C., 358-359
Lord, Nathaniel, 533
Lord, Otis P., 554, 563, 568, 690
Loring, Charles G., 39, 43, 56, 60-61, 92, 160, 432; courtroom manner, 146-147; ether controversy, 331; Sims counsel, 420-421, 423, 426; Franklin Haven controversy, 429; Webster's death, 513-514; Dana dreams of, 599; Greenleaf memorial, 600; Burns case, 628; anecdote of Webster, 659-661; opinion of English juries, 662; *Younger v. Gloucester*, 668; Dana dines with, 833
Loring, Edward G., 59, 339, 626-627, 631-633, 671-674
Loring, Ellis G., 60-61, 411

Loring, Francis C., 44
Lorn, Marquis of, 732
Lothrop, Samuel K., 52, 110, 469-471, 556, 564, 598
Lott, Captain, 74
Louise, Queen of Prussia, 744
Lovejoy, Elijah P., 161
Lovering, Joseph, 834
Lovering, Warren, 601
Low, Gorham P., 295
Lowell, Mrs., 707
Lowell, James Russell, xvii; at Longfellow's, 432; gives dinner, 529; Dana's guest, 539, 829, 833; character of, 615; Saturday Club, 666, 669, 830; Palfrey dinner, 830
Lowell, Mrs. James Russell, 432
Lowell, John, 70
Lowndes, Charles, 1060
Lucas, Mr., 614
Lucy, Mrs., 781
Ludlow, Augustus C., 621
Lumpkin, Robert, 639
Lunt, Miss, 525
Lunt, George, 414-415, 431, 509, 514, 531-533
Lunt, William Parsons, 525
Lushington, Stephen, 663
Luther v. Ocean Ins. Co., 56
Lyell, Charles, 71, 74
Lyle, Reverend (China), 995-997, 1033-1044, 1058-1059
Lyman, Arthur Theodore, 583, 818-819
Lyman, Charles, 229
Lyman, David Belden, Sr., 875, 878-879, 890, 918, 1027
Lyman, Mrs. David Belden, Sr. (Sarah Joiner), 878-880
Lyman, David Belden, Jr., 878-880, 883
Lyman, Ellen, 878
Lyman, Emma W., 878-881
Lyman, Frank, 878
Lyman, Frederick S., 875-880
Lyman, Henry Munson, 878
Lyman, Rufus Anderson, 878
Lyman, Theodore, 131, 230, 459
Lynch, Adele, 153, 990. *See also* Watson, Mrs. William
Lynch, Dominick, 990
Lyndhurst, Lord (John Singleton Copley), 747-748, 750, 757-759
Lyon, Mr., 367
Lyon, Henry, 90, 319

Macaulay, Thomas B., xvii, 143, 772-774, 882, 1135-1136
Macbeth, 290-291
Macedonian (ship), 127
Macgregor, John, 768-769
Maclagan, Mr., 553
Macondray, Frederick W., 909
Macondray, Mrs. Frederick W., 914
Mackenzie, Alexander Slidell: the *Somers* mutiny affair, xix-xx, 112-113, 117-119, 122, 124-125, 143, 148, 152, 160, 168-169, 215, 218, 398-399
Mackenzie, Mrs. Alexander Slidell, 118-119
Mackenzie, Ranald Slidell, 118
Mackintosh, Robert, 49, 526, 749, 788
Mackintosh, Mrs. Robert (Miss Appleton), 49, 493
Macready, William C., xvii-xviii, 224-225, 287-291, 340
Macy, Mr., 868
Madhavadras, Karsandros, 1090
Madison, President James, 601
Maguire, Captain, 1045-1046
Maine Law, 505-506
Malins, Mr., 726
Mallett, Captain, 867-868
Man, Sir C., monument of, 526
"Man of the Mountain" (Franconia, N.H.), 278
Manchester (Mass.): purchase of Dana land in, 304
Mandan, Mrs. (Miss O'Sullivan), 834
Mangum, William P., 240
Mann, Horace, 93, 334-336, 424, 506, 533, 732
Manners, Lord John, 159
Mansfield, Sir William Rose, 1099
Manter, Captain, 868
March, Charles Wainwright, 379-380, 383
March, Nathaniel B., 606
March, Sarah Drisko, 606
Marcy, William Leonard, 366
Mario, Guiseppe, 669-670
Marion v. Moody, 616
Mariotti, Professor, 76
Marlborough, Duke of, 726
Marquand, J. P., xviii
Marsh, Abigail ("Aunt Abby"), 95, 124, 158, 305, 832
Marsh, Eben, 831
Marsh, Frances Ann ("Fanny"), 684
Marsh, George P., 338
Marsh, James, 30, 376
Marsh, John, 40, 217, 261
Marsh, John S., 319

Marsh, Rev. John T., 47, 138, 158, 475; in Brooklyn, 306, 333, 390, 408, 684; death of John Watson, 359-360; Wethersfield, 389; rescue trials, 415; in Bangor, 446; death of Nancy Marsh, 831
Marsh, Mrs. John T., 116, 118, 327, 332, 527
Marsh, Laura, 453
Marsh, Lydia, 49, 95, 124, 305, 389, 490-491, 494, 832, 1119
Marsh, Mary, 831
Marsh, Nancy, 40-41, 95, 124, 130; visits Boston, 225-227, 416, 526; at Niagara Falls, 305-306, 313; at Rochester, 311; at Albany, 316-317; death of, 831-832
Marshall, Edward Colston, 924
Marshall, Justice John, 518, 616
Marshall, Marian, 135, 138
Marten, Capt. Francis, 1044-1046, 1058, 1061
Martin, Mr., 184-185
Martha, Aunt. *See* Allston, Mrs. Washington
Martineau, Harriet, 665, 937
Martyn, Henry, 89
Mary Ellen (ship): loss of, 1001-1002
Mary Pauline case, 132
Mason, the Misses, 253
Mason, Mr., 439
Mason, Reverend, 295
Mason, George, 253
Mason, James M., 398, 503-504
Mason, Jeremiah, 102, 160, 225, 1124-1125; anecdote of, 229; political position, 285-286; Story memorial, 321; Dartmouth College case, 518
Mason, Jonathan, 226
Mason, Lowell, 130
Mason, Thomas, 253
Massachusetts Constitutional Convention. *See* Constitutional Convention of Massachusetts
Massachusetts Historical Society, 28
Massachusetts Ploughman, 90
Mastiff (ship), 837, 857-862
Matson, Mrs. (Elizabeth Strong), 95-96
Matthews, Robert, 72
Matthias. *See* Matthews, Robert
Maurice, Fredrick Denison, 579
Maxey, Virgil, 242-243
May, Charles A., 339
May, Samuel J., 161-162
Mayer, Brantz, 257, 259
Mayo, Mr., 534
McAllister, Hall, 844-845, 855

McAllister, Matthew Hall, 844-845, 855
McAllister, Samuel W., 844-845, 909
McCall, Peter, 262
McCall, Mrs. Peter, 264
McCarty, Rev. Dr., 1050, 1056
McCarty, Mrs., 1056
McCoy, Reverend, 293
McCoy, Tom, 105
McCullough, Mr., 719, 776, 815
McCurdy, Mr., 479
McDaniel, Mr., 673
McDonald, William, 906
McDonald, Mrs. William, 906-907
McDougal, Capt. David Stockton, 903, 909
McDougall, James Alexander, 915, 922, 924
McDougall, Mrs. James Alexander, 919-920, 922, 924
McGowan, Ellen, 444
McGowen, Edward ("Ned"), 924
McGregor, Mrs., 390
McHenry, James, 257, 258
McHenry, James Howard, 257
McKay, Rev. Mr., 1071
McKay, Donald, 857
McKean, Henry Swazey, 14
McKean, John George, 338
McKee, William R., 343
McKeen, John, 652-653
McKeen, Joseph, 651-652
McKill, Dr., 581
McKinley, Justice John, 241, 245, 256-257, 844
McKinnon, Captain, 761
McLane, Louis, 257, 259
McLane, Robert M., 259-260, 264
McLaughlin v. Calahan, 535
McLean, Mr., 305, 312
McLean, Mrs., 312
McLean, Justice John, 38, 241, 245, 347-348, 350, 471
McLean, Mrs. John, 245
McLeod v. Peterson, 65
McLeod, Kate, 991. *See also* Bourbulon, Mme. de
McMurtie, Henry, 326
McNary, James M. Beach, 598
Meade, Dr., 1078-1081, 1095
Meade, Miss, 571
Meadows, Thomas Taylor, 999, 1033
Medici, Marquis Simone Peruzzi de, 693
Meigs, Ann, 277
Melcy, Mme. Girard de (Grisi), 669-670
Mellen, Mr., 892
Mellus, Francis, 848-849
Mellus, Henry, 848–849, 924

Melville, Herman, 112, 399, 441; *Redburn*, xxxv; *Typee*, xxxvi; Russell party, 336; friendship with Dana, 336-337; Dana's guest, 348
Melvin, Olive (Mrs. Joseph Baldwin), 106
Memoir of Rev. Henry Martyn (Sargent), 67
Memoirs and Confessions (Reinhard), 62
Memoirs of the Life of Sir Samuel Romilly, 654-655
Memorial of Daniel Webster from the City of Boston, A, 521
Mendelssohn, Felix, 743
Merchant, Charles Spencer, 849, 899
Merchant of Venice, The, 289-290, 1117
Meritens, Baron de, 1044, 1046-1047
Mermet, Abbé, 1027-1028
Merriam, Miss, 721-722
Merrick, Judge Pliny, 616, 690
Merrimac (frigate), 677
Merwanjee, Dossabhoy, 1080, 1083
Metcalf, George, 433
Metcalf, Julia. *See* Metcalf, Mrs. Thernon
Metcalf, Theodore, 360, 362, 366-367, 369, 371-375, 606, 692
Metcalf, Judge Thernon, 174, 521, 1069; Episcopal convention, 304; Dana's guest, 348; on Lemuel Shaw, 415, 689; at Plymouth, 428; his memory, 533; Constitutional Convention, 556; death of wife, 821
Metcalf, Mrs. Thernon (Julia), 165, 174-175, 190, 329, 821-822
Metcalfe, Sir Charles, 141
Metropolitan Police case, 825
Metzdorf, Robert F.: editorial work, 3, 8, 11-13, 15, 17, 23, 34, 36
Mexico as it Is and Was (Mayer), 257
Meyer, Mrs., 553
Meyers, William H., 220
Miantonomo, 63
Middle Kingdom, The (Williams), 925, 930
Might, John, 366, 368-369
Might, Mrs. John, 366
Mildmacy, Sir Henry St. John, 582
Mill, James, 1096
Miller, Captain, 1096
Miller, Mr., 881
Miller, Mrs. (Captain), 1096
Miller, Jacob W., 245
Miller, James, 311
Miller, Peter, 98
Millerite movement, 106, 130, 142-143, 216
Mills, Charles H., 217
Mills, Mrs. Charles H., 217

Mills, Elijah Hunt, 601
Mills, John, 349
Millspaugh, Mr., 631
Milton, John, 376, 472, 478, 1133, 1136
Minot, Francis, 169
Minot, George, 416
Minot, George Francis, 129
Minot, Julia, 143, 169, 667-668
Minot, William, Sr., (1783–1873), 108, 129, 169, 217, 317, 624-625
Minot, Mrs. William, Sr. (Louisa Davis), 217, 286, 436
Minot, William, Jr. (1817–1894), 108, 139, 143, 169, 429-430, 480, 533
Minot, Mrs. William, Jr. (Katharine M. Sedgwick), 128-129, 139, 143, 158, 169, 223, 480
Missouri Compromise, xxviii
Mitchell, Judge, 96, 193
Mitchell, Mrs., 193
Mitchell, James, 529
Mitchell, John Murray, 1087
Mitford, William, 127, 136
Mito, Prince of, 1017
Mole, Reverend, 1050
Moliere, 808-809
Montagneux, Père, 1047
Montague, Basil, 755
Montauban, Gen. Charles A. Cousin, 1001, 1032-1034
Montcalm, Marquis Louis Joseph de, 575
Monteagle, Lord, 743, 746, 758
Monterey, battle of, 155, 605
Montgomery, Mr., 864
Montgomery, Richard, 574
Montgomery, Richard Roger, 320
Montgomery, Mrs. Richard Roger, 320
Moore, J. H., 27
Moore, Michael, 826, 828
Moore, Nathaniel F., 264, 400
Moore, Thomas, 50, 541, 615, 897
Morgan, Captain, 894
Morgan, Julius S., 761
Morgan, Mary Ann, 138
Morison, Dr., 895
Morison, Reverend, 895
Mormon meeting, 142
Morpeth, Lord, 50, 52-54, 59, 179
Morricay, Kitty, 80, 83
Morrill, Lot Myrick, 604
Morris, Charles, 621-622
Morris, Charles D., 510
Morris, Gouveneur, 682, 909
Morris, Henry W., 61
Morris, Sir James Nicoll, 510
Morris, Robert, 411, 432, 466, 469, 472, 478

Morrisey, John, 844
Morrison, Mrs., 914
Morrison, John Robert, 985, 1004
Morrison, Robert, 985, 1050
Morse, Jeremiah, 659-660
Morse, Samuel F. B., 188-191, 193, 286
Morton, Judge, 490
Morton, Elbridge G., 570
Morton, Marcus, Sr. (1784–1864), 406, 551, 556, 559, 566, 690
Morton, Marcus, Jr. (1819–1891), 559, 562
Morton, William T. G., 330-332, 345, 519
Moseley, Mr., 316
Motley, John Lothrop, 830, 986
Mount Vernon, 245-251
Mountford, William, 539
Mowatt, Anna C. O., 463
Mowry, Sylvester, 844
Moxon, Edward, 49-50, 55, 92, 169
Muckie (Sumatra), destruction of, 210
Mullins, Mr., 726
Mulock, Dinah, 936
Murad, Lazarus L., 520
Murdoch, Beamish, 440
Murietta, Joaquin, 854
Murphy, Mr., 623
Murray, B. B., 540
Murray, Charles August, 309
Murray, John, 897, 1120
Myers, Lt. Williams, 841

Naosuke, II, 1017
Napier, Lord Francis, 693
Napier, Sir Joseph, 726
Napier, Sir Robert John M., 1047
Napier, William: Atlantic crossing, 693-698, 703, 706-709, 733
Napoleon, 70, 472, 607
Narrative of a Mission to China and Japan in 1857-59 (Oliphant), 1012
Narrative of the Expedition of an American Squadron to the China Seas and Japan (Perry), 939
Nash, Mr., 364
Nash, Lonson, 295
"Nativity Hymn" (Milton), 478
Natural History of Enthusiasm (Taylor), 1079-1080
Naval Expedition to Japan (1853), 617
Nayson, Jonathan, 569-570
Neal, John, 655
Nebraska: free soil question, 617-618
Neilson, Mr., 861-864
Nelson v. Richardson, 542

Nelson, Lord, 766-767, 769-770, 788, 803-804, 835

Nestorians, 1049

Nevius, Rev. John Livingston, 1050, 1052-1054, 1056-1057

Nevius, Mrs. John Livingston, 1056-1057

New American Practical Navigator, The (Bowditch), 27, 929

New Haven: railroad accident (1853), 546-547

New York Copyright Club, 214

New Zealand, Bishop of. *See* Selwyn, George Augustus

Newall, Reverend, 609

Newell, Charles Stark, 319

Newman, Mr., 860

Newman, John Henry, 287, 777

Newton, Miss, 340

Newton, Mr., 208

Newton, Edward A., 340, 433

Newton, Isaac, 1137

Newton, John, 121-122

Niagara Falls, 305-316

Niblo, William, 306, 405

Niblo's garden. *See* Niblo, William

Nicholas ("the big French man"), 155

Nicholas, Commodore John, 540-541

Nicholas Nickleby (Dickens), 59, 204

Nichols, Dr., 531

Nichols, Dr. (of Savannah), 598

Nichols, Mrs., 544, 551, 1009

Nicholson, Mrs., 428

Nicholson, John, 1099

Nicholson, Commodore John B., 110-111, 127, 223, 229

Nicoll, Henry, 117, 408

Nightingale, Florence, 799-800

Niphon, case of, 574

Noble, William Henry, 580

Noel, Gerard Thomas, 793

Norfolk, Duke of, 750, 774

Norma, 669-670

North Carolina (ship), 117-118

Northcote, Sir Stafford Henry, 726

Norton, Andrews, 102, 129; death of Allston, 174; gives large party, 266, 482; at theater, 287, 290; at Macready benefit, 291; Dana's host, 476; Dana's guest, 543; death of, 600; recollection of, 682

Norton, Mrs. Andrews, 56, 131, 218, 287, 482, 807-809

Norton, Caroline Sheridan, 744

Norton, Charles Eliot, 56; at Robert Wheaton's funeral, 464; visits Himalayas, 467; at opera, 482; Scherb

lecture, 487; Dana's guest, 489, 526; at children's party, 492-493; with Lord Acton, 553; death of father, 600; in Paris, 807-809

Norton, Judge Edward, 895, 899

Norton, Grace, 56, 286, 290, 526, 807

Norton, Jane, 56, 286-287, 290; at Sears party, 229; at Ticknor party, 265; at opera, 482; Dana's guest, 489, 526; her appearance, 775; Paris, 807-810

Nouise, Miss, 571

Noyes family, 646

Nugent v. Oden, 65

Nunnery Committee, 674

Nutford's, 210

Nye, Mr. (at Macao), 983-984, 986-987, 1063

Oatley, Anne (Mrs. Stubbs), 419

Oatley, Rev. George Kinnaird, 418-419

Oatley, Mrs. George Kinnaird (Helen Kinnaird Dana), 418

Oatley, Helen Kinnaird (Mrs. Parsons), 419

Oatley, John, 418-419

Oatley, Joseph, 419, 786-787

Oatley, William Henry, 419

O'Brien, Reverend, 75-76

O'Brien, Mr., 444

O'Brien, John P. J., 344, 657

O'Connor, Charles, 475

"O'Connor's Child" (Campbell), 291

"Ode on the Intimations of Immortality" (Wordsworth), 36, 1119

"Ode to Georgiana" (Coleridge), 813

Odenheimer, William Henry, 262

Odyssey (tr. Cowper), 227

Ogle, Capt. Charles, 698, 700, 703, 706, 749

"Old Cumberland Beggar" (Wordsworth), 291

Old Curiosity Shop, The (Dickens), 64

Old Robert (Catalina), 154

Oliphant, Laurence, 1012, 1025

Olive, 89, 96, 101, 163

Oliver family, 330

Oliver, Mr. (Prescott case), 483

Oliver, Mr. (of Middletown, Conn.), 598

Oliver, Mrs. (Elizabeth Shaw), 361

Oliver, Andrew, 333

Oliver, James, 153

Oliver Twist (Dickens), 57

Olmsted, Professor Denison, 123, 227

Olney, James N., 898
Olyphant, David W. C., 1061
Olyphant, Robert, 1061-1062
Olyphant, Robert Morrison, 310, 1061-1062
Olyphant, Mrs. Robert Morrison, 1061-1062
"On the Removal of Judge Woodbury Davis" (Dana), 687
"On This Day I Complete My Thirty Sixth Year" (Byron), 897
Ordway, Alfred T., 594-595
Oregon: boundary question, 136-137
Oregon Trail, The (Parkman), 758
Orne, Mr. (China), 947, 949-950, 967, 971-972, 977, 981-982
Osborn, William Henry, 617
Osgood, Mr., 364, 373-374
Osprey, case of, 662-663
O'Sullivan, Mr., 1068
O'Sullivan, John L., 117-118, 232
Otey, Bishop James Hervey, 297-298
Othello, 340, 460
Otis, Edmund D., 925
Otis, Harrison Gray, Sr., 52-53, 146, 164, 291, 485
Otis, Harrison Gray, Jr., 223, 230, 469
Otis, William F., 230, 410, 595
Outram, Sir James, 1098-1099
Owen, Mr., 406
Owen, Mr. (China), 961
Oxford, Mr., 638
Oxford, Bishop of. *See* Wilberforce, Bishop Samuel
Oxford Tracts, 146
Oxford University Act of 1854, 510

Packard, Reverend, 480
Packard, Alpheus Spring, 652-653
Page, John H. W., 158
Paige, James W., 563
Paine, Judge Elijah, 825
Paine, Henry W., 687
Pakenham, Sir Richard, 253
Paki, Bernice Pauahi (Mrs. C. R. Bishop), 862-863, 865, 885, 889
Palanjee, Mr., 1078
Palfray, Charles W., 90, 197, 319, 337
Palfrey, Miss, 526
Palfrey, Francis Winthrop, 570, 1062
Palfrey, John G., xxiii, xxx, 59, 91, 354, 551; Dana speaks in support of, 392, 394, 419; political views of, 389, 391, 479; Free Soil Convention (1850), 395; Free Soil party meeting (1850),

406; Sims case, 424; Homer party, 471; Dana's host, 477, 547; Dana's guest, 485, 503, 821, 829, 833; on Whig Convention of 1847, 486; on Edward Everett, 497; anecdotes of Congress, 505; Lowell Convention (1852), 505-506; Cambridge meeting (1852), 508; loses Congressional nomination (1852), 511; at Murray dinner, 540; at Hale dinner, 545; on proposed constitution, 602; and Sumner-Adams reconciliation, 603; excluded from Free Soil meeting, 618; in England (1856), 728, 731, 733, 735, 743, 753, 755-756, 815; Dana's correspondence with, 899
Palmer v. Stetson, 137
Palmer, Mrs., 892-894
Palmer, Sir Roundell, 725
Palmerston, Lord (H. J. Temple), 394, 470, 725-726, 746, 751, 756, 1058
Palmerston, Lady, 756-757
Palo Alto, battle of, 339
Panama: Dana crosses, 842-843
Panchard v. Mallory, 487
Papal Nuncio. *See* Bedini, Cajetan
Paradise Lost (Milton), 132, 764
Paris, Mr., 871
Paris, Rev. Thomas, 871, 873, 890
Parish, Mr., 307
Parish, Daniel, 825
Parish, Henry, 825
Parish, Mrs. Henry, 825
Parish, James, 825
Parish Will case, 825
Park, John C., 129
Parker, Captain, 61
Parker, Mr., 130
Parker, Benjamin W., 866, 890, 918
Parker, Charles Henry, 319
Parker, Edward Griffith, 626, 629
Parker, Francis E., xxxiv, 410, 684, 1129; Dana's guest, 333, 479, 526, 544; legal business, 385, 409; advises Dana, 425; and Franklin Haven controversy, 429; Prescott trial, 481; Dana discusses with Boutwell, 486; in England, 497; correspondence with Dana, 499, 588, 902; on Europe, 506-507; at H. T. Parker dinners, 510, 541, 675; Constitutional Convention, 556; on vacation, 598, 822; at funeral of Francis Dana, 609; Burns case, 629; sees Dana off to England, 692; on Harriet Martineau, 665; and Federal Street Church case, 665-666; trip to

Europe, 829; legal partnership, 832; Dana's Cuba trip, 834

Parker, Mrs. Francis E., 609

Parker, Henry Melville, 222, 277, 292-294, 296-297, 625, 675

Parker, Henry Tuke, 692; death of Dr. Croswell, 467-468; rescue cases, 472; visit to England, 478; Dana's guest, 489; Dana's host, 491, 510, 541; dinner for, 674-675; with Dana in England, 714-720, 724, 728, 735, 755-756, 760-761, 766, 768, 776, 778, 815, 1129-1130, 1137

Parker, Mrs. Henry Tuke, 728, 756, 815

Parker, Isaac, 542

Parker, Judge Joel, 397, 533, 548, 557, 562, 567

Parker, John, 223

Parker, Levi, 10

Parker, Theodore, 283, 488, 517, 522, 525, 629, 674, 984

Parkes, Miss, 485

Parkes, Harry Smith, 957, 980-981, 994, 999

Parkes, Joseph, 720, 734-735, 753, 755, 815, 1129

Parkman, Mr., 598, 1138

Parkman, Francis (1788–1852), 520-521

Parkman, Francis (1823–1893), xvi, 520, 758

Parkman, George: Webster murder victim, xix, 39, 55, 174, 182, 329, 392-393, 520, 586

Parks, Miss, 684

Parmpelli, Mr., 306, 317

Parodi, Madame, 409

Parr, Samuel, 392, 755

Parsons, Mr., 107

Parsons, Ellen, 598

Parsons, Judge Levi, 844-845, 855, 898

Parsons, Theophilus, 109, 164, 338

Patmore, George, 1136

Patsy, Mrs., 889

Patterson, Elizabeth, 337, 383

Paul Clifford (Bulwer-Lytton), 35

Paul Jones, U.S.S., 111

Paulet, Lord George, 163

Paulk, Edward, 605-606

Payne, Miss, 841

Peabody, Mr., 320, 331

Peabody, Rev. Andrew P., 320

Peabody, Miss E. G., 174, 182, 188, 190

Peabody, George, 760-761

Peabody, Miss Lucia, 595

Peacock (brig), 622

Pearce, James Alfred, 540

Pearson, J. H., 425

Pease, Mr., 94

Pease, Henry, 700

Peck, George W., 46, 71, 169, 197, 212, 435, 501-502, 516, 533

Peck, William Dandridge, 524

Peel, Sir Frederick, 726

Peel, Sir Robert (1788–1850), 36, 74, 137, 394, 579, 716, 723, 788

Peel, Sir Robert (1822–1895), 726, 1045

Peel, Sir William, 1045

Peirce, Miss, 356

Peirce, Benjamin, 539, 686, 689, 830

Pelden, Dudley, 660

Pelham (Bulwer-Lytton), 35

Pendexter, Mr., 277

Pepys, Samuel, xv

Perkins v. Easton, 549

Perkins, Captain, 107

Perkins, Major, 63

Perkins, Mr., 637

Perkins, Mr. (Hawaii), 883

Perkins, George William, 13

Perkins, Louisa, 399-400

Perkins, T. C., 487

Perkins, Thomas H., 176, 256, 398-399, 549

Perry cases, 338

Perry Co. v. Brown et al., 332

Perry Co., Matthew Calbraith, Sr. (1794–1858), 118, 151, 617, 936, 1003, 1006, 1025, 1033, 1063

Perry, Matthew Calbraith, Jr., 118

Perry, Oliver Hazard, 118, 1062

Persia (ship), 1137-1138

Peters, Mr., 1123

Peters, Richard, 245, 1123

Pettes, Samuel, 377

Peyton, Bayley, 844-845

Phèdre, 681

Phelps, William D., 153

Philadelphia: Dana visits, 235-236, 260-264

Philip, Mr., 167

Phillips, Judge, 135, 229, 447

Phillips, Mr., 447-448

Phillips, Adelaide, 467

Phillips, George W., 298

Phillips, Jonathan, 591

Phillips, Stephen Henry, 581

Phillips, Steven Clarendon, 349-351, 395-397, 406, 540

Phillips, Wendell, 161-162, 634, 574, 599, 626-627

Phillips, William, 591

Philosophy of Comte, The (Martineau), 665

Pickering, Charles, 221

Pickering, John, 129, 682-683
Pico, Don Andres, 919, 921, 923
Pico, Tomasa, 848
Pierce, President Franklin, xxviii, 414, 491, 516, 584, 597
Pierce, John, 36
Pierpont, John, 312-313, 438
Pilgrim (brig), 27, 29, 111, 525, 1071
Pinckney, C. C., 253
Pinkney, William, 686
Pitman, Captain, 666
Pitt, Mr., 439
Pitt, William, Sr. (1708–1778), xxi, 115, 388, 472-473, 603, 682-683, 723, 788, 835
Pitt, William, Jr. (1759–1806), 788
Pitts, Coffin, 626-627, 634
Plan of the Founder of Christianity (Reinhard), 62
Plea for National Holy Days, A (Manners), 159
Plitt, Mrs., 399-400
Plummer, George H., 938-939
Pocahontas, 240
Poe, Edgar Allan, 370, 1072
Poems on Slavery (Longfellow), 107
Poets and Poetry of America, The (Griswold), 169
Point Conception, California, 847
Police Riots: New York City, 823-826
Polk, President James K., 295, 366, 404-405
Pollard, Reverend, 296, 318, 322
Pollock, Mr., 1095-1096, 1111, 1117
Pollock, Mrs., 1096, 1111, 1117
Pollock, Sir David, 1095-1096
Pollock, Sir George, 1095-1096
Pollock, Sir Jonathan Frederick, 1095-1096
Pomeroy, George, 118, 158, 232, 327
Pond, Enoch, 606
Poor, Capt. Charles Henry, 841-842
Pope, Mr. (of Washington, D.C.), 660
Pope, Mr. (of San Francisco), 841
Pope, Alexander, 244, 335, 527, 552, 897
Popoff, Com., 902
Portens, Mr., 366
Porter, Miss, 398
Porter, Mr., 507
Porter, David R., 262, 439
Porter, James H., 166
Porter, Noah, 683
Porter, Sarah, 546, 555, 1024
Porter, Z. D., 509
Porteus, Mr., 398
Portland, Duke of, 1046
Potter, Alonzo, 45, 298-299, 325, 348

Potter, Elisha R., 110
Potter, William, 110
Powell, Mr. (Atlantic crossing), 707
Powell, Mr. (of Philadelphia), 320
Powell, Elizabeth, 320
Powell, John Hare, 320
Powers, Earl, 757
Powers, Hiram, 326, 340, 503, 761
Practical Navigator, The, 27
Practical View of the Prevailing Religious System of Professed Christians, A (Wilberforce), 136
Pratt, Miss, 880-882
Pratt, Josiah, IV, 122
Pratt, Orson, 709-710
Prentiss, Seargent Smith, 896
Prescott, Judge, 11
Prescott, Eustis, 83
Prescott, Oliver S.: heresy trial, 493-494, 499
Prescott, William, 11
Prescott, William H., xvi, 11, 57-59, 102, 131, 229, 265, 542
Prescott, William Oliver, 11
Prestman, Benjamin C., 259
Preston, Rev. Charles Finney, 948-951, 962-966, 969-971, 977, 982
Preston, Mrs. Charles Finney, 948, 969-970
Price, Miss, 841
Priestly, Joseph, 735
Prigg v. State of Pennsylvania, 115
Prigg, Mr., 653
Prime, Mr., 320, 1102
Primrose, Archibald John (Earl of Roseberry), 582
Primrose, Francis Ward, 582
Prince, Miss, 362
Prince, Henry, 571-572
Prince Regent of Japan. *See* Naosuke II
Princeton, U.S.S.: explosion on, 242-245
Pringle, Mr., 495
Pringle, Edward J., 844-845, 901
Prinibac, Miss, 258
Prior, Matthew, 527
Proctor, Adelaide Anne, 755
Proctor, Bryan Waller ("Barry Cornwall"), 755, 1031
Proctor, Mrs. Bryan Waller, 755
Pryor, Dr., 693
Pulaski (steam packet): wreck of, 26
Pulszky, Ferenez, 488-489
Pulszky, Mme. Ferenez, 488
Pulteney, Sir William, 419, 473, 784
Punch, 749
Puntinqua, 952-953
Purdy, S., 918, 920

Pusey, Edward B., 194, 222, 294, 777, 779
Putnam, Dr., 356
Putnam, Mrs., 437
Putnam, Israel, 168
Putnam, John P., 95, 135, 220, 513
Putnam, Mrs. John P. (Harriet Day), 135

Quarterly Review, The, 149, 507, 682
Quincy, Edmund, 337, 529
Quincy, Josiah, Sr. (1772–1864), xxvi, 337, 338, 558; Harvard president, 20; at Dickens dinner, 59; his *History of Harvard University,* 91; Allston's death, 174; at Macready's benefit, 291; at Phi Beta Kappa dinner, 320; at Quincy, 386; correspondence, 426; advises Dana, 428; Hillard attacks, 437-438; oration by, 438-439; at anti-Nebraska meeting, 618-619; and Loring removal, 671-673
Quincy, Josiah, Jr. (1802–1882), 52, 59, 102
Quincy, Josiah P., 624-625
Quiner v. Gregory, 541
Quitman, John Anthony, 902

Races of Men and Their Geographic Distribution (Anderson), 221
Rachel (Elizabeth Rachel Felix), 191-192, 231, 669, 681, 704, 912
Racine, 681
Radnor, Earl of, 765-766
Radstock, Lord, 833-834
Ralph, Alexander, 366-368
Ralston, Mrs., 261
Ramsay, Mr., 653
Rand v. Mather, 536, 538
Rand, E. S., 222, 292-297
Randall, George M., 483
Randlett, Captain, 926
Randolph, David C., 239-240
Randolph, Edmund, 845
Randolph, George W., 653
Randolph, John, xxiii, 386, 616, 618-619, 909
Rankin, Mr., 1049-1050, 1055-1056
Rankin, Mrs., 1056
Ransom, Mr., 766
Rantoul, Robert, Sr. (1778–1858), 534-535
Rantoul, Robert, Jr. (1805–1852), 100, 420, 423, 534, 539

Rantoul, Robert S., 534
Rathbone, William, 361
Ratification Meeting of Pittsburgh Convention, 502
Ray, Martha, 755
Raymer, Robert, 925, 927, 929
Raymond, Henry J., 497, 521
Read family: in Donner party, 905
Read, George C., 210
Recollections of Eminent Men (Whipple), 338
Redburn (Melville), xxxv
Redesdale, Lord, 727, 743
Reed, Mr., 146-147
Reed, Benjamin T., 292-293, 296-297, 600
Reed, Henry H., 92, 326
Reed, William B., 91-92, 264, 325, 398, 942, 986
Reeve, Henry, 736
Reeves, Colonel, 1046
"Reflections on the Revolution in France" (Burke), 250
Register, The, 535
Reinhard, Franz, 62
Remarks on the Classical Education of Boys (Cleveland), 682
Remington, Judge Jonathan, 156, 213
Remond, Charles L., 161
Republican Party: formation of, 680-681
Repudiation: British bonds, 73
Reynolds, Dr., 187-188
Reynolds, Reverend, 529
Reynolds, Lt. William, 865, 885
Reynolds, William B., 222, 292-297
Rhode Island American (ed. Goddard), 110
Rice, Mr., 1029
Rice, Richard Drury, 604
Rice, Thomas D. (Jim Crow), 532
Rich, Lt. G. Whitworth Talbot, 588
Richards, Mr., 1023
Richardson, Captain, 541
Richardson, Edgar P., 187
Richelieu de, Cardinal, 229
Richmond, George M., 109
Richmond, Mrs. George M., 109
Richmond, James H. C., 857
Ricker, Moses, 148
Ricketson, Joseph, 319, 603
Ridgely, Randolph, 344
Ridgely, Samuel C., 630
Ridington, Thomas, 154
Riedel v. Kessler, 99-100, 137, 267

Riley, Patrick, 410-412, 425-426
Riots, anti-Catholic, 584
Ripley, George: Dana's tutor, 9; mourns nephew, 156; religious views, 283; Allston's death, 174; in New York, 390, 408, 434, 841; at Mrs. Allston's, 503; letter from Carlyle, 662
Ripley, Mrs. George (Sophia Willard Dana), 9, 29, 104, 135, 137, 596; mourns nephew, 156; Allston's death, 174, 182; at Rockport, 210-211; at Manchester, 336; on Mary Rosamund Dana, 357; in New York, 390, 408-409, 434, 476; on Archbishop Hughes, 435, 585; at Mrs. Allston's, 503; Dana's guest, 509; at Lewis Gray funeral, 511; death of father, 608-609; and Dana's Cuba trip, 834
Ripon, Earl of, 726
Rise of the Dutch Republic (Motley), 830, 986
Ritchie, James, 90, 319
Ritchie, John William, 440
Rivers, George, 110, 336, 618
Rivers, Mrs. George (Geraldine Russell), 110, 336, 618
Rives, William C., 244, 320
Robb, Miss, 761
Robb, Mr., 761
Robbins, Eliza, 114, 116
Roberts v. Roberts, 215
Roberts, George, 196, 242
Robertson, Judge, 861, 864, 867, 885, 1087
Robertson, Lieutenant, 1046
Robeson, William R., 90, 319, 391
Robinson, Mr. (of Hartford), 96
Robinson, Mr. (of London), 769-770
Robinson, Mr. (of Philadelphia), 399
Robinson, Mr.: former slave, 639-641
Robinson, Lieutenant, 126
Robinson, Alfred, 847-848
Robinson, Gov. Charles, 688
Robinson Crusoe (Defoe), 335
Robinson, Henry R., Sr., 274-277
Robinson, Henry R., Jr., 274-275, 277
Robinson, Sir Hercules, 1063
Robinson, Rev. J. P., 490
Robinson, John, 218
Robinson, Lucius, 408
Robinson, Morris, 118
Robinson, Miss S., 397
Robles, Don Secundio, 910
Rochester, Nathaniel, 310
Rockwell, Mr., 135
Rockwell, Julius, 568

Roderick, the Last of the Goths (Southey), 192
Roebuck, John Arthur, 725, 745
Roelker, Bernard, 692
Rogers, Mrs., 339
Rogers, David L., 348
Rogers, Robert P., 685, 692
Rogers, Mrs. Robert P., 97, 174, 182
Rogers, Samuel, 107, 334, 541, 686, **716**
Rogers, William Barts, 410
Rogers, William S., 143, 173-174
Rolfe, Robert Monsey. *See* Cranworth, Lord
Romilly, Sir Samuel, 654-655, 788
Rooney, Sir Cusac Patrick, 655
Roosevelt, Franklin D., 941
Roosevelt, James, 941
Roper, Mr., 391
Rose, Hugh Henry, 1099
Roseberry, Lord (Archibald J. Primrose): divorce case, 582
Rosebrook, Mr., 594
Rosebrook, Eleazer, 594
Ross, Mr., 655, 706
Rotch, Madame, 721, 772
Rotch, Miss, 336
Rotch, Benjamin S., 131, 286, 320
Rousseau, Jean Jacques, 550, 652
Rowan, William, 578-580
Rowell, Mr., 449-451, 456-457
Rugg, Augustus Kendall, 20
Ruggles et al. v. Sheldon, 614-615
Ruggles, Otis Taft, 614-615
Ruggles, Mrs. Otis Taft, 615
Rush, Mrs., 398-400
Ruskin, John, 713, 749
Russ, Mrs. John, 191-193
Russell v. Russell, 832
Russell, Judge, 540, 627
Russell, Major and Mrs. (Trieste), 1111
Russell, Mr. (San Diego), 154
Russell, Mr. and Mrs. (New York), 333
Russell, Andrew, 530
Russell, Lord Charles, 745
Russell, Sir Charles, 772-773
Russell, C. T., 56, 537, 685
Russell, George Robert, 471, 557
Russell, Geraldine, 110, 557, 670. *See also* Rivers, Mrs. George
Russell, Ida, 638-639; travels with Dana, 348; at New Year's party, 478; in Cambridge, 480; Dana's guest, 492, 539; at Milton, 502-503; illness of, 603; Abby Wheaton wedding, 615; on Abby Wheaton, 618; death of, 670; compared to Duchess of Argyll, 732
Russell, James Dutton, 705

Russell, Capt. John, 386, 428, 530
Russell, Lord John, 36, 394, 725
Russell, John Scott, 766
Russell, Jonathan, Sr. (1771–1832), 336, 471, 499, 601
Russell, Mrs. Jonathan, Sr. (Lydia Russell), 62, 97, 110, 285, 336, 348, 354, 502-503, 557, 615, 670, 988
Russell, Jonathan, Jr. (1825–1875), 988
Russell, Laura, 669
Russell, Lucia (Mrs. George W. Briggs), 530
Russell, Mrs. Lucy, 218, 332
Russell, Nathaniel, Sr. (1769–1852), 385, 428
Russell, Nathaniel, Jr. (1801–1875), 385, 530
Russell, Nathaniel P., 195
Russell, Rosalie G. ("Rose"), 285, 290, 348, 499, 502-503, 615, 670
Russell, Thomas, 385-386, 428, 530
Russell, Rev. William Armstrong, 1049-1051, 1055-1056
Russell, Mrs. William Armstrong, 1056
Russell, William C., 97, 232, 327, 332, 408, 476, 685
Rutherford, Walter, 571-572, 598
Rutherford, Mrs. Walter, 571-572
Ryan, Mr., 860
Ryan, James T., 915, 919
Rye, Mr., 707-708

Salem, Massachusetts: inhospitable reputation of, 690
Salisbury, Edward E., 286-287, 488, 683
Salisbury, Mrs. Edward E. (Abigail S. Phillips), 286-287, 683
Salter, Dr., 153, 230, 332, 467-468, 483, 636, 1171
Salter, Emily Otis, 467
Salter, William, 462
Saltonstall, Leverett, 223
Sampson v. Wilder, 135
Samson Agonistes (Milton), 1113
San Francisco: Dana's arrival in, 843-844, 895
San Juan de Nicaragua: destruction of, 658
Sanborn, Franklin Benjamin, 666
Sandford, Mr., 542-543
Sandford, Edward, 476
Sandford, Henry Shelton, 670
Sandford, William H., 13-14
Sandwich, Earl of, 755
Sanger, George Partridge, 532
Santa Anna, Antonio López de, 343

Santa Barbara, 847
Sarah Jane (ship), 541
Saratoga (sloop), 126
Sargent, Epes, 97
Sargent's New Monthly Magazine, 97
Sargent, John (*A Memoir of Rev. Henry Martyn, B.D.*), 67
Sargent, John (Cambridge, Mass.), 567, 569
Sargent, L. M., 101, 288, 427
Sartin, Madame, 439
Saturday Club, 507, 658-659, 666-667, 669, 830
Savage, James S., 542
Sawin, Mr., 542
Say, Lord, 464
"Scape Goat, The" (Hunt), 752-753
Schell, Mr., 408
Schenck, James Findlay, 1060
Schenck, Robert, xl
Schenck, Robert C., 1060
Scherb, Mr., 478, 482
Schlafter, Mr., 293, 305
School District Library of New York, 45
Schoolcraft, John L., 504
Schouler, William, 561, 568-569
Scientific Witness, the, 835
Scott, James, 429-431, 531
Scott, Sir Walter, xvi, 57, 124, 446, 686, 723, 782, 784
Scott, Gen. Winfield T., 252, 341, 493, 504, 516
Scribe, Augustin, 681
Scudder, Charles, 593
"Sea, The" (Proctor), 1031
Seabrook, Miss, 598
Seabury, Samuel, 306, 327-328
Seaman's Friend, The (Dana), xxxiii, xxxviii, 50
Searle, Mr., 135
Sears, David, 52, 110, 229, 265, 291
Sears, Mrs. David, 111
Sears, Joshua, 525
Sears, Philip H., 583
Seccomb v. Provincial Ins. Co.: "Smyrna" case, 833, 836
Second Visit to the United States (Lyell), 71
Sectarian Schools: state aid for, 602
Sedgwick, Adam, 739-740
Sedgwick, Catherine Maria, 108, 116-117, 119, 135, 158, 169, 232; helps Mackenzie, 124-125; on Cooper and Mackenzie, 168; at Channing party, 287;

at Stockbridge, 317; in New York, 408; at Manchester, 599; in Trenton Falls, 828

Sedgwick, Charles, 108, 128, 185, 317, 339, 352, 354, 533

Sedgwick, Mrs. Charles (Elizabeth B. Dwight), 108, 339, 488

Sedgwick, Charles B., 435

Sedgwick, Elizabeth Dwight ("Bessy"), 129, 339

Sedgwick, Elizabeth Ellery ("Lizzy"), 116, 137, 139, 143, 148-149, 232, 327, 478-480. *See also* Child, Mrs. James Francis

Sedgwick, Harriet, 599

Sedgwick, Mrs. Harry, 232, 339

Sedgwick, Helen, 116, 286, 339, 408-409, 433-434

Sedgwick, Katherine M., 108, 139, 232, 286. *See also* Minot, Mrs. William, Jr.

Sedgwick, Katherine M. (daughter of Harry Sedgwick), 339

Sedgwick, Mrs. Robert (Elizabeth Dana Ellery), 29-30, 93, 108, 112, 116-122, 125, 135, 158, 196, 221, 232, 234-235, 264, 286-288, 327, 333, 390, 408-409, 433-435, 476, 599-600, 665

Sedgwick, Robert (b. 1852, son of William Ellery Sedgwick), 476

Sedgwick, Roderick, 818

Sedgwick, Susan Ridley, 286, 288-289, 327, 476, 526-528

Sedgwick, Theodore, Sr. (1780–1839), 117

Sedgwick, Mrs. Theodore, Sr. (Susan A. L. Ridley), 232

Sedgwick, Theodore, Jr. (1811–1859), 117, 158, 398-400

Sedgwick, Mrs. Theodore, Jr. (Sarah M. Ashburner), 232, 339

Sedgwick, William Ellery, 116, 152, 354, 409, 429-430, 434, 476, 479, 685

Sedgwick, Mrs. William Ellery (Constance I. Brevoort), 409, 429

Segrave, Lt. William Francis, 588-589

Seid, Pacha, 1103

Selden, William Cary, 250

Sele, Lord, 463

Selection of Leading Cases, A (Smith), 263

Selkirk, Lord (James Dunbar Douglas), 54

Selwyn, Bishop George Augustus of New Zealand, 742

Selwyn, William, 742

Senior, William N., 720, 735, 743-744, 753, 758, 815, 831, 1129

Sergeant, Miss (Mrs. H. A. Wise), 255

Sergeant, John, 254-256

Serre, Rebecca Ann, de la, 247

Sever, Mrs. Charles, 385, 428, 530

Sever, Jane, 531

Sever, Col. John, 531

Sever, Kate, 530

Sever, William Russell, 531, 1013

Severance, Mrs. Luther, 890

Sevier, Ambrose H., 240

Sewall, Samuel, xv

Sewall, Samuel Edmund, 420-423, 627

Seward, William Henry, 424, 504-505, 528, 670, 681, 1058, 1078

Sewell, Mr., 778

Sewell, Elizabeth Missing, 778

Sewell, Mary, 664

Seymour, Captain, 442

Seymour, Edward A. S., 73

Seymour, Lady, 73

Seymour, Sir George Francis, 440

Seymour, Henry George, 440

Seymour, Horatio, 829, 833-834

Seymour, Sir Michael, 1058

Shackford, Charles C., 90

Shadrack (Frederick Jenkins), xxvi, xxviii-xxix, 429-430, 432, 511-512

Shaftesbury, Lord (Anthony A. Cooper), 727, 742, 746, 757

Shanburn, Mr., 857

Shannon, U.S.S., 391, 621-622

Shapiro, Samuel, 333, 347, 545, 832

Shattuck, George C., Sr. (1783–1854), 68, 70, 174, 285

Shattuck, George C., Jr. (1813–1893), 68, 114, 128, 137, 322; death of Allston, 173-174; Church of the Advent, 230; attends Mrs. Dana, 266; Dana's host, 320; in England, 790

Shattuck, Mrs. George C., Jr., 410

Shaw, Elizabeth (Mrs. Oliver), 361

Shaw, Frederick Plummer, 332-333

Shaw, Joseph Coolidge, 336, 586

Shaw, Chief Justice Lemuel, 90-91, 415; Webster murder trial, xix, 397; Allston's death, 174; at Macready benefit, 291; Story memorial, 321; Russell party, 336; in Cambridge, 337; Shadrack case, 411-413; Sims case, 418, 424; Dempster murder case, 613; Burns case, 631; Federal Street Church case, 688-689

Shaw, Robert Gould, 52, 59, 336

Shaw-Lefevre, Sir John, 772-774, 796

Sheafe, Mr., 209, 399-400

Sheckll v. Jackson, 461, 479

Shelburne, Lord, 757-758

Shelburne, Lady, 757, 759
Shelley, Percy B., xli, 686
Shepard, Charles Upham, 464
Shepard, George, 93
Shepley, George F., 125, 648-650, 653-658
Sheppard, Mr., 947, 949, 971
Sherborne, Pulteney, 418
Sherborne, Mrs. Pulteney, 418
Sheridan, Charles, 73-74
Sheridan, Jane Georgiana (Lady Seymour), 73
Sheridan, Richard, 73
Sheridan, Richard B., 107, 472-473, 603, 715
Sheridan's gymnasium, 92, 136
Sherman, Mr., 883, 892
Sherman, Thomas West, 657
Sherwood, Mary Martha, 31
Shields, James, 902
Shiman, Francis, 339
Shipley, Horatio, 11
Shipman, Reverend, 874-876
Shipman, Mrs., 874-875
Shippen, Mr., 108
Shirley (Charlotte Brontë), 937
Shirley, Evelyn John, 791, 793, 797
Shirley, Mrs. Evelyn John, 802
Shirley, Evelyn Phillip, 791
Shultz v. Welch, 135
Sibthorp, Charles de L. W., 1135
Sibthorp, Humphrey, 1135
Siddons, Sarah, 704, 835
Sigourney, Charles, 55
Sigourney, Mrs. Charles (Lydia Howard Huntley), 55, 95, 106, 108, 228, 360
Silliman, Mr., 306
Silliman, Benjamin, Sr. (1779–1864), 123, 135, 137-138, 227, 260, 835
Silliman, Mrs. Benjamin, Sr. (Harriet Trumbull), 123
Silliman, Benjamin, Jr., 135, 137-138, 227
Simmons, Rev. Dr., 1022
Simms, William Gilmore, 213
Simpson, Sir James, 708-709
Sims, Thomas, fugitive slave: case of, xxvi, xxviii-xxix, 420-425, 628-629, 638, 653
Singleton, Mr., 107
Sketch of China (Davis), 933
Slafter, Rev. Edmund Farwell, 480
Sleeper, Mr., 885
Sleeper, John Sherburne, 885
Slidell, John, 398-399
Slidell, Mrs. John, 399-400
Smith, Captain, 882

Smith, the Misses, 603
Smith, Mr. (Boston caterer), 639
Smith, Reverend (Hawaii), 861, 863, 886
Smith, Mrs. Rev. (Miss Patsy): Hawaii, 890
Smith, Reverend (China), 995, 1033-1034, 1044
Smith, Mrs. Rev. (China), 1050
Smith, Albert Richard, 724
Smith, Alfred, 96
Smith, Barney, 62
Smith, Canning, 923
Smith, F. O. J., 687
Smith, Floyd, 328
Smith, Bishop George, 999, 1001, 1004
Smith, Henry Boynton, 285
Smith, I. V. C., 541
Smith, J. W., 263
Smith, Jeremiah, 518
Smith, Jerome Van Crowninshield, 629, 632, 635, 638
Smith, John Wilson, 62, 101, 270
Smith, Joseph, 709-710
Smith, Joseph Emerson, 652
Smith, Mrs. Kitty, 285
Smith, Oliver, 607
Smith, Persifor F., 902
Smith, Phily (RHD, Jr.'s aunt), 1061-1062
Smith, Richard Penn, 480
Smith, Sidney, 758, 775-776
Smith, D. Talcott, 606
Smith, William, 30
Smith, William (RHD, Jr.'s uncle), 109-110
Snell, Mr., 607
Snyder, Antoine, 368
Sohier, Edward D., 674
"Some Account of Letheon" (Warren), 332
Somers, statue of, 240
Somers (brig), 118, 122
Somers mutiny, 112-113, 117-119, 125
Somers Mutiny Affair, The (ed. Hayford), 112
"Son, The" (Dana), 11
"Song for St. Cecila's Day" (Dryden), 291
Soule, Nicholas Emery, 645
Soulé, Pierre, 503
Southey, Robert, 192, 782
Southgate, Reverend, 284
Southgate, Bishop Horatio, 490, 538, 603, 624, 822
Southerland, Dr., 766
Sparks' American Biography, 45, 196
Sparks, Major, 442

Sparks, Jared, 57, 59, 136, 286, 490, 539, 821, 833
Sparks, Mrs. Jared, 286, 833
Sparrow, Patrick J., 1050
Spaulding, C. W., 408-409, 646
Spear, Thomas, 328-329
Spear, Thomas R., Jr., 358
Speidon, Mr., 925, 927, 929-930, 1063
Spencer, Miss, 401
Spencer, Aubrey George, 401
Spencer, Lord Charles, 401, 830
Spencer, Frederick, 388
Spencer, George John (2nd Earl Spencer), 388
Spencer, John Canfield, 112, 117, 124, 150-152, 166
Spencer, John Charles, 388
Spencer, Philip, 112, 117, 150-152, 399
Spencer, William Ambrose, 150-151
Spooner, Miss, 1068-1069, 1071-1072
Spooner, Mr., 774
Spooner, Allen C., 90, 319, 348
Sprague, Judge Peleg, 98, 132, 139, 681; Story memorial, 321; Sims case, 421-422; Scott trial, 430-431, 466; *Webb v. Peirce*, 484-485; Webster memorial, 514; rescue cases, 532; Constitutional Convention, 548; Captain Hotchkiss case, 616; Burns case, 627; *Osprey* case, 662-663
Sprague, William Buell, 317, 438-439, 472
Springfield Whig Convention, 486
Stack, Col. Nathaniel Massy, 588-590
Stacy, Margaret Black (Mrs. John Brooks), 577
Stafford, Marquis of, 186, 750
Staigg, Richard M., 431-432
Stallknecht, Frederic S., 327
Standish, Miles, 218
Stanley, Edward Johns, 727
Stanly, Edward, 902, 904-908, 924
Stanly, Mrs. Edward, 907-908, 924
Stanow, Nancy, 361
Stanton, Henry Brewster, 350
Starr, Mrs., 440
Stearns, Mr., 1016
Stearns, Abel, 154, 848
Stearns, Jonathan P., 126
Stearns, William Augustus, 1078
Stearns, William French, 1078-1079, 1081-1082, 1086-1090, 1095-1096
Stearns, Mrs. William French, 1081-1082, 1095-1096
Stebbins, Rufus P., 410
Stedman, Charles H., 137-138, 182, 675, 738

Stedman, Francis D., 182, 406, 609
Stedman, William, 98, 738
Stege, Mr., 892
Stephens, Mr., 158
Stetson, Mr., 337
Stetson, Caleb, 566
Stevens v. Rodson, 530
Stevens, Mr., 447
Stevens, Isaac I., 209
Stevenson, Mr., 280
Stevenson, Joshua Thomas, 568
Stevenson, Theodore, 59, 160
Stewart, Charles, 117-118
Stewart, David, 259
Stewart, Jack, 154, 848-849
Stewart, William Morris, 919-920
Stickney, Mr., 410, 822
Stien, Mr., 898
Stimson, Benjamin G., 28, 220, 525, 849
Stimson-Cook family, 598
Stinchfield, Anson G., 605
Stockbridge, Massachusetts: described, 339
Stockton, Robert F., 243-244
Stoddard, Mr., 378
Stoddard, Mrs. (Martha Thomas), 428, 530
Stone, James W., 680
Stone, John Seely, 167, 303, 549
Stores, Mrs., 652
Storey, Charles W., 90, 319
Storrow, Charles S., 480
Story Association, 438-439
Story, Mr., 279
Story, Edith, 693, 703, 707
Story, Judge Joseph, xvii, 37-40, 196, 215, 223, 279, 660, 700; at Lawrence party, 52-54; Harvard oration, 90; Allston's death, 176; anecdote of, 229; and U. S. Supreme Court, 241, 244-245; death of, 320-321; Dartmouth College case, 517-518; Constitutional Convention of 1820, 542; Ludlow-Lawrence funeral oration, 621; with Sumner, 661-662
Story, Waldo, 694-695, 703, 705, 709
Story, William Wetmore, xxvi; Dana recalls his father, 427; at Brattle House, 428, 431; at Longfellow's, 432; leaves Boston, 433; Story Association affair, 438-439; on Lewis Cass, Jr., 653-654; in Boston, 464; Webster poem, 512; Atlantic crossing, 693-696, 698-700, 703, 707-711; in England, 731, 805
Story, Mrs. William Wetmore (Emelyne Eldredge), 431; described, 432; Bos-

ton theater, 463; Atlantic crossing, 693-696, 699, 703, 706, 709, 711; in England, 731, 805
Stowe, Harriet Beecher, 487, 518
St. Paul's Church: board meeting, 292-297
Strathmore, Earl of, 73
Stribling, Cornelius K., 1060-1061
Strong, Miss, 400
Strong, Caleb, 95
Strong, Mrs. Caleb, 193
Strong, Lewis, 354
Strong, Mrs. Lewis, 193
Strong, Titus, 469
Strutt, Edward (Baron Belper), 766
Stuart, Professor, 88-89
Stuart, George Okill, Jr., 576-577, 581-582, 592
Stuart, Gilbert, 177
Stuart, Mrs. Isaac, 89
Stuart, Mrs. J. W., 97
Stuart, Mrs. Lucy, 577
Stuart, Sarah, 89
Sturgis, Caroline, 339
Sturgis, Harriet, 280, 283-284
Sturgis, Jonathan, 617
Sturgis, Russell, 280, 718, 736, 768, 805, 1129
Sturgis, Mrs. Russell, 736
Sturgis, William, 160, 197
Suchow: trip to, 1034-1044
Suffield, Lord, 589
Suffren, Miss, 390
Suliman, Pacha, 1103
Sullivan, Mr., 105
Sullivan, George, 160, 313
Sullivan, Mrs. George, 313
Sullivan, Gov. James, 313
Sullivan, Olivia (Mrs. John E. Ward), 983
Sullivan, William, 160
Sumner, Mrs. Albert, 598
Sumner, Charles, xxi, xxiii, xxvi, xxix-xxx, 49-50, 52, 93, 135, 161, 169, 223-225, 392, 425, 463, 491, 575, 737; with Dickens, 56; characterized, 59; Allston's death, 174, 176; 4th of July oration, 314, 319; Russell party, 336; political position of, 347, 389, 391; ratification meeting, Free Soil party, 354; Free Soil convention, 395; ostracism of, 408; elected to U. S. Senate, 409, 426-427, 469; on fugitive slave cases, 413; Personal Liberty law, 416; Sims case, 422; Dana's Worcester speech, 428; letter to newspapers, 428; Story Association affair, 438; Homer party, 471; "Freedom National"
speech, 503-505; Parker party, 510; on George Sumner, 525; letter to Dana, 527; Constitutional Convention, 536, 548, 551, 553, 557, 565; on conditions in Washington, D.C., 544; Hale dinner, 545; reputation in Canada, 579; Lord Elgin on, 580; at Manchester, 599; Dana's guest, 602; quarrel with C. F. Adams, Sr., 603; on newspaper practices, 653-654; on U. S. Senate, 659; early life of, 661-662; on election expenses, 675; Republican meeting, 680; letter to Ingham, 719; letter to Earl of Carlisle, 721; reputation in England, 744, 757; assaulted in U. S. Senate, 773; re-elected to U. S. Senate, 821; introduces Lord Althorp, 829; state of health, 831-832; reputation in Hawaii, 867
Sumner, Charles Pinckney, 661-662
Sumner, George, 488, 491, 525
Sumner, Increase, 570
Sutherland, Duke of, 744, 1129
Sutherland, Duchess of, 179, 732, 737, 743-744, 749-750, 754, 756-757, 831, 1079, 1129
Suttle, Colonel, xxviii-xxix, 626-627, 631, 633, 673
Swan, Dr., 406
Sweetser, Moses F., 187
Swift, Mr., 495
Symonds, Sir William, 441

Table Talk (Hazlitt), 827
Talbot, Mr., 655
Talbot, Mr. (Japan), 1020
Talfourd, Thomas Noon, 507, 662
Taming of the Shrew, 129
Tankerville, Lord, 805
Tappan, Miss, 138
Tappan, Benjamin, 604
Tappan, Charles, 47
Tappan, John G., 138
Tappan, John S., 221
Tattnall, Com. Josiah, 994, 1057-1058
Taylor v. Edwards, 428
Taylor, Major (China), 980
Taylor, Mr. (Andover), 89
Taylor, Mrs. (Miss Thurston), 870-871
Taylor, Reverend, 510
Taylor, Bayard, 408, 617, 855, 1033, 1051
Taylor, Edward T., 62

Taylor, Isaac, 1079-1080
Taylor, Jeremy, 89, 93, 104, 127
Taylor, Oliver, 62
Taylor, Gen. Zachary, xxiii-xxiv, xxvi, 342-344, 486, 656-657
Tecumseh (Colton), 123
Temple, John, 848
Tenny, John S., 649-650, 653
Tennyson, Alfred, 394, 882
Terry, Catherine E. ("Kate"), 95, 683. *See also* Bacon, Mrs. Leonard P.
Terry, Mrs. Charles, 95
Terry, David S., 916
Terry, Job, 304
Texas, annexation of, xxiii
Thacher, James, 12, 19, 25, 385, 682
Thackeray, William M., xvii, 527, 529, 682, 693, 749, 991, 994
Thatcher, Judge Peter O., 54, 69-70, 93-94, 103-104
Thayer, Alexander Wheelock, 633, 644
Thayer, Christian T., 534
Thayer, John E., 948
Thayer, Mrs. John E., 948
Thayer, Nathaniel, 948
Thayer, Mrs. Nathaniel, 948
Thellusson Will case, 584
Thellusson, Capt. Alexander Dalton, 584
Thellusson, Charles S. A., 584
Thellusson, Frederick W. B. (Lord Randlesham), 584
Thellusson, Peter, 584
Thomas, Captain, 899
Thomas, Mr., 706
Thomas, Judge Benjamin F., 533, 685, 689
Thomas, George Henry, 290
Thomas, Col. Seth J., 385, 420, 423, 428, 629, 632, 638
Thomas, Mrs. Seth J., 530
Thompson, Mrs., 914
Thompson, Charles, 566
Thompson, Capt. Francis, 29, 1071
Thompson, George, 844
Thompson, J. A., 416
Thompson, James, 760
Thompson, Judge Smith, 96
Thompson, William, 23
Thoms, William, 931
Thorvaldsen, Bertel, 739
Thrall, Stephen C., 901
Thumping Legacy, The, 543-544
Thurston, Mr., 871
Thurston, Mrs., 871
Thurston, Rev. Asa, 869-871
Thurston, Mrs. Asa, 870

Ticknor, Anna, 102, 135, 229, 265, 309, 554
Ticknor, George, xvii-xviii, xxv-xxvi, 52, 57, 129, 131-132, 139; characterized, 59; on Byron, 70; Dana's host, 102, 228-229, 265, 290, 388-389; on Canning, 140; on Allston, 191, 226; at theater, 287, 290; Macready benefit, 291; in Genesee Valley, 311; at Niagara Falls, 314; at Manchester, 347; on Gallatin and Fanny Kemble, 389; tries to ostracize Sumner, 408; Franklin Haven controversy, 429; newspaper attacks on Dana, 437; Dana dreams of, 451; influence on Hillard, 553-554; house of, 554; Constitutional Convention, 558; London, 720-721
Ticknor, Mrs. George, 56, 102, 139-140, 228-229, 265, 311, 314, 347, 554
Tiffany, Mrs. Henry, 257-258
Tilden, Mr., 361
Tildon, Mr., 408
Tillinghast, Miss, 339
Tillinghast, Joseph L., 262, 339
Tillinghast, Rev. N., 339
"Titania's Court" (Allston), 179
"To a Mountain Daisy" (Burns), 1015
To Cuba and Back (Dana), xxxviii, 835, 1002
Tocqueville, Alexis de, 890
Toppan, Mr., 1076
Torrey, Mr., 941, 944
Torrey, Henry Warren, 277
Torrey, Samuel, 280-281, 941
Totten, Joseph Gilbert, 405
Toucey, Isaac, 1060
Tower, Charlemagne, 338
Towers, Mr., 65-66
Townsend, Dr., 536
Townsend, Mr., 398
Tracy, Judge T. P., 922
Train, Charles Russell, 569
Trask, Colonel, 279
Trask, Edward, 279
Treatise on the Law of Evidence, A (Greenleaf), 136
Treatise on the Measure of Damages, A (Sedgwick), 117
Trent Affair, 398
Trevelyan, Sir Charles Edward, 1076, 1080
Tribune, New York, 9
Trofater, Edward, 859
Trott, Mr., 492
Trowbridge, Mrs., 496
Trowbridge, Lydia (Mrs. Richard Dana), 186

Trowbridge, Judge Thomas, 138, 185-186, 215
Troyon, Constant, 595
"True American, The" (ed. Clay), 545
True, Charles Kittridge, 388, 634
Trumbull Gallery, 487
Trumbull, Captain, 1096
Trumbull, Harriet, 123
Tuck, Amos, 433
Tucker, Dr., 346, 354, 360
Tucker, Miss, 400
Tucker, Mr., 166
Tucker, Luther, 379
Tucker, Mrs. Luther, 379
Tuckerman, Samuel Parkman, 361, 828
Tuckett, Capt. Harvey G. P., 584
Tudor, Jane, 360
Tudor, Frederic, 1076
Tudor, Samuel ("Uncle"), 193, 227, 305, 346, 360, 388
Tudor, Mrs. Samuel ("Aunt"), 47, 95, 193, 305, 318
Tudor, William, 360, 1076
Tufts, Mrs., 265
Tukey, Marshal, 921
Tukugawa, Mariaki (Prince Mito), 1017
Turgeon, Archbishop Pierre Flavien, 581-582
Turner v. Gregory, 489
Turner, Daniel, 845, 903
Turner, Mrs. Daniel, 845, 903
Turner, Sir James, 770
Turner, Sharon, 784
Turno, Lord, 470
Twisleton, Edward T. B., 463
Two Gentlemen of Verona, The, 126
Two Years Before the Mast, xv-xvii, xxxii, xxxv-xxxvi, 9, 13, 28, 33, 49, 68, 73, 89, 107-108, 111, 117, 154, 159, 220, 265, 334-336, 732, 758, 835, 843, 847-850, 902
Tyler, Daniel, 62
Tyler, Mrs. Daniel, 62-63
Tyler, Edward Royall, 13
Tyler, President John, 162, 165-166, 203, 242, 244, 253-254, 414
Tyler, Robert, 166, 242
Tyng, Stephen H., 158
Tyran de Padoue (Hugo), 480
Tyrrell, Albert J., 630
Tyson, Mr., 941
Tzuiken, Kusimoto, 1030

Uncas, 63
Uncle Tom's Cabin (Stowe), 487, 518
Underwood, Joseph Rogers, 504, 540

Uniacke, Crofton, 443
Uniacke, Richard John, 443
United States v. LeCraw, 144
United States (ship), 127
Upham, Mr., 292, 675
Upham, Charles W., 425, 568
Upham, Mrs. H., 361
Upsher, Abel P., 166, 242-244, 254
Upton, Bruce, 925
"Uriel" (Allston), 187

Valignano, Alessandro, 1003
Vallejo, Guadaloupe, 155, 902-903, 905
Vallejo, Josita, 903
Vallejo, Rosalia Estrada, 155
Vallejo, Salvador, 903
Van Buren, John, 348, 351-354, 391-392, 475
Van Buren, Martin, xxiv, 203, 348, 491
Vandervort, Mr., 400
Van Lennep, Henry J., 217, 220-221
Van Lennep, Mrs. Henry J., 217, 221
Van Rensselaer, Courtlandt, 193, 948
Van Rensselaer, Mrs. Courtlandt (Catherine Cogswell), 193, 948
Van Rensselaer, Solomon, 948
Van Rensselaer, Stephen, 193, 948
Van Vleck, Mr., 402
Vega, General, 339
Venice: visit to, 1114-1118
Verbeck, Rev. Guido H., 1004-1011, 1016
Verbeck, Mrs. Guido H., 1006-1007
Vernon, Anna. See Olyphant, Mrs. Robert Morrison
Vernon, Sophia. See Olyphant, Mrs. Robert Morrison
Vernon, William, 1061
Vethake, Henry, 326
Victor, Prince, 441, 804-805
Victoria, Bishop of. See Smith, Bishop George
Victoria, Queen, 163, 441, 443, 722, 761-763, 798-801
Vigilance, Committee of: California, 846, 856
Villiers, Bishop, 765-766
Vinton, Rev. Alexander H., 102, 104, 106, 136; Allston's death, 175; sermon of, 219; church controversy, 222; in Philadelphia, 263; baptism of Mary Rosamund C. Dana, 285; St. Paul's meeting, 292-297; religious views, 303; at Niagara Falls, 312-313; death of William E. Dana, 329; at Episcopal convention, 490
Viri Romae (ed. Lhomond), 19

Visit to India, China and Japan, A (Taylor), 1033
Visit to the Philippine Islands, A (Bowring), 1067
Viviparous Quadrupeds of North America (Audubon), 382
Voltaire, 652
Von Amburgh, 190
Vyse, Richard H., 1104

Wade, Benjamin F., 505
Wade, Thomas Francis, 999, 1033
Wadsworth, Miss (Mrs. C. A. Murray), 309, 311, 314
Wadsworth, Daniel, 55, 95, 193, 227-228, 305, 346
Wadsworth, Mrs. Daniel, 55, 95
Wadsworth, James, 309-310
Wadsworth, James Samuel, 309
Wadsworth, Jeremiah, 310
Wagland, Dr., 308, 315
Wainwright, Jonathan M., 264, 468
Wainwright, Mr. P., 361
Wainwright, Mrs. P., 361
Wait, Mrs., 364
Wakefield, Mr., 678
Walcott, Captain, 944
Walden, Lord Howard de, 1045
Waldo, Mr., 400
Waldron, Mr., 209, 284, 985
Wales, Mr., 526
Walker, Reverend, 539
Walker, Amasa, 506, 569
Walker, Sir Baldwin Wake, 757-758
Walker, D. B., 432, 466
Walker, James, 148
Walker, Robert J., 240
Wallace, Horace Binney, 262-263, 320, 325-326, 530
Wallace, John Bradford, 326
Wallace, Mrs. John Bradford (Susan Binney), 326
Walpole, Spencer Horatio, 725, 745, 772-774
Walsh, Mrs. (Miss Church), 1006
Walter, Miss, 329-330
Walter, Arthur Maynard, 472
Walton, Izaak, 774
Warburton, William, 244
Ward, Captain, 439
Ward, Sir Henry George, 1076
Ward, John Elliott, 943, 982-985, 987-988, 1023, 1058, 1061
Ward, Mrs. John Elliott (Olivia Sullivan), 983
Ward, Julia, 93, 118, 131, 135, 149. See also Howe, Mrs. Samuel Gridley

Ward, Mary, 135, 265, 339
Ward, Samuel G., 339, 830, 1002
Ward, Mrs. Samuel G., 1002
Wardell, Mr., 1060
Ware, Mr., 508
Ware, Ashur, 681-682
Ware, Charles Eliot, 326
Ware Henry ("Hy"), 20, 187, 478
Warner, Jonathan Trumbull, 848
Warren, Judge, 320, 513-514
Warren, Mr. (California), 923
Warren, Mr. (Troy, N.Y.), 400
Warren, Edward, 332
Warren, Joseph, 426-427
Warren, William, 462, 480, 543-544
Warrener's restaurant, 96, 130, 191, 215-216, 231
Warspite (frigate), 91
Warwick, Earl of, 780
Washburn, Gov. Emory, 615-617, 676
Washington Allston (Richardson), 187
Washington, Benjamin F., 915
Washington, Bushrod, 249-251
Washington, D. C.: visit to, 238-245
Washington, George, 12, 248-251, 253, 309-310, 474, 497-498, 615-616, 935
Washington, John A., Sr., 249
Washington, Mrs. John A., Sr., 249-251
Washington, John A., Jr., 248-251
Washington, Mrs. John A., Jr., 250
Washington, John Macrae, 342
Waterson, Robert C., 531
Waterston, Mr., 174
Waterston, Mrs., 174
Watkinson, Mrs. David, 95
Watkinson, Maria, 221
Watson, Captain, 98
Watson, Reverend (Trinity Church, Boston), 305
Watson, the Misses, 571
Watson, Mr., 380
Watson, Mrs., 380
Watson, Benjamin Marston, 415, 530, 1013
Watson, Mrs. Benjamin Marston, 415
Watson, Elizabeth, 40, 46. See also Daggett, Mrs. Oliver E.
Watson, John M., 54, 116-117, 306, 327, 333, 349, 359-360
Watson, Mary, 49, 103-104, 112, 124, 127-128, 135, 141, 158-159, 192, 216, 228, 267, 307, 311, 313, 332. See also Wilson, Mrs. Jared
Watson, Sarah, xxxvi-xxxvii, 40. See also Dana, Mrs. Richard Henry, Jr.
Watson, Mrs. William (Sarah's mother), 54, 68, 71, 88, 95, 124, 130, 158, 192,

216, 267, 285, 305-306, 349, 356, 360, 384, 387, 496, 507, 519, 526, 528, 543, 599, 832

Watson, William B., 42, 116-117, 135, 153, 158, 223-224; takes letter to Dickens, 61; wedding of, 222; Dana visits in New York, 233, 235, 263, 306, 327, 332-333, 390, 405, 434, 476; death of brother, 360; legal problems of, 407-409; visits Dana, 493-494; at Brattleboro, 570; at Mt. Washington, 647-648; at Albany, 684; godparent of Angela H. C. Dana, 822; death of Nancy Marsh, 831

Watson, Mrs. William B. (Adele Lynch), 222-223, 233, 235, 306, 327, 409, 434, 476, 822, 940, 990

Watts, Mr., 292-297

Watts, Isaac, 875

Wayland, Reverend, 480

Wayland, Francis, 833, 1125-1126

Waync, Justice, 241

Webb v. Peirce, 484

Webb, Miss, 380

Webb, the Misses, 305, 346, 360

Webb, Mr. (in Orient), 1001, 1023, 1033, 1060

Webb, Mrs., former slave, 756

Webb, Henry, 217, 380, 540, 948

Webb, John, 138, 193, 227, 305, 948

Webster, the Misses, 601

Webster-Ashburton treaty, 91, 136-137

Webster, Daniel, xxiv-xxv, xxvii-xxviii, 68, 90, 225, 323, 429, 437, 475, 528, 577, 628, 865, 1064; on Clay's Compromise, xxvi; Bunker Hill orations, 12, 167; education, 69-70; on British Empire, 75; in U. S. Senate, 93, 675; speech at Faneuil Hall, 96-97; Ashburton treaty speech, 102; Oregon boundary question, 131, 136, 140; honored, 160; in Constitutional Convention of 1820, 164, 542-543; in Supreme Court, 241; *Princeton* explosion, 253; Macready benefit, 291; Story memorial, 321; Texas convention, 395-397; Fugitive Slave Law, 408; railroad celebration, 462, 580; helps B. R. Curtis, 465; Springfield convention, 486; Whig convention, 493; at Sumner speech, 504; poem on, 512; death of, 512-517; Dartmouth College case, 518; memorial service, 521; Everett eulogy, 530; rescue cases, 531-532; on Mr. Lunt, 533; article on, 535; son's defeat, 536; Ticknor's support of, 553; correspondence with J. C. Chamberlain, 598; anecdotes of, 607, 660-661, 855; anti-Nebraska meeting, 618; influence of, 637-638; on G. T. Curtis, 644; political position, 650; oratory, 689; reputation in England, 831; *Works* edited by Everett, 1064

Webster, Mrs. Daniel, 660

Webster, Fletcher, 644

Webster, John White, xix-xx, 39, 392-393, 397

Webster, Mrs. John White, 600

Webster, Noah, 865

Webster, Sidney, 597

Weir, Robert W., 218-219, 404-405, 595

Welch, Dr., 354

Welch, John H., 90, 319

Weld, the Misses, 652

Weld, Francis Minot, 319

Welford, Mr., 818-819

Weller, Gov. John B., 921, 923-924

Welles, Benjamin, 173-174, 229, 836

Welles, Mrs. John, 223

Wellington, Duke of, 54, 70, 470-471, 588, 694, 714, 729, 747, 788, 1088

Wells, Judge, 346, 354, 384, 390, 392, 424, 831

Wells, Rev. Dr., 490, 499

Wells, Judge Alexander (California), 844, 896

Wells, George, 828

Wells, John S., 274-275

Wells, Gov. Samuel, 687

Wells, William, 17-19, 148-149

Wensleydale, Lord (James Parke), 747-750, 760

Wentworth v. Nickerson, 98

Wentworth, Miss, 693-694

Wesley, Samuel S., 789

Wesselhoeft, Robert, 387

West, Miss., 841, 902, 909

West, Mr., 408, 434

West Point: visited, 402-405

Weston, Mr., 351

Weston, Nathan, Sr. (1782–1872), 604-605

Weston, Nathan, Jr. (1813–1889), 604-605

Wethered, Miss, 243

Wetherell, Sir Charles, 36

Wetmore, Mrs., 400

Wetmore, Dr. C. H., 881-882

Wharncliffe, Lord, 726

Wharton, Eliza, 690-691

Whatley, Richard, 777

Wheaton, Abigail (Abby), 463, 526, 538, 615, 618-619, 653, 919. *See also* Little, Mrs. Charles Coffin
Wheaton, Henry, 336, 463-465, 615
Wheaton, Mrs. Henry, xxxix
Wheaton, Martha, 502-503
Wheaton, Robert, 245, 463-465, 530, 600
Wheaton's Elements of International Law, xxxix-xl
Wheeler, Charles Stearns, 36, 210-211
Wheeler, Mrs. Charles Stearns, 48, 210
Wheeler, Hugh Massy, 1099
Wheeler, John, 376
Wheeler, Mrs. John, 376
Whewell, Dr. William, 738-739
Whig anti-Nebraska meeting, 618-619
Whig National Conventions, 285, 493
Whipple, Edwin P.: Phi Beta Kappa, 338; Dana's guest, 348, 485, 497; traveling companion, 474; Parker party, 491, 541, 675; Powers joke, 503; dinner parties, 521, 617, 686; Saturday Club, 658, 669, 830
Whitcomb, Mr., 844, 855
White v. Braintree, 536-537, 616, 671, 685
White Jacket (Melville), xxxv
White, Judge, 62
White, Mr., 603
White, Ferdinand E., 114, 386
White, Henry, 111
White, I. L., 353
White, Maria, 432
White Mountains: trips to, 268-277, 592-597, 641-648
White, Richard Grant, 826
White, William Abijah, 419
Whiting, Captain, 843
Whitney, Mr., 471
Whitney, Mrs. (Miss Train), 339
Whitney, James S., 562, 570
Whittemore, the Misses, 101
Whittemore, Thomas, 492
Whittlesey, Elisah, 504
Whittlesey, Hannah, 317-318, 346
Whitwell, Mrs., 245
Wickliffe, Charles A., 254
Wigfall, Mrs., 182
Wiggin v. Arkenburgh, 474
Wilberforce, Bishop Samuel, 470, 727, 831
Wilberforce, William, 136, 470
Wilde, Hamilton Gibbs, 594
Wilde, Kate, 598
Wilde, Samuel S., 56, 298, 499, 600, 677
Wilder, Mr., 154

Wilderness, Battle of, 309
Wilkes, Charles, 398
Wilkes Exploring Expedition, 68
Wilkie, Sir David, 613
Wilkinson, Ezra, 568
Willard, the Misses, 135
Willard, Augustus, 185
Willard, Ellery V., 492
Willard, James, 106
Willard, Joseph, 46, 104, 329, 388, 492, 519, 609, 836
Willard, Mrs. Joseph, 388, 609
Willard, Samuel, 319
Willard, Rev. Samuel, 319
Willard, Sidney, 40-41, 174-175, 185, 329, 492, 524, 609
Willard, Mrs. Sidney (Theodora Dana), 185
Willey, Dr., 398-400
Willey, Samuel, Jr., 274, 378-379
Willey, Tolman, 513
William I of Prussia, 1074
William IV of Prussia, 1074
Williams, Captain, 925, 927, 929, 938-939, 944
Williams, Miss, 305
Williams, Mr. (of Boston), 630
Williams, Mr. (of New York), 834
Williams, Mrs. (of Wethersfield), 346
Williams, Channing M., 1003-1005, 1016
Williams, F. D., 1061
Williams, Henry, 566, 568
Williams, Bishop John, 468
Williams, Joseph H., 604
Williams, Reuel, 604
Williams, Roger, 160
Williams, Samuel Wells, 925, 930, 932-933, 969, 1050, 1096
Williams, Thomas H., 915
Williams, Thomas L., 94-95
Williams, Thomas Scott, 55, 94, 100, 137, 193, 831
Williams, Sir Walter F., 757-758
Williamson, Mr., 442
Willian, William Mortimer, 606
Willing, Charles, 262, 339
Willing, Mrs. Charles, 262-263, 339
Willis, Nathaniel P., 391, 826
Wilmot Proviso, 394-395
Wilson, Clara, 496
Wilson, Elizabeth, 308
Wilson, George, 308, 496, 527
Wilson, Mrs. George, 596
Wilson, Henry, 502, 506, 511, 534, 555-558, 561, 565-566, 599, 614-615, 617, 670

Wilson, James, 363, 406, 678
Wilson, Jared, 49, 308, 315, 332, 349, 384
Wilson, Mrs. Jared (Mary Watson), 332, 349, 360, 384, 496, 527, 555, 676, 831
Wilson, Capt. John, 154, 846-847, 849
Wilson, Mrs. John, 847
Wilson, Julia, 432
Wilson, Richard Dana, 360, 496
Wilson, Samuel M., 898-899
Wilson, William Dexter, 495-496
Wilson, Mrs. William Dexter, 496
Windham, Sir Charles A., 709
Windham, William, 472-473
Wingard, Captain, 1061
Winslow, Edward, 218
Winslow, Mrs. Edward, 218
Winsor v. Sampson, 541-542
Winter's Tale, The, 126
Winthrop, Robert C., xxiv, xxviii; in Washington, D. C., 243-245, 256; ether controversy, 359; defeat of, 469, 479; Whig convention, 486; Harvard address, 497; anti-Nebraska meeting, 618-619
Wirt, William, 517, 686
Wise, Henry A., 255
Wo Lung, 986-987
Wolcott, Oliver, 119
Wolfe, James, 575
Wood, Mr., 428, 557
Wood, Mr. (of Canandaigua, N.Y.), 308, 496
Wood, Sir Charles, 725-726
Wood, Charles E. P., 419
Wood, Fernando, 825
Wood, George, 475
Wood, Horatio, 14-16
Wood, James George, 419
Wood, Mrs. John Asprey, 419
Wood, Nathaniel, 614
Wood, William Henry, 784-785, 787
Wood, Mrs. William Henry, 418, 784, 787, 815
Woodbridge, Caroline, 92
Woodbury v. Ober, 689-690
Woodbury, Levi, 201, 284-285, 338, 422-423, 425, 622-623
Woodbury, Obediah, 689-690
Woodbury, Tebulor, 690
Woodman, Horatio, 340, 348, 521, 600, 617, 658-659, 666, 675, 686, 689, 830
Woods, Leonard, Jr., 23, 25, 34, 55, 88-90, 129, 131, 135, 215, 863; Dana's tutor, 22; character of, 24; cleverness of, 128; sermon analyzed, 132-134; on religious holidays, 159-160; circus anecdote, 163; religious views, 218, 285; in Cambridge, 480; described, 485; at Bowdoin, 651-652; Dana's guest, 490
Woods, Sarah A., 34, 89
Woodville, Richard C., 114
Woodward, Rufus, 194
Woodward, Samuel B., 194
Woodward, William, 194
Wool, John Ellis, 344
Woolsey, Mrs., 260, 264, 325
Woolsey, Theodore D., 160, 488, 683
Wordsworth, Rev. Christopher, 754-755
Wordsworth, William, xvi, 10, 36, 64, 92, 291, 394, 464, 501, 519, 686, 748, 774, 835
Wortley, James Stuart, 725-726
Wreck of the Glide (Oliver), 153
Wright, Elizur: Shadrack rescue case defendant, 413-414, 492, 511-513
Wright, John, 10, 13
Wrightington, Tom, 849
Writings of George Washington (Sparks), 57
Wyckoff, Mr., 71
Wyeth, Mr., 437
Wylie, Mr., 861, 864-865, 928
Wyman, Jeffries, 635
Wyman, William, 202, 607
Wyndham, Mr., 994

Yale College, 488
Yeh, Commissioner, 963
Yell, Archibald, 343
Yesterdays with Authors (Fields), 507
Yonge, Charlotte M., 663-664, 795
Yonge, William C., 795
Yonge, Mrs. William C., 795
York, Peter, 298
Young, Captain, 635
Young, Mrs., 446
Young, Brigham, 709
Young, George R., 71, 74-76, 82, 169, 440, 442-443, 446, 479
Young, Sir William, 71, 75-76, 81-82, 214, 440, 446, 462
Younger v. Gloucester Ins. Co., 668
Yount, George C., xxii, 902-908, 913
Yount, Mrs. George C., 904, 907
Yount, Lilly, 904, 907
Yung Ting, 977-979, 981-982

Zabriskie, Annie, 920
Zabriskie, Col. J. C., 920
Zabriskie, Mrs. J. C., 920
Zipcey v. Thompson, 537